CW00420452

THE SAVE
RUGBY UNION WHO'S WHO
1995/96

—THE—
SAVE & PROSPER RUGBY UNION WHO'S WHO 1995/96

Compiled and edited by
Alex Spink

CollinsWillow
An Imprint of HarperCollins*Publishers*

This edition published in 1995 by
CollinsWillow
an imprint of HarperCollins*Publishers*
London

A CIP catalogue record for this book
is available from the British Library

ISBN 0 00 218540 7

Photographs courtesy of Allsport Photographic

Printed in Great Britain by The Bath Press

CONTENTS

**ALWAYS ONE TO SPOT A GOOD OPENING,
ONCE ARCHIE HEARD ABOUT SAVE & PROSPER
UNIT TRUSTS, THERE WAS NO STOPPING HIM**

If you'd like to hear more about Save & Prosper Unit Trusts, just ring
us on our free Moneyline: 0800 282 101. It could be just the break you need.

© RFU 1990

THE INVESTMENT HOUSE
SPONSORS OF ENGLISH RUGBY

SAVE & PROSPER GROUP ONLY MARKETS ITS OWN PRODUCTS AND IS REGULATED BY
THE PERSONAL INVESTMENT AUTHORITY AND IMRO.

PREFACE

RUGBY UNION had for so long been anchored firm against the gale force squalls and storm tossed seas of professionalism that it was only a matter of time before the Good Ship Amateurism broke free of its mooring.

Yet here we are out on the open seas, after the International Rugby Football Board's momentous decision to finally take a decision. One moment it was taboo to mention money, now it's suddenly the currency in which the sport deals. From Blackmarket to Bank of England in one fell swoop.

It had to happen of course. But even the most enthusiastic peddlers of a cash-backed future were surprised when the IRFB, for so long a bastion of total ineffectiveness, grasped the nettle so wholeheartedly. Put another way the sport finally came clean, having lived a lie for too long in too many parts of the world.

Shamateurism was killing rugby union. As I wrote in last year edition: 'Rugby Union is in a right mess. The players don't know if they are coming or going. Off the field there is a great dichotomy in what countries permit their players to get up to. Confusion is the name of the game, inconsistency the cancer endangering its soul.'

The IRFB have attempted to take a knife to the diseased area by repealing all regulations relating to amateurism. Rugby will become an open game, with no prohibition on payment or provision of other material benefit to any person involved in it. In theory anyone, anywhere at whatever level of the game can now cash in on his talent. No pay ceiling will be imposed, neither will win bonuses be frowned upon.

There is a get-out clause for Unions who can't quite believe what they have heard. Regulations will not be mandatory. Any union may put in place domestic regulations which can be more restrictive and certain countries have already taken up that option. But it will take a brave administrator to block the path to El Dorado.

What rugby union now requires is a maturity to deal with these changes. It is worth remembering that all was not sweetness and light in Germany immediately once the cursed Wall came down. Change spawns its own problems.

As Tony Hallett, secretary of the Rugby Football Union, acknowledged: 'The decision to open the game is as momentous as it is challenging. It is not without the many dangers that professionalism brings in its train. There is the obvious concern that the floodgates have been opened too wide, and all at once. The RFU, together with all in the game, must decide the professional code of conduct to be employed in this new "open game".'

DIARY OF DISCONTENT
(as kept by the RUWW)

1989/90: 'The overwhelming majority have made it abundantly clear that they do not expect to be paid to play, nor would they seek such a scenario. But from top to bottom they ask with one voice why they cannot be reimbursed for working time lost to rugby, and why they should not be permitted to benefit financially from their rugby success away from the field.'

1991/92: 'Away from the playing fields the players want the amateurism wrangle straightened out, with some form of reward for their professional levels of commitment to the sport. The RUWW has expunged the theory that players are not interested in financial gain from activities peripheral to the sport.'

1992/93: 'For 99.9% of rugby's worldwide playing community the opportunity to make money from rugby does not present itself. The opportunity to lose money does. For them, the worry concerns the amount of money leaving rather than entering their wallets as a result of increased commitment to the sport.'

1993/94: 'Top grade rugby union is now a professional game, in all but name. Yet rugby continues to be played by men who are expected, basically, to fend for themselves financially. Many leading players feel they are being exploited and do not care for it.'

1994/95: 'Rugby Union is in a right mess. The players don't know if they are coming or going. Off the field there is a great dichotomy in what countries permit their players to get up to. Confusion is the name of the game, inconsistency the cancer endangering its soul.'

The future for the sport might be as clear as mud, but at least it's rulers have finally shown a willingness to accept that things ain't what they used to be. At the top end it ceased to be about a pie, a pint and a load of free kit long, long ago. The only thing the higher echelons promised was a demand for suffocating commitment.

That was why the *Save & Prosper Rugby Union Who's Who* campaigned so vociferously for change through it's spokesmen, the world's very best players. The message, shouted from the rooftops, never really changed; only the chorus grew louder.

From Twickenham to Cardiff to Dublin to Edinburgh and onwards east and south east, through Paris, Johannesburg, Sydney to Auckland, rugby's biggest names implored: 'Do something for us before we do it for ourselves'.

Sympathetic noises emanated from the game's bosses, some even went as far as actually talking about doing something, but at the end of the day front-line rugby union remained a wolf in sheep's clothing. A professional sport masquerading as a corinthian pastime.

So who could genuinely have been surprised by the momentous developments of this summer? Exasperated from watching the Golden Goose, that is top-end rugby union, laying lucrative eggs for everyone but them, the players were driven to confrontation.

The rebellion was led by the generals. Will Carling, the England captain, and François Pienaar, skipper of the world champion Springboks. Each supplemented outstanding campaigns on the field by prodding at their bosses with a metaphorical stick until they got a reaction.

Carling described the committee of the Rugby Football Union as '57 old farts' in the company of a television crew, while Pienaar tried effectively to hold the Transvaal Union to ransom by witholding the services of the province's myriad Springboks over 'better pay and conditions'.

England's high-profile skipper was damn lucky to survive his dig at the establishment and it took a remarkable show of solidarity from both his international comrades and the public at large to get him his job back after he had been sacked by the RFU. Pienaar might not be so lucky. At the time of going to print, he is in the doghouse, accused of acting as a highly paid agent for Kerry Packer in the extraordinary and bitter conflict with rival Australian tycoon Rupert Murdoch over control of the sport.

Packer's World Rugby Corporation flooded the market place, post-World Cup, with big-money offers to join a 900-player rebel circuit, with the aim of filling 30 teams and dividing them into three groups. The top players were purportedly promised a signing-on fee of

£176,000 plus an income of £144,000, although a major sticking point was that only 10% was being offered up front.

All of this came in hurried response to the earth-shattering news, on the eve of the World Cup final, that media mogul rival Murdoch had effectively bought up Southern Hemisphere rugby in a £366 million, ten-year broadcast deal which guaranteed:

- A new tri-nation championship, to be played on a home and away basis, involving South Africa, Australia and New Zealand.
- A new inter-provincial round-robin competition (69 matches over 13 weeks) involving five Kiwi teams, four from South Africa and three from Oz.
- Exclusive coverage of all in-bound tours to the Southern Hemisphere, including British Lions visits, plus all major domestic provincial competitions in the Big Three nations.

With this development Rugby Union took an irrevocable step forward into a new era. Murdoch's money might have been directed into Southern Hemisphere bank accounts – indeed, he reportedly said: 'They will have to learn to play better rugby in the Northern Hemisphere if they want to sign up' – but once Europe cottoned on there was absolutely no way its stars were about to continue playing for peanuts. And quite right too.

Jonah Lomu towers over England during the pre-match Haka. Nothing changed during the World Cup semi-final with Lomu bagging four tries.

Murdoch, of course, could afford to make such a provocative remark, knowing that increased dissatisfaction with Union north of the great divide would only play into his other hand – that of Rugby League.

In a previous barnstorming move, Murdoch had stolen the thunder from Packer's TV deal with the Australian Rugby League by giving birth to his own Super League with a wave of his cheque book. Thus, even before the watershed that was the Rugby Union World Cup, leading Union stars were being headhunted by Murdoch's recruiters and offered small fortunes to defect.

The advice from Union chiefs was to wait. The IRFB would implement sweeping changes in their forthcoming August meeting. To their credit, the players took heed, even if they did use the spectre of League lucre, and the very real threat of teaming up with Packer, to effectively hold a gun to the head of the Unions.

Even before the IRFB pronouncement major concessions had been made by the Unions. The All Blacks, Wallabies and Springboks were already assured of coining in upwards of £100,000 per player per annum. England's players had opened discussions at £30,000 but made it abundantly clear they would not even get out of bed for that.

The sad commentary on all this is that the powers-that-be only acquiesced to player demands when they were forced into a corner. 'Five years ago we sat down with them and tried to work out a way to manage the situation,' said England hooker Brian Moore. 'They refused point blank. Now they must think big.'

For most rugby fans thinking big meant only one thing in 1995. And his name was Jonah Lomu. The giant All Black wing was the star of the World Cup, his four-try display in the semi-final against England, the most compelling sight the sport has seen in years.

After the dull fare served up around the globe in 1993/94, Lomu's contribution alone elevated last season to a higher plain. Events in South Africa might not have lived up to Lomu's example across the board, but a World Cup in one country, and one country making such an effort, was a wonderous sight. Never again should the tournament be shared, although it will, of course. Money talks louder than commonsense.

The stars of the show (those capped between June 1994–95) are all featured in this sixth edition of the *Save & Prosper Rugby Union Who's Who* on pages 133–389, with an overflow into the Appendix (pages 391–397). And once again, the world's leading international captains, plus England supremo Jack Rowell have each reviewed the season for the RUWW. Michael Lynagh (Australia), Philippe Saint-Andre (France), Terry Kingston (Ireland), Sean Fitzpatrick (New Zealand), Gavin Hastings (Scotland) and François Pienaar (South Africa) give their exclusive verdicts while, in the absence of a leader in crisis-torn Wales, respected Welsh journalist Robert Cole spells out a few home truths.

Players have not this year been grilled on what they think of what has been going on in rugby union during this turbulent period, simply because with events changing by the day the general consensus is that nobody has a clue what exactly is going on. Suffice to say that the *Suggestions To Improve Rugby* proffered in previous editions have acted as a catalyst for the change we are now witnessing.

The most up-to-date global results service available is situated at the rear of the book (pages 423–453), charting the campaign in chronological order up until the World Cup, a tournament which is featured in full detail on pages 399–422. New Zealand's Bledisloe Cup triumph appears on page 97, although caps won in those two Tests have not been credited to players in this edition.

I am once again indebted to the players and, especially, the skippers and Jack Rowell, for their continued co-operation and indeed enthusiasm. The same applies to my top team of contributors, Greg Campbell, Wynne Gray, Chris Thau, Jonathan Goslett, Robert Cole, the Big Eight unions, Westgate Sports, Michael Humphrey & Partners, Slattery PR, *Rugby World*, *Rugby News*, Bill Cotton and Programme Publications, Tom Whiting, Rachel Smyth, the Allsport photographic team, *Today* newspaper, my other colleagues in the world media and to the ever-tolerant Karen, Tom and Jenny.

Alex Spink
August 1995

FOREWORD

PAUL BATEMAN
Chief Executive, Save & Prosper Group

Once more, it is a pleasure to pen this foreword to the *Save & Prosper Rugby Union Who's Who*. I offer my congratulations to the author, Alex Spink, who has continued to maintain a high degree of accuracy within the publication coupled with many thought-provoking and amusing entries.

Save & Prosper continues its sponsorship of International Rugby at Twickenham this season with matches against the new World Champions South Africa, then Western Samoa, Wales and Ireland. Despite the disappointment of their World Cup, England will, as ever, be looking to impress at home and what better theatre than at the newly completed stadium at Twickenham.

With hindsight, the World Cup may have marked the end of the amateur game we have known for so long. However, it is crucial that the game at all levels continues to adapt to the conditions of the modern world. My wish is that adapting to these conditions is done in such a way as not to fragment the international scene or change the spirit in which games are played.

REVIEW OF
THE 1994/95 SEASON

 ## ENGLAND

Jack Rowell
(with Alex Spink)

A YEAR of unrivalled drama, commitment, controversy and change brought England the elation of a Grand Slam but also the crushing disappointment of failing to bring home the World Cup.

England overcame the best our Five Nations rivals could serve up, survived the most highly structured domestic season ever and even weathered the 'Old Farts' affair. But Jonah Lomu proved to be one challenge too far.

New Zealand's performance against us in the World Cup semi-final was the most devastating by any side I have ever come up against. They fizzed around, playing a pace of rugby our players just were not used to. But it was Mr Lomu who made the big difference.

We always imagined there would be a Lomu effect but we thought if we closed his space down, as South Africa were subsequently to do in the final, we could contain him. It obviously didn't happen like that. The pace of New Zealand's game, the handling, movement and power

15

of it, pulled England out of their defensive patterns. The All Blacks were 12–0 up after four minutes, 25–0 ahead after twenty-six, and Lomu ended up with four tries.

Defeat that day was very painful, not least because we had almost forgotten what it was like to lose. Since going down against South Africa on the same Newlands pitch in Cape Town a year and seven days earlier, England had strung together ten victories and, in so doing, embraced a new style of play.

In the previous seven years England had developed a style that was set-piece orientated and relatively static. It had been successful in the northern hemisphere, bringing Grand Slams in 1991 and 1992. But by the time I became involved, midway through 1994, I felt England were running out of tries.

With few immediate challenges to positions in the England team, I decided to hold the team stable and work on a change of style. The tour to South Africa had underpinned the need to change, particularly on firm surfaces, and we set out to do that.

That autumn we worked at Marlow, helped by Pierre Villepreux, on moving the ball quickly, preferably before contact. This was diametrically opposite to the way England had played and I was warned by Villepreux that such a change would take several years to fully implement.

> 'New Zealand's performance against us in the World Cup semi-final was the most devastating by any side I have ever come up against. They fizzed around, playing a pace of rugby our players just were not used to. But it was Lomu who made the big difference'

Still, the pre-Christmas internationals against Romania and Canada allowed us the opportunity to gauge our progress and the results were most encouraging. Having managed only two tries throughout the 1994 Five Nations Championship, we ran in 12 in our two Tests.

Against Romania (won 54–3), even accepting the calibre of the opposition, we moved the ball well in testing conditions. We followed up with 60 points against Canada (won 60–19), producing a display of very fluent rugby and, as against Romania, claimed six tries. Our performance was augmented by an outstanding kicking display by

Rob Andrew, demonstrating that he had made the breakthrough to a much higher level in that area of his game.

Going into the Five Nations series we had developed a game of greater flexibility, greater movement of the ball, more an integrated backs and forwards XV-man-game. And we were confident enough in what we were doing to accord this dynamic style of rugby Plan A status.

That was before we woke up to a howling gale in Dublin on the opening day of the championship. Such potentially disruptive conditions were hardly ideal for test driving Plan A in the Five Nations arena but the players insisted on doing so, despite being given the option to revert to a tighter game.

Such self-confidence was mirrored by the performance the team produced, both in the first half, when they won the game (20–8), and in the second-half, when they consolidated against the wind. Such a collective game of rugby inspired everyone. The belief was growing that we could play a game of greater flexibility.

Next was France and a challenge of even greater proportions than usual, given that they had won a Test series 2–0 in New Zealand. To my absolute delight England (won 31–10) produced a storming performance at Twickenham. The French have a renowned defence, difficult to play against, but we ran in three tries and were never really threatened.

On to Wales in Cardiff where there was a lot of historical pressure on Rory Underwood. Rory had committed one or two costly mistakes previously and felt he had a monkey to get off his back. Two tries in a 23–9 win did very nicely and he had every reason to feel proud of his effort.

> '*All season long the domestic structure had given me a headache. It was most unfortunate that England going into the World Cup coincided with the most highly structured season ever. We knew well what would be the consequences, having toured South Africa the summer before and found that the players were worn out physically and mentally by the time we got there*'

Judging by some reports we could have been given the Grand Slam there and then but a born-again Scotland side had something to say about that. Written off after failing to win in nine Tests, the Scots had bounced back splendidly to win in Parc des Princes for the first time. They too had three wins and high expectations.

Yet despite the obvious danger I had the utmost confidence in my team: in each player and the rugby we were playing. The Scots made it difficult, closing us down a lot and giving a number of penalties away in the process, and for the first time in the championship we had to rely on Rob's boot rather than tries (won 24–12). With seven penalty goals and a dropped goal, he let nobody down.

To win a Grand Slam at my first attempt was hugely satisfying, but I knew that to transfer European glory onto a global podium was going to take an altogether greater effort – not least because of the hurdles we had to overcome simply to get the squad to South Africa in optimum physical and mental shape.

All season long the domestic structure had given me a headache. It was most unfortunate that England going into the World Cup coincided with the most highly structured season ever. We knew well what would be the consequences, having toured South Africa the summer before and found that the players were worn out physically and mentally by the time we got there.

My view was that players had to be fit and fresh going into the World Cup for us to have a chance. After all, the Southern Hemisphere players were just going into their season. But the onus was very much on us to do this for ourselves, which was regrettable. It caused understandable tension among the players, because of their club loyalties. Naturally enough, they did not want to abandon them in their hours of need.

We managed to muddle by, albeit unsatisfactorily, but just when I thought we could finally extinguish all other matters from our minds and focus on the World Cup came that television programme containing Will Carling's unflattering observation about members of the Rugby Football Union committee.

The whole affair saddened me, not least because of its timing. My immediate reaction was that it was yet another barrier to England getting to the World Cup in the right frame of mind. But then it blew up into a very major issue, with Will being sacked and then reinstated.

Mr Carling rather put his foot in it. And the Powers-that-be felt obliged to react. It was a unique situation and the level of public uproar was incredible. Fortunately for England, Will and RFU president Dennis Easby found a way through it. And an episode which at one stage had threatened to cause great damage, ultimately had the effect of bonding the squad closer together. From domestic tension to international apprehension as England took a while to get their feet under the table at the World Cup. There were very few easy games in the tournament and certainly we did not have any. Argentina had a very fine scrummaging pack, Italy had made such advances that people were suggesting the Five Nations Championship should expand to accommodate them, while Western Samoa, having had made a huge impact in the 1991 World Cup, were always going to be dangerous through their style of play.

> '*Just when I thought we could finally extinguish all other matters from our minds and focus on the World Cup came that television programme containing Will Carling's unflattering observation about members of the RFU committee. Mr Carling rather put his foot in it and the Powers-that-be felt obliged to react*'

Having been denied the luxury of a warm-up game by our claustrophobic season, our error-rate was high against Argentina (won 24–18) and that stopped us building any rhythm at all. On top of that the South Americans were the best scrummaging side and one of the best lineout sides in the tournament. They put up a formidable fight.

Against Italy (won 27–20) England were better – although not markedly. We had settled down a bit, halved our error-rate and played some good running rugby at times. Italy were sharp and well organised and made it difficult for us, but we won with more to spare than the scoreline suggested.

With a quarter-final place assured, certain players were rested against Western Samoa (won 44–22). I brought in the likes of Ian Hunter, Neil Back, Richard West, Graham Dawe and Jon Callard, and moved Mike Catt to fly-half. Helped greatly by the immense enthusiasm of these players coming in, England produced their most convincing Pool performance.

Into the knockout stages and my personal view was that if England played well they could beat anyone on their day. But if they didn't, against the likes of Australia and New Zealand, they could well lose ... and by a number points.

This theory was put to the test against the world champion Wallabies (won 25–22), on an afternoon of unbelievable tension in Cape Town. We were very much up for Australia psychologically and, although they had more possession than England, thanks in no small measure to John Eales' breathtaking lineout work, England had the final say. Rob Andrew's dropped goal provided a staggeringly sweet moment in the rugby lives of all concerned; players, management and supporters alike.

> 'Prior to kick-off against New Zealand I reminded myself of my earlier fear that if we did not play well we could ship points. It proved prophetic as England got off to an appalling start. You can be as fit as you want, you can practice as much as you want, but when you start like that and give the cup favourites a 12-point start, you are going to have problems'

And so to New Zealand. Only 80 minutes stood between England and a place in the World Cup final. But I felt the All Blacks posed a bigger threat than had Australia. They were playing the most striking rugby in the tournament, mixing traditional forward skills with some very exciting backs: Mehrtens, Osborne and that man Lomu.

Prior to kick-off I reminded myself of my earlier fear that if we did not play well we could ship points. It proved prophetic as England got off to an appalling start. You can be as fit as you want, you can practice as much as you want, but when you start like that and give the cup favourites a 12-point start through two errors, you are going to have problems.

All credit to New Zealand who played with a great deal of movement, the like of which we do not see in the Northern Hemisphere. I have not see any international team play with the ease, the power and the pace which New Zealand did. They beat all the Four Home Unions handsomely.

We had planned that there would always be someone right up on Lomu before he got into his stride. But it did not work. We allowed him too much room. Once England finally stopped bringing New Zealand into the game, we played some stunning rugby ourselves, but by the second half it was too late.

To have to play France three days later was every bit as hard as All Black skipper Sean Fitzpatrick warned. He said they had found it incredibly tough in 1991 when pitted against Scotland. 'While no-one really wants to play in it,' he advised, 'spectators and critics still turn up with expectations.' Sean was absolutely right. The players were physically and mentally drained and we failed to do ourselves justice.

Against France, you have to get a drive going to create space for your backs to play in. We managed that at Twickenham but in Pretoria we were never able to. We barely, if ever, won two balls in a row. England did not play anywhere near their potential.

But the future is exciting. Rugby union was on a crest of a wave before the International Board turned the sport professional. What is now important is that it catches the next wave. And to that end the Northern Hemisphere must follow the Southern Hemisphere's lead and make rugby union a game of more movement.

England will do her bit.

Kyran Bracken hands off Garin Jenkins as England triumph in Cardiff.

ENGLAND (P12 W10 D0 L2 F370 A207)

(H) v Romania	(Twickenham, 12.11.94)	won	54–3
(H) v Canada	(Twickenham, 10.12.94)	won	60–19
(A) v Ireland	(Dublin, 21.1.95)	won	20–8
(H) v France	(Twickenham, 4.2.95)	won	31–10
(A) v Wales	(Cardiff, 18.2.95)	won	23–9
(H) v Scotland	(Twickenham, 18.3.95)	won	24–12
(–) v Argentina*	(Durban, 27.5.95)	won	24–18
(–) v Italy*	(Durban, 31.5.95)	won	27–20
(–) v Western Samoa*	(Durban, 4.6.95)	won	44–22
(–) v Australia*	(q/f: Cape Town, 11.6.95)	won	25–22
(–) v New Zealand*	(s/f: Cape Town, 18.6.95)	lost	29–45
(–) v France*	(3/4: Pretoria, 22.6.95)	lost	9–19

* World Cup

England A (P6 W4 D0 L2 F160 A149):

(A) v Ireland A	(Dublin, 20.1.95)	won	21–20
(H) v France A	(Leicester, 3.2.95)	won	29–9
(H) v Italy A	(Gloucester, 19.2.95)	won	33–9
(A) v Natal	(Durban, SA, 18.3.95)	lost	25–33
(A) v Australia XV	(Brisbane, 7.6.95)	won	27–19
(A) v Fiji	(Suva, 10.6.95)	lost	25–59

England A to Australia and Fiji (tour record: P7 W3 D0 L4 F263 A186):

(A) v South Australia	(Adelaide, 20.5.95)	won	66–9
(A) v Victoria	(Melbourne, 24.5.95)	won	76–19
(A) v Queensland XV	(Brisbane, 28.5.95)	lost	15–20
(A) v Australian Universities	(Sydney, 31.5.95)	lost	30–32
(A) v NSW Country	(Gosford, 4.6.95)	lost	24–28

England Emerging XV (P3 W2 D0 L1 F134 A39):

(H) v Canada	(Bath, 6.12.94)	won	34–6
(H) v Romania	(Bristol, 8.3.95)	won	97–14
(H) v Northern Transvaal	(West Hartlepool, 17.2.95)	lost	3–19

England U-21 (P3 W2 D0 L1 F66 A24):

(H) v RN New Zealand U-21	(Northampton, 13.12.94)	won	15–6
(A) v Ireland	(Belfast, 8.11.94)	lost	8–12
(A) v Italy	(Palma, 13.5.95)	won	43–6

England Students (P3 W3 D0 L0 F110 A31):

(A) v Ireland	(Port Laoise, 20.1.95)	won	40–3
(H) v France	(Blackheath, 3.2.95)	won	14–10
(H) v Italy	(Leicester, 17.3.95)	won	56–18

England Colts (P4 W3 D0 L1 F98 A46):

(H) v Italy	(Camborne, 4.3.95)	won	29–0
(H) v Wales	(Twickenham, 26.3.95)	lost	12–23
(A) v Scotland	(Stirling, 1.4.95)	won	32–13
(A) v France	(La Teste, 22.4.95)	won	25–10

England 18 Group (P6 W5 D0 L1 F109 A57):

(H) v Australia	(Gloucester, 25.1.95)	won	30–3
(H) v New Zealand	(Leicester, 1.2.95)	lost	12–22
(H) v Scotland	(Twickenham, 25.3.95)	won	19–14
(A) v Wales	(Llanelli, 29.3.95)	won	9–6
(A) v Ireland	(Galway, 15.4.95)	won	17–6
(H) v France	(Cambridge, 19.4.95)	won	22–6

England 16 Group (P2 W1 D0 L1 F18 A10):

(A) v Portugal	(Lisbon, 15.4.95)	won	15–0
(A) v Wales	(Pontypridd, 22.4.95)	lost	3–10

England 16 Group A (P2 W2 D0 L0 F69 A25):

(H) v Scotland	(Wolverhampton, 9.4.95)	won	46–18
(A) v Wales	(Maesteg, 21.4.95)	won	23–7

DOMESTIC RUGBY

COURAGE CLUB CHAMPIONSHIP

Division One	P	W	D	L	F	A	Pts
Leicester	18	15	1	2	400	239	31
Bath	18	12	3	3	373	245	27
Wasps	18	13	0	5	470	313	26
Sale	18	7	2	9	327	343	16
Orrell	18	6	3	9	256	326	15
Bristol	18	7	0	11	301	353	14
Gloucester	18	6	1	11	269	336	13
Harlequins	18	6	1	11	275	348	13
West Hartlepool	18	6	1	11	312	412	13
Northampton	18	6	0	12	267	335	12

champions: Leicester; **relegated:** Northampton.

Division Two	P	W	D	L	F	A	Pts
Saracens	18	15	1	2	389	213	31
Wakefield	18	12	1	5	354	261	25
Newcastle Gosforth	18	8	2	8	373	281	18
London Scottish	18	9	0	9	351	321	18
London Irish	18	9	0	9	363	381	18
Moseley	18	8	1	9	299	303	17
Nottingham	18	8	1	9	299	322	17
Waterloo	18	8	0	10	287	331	16
Fylde	18	8	0	10	250	329	16
Coventry	18	2	0	16	213	436	4

champions: Saracens; **relegated:** Coventry, Fylde.

Div 3 – promoted: Bedford (c), Blackheath; relegated: Exeter, Clifton.
Div 4 – promoted: Rotherham (c), Reading; relegated: Broughton Park, Askeans.

CUP FINALS:

Pilkington Cup
Bath 36, Leicester 16 (Twickenham, 6 May)
Bath: J Callard; A Swift, P de Glanville (capt), J Guscott, A Adebayo; R Butland, I Sanders; K Yates, G Adams, V Ubogu (J Mallett 67), M Haag, N Redman, A Robinson, B Clarke, S Ojomoh.
   Scorers – Tries: Haag 2, Clarke, Swift, Callard. *Conversions:* Callard 4. *Penalty goal:* Callard.
Wasps: J Ufton; P Hopley, D Hopley, G Childs, N Greenstock; R Andrew, S Bates; D Molloy, K Dunn, I Dunston, M Greenwood, N Hadley, L Dallaglio, D Ryan (capt), M White.
   Scorers – Tries: Dunston, D Hopley. *Penalty goals:* Andrew 2.
Referee: J Pearson (Durham).

CIS County Championship
Warwickshire 15, Northumberland 9 (Twickenham, 22 April)

U-21 County Championship
Yorkshire 20, Buckinghamshire 6 (Twickenham, 22 April)

Pilkington Shield
Bedford Queens 11, St Albans 10 (Twickenham, 6 May)

Vladivar Women's National Cup:
Richmond 27, Wasps 0

Captains unite: Will Carling eludes fellow skipper Gavin Hastings during England's 24–12 defeat of Scotland at Twickenham.

1980:

I	W24–9	Twickenham	19 Jan	**t:** Scott, Slemen, SJ Smith **c:** Hare 3 **p:** Hare 2
F	W17–13	Paris	2 Feb	**t:** Carleton, Preston **p:** Hare **dg:** Horton 2
W	W 9–8	Twickenham	16 Feb	**p:** Hare 3
S	W30–18	Edinburgh	15 Mar	**t:** Carleton 3, Slemen, Smith **c:** Hare 2 **p:** Hare 2

1981:

W	L19–21	Cardiff	17 Jan	**t:** Hare **p:** Hare 5
S	W23–17	Twickenham	21 Feb	**t:** Davies, Slemen, Woodward **c:** Hare **p:** Hare 3
I	W10–9	Dublin	7 Mar	**t:** Dodge, Rose **c:** Rose
F	L12–16	Twickenham	21 Mar	**p:** Rose 4
Arg(1)	D19–19	Buenos Aires	30 May	**t:** Woodward 2, Davies **c:** Hare 2 **p:** Hare
Arg(2)	W12–6	Buenos Aires	6 Jun	**t:** Davies **c:** Hare **p:** Hare 2

1982:

A	W15–11	Twickenham	2 Jan	**t:** Jeavons **c:** Dodge **p:** Rose 3
S	D 9–9	Edinburgh	16 Jan	**p:** Dodge 2, Rose
I	L15–16	Twickenham	6 Feb	**t:** Slemen **c:** Rose **p:** Rose 3
F	W27–15	Paris	20 Feb	**t:** Woodward, Carleton **c:** Hare 2 **p:** Hare 5
W	W17–7	Twickenham	6 Mar	**t:** Carleton, Slemen **p:** Hare 3
US[+]	W59–0	Hartford	19 Jun	**t:** SJ Smith 2, Swift 2, Scott 2, Carleton, Rendall, Wheeler **c:** Hare 7 **p:** Hare 2 **dg:** Cusworth
Fj[+]	W60–19	Twickenham	16 Oct	**t:** Trick 3, Swift 2, Gadd 2, Scott, SJ Smith, Cusworth, Dodge, Colclough **c:** Hare 6

1983:

F	L15–19	Twickenham	15 Jan	**p:** Hare 4
				dg: Cusworth
W	D13–13	Cardiff	5 Feb	**t:** Carleton
				p: Hare 2
				dg: Cusworth
S	L12–22	Twickenham	5 Mar	**p:** Hare 3
				dg: Horton
I	L15–25	Dublin	19 Mar	**p:** Hare 5
NZ	W15–9	Twickenham	19 Nov	**t:** Colclough
				c: Hare
				p: Hare 3
C+	W27–0	Twickenham	15 Oct	**t:** Youngs, Winterbottom, penalty try
				c: Hare 3
				p: Hare 3

1984:

S	L 6–18	Edinburgh	4 Feb	**p:** Hare 2
I	W12–9	Twickenham	18 Feb	**p:** Hare 3
				dg: Cusworth
F	L18–32	Paris	3 Mar	**t:** R Underwood, Hare
				c: Hare 2
				p: Hare 2
W	L15–24	Twickenham	17 Mar	**p:** Hare 5
SA(1)	L15–33	Port Elizabeth	2 Jun	**p:** Hare 4
				dg: Horton
SA(2)	L 9–35	Johannesburg	9 Jun	**p:** Hare 3
A	L 3–19	Twickenham	3 Nov	**p:** Barnes

1985:

F	D 9–9	Twickenham	2 Feb	**p:** Andrew 2
				dg: Andrew
W	L15–24	Cardiff	20 Apr	**t:** Smith
				c: Andrew
				p: Andrew 2
				dg: Andrew
S	W10–7	Twickenham	16 Mar	**t:** Smith
				p: Andrew 2
I	L10–13	Dublin	30 Mar	**t:** R Underwood
				p: Andrew 2
NZ(1)	L13–18	Christchurch	1 Jun	**t:** Harrison, Teague
				c: Barnes
				p: Barnes
NZ(2)	L15–42	Wellington	8 Jun	**t:** Hall, Harrison
				c: Barnes 2
				dg: Barnes
R	W22–15	Twickenham	5 Jan	**t:** S T Smith
				p: Andrew 4
				dg: Andrew 2

1986:

W	W21–18	Twickenham	17 Jan	**p:** Andrew 6
				dg: Andrew

S	L 6–33	Edinburgh	15 Feb	p: Andrew 2
I	W25–20	Twickenham	1 Mar	t: Richards 2, penalty try, Davies
				c: Andrew 3
				p: Andrew
F	L10–29	Paris	15 Mar	t: Dooley
				p: Barnes 2
J[+]	W39–12	Twickenham	11 Oct	t: R Underwood, Hall, Bailey, Richards, Rees, Salmon
				c: Rose 6
				p: Rose

1987:

I	L 0–17	Dublin	7 Feb	
F	L15–19	Twickenham	21 Feb	p: Rose 4
				dg: Andrew
W	L12–19	Cardiff	7 Mar	p: Rose 4
S	W21–12	Twickenham	4 Apr	t: penalty try, Rose
				c: Rose 2
				p: Rose 3
A*	L 6–19	Sydney	23 May	t: Harrison
				c: Webb
J*	W60–7	Sydney	30 May	t: R Underwood 2, Rees, Salmon, Richards, Simms, Harrison 3, Redman
				c: Webb 7
				p: Webb 2
US*	W34–6	Sydney	3 Jun	t: Winterbottom 2, Harrison, Dooley
				c: Webb 3
				p: Webb 4
W*	L 3–16	Brisbane	8 Jun	p: Webb

1988:

F	L 9–10	Paris	16 Jan	p: Webb 2
				dg: Cusworth
W	L 3–11	Twickenham	6 Feb	p: Webb
S	W 9–6	Edinburgh	5 Mar	p: Webb 2
				dg: Andrew
I(a)	W35–3	Twickenham	19 Mar	t: Oti 3, R Underwood 2, Rees
				c: Webb, Andrew 3
				p: Webb
I(b)^	W21–10	Dublin	23 Apr	t: R Underwood, Harding
				c: Webb 2
				p: Webb 3
A(a1)	L16–22	Brisbane	29 May	t: R Underwood, Bailey
				c: Webb
				p: Webb 2
A(a2)	L 8–28	Sydney	12 Jun	t: Richards, R Underwood
Fj	W25–12	Suva	17 Jun	t: R Underwood 2, Barley
				c: Barnes 2
				p: Barnes 3
A(b)	W28–19	Twickenham	5 Nov	t: R Underwood 2, Morris, Halliday
				c: Webb 3
				p: Webb 2

1989:

S	D12–12	Twickenham	4 Feb	**p:** Andrew 2, Webb 2
I	W16–3	Dublin	18 Feb	**t:** Moore, Richards **c:** Andrew **p:** Andrew 2
F	W11–0	Twickenham	4 Mar	**t:** Carling, Robinson **p:** Andrew
W	L 9–12	Cardiff	18 Mar	**p:** Andrew 2 **dg:** Andrew
R	W58–3	Bucharest	13 May	**t:** Oti 4, Guscott 3, Probyn, Richards **c:** Hodgkinson 8 **p:** Hodgkinson **dg:** Andrew
Fj	W58–23	Twickenham	4 Nov	**t:** R Underwood 5, Skinner, Bailey, Linnett, Ackford, Guscott **c:** Hodgkinson 5, Andrew **p:** Hodgkinson 2

1990:

I	W23–0	Twickenham	20 Jan	**t:** R Underwood, Probyn, Egerton, Guscott **c:** Hodgkinson 2 **p:** Hodgkinson
F	W26–7	Paris	3 Feb	**t:** R Underwood, Guscott, Carling **c:** Hodgkinson **p:** Hodgkinson 4

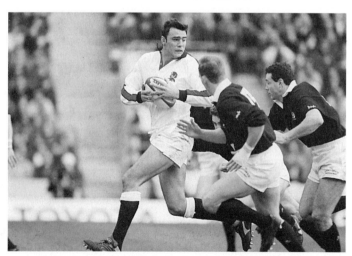

England's Ben Clarke shows Scotland his heels at Twickenham.

W	W34–6	Twickenham	17 Feb	**t:** Carling, R Underwood 2, Hill
				c: Hodgkinson 3
				p: Hodgkinson 4
S	L 7–13	Edinburgh	17 Mar	**t:** Guscott
				p: Hodgkinson
It+	W33–15	Rovigo	1 May	**t:** Oti, Buckton, Back, Andrew
				c: Hodgkinson 4
				p: Hodgkinson 2
				dg: Andrew
Arg(a1)	W25–12	Buenos Aires	28 Jul	**t:** Ryan, Oti
				c: Hodgkinson
				p: Hodgkinson 5
Arg(a2)	L13–15	Buenos Aires	4 Aug	**t:** Hodgkinson, Heslop
				c: Hodgkinson
				p: Hodgkinson
Ba+	W18–16	Twickenham	29 Sep	**t:** Richards, Hodgkinson
				c: Hodgkinson 2
				p: Hodgkinson 2
Arg(b)	W51–0	Twickenham	3 Nov	**t:** R Underwood 3, Guscott 2, Hill, Hall
				c: Hodgkinson 7
				p: Hodgkinson 3

1991:

W	W25–6	Cardiff	19 Jan	**t:** Teague
				p: Hodgkinson 7
S(a)	W21–12	Twickenham	16 Feb	**t:** Heslop
				c: Hodgkinson
				p: Hodgkinson 5
I	W16–7	Dublin	2 Mar	**t:** R Underwood, Teague
				c: Hodgkinson
				p: Hodgkinson 2
F	W21–19	Twickenham	16 Mar	**t:** R Underwood
				c: Hodgkinson
				p: Hodgkinson 4
				dg: Andrew
Fj	W28–12	Suva	20 Jul	**t:** Probyn, R Underwood, Andrew
				c: Webb 2
				p: Webb 2
				dg: Andrew 2
A(a)	L15–40	Sydney	27 Jul	**t:** Guscott
				c: Webb
				p: Webb 3
USSR+	W53–0	Twickenham	7 Sep	**t:** Oti 2, Guscott 2, R Underwood 2, Skinner 2, Andrew
				c: Andrew 4, Hodgkinson 3
				p: Hodgkinson
NZ*	L12–18	Twickenham	3 Oct	**p:** Webb 3
				dg: Andrew
It*	W36–6	Twickenham	8 Oct	**t:** R Underwood, Guscott 2, Webb
				c: Webb 4
				p: Webb 4

US*	W37–9	Twickenham	11 Oct	**t:** R Underwood 2, Carling, Skinner, Heslop **c:** Hodgkinson 4 **p:** Hodgkinson 3
F*	W19–10	Paris	19 Oct	**t:** R Underwood, Carling **c:** Webb **p:** Webb 3
S(b)*	W 9–6	Edinburgh	26 Oct	**p:** Webb 2 **dg:** Andrew
A(b)*	L 6–12	Twickenham	2 Nov	**p:** Webb 2

1992:

S	W25–7	Edinburgh	18 Jan	**t:** R Underwood, Morris **c:** Webb **p:** Webb 4 **dg:** Guscott
I	W38–9	Twickenham	1 Feb	**t:** Webb 2, Morris, Guscott, R Underwood, Halliday **c:** Webb 4 **p:** Webb 2
F	W31–13	Paris	15 Feb	**t:** Webb, R Underwood, Morris, penalty try **c:** Webb 3 **p:** Webb 3
W	W24–0	Twickenham	7 Mar	**t:** Carling, Skinner, Dooley **c:** Webb 3 **p:** Webb 2
C †	W26–13	Wembley	17 Oct	**t:** Hunter 2, Guscott, Winterbottom **p:** Webb 2
SA	W33–16	Twickenham	14 Nov	**t:** T Underwood, Guscott, Morris, Carling **c:** Webb 2 **p:** Webb 3

1993:

F	W16–15	Twickenham	16 Jan	**t:** Hunter **c:** Webb **p:** Webb 3
W	L 9–10	Cardiff	6 Feb	**p:** Webb 2 **dg:** Guscott
S	W26–12	Twickenham	6 Mar	**t:** Guscott, R Underwood, T Underwood **c:** Webb **p:** Webb 3
I	L 3–17	Dublin	20 Mar	**p:** Webb
NZ	W15–9	Twickenham	27 Nov	**p:** Callard 4 **dg:** Andrew

1994

S	W15–14	Edinburgh	5 Feb	**p:** Callard 5
I	L12–13	Twickenham	19 Feb	**p:** Callard 4
F	W18–14	Paris	5 Mar	**p:** Andrew 5

				dg: Andrew
W	W15–8	Twickenham	19 Mar	**t:** R Underwood, Rodber
				c: Andrew
				p: Andrew
SA(1)	W33–15	Pretoria	4 Jun	**t:** Clarke, Andrew
				c: Andrew 2
				p: Andrew 5
SA(2)	L 9–27	Cape Town	11 Jun	**p:** Andrew 3
R	W54–3	Twickenham	12 Nov	**t:** T Underwood 2, Carling, Rodber, R Underwood, penalty try
				c: Andrew 6
				p: Andrew 4
C	W60–19	Twickenham	xx Nov	**t:** R Underwood 2, Catt 2, Bracken, T Underwood
				c: Andrew 6
				p: Andrew 6

1995

I	W20–8	Dublin	21 Jan	**t:** Carling, T Underwood, Clarke
				c: Andrew
				p: Andrew
F(a)	W31–10	Twickenham	4 Feb	**t:** T Underwood 2, Guscott
				c: Andrew 2
				p: Andrew 4
W	W23–9	Cardiff	18 Feb	**t:** Ubogu, R Underwood 2
				c: Andrew
				p: Andrew 2
S	W24–12	Twickenham	18 Mar	**p:** Andrew 7
				dg: Andrew
Arg*	W24–18	Durban	27 May	**p:** Andrew 6
				dg: Andrew 2
It*	W27–20	Durban	31 May	**t:** T Underwood, R Underwood
				c: Andrew
				p: Andrew 5
WS*	W44–22	Durban	4 Jun	**t:** R Underwood 2, Back, penalty try
				c: Callard 3
				p: Callard 5
				dg: Catt
A*	W25–22	Cape Town	11 Jun	**t:** T Underwood
				c: Andrew
				p: Andrew 5
				dg: Andrew
NZ*	L29–45	Cape Town	18 Jun	**t:** R Underwood 2, Carling 2
				c: Andrew 3
				p: Andrew
F(b)*	L 9–19	Pretoria	22 Jun	**p:** Andrew 3

* World Cup
+ Non-cap
† Five-point try introduced from this game onwards
^ Non-championship

IRELAND

Terry Kingston
(with Alex Spink)

IRELAND did not win the World Cup, nor did we lift the Five Nations Cup, but only a harsh judge would say we ended the 1994/95 season in worse shape than we started it.

Two months before the World Cup you could have got good odds on us, rather than Wales, taking the Wooden Spoon and then failing to reach the knockout stages in South Africa. For all the promise we had shown in Australia the previous summer, we had nothing tangible to show for our efforts. We had lost our first three championship games and badly needed a lift.

In that respect we have much for which to be thankful to Wales. Not only did we win the Battle of the Basement in Cardiff, to inflict on them an inglorious whitewash, we then beat them again in South Africa in the World Cup to achieve our declared pre-tournament aim of making the quarter-finals.

But the difference between being relatively successful ultimately and finishing the campaign on the international garbage dump came down to the resolve within our squad, rather than any failing in a rival camp. We won those two games against Wales because we demanded it of ourselves. If only we had started out with such self-expectation.

Sure, we were optimistic after the tour Down Under. We had lost both Tests but otherwise played very well. And a number of young players – Jonathan Bell, David Corkery, Gabriel Fulcher and Keith Wood among them – had given us cause to enthuse over the future.

To then fail to deliver in our first international back, against the United States, was a big disappointment. Yes, we were always going to be on a hiding to nothing, but even though we won (26–15) we didn't do ourselves justice, and that was what mattered.

I think players were tired going into that game, after a series of important domestic fixtures in the preceding weeks. It is just not realistic for guys to play big competitive games week after week with no rest. With hindsight I don't think players took enough rest after the Australia tour.

> *'Scotland were a useful side but it was a game Ireland should have won, absolutely no doubt about that. We ran out of puff and we ran out of ball. The alarm bells were beginning to ring'*

In spite of that disappointment, going into the championship the feeling was very positive. England (lost 8–20) were our first opponents and we were going for our third consecutive win against them – what greater motivation could there be? But in the event we found it very difficult to play against them. They were dominant and we only really got into the game once or twice.

Yet the Scotland game, next up, was much more disappointing in that we put ourselves into a winning position. After a great first half display the game was ours to lose, and we did just that (13–26). Johnny Bell's try early in the second half put us firmly in the driving seat but we did not kick our goals and things suddenly collapsed around us. Scotland were a useful side but it was a game Ireland should have won, absolutely no doubt about that. We ran out of puff and we ran out of ball.

After those defeats and knowing that next were France, who we had not beaten in quite a while, the alarm bells were beginning to ring. There was a great fear of the Wooden Spoon and something needed to be done. A number of the players who had performed so encouragingly in Australia had not reproduced that form. The side was not getting the results and so changes were necessary.

We actually performed fairly well against France, especially our lineout men Gabriel Fulcher and Davy Tweed. But the end result was the same. It's always tough to chase a game against the French because when they get confident you're in trouble.

We felt we had a good squad but things weren't clicking. Perhaps it was down to lack of fitness but we also had a spate of injuries disrupting our preparations throughout the championship so continuity, or rather lack of it, was a constant problem. These relatively minor things weren't the sole reason for us losing games but they were most definitely contributory factors.

For the Wooden Spoon game in Cardiff, I was awarded the captaincy. It was unfortunate for Michael Bradley that results went against him, but obviously I was delighted and honoured to get the call. It was a shock, only one game after getting back into the side, but I did have experience on my side and had led the pack in the last two championships.

To go to the Welsh capital and win in my first game was a dream start, although it is fair to say Cardiff is one of the away venues of which we don't have a great fear. Our record there is a belter, not that we travelled in any way overconfident. How could we be? Wales have a habit of biting back when things are not going for them, but on this occasion they didn't.

> 'You couldn't say our Five Nations win over Wales was the most exciting game in the world. If you were looking for running rugby you were in the wrong place. But the result was vitally important for us so close to the World Cup'

Some people say the past counts for nothing but we obviously felt a psychological edge. There were a number of our team able to pass down positive experiences to the younger members. That counted for a lot. We told them not to worry about the Welsh *Hwyl*, that there was no reason to feel any great fear.

You couldn't say it was the most exciting game in the world. If you were looking for running rugby you were in the wrong place. But the result was vitally important for us so close to the World Cup, where we knew we would meet again for a place in the quarter-finals.

To go from that high to the low of becoming the first major nation ever to lose to Italy (12–22) was a major disappointment. The timing was just awful. But looking back it probably wasn't such a bad thing to have happened to us. Because going to Treviso having beaten Wales we were probably a bit too confident in our own ability. I felt we hadn't worked enough on becoming a good side.

In defeat we suddenly realised we still had an awful lot of work to do, just to get the basics right. And in the light of that defeat we covered a lot of work we might not otherwise have done.

What worked in our favour going into the World Cup was that for the first time all season we actually had time together to devise gameplans and fitness regimes. Consequently, the self-doubt over our fitness was removed and we felt we knew what we had to do to compete with the southern hemisphere sides.

That was handy seeing as we opened our Cup account against New Zealand (lost 19–43). Our attitude was that there was no point trying to contain the All Blacks. We may as well try to beat them. We went out with all guns blazing. We were always going to be the underdogs but we gave it our best shot and can look back with pride on that result.

There was even a point in that game when we felt we could beat the All Blacks. Even turning round at half-time after giving away two soft tries we agreed that: 'these guys aren't as awesome as they've been made out'. Against sides like New Zealand you can be beaten before you take the field, but we never thought they were unbeatable.

'Where Irish rugby goes from here is very difficult to say. All European nations must try and compete with the southern hemisphere sides, both on and off the pitch. If we don't then come the next World Cup we will see two-tier rugby and you will confidently be able to predict who will finish 1–2–3'

Unfortunately for us they brought Jonah Lomu more into the second half. and that effectively was the end of that. He was some player, wasn't he? The player of the championship without doubt.

Japan next (won 50–28) was never going to be an easy game. We knew they would play a sevens style of rugby in the heat of the midday sun. They never gave up, they played with a lot of pride, and we certainly weren't 100% happy with the way we let them back into the contest towards the end. We should have killed them off. Manager Noel Murphy banned the booze after that game, partly because of dissatisfaction over the result and partly because everyone knew the next engagement against Wales was the big one, with qualification resting on it.

As we had done against the All Blacks we set a lot of store in the first 20 minutes against the Welsh (won 24–23). But it still came as much a surprise to us as anyone else that we went into a 14-point lead so early. So much so that we didn't know whether to start closing down the game and try to build on our lead. We never quite did either.

That said it was never a one-point match. We were a better side than them, better organised. I have to admit the referee did tell us, before the move that led to Hemi Taylor's last-gasp try, that it was the final passage of the game and therefore irrelevant.

Qualifying for the last eight was hugely satisfying. But having achieved that we were very disappointed not to then give France (lost 12–36) more of a game down in Durban. We honestly felt we had the capability in the squad to make the semi-finals. But France dominated the lineouts and loose phases of play. They got their big men running at us when it had been our plan for our big men to run at them.

You can never be happy when you enter a tournament and don't win it, but there has to be a degree of satisfaction having achieved what we did from the tough Pool we were in. Even more pleasure from the forwards point of view because we scored nearly all the tries.

Where Irish rugby goes from here is very difficult to say. All northern hemisphere countries must try and compete with the southern hemisphere sides, both on and off the pitch. If we don't then come the next World Cup in four years time, we will see two-tier rugby and you will confidently be able to predict who will finish 1–2–3. If northern hemisphere countries want rugby to come first then the players have to be looked after.

IRELAND (P10 W4 D0 L6 F187 A249)

(H) v United States	(Dublin, 5.11.94)	won	26–15
(H) v England	(Dublin, 21.1.95)	lost	8–20
(A) v Scotland	(Edinburgh, 4.2.95)	lost	13–26
(H) v France	(Dublin, 4.3.95)	lost	7–25
(A) v Wales	(Cardiff, 18.3.95)	won	16–12
(A) v Italy	(Treviso, 6.5.95)	lost	12–22
(–) v New Zealand*	(Johannesburg, 27.5.95)	lost	19–42
(–) v Japan*	(Bloemfontein, 31.5.95)	won	50–28
(–) v Wales*	(Johannesburg, 4.6.95)	won	24–23
(–) v France*	(q/f: Durban, 10.6.95)	lost	12–36

* World Cup

Ireland A (P3 W0 D0 L3 F57 A75):

(H) v England	(Dublin, 20.1.95)	lost	20–21
(A) v Scotland	(Edinburgh, 3.2.95)	lost	18–24
(A) v Wales	(Pontypridd, 17.3.95)	lost	19–30

Ireland U-21 (P3 W2 D0 L1 F45 A46):

(H) v England	(Belfast, 8.11.94)	won	12–8
(A) v Scotland	(Edinburgh, 3.2.95)	won	24–22
(A) v Wales	(Glamorgan Wanderers, 17.3.95)	lost	9–16

Ireland Students (P2 W0 D0 L2 F21 A60):

(H) v England	(Port Laoise, 20.1.95)	lost	3–40
(H) v France	(Longford, 3.3.95)	lost	18–20

Ireland Schools U-18 (P4 W1 D0 L3 F58 A95):

(H) v Australia	(Dublin, 17.1.95)	lost	3–27
(A) v England	(Galway, 15.4.95)	lost	6–17
(A) v Scotland	(Balgary, 8.4.95)	won	29–23
(A) v Wales	(Dunvant, 21.4.95)	lost	20–28

Ireland Youth (P2 W1 D0 L1 F27 A28):

(H) v Wales	(Limerick, 2.4.95)	lost	12–17
(A) v Scotland	(Ayr, 8.4.95)	won	15–11

DOMESTIC RUGBY

SMITHWICK'S INTER-PROVINCIAL CHAMPIONSHIP

	P	W	D	L	F	A	Pts
Munster	4	4	0	0	159	58	8
Ulster	4	2	0	2	84	51	4
Leinster	4	2	0	2	65	80	4
Irish Exiles	4	1	0	3	77	117	2
Connacht	4	1	0	3	55	134	2

ALL IRELAND LEAGUE

Division One:	P	W	D	L	F	A	Pts
Shannon	10	10	0	0	162	60	20
Blackrock College	10	7	0	3	228	135	14
St Mary's College	10	7	0	3	151	137	14
Garryowen	10	6	0	4	160	113	12
Cork Constitution	10	6	0	4	148	129	12
Old Wesley	10	5	0	5	131	171	10
Lansdowne	10	3	1	6	150	225	7
Young Munster	10	3	0	7	115	153	6
Instonians	10	3	0	7	111	160	6
Sunday's Well	10	2	1	7	119	165	5
Dungannon	10	2	0	8	114	141	4

champions: Shannon; relegated: Dungannon, Sunday's Well.

Division Two:	P	W	D	L	F	A	Pts
Old Belvedere	10	8	0	2	157	123	16
Ballymena	10	7	1	2	191	122	15
Wanderers	10	6	1	3	151	133	13
Terenure College	10	6	0	4	187	171	12
Bective Rangers	10	5	1	4	181	135	11
Malone	10	5	0	5	143	141	10
Old Crescent	10	4	1	5	179	173	9
Greystones	10	4	1	5	173	191	9
Dolphin	10	3	1	6	102	144	7
Univ. College Dublin	10	2	2	6	141	157	6
Bangor	10	1	0	9	90	205	2

promoted: Old Belvedere (c), Ballymena; **relegated:** Bangor, UCD.

Div 3 – promoted: NIFC (c), Clontarf; **relegated:** Ballina, Galway Cs.
Div 4 – promoted: Bohemians (c), Skerries; **relegated:** None.

SENIOR CUP WINNERS
Connacht: Buccaneers
Leinster: St Mary's College
Munster: Garryowen
Ulster: Dungannon

1980:

E	L 9–24	Twickenham	19 Jan	**p:** Campbell 3
S	W22–15	Dublin	2 Feb	**t:** Keane, Kennedy
				c: Campbell
				p: Campbell 3
				dg: Campbell
F	L18–19	Paris	1 Mar	**t:** McLennan
				c: Campbell
				p: Cambell 3
				dg: Campbell
W	W21–7	Dublin	15 Mar	**t:** Irwin, O'Driscoll, C Fitzgerald
				c: Campbell 3
				p: Campbell
R[+]	D13–13	Dublin	18 Oct	**t:** F Quinn
				p: Campbell 3

1981:

F	L13–19	Dublin	7 Feb	**t:** MacNeill
				p: Campbell 3
W	L 8–9	Cardiff	21 Feb	**t:** Slattery, MacNeill
E	L 6–10	Dublin	7 Mar	**dg:** Campbell, MacNeill
S	L 9–10	Edinburgh	21 Mar	**t:** Irwin
				c: Campbell
				p: Campbell
SA(1)	L15–23	Cape Town	30 May	**t:** McGrath, McLennan
				c: Campbell 2
				p: Campbell
SA(2)	L10–12	Durban	6 Jun	**t:** O'Brien
				p: Quinn 2
A	L12–16	Dublin	21 Nov	**p:** Ward 4

1982:

W	W20–12	Dublin	23 Jan	**t:** Ringland, Finn 2
				c: Campbell
				p: Campbell 2
E	W16–15	Twickenham	6 Feb	**t:** MacNeill, McLoughlin
				c: Campbell
				p: Campbell 2
S	W21–12	Dublin	20 Feb	**p:** Campbell 6
				dg: Campbell
F	L 9–22	Paris	20 Mar	**p:** Campbell 3

1983:

S	W15–13	Edinburgh	15 Jan	**t:** Kiernan
				c: Campbell
				p: Campbell 3
F	W22–16	Dublin	19 Feb	**t:** Finn 2
				c: Campbell
				p: Campbell 4

39

W	L 9–23	Cardiff	5 Mar	**p:** Campbell 2, MacNeill
E	W25–15	Dublin	19 Mar	**t:** Slattery, Campbell
				c: Campbell
				p: Campbell 5

1984:

F	L12–25	Paris	21 Jan	**p:** Campbell 4
W	L 9–18	Dublin	4 Feb	**p:** Campbell 3
E	L 9–12	Twickenham	18 Feb	**p:** Ward 3
S	L 9–32	Dublin	3 Mar	**t:** Kiernan
				c: J Murphy
				p: J Murphy
A	L 9–16	Dublin	10 Nov	**p:** Kiernan 3

1985:

S	W18–15	Edinburgh	2 Feb	**t:** Ringland 2
				c: Kiernan 2
				p: Kiernan
				dg: Kiernan
F	D15–15	Dublin	2 Mar	**p:** Kiernan 5
W	W21–9	Cardiff	16 Mar	**t:** Crossan, Ringland
				c: Kiernan 2
				p: Kiernan 3
E	W13–10	Dublin	30 Mar	**t:** Mullin
				p: Kiernan 2
				dg: Kiernan
J(1)[+]	W48–13	Osaka	26 May	**t:** Ringland 3, Matthews 2, Kiernan, MacNeill, C Fitzgerald
				c: Kiernan 5
				p: Kiernan 2
J(2)[+]	W33–15	Tokyo	2 Jun	**t:** Kiernan 2, Mullin, Anderson
				c: Kiernan 4
				p: Kiernan 3

Ireland centre Maurice Field gets his man in the Bloemfontein defeat of Japan.

Fj[+]	W16–15	Dublin	19 Oct	t: Bradley p: Kiernan 4

1986:

F	L 9–29	Paris	1 Feb	p: Kiernan 3
W	L12–19	dublin	15 Feb	t: Ringland c: Kiernan p: Kiernan 2
E	L20–25	Twickenham	1 Mar	t: Ringland, Mullin, McCall c: Kiernan p: Kiernan 2
S	L 9–10	Dublin	15 Mar	t: Ringland c: Kiernan p: Kiernan
R	W60–0	Dublin	1 Nov	t: Crossan 3, Mullin 2, Dean 2, Anderson, Bradley, MacNeill c: Kiernan 7 p: Kiernan 2

1987:

E	W17–0	Dublin	7 Feb	t: Kiernan, Matthews, Crossan c: Kiernan p: Kiernan
S	L12–26	Edinburgh	21 Feb	t: Lenihan c: Kiernan p: Kiernan dg: Kiernan
F	L13–19	Dublin	21 Mar	t: Ringland, Bradley c: Kiernan p: Kiernan
W(a)	W15–11	Cardiff	4 Apr	t: Dean, Mullin c: Kiernan 2 p: Kiernan
W(b)*	L 6–13	Wellington	25 May	p: Kiernan 2
C*	W46–19	Dunedin	30 May	t: Bradley, Crossan 2, Spillane, Ringland, MacNeill c: Kiernan 5 p: Kiernan 2 dg: Kiernan, Ward
T*	W32–9	Brisbane	3 Jun	t: MacNeill 2, Mullin 3 c: Ward 3 p: Ward 2
A*	L15–33	Sydney	7 Jun	t: MacNeill, Kiernan c: Kiernan 2 p: Kiernan

1988:

S	W22–18	Dublin	16 Jan	t: Mullin, MacNeill, Bradley c: Kiernan 2 p: Kiernan dg: Kiernan

41

F	L6–25	Paris	20 Feb	p: Kiernan 2
W	L9–12	Dublin	5 Mar	t: Kingston
				c: Kiernan
				p: Kiernan
E(a)	L 3–35	Twickenham	19 Mar	dg: Kiernan
E(b)^	L 10–21	Dublin	23 Apr	t: S Smith, MacNeill
				c: Kiernan
WS	W49–22	Dublin	29 Oct	t: Crossan 2, Kiernan, Matthews, Mullin, Francis, McBride, Sexton
				c: Kiernan 4
				p: Kiernan 2
				dg: Sexton
It	W31–15	Dublin	31 Dec	t: Crossan 2, Matthews 2, Aherne
				c: Cunningham
				p: Danaher 2
				dg: Dean

1989:

F	L21–26	Dublin	21 Jan	t: Mullin
				c: Kiernan
				p: Kiernan 5
W	W19–13	Cardiff	4 Feb	t: Mannion, Dean
				c: Kiernan
				p: Kiernan 3
E	L 3–16	Dublin	18 Feb	p: Kiernan
S	L21–37	Dublin	4 Mar	t: Mullin 2, Dunlea
				c: Kiernan 3
				p: Kiernan
C[+]	W24–21	Victoria	2 Sep	t: Dunlea, Sexton
				c: Kiernan 2
				p: Kiernan 4
US[+]	W32–7	New York	9 Sep	t: Dunlea, Mannion, Crossan, Bradley
				c: Kiernan 2
				p: Kiernan 3
				dg: B Smith
NZ	L 6–23	Dublin	18 Nov	p: B Smith 2

1990:

E	L 0–23	Twickenham	20 Jan	
S	L10–13	Edinburgh	3 Feb	t: J Fitzgerald
				p: Kiernan 2
F	L12–31	Paris	3 Mar	p: Kiernan 4
W	W14–8	Dublin	24 Mar	t: S Smith, McBride, Kingston
				c: Kiernan
Arg	W20–18	Dublin	27 Oct	t: Hooks, Kiernan
				p: Kiernan 4

1991:

F	L13–21	Dublin	2 Feb	t: S Smith
				p: Kiernan 3
W	D21–21	Cardiff	18 Feb	t: Clarke, Mullin, Geoghegan, Staples

				c: B Smith
				p: B Smith
E	L 7–16	Dublin	2 Mar	**t:** Geoghegan
				p: B Smith
S	L25–28	Edinburgh	16 Mar	**t:** Crossan, Robinson, Geoghegan, Mullin
				c: B Smith 3
				dg: B Smith
Na(1)	L 6–15	Windhoek	20 Jul	**t:** penalty try
				c: Mullin
Na(2)	L15–26	Windhoek	27 Jul	**t:** Staples, Cunningham
				c: Staples 2
				dg: Curtis
Z*	W55–11	Dublin	6 Oct	**t:** Robinson 4, Geoghegan, Popplewell 2, Curtis
				c: Keyes 4
				p: Keyes 5
J*	W32–16	Dublin	9 Oct	**t:** O'Hara, Mannion 2, Staples
				c: Keyes 2
				p: Keyes 4
S(b)*	L15–24	Edinburgh	12 Oct	**p:** Keyes 4
				dg: Keyes
A*	L18–19	Dublin	20 Oct	**t:** Hamilton
				c: Keyes
				p: Keyes 3
				dg: Keyes
1992:				
W	L 15–16	Dublin	18 Jan	**t:** Wallace
				c: Keyes
				p: Keyes 3
E	L 9–38	Twickenham	1 Feb	**t:** Keyes
				c: Keyes
				p: Keyes
S	L10–18	Dublin	15 Feb	**t:** Wallace
				p: Keyes 2
F	L12–44	Paris	21 Mar	**p:** McAleese 4
NZ(1)	L21–24	Dunedin	30 May	**t:** Cunningham 2, Staples
				c: Russell 3
				p: Russell
NZ(2)	L 6–59	Wellington	6 Jun	**t:** Furlong
				c: Russell
A†	L17–42	Dublin	31 Oct	**t:** Wallace
				p: Russell 4
1993:				
S	L 3–15	Edinburgh	16 Jan	**p:** Malone
F	L 6–21	Dublin	20 Feb	**p:** Malone 2
W	W19–14	Cardiff	6 Mar	**t:** Robinson
				c: Elwood
				p: Elwood 3
				dg: C Clarke

E	W17–3	Dublin	20 Mar	t: Galwey
				p: Elwood 2
				dg: Elwood 2
R	W25–3	Dublin	14 Nov	t: Geoghegan
				c: Elwood
				p: Elwood 6

1994

F	L15–35	Paris	15 Jan	p: Elwood 5
W	L15–17	Dublin	5 Feb	p: Elwood 5
E	W13–12	Twickenham	19 Feb	t: Geoghegan
				c: Elwood
				p: Elwood 2
S	D 6–6	Edinburgh	5 Mar	p: Elwood 2
A(1)	L13–31	Brisbane	5 Jun	t: Johns
				c: Elwood
				p: Elwood, O'Shea
A(2)	L18–32	Sydney	11 Jun	t: Francis, Clohessy
				c: O'Shea
				p: O'Shea
				dg: O'Shea
US	W26–15	Dublin	5 Nov	t: Geoghegan, Bradley
				c: McGowan 2
				p: McGowan 3, O'Shea

1995

E	L 8–20	Dublin	21 Jan	t: Foley
				p: Burke
S	L13–26	Edinburgh	4 Feb	t: Mullin, Bell
				p: Burke
F(a)	L 7–25	Dublin	4 Mar	t: Geoghegan
				c: Elwood
W(a)	W16–12	Cardiff	18 Mar	t: Mullin
				c: Burke
				p: Burke 2
				dg: Burke
It	L12–22	Treviso	8 May	p: Burke 4
NZ*	L19–43	Johannesburg	27 May	t: Halpin, McBride, Corkery
				c: Elwood 2
J*	W50–28	Bloemfontein	31 May	t: Halvey, Francis, Corkery, Hogan, Geoghegan, penalty tries 2
				c: Burke 6
				p: Burke
W(b)*	W24–23	Johannesburg	4 Jun	t: Popplewell, McBride, Halvey
				c: Elwood 3
				p: Elwood
F(b)*	L12–36	Durban	10 Jun	p: Elwood 4

* World Cup
\+ Non-cap
† Five-point try introduced from this game onwards
^ Non-championship

SCOTLAND

Gavin Hastings
(with Alex Spink)

THE French connection held the key to Scotland's fortunes in 1994/95 and if ever a season could be summed up by two matches then this was it. The incredible joy of winning in Paris for the first time in 26 years was matched only by the despair felt when losing in injury-time to France at the World Cup.

The first result confirmed Scotland's recuperation after a year or so on the sick bed of international rugby. It gave the squad and the whole nation such a shot of confidence, which manifested itself by our feat in going on to contest a Grand Slam decider with England at Twickenham the following month.

Despite losing that contest to our Auld Enemy, self-belief was still rushing through our veins by the time we came across the French again in South Africa. We had destroyed Cote d'Ivoire and Tonga and had our sights firmly fixed on a place in the semi-finals. To be leading 19–15 four minutes into injury time and then be beaten remains to this day hard to accept.

I still can't really believe how we contrived to lose that match. We were all over France for the vast majority of the game. Everything was just going so well. It was just right for us to win. Yet in the last seconds France stole it away from us with Emile NTamack's desperately late try. It was a terribly disappointing moment for all of us involved, not least as, for all our best efforts it effectively cost us a place in the last four.

Had we won we would have qualified as Pool D winners for a quarter-final tie against Ireland whom we had beaten convincingly during the Five Nations Championship months earlier. By losing our fate was a match-up against the New Zealand All Blacks. A different kettle of fish altogether.

But heck we shouldn't complain, bearing in mind the parlous state of the Scottish game at the turn of the year. Nine internationals had come and gone, and we had not won any of them. Our latest Test, against South Africa, to mark the official opening of the new-look Murrayfield, had ended in a comprehensive 34–10 defeat.

Our preparation had gone well but on the day we flattered to deceive. At times during the second half the game was really going against us. We gave the Springboks too many soft tries and they really exploited our generosity, with Joost van der Westhuizen especially ruthless.

> 'Never before had Scotland won in the Parc des Princes, so to go there with the young side that we did and triumph 23–21 was a wonderful achievement. The win gave Scottish rugby it's biggest boost since the Grand Slam in 1990, without a doubt'

But I told the guys not to get down on themselves. You have to remember that we went through the season without Gary Armstrong, Andy Reed, Andy Nicol and Alan Sharp; all key members of our squad. I don't think any side can afford to lose three or four key players and not suffer.

From that very disappointing match we made ten changes for the visit of Canada. It was awfully cold but the guys were very patient in the way they played. It was well into the second half before we broke the game open with Damian Cronin's try and, with me kicking my penalties, we at last had a victory (22–6) to celebrate.

It was a mighty relief because there was quite a bit of pressure on the Scottish side, although to my mind it came from the media. But I was always confident we would find our way out of the forest provided we didn't lose sight of what we were doing. I came in for some stick personally, but I felt I had only one poor game, against South Africa.

So I didn't harbour any worries about my form or indeed my fitness. If people wanted to write me off then that was up to them. It only made me more determined to prove the critics wrong.

But I wouldn't give the Press the credit for motivating me because I didn't think I needed their help. I was always gearing myself up for the Five Nations and the World Cup and with the benefit of years of experience I felt I was doing the right thing.

By spending our blank Five Nations weekend entertaining Canada we ensured we were warmed up and raring to get stuck into our first championship opponents, Ireland (won 26–13). That said, a wee bit too much indiscipline in the first half gave the Irish a great chance to take control. Fortunately, Paul Burke was wayward in his goalkicking whereas I got a few over. Ultimately, I think we showed a ruthless streak and ran out worthy winners.

What happened next will live forever in my memory. Never before had Scotland won in the Parc des Princes, so to go there with the young side that we did and triumph 23–21 was a wonderful achievement. The win gave Scottish rugby it's biggest boost since the Grand Slam in 1990, without a doubt.

> *'My last-minute try against France was Boy's Own stuff and has to go down as the most memorable moment of my career. For the conversion to then win the game was just fantastic. We started the game as boys and finished it as men'*

I don't know what it was about that weekend but I went over there with enormous confidence. It was my 13th game as Scottish captain. It was also Scotland's 13th attempt to win a match in Paris. Yet I honestly believe that had we converted our chances, as we did in that particular game, we'd have won on any of my previous visits to Paris.

My last-minute try was Boy's Own stuff and has to go down as the most memorable moment of my career. For the conversion to then win the game was just fantastic. It's amazing how much you can grow in confidence and stature in a period of 80 minutes. We started the game as boys and finished it as men.

It helped that we were away from home, on our own so to speak. The surroundings were conducive to preparing ourselves mentally as much as physically and the French maybe underestimated us a little bit.

But it's funny how things change, isn't it? One moment we were Wooden Spoon certainties, the next Grand Slam likely lads. But that's sport. You win a golf tournament and suddenly you're the best golfer. That's what's so compelling about sport.

The following game against Wales (won 26–13) was the hardest we had all season. As far as I was concerned, if we hadn't performed at Murrayfield that day we would have undone all our good work. Wales had nothing to lose. They'd lost to France and England so they weren't going to win the championship. But they hadn't won in Edinburgh for a long time so there was always the chance they might end their drought, as we had in Paris.

They took the lead very early, but maybe that worked in our favour. Save for that early lapse in concentration, we basically carried on from where we had left off in Paris. And some of our tries were very special, especially the one by Eric Peters.

And so to Twickenham for the Grand Slam showdown. I told the boys to go down and enjoy it. They'd earned the right to be there. And there was certainly no disgrace in the way we performed. I felt confident we could really cause England some problems. Everyone was talking about 1990 but I didn't see it that way at all because there were so few players from either side that had been involved five years earlier.

I was almost more glad the game was at Twickenham than Murrayfield because in Edinburgh the hype and pressure would have been so much greater on Scotland. England's feet were far more on the ground this time, no question about that. In fact, England's feet have been on the ground for the last two or three years. Games they might have lost in the past they've not been losing in recent times.

'Brian Moore's after-match comments were disgraceful and totally out of order. I don't know why people interview him … or rather I do. Brian Moore is not the captain of the side. He was obviously upset with the way Scotland played but what did he expect us to do – lie down and die?'

I don't think we played that badly and in many respects I don't think we'd have had to play a lot better to have beaten Will Carling's side. But we gave away too many penalties and didn't convert the opportunities that came our way, as we had done in Paris.

Brian Moore's after-match comments, basically accusing of us of killing the game as a spectacle, were disgraceful and totally out of order. I don't know why people interview him ... or rather I do. Brian Moore is not the captain of the side and it struck me that the captain, Will Carling, and Rob Andrew took a far more sensible view of the game. Brian was obviously upset with the way that Scotland played but what did he expect us to do – lie down and die?

Of course by the World Cup we had weightier matters on our mind. It was difficult to start against Cote d'Ivoire and I thought at the time 89–0 was a huge score, especially for a world competition. We played extremely well at Rustenburg. It was an extremely disciplined performance and we were really quite ruthless. To have that score simply demolished by the All Blacks (145–17 versus Japan) put everything into perspective. I don't think scores like that are good for the World Cup.

Next up were Tonga and what a bruising challenge they gave us. I said at the time it was not a dirty game although I am sometimes distanced from events at fullback. I don't see the close-quarter action stuff. But I'm also quite a diplomat at times. We'd won the game fair and square and to me there were more important things to worry about than commenting on the physical nature of the game. We didn't suffer any serious injuries so I didn't feel justified in commenting. I still don't really have much comment to make. That's the way that they play. These people like to show their physical strengths.

There then followed *that* game against France, with NTamack's cruel late try and Thierry Lacroix's faultless goalkicking. But I would love to go back to the moment I kicked a penalty to extend our lead to 19–12. At that point I thought we'd won the game. But then we gave away a penalty, which Lacroix kicked for 19–15 and after that I thought 'we'll have to do some defending'.

Maybe we sat back a wee bit and waited for France to come to us instead of really continuing to play the way we'd played to get into what I considered a winning position. But that's just the way it is. I don't think France looked like scoring until they did. If you are not under any enormous amount of pressure you just do what you feel is best. You could argue we kicked a bit more than we needed to but *c'est la vie*.

So we were set on a collision course with New Zealand (lost 30–48) and I was delighted with the way we played in the last 15–20 minutes. I wasn't so delighted with the way we played in the first five minutes after half-time and, sadly, that was when the game went away from us. You can't afford to give away soft tries to the All Blacks and we handed them two on a plate.

But that's typical of All Black rugby. Coping with the pressure and then getting upfield and forcing mistakes in the opposition. I was not overly upset about our performance, it was just one or two areas that let us down. The dejection was in thinking of what might have been had we beaten France.

Gregor Townsend walks tall during Scotland's defeat of Ireland at Murrayfield.

SCOTLAND (P12 W8 D0 L4 F410 A209):

(H)	v South Africa	(Edinburgh, 19.11.94)	lost	10–34
(H)	v Canada	(Edinburgh, 21.1.95)	won	22–6
(H)	v Ireland	(Edinburgh, 4.2.95)	won	26–13
(A)	v France	(Paris, 18.2.95)	won	23–21
(H)	v Wales	(Edinburgh, 4.3.95)	won	26–13
(A)	v England	(Twickenham, 18.3.95)	lost	12–24
(H)	v Romania	(Edinburgh, 22.4.95)	won	49–16
(A)	v Spain+	(Madrid, 6.5.95)	won	62–7
(–)	v Cote d'Ivoire*	(Rustenburg, 26.5.95)	won	89–0
(–)	v Tonga*	(Pretoria, 30.5.95)	won	41–5
(–)	v France*	(Pretoria, 3.6.95)	lost	19–22
(–)	v New Zealand*	(q/f: Pretoria, 11.6.95)	lost	30–48

* World Cup; + non-cap

Springboks in Scotland (Scottish tour record: P4 W3 D0 L1 F119 A41):

(–)	v Combined Scottish Districts	(Glasgow, 12.11.94)	won	33–6
(–)	v Scottish Select	(Aberdeen, 15.11.94)	won	35–10

SCOTLAND A (P2 W1 D0 L1 F39 A35):

(H)	v South Africa	(Melrose, 9.11.94)	lost	15–17
(H)	v Ireland	(Edinburgh, 3.2.95)	won	24–18

SCOTLAND U-21 (P2 W1 D0 L1 F37 A33):

(H)	v Ireland	(Edinburgh, 3.2.95)	lost	22–24
(H)	v Wales	(Inverleith, 3.3.95)	won	15–9

SCOTLAND UNIVERSITIES (P1 W1 D0 L0 F23 A14):

(H)	v Wales	(Edinburgh, 3.3.95)	won	23–14

SCOTLAND U-19 (P3 W0 D0 L3 F32 A83):

(H)	v England	(Stirling, 1.4.95)	lost	13–32
(H)	v Ireland	(Ayr, 8.4.95)	lost	11–15
(A)	v Wales	(Llanelli, 29.4.95)	lost	8–36

SCOTLAND U-18 (P5 W1 D0 L4 F87 A109):

(A)	v France	(Flers, 17.12.94)	lost	13–25
(H)	v Australia	(Edinburgh, 31.12.94)	lost	17–18
(H)	v Wales	(Edinburgh, 7.1.95)	won	20–18
(A)	v England	(Twickenham, 25.3.95)	lost	14–19
(A)	v Ireland	(Balgray, 8.4.95)	lost	23–29

SCOTLAND SCHOOLS (P1 W0 D0 L1 F16 A29):

(A)	v Wales	(Llanelli, 29.4.95)	lost	16–29

SCOTLAND U-16 (P1 W0 D0 L1 F18 A46):

(A)	v England	(Wolverhampton, 9.4.95)	lost	46–18

McEWAN'S INTER DISTRICT CHAMPIONSHIP

	P	W	D	L	F	A	Pts
Scottish Exiles	4	4	0	0	119	51	8
Edinburgh	4	1	2	1	62	62	4
North & Midlands	4	1	1	2	69	84	3
South	4	1	1	2	61	81	3
Glasgow	4	1	0	3	62	95	2

SCOTLAND/IRELAND DISTRICT/PROVINCE MATCHES

22.10.94: South 20, Ulster 19; Glasgow 19, Leinster 19; Connacht 26, North & Midlands 28; Munster 16, Edinburgh 13. 29.10.94: Leinster 3, South 28; Ulster 18, Glasgow 8; North & Midlands 9, Munster 19; Edinburgh 28, Connacht 22.

McEWAN'S CLUB CHAMPIONSHIP

Division One:	P	W	D	L	F	A	Pts
Stirling County	13	11	1	1	234	162	23
Watsonians	13	9	0	4	296	212	18
Edinburgh Academicals	13	7	2	4	214	141	16
Hawick	13	7	2	4	215	199	16
Boroughmuir	13	7	1	5	325	226	15
Heriot's FP	13	7	1	5	199	195	15
Gala	13	7	1	5	226	245	15
Melrose	13	7	0	6	308	261	14
Glasgow High/Kelvinside	13	6	1	6	228	183	13
Jed-Forest	13	6	0	7	221	256	12
West of Scotland	13	5	0	8	166	233	10
Dundee HSFP	13	3	1	9	200	264	7
Currie	13	3	0	10	188	280	6
Stewart's-Melville FP	13	1	0	12	158	321	2

champions: Stirling County; **relegated:** Stewart's-Melville FP, Currie, Dundee HSFP, West of Scotland, Jed-Forest, GHK.

Division Two:	P	W	D	L	F	A	Pts
Kelso	13	11	0	2	318	159	22
Selkirk	13	10	2	1	336	184	22
Kirkcaldy	13	8	1	4	271	230	17
Bigger	13	7	2	4	180	173	16
Preston Lodge FP	13	7	1	5	269	214	15
Glasgow Academicals	13	7	0	6	199	239	14
Peebles	13	7	0	6	175	204	14
Musselburgh	13	6	1	6	203	196	13
Grangemouth	13	6	0	7	223	246	12
Corstorphine	13	5	1	7	180	212	11
Edinburgh Wanderers	13	5	0	8	210	261	10
Wigtownshire	13	3	0	10	173	265	6
Gordonians	13	3	0	10	145	300	6
Haddington	13	2	0	11	178	277	4

promoted (to new Div 2): Kelso (champions), Selkirk; **relegated (to new Div 4):** Haddington, Gordonians, Wigtownshire, Edinburgh Wanderers.

Three more points for captain Gavin Hastings.

1980:

I	L 15–22	Dublin	2 Feb	**t:** Johnston 2 **c:** Irvine 2 **p:** Irvine
F	W 22–14	Edinburgh	16 Feb	**t:** Rutherford, Irvine 2 **c:** Irvine, Renwick **p:** Irvine 2
W	L 6–17	Cardiff	1 Mar	**t:** Renwick **c:** Irvine
E	L 18–30	Edinburgh	15 Mar	**t:** Tomes, Rutherford **c:** Irvine 2 **p:** Irvine 2

1981:

F	L 9–16	Paris	17 Jan	**t:** Rutherford **c:** Renwick **p:** Irvine
W	W 15–6	Edinburgh	7 Feb	**t:** Tomes, penalty try **c:** Renwick 2 **p:** Renwick
E	L 17–23	Twickenham	21 Feb	**t:** Monro 2, J Calder **c:** Irvine **p:** Irvine
I	W 10–9	Edinburgh	21 Mar	**t:** Hay **p:** Irvine **dg:** Rutherford
NZ(1)	L 4–11	Dunedin	13 June	**t:** Deans
NZ(2)	L 15–40	Auckland	20 Jun	**t:** Hay **c:** Irvine **p:** Irvine 2 **dg:** Renwick
R	W 12–6	Edinburgh	26 Sep	**p:** Irvine 4
A	W 24–15	Edinburgh	19 Dec	**t:** Renwick **c:** Irvine **p:** Irvine 5 **dg:** Rutherford

1982:

E	D 9–9	Edinburgh	16 Jan	**p:** Irvine 2 **dg:** Rutherford
I	L 12–21	Dublin	20 Feb	**t:** Rutherford **c:** Irvine **p:** Renwick 2
F	W 16–7	Edinburgh	6 Mar	**t:** Rutherford **p:** Irvine 3 **dg:** Renwick
W	W 34–18	Cardiff	20 Mar	**t:** J Calder, Renwick, Pollock, White, Johnston **c:** Irvine 4 **dg:** Renwick, Rutherford

A(1)	W12–7	Brisbane	3 Jul	t: Robertson
				c: Irvine
				p: Irvine
				dg: Rutherford
A(2)	L 9–33	Sydney	10 Jul	p: Irvine 3
Fj+	W32–12	Edinburgh	25 Sep	t: Dods 2, Johnston, F Calder, Beattie
				c: Dods 3
				p: Dods
				dg: Rutherford

1983:

I	L13–15	Edinburgh	15 Jan	t: Laidlaw
				p: Dods 2
				dg: Renwick
F	L15–19	Paris	5 Feb	t: Robertson
				c: Dods
				p: Dods
				dg: Gossman 2
W	L15–19	Edinburgh	19 Feb	t: Renwick
				c: Dods
				p: Dods 3
E	W22–12	Twickenham	5 Mar	t: Laidlaw, Smith
				c: Dods
				p: Dods 3
				dg: Robertson
NZ	D25–25	Edinburgh	12 Nov	t: Pollock
				p: Dods 5
				dg: Rutherford 2

1984:

W	W15–9	Cardiff	21 Jan	t: Paxton, Aitken
				c: Dods 2
				p: Dods
E	W18–6	Edinburgh	4 Feb	t: Johnston, Kennedy
				c: Dods 2
				p: Dods 2
I	W32–9	Dublin	3 Mar	t: Laidlaw 2, penalty try, Robertson, Dods
				c: Dods 3
				p: Dods 2
F	W21–12	Edinburgh	17 Feb	t: J Calder
				c: Dods
				p: Dods 5
R	L22–28	Bucharest	12 May	t: Leslie, Dods
				c: Dods
				p: Dods 3
				dg: Robertson
A	L12–27	Edinburgh	8 Dec	p: Dods 4

1985:

| I | L15–18 | Edinburgh | 2 Feb | p: Dods 4 |
| | | | | dg: Robertson |

F	L 3–11	Paris	16 Feb	**p:** Dods
W	L21–25	Edinburgh	2 Mar	**t:** Paxton 2
				c: Dods 2
				p: Dods
				dg: Rutherford 2
E	L 7–10	Twickenham	16 Mar	**t:** Robertson
				p: Dods

1986:

F	W18–17	Edinburgh	17 Jan	**p:** G Hastings 6
W	L15–22	Cardiff	1 Feb	**t:** Duncan, Jeffrey, G Hastings
				p: G Hastings
E	W33–6	Edinburgh	15 Feb	**t:** Duncan, Rutherford, S Hastings
				c: G Hastings 3
				p: G Hastings 5
I	W10–9	Dublin	12 Mar	**t:** Laidlaw
				p: G Hastings 2
R	W33–18	Bucharest	30 Mar	**t:** Jeffrey, S Hastings, Deans
				c: G Hastings 3
				p: G Hastings 5

1987:

I	W16–12	Edinburgh	21 Feb	**t:** Laidlaw, Tukalo
				c: G Hastings
				dg: Rutherford 2
F(a)	L22–28	Paris	7 Mar	**t:** Beattie, S Hastings
				c: G Hastings
				p: G Hastings 4
W	W21–14	Edinburgh	21 Mar	**t:** Beattie, Jeffrey
				c: G Hastings 2
				p: G Hastings 2
				dg: Rutherford
E	L12–21	Twickenham	4 Apr	**t:** Robertson
				c: G Hastings
				p: G Hastings 2
Sp[+]	W25–7	Edinburgh	19 Apr	**t:** Duncan, Tukalo, Deans, Paxton
				c: G Hastings 3
				p: G Hastings
F(b)*	D20–20	Christchurch	23 May	**t:** White, Duncan
				p: G Hastings 4
Z*	W60–21	Wellington	30 May	**t:** Tait 2, Duncan 2, Tukalo 2, Paxton 2, Oliver, G Hastings, Jeffrey
				c: G Hastings 8
R*	W55–28	Dunedin	2 Jun	**t:** G Hastings 2, Tukalo, Duncan Tait 2, Jeffrey 3
				c: G Hastings 8
				p: G Hastings
NZ*	L 3–30	Christchurch	6 Jun	**p:** G Hastings

1988:

I	L18–22	Dublin	16 Jan	**t:** Laidlaw, S Hastings
				c: G Hastings 2
				p: G Hastings 2

56

F	W23–12	Edinburgh	6 Feb	**t:** G Hastings, Tukalo
				p: G Hastings 4
				dg: Cramb
W	L20–25	Cardiff	20 Feb	**t:** F Calder, Duncan
				p: G Hastings 4
E	L 6–9	Edinburgh	5 Mar	**p:** G Hastings 2
A	L13–32	Edinburgh	19 Nov	**t:** G Hastings, Robertson
				c: G Hastings
				p: G Hastings

1989:

W	W23–7	Edinburgh	21 Jan	**t:** Armstrong, White, Chalmers
				c: Dods
				p: Dods 2
				dg: Chalmers
E	D12–12	Twickenham	4 Feb	**t:** Jeffrey
				c: Dods
				p: Dods 2
I	W37–21	Edinurgh	4 Mar	**t:** Tukalo 3, Jeffrey, Cronin
				c: Dods 4
				p: Dods 3
F	L 3–19	Paris	19 Mar	**p:** Dods
Fj	W38–17	Edinburgh	28 Oct	**t:** Stanger 2, K Milne, Gray, G Hastings, Tukalo
				c: G Hastings 4
				p: G Hastings 2
R	W32–0	Edinburgh	9 Dec	**t:** Stanger 3, White, Sole
				c: G Hastings 3
				p: G Hastings 2

1990:

I	W13–10	Dublin	3 Feb	**t:** White 2
				c: Chalmers
				p: Chalmers
F	W21–0	Edinburgh	17 Feb	**t:** F Calder, Tukalo
				c: Chalmers 2
				p: Chalmers 2, G Hastings
W	W13–9	Cardiff	3 Mar	**t:** Cronin
				p: Chalmers 3
E	W13–7	Edinburgh	17 Mar	**t:** Stanger
				p: Chalmers 3
NZ(1)	L16–31	Dunedin	16 Jun	**t:** Lineen, Gray, Sole
				c: G Hastings 2
NZ(2)	L18–21	Auckland	23 Jun	**t:** Stanger, Moore
				c: G Hastings 2
				p: G Hastings 2
Arg	W49–3	Edinburgh	10 Nov	**t:** Stanger 2, K Milne 2, Moore, Armstrong, Gray, G Hastings, Chalmers
				c: G Hastings 5
				p: G Hastings

1991:

F	L 9–15	Paris	19 Jan	**p:** Chalmers 2
				dg: Chalmers
W	W32–12	Edinburgh	2 Feb	**t:** Chalmers, White 2, Armstrong
				c: Chalmers, G Hastings
				p: Chalmers, G Hastings 2
				dg: Chalmers
E(a)	L12–21	Twickenham	16 Feb	**p:** Chalmers 4
I(a)	W28–25	Edinburgh	16 Mar	**t:** G Hastings, Stanger, S Hastings
				c: Chalmers 2
				p: Chalmers 3, G Hastings
R	L12–18	Bucharest	31 Aug	**t:** Tukalo
				c: Dods
				p: Dods 2
J*	W47–9	Edinburgh	5 Oct	**t:** S Hastings, Stanger, Chalmers, penalty try, White, Tukalo, G Hastings
				c: G Hastings 5
				p: Chalmers, G Hastings 2
Z*	W51–12	Edinburgh	9 Oct	**t:** Tukalo 3, Turnbull, Stanger, S Hastings, Weir, White
				c: Dods 5
				p: Dods 2
				dg: Wyllie
I(b)*	W24–15	Edinburgh	12 Oct	**t:** Shiel, Armstrong
				c: G Hastings 2
				p: G Hastings 3
				dg: Chalmers
WS*	W28–6	Edinburgh	19 Oct	**t:** Jeffrey 2, Stanger
				c: G Hastings 2
				p: G Hastings 4
E(b)*	L 6–9	Edinburgh	26 Oct	**p:** G Hastings 2
NZ*	L 6–13	Cardiff	30 Oct	**p:** G Hastings 2

1992:

E	L 7–25	Edinburgh	18 Jan	**t:** White
				p: G Hastings
I	W18–10	Dublin	15 Feb	**t:** Stanger, Nicol
				c: G Hastings 2
				p: G Hastings 2
F	W10–6	Edinburgh	7 Mar	**t:** Edwards
				p: G Hastings 2
W	L12–15	Cardiff	21 Mar	**p:** G Hastings, Chalmers 2
				dg: Chalmers
A(1)	L12–27	Sydney	13 Jun	**t:** Wainwright
				c: G Hastings
				p: G Hastings 2
A(2)	L13–37	Brisbane	21 Jun	**t:** Lineen, Sole
				c: Chalmers
				p: Chalmers

1993:

I†	W15–3	Edinburgh	16 Jan	t: Stark, Stanger
				c: G Hastings
				p: G Hastings
F	L 3–11	Paris	6 Feb	p: G Hastings
W	W20–0	Edinburgh	20 Feb	t: Turnbull
				p: G Hastings 5
E	L12–26	Twickenham	6 Mar	p: G Hastings 3
				dg: Chalmers
NZ	L15–51	Edinburgh	20 Nov	p: G Hastings 4, Chalmers

1994

W	L 6–29	Cardiff	15 Jan	p: G Hastings 2
E	L14–15	Edinburgh	5 Feb	t: Wainwright
				p: G Hastings 2
				dg: Townsend
I	D 6–6	Dublin	5 Mar	p: G Hastings 2
F	L12–20	Edinburgh	19 Mar	p: G Hastings 4
Arg(1)	L15–16	Buenos Aires	4 Jun	p: M Dods 5
Arg(2)	L17–19	Buenos Aires	11 Jun	t: Logan
				p: Shiel 2, M Dods
				dg: Townsend
SA	L10–34	Edinburgh	19 Nov	t: Stanger
				c: G Hastings
				p: G Hastings

1995

C	W22–6	Edinburgh	21 Jan	t: Cronin
				c: G Hastings
				p: G Hastings 5
I	W26–13	Edinburgh	4 Feb	t: Joiner, Cronin
				c: G Hastings 2
				p: G Hastings 4
F(a)	W23–21	Paris	18 Feb	t: Townsend, G Hastings
				c: G Hastings 2
				p: G Hastings 3
W	W26–13	Edinburgh	4 Mar	t: Peters, Hilton
				c: G Hastings 2
				p: G Hastings 4
E	L12–24	Twickenham	18 Mar	p: G Hastings 4
R	W49–16	Murrayfield	22 Apr	t: Stanger 2, G Hastings, Shiel, Logan, Joiner, Peters
				c: G Hastings 4
				p: G Hastings 2
Sp+	W62–7	Madrid	6 May	t: Joiner 3, Wainwright 2, G Hastings 2, Logan, Chalmers, Morrison
				c: G Hastings 6
IC*	W89–0	Rustenburg	26 May	t: G Hastings 4, Walton 2, Logan 2, Stanger, Chalmers, Shiel, Burnell, Wright
				c: G Hastings 9
				p: G Hastings 2

T*	W41–5	Pretoria	30 May	t: G Hastings, Peters, S Hastings
				c: G Hastings
				p: G Hastings 8
F(b)*	L19–22	Pretoria	3 Jun	t: Wainwright
				c: G Hastings
				p: G Hastings 4
NZ*	L30–48	Pretoria	11 Jun	t: Weir 2, S Hastings
				c: G Hastings 3
				p: G Hastings 3

* World Cup
+ Non-cap
† Five-point try introduced from this game onwards

Scott Hastings splits the English cover at Twickenham.

WALES

*Clockwise from top left: Ieuan Evans, Gareth Llewellyn,
Mike Hall and Jonathan Humphreys, four players who have
captained Wales during 1994/95*

(by Robert Cole)

WELSH rugby used to be famous for its daring and its cunning. Now
it is renowned for tearing itself to shreds.

The events in the build-up to the 1995 World Cup epitomised the
disease that is endemic to the national sport of Wales. If in doubt,
throw someone out.

Two years earlier it had been the secretary of the Welsh Rugby
Union, Denis Evans, who had been cut from the heart of Welsh rugby,
with his chief aide, the commercial executive Jonathan Price, hounded
out shortly after.

In 1995, the scapegoats for a lack of success became the national managament team, Robert Norster, Alan Davies and Gareth Jenkins. Although the three men who had delivered a first victory over France in 12 years and the Five Nations trophy a year earlier, not to mention clinching the top qualifying slot for South Africa from the European World Cup zone, they were hung out to dry by the Union's general committee.

They were brought before the 32 wise men of Welsh rugby accused of letting standards slip due to five successive defeats – South Africa and a second Five Nations whitewash of the nineties. No-one was more dismayed than the trio who had worked so hard on dragging Welsh rugby out of the international mire since the disasters of the 1991 World Cup, yet it was their contention they were offered little or no support.

They put that to the test by saying that unless they had the full backing of the general committee they would tender their resignations. The silence was deafening in their defence and they departed, with little or no thanks, on 27 March 1995.

'The more I look back at what went on the happier I am that we tended our resignations,' said Davies. 'We told the committee we wouldn't stay unless they backed us and they didn't.'

'Had we tried to play a more political game, and sucked up more to the Union members, perhaps we would have had a better chance of survival. It was as though some people wanted to see us undermined'– former Wales coach Alan Davies

'It was more or less the same following the game against the Springboks last year. After that game we presented an action plan to the National Player Development Committee that would have taken us through to the World Cup.

'We were asking for their support on a number of major points and calling on them to back the team. We could see problems emerging and identified them, yet the NPDC did little or nothing until just prior to the final Five Nations game against Ireland.

'By then it was too late – we all felt disappointed and let down. Had we tried to play a more political game, and sucked up more to the Union members, perhaps we would have had a better chance of survival.

'For the first two years of our four-year tenure things seemed to be moving in the right direction. Then came the change in the general committee and Denis Evans and Jonathan Price left the scene.

'For the last two years it seemed to be a constant battle against the WRU, rather than a joint effort between us all. It was as though some people wanted to see us undermined.

'I honestly think that had we been given the level of support we asked for that we could have gone on to the 1999 World Cup and done a much better job. There are lots of thoughts, and regrets, about what might have been,' said Davies.

'My main concern for the man who comes in and takes over as national coach, whether as a paid official or not, is that he won't have the system in place that is needed to enable him to make a success of the job.

'The same could be true of the new director of national squads. There is a lot of work that needs to be done, but those people in charge must be allowed to use their expertise to effect the necessary change.

'We don't seem to be any further down the road than we were when I took over just prior to the 1991 World Cup. Unless the system in which national coaches have to operate is changed drastically, and everyone supports them rather than works against them, it will just stay the same '– Davies

'I still feel that had we been backed properly after the defeat by Ireland in the Five Nations series that we could have regrouped and got the Welsh team into the quarter-finals at the World Cup.

'I watched all the games involving Wales in South Africa and the players looked very, very tired by the time the Irish match came around. They never realled looked like winning it.

'The worrying thing is that we don't seem to be any further down the road than we were when Rob and I took over just prior to the 1991 World Cup. And unless the system in which national coaches have to operate is changed drastically, and everyone begins to support them rather than work against them, it will just stay the same.'

The man most likely to require that support is Australian-born Alex Evans. He started the year as Cardiff RFC's paid coaching organiser and ended it by serving both club and country with a second appointment as caretaker Wales coach.

And he is favourite to fill a proposed new role of overseeing all the five national squads from under-18 to full international levels. Wales are clearly contemplating putting virtually all their eggs in one Aussie basket. But Evans, after the high of guiding Cardiff to a first Heineken League crown, saw just how deep the national problems were when he took Wales to the World Cup in South Africa.

He had barely six weeks to try and turn things around and get things to be done his way but, in the end, it all ended in another humiliation on the world stage as Wales flew home early in the company of Cote d'Ivoire, Japan, Tonga, Italy, Argentina, Romania and Canada while the big guns stayed on to contest the prizes.

It was 1991 revisited, with Ireland replacing Western Samoa as the ones to prove a hurdle too high for the once feared Welsh. The fall from grace has gone into freefall, with few signs of it being halted, let alone reversed.

> '*Wales now have four years to sort out the sorry mess they have sunk ever deeper into before they host the 1999 World Cup finals. Their recent track record may not inspire any great confidence but, surely, things cannot get any worse. Or can they?*'

The chaos off the field was matched by that on it, epitomised by Wales naming an unprecedented four captains during the course of the year. Any captain's log would have to have been a strictly joint affair. Neath lock Gareth Llewellyn led Wales against France in January and then handed the reins back to a fit-again Ieuan Evans for the rest of the Five Nations.

Llanelli wing Evans was then demoted when the old management team jumped before they were pushed, with new coach Evans opting for his Cardiff skipper Mike Hall to take Wales to the World Cup.

Hall lasted just three games before quitting international rugby in the acrimonious fallout from the tournament flop, with Cardiff hooker Jonathan Humphreys then installed as the new captain for the return trip to South Africa.

While Humphreys' rise was meteoric, Llewellyn's fall was equally dramatic: from captain in January to surplus to requirements by July

... that just about summed up Welsh rugby perfectly. The chopping and changing was not confined to the management and captains. Players also came and went with alarming alacrity.

A staggering 34 players were used in the ten internationals during the season so it hardly came as any great surprise that there was a marked lack of consistency and continuity. The uncertainty was underlined by 11 players making their debuts during those turbulent times: Derwyn Jones, Mark Taylor, Matthew Back, Greg Prosser, Spencer John, Andrew Gibbs, Gareth Thomas, Andrew Moore, Stuart Roy, Mark Bennett and Humphreys.

But however many changes Wales made, things simply got progressively worse as the players suffered a crisis of confidence and retreated into their shells.

World Cup ranking match victories over Romania (16–9) in Bucharest and Italy (29–19) in Cardiff proved to be merely the calm before the storm. Wales showed plenty of guts against South Africa at the Arms Park, tackling their hearts out, but still went down 12–20 and were unable to manage a try.

That set the tone for a championship whitewash, a try from scrum-half Robert Jones against Scotland all they could manage with the ball in hand as they otherwise relied exclusively on the boot of Neil Jenkins.

And the home defeat at the hands of the Irish in the Wooden Spoon decider was the last thing Wales needed before heading for the Republic and, though Japan proved no physical match for Wales up front when they clashed in Bloemfontein, the 57–10 win only served to paper over the cracks.

The cracks became chasms as New Zealand won 34–9, with plenty to spare, before the Irish provided the coup de grace, final humiliation and tickets for that early flight home.

Wales now have four years to sort out the sorry mess they have sunk ever deeper into before they host the 1999 World Cup finals. Their recent track record may not inspire any great confidence but, surely, things cannot get any worse. Or can they?

WALES (P10 W3 D0 L7 F189 A199):

(A)	v Romania**	(Bucharest, 17.9.94)	won	16–9
(H)	v Italy**	(Cardiff, 12.10.94)	won	29–19
(H)	v South Africa	(Cardiff, 26.11.94)	lost	12–20
(A)	v France	(Paris, 21.1.95)	lost	9–21
(H)	v England	(Cardiff, 18.2.95)	lost	9–23
(A)	v Scotland	(Edinburgh, 4.3.95)	lost	13–26
(H)	v Ireland	(Cardiff, 18.3.95)	lost	12–16
(–)	v Japan*	(Bloemfontein, 27.5.95)	won	57–10
(–)	v New Zealand*	(Johannesburg, 31.5.95)	lost	9–34
(–)	v Ireland*	(Johannesburg, 4.6.95)	lost	23–24

* World Cup; ** World Cup qualifiers

WALES A (P3 W2 D0 L1 F64 A59):

(H)	v South Africa	(Newport, 26.10.94)	lost	13–25
(A)	v France	(Paris, 26.1.95)	won	21–15
(H)	v Ireland	(Pontypridd, 17.3.95)	won	30–19

WALES U-21 (P5 W3 D0 L2 F125 A102):

(H)	v Romania	(Bridgend, 25.11.94)	won	20–8
(A)	v Scotland	(Inverleith, 3.3.95)	lost	9–15
(H)	v Ireland	(Glamorgan Wanderers, 17.3.95)	won	16–9
(A)	v Netherlands	(Hilversum, 9.5.95)	won	63–0
(A)	v France	(Rouen, 13.5.95)	lost	17–70

WALES STUDENTS (P6 W3 D0 L3 F124 A102):

(A)	v France	(Le Creusot, 20.1.95)	won	18–9
(H)	v England	(Swansea, 17.2.95)	lost	10–27
(–)	FIRA Student Tournament	(Bucharest, 9–14.4.95):		
	v France		lost	10–31
	v Romania		lost	15–22
	v Portugal		won	28–3
	v Russia		won	43–10

WALES UNIVERSITIES (P3 W2 D0 L1 F60 A33):

(H)	v England	(Newport, 17.2.95)	won	32–7
(A)	v Scotland	(Edinburgh, 3.3.95)	won	23–14
(H)	v Ireland	(Llanwern, 17.3.95)	lost	5–12

WALES DISTRICTS (P5 W4 D0 L1 F161 A23):

(H)	v Denmark	(Maesteg, 17.3.95)	lost	3–6
(A)	Tour of Sri Lanka	(April 1995):		
	v Western Provinces		won	27–11
	v Central Provinces		won	47–0
	v Sri Lanka (1)		won	43–3
	v Sri Lanka (2)		won	41–3

WALES SENIOR SCHOOLS (P7 W4 D0 L3 F113 A124):

(A)	v Australia	(Brisbane, 24.8.94)	won	19–12

(A)	v Scotland	(Edinburgh, 7.1.95)	lost	18–20
(H)	v New Zealand	(Cardiff, 14.1.95)	lost	6–42
(A)	v France	(Viry-Chatillon, 25.2.95)	won	15–3
(H)	v Japan	(Aberavon, 15.3.95)	won	21–18
(H)	v England	(Llanelli, 29.3.95)	lost	6–9
(H)	v Ireland	(Dunvant, 21.4.95)	won	28–20

Wales Senior Schools to Australia (tour record: P7 W7 D0 L0 F275 A61):

(A)	v Western Australia	(Perth, 3.8.94)	won	49–6
(A)	v ACT Schools	(Canberra, 6.8.94)	lost	27–29
(A)	v NSW Schools	(Sydney, 10.8.94)	won	55–3
(A)	v NSW Country Schools	(Coonambie, 13.8.94)	won	32–0
(A)	v NSW Indp. Schools	(Sydney, 17.8.94)	won	40–6
(A)	v Queensland Schools	(Sunshine Coast, 20.8.94)	won	53–5

WALES YOUTH (P4 W4 D0 L0 F117 A27):

(A)	v Italy	(Naples, 25.2.95)	won	33–7
(H)	v France	(Cardiff, 12.3.95)	won	26–0
(A)	v England	(Twickenham, 26.3.95)	won	22–12
(H)	v Scotland	(Llanelli, 29.4.95)	won	36–8

WALES U-18 (P4 W3 D0 L1 F66 A68):

(H)	v New Zealand	(Swansea, 8.1.95)	lost	3–29
(H)	v Japan	(Neath, 19.3.95)	won	17–11
(A)	v Ireland	(Limerick, 2.4.95)	won	17–12
(H)	v Scotland	(Llanelli, 29.4.95)	won	29–16

WALES U-16 (P3 W2 D0 L1 F49 A35):

(A)	v Portugal	(Lisbon, 9.4.95)	won	32–9
(H)	v England	(Pontypridd, 22.4.95)	won	10–3
(H)	v England A	(Maesteg, 21.4.95)	lost	7–23

DOMESTIC RUGBY

HEINEKEN CLUB CHAMPIONSHIP

Division One:	P	W	D	L	F	A	Pts
Cardiff	22	18	0	4	672	269	36
Pontypridd	22	17	0	5	555	255	34
Treorchy	22	13	0	9	479	312	26
Neath	22	12	2	8	379	398	26
Bridgend	22	12	1	9	518	451	25
Swansea	22	12	0	10	475	400	24
Llanelli	22	10	0	12	459	409	20
Newport	22	9	0	13	366	433	18
Newbridge	22	8	0	14	302	452	16
Abertillery	22	8	0	14	349	604	16
Dunvant	22	7	1	14	333	542	15
Pontypool	22	4	0	18	293	655	8

champions: Cardiff; **relegated:** Pontypool, Dunvant.

Division One:	P	W	D	L	F	A	Pts
Aberavon	22	17	0	5	506	263	34
Ebbw Vale	22	16	1	5	447	283	33
Abercynon	22	16	1	5	368	260	33
South Wales Police	22	12	2	8	413	357	26
Bonymaen	22	11	1	10	370	312	23
Maesteg	22	10	1	11	365	388	21
Tenby United	22	10	0	12	290	374	20
Llandovery	22	9	0	13	313	363	18
Llanharan	22	9	0	13	316	319	18
Cross Keys	22	8	0	14	292	438	16
Narbeth	22	6	2	14	299	446	14
Penarth	22	4	0	18	289	477	8

promoted: Aberavon (champions), Ebbw Vale; **relegated:** Penarth, Narbeth.

Div 3 – promoted: Ystradgynlais (c), Caerphilly; **relegated:** Pontypool United, Aberavon Quins.
Div 4 – promoted: Cardiff Institute (c), Pyle; **relegated:** Kidwelly, Oakdale.
Div 5 – promoted: Rumney (c), Merthyr; **relegated:** Wrexham, Pwllheli, Cardigan.

SWALEC CUP FINAL:
Swansea 17, Pontypridd 12 (Cardiff, 6.5.95)

Swansea: A Clement (capt); A Harris, R Boobyer, D Weatherley, Simon Davies; A Williams, R Jones; C Loader, G Jenkins, K Colclough, P Arnold, A Moore, A Reynolds, R Appleyard, Stuart Davies.
Scorers – Tries: Appleyard, Stuart Davies. *Conversions:* Williams 2. *Penalty goal:* Williams.

Pontypridd: C Cormack; D Manley, J Lewis, S Lewis, O Robins (G Jones 7); N Jenkins, P John; N Bezani (capt), P John, A Metcalfe, G Prosser, N Rowley, M Lloyd (M Spiller 69), R Collins, D McIntosh.
Scorers – Tries: Manley 2. *Conversion:* Jenkins (missed 4 of 4 penalty attempts).

Referee: C Thomas.

Heineken Division One Dream Team: A Clement (Swansea); I Evans (Llanelli), G Thomas (Bridgend), J Lewis (Pontypridd), S Ford (Cardiff); N Jenkins, P John; N Benzani (all Pontypridd), J Humphreys (Cardiff), J Davies, G Llewellyn (both Neath), D Jones (Cardiff), A Gibbs (Newbridge), R Collins (Pontypridd), O Williams (Cardiff).

1980:

F	W18–9	Cardiff	19 Jan	**t:** E Rees, Holmes, D S Richards, G Price
				c: G Davies
E	L 8–9	Twickenham	16 Feb	**t:** E Rees, Squire
S	W17–6	Cardiff	1 Mar	**t:** Holmes, Keen, D S Richards
				c: Blyth
				p: Fenwick
I	L 7–21	Dublin	15 Mar	**t:** Blyth
				p: Fenwick
NZ	L 3–23	Cardiff	1 Nov	**p:** Fenwick

1981:

E	W21–19	Cardiff	17 Jan	**t:** G Davies
				c: Fenwick
				p: Fenwick 4
				dg: G Davies
S	L 6–15	Edinburgh	7 Feb	**dg:** Fenwick 2
I	W 9–8	Cardiff	21 Feb	**p:** G Evans 2
				dg: Pearce
F	L15–19	Paris	7 Mar	**t:** D S Richards
				c: G Evans
				p: G Evans 3
A	W18–13	Cardiff	5 Dec	**t:** R Moriarty
				c: G Evans
				p: G Evans 3
				dg: G Davies

1982:

I	L12–20	Dublin	23 Jan	**t:** Holmes
				c: G Evans
				p: G Evans
				dg: Pearce
F	W22–12	Cardiff	6 Feb	**t:** Holmes
				p: G Evans 6
E	L 7–17	Twickenham	6 Mar	**t:** JR Lewis
				dg: G Davies
S	L18–34	Cardiff	20 Mar	**t:** Butler
				c: G Evans
				p: G Evans 4

1983.

E	D13–13	Cardiff	5 Feb	**t:** Squire
				p: Wyatt 2
				dg: Dacey
S	W19–15	Edinburgh	19 Feb	**t:** S Jones, E Rees
				c: Wyatt
				p: Wyatt 3
I	W23–9	Cardiff	5 Mar	**t:** Wyatt, Holmes, E Rees
				c: Wyatt
				p: Wyatt 3

F	L 9–16	Paris	19 Mar	**t:** Squire **c:** Wyatt **p:** G Evans
J[+]	W29–24	Cardiff	22 Oct	**t:** Hadley, Brown, Dacey, Bowen, Giles **c:** Wyatt 3 **p:** Wyatt
R	L 6–24	Bucharest	12 Nov	**p:** G Evans 2

1984:

S	L 9–15	Cardiff	21 Jan	**t:** Titley **c:** H Davies **p:** H Davies
I	W18–9	Dublin	4 Feb	**t:** Ackerman **c:** H Davies **p:** H Davies 2, Bowen 2
F	L16–21	Cardiff	18 Feb	**t:** H Davies, Butler **c:** H Davies **p:** H Davies 2
E	W24–15	Twickenham	17 Mar	**t:** Hadley **c:** H Davies **p:** H Davies 4 **dg:** Dacey 2
A	L 9–28	Cardiff	24 Nov	**t:** Bishop **c:** Wyatt **p:** Wyatt

1985:

S	W25–21	Edinburgh	2 Mar	**t:** Pickering 2 **c:** Wyatt **p:** Wyatt 4 **dg:** G Davies
I	L 9–21	Cardiff	16 Mar	**t:** P Lewis **c:** G Davies **p:** G Davies
F	L 3–14	Paris	30 Mar	**p:** Thorburn
E	W24–15	Cardiff	20 Apr	**t:** J Davies, Roberts **c:** Thorburn 2 **p:** Thorburn 3 **dg:** J Davies
Fj	W40–3	Cardiff	9 Nov	**t:** P Davies 2, Titley, Holmes, Hadley, James, Pickering **c:** Thorburn 3 **p:** Thorburn 2

1986:

E	L18–21	Twickenham	17 Jan	**t:** Bowen **c:** Thorburn **p:** Thorburn 3 **dg:** J Davies
S	W22–15	Cardiff	1 Feb	**t:** Hadley **p:** Thorburn 5 **dg:** J Davies

I	W19–12	Dublin	15 Feb	**t:** P Lewis, P Davies
				c: Thorburn
				p: Thorburn 3
F	L15–23	Cardiff	1 Mar	**p:** Thorburn 5
Fj	W22–15	Suva	31 May	**t:** J Davies, Bowen
				c: Bowen
				p: Dacey 3
				dg: J Davies
T	W15–7	Nuku'alofa	12 Jun	**t:** P Moriarty
				c: Dacey
				p: Bowen 2, Dacey
WS	W32–14	Apia	14 Jun	**t:** Titley 2, Bowen, R Moriarty
				c: Dacey 2
				p: Dacey 3
				dg: J Davies

1987:

F	L 9–16	Paris	7 Feb	**p:** Thorburn 3
E	W19–12	Cardiff	7 Mar	**t:** S Evans
				p: Wyatt 5
S	L15–21	Edinburgh	21 Mar	**t:** M Jones
				c: Wyatt
				p: Wyatt 2
				dg: J Davies
I	L11–15	Cardiff	4 Apr	**t:** I Evans, Norster
				p: Wyatt
I(b)*	W13–6	Wellington	25 May	**t:** Ring
				p: Thorburn
				dg: J Davies 2
T*	W29–16	Palmerston North	29 May	**t:** Webbe 3, Hadley
				c: Thorburn 2
				p: Thorburn 2
				dg: J Davies
C*	W40–9	Brisbane	3 Jun	**t:** I Evans 4, Bowen, Hadley, Devereux, A Phillips
				c: Thorburn 4
E(b)*	W16–3	Brisbane	8 Jun	**t:** Roberts, Jones, Devereux
				c: Thorburn 2
NZ*	L 6–49	Brisbane	14 Jun	**t:** Devereux
				c: Thorburn
A*	W22–21	Rotorua	18 Jun	**t:** Roberts, P Moriarty, Hadley
				c: Thorburn 2
				p: Thorburn 2
US	W46–0	Cardiff	7 Nov	**t:** Bowen 2, Clement 2, Webbe, Young, P Moriarty, Norster
				c: Thorburn 4
				p: Thorburn 2

1988:

E	W11–3	Twickenham	6 Feb	**t:** Hadley 2
				dg: J Davies

S	W25–20	Cardiff	20 Feb	**t:** J Davies, I Evans, Watkins
				c: Thorburn 2
				p: Thorburn
				dg: J Davies 2
I	W12–9	Dublin	5 Mar	**t:** P Moriarty
				c: Thorburn
				p: Thorburn
				dg: J Davies
F	L 9–10	Cardiff	19 Mar	**t:** I Evans
				c: Thorburn
				p: Thorburn
NZ(1)	L 3–52	Christchurch	28 May	**p:** Ring
NZ(2)	L 9–54	Auckland	11 Jun	**t:** J Davies
				c: Ring
				p: Ring
WS	W24–6	Cardiff	12 Nov	**t:** N Davies 2, J Davies, C Davies
				c: Thorburn 4
R	L 9–15	Cardiff	10 Dec	**t:** Devereux
				c: Thorburn
				p: Thorburn

1989:

S	W23–7	Edinburgh	21 Jan	**t:** Hall
				p: Bowen

Neil Jenkins feeds Anthony Clement during Wales' 57–10 defeat of Japan in Bloemfontein during the World Cup.

I	L13–19	Cardiff	4 Feb	t: M Jones
				p: Thorburn 3
F	L12–31	Paris	18 Feb	p: Thorburn 4
E	W12–9	Cardiff	18 Mar	t: Hall
				c: Thorburn
				p: Thorburn 2
NZ	L 9–34	Cardiff	4 Nov	p: Thorburn 3

1990:

F	L19–29	Cardiff	20 Jan	t: Titley
				p: Thorburn 4
				dg: D Evans
E	L 6–34	Twickenham	17 Feb	t: P Davies
				c: Thorburn
S	L 9–13	Cardiff	3 Mar	t: Emyr
				c: Thorburn
				p: Thorburn
I	L 8–14	Dublin	24 Mar	t: Ford, G O Llewellyn
Na(1)	W18–9	Windhoek	2 Jun	t: Thorburn, Bridges
				c: Thorburn 2
				p: Thorburn 2
Na(2)	W34–30	Windhoek	9 Jun	t: Emyr 2, O Williams, penalty try
				c: Thorburn 3
				p: Thorburn 3
				dg: Clement
Ba	L24–31	Cardiff	6 Oct	t: Thorburn
				c: Thorburn
				p: Thorburn 5
				dg: D Evans

1991:

E	L 6–25	Cardiff	19 Jan	p: Thorburn, N Jenkins
S	L12–32	Edinburgh	2 Feb	t: Ford
				c: Thorburn
				p: Thorburn 2
I	D21–21	Cardiff	16 Feb	t: Arnold, N Jenkins
				c: Thorburn 2
				p: Thorburn 2
				dg: N Jenkins
F(a)	L 3–36	Paris	2 Mar	p: Thorburn
A(a)	L 6–63	Brisbane	21 Jul	p: Thorburn
				dg: A Davies
F(b)	L 9–22	Cardiff	4 Sep	t: Collins
				c: Ring
				p: Ring
WS*	L13–16	Cardiff	6 Oct	t: Emyr, I Evans
				c: Ring
				p: Ring
Arg*	W16–7	Cardiff	9 Oct	t: Arnold
				p: Ring 3, Rayer
A(b)*	L 3–38	Cardiff	12 Oct	p: Ring

1992:

I	W16–15	Dublin	18 Jan	**t:** S Davies
				p: N Jenkins 3
				dg: C Stephens
F	L 9–12	Cardiff	1 Feb	**p:** N Jenkins 3
E	L 0–24	Twickenham	7 Mar	
S	W15–12	Cardiff	21 Mar	**t:** Webster
				c: N Jenkins
				p: N Jenkins 3
It[+]	W43–12	Cardiff	7 Oct	**t:** Clement, I Evans, Gibbs, C Stephens, Webster, S Davies, Rayer
				c: C Stephens 4
A	L 6–23	Cardiff	21 Nov	**p:** C Stephens 2

1993:

E	W10–9	Cardiff	6 Feb	**t:** I Evans
				c: N Jenkins
				p: N Jenkins
S	L 0–20	Edinburgh	20 Feb	
I	L14–19	Cardiff	6 Mar	**t:** I Evans
				p: N Jenkins 3
F	L10–26	Paris	20 Mar	**t:** Walker
				c: N Jenkins
				p: N Jenkins
Z(1)	W35–14	Bulawayo	22 May	**t:** Moon, Hill, Proctor, P Davies
				c: N Jenkins 3
				p: N Jenkins 2
				dg: A Davies
Z(2)	W42–13	Harare	29 May	**t:** G O Llewellyn 2, Bidgood, J Davies, N Jenkins, S Davies
				c: N Jenkins 3
				p: N Jenkins 2
Na	W38–23	Windhoek	5 Jun	**t:** Lewis 2, Hill, Proctor, Moon
				c: N Jenkins 2
				p: N Jenkins 3
J	W55–5	Cardiff	16 Oct	**t:** I Evans 2, Gibbs 2, Moon, Clement, Lewis, Rayer, N Jenkins
				c: N Jenkins 5
C	L24–26	Cardiff	10 Nov	**p:** N Jenkins 8

1994

S	W29–6	Cardiff	15 Jan	**t:** Rayer 2, I Evans
				c: N Jenkins
				p: N Jenkins 4
I	W17–15	Dublin	5 Feb	**t:** N Jenkins
				p: N Jenkins 4
F	W24–15	Cardiff	19 Feb	**t:** Quinnell, Walker
				c: N Jenkins
				p: N Jenkins 4
E	L 8–15	Twickenham	19 Mar	**t:** Walker
				p: N Jenkins

74

P=	W102–11	Lisbon	18 May	t: Walker 4, I Evans 3, Hall 3, R Jones 2, Taylor, Quinnell, Llewelyn, penalty try
				c: N Jenkins 11
S=	W54–0	Madrid	21 May	t: Quinnell, I Evans 3, Walker, G Jenkins, penalty try
				c: N Jenkins 5
				p: N Jenkins 3
C	W33–15	Toronto	11 Jun	t: I Evans, Hall 2
				c: N Jenkins 3
				p: N Jenkins 4
Fj	W23–8	Suva	18 Jun	t: Rayer, Collins
				c: A Davies 2
				p: A Davies 3
T	W 18–9	Nuku'alofa	22 Jun	p: N Jenkins 6
WS	L 9–34	Apia	25 Jun	p: N Jenkins 3
R=	W16–9	Bucharest	17 Sep	t: I Evans
				c: N Jenkins
				p: N Jenkins 3
It=	W29–19	Cardiff	12 Oct	t: N Davies
				p: N Jenkins 7
				dg: N Jenkins
SA	L12–20	Cardiff	26 Nov	p: N Jenkins 4

1995

F	L 9–21	Paris	21 Jan	p: N Jenkins 3
E	L 9–23	Cardiff	18 Feb	p: N Jenkins 3
S	L13–26	Edinburgh	4 Mar	t: R Jones
				c: N Jenkins
				p: N Jenkins 2
I(a)	L12–16	Cardiff	18 Mar	p: N Jenkins 4
J*	W57–10	Bloemfontein	27 May	t: Thomas 3, I Evans 2, Griffiths, Moore
				c: N Jenkins 5
				p: N Jenkins 4
NZ*	L 9–34	Johannesburg	31 May	p: N Jenkins 2
				dg: N Jenkins
I(b)*	L23–24	Johannesburg	4 Jun	t: Humphreys, Taylor
				c: N Jenkins 2
				p: N Jenkins 2
				dg: A Davies

* World Cup
= World Cup qualifier
+ Non-cap
| Five-point try introduced from this game onwards

FRANCE

Philippe Saint-Andre
(with Chris Thau)

WHAT a way to lose. Ten centimetres between a place in the World Cup final and a dignified, but heartbreaking exit on a day when our dream was washed away in the Durban downpour.

Initially I thought Abdel Benazzi had scored to turn the semi-final decisively in our favour and break South African hearts. I was down on the ground and when he surged forward he tripped over my legs and grounded the ball near the line. From where I was I could not see the ball, but I realised from the body language of those surrounding him that actually he did not score. So near, yet so far. Surely, this must be the most significant tackle of my career.

At the time I was sizzling with frustration. It felt like we had been denied something we deserved and when I saw the Springboks running out onto Ellis Park for the final the following week I felt a lump in my throat. There is a difference between water polo and rugby. The weather had played havoc with our gameplan and deprived us of what we thought was our main weapon; running the ball and threatening their line.

But now I am more philosophical. We might argue that the deluge in Durban had affected us more than South Africa, but on a sunny and dry afternoon in the final New Zealand ran every ball at them without any real success. We might also claim that in similar circumstances we might have been able to vary our game a bit more than the All Blacks, but at the end of the day one has to give credit to the Springboks for their performance. They beat Australia, Romania, Canada, Western Samoa, France and New Zealand to become world champions, so they deserve it.

There was also a bit of divine justice in our loss to South Africa, perhaps, as we had won a lot of matches with last-minute tries. Serge Blanco's last-gasp try against Australia which won France a place in the 1987 final. Emile NTamack repeating the trick to see off Scotland (22–19) and give us a more favourable quarter-final tie against Ireland (35–12) in 1995. And of course Jean-Luc Sadourny's late, late try in Auckland (1994), the try from the end of the world, which beat the All Blacks (23–20) and made us the first northern hemisphere nation ever to win a series in New Zealand. Against South Africa we went to the well once too often.

But at least we knew that in defeat we had played well. Prior to the semi, we had produced our best form only in patches. That was, I think, because we had been slow in building up for the final stages. Many of the players were already exhausted by the time we reached South Africa after a demanding season. Resting the players became as significant as finding the optimum combinations. This was why after two games all 26 players had had a go.

Our build-up, though a bit slow, was nevertheless adequate. Physically we were in good shape. It was our concentration that let us down. Difficult to say but a great game against Scotland or Ireland would have helped us to peak against South Africa.

> *'French flair is based on an intense perfectionist streak at individual level. We are also Latins, which means that sometimes we need to find an event within the event in order to be able to motivate ourselves'*

It was a difficult campaign bearing in mind that in the two years prior to the World Cup we had rid France of the 'bad traveller' tag. We won the series in South Africa in 1993 and returned home with the scalp of the All Blacks in 1994. It had become obvious to us all that we play better on tour, when we train together for a long period of time.

Do not forget this is French rugby. We are coming from clubs which play different types of rugby. Coaching has been the cornerstone of

French rugby since time immemorial. I Don't know what the so-called French flair means. But whatever, most of it is based on an intense perfectionist streak at individual level. We are also Latins, which means that sometimes we need to find an event within the event in order to be able to motivate ourselves.

Early on in the tournament it was hard to really get going. We started off with matches against Tonga (won 38–10) and Cote d'Ivoire (won 54–18) and were staying in a hotel in the middle of nowhere, living and training like inmates of a penal colony. The decision to shave our heads reflected this aspect of our existence. I had the additional trauma of learning from a press cutting that our coach Pierre Berbizier wanted to replace me as captain.

It was obvious from the first game that we were not quite ready. Mind you, that should not detract from the quality of the Tongan challenge. In the early stages they played very well and we did not which, to an extent, was a trend noticeable throughout the competition. Irrespective of standards, the emerging nations would play very well for 30–40 minutes.

We lacked control even if we did improve the longer the game wore on. Mind you it is very difficult to exercise control against a side playing with such enthusiasm and lack of discipline. We only really bossed the contest once one of their forwards had been sent-off. A forgettable game perhaps, but a memorable milestone for Thierry Lacroix, who scored try number 1000 in the history of French rugby.

> 'Our World Cup hotel was in the middle of nowhere. We lived and trained like inmates of a penal colony and the decision to shave our heads reflected this aspect of our existence. I had the additional trauma of learning that Pierre Berbizier wanted to replace me as captain'

The problem was to motivate our players for the game against Cote d'Ivoire, annihilated 89–0 by Scotland in the opening game. Berbizier believed that the best way to maintain the edge was to create a competitive self-interest among the 26 players. So he made a lot of changes. It didn't work. I can't say who or what was responsible but we were even worse than against Tonga.

Many of the Ivorian players play in France in the second and third divisions and were very much on a learning curve in South Africa.

Theoretically, there should be a huge quality gap between them and us. But their enthusiasm and pride, combined with our greed, lack of respect for them and lack of concentration, made us look distinctly poor. The only positive aspect of the debacle was the fact we had secured our place in the last eight, which was our declared aim before the World Cup.

At the time I was a bit irritated by the criticism of the media, but with hindsight that was not too bad. In a way they helped us better focus on the tasks ahead. And of course Scotland, who had only months earlier beaten us in Paris (23–21) for the first time in 26 years, were a far bigger nut to crack. The Scottish forwards were superb early on and forced us to tackle desperately. Credit to our back row and virtually everybody else who kept them at bay.

It was a titanic, physical battle – witness the fractured arms suffered by Philippe Benetton and Guy Accoceberry – and our winning try by N'Tamack, four minutes into injury time, will live long in the memory of everyone concerned. It was another one of those tries, a la Francaise, manufactured out of thin air. But it was Lacroix, with a 100% goalkicking record, who secured us the win.

We failed again to fire on all cylinders in the quarter-final against Ireland. But at no stage did I really feel they could beat us. Maybe that was what was wrong with us. We never really believed that we needed to apply ourselves 100% in order to win the game and that showed. It was not pretty to watch, but we were efficient and composed.

It was very difficult to remotivate our players after the subsequent defeat in Durban, but having to play against England for third place helped. The history of the 1991 World Cup, when we were knocked out by the English in Paris, was still fresh in our minds, not to mention that England were the only team we had failed to beat during the previous four seasons.

I would have preferred to play them in the final but taking them on for the bronze medal was good enough. There were not many players in our team, other than perhaps Philippe Sella, Franck Mesnel, Marc Cecillon and myself, who knew what it was like to beat the English. It was not a great game, but who cares. We won and England didn't. We haven't been able to say that for a while.

FRANCE (P12 W9 D0 L3 F323 A181)

(H) v Canada	(Besancon, 17.12.94)	won	28–9
(H) v Wales	(Paris, 21.1.95)	won	21–9
(A) v England	(Twickenham, 4.2.95)	lost	10–31
(H) v Scotland	(Paris, 18.2.95)	lost	21–23
(A) v Ireland	(Dublin, 18.3.95)	won	25–7
(A) v Romania	(Bucharest, 7.4.95)	won	24–15
(–) v Tonga*	(Pretoria, 26.5.95)	won	38–10
(–) v Cote d'Ivoire*	(Rustenburg, 30.5.95)	won	54–18
(–) v Scotland*	(Pretoria, 3.6.95)	won	22–19
(–) v Ireland*	(q/f: Durban, 10.6.95)	won	36–12
(–) v South Africa*	(s/f: Durban, 17.6.95)	lost	15–19
(–) v England*	(3/4: Pretoria, 22.6.95)	won	19–9

* World Cup

France in New Zealand (tour record: P8 W6 L2 F253 A160):

(–) v Northland	(Whangarei, 9.6.94)	won	28–23
(–) v North Harbour	(Auckland, 12.6.94)	lost	23–27
(–) v Wairarapa Bush	(Masterton, 15.6.94)	won	53–9
(–) v New Zealand XV	(Wanganui, 18.6.94)	won	33–25
(–) v Nelson Bays	(Nelson, 22.6.94)	won	46–18
(–) v Hawke's Bay	(Napier, 29.6.94)	lost	25–30

FRANCE A (P W D L F A):

(H) v Wales A	(Paris, 26.1.95)	lost	15–21
(A) v England A	(Leicester, 3.2.95)	lost	9–29

FRANCE U-21 (P W D L F A):

(H) v Wales	(Rouen, 13.5.95)	won	70–17

FRANCE STUDENTS (P W D L F A):

(H) v England	(Paris)	lost	10–14
(A) v Ireland	(Longford, 3.3.95)	won	20–18

FRANCE JUNIORS (P W D L F A):

(A) v Wales Youth	(Cardiff, 12.3.95)	lost	0–26
(H) v England Colts	(La Teste, 22.4.95)	lost	10–25

FRANCE 18-GROUP (P W D L F A):

(H) v Scotland	(Fliers, 17.12.94)	won	25–13
(H) v Wales	(Viry-Chatillon, 25.2.95)	lost	3–15
(A) v England	(Cambridge, 198.4.95)	lost	6–22

FIRA CHAMPIONSHIP 1994

RESULTS: France 51, Romania 0 (Brive 17.10.93); Russia 19, Italy 30 (Moscow, 6.11.93); Italy 16, France 9 (Treviso, 11.11.93); France 49, Spain 3 (Sarlat, 20.3.94); Spain 9, Russia 16 (Madrid, 10.4.94); Spain 3, Romania 11 (Zaragoza, 24.4.94); Romania 30, Russia 0 (Bucharest, 7.5.94); Italy 62, Spain 15 (Parma, 7.5.94); Romania 26, Italy 12

(Bucharest, 14.5.94); Russia 9, France 11 (Moscow, 28.5.94).

	P	W	D	L	F	A	Pts
France	4	3	0	1	120	28	10
Italy	4	3	0	1	120	69	10
Romania	4	3	0	1	67	66	10
Russia	4	1	0	3	44	80	6
Spain	4	0	0	4	30	138	4

DOMESTIC RUGBY

Club Championship Final
Toulouse (6) 31 Castres (16) 16 (Parc des Princes, Paris)

Toulouse: S Ougier; E NTamack, P Carbonneau, T Castaignede, D Berty; C Deylaud, J Cazalbou; C Califano, P Soula, C Portolan, H Miorin, F Belot, D Lacroix, R Sonnes, A Cigagna.

 Scorers – Try: Ougier. *Conversion:* Deylaud. *Penalty goals:* Deylaud 7. *Dropped goal:* Deylaud.

Castres: C Savy; P Escalle, A Hyardet, J-M Aue, C Lucquiaud; F Rui, F Seguier; L Touissant, C Batut, T Lafforgue, G Jennard (Gaston 31), J-F Gourragne, J Diaz, G Pages, J-P Swiadek.

 Scorers – Try: Seguier. *Conversion:* Savy. *Penalty goals:* Savy 2. *Dropped goal:* Rui.

Referee: M Pascal.

French flanker Laurent Cabannes sizes up the opposition,
supported by Thierry Lacroix.

1980:

W	L 9–18	Cardiff	19 Jan	**t:** Marchal
				c: Caussade
				dg: Caussade
E	L13–17	Paris	2 Feb	**t:** Averous, Rives
				c: Caussade
				p: Caussade
S	L14–22	Edinburgh	16 Feb	**t:** Gallion, Gabernet
				p: Gabernet
				dg: Caussade
I	W19–18	Paris	1 Mar	**t:** Gourdon 2
				c: Aguirre
				p: Aguirre 2
				dg: Pedeutour
SA	L15–37	Pretoria	8 Nov	**t:** Dintrans
				c: Vivies
				p: Vivies 3
R	L 0–15	Bucharest	23 Nov	

1981:

S	W16–9	Paris	17 Jan	**t:** Blanco, Bertranne
				c: Caussade
				p: Vivies, Gabernet
I	W19–13	Dublin	7 Feb	**t:** Pardo
				p: Laporte 2, Gabernet
				dg: Laporte 2
W	W19–15	Paris	7 Mar	**t:** Gabernet
				p: Laporte 3, Gabernet 2
E	W16–12	Twickenham	21 Mar	**t:** Lacans, Pardo
				c: Laporte
				dg: Laporte 2
A(1)	L15–17	Brisbane	5 Jul	**t:** Mesny
				c: Gabernet
				p: Blanco, Gabernet
				dg: Vivies
A(2)	L14–24	Sydney	11 Jul	**t:** Lacas, Elissalde
				dg: Elissalde, Sallefranque
R	W17–9	Narbonne	1 Nov	**t:** Elissalde 2, Blanco
				p: Gabernet 2
				dg: Laporte
NZ(1)	L 9–13	Toulouse	14 Nov	**p:** Laporte 2
				dg: Gabernet
NZ(2)	L 6–18	Paris	21 Nov	**p:** Laporte, Blanco

1982:

W	L12–22	Cardiff	6 Feb	**t:** Blanco
				c: Sallefranque
				p: Sallefranque, Martinez
E	L15–27	Paris	20 Feb	**t:** Pardo

				c: Sallefranque
				p: Sallefranque 2
				dg: Lescarboura
S	L 7–16	Edinburgh	6 Mar	t: Rives
				p: Sallefranque
I	W22–9	Paris	20 Mar	t: Blanco, Mesny
				c: Gabernet
				p: Blanco 2, Gabernet 2
R	L 9–13	Bucharest	31 Oct	t: Fabre
				c: Camberabero
				dg: Camberabero
Arg(1)	W25–12	Toulouse	14 Nov	t: Sella 2, Esteve, Blanco
				p: Blanco, Camberabero
				dg: Camberabero
Arg(2)	W13–6	Paris	20 Nov	t: Begu, Blanco
				c: Camberabero
				p: Camberabero

1983:

E	W19–15	Twickenham	15 Jan	t: Esteve, Sella, Paparemborde
				c: Blanco 2
				p: Camberabero
S	W19–15	Paris	5 Feb	t: Esteve 2
				c: Blanco
				p: Blanco 3
I	L16–22	Dublin	19 Feb	t: Blanco, Esteve
				c: Blanco
				p: Blanco 2
W	W16–9	Paris	19 Mar	t: Esteve
				dg: Camberabero
				p: Blanco 3
A(1)	D15–15	Clermont-Ferrand	13 Nov	p: Lescarboura 3
				dg: Lescarboura, Lafond
A(2)	W15–6	Paris	20 Nov	t: Esteve
				c: Lescarboura
				p: Gabernet, Lescarboura 2

1984:

I	W25–12	Paris	21 Jan	t: Gallion, Sella
				c: Lescarboura
				p: Lescarboura 4
				dg: Lescarboura
W	W21–16	Cardiff	18 Feb	t: Sella
				c: Lescarboura
				p: Lescarboura 4
				dg: Lescarboura
E	W32–18	Paris	3 Mar	t: Cordorniou, Sella, Esteve, Bergu, Gallion
				c: Lescarboura 3
				p: Lescarboura
				dg: Lescarboura

S	L12–21	Edinburgh	17 Mar	t: Gallion
				c: Lescarboura
				p: Lescarboura
				dg: Lescarboura
NZ(1)	L 9–10	Christchurch	16 Jun	t: Blanco
				c: Lescarboura
				p: Lescarboura
NZ(2)	L18–31	Auckland	23 Jun	t: Lescarboura 2, Bonneval
				p: Lescarboura 2
R	W18–3	Bucharest	11 Nov	t: Sella, Lescarboura
				c: Lescarboura 2
				p: Lescarboura 2

1985:

E	D 9–9	Twickenham	2 Feb	dg: Lescarboura 3
S	W11–3	Paris	16 Feb	t: Blanco 2
				p: Lescarboura
I	D15–15	Dublin	2 Mar	t: Esteve, Codorniou
				c: Lescarboura 2
				p: Lescarboura
W	W14–3	Paris	30 Mar	t: Esteve, Gallion
				p: Lescarboura 2
Arg(1)	L16–24	Buenos Aires	22 Jun	t: Blanco, Bonneval
				c: Lescarboura
				p: Lescarboura 2
Arg(2)	W23–15	Buenos Aires	29 Jun	t: Codorniou, Erbani, Berbizier, Blanco
				c: Lescarboura 2
				p: Lescarboura
J(1)+	W50–0	Dax	19 Oct	t: Lafond 4, Fabre, Cassagne,
				Codorniou, Rodriguez, Detrez, dubroca
				c: Camberabero 5
J(2)+	W52–0	Nantes	26 Oct	t: Camberabero 2, Lafond 2, Charvet 2,
				Dintrans 2, Fabre, Rodriguez
				c: Camberabero 6

1986:

S	L17–18	Edinburgh	17 Jan	t: Berbizier, Sella
				p: Laporte 2
				dg: Laporte
I	W29–9	Paris	1 Feb	t: Berbizier, Marocco, Sella
				c: Laporte
				p: Laporte 3, Blanco
				dg: Lafond
W	W23–15	Cardiff	1 Mar	t: Sella, Lafond 2, Blanco
				c: Laporte 2
				dg: Laporte
E	W29–10	Paris	15 Mar	t: Sella, Blanco, penalty try, Laporte
				c: Laporte 2
				p: Laporte 3
R(a)	W25–13	Lille	12 Apr	t: Charvet, Bonneval, Sella, Erbani,
				Lagisquet

				c: Laporte
				p: Laporte
Arg(1)	L13–15	Buenos Aires	31 May	t: Bonneval
				p: Laporte 3
Arg(2)	W22–9	Buenos Aires	7 Jun	t: Lescarboura, Sella, Debroca
				c: Lescarboura 2
				p: Lescarboura 2
A	L14–27	Sydney	21 Jun	t: Blanco 2, Sella
				c: Lescarboura
NZ(a)	L 9–18	Christchurch	28 Jun	dg: Lescarboura 3
R(b)	W20–3	Bucharest	25 Oct	t: Andrieu, Blanco, Berot
				c: Berot
				p: Berot 2
NZ(b1)	L 7–19	Toulouse	8 Nov	t: Sella
				p: Berot
NZ(b2)	W16–3	Nantes	15 Nov	t: Charvet, Lorieux
				c: Berot
				p: Berot 2

1987:

W	W16–9	Paris	7 Feb	t: Mesnel, Bonneval
				c: Berot
				p: Berot 2
E	W19–15	Twickenham	21 Feb	t: Bonneval, Sella
				c: Berot
				p: Berot 2
				dg: Mesnel
S(a	W28–22	Paris	7 Mar	t: Bonneval 3, Berot
				p: Berot 3
				dg: Mesnel
I	W19–13	Dublin	21 Mar	t: Champ 2
				c: Berot
				p: Berot 3
S(b)*	D20–20	Christchurch	23 May	t: Sella, Berbizier, Blanco
				c: Blanco
				p: Blanco 2
R(a)*	W55–12	Wellington	28 May	t: Charvet 2, Lagisquet 2, Sella, Andrieu, Camberabero, Erbani, Laporte
				c: Laporte 8
				p: Laporte
Z*	W70–12	Auckland	2 Jun	t: Modin 3, Camberabero 3, Charvet 2, Dubroca, Rodriguez 2, Esteve, Laporte
				c: Camberabero 9
Fj*	W31–16	Auckland	7 Jun	t: Lorieux, Rodriguez 2, Lagisquet
				c: Laporte 3
				p: Laporte 2
				dg: Laporte
A*	W30–24	Sydney	13 Jun	t: Lorieux, Sella, Lagisquet, Blanco
				c: Camberabero 4
				p: Camberabero 2

NZ*	L 9–29	Auckland	20 Jun	**t:** Berbizier
				c: Camberabero
				p: Camberabero
S(c)+	L12–15	Galashiels	26 Sep	**t:** Mesnel
				c: Bianchi
				p: Bianchi 2
R(b)	W49–3	Agen	11 Nov	**t:** Berot, Lagisquet 2, Andrieu 2, Ondarts, penalty try
				c: Berot 6
				p: Berot 3

1988:

E	W10–9	Paris	16 Jan	**t:** Rodriguez
				p: Berot 2
S	L12–23	Edinburgh	6 Feb	**t:** Lagisquet
				c: Berot
				p: Berot
				dg: Lescarboura
I	W25–6	Paris	20 Feb	**t:** Blanco, Lagisquet, Sella, Camberabero, Carminati
				c: Camberabero
				dg: Berot
W	W10–9	Cardiff	19 Mar	**t:** Lescarboura
				p: Lafond 2
Arg(a1)	W18–15	Buenos Aires	18 Jun	**t:** Dintrans
				c: Berot
				p: Berot 4
Arg(a2)	L 6–18	Buenos Aires	25 Jun	**p:** Berot 2
Arg(b1)	W29–9	Nantes	5 Nov	**t:** Blanco 2, Cecillon, Lagisquet, Rodriguez
				c: Berot 3
				p: Berot
Arg(b2)	W28–18	Lille	11 Nov	**t:** Sanz, Cecillon, Andrieu, Sella
				c: Berot 3
				p: Berot 2
R	W16–12	Bucharest	26 Nov	**t:** Blanco, Lagisquet
				c: Berot
				p: Berot 2

1989:

I	W26–21	Dublin	21 Jan	**t:** Lagisquet 2, Blanco, Lafond
				c: Lafond 2
				p: Lafond 2
W	W31–12	Paris	18 Feb	**t:** Blanco 2, Berbizier, Dintrans
				c: Lafond 3
				p: Lafond 2
				dg: Mesnel
E	L 0–11	Twickenham	4 Mar	
S	W19–3	Paris	19 Mar	**t:** Berbizier, Blanco, Lagisquet
				c: Berot 2
				p: Berot

USSR[+]	W18–16	Valence	20 May	t: Roumat
				c: Lafond
				p: Lafond 3, Camberabero
NZ(1)	L17–25	Christchurch	17 Jun	t: Blanco 2, Cecillon
				c: Berot
				p: Berot
NZ(2)	L20–34	Auckland	1 Jul	t: Rouge-Thomas, Cecillon
				p: Blanco 4
BL	L27–29	Paris	4 Oct	t: Blanco, Benetton, Camberabero
				c: Camberabero 3
				p: Camberabero 3
A(1)	L15–32	Strasbourg	4 Nov	p: Camberabero 4
				dg: Camberabero
A(2)	W25–19	Lille	11 Nov	t: Lagisquet, Andrieu
				c: Lacroix
				p: Lacroix 5

1990:

W	W29–19	Cardiff	20 Jan	t: Lafond, Sella, Camberabero,
				Lagisquet, Rodriguez
				c: Camberabero 3
				p: Camberabero
E	L 7–26	Paris	3 Feb	t: Lagisquet
				p: Charvet
S	L 0–21	Edinburgh	17 Feb	
I	W31–12	Paris	3 Mar	t: Mesnel 2, Lagisquet
				c: Camberabero 2
				p: Camberabero 5
R	L 6–12	Auch	24 May	p: Lescarboura 2
A(1)	L 9–21	Sydney	9 Jun	p: Camberabero 3
A(2)	L31–48	Brisbane	24 Jun	t: Blanco 2, Armary, Lacombe
				c: Camberabero 3
				p: Camberabero 3
A(3)	W28–19	Sydney	30 Jun	t: Camberabero, Mesnel
				c: Camberabero
				p: Camberabero 2, Blanco
				dg: Camberabero 3
NZ(1)	L 3–24	Nantes	3 Nov	p: Camberabero
NZ(2)	L12–30	Paris	10 Nov	p: Camberabero 3
				dg: Camberabero

1991:

S	W15–9	Paris	19 Jan	p: Camberabero 2
				dg: Blanco, Camberabero 2
I	W21–13	Dublin	2 Feb	t: Lagisquet, Cabannes
				c: Camberabero 2
				p: Camberabero 3
W(a)	W36–3	Paris	2 Mar	t: Blanco, Saint-Andre, Mesnel,
				Roumat, Sella, Lafond
				c: Blanco, Camberabero 2
				p: Camberabero 2

87

E	L19–21	Twickenham	16 Mar	t: Saint-Andre, Camberabero, Mesnel c: Camberabero 2 p: Camberabero
R(a)	W33–21	Bucharest	22 Jun	t: Blanco, Camberabero, Cecillon, Simon c: Camberabero p: Camberabero 5
US(1)	W41–9	Denver	13 Jul	t: Blanco 2, Lafond, Saint-Andre, Champ, Courtiols, Cecillon, Mesnel c: Camberabero 3 p: Camberabero
US(2)	W10–3	Colorado Springs	20 Jul	t: Mesnel, Blanco c: Camberabero
W(b)	W22–9	Cardiff	4 Sep	t: Blanco, Camberabero, Saint-Andre c: Camberabero 2 p: Camberabero 2
R(b)*	W30–3	Beziers	4 Oct	t: penalty try, Saint-Andre, Roumat, Lafond c: Camberabero p: Camberabero 4
Fj*	W33–9	Grenoble	8 Oct	t: Lafond 3, Sella 2, Camberabero c: Camberabero 3 p: Camberabero
C*	W19–13	Agen	13 Oct	t: Lafond, Saint-Andre c: Camberabero p: Camberabero, Lacroix 2
E*	L10–19	Paris	19 Oct	t: Lafond p: Lacroix 2

1992:

W	W12–9	Cardiff	1 Feb	t: Saint-Andre c: Lafond p: Viars dg: Penaud
E	L13–31	Paris	15 Feb	t: Viars, Penaud c: Viars p: Viars
S	L 6–10	Edinburgh	7 Mar	p: Lafond 2
I	W44–12	Paris	21 Mar	t: Penaud 2, Viars 2, Cecillon, Cabannes, Sadourny c: Viars 5 p: Viars 2
R	W25–6	Le Havre	28 May	t: Saint-Andre, Cadieu, Galthie, penalty try c: Viars, Lacroix 2 p: Viars
Arg(a1)†	W27–12	Buenos Aires	4 Jul	t: Deylaud, Viars c: Deylaud p: Viars 4 dg: Penaud
Arg(a2)	W33–9	Buenos Aires	11 Jul	t: Saint-Andre, Viars, Hueber

				c: Viars 3
				p: Viars 3
				dg: Hueber
SA(1)	L15–20	Lyon	17 Oct	t: Penaud 2
				c: Viars
				p: Viars
SA(2)	W29–16	Paris	24 Oct	t: Penaud, Roumat
				c: Lacroix 2
				p: Lacroix 5
Arg(b)	L20–24	Nantes	14 Nov	t: Gonzalez, Galthie, Sella
				c: Viars
				p: Viars

1993:

E	L15–16	Twickenham	16 Jan	t: Saint-Andre 2
				c: Camberabero
				p: Camberabero
S	W11–3	Paris	6 Feb	t: Lacroix
				p: Camberabero 2
I	W21–6	Dublin	20 Feb	t: Saint-Andre, Sella
				c: Camberabero
				p: Camberabero 2
				dg: Camberabero

Abdel Benazzi heads for glory at Lansdowne Road.

W	W26–10	Paris	20 Mar	t: Benetton 2, Lafond
				c: Lafond
				p: Lacroix 3
R(a)	W37–20	Bucharest	20 May	t: Bernat-Salles 3, Cecillon
				c: Viars 4
				p: Viars 3
SA(1)	D20–20	Durban	26 Jun	t: Saint-Andre
				p: Lacroix 5
SA(2)	W18–17	Johannesburg	3 Jul	p: Lacroix 4
				dg: Lacroix, Penaud
R(b)	W51–0	Brive	9 Oct	t: Bernat-Salles 3, Sella, Loppy, Merle
				c: Lacroix 6
				p: Lacroix 3
A(1)	W16–3	Bordeaux	30 Oct	t: Hueber
				c: Lacroix
				p: Lacroix
				dg: Penaud, Sadourny
A(2)	L 3–24	Paris	6 Nov	p: Lacroix

1994

I	W35–15	Paris	15 Jan	t: Benetton, Saint-Andre, Lacroix, Merle
				c: Lacroix 3
				p: Lacroix 3
W	L15–24	Cardiff	19 Feb	t: Roumat, Sella
				c: Lacroix
				p: Lacroix
E	L14–18	Paris	5 Mar	t: Benazzi
				p: Lacroix 3
S	W20–12	Edinburgh	19 Mar	t: Sadourny, Saint-Andre
				c: Lacroix, Montlaur
				p: Lacroix 2
C(a)	L16–18	Ottawa	5 Jun	t: NTamack
				c: Lacroix
				p: Lacroix 3
NZ(1)	W22–8	Christchurch	26 Jun	t: Benetton
				c: Lacroix
				p: Lacroix 2
				dg: Deylaud 2
NZ(2)	W23–20	Auckland	3 Jul	t: NTamack, Sadourny
				c: Lacroix, Deylaud
				p: Lacroix 2, Deylaud
C(b)	W28–9	Besancon	17 Dec	t: Sadourny, Sella, Benetton
				c: Lacroix 2
				p: Lacroix 2
				dg: Delaigue

1995

W	W21–9	Paris	21 Jan	t: NTamack, Saint-Andre
				c: Lacroix
				p: Lacroix 3

E(a)	L10–31	Twickenham	4 Feb	**t:** Viars **c:** Lacroix **p:** Lacroix
S(a)	L21–23	Paris	18 Feb	**t:** Saint-Andre 2, Sadourny **p:** Lacroix **dg:** Deylaud
I(a)	W25–7	Dublin	4 Mar	**t:** Delaigue, Cecillon, NTamack, Saint-Andre **c:** NTamack **p:** NTamack
R	W24–15	Bucharest	7 Apr	**t:** Sadourny, penalty try **c:** Lacroix **p:** Lacroix 4
T*	W38–10	Pretoria	26 May	**t:** Lacroix 2, Saint-Andre, Hueber **c:** Lacroix 3 **p:** Lacroix 3 **dg:** Delaigue
IC*	W54–18	Rustenburg	30 May	**t:** Lacroix 2, Saint-Andre, Accoceberry, Benazzi, Techoueyres, Costes, Viars **c:** Lacroix 4 **p:** Lacroix 2
S(b)*	W22–19	Pretoria	3 Jun	**t:** NTamack **c:** Lacroix **p:** Lacroix 5
I(b)*	W36–12	Durban	10 Jun	**t:** Saint-Andre, NTamack **c:** Lacroix **p:** Lacroix 8
SA*	L15–19	Durban	17 Jun	**p:** Lacroix 5
E(b)*	W19–9	Pretoria	22 Jun	**t:** Roumat, NTamack **p:** Lacroix 3

* World Cup
+ Non-cap
† Five-point try introduced from this game onwards

Australia

Michael Lynagh
(with Greg Campbell)

THE 1995 World Cup will go down as one of the greatest disappointments for the Wallabies. To have won the Webb Ellis Cup in 1991 and to have lived up to our reputation as world champions over the ensuing three years took a tonne of effort, dedication, determination, courage and, in particular, skill.

But then to see us eliminated in the dying minutes of the quarter-final against England was a terrible blow because we felt, had we overcome that hurdle, we could have gone on successfully to defend the cup.

Our disappointment was deepened by the fact that we had such high expectations going into the tournament, yet were unable to attain those goals. Furthermore, we knew we could play a lot better than we did during our stay in South Africa. The inability to play to our potential was particularly frustrating for all of us.

Looking back, maybe we tried too hard. We possibly put ourselves under too much pressure because we were the defending world champions. But, in saying that, all teams were under pressure, no more than South Africa having to play in front of their expectant home crowd.

I liken the pressure we placed on ourselves to a golfer trying to reach the green. He knows what shot he wants to play and how to hit it. But in the process he tenses up and his skill is not as sharp as it is normally and the shot is not as good as he hoped. This is the fine line between success and failure which I believe the Wallabies crossed during the 1995 World Cup.

There was little difference between the top eight teams and it was a case of who could deliver the goods on the day. The competition at the top is very close while many of the other nations, such as Canada and Romania, who played in our Pool matches, demonstrated that they are not far behind the world leaders.

> *'I could actually feel the wind of the ball on my fingers as Rob Andrew launched it. It was never going to miss and I didn't want to open my eyes. The next thing I heard was Rob shouting "Yes!" near my right ear as he drove the ball home'*

I am the first to admit we didn't play consistently well during the Cup but there were segments of games where we put together some very good pieces of rugby. There were solid patches against South Africa, the first half against Canada was good, as was the second half against Romania. And I felt there were times in the second half against England when we were starting to take control. But suddenly we would make an error or concede a penalty and the next thing we knew we were hard on defence instead of being on attack.

It is these periods in these games which convinced me that we were on the cusp of something great and that we could have gone all the way. That's why it was so disappointing that we failed to progress beyond the last eight.

After we lost to South Africa in the opening match I felt we would meet them in the final. They played very well against us and I felt, given the side of the draw in which they were located, they would qualify for the final. They were well organised and played committed rugby.

In the quarter-final against England, we fought back from a 16–3 half-time deficit to finally get in front – a position from where I believed we would hang on and win. But Rob Andrew kept pegging us back with his great kicking and then there was his match-winning field goal.

As soon as the lineout formed in our half, I knew the field goal would be attempted. Rob stood deep and the English forwards successfully rolled the maul forwards to pick up vital yards. I charged Rob as hard as I could and I could actually feel the wind of the ball on my fingers as he launched it. But it was never going to miss and I didn't want to open my eyes.

But I can remember turning around just as the ball went through the posts. That image is framed in my mind. The next thing I heard was Rob shouting 'Yes!' near my right ear as he drove the ball home.

> *'I am the first to admit we didn't play consistently well during the World Cup but there were segments of games where we put together some very good pieces of rugby. After we lost to South Africa in the opening match I felt we would meet them in the final'*

Like in the quarter-final against Ireland in 1991, we still had limited time to pull off a last-second victory but this was different as we didn't have field position and anyway the English defence was a lot better. The guys were terribly disappointed afterwards. I just went round to each player individually and thanked them for their effort. Not a lot was said there but we spoke more about it at our traditional 'Happy Hour' later that night.

Like all teams, we suffered injuries along the way. We had a number of players who were carrying injuries and the decision had to be made as to whether these players could play better and offer more to the team than those who were being considered as their replacements. That's a judgmental decision at the time and one which the selectors deeply considered before announcing the final teams.

But we certainly had more injury problems this time around compared to 1991. I still maintain one of the reasons why we were successful in 1991 was because we had all players fully fit and available for selection for all games with the obvious exception being Nick Farr-Jones. But when he missed the game against Wales and came off injured against Western Samoa and Ireland, Peter Slattery did a great job as his replacement.

We certainly were well prepared for the Cup. Great care and research was taken throughout the preparation with several summer Cup squad training camps and two Tests against Argentina. At the time, we felt we could not have done anything better.

Our first half performance against Argentina, where we were 30 points up at half-time, was tremendous and lifted our confidence sky high. Then in the second half we tried to do too many things and, as a consequence, spoiled much of our earlier good work. By contrast, the second Test started badly and got better. The Pumas gave us a real scare and we had to come from behind after half-time to win.

> 'I received many letters from people saying what a great job we had done, how we conducted ourselves with class and how we accepted our defeat to England with grace. I remember one from a guy who had told his 10-year-old son that the team with the best players doesn't always win'

Argentina's subsequent performances in the World Cup came as no surprise to me. But how they did not win any of their three games I just don't know. They were the unluckiest team in South Africa without a shadow of a doubt.

Throughout all this preparation and during the Cup itself, there was all this distracting talk about Rupert Murdoch's Super League. It didn't help us at all as different rumours were flying around each day. I never received an offer, either directly or indirectly. They probably felt that at 31 years of age they would be better advised spending their money on a player with a longer playing career ahead of him.

I thought the Cup, from a players' viewpoint, was exceptionally well organised. Everything we asked for was made available and all the hotels were most co-operative. We received fantastic support from our fellow Australians throughout. Thousands of faxes arrived during the Cup but what was particularly pleasing was the letters and messages we received when we arrived home.

I received many letters from people saying what a great job we had done over the past four years, how we conducted ourselves with class during that period and how we accepted our defeat to England with grace. I can remember one letter from a guy who had told his 10-year-old son that the team with the best players doesn't always win and that it is important to accept defeat when the time comes.

It is also important to accept retirement when the time comes. Prior to the Cup, I had made my decision to retire from international rugby at the end of the competition, whenever that came. However, I will continue to play in Italy with Benetton this winter. I had only communicated this decision to a few close friends and after the World Cup Australian Rugby Football Union chairman Leo Williams asked me to delay making any public statement until we had spoken following his return from South Africa.

But my decision is final and I'm very proud to have achieved so much during my career. I've been fortunate to have played with many great players in many great teams and I am proud to have made a contribution to each of those teams. The career highlights are the 1991 World Cup, particularly the quarter-final win over Ireland, the 1984 Grand Slam and the 1986 Bledisloe Cup series win in New Zealand.

I've always sought to leave the game with the same character and excited anticipation for the future as when my career began, and this I intend to do.

Michael Lynagh takes aim.

AUSTRALIA (P12 W10 D0 L2 F393 A163):

(H)	v Ireland	(Brisbane, 5.6.94)	won	33–13
(H)	v Ireland	(Sydney, 11.6.94)	won	32–18
(H)	v Italy	(Brisbane, 18.6.94)	won	23–20
(H)	v Italy	(Melbourne, 26.6.94)	won	20–7
(H)	v Western Samoa	(Sydney, 6.8.94)	won	73–3
(H)	v New Zealand	(Sydney, 17.8.94)	won	20–16
(H)	v Argentina	(Brisbane, 29.4.95)	won	53–7
(H)	v Argentina	(Sydney, 6.5.95)	won	30–13
(–)	v South Africa*	(Cape Town, 25.5.95)	lost	18–27
(–)	v Canada*	(Port Elizabeth, 31.5.95)	won	27–11
(–)	v Romania*	(Stellenbosch, 3.6.95)	won	42–3
(–)	v England*	(q/f: Cape Town, 11.6.95)	lost	22–25

1995 BLEDISLOE CUP
(New Zealand win series 2–0)

New Zealand 28, Australia 16
first Test: Auckland, 22 July 1995

New Zealand: G Osborne; J Wilson, F Bunce, W Little, J Lomu; A Mehrtens, G Bachop; C Dowd, S Fitzpatrick (capt), O Brown, I Jones, R Brooke, M Brewer, J Kronfeld, Z Brooke (M Jones 50).

Scorers – Try: Lomu. *Conversion:* Mehrtens. *Penalty goals:* Mehrtens 5. *Dropped goals:* Mehrtens 2.

Australia: M Burke (P Howard 28); D Smith, J Little, T Horan, J Roff; S Bowen, S Merrick; D Crowley, P Kearns (capt), M Hartill, W Waugh, J Eales, W Ofahengaue, D Manu, T Gavin.

Scorers – Try: Ofahengaue. *Conversion:* Roff. *Penalty goals:* Roff 2, Burke.

Referee: R Megson (Scotland).

Series score: Played 99, New Zealand 67, Australia 27, Drawn 5.

Australia 23, New Zealand 34
second Test: Sydney, 29 July 1995

Australia: M Burke; D Smith (D Campese 40), J Little, T Horan, J Roff; S Bowen, S Merrick; E McKenzie, P Kearns (capt), M Hartill, W Waugh, J Eales, W Ofahengaue, D Manu, T Gavin.

Scorers – Tries: Smith, Ofahengaue. *Conversions:* Burke 2. *Penalty goals:* Burke 3.

New Zealand: G Osborne; J Wilson, F Bunce, W Little, J Lomu; A Mehrtens, G Bachop; C Dowd, S Fitzpatrick (capt), O Brown, I Jones, R Brooke, M Brewer, M Jones (J Kronfeld 40), Z Brooke.

Scorers – Tries: Bunce 2, Mehrtens, Lomu, Wilson. *Conversions:* Mehrtens 3. *Penalty goal:* Mehrtens.

Referee: S Hilditch (Ireland).

Series score: Played 100, New Zealand 68, Australia 27, Drawn 5.

1994 SUPER TEN TOURNAMENT
FINAL: Natal 10, Queensland 21
Kings Park, Durban, 14 May 1994

POOL A: Queensland 21, Transvaal 10; Transvaal 35, Eastern Province 15; Eastern Province 10, Queensland 41; Transvaal 44, Otago 19; Otago 24, Queensland 18; Eastern Province 21, North Harbour 31; North Harbour 23, Otago 19; Otago 57, Eastern Province 24; North Harbour 19, Transvaal 6; Queensland 13, North Harbour 10.

POOL A	P	W	D	L	F	A	Pts
Queensland	4	3	0	1	85	61	12
North Harbour	4	3	0	1	83	59	12
Otago	4	2	0	2	119	109	8
Transvaal	4	2	0	2	95	74	8
Eastern Province	4	0	0	4	70	164	0

POOL B: Waikato 16, New South Wales 43; New South Wales 25, Western Samoa 23; Auckland 27, Waikato 10; Waikato 16, Western Samoa 32; Natal w/o New South Wales; Auckland 13, Western Samoa 15; Natal 30, Waikato 24; Natal 48, Western Samoa 26; New South Wales 22, Auckland 19; Natal 14, Auckland 12.

POOL B	P	W	D	L	F	A	Pts
Natal	4	4	0	0	92	62	16
New South Wales	4	3	0	1	90	58	12
Western Samoa	4	2	0	2	96	104	8
Auckland	4	1	0	3	71	61	4
Waikato	4	0	0	4	66	132	0

DOMESTIC RUGBY

Sydney Premiership Grand Final
Randwick 36, Warringah 16 (Concord Oval, 19.9.94)

AUSTRALIA TEST RESULTS AND SCORERS SINCE 1980

1980:				
Fj	W22–9	Suva	24 May	**t:** Martin, Moon **c:** P E McLean **p:** P E McLean 3 **dg:** P E McLean
NZ(1)	W13–9	Sydney	21 Jun	**t:** Hawker, Martin **c:** Gould **dg:** M Ella
NZ(2)	L 9–12	Brisbane	28 Jun	**t:** Moon **c:** Gould **p:** Gould
NZ(3)	W26–10	Sydney	12 Jul	**t:** Grigg 2, O'Connor, Carson **c:** Gould 2 **p:** Gould **dg:** M Ella
1981:				
F(1)	W17–15	Brisbane	5 Jul	**t:** Poidevin, O'Connor, Moon **c:** P McLean **p:** Richards
F(2)	W24–14	Sydney	11 Jul	**t:** Hall, O'Connor **c:** P McLean 2 **p:** P McLean 4
I	W16–12	Dublin	21 Nov	**t:** O'Connor **p:** P McLean 3 **dg:** Gould
W	L13–18	Cardiff	5 Dec	**t:** Slack, M Cox **c:** P McLean **p:** P McLean
S	L15–24	Edinburgh	19 Dec	**t:** Poidevin, Moon, Slack **p:** P McLean
1982:				
E	L11–15	Twickenham	2 Jan	**t:** Moon 2 **p:** P McLean
S(1)	L 7–12	Brisbane	3 Jul	**t:** Hawker **p:** Hawker
S(2)	W33–9	Sydney	10 Jul	**t:** Gould 2, O'Connor **c:** P McLean 3 **p:** P McLean 5
NZ(1)	L16–23	Christchurch	14 Aug	**t:** Hawker, Campese **c:** Gould **p:** Gould 2
NZ(2)	W19–16	Wellington	28 Aug	**t:** G Ella, Campese **c:** Gould **p:** Gould 3
NZ(3)	L18–33	Auckland	11 Sep	**t:** Gould **c:** Gould **p:** Gould 3 **dg:** Hawker

1983:

US	W49–3	Sydney	9 Jul	**t:** Campese 4, Slack 2, Ross, Roche, Hanley **c:** Gould 4, Campese **dg:** M Ella
Arg(1)	L 3–18	Brisbane	31 Jul	**dg:** Campese
Arg(2)	W29–13	Sydney	8 Aug	**t:** Moon 2, Roche, Campese, penalty try **c:** Campese 3 **p:** Campese
Fj	W16–3	Suva	xx Aug	**t:** Campese **p:** Lynagh 4
NZ	L 8–18	Sydney	20 Aug	**t:** Slack, Poidevin
It	W29–7	Padova	22 Oct	**t:** Hawker 2, Moon, Williams, M Ella **c:** M Ella 3 **p:** M Ella
F(1)	D15–15	Clermont-Ferrand	13 Nov	**t:** Roche **c:** Campese **p:** Campese **dg:** M Ella, Hawker
F(2)	L 6–15	Paris	20 Nov	**p:** Campese **dg:** M Ella

1984:

NZ(1)	W16–9	Sydney	21 Jul	**t:** Reynolds, Moon **c:** M Ella **p:** M Ella **dg:** Gould
NZ(2)	L15–19	Brisbane	4 Aug	**t:** M Ella **c:** M Ella **p:** M Ella 2, Campese
NZ(3)	L24–25	Sydney	18 Aug	**t:** Campese **c:** M Ella **p:** M Ella 5, Campese
E	W19–3	Twickenham	3 Nov	**t:** M Ella, Poidevin, Lynagh **c:** Lynagh 2 **p:** Lynagh
I	W16–9	Ireland	10 Nov	**t:** M Ella **p:** Lynagh **dg:** M Ella 2, Lynagh
W	W28–9	Cardiff	24 Nov	**t:** Lawton, Tuynman, M Ella, Lynagh **c:** Gould 3 **p:** Gould 2
S	W37–12	Edinburgh	8 Dec	**t:** Campese 2, Farr-Jones, M Ella **c:** Lynagh 3 **p:** Lynagh 5

1985:

C(1)	W59–3	Sydney	15 Jun	**t:** Burke 2, Lane 2, Grigg 2, Calcraft, Farr-Jones, Kassulke **c:** Lynagh 7 **p:** Lynagh 3

C(2)	W43–15	Brisbane	23 Jun	**t:** Burke 3, Grigg, Cutler, Tuynman, Farr-Jones **c:** Lynagh 3 **p:** Lynagh 2 **dg:** Lynagh
NZ	L 9–10	Auckland	29 Jun	**t:** Black **c:** Lynagh **p:** Lynagh
Fj(1)	W52–28	Brisbane	10 Aug	**t:** Farr-Jones 2, Reynolds, Cutler, Lawton, Papworth, Grigg **c:** Knox 3 **p:** Knox 3 **dg:** Knox 2, Campese
Fj(2)	W31–9	Sydney	17 Aug	**t:** Campese 2, Grigg, McIntyre, Cutler **c:** Knox **p:** Knox 3

1986:

It	W39–18	Brisbane	1 Jun	**t:** Campese 2, Tuynman, McIntyre, Moon, Burke **c:** Lynagh 6 **p:** Lynagh
F	W27–14	Sydney	21 Jun	**t:** Campese **c:** Lynagh **p:** Lynagh 6 **dg:** Lynagh
Arg(1)	W39–19	Brisbane	6 Jul	**t:** Papworth 2, Grigg, Campese **c:** Lynagh 4 **p:** Lynagh 5
Arg(2)	W26–0	Sydney	12 Jul	**t:** Campese 2, Tuynman **c:** Lynagh **p:** Lynagh 4
NZ(1)	W13–12	Wellington	9 Aug	**t:** Campese, Burke **c:** Lynagh **p:** Lynagh
NZ(2)	L12–13	Dunedin	23 Aug	**p:** Lynagh 3 **dg:** Lynagh
NZ(3)	W22–9	Auckland	6 Sep	**t:** Leeds, Campese **c:** Lynagh **p:** Lynagh 4

1987:

SK	W65–18	Brisbane	17 May	**t:** Burke 3, Grigg 2, Slack 2, Cook, Gould, B Smith, Miller, James, Farr-Jones **c:** Smith 5 **p:** Smith
E*	W19–6	Sydney	23 May	**t:** Campese, Poidevin **c:** Lynagh **p:** Lynagh 3
US*	W47–12	Brisbane	31 May	**t:** penalty try, Smith, Slack, Leeds 2,

				Papworth, Campese, Codey
				c: Lynagh 6
				p: Lynagh
J*	W42–23	Sydney	3 Jun	t: Slack 2, Tuynman, Burke 2, Grigg, Hartill, Campese
				c: Lynagh 5
I*	W33–15	Sydney	7 Jun	t: McIntyre, Smith, Burke 2
				c: Lynagh 4
				p: Lynagh 3
F*	L24–30	Sydney	13 Jun	t: Campese, Codey
				c: Lynagh 2
				p: Lynagh 3
				dg: Lynagh
W*	L21–22	Rotorua	18 Jun	t: Burke, Grigg
				c: Lynagh 2
				p: Lynagh 2
				dg: Lynagh
NZ	L16–30	Sydney	25 Jul	t: Papworth
				p: Leeds 3
				dg: Hawker
Arg(1)	D19–19	Buenos Aires	31 Oct	t: Williams, Cutler, Lynagh
				c: Lynagh 2
				p: Lynagh
Arg(2)	L19–27	Buenos Aires	7 Nov	t: Williams 2
				c: Lynagh
				p: Lynagh 3

1988:

E(a1)	W22–16	Brisbane	29 May	t: Williams
				p: Lynagh 6
E(a2)	W28–8	Sydney	12 Jun	t: Campese, G Ella, Lynagh, Carter
				c: Lynagh 3
				p: Lynagh 2
NZ(1)	L 7–32	Sydney	3 Jul	t: Williams
				p: Lynagh
NZ(2)	D19–19	Brisbane	16 Jul	t: Grant, Williams
				c: Leeds
				p: Leeds 3
NZ(3)	L 9–30	Sydney	30 Jul	t: Walker
				c: Lynagh
				p: Leeds
E(b)	L19–28	Twickenham	5 Nov	t: Leeds, Campese, Grant
				c: Lynagh 2
				p: Lynagh
S	W32–13	Edinburgh	19 Nov	t: Lawton 2, Campese 2, Gourley,
				c: Lynagh 3
				p: Lynagh 2
It	W55–6	Milan	3 Dec	t: Campese 3, Niuqila 3, Leeds, Gourley, Lynagh
				c: Lynagh 8
				p: Lynagh

1989:

BL(1)	W30–12	Sydney	1 Jul	**t:** Walker, Gourley, Maguire, Martin
				c: Lynagh 4
				p: Lynagh
				dg: Lynagh
BL(2)	L12–19	Brisbane	8 Jul	**t:** Martin
				c: Lynagh
				p: Lynagh 2
BL(3)	L18–19	Sydney	15 Jul	**t:** Williams
				c: Lynagh
				p: Lynagh 4
NZ	L12–24	Auckland	5 Aug	**t:** Campese
				c: Lynagh
				p: Lynagh 2
F(1)	W32–15	Strasbourg	4 Nov	**t:** Horan 2, Williams, Campese
				c: Lynagh 2
				p: Lynagh 4
F(2)	L19–25	Lille	11 Nov	**t:** Kearns, Farr-Jones
				c: Lynagh
				p: Lynagh 3

1990:

F(1)	W21–9	Sydney	9 Jun	**t:** Martin
				c: Lynagh
				p: Lynagh 5
F(2)	W48–31	Brisbane	24 Jun	**t:** Carozza, Cornish, Gavin, Little, penalty try, Campese
				c: Lynagh 6
				p: Lynagh 4
F(3)	L19–28	Sydney	30 Jun	**t:** Campese, Daly
				c: Lynagh
				p: Lynagh 2
				dg: Lynagh
US	W67–9	Brisbane	8 Jul	**t:** Lynagh 2, Williams 2, Daly, McKenzie, Kearns, Gavin, Little, Farr-Jones, Slattery, Campese
				c: Lynagh 8
				dg: Campese
NZ(1)	L 6–21	Christchurch	21 Jul	**p:** Lynagh 2
NZ(2)	L17–27	Auckland	4 Aug	**t:** Horan, Ofahengaue
				p: Lynagh 2
				dg: Lynagh
NZ(3)	W21–9	Wellington	18 Aug	**t:** Kearns
				c: Lynagh
				p: Lynagh 5

1991:

W(a)	W63–6	Brisbane	21 Jul	**t:** Lynagh 2, Kearns 2, Gavin 2, Ofahengaue, Horan, Roebuck, Campese, Egerton, Little
				c: Lynagh 6

				p: Lynagh
E(a)	W40–15	Sydney	27 Jul	t: Campese 2, Ofahengaue 2, Roebuck
				c: Lynagh 4
				p: Lynagh 4
NZ(a1)	W21–12	Sydney	10 Aug	t: Gavin, Egerton
				c: Lynagh 2
				p: Lynagh 3
NZ(a2)	L 3–6	Auckland	24 Aug	p: Lynagh
Arg*	W32–19	Llanelli	4 Oct	t: Campese 2, Horan 2, Kearns
				c: Lynagh 3
				p: Lynagh 2
WS*	W 9–3	Pontypool	9 Oct	p: Lynagh 3
W(b)*	W38–3	Cardiff	12 Oct	t: Roebuck 2, Slattery, Campese, Horan,
				Lynagh
				c: Lynagh 4
				p: Lynagh 2
I*	W19–18	Dublin	20 Oct	t: Campese 2, Lynagh
				c: Lynagh 2
				p: Lynagh
NZ(b)*	W16–6	Dublin	27 Oct	t: Campese, Horan
				c: Lynagh
				p: Lynagh 2

South Africa's Gavin Johnson is trapped by hungry Romanians in Cape Town.

E*	W12–6	Twickenham	2 Nov	t: Daly
				c: Lynagh
				p: Lynagh 2

1992:

S(1)	W27–12	Sydney	13 June	t: Campese 2, Carozza, Lynagh
				c: Lynagh
				p: Lynagh 3
S(2)	W37–13	Brisbane	21 Jun	t: Carozza 2, Horan 2, Eales
				c: Lynagh
				p: Lynagh 5
NZ(1)†	W16–15	Sydney	14 Jul	t: Campese, Horan
				p: Lynagh 2
NZ(2)	W19–17	Brisbane	19 Jul	t: Carozza 2
				p: Lynagh 3
NZ(3)	L23–26	Sydney	25 Jul	t: Farr-Jones, Herbert
				c: Lynagh 2
				p: Lynagh 3
SA	W26–3	Cape Town	23 Aug	t: Carozza 2, Campese
				c: Lynagh
				p: Lynagh 3
I	W42–17	Dublin	31 Oct	t: Campese, McKenzie, Little, Kelaher, Horan
				c: Roebuck 4
				p: Roebuck 3
W	W23–6	Cardiff	21 Nov	t: Wilson, McCall, Campese
				c: Roebuck
				p: Roebuck 2

1993

T	W52–14	Brisbane	3 Jul	t: Campese 2, Carozza, Little, Gavin, Morgan, Johnstone
				c: Roebuck 3, Lynagh
				p: Roebuck 3
NZ	L10–25	Dunedin	17 Jul	t: Horan
				c: Kelaher
				p: Kelaher
SA(1)	L12–19	Sydney	31 Jul	p: Roebuck 4
SA(2)	W28–20	Brisbane	14 Aug	t: Little 2, Horan
				c: Roebuck 2
				p: Roebuck 3
SA(3)	W19–12	Sydney	21 Aug	t: Horan
				c: Roebuck
				p: Roebuck 4
US⁺	W26–22	California	2 Oct	t: Wilson, Howard, Tabua, Lea
				c: Lynagh 3
C	W43–16	Calgary	9 Oct	t: Campese 3, Horan, Daly, D Smith
				c: Lynagh 2
				p: Lynagh 3
F(1)	L13–16	Bordeaux	30 Oct	t: Gavin
				c: Lynagh
				p: Lynagh 2

F(2)	W24–3	Paris	6 Nov	t: Roebuck, Gavin c: Roebuck p: Roebuck 4

1994

I(1)	W33–13	Brisbane	5 Jun	t: Tabua, Lynagh, Campese, Burke, D Smith c: Lynagh p: Lynagh 2
I(2)	W32–18	Sydney	11 Jun	t: D Herbert, Wilson, Tabua c: Lynagh p: Lynagh 5
It(1)	W23–20	Brisbane	18 Jun	t: Burke, D Herbert c: Lynagh, Wallace p: Lynagh 2, Wallace
It(2)	W20–7	Melbourne	26 Jun	t: Campese p: Wallace 5
WS	W73–3	Brisbane	6 Jul	t: D Smith 2, Little 2, Campese, Gavin, Pini, Junee, Howard, Ofahengaue, Gregan c: Knox 6 p: Knox 2
NZ	W20–16	Sydney	17 Aug	t: Kearns, Little c: Knox 2 p: Knox 3

1995

Arg(1)	W53–7	Brisbane	29 Apr	t: Lynagh 2, D Smith, Campese, Pini, Eales, Ofahengaue c: Lynagh 3 p: Lynagh 4
Arg(2)	W30–13	Sydney	6 May	t: Campese 2, Wilson p: Lynagh 5
SA*	L18–27	Cape Town	25 May	t: Lynagh, Kearns c: Lynagh p: Lynagh 2
C*	W27–11	Port Elizabeth	31 May	t: Tabua, Roff, Lynagh c: Lynagh 3 p: Lynagh 2
R*	W42–3	Stellenbosch	3 Jun	t: Roff 2, D Smith, Wilson, Burke, Foley c: Burke 2, Eales 4
E*	L22–25	Cape Town	11 Jun	t: D Smith c: Lynagh p: Lynagh 5

* World Cup
+ Non-cap
† Five-point try introduced from this game onwards

New Zealand

Sean Fitzpatrick
(with Wynne Gray, *New Zealand Herald*)

IT WAS crushing not to win the third World Cup against the Springboks, worse even than our loss in the semi-final to Australia in 1991. Final defeat at Ellis Park in Johannesburg hurt more than that miserable afternoon in Dublin four years ago.

Perhaps the pain was more intense because the new-look All Blacks had even exceeded our own expectations in 1995. We hoped we would perform well and knew we had the potential but I must admit I was surprised how well we came together and how some of the individuals played.

There was a confidence starting to ooze through the squad, a quality which manifested itself most in the run-up to our semi-final against England (won 45–29). We had already beaten Ireland (42–19), Wales (34–9) and Japan (145–17) in the pool matches without any real dramas. There were a few hiccups from the tight forwards against Scotland (won 48–30) but it was not a Test we were going to lose.

Then we really started to get it together in the week leading up to the semi with England. They had been unbeaten in ten Tests and had shown an imposing forward effort early against the defending champions Australia in the previous round before Rob Andrew booted them to a late victory.

Even so, we fancied our chances of halting England's Sweet Chariot

107

at Newlands in Cape Town. And our confidence was not misplaced. It was a huge game but for the first time in about two or three seasons with the All Blacks I was 100% confident we would triumph and go through to the final.

For the first time in a long while I knew we had the team to do it. The All Blacks were strong in most, if not all, positions and when we won so well I really thought we could repeat that style one more time in the final.

> *'Food poisoning played a part in our lacklustre final performance. I find it hard to fathom how 18 out of 26 in the squad had been sick two days before the game. I accept it could have been an accident but it was a strange coincidence'*

To then lose out, 12–15 in extra-time, after a mind-numbing, leg-sapping extra-time duel with South Africa, was almost unreal. Even though many in the side had been hit by food poisoning we still thought we could win the Webb Ellis Cup.

But it was one of those days, one of enormous emotion, though we did not choke or anything like that. In fact most of us revelled in the huge occasion. It really was some atmosphere.

It is hard to say when you lose, but I think the food poisoning played a part in our lacklustre performance. I find it hard to fathom how 18 out of 26 in the squad had been sick two days before the game. I accept it could have been an accident but it was a strange coincidence.

I suffered from diarrhoea myself a few days before the game and felt flat during the final. A number of my team mates complained of the same problems and poor Jeff Wilson had to leave the park before he was sick.

It was distressing to see others, like Andrew Mehrtens, throwing up the day before the final and we spent a lot of energy wondering whether our mates would be 100% for the biggest game of the tournament. I think the sickness left us all with some psychological weaknesses.

We had come to the World Cup on the back of a great build-up. Plenty of trial games and then a Test against Canada (won 73–7) had given us some great preparation and worked a lot of our new players into the All Blacks. Our series of camps during the summer combined with torrid fitness sessions had honed us for the tournament, which made it all the more horrific to be so badly affected at the moment we needed to be at our best.

The planning had all gone to schedule. We had thought out our campaign well and it was just unfortunate we did not carry it through to the end. We were a happy team, we loved the new style we brought, it was a great way to play rugby.

> 'If you ask me the 1995 All Blacks have the potential to be even better than the great 1987 side which won the World Cup. They have probably got more talent and skill than their predecessors – they could go on to be a great side'

At some stages of the final perhaps we could have consolidated and played some more percentage rugby but that is something you learn with a lot of experience. Many of our guys had only just been introduced to Test rugby so it was a marvellous feat to do as well as we did.

But I know that the final was there for the taking, although you must give the Springboks credit for their courage and conviction. They never gave in, they never cracked and were better on the day.

We were disappointed for ourselves, for the coach Laurie Mains, manager Colin Meads and campaign manager Brian Lochore who had done so much work to get us right. So too the rest of the coaching, fitness and support staff. We were also disappointed for the whole of New Zealand who had supported us so strongly.

It was a pity we could not emulate the 1987 All Blacks who won the first tournament, but if you ask me this 1995 side has the potential to be even better than that great combination.

We were probably beaten in 1991 by a better side than the Springboks who just nailed us this year. But I think this squad is maybe on the threshold of something special. It could go on to be a great side, and I do not use that description of teams too often.

The 1987 All Blacks fitted that category as they showed in their incredible unbeaten run through to late 1990. The side clearly had talent but its strength was in the burning drive of players like Murray Pierce and Buck Shelford. The way they gave their guts every game was the basis of the unyielding passion in that side.

The 1995 All Blacks have probably got more talent and skill than our predecessors. Lots of that individual talent has not been fully exposed yet but when it is, look out world.

I am amazed at the class already of people like Mehrtens, Glen Osborne at fullback, Jonah Lomu, who hit the headlines in South Africa, and Robin Brooke, who to my mind is a pretty special player.

> *'During the World Cup there were not many in the New Zealand team that I would have swapped for any opposition players. These All Blacks are the team for the future'*

Before each Test I always go through my team to look for the strengths and weaknesses and during the World Cup there were not many All Blacks I would have swapped for any opposition players. That is incredibly encouraging for a captain and I think this 1995 All Black model is on the verge of a special era.

We had our rough times in 1993–94, some of the results were not too good and last year was probably the toughest when we only won two of six Tests against France, South Africa and Australia.

That list of opponents is as tough as you will get but we did not play well enough, consistently. However, we were always confident that the right preparation and selection would give us a real crack at the third World Cup.

It worked out that way except for the final hurdle, but this team will go on to even better deeds – these All Blacks are the team for the future.

NEW ZEALAND (P13 W8 D1 L4 F497 A232):

(H) v France	(Christchurch, 26.6.94)	lost	8–22	
(H) v France	(Auckland, 3.7.94)	lost	20–23	
(H) v South Africa	(Dunedin, 9.7.94)	won	22–14	
(H) v South Africa	(Wellington, 23.7.94)	won	13–9	
(H) v South Africa	(Auckland, 6.8.94)	drew	18–18	
(A) v Australia	(Sydney, 17.8.94)	lost	16–20	
(H) v Canada	(Auckland, 22.4.95)	won	73–7	
(–) v Ireland*	(Johannesburg, 27.5.95)	won	43–19	
(–) v Wales*	(Johannesburg, 31.5.95)	won	34–9	
(–) v Japan*	(Bloemfontein, 4.6.95)	won	145–17	
(–) v Scotland*	(q/f: Pretoria, 11.6.95)	won	48–30	
(–) v England*	(s/f: Cape Town, 18.6.95)	won	45–29	
(–) v South Africa*	(f: Johannesburg, 24.6.95)	lost	12–15 (aet)	

* World Cup

Tonga to New Zealand (tour record: P4 W3 D1 L0 F98 A52):

(–) v Taranaki	(New Plymouth, 7.5.94)	won	23–16
(–) v Wanganui	(Wanganui, 11.5.94)	won	42–13
(–) v Manawatu	(Palmerston North, 14.5.94)	won	19–9
(–) v Hawke's Bay	(Napier, 17.5.94)	drew	14–14

Fiji to New Zealand (tour record: P6 W3 D0 L3 F183 A128):

(–) v Thames Valley	(Paeroa, 18.5.94)	won	35–16
(–) v East Coast	(Ruatoria, 21.5.94)	won	62–6
(–) v Bay of Plenty	(Rotorua, 24.5.94)	lost	26–36
(–) v NZ Universities	(Palmerston North, 27.5.94)	lost	5–11
(–) v Horowhenua	(Levin, 1.6.94)	won	42–25
(–) v NZ Maoris	(Christchurch, 4.6.94)	lost	13–34

New Zealand Development XV to Argentina (P7 W5 D0 L2 F304 A136):

(A) v Rosario Selection	(Rosario, 19.3.94)	lost	20–25
(A) v Entre Rios Selection	(Parana, 22.3.94)	won	78–12
(A) v Cordoba Selection	(Cordoba, 26.3.94)	won	38–23
(A) v Cuyo Selection	(Mendoza, 29.3.94)	won	45–17
(A) v Combined South Selection	(Trelew, 2.4.94)	won	75–16
(A) v North East Selection	(Resistencia, 5.4.94)	won	22–5
(A) v Buenos Aires Selection	(Buenos Aires, 9.4.94)	lost	26–38

New Zealand Colts to Australia (P3 W3 D0 L0 F177 A44):

(A) v NSW Country U-21s	(Port Macquarie, 31.7.94)	won	76–3
(A) v NSW U-21 Dev. XV	(Sydney, 3.8.94)	won	60–10
(A) v Australia U-21	(Sydney, 6.8.94)	won	41–31

New Zealand Universities (P4 W2 D0 L2 F154 A62):

(–) v Wairarapa Bush	(Masterton, 24.5.94)	lost	23–24
(H) v Fiji	(Palmerston North, 27.5.94)	won	11–5
(H) v Japan Under-23	(Wellington, 14.8.94)	won	106–9
(A) v Australia Universities	(Sydney, 17.8.94)	lost	14–24

New Zealand Under-19 (P1 W1 D0 L0 F55 A6):
(H) v Australia U-19   (Wellington, 23.7.94)   won   55–6

New Zealand Schools (P1 W1 D0 L0 F52 A5):
(H) v Japan Schools   (Palmerston North, 6.4.94)   won   52–5

New Zealand Under-16 (P1 W0 D1 L0 F10 A10):
(A) v Australia U-16   (Brisbane, 24.9.94)   drew   10–10

1994 SUPER TEN TOURNAMENT
'North Harbour' squeezed out of place in final by Queensland' – see page 97

DOMESTIC RUGBY

AIR NEW ZEALAND NATIONAL PROVINCIAL CHAMPIONSHIP

Division One:	P	W	D	L	F	A	Pts
Auckland	8	7	0	1	319	164	29
North Harbour	8	7	0	1	294	165	28
Canterbury	8	6	0	2	230	194	24
Otago	8	4	0	4	241	205	18
Counties	8	4	0	4	179	166	17
Wellington	8	4	0	4	200	262	16
Waikato	8	3	0	5	191	202	13
King Country	8	1	0	7	136	324	4
Taranaki	8	0	0	8	153	261	4

FINAL: Auckland 22, North Harbour 16 (Takapuna, 16.10.94). **Semi-finals:** North Harbour 59, Canterbury 27 (Takapuna, 8.10.94); Auckland 33, Otago 16 (Dunedin, 9.10.94).

Division Two:	P	W	D	L	F	A	Pts
Hawke's Bay	8	8	0	0	399	172	32
Southland	8	7	0	1	284	177	28
Northland	8	6	0	2	343	166	24
Bay of Plenty	8	5	0	3	314	227	21
Manawatu	8	4	0	4	260	222	17
Nelson Bays	8	3	0	5	156	279	12
South Canterbury	8	2	0	6	218	269	10
Wairarapa Bush	8	1	0	7	107	420	4
Horowhenua	8	0	0	8	155	304	1

FINAL: Southland 20, Hawke's Bay 18 (Invercargill, 15.10.94). **Semi-finals:** Southland 29, Northland 22 (Whangarei, 8.10.94); Hawke's Bay 65, Bay of Plenty 18 (Napier, 9.10.94).

Division Three:
Promoted: Mid Canterbury. **Final:** Mid Canterbury 26, Poverty Bay 16 (Ashburton, 15.10.94). **Semi-finals:** Poverty Bay 40, Thames Valley 20 (Gisborne, 8.10.94); Mid Canterbury 22, Wanganui 13 (Wanganui, 9.10.94).

National Sevens (final): Counties 36*, Waikato 19 (Palmerston North, 6.3.94).
* Jonah Lomu 3 tries.

RANFURLY SHIELD
Holders – Canterbury (3 wins).
Waikato 74, Thames Valley 3 (Napier, 6.6.94); Waikato 26, Manawatu 11 (Hamilton, 2.7.94); Waikato 98, South Canterbury 22 (Hamilton, 30.7.94); Waikato 45, King Country 10 (Hamilton, 13.8.94); Waikato 26, Counties 29 (Hamilton, 3.9.94); Canterbury 42, Counties 16 (Christchurch, 18.9.94); Canterbury 22, Otago 20 (Christchurch, 1.10.94).

The most fearsome sight in rugby: Jonah Lomu ready to rumble.

1980:

A(1)	L 9–13	Sydney	21 Jun	**p:** Codlin 3
A(2)	W12–9	Brisbane	28 Jun	**t:** Reid
				c: Codlin
				p: Codlin 2
A(3)	L10–26	Sydney	12 Jul	**t:** Fraser
				p: Codlin 2
Fj(a)[+]	W30–6	Suva	23 Jul	**t:** Fraser 3, Allen, B Robertson
				c: Codlin 2
				p: Codlin 2
Fj(b)[+]	W33–0	Auckland	30 Sep	**t:** Osborne 2, K Taylor 2, Wylie, Woodman
				c: Valli 3
				p: Valli
C[+]	W43–10	Vancouver	11 Oct	**t:** M Shaw 3, Mourie, Haden, Osborne, S Wilson, Fraser
				c: Rollerson 4
				p: Rollerson
US[+]	W53–6	San Diego	Oct	**t:** Woodman 3, Osborne 2, Wilson, Allen, Old
				c: Codlin 6
				p: Codlin 3
W	W23–3	Cardiff	1 Nov	**t:** Mourie, Fraser, Allen, Reid
				c: Rollerson 2
				p: Rollerson

1981:

S(1)	W11–4	Dunedin	13 Jun	**t:** Wilson, Loveridge
				p: Hewson
S(2)	W40–15	Auckland	20 Jun	**t:** Wilson 3, Hewson 2, Robertson, Mourie
				c: Hewson 6
SA(1)	W14–9	Christchurch	15 Aug	**t:** Rollerson, Wilson, Shaw
				c: Rollerson
SA(2)	L12–24	Wellington	29 Aug	**p:** Hewson 4
SA(3)	W25–22	Auckland	12 Sep	**t:** Wilson, Knight
				c: Rollerson
				p: Hewson 3, Rollerson
				dg: Rollerson
R	W14–6	Bucharest	24 Oct	**t:** Salmon, Dalton
				p: Hewson
				dg: Rollerson
F(1)	W13–9	Toulouse	14 Nov	**t:** Wilson
				p: Hewson 2
				dg: Hewson
F(2)	W18–6	Paris	21 Nov	**t:** penalty try, Wilson
				c: Hewson 2
				p: Hewson 2

1982:

A(1)	W23–16	Christchurch	14 Aug	**t:** Mexted, Mourie, Pokere, Fraser
				c: Hewson 2
				p: Hewson
A(2)	L16–19	Wellington	28 Aug	**t:** Shaw, Fraser
				c: Hewson
				p: Hewson 2
A(3)	W33–18	Auckland	11 Sep	**t:** Hewson, Shaw
				c: Hewson 2
				p: Hewson 5
				dg: Hewson, Smith

1983:

BL(1)	W16–12	Christchurch	4 Jun	**t:** Shaw
				p: Hewson 3
				dg: Hewson
BL(2)	W 9–0	Wellington	18 Jun	**t:** Loveridge
				c: Hewson
				p: Hewson
BL(3)	W15–8	Dunedin	2 Jul	**t:** Wilson
				c: Hewson
				p: Hewson 3
BL(4)	W38–6	Auckland	16 Jul	**t:** Wilson 3, Hewson, Hobbs, Haden
				c: Hewson 4
				p: Hewson 2
A	W18–8	Sydney	20 Aug	**t:** Taylor
				c: Hewson
				p: Hewson 4
S	D25–25	Edinburgh	12 Nov	**t:** Fraser 2, Hobbs
				c: Deans 2
				p: Deans 3
E	L 9–15	Twickenham	19 Nov	**t:** Davie
				c: Deans
				p: Deans

1984:

F(1)	W10–9	Christchurch	16 Jun	**t:** Taylor
				p: Hewson 2
F(2)	W31–18	Auckland	23 Jun	**t:** B Smith, Dalton, Taylor
				c: Hewson 2
				p: Hewson 5
A(1)	L 9–16	Sydney	21 Jul	**p:** Hewson 2
				dg: Hewson
A(2)	W19–15	Brisbane	4 Aug	**t:** Pokere
				p: Deans 5
A(3)	W25–24	Sydney	18 Aug	**t:** Clamp, Stone
				c: Deans
				p: Deans 5

1985:

E(1)	W18–13	Christchurch	1 Jun	**p:** Crowley 6

E(2)	W42–15	Wellington	8 Jun	t: Green 2, Kirwan, Mexted, Hobbs, Shaw c: Crowley 3 p: Crowley 3 dg: Smith
A	W10–9	Auckland	29 Jun	t: Green p: Crowley 2
Arg(1)	W33–20	Buenos Aires	26 Oct	t: Kirwan 2, Hobbs, Crowley c: Crowley p: Crowley 4 dg: Fox
Arg(2)	D21–21	Buenos Aires	2 Nov	t: Kirwan 2, Mexted, Green c: Crowley. p: Crowley

1986:

F(a)	W18–9	Christchurch	28 Jun	t: Brewer c: G Cooper p: G Cooper dg: Botica 2, G Cooper
A(1)	L12–13	Wellington	9 Aug	t: Brooke-Cowden c: G Cooper p: G Cooper 2
A(2)	W13–12	Dunedin	23 Aug	t: Kirk p: G Cooper 2 dg: G Cooper
A(3)	L 9–22	Auckland	6 Sep	p: Crowley 3
F(b1)	W19–7	Toulouse	8 Nov	t: Shelford p: Crowley 3 dg: Stone, Crowley
F(b2)	L 3–16	Nantes	15 Nov	p: Crowley

1987:

It*	W70–6	Auckland	22 May	t: Kirk 2, Kirwan 2, Green 2, M Jones, Taylor, McDowell, Stanley, A Whetton, penalty try c: Fox 8 p: Fox 2
Fj*	W74–13	Christchurch	27 May	t: Green 4, Gallagher 4, Kirk, Kirwan, A Whetton, penalty try c: Fox 10 p: Fox 2
Arg*	W46–15	Wellington	1 Jun	t: Kirk, Z Brooke, Stanley, Earl, Crowley, A Whetton c: Fox 2 p: Fox 6
S*	W30–3	Christchurch	6 Jun	t: Gallagher, A Whetton c: Fox 2. p: Fox 6
W*	W49–6	Brisbane	14 Jun	t: Kirwan 2, Shelford 2, Drake, Brooke-Cowden, Stanley, A Whetton

116

				c: Fox 7
				p: Fox
F*	W29–9	Auckland	20 Jun	**t:** Kirk, Kirwan, M Jones
				c: Fox
				p: Fox 4
				dg: Fox
A	W30–16	Sydney	25 Jul	**t:** Fitzpatrick 2, Kirwan, Green
				c: Fox
				p: Fox 3
				dg: Fox

1988:

W(1)	W52–3	Christchurch	28 May	**t:** Kirwan 4, Wright 2, Gallagher, Deans, Shelford, G Whetton
				c: Fox 6
W(2)	W54–9	Auckland	11 Jun	**t:** Kirwan 2, Wright 2, Taylor, Deans, M Jones, McDowell
				c: Fox 8
				p: Fox 2
A(1)	W32–7	Sydney	3 Jul	**t:** Kirwan 2, McDowell, A Whetton, Schuster
				c: Fox 3
				p: Fox 2
A(2)	D19–19	Brisbane	16 Jul	**t:** M Jones, Wright, Kirwan
				c: Fox 2
				p: Fox
A(3)	W30–9	Sydney	30 Jul	**t:** Deans, Gallagher, Kirwan
				c: Fox 3
				p: Fox 4

1989:

F(1)	W25–17	Christchurch	18 Jun	**t:** Wright 2, A Whetton
				c: Fox 2
				p: Fox 3
F(2)	W34–20	Auckland	1 Jul	**t:** Stanley, Deans, Fitzpatrick, A Whetton
				c: Fox 3
				p: Fox 4
Arg(1)	W60–9	Dunedin	15 Jul	**t:** Gallagher 3, Kirwan 2, Wright 2, penalty try, M Jones 2
				c: Fox 7
				p: Fox 2
Arg(2)	W49–12	Wellington	29 Jul	**t:** Wright 2, Deans 2, Gallagher, Kirwan, A Whetton
				c: Fox 6
				p: Fox 3
A	W24–12	Auckland	5 Aug	**t:** Gallagher, Loe
				c: Fox 2
				p: Fox 4
W	W34–9	Cardiff	4 Nov	**t:** Innes 2, Bachop, Wright
				c: Fox 3

I	W23–6	Dublin	18 Nov	**p:** Fox 4 **t:** Gallagher, Wright, Shelford **c:** Fox **p:** Fox 3

1990:

S(1)	W31–16	Dunedin	16 Jun	**t:** Kirwan 2, Crowley, I Jones, Fox **c:** Fox 4 **p:** Fox
S(2)	W21–18	Auckland	23 Jun	**t:** Loe **c:** Fox **p:** Fox 5
A(1)	W21–6	Christchurch	21 Jul	**t:** Fitzpatrick, Crowley, Innes, Kirwan **c:** Fox **p:** Fox
A(2)	W27–17	Auckland	4 Aug	**t:** Fitzpatrick, Z Brooke, G Bachop **c:** Fox 3 **p:** Fox 2 **dg:** Fox
A(3)	L 9–21	Wellington	18 Aug	**p:** Fox 2 **dg:** Fox
F(1)	W24–3	Nantes	3 Nov	**t:** Innes, A Whetton **c:** Fox 2 **p:** Fox 3 **dg:** Fox
F(2)	W30–12	Paris	10 Nov	**t:** Crowley, M Jones **c:** Fox 2 **p:** Fox 6

1991:

Arg(1)	W28–14	Buenos Aires	6 Jul	**t:** Wright, Earl **c:** Fox **p:** Fox 5 **dg:** Crowley
Arg(2)	W36–6	Buenos Aires	13 Jul	**t:** Z Brooke, M Jones, Kirwan, Wright **c:** Fox 4 **p:** Fox 4
A(a1)	L12–21	Sydney	10 Aug	**t:** I Jones **c:** Fox **p:** Fox 2
A(a2)	W 6–3	Auckland	24 Aug	**p:** Fox 2
E*	W18–12	Twickenham	3 Oct	**t:** M Jones **c:** Fox **p:** Fox 4
US*	W46–6	Gloucester	8 Oct	**t:** Wright 3, Timu, Earl, Purvis, Tuigamala, Innes **c:** Preston 4 **p:** Preston 2
It*	W31–21	Leicester	13 Oct	**t:** Z Brooke, Tuigamala, Hewitt, Innes **c:** Fox 3 **p:** Fox 3

118

C*	W29–13	Lille	20 Oct	t: Timu 2, McCahill, Kirwan, Z Brooke
				c: Fox 3
				p: Fox
A(b)*	L 6–16	Dublin	27 Oct	p: Fox 2
S*	W13–6	Cardiff	30 Oct	t: Little
				p: Preston 3

1992:

Wd(1)	L14–28	Christchurch	18 Apr	t: Turner, Tuigamala
				p: Fox 2
Wd(2)	W54–26	Wellington	22 Apr	t: G Cooper 2, Loe 2, Pene, Clarke 2,
				Tuigamala, Larsen, Strachan
				c: G Cooper 6, Fox
Wd(3)	W26–15	Auckland	25 Apr	t: Pene, Kirwan, Loe, Clarke
				c: G Cooper 2
				p: G Cooper 2
I(1)	W24–21	Dunedin	30 May	t: Henderson, Bunce 2, Clarke
				c: G Cooper 4
I(2)	W59–6	Wellington	6 Jun	t: Bunce 2, Pene 2, I Jones, Clarke,
				Timu, M Cooper 2, Kirwan, Strachan
				c: M Cooper 6
				p: M Cooper
A(1)	L15–16	Sydney	14 Jul	t: Tuigamala, Bunce
				c: Fox
				p: Fox
A(2)	L17–19	Brisbane	19 Jul	t: Timu, Kirwan
				c: Fox 2
				p: Fox
A(3)	W26–23	Sydney	25 Jul	t: Bunce, Joseph
				c: Fox 2
				p: Fox 3
				dg: Fox
SA	W27–24	Johannesburg	15 Aug	t: Z Brooke, Kirwan, Timu
				c: Fox 3
				p: Fox 2

1993

BL(1)	W20–18	Christchurch	12 Jun	t: Bunce
				p: Fox 5
BL(2)	L 7–20	Wellington	26 Jun	t: Clarke
				c: Fox
BL(3)	W30–13	Auckland	3 Jul	t: Bunce, Fitzpatrick, Preston
				c: Fox 3
				p: Fox 3
A	W25–10	Dunedin	17 Jul	t: Fitzpatrick, Bunce
				p: Fox 5
WS	W35–13	Auckland	31 Jul	t: Stensness, Z Brooke
				c: Fox 2
				p: Fox 7
S	W51–15	Edinburgh	20 Nov	t: Wilson 3, Ellis 2, Bunce, Z Brooke
				c: Cooper 4, Wilson

| | | | | **p:** Cooper 2 |
| E | L 9–15 | Twickenham | 27 Nov | **p:** Wilson 3 |

1994

F(1)	L 8–22	Christchurch	26 Jun	**t:** Bunce
				p: M Cooper
F(2)	L20–23	Auckland	3 Jul	**t:** Fitzpatrick
				p: M Cooper 5
SA(1)	W22–14	Dunedin	9 Jul	**t:** Kirwan
				c: Howarth
				p: Howarth 5
SA(2)	W13–9	Wellington	23 Jul	**t:** Timu, Z Brooke
				p: Howarth
SA(3)	D18–18	Auckland	6 Aug	**p:** Howarth 6
A	L16–20	Sydney	17 Aug	**t:** Howarth
				c: Howarth
				p: Howarth 3

1995

C	W73–7	Auckland	22 Apr	**t:** Osborne 2, Bunce 2, Ellis 2, Wilson, Mehrtens, G Bachop, Brown
				c: Mehrtens 7
				p: Mehrtens 3
I*	W43–19	Johannesburg	27 May	**t:** Lomu 2, Kronfeld, Bunce, Osborne
				c: Mehrtens 3
				p: Mehrtens 4
W*	W34–9	Johannesburg	31 May	**t:** Kronfeld, Little, Ellis
				c: Mehrtens 2
				p: Mehrtens 4
				dg: Mehrtens
J*	W145–17	Bloemfontein	4 Jun	**t:** Ellis 6, Wilson 3, Rush 3, Osborne 2, R Brooke 2, Dowd, Loe, Ieremia, Culhane, Henderson
				c: Culhane 20
S*	W48–30	Pretoria	11 Jun	**t:** Little 2, Lomu, Bunce, Mehrtens, Fitzpatrick
				c: Mehrtens 6
				p: Mehrtens 2
E*	W45–29	Cape Town	18 Jun	**t:** Lomu 4, Kronfeld, G Bachop
				c: Mehrtens 3
				p: Mehrtens
				dg: Mehrtens
SA*	L12–15^	Johannesburg	24 Jun	**p:** Mehrtens 3
				dg: Mehrtens

* World Cup matches
^ after extra time
† Five-point try from here onwards
+ Non-cap Tests

120

SOUTH AFRICA

François Pienaar
(with Chris Thau)

WHATEVER the future may hold for me personally and the sport of rugby union in general, nothing will ever compare with the experience of leading South Africa to World Cup glory and of President Nelson Mandela handing me the trophy dressed in my No 6 Springbok jersey.

The World Cup was so important to my country for so many reasons. Of course the rugby aspect, but more the unifying qualities that came with the occasion. One Team, One Country was our slogan. By the end of the tournament I really think most of the world believed in it.

It was not enough for us to win the World Cup. The month-long competition offered the nation a once-in-a-lifetime opportunity to come together after too many years split apart. So when we beat New Zealand, our greatest rivals, on that never-to-be-forgotten final afternoon in Johannesburg, the victory belonged to every person in South Africa.

When President Mandela gave me the trophy he said: 'Thank-you for what you have done for South Africa. You have been a shining example of dignity and fortitude.' But I told him that nobody has done as much for our country as him.

The seeds of that triumph had been sown in the United Kingdom at the tail-end of 1994. By any standard it could be described as a successful tour, winning 11 of our 13 matches including both Tests. By recent South African standards it was exceptional. It ranked as the most successful tour since our return to international action in 1992.

The secret of our success was two-fold. Firstly, once we found a winning side we stuck to it. There was no chopping or changing for the sake of it. That line-up became the backbone of our World Cup team. Secondly, and arguably the most significant factor in our development, was the appointment as coach of Kitch Christie.

My relationship with Kitch, which started while he coached Transvaal, blossomed during the tour. Based on respect and mutual trust, it goes back a long time. We have a partnership of about 50 games without defeat and I rate him an excellent selector as well as a fitness freak.

He is a very thorough man and a deep thinker. I can safely say he was the architect of our success in the World Cup. Without him we would not have been able to make it. But he pushed us to the limit in the UK and some of the guys nearly cracked up during the early part of the tour. Thankfully we all persevered as the longer the tour wore on we started to play better and feel more confident.

> 'When President Mandela gave me the trophy he said: "Thank-you for what you have done for South Africa. You have been a shining example of dignity and fortitude." But I told him that nobody has done as much for our country as him'

I suffered tendenitis in my knee during the trip and was advised to rest on our return with the scalps of Scotland (won 34–10) and Wales (won 20–12). The injury was a legacy of having played some 85 games in the previous two seasons. All these were tough representative matches at provincial and international level. Not one was for my club.

But I returned to international action against Western Samoa (won 60–8) in the M-Net series five months later. We won easily with a nine-try performance that would stand us in good stead when we came across the Samoans in the World Cup two months later.

The first thing to strike me when our squad gathered for the Big One was how much fitter than the rest were the Transvaal players. This was because both Kitch and his former Transvaal assistant Ray Mordt are strong believers in physical fitness rather than aerobic fitness. They believe the key is leg power rather than lung power. And although their methods might look old fashioned I can assure you they are very effective.

We only came together about a fortnight before the start of the tournament. And the speed with which we had to prepare drew criticism from observers. We trained every day, twice a day. We even trained in the mornings before trial games against Western Province and Natal. We would train for two hours in the morning, mostly fitness, followed by two and a half hours of skill work in the afternoon.

Naturally enough, training before matches, we were less than impressive in the games themselves. The media savaged us but what they did not understand, or refused to, was that we were preparing for the World Cup, not the Currie Cup. Thrashing Western Province or Natal was not as important as how we played together. And we did learn.

> 'We came to the conclusion that George Gregan and David Campese could be the chinks in the Australian armour. Both seemed suspect under severe pressure and so we decided to play on them a lot. The plan worked a treat'

For example, after the Western Province game, which we won in injury time with a Joel Stransky dropped goal, I said: 'What Joel has proved today is that he can win a game in injury-time. He has the skill, the mental steel and the capability to win a game when the chips are down.' Prophetic words, eh? A little over a month later he repeated the trick to beat the All Blacks in Ellis Park.

But before then there was the small matter of the world champions to remove from our path. Kitch is a very astute observer and a fine analyst. He dismantles the opposition game to its finest detail and identifies their perceived strengths and weaknesses. But once the game is on he allows the players and his captain to take over. He provides the overall strategic approach and the means to beat the opposition, skill-wise, fitness-wise and in terms of game management. The rest is our business.

So it was that we picked through Australia's challenge with a fine tooth comb, coming to the conclusion that the new Wallaby scrum-half George Gregan and ageing wing maestro David Campese could be the chinks in the Aussie armour. Both seemed suspect under severe pressure and so we decided to play on them a lot. The plan worked a treat (won 27–18). In addition, we defended well and ran at them at every opportunity. Having played Australia three times in 1993 we knew what was required to beat them.

We were painfully aware that there were two routes through the World Cup. An easy route, if we beat Australia, and a hard one, if we did not. Nobody needed to tell us that victory over the holders would give us both confidence and the easier passage. But we truly earned both.

The second game against Romania (won 21–8) was a different story altogether. We had selected the team for the game long in advance. We planned the campaign in detail. If we won against Australia than Kitch would give the rest of the squad a game, because we felt it was important everyone had an outing under their belts by the time we reached the knockout stages.

With the Wallabies safely in the bag we could afford to be adventurous. But the Romanians surprised us by playing their running fly-half rather than their kicking one and, unfortunately, our second string were not particularly motivated for the game, I felt. They had sensed that after the win against Australia there was going to be one side playing in all the big games, while they had to appear in the less glamorous ones. However, credit to Romania who showed they are a tough rugby nation and deserve respect for their spirited performance.

Against Canada (won 20–0), the sole objective was to win the game with as few casualties as possible. In the event it turned out to be a watershed in our World Cup campaign. The outcome of the game, with its explosion of mindless violence early in the second-half, upset our plans, and nearly destroyed our Cup bid.

We believed we were unjustly singled out. We thought the Canadians went out trying to disrupt and intimidate us, regardless of the outcome. It was the same tactic they had employed against Australia. It did not work with the Wallabies and it did not work with us either. They grew increasingly frustrated as the game wore on but it harmed us far more than it harmed them.

The flare-up immediately cost us our hooker James Dalton, sent-off along with Canadians Gareth Rees and Rod Snow, and later, wing Pieter Hendriks, cited and banned by organising chiefs. I still believe that Dalton was innocent of any crime.

In the aftermath, team morale plummeted to its lowest ebb. We were so shattered we could hardly train. I had a word with Kitch and told him we must do something to rebuild team spirit otherwise we would be finished. We turned to a golf day, one in which everyone had to take part. It seemed to work. We had a superb day and it helped us forget the nonsense of the previous encounter.

> 'We believed we were unjustly singled out. We thought the Canadians went out trying to disrupt and intimidate us, regardless of the outcome. They grew increasingly frustrated as the game wore on but it harmed us far more than it harmed them. I still believe James Dalton was innocent of any crime'

The way the team trained the following morning told me we were ready for our quarter-final test against Western Samoa (won 42–14). We knew we were going to win, no disrespect intended, after having stuck 60 points on them in the M-Net series. Complacency was the only worry. We decided to start hard, fast and get points on the board early. That's what we did and the rest is history.

The only concern on the day was Andre Joubert's broken hand. And it was a big worry. He was a vital cog in our gameplan. As captain, when you have a left-footed fullback and right-footed fly-half you are sailing – you have so many options. When you lose one of them you struggle. When Andre told me he thought he would be able to play in the semi-final against France I thought he was joking. How could he play? But he did and his presence made the difference in Durban (won 19–15).

I had never before seen anything like the rain that submerged Durban that afternoon. Interestingly enough it did not bother us unduly. We had already experienced these types of conditions during our 1994 New Zealand tour. The fear was that the game could be called off during the first half as the rain continued to pour from the skies. Had referee Derek Bevan pulled the plug before half-time we would have been eliminated from the tournament by virtue of an inferior disciplinary record to that of France.

In the event, the atmosphere was fantastic and we played a great game. That said, the number of mistakes we made could have cost us dearly. Every time we took the lead, somehow we slowed down and

125

allowed France back into the game. The last ten minutes were epic. The French were exceptionally hard and I cannot put into words my relief on hearing the final whistle.

We returned to Johannesburg immediately after the game to give ourselves as long as possible at altitude to prepare for the final. Again we were billed as underdogs, with the All Blacks having destroyed England but we battled and battled and then battled some more (won 15–12 aet). Our defence absorbed everything they threw at us, including Jonah Lomu. The team was in heroic mood and I was utterly inspired by President Mandela's decision to wear my jersey. I don't really know what impact it had on the other guys, but to me it was like a personal vote of confidence. I wanted to show him that we could do it.

I remember thinking of the President as Andrew Mehrtens landed a penalty goal to take New Zealand 12–9 ahead late in the game. Suddenly I became confident that we were going to win. In the French game, every time we took the lead we had slowed down. This time around Mehrtens' go-ahead score provoked us to really dig in.

Joel Stransky kicked us into extra-time and then produced the late winning dropped goal he had perfected in the warm-up game against Western Province. As soon as it sailed through the posts I knew we had won. Only later did I remember sinking to my knees and praying with my team mates.

I thanked the Lord for giving us the talent and the ability to express it. I am still smiling at the memory of it all and am still not so sure this is not a dream. If it is, I hope I never wake up.

SOUTH AFRICA (P16 W12 D1 L3 F431 A255):

(H)	v England	(Pretoria, 4.6.94)	lost	15–32
(H)	v England	(Cape Town, 11.6.94)	won	27–9
(A)	v New Zealand	(Dunedin, 9.7.94)	lost	14–22
(A)	v New Zealand	(Wellington, 23.7.94)	lost	9–13
(A)	v New Zealand	(Auckland, 6.8.94)	drew	18–18
(H)	v Argentina	(Port Elizabeth, 8.10.94)	won	42–22
(H)	v Argentina	(Johannesburg, 15.10.94)	won	46–26
(A)	v Scotland	(Edinburgh, 19.11.94)	won	34–10
(A)	v Wales	(Cardiff, 26.11.94)	won	20–12
(H)	v Western Samoa	(Johannesburg, 12.4.95)	won	60–8
(–)	v Australia*	(Cape Town, 25.5.95)	won	27–18
(–)	v Romania*	(Cape Town, 30.5.95)	won	21–8
(–)	v Canada*	(Port Elizabeth, 3.6.95)	won	20–0
(–)	v Western Samoa*	(q/f: Johannesburg, 10.6.95)	won	44–28
(–)	v France*	(s/f: Durban, 17.6.95)	won	19–15
(–)	v New Zealand*	(f: Johannesburg, 24.6.95)	won	15–12 (aet)

* World Cup

South Africa in New Zealand (P14 W10 D1 L3 F445 A241):

(A)	v King Country	(Taupo, 23.6.94)	won	46–10
(A)	v Counties	(Pukekohe, 25.6.94)	won	37–26
(A)	v Wellington	(Wellington, 28.6.94)	won	36–26
(A)	v Southland	(Invercargill, 2.7.94)	won	51–15
(A)	v Hanan Shield Districts	(Timaru, 5.7.94)	won	67–19
(A)	v Taranaki	(New Plymouth, 13.7.94)	won	16–12
(A)	v Waikato	(Hamilton, 16.7.94)	won	38–17
(A)	v Manawatu	(Palmerston North, 19.6.94)	won	47–21
(A)	v Otago	(Dunedin, 27.7.94)	lost	12–19
(A)	v Canterbury	(Christchurch, 30.7.94)	won	21–11
(A)	v Bay of Plenty	(Rotorua, 2.8.94)	won	33–12

Argentina in South Africa (P6 W3 D0 L3 F216 A216):

(–)	v SA Development XV	(Wellington, 27.9.94)	won	51–20
(–)	v Border	(East London, 30.9.94)	won	41–25
(–)	v South Africa A	(Brakpan, 4.10.94)	lost	12–56
(–)	v Northern OFS	(Welkom, 11.10.94)	won	64–27

PROVINCIAL INTERNATIONAL RUGBY
'Natal come to grief in Super-10 final' – see page 98

BANKFIN CURRIE CUP
Final: Transvaal (31) 56, Free State (16) 33 (Springbok Park, Bloemfontein, 1.10.94)

	P	W	D	L	F	A	Pts
Orange Free State	10	7	0	3	283	265	14
Transvaal	10	6	0	4	276	237	12
Western Province	10	5	0	5	277	190	10
Natal	10	4	0	6	231	208	8
Northern Transvaal	10	4	0	6	245	321	8
Eastern Province	10	4	0	6	236	317	8

Currie Cup roll of honour (since 1980):

1980 Northern Transvaal
1981 Northern Transvaal
1982 Western Province
1983 Western Province
1984 Western Province
1985 Western Province
1986 Western Province
1987 Northern Transvaal
1988 Northern Transvaal
1989 Western Province
1990 Natal
1991 Northern Transvaal
1992 Natal
1993 Transvaal
1994 Transvaal

Previous winners: 24 –Western Province (4 draws); 14 –Northern Transvaal (3 draws); 7 –Transvaal (1 draw); 3 –Griquas; 2 –Natal, Border; 1 –Orange Free State.

PERCY FRAMES CUP (Cross Section League)

	P	W	D	L	F	A	Pts
Transvaal	4	4	0	0	275	81	8
Northern Transvaal	4	4	0	0	279	87	8
Western Province	4	4	0	0	225	113	8
Eastern Province	4	4	0	0	196	104	8
Natal	4	4	0	0	181	104	8
Orange Free State	4	3	0	1	167	105	8

Winners: Transvaal.

Bankfin Cup final (Central Unions): Griqualand West 24, Western Transvaal 11.

1980:

SAm(a1)	W24–9	Johannesburg	26 Apr	**t:** T du Plessis, Mordt, Germishuys **c:** Botha 3 **p:** Botha **dg:** Botha
SAm(a2)	W18–9	Durban	3 May	**t:** M du Plessis **c:** Botha **p:** Botha **dg:** Botha 3
BL(1)	W26–22	Cape Town	31 May	**t:** Louw, W du Plessis, Van Heerden, Germishuys, Serfontein **c:** Botha 3
BL(2)	W26–19	Bloemfontein	14 Jun	**t:** Louw, Stofberg, Germishuys, Pienaar **c:** Botha 2 **p:** Botha 2
BL(3)	W12–10	Port Elizabeth	28 Jun	**t:** Germishuys **c:** Botha **p:** Botha **dg:** Botha
BL(4)	L13–17	Pretoria	12 Jul	**t:** W du Plessis **p:** Pienaar 2, Botha
SAm(b1)	W22–13	Montevideo	18 Oct	**t:** Stofberg, Gerber, Berger **c:** Botha 2 **p:** Botha **dg:** Botha
SAm(b2)	W30–16	Santiago	26 Oct	**t:** Mordt 2, Germishuys 2, Gerber, M du Plessis **c:** Botha 3
F	W37–15	Pretoria	8 Nov	**t:** Pienaar, Germishuys, Serfontein, Stofberg, Kahts **c:** Botha 4 **p:** Botha 3

1981:

I(1)	W23–15	Cape Town	30 May	**t:** Gerber 2, Louw **c:** Botha **p:** Botha 3
I(2)	W12–10	Durban	6 Jun	**p:** Botha **dg:** Botha 3
NZ(1)	L 9–14	Christchurch	15 Aug	**t:** Bekker **c:** Botha **dg:** Botha
NZ(2)	W24–12	Wellington	29 Aug	**t:** Germishuys **c:** Botha **p:** Botha 5 **dg:** Botha
NZ(3)	L22–25	Auckland	12 Sep	**t:** Mordt 3 **c:** Botha 2 **p:** Botha 2

US	W38–7	Glenville		**t:** Mordt 3, Geldenhuys, Germishuys 2, Beck, Berger **c:** Botha 3

1982:

SAm(1)	W50–18	Pretoria	27 Mar	**t:** Gerber 3, Mordt 2, Oosthuizen, C du Plessis, W du Plessis **c:** Botha 6 **p:** Heunis **dg:** Botha
SAm(2)	L12–21	Bloemfontein	3 Apr	**t:** Gerber **c:** Botha **p:** Botha 2

1984:

E(1)	W33–15	Port Elizabeth	2 Jun	**t:** Gerber, C du Plessis, Louw **c:** Heunis 3 **p:** Heunis 5
E(2)	W35–9	Johannesburg	9 Jun	**t:** Gerber 3, Stofberg, Sonnekus, Tobias **c:** Heunis 3, Tobias **p:** Heunis
SAm(1)	W32–15	Pretoria	20 Oct	**t:** Louw, Gerber, Serfontein, Heunis, Mallet **c:** Tobias 2, Gerber **p:** Tobias 2
SAm(2)	W22–13	Cape Town	27 Oct	**t:** C du Plessis, Ferreira, Mordt, Gerber **p:** Tobias 2

1986:

Cv(1)	W21–15	Cape Town	10 May	**t:** C du Plessis **c:** Botha **p:** Botha 3 **dg:** Botha 2
Cv(2)	L18–19	Durban	17 May	**t:** Reinach **c:** Botha **p:** Botha 4
Cv(3)	W33–18	Pretoria	24 May	**t:** Schmidt, Botha, Gerber, Reinach **c:** Botha 4 **p:** Botha 3
Cv(4)	W24–10	Johannesburg	31 May	**t:** Wright **c:** Botha **p:** Botha 5 **dg:** M du Plessis

1989:

Wd(1)	W20–19	Cape Town	26 Aug	**t:** Knoetze, Botha, Smal **c:** Botha **p:** Botha 2
Wd(2)	W22–16	Johannesburg	1 Sep	**t:** Heunis, M du Plessis **c:** Botha **p:** Botha 3 **dg:** Botha

130

1982:

NZ [†]	L24–27	Johannesburg	15 Aug	**t:** Gerber 2, P Muller
				c: Botha 3
				p: Botha
A	L 3–26	Cape Town	22 Aug	**p:** Botha
F(1)	W20–15	Lyon	17 Oct	**t:** Gerber, Small
				c: Botha 2
				p: Botha
				dg: Botha
F(2)	L16–29	Paris	24 Oct	**t:** Gerber
				c: Botha
				p: Botha 2
				dg: Botha
E	L16–33	Twickenham	14 Nov	**t:** Smit
				c: Botha
				p: Botha 2
				dg: Botha

1993

F(1)	D20–20	Durban	26 Jun	**t:** Schmidt
				p: van Rensburg 5
F(2)	L17–18	Johannesburg	3 Jul	**t:** Small
				p: van Rensburg 4
A(1)	W19–12	Sydney	31 Jul	**t:** Small 2, Muller
				c: van Rensburg 2
A(2)	L20–28	Brisbane	14 Aug	**t:** Olivier, Stransky
				c: Stransky 2
				p: Stransky 2
A(3)	L12–19	Sydney	21 Aug	**t:** Small, Pienaar
				c: Stransky
Arg(a1)	W29–26	Buenes Aires	6 Nov	**t:** Small 2, van der Westhuizen, Joubert
				c: Stransky 3
				p: Stransky
Arg(a2)	W52–23	Buenes Aires	13 Nov	**t:** Strauss 2, Small 2, Williams, van der Westhuizen, Johnson
				c: Johnson 4
				p: Johnson 3
E(1)	L15–32	Pretoria	4 Jun	**p:** Joubert 5
E(2)	W27–9	Cape Town	11 Jun	**t:** H le Roux, Joubert
				c: Joubert
				p: Joubert 2, H le Roux 3
NZ(1)	L14–22	Dunedin	9 Jul	**t:** Straeuli
				p: Joubert 3
NZ(2)	L 9–13	Wellington	23 Jul	**p:** T van Rensburg
NZ(3)	D18–18	Auckland	6 Aug	**t:** Johnson, Venter
				c: Johnson
				p: Johnson 2
Arg(b1)	W42–22	Port Elizabeth	8 Oct	**t:** Roux 2, Stransky, Strauss, Williams
				c: Stransky 4
				p: Stransky 3
Arg(b2)	W46–26	Johannesburg	15 Oct	**t:** Badenhorst 2, Stransky, Andrews,

				Straeuli, Williams, J van der Westhuizen
				c: Stransky 4
				p: Stransky
S	W34–10	Edinburgh	19 Nov	t: J van der Westhuizen 2, Williams, Mulder, Straeuli
				c: Joubert 3
				p: Joubert
W	W20–12	Cardiff	26 Nov	t: Straeuli, Williams, Joubert
				c: H le Roux
				p: H le Roux

1995

WS(a)	W60–8	Johannesburg	xx Apr	t: Johnson 3, Williams 2, Small, M Andrews, Rossouw, Stransky
				c: Johnson 5, Stransky
				p: Johnson
A*	W27–18	Cape Town	25 May	t: Hendriks, Stransky
				c: Stransky
				p: Stransky 4
				dg: Stransky
R*	W21–8	Cape Town	30 May	t: Richter 2
				c: Johnson
				p: Johnson 3
C*	W20–0	Port Elizabeth	3 Jun	t: Richter 2
				c: Stransky 2
				p: Stransky 2
WS(b)*	W42–14	Johannesburg	10 Jun	t: Williams 4, M Andrews, Rossouw
				c: Johnson 3
				p: Johnson 2
F*	W19–15	Durban	17 Jun	t: Kruger
				c: Stransky
				p: Stransky 4
NZ*	W15–12^	Johannesburg	24 Jun	p: Stransky 3
				dg: Stransky 2

* World Cup
^ after extra time
† Five-point try from this game onwards

THE PLAYERS A–Z

Take the case of Tom Giles (right) as an example*. Tom was first capped at senior level for England in 1984, won 8 caps last season, and has 35 caps in all, with 60 points to his credit. He played in the 1986 IRB Centenary match in Cardiff (Lions 7, The Rest 15) which has been included as a Lions cap. And in 1993 Tom played two Tests in the series against New Zealand.

Each player has his caps listed in order, plus a breakdown of his points tally, again in chronological order. For example, Tom marked his debut against Wales in 1984 with one try. If

England (1984)		
Last Season	8 caps	18 pts
Career	35 caps	60 pts
Lions 1986		
1993	2 Tests	0 pts
Caps	(35): **1984** W, F, E, S, Fj **1987** S, I, W(a), wc–T, W(b), A **1989** W, S, I, F, Arg(1,2), Fj **1991** F, S, J, W **1993** I, F. Lions–NZ(1,2) **1994** F, S, W, SA(1) **1995** I, F(a), W, S, wc–Arg, NZ, F(b)	
Points	(60 – 9t, 4p, 1dg) **1984** W(1t) **1991** F(1t), W(2t) **1993** F(1p) **1994** S(2t, 1p), SA(1:1t) **1995** F(a:1dg), wc–Arg(2t)	

a nation is played more than once in the same year, the statistic is recorded in one of two ways. For a 3-match series against, say, Australia, the statistic reads: A(1,2,3). If our player has previously turned out against the Aussies in the same year, that statistic reads: A(a), followed by A(b1,b2,b3). This makes identification possible when it comes to points scored, e.g. A(b3:1t) means that our player has scored a try against Australia in the third Test of the second series.

* The qualification for entry in *The Save & Prosper Rugby Union Who's Who* is involvement in any Test match of any player from the Big Eight nations during the 1994/95 season (June 1994–June 1995). Players' statistics *do* include World Cup matches, but not Bledisloe Cup and South Africa v Wales matches. Details of A-team players are logged in the Appendix section (pp 391–397).

Accoceberry, G.   France

Full Name: Guy Accoceberry
Club: Begles-Bordeaux
Position: Scrum-half
Height: 5ft 11½in (1.82m)
Weight: 12st 5lb (76kg)
Occupation: Pharmacist
Born: Vittel, 5.5.67
Family: Married
Former club: Tyrosse
International debut: New Zealand 8, France 22, 1994
Five Nations debut: France 21, Wales 9, 1995
Notable landmarks in rugby career:
One of ten French backs to shave their heads during last summer's World Cup, Guy will remember the campaign more for the broken arm he suffered 33 minutes into France's extraordinary 22–19 defeat of Scotland (Pretoria, 3.6.95), an injury which ended his participation. His only other outing in South Africa had come in the 54–18 win over Cote d'Ivoire (Rustenburg, 30.5.95)

France (1994)

Last Season	10 caps	5 pts
Career	10 caps	5 pts

Caps (10): **1994** NZ(1,2), C(b) **1995** W, E, S, I, R wc-IC, F
Points (5 – 1t): **1995** wc-IC(1t)

when he claimed a try. Rose to prominence as a member of the French side that won the 1992 Students World Cup, but it was not until France toured New Zealand two summers later that he really hit the big time. A visit that has gone down in history as France's most successful ever, saw Guy make his debut in the 22–8 shock first Test win and retain it in the heroic 23–20 second Test triumph. The tallest French scrum-half since Jean-Michel Aguirre in 1972, Guy was also a member of the Cote Basque XV which beat the 1990 All Blacks. Tyrosse captain for three seasons before switching to Begles at the start of last season, where he found himself at the heels of a powerful pack, the former French Universities No.9 graduated to the France A side against their English counterparts at Leicester in 1993 as a prelude to a brief tour of duty on the Five Nations bench in place of the unavailable Jerome Cazalbou. No second best for Guy in 1995, however, as the Bordeaux pharmacist held onto his place throughout the championship

Allan, J.   South Africa

Full Name: John Allan
Province: Natal
Club: Glenwood Old Boys (SA)
Position: Hooker
Height: 6ft (1.83m)
Weight: 15st (91kg)
Occupation: Computer consultant with ABS Computers
Born: Glasgow, Scotland, 25.11.63
Family: Claire (wife)
Family links with rugby: Brothers both play – William in Italy and Richard for Empangeni in Durban, SA
Former clubs: Northern Transvaal Defence (SA), Edinburgh Academicals
International debut (for Scot): New Zealand 31, Scotland 16, 1990
International debut (for SA): Australia 12, South Africa 19, 1993
Five Nations' debut: Scotland 32, Wales 12, 1991
Other sporting achievements: Softball for Scotland Schools
Suggestions to improve rugby: Penalise players for killing opposition ball anywhere by award of automatic penalty in front of posts.

Scotland (1990)		
Career	9 caps	0 pts
South Africa (1993)		
Last Season	5 caps	0 pts
Career	8 caps	0 pts

Caps	(Scotland-9): **1990** NZ(1) **1991** W, I, R wc-J, I, WS, E, NZ
Caps	(S Africa-8): **1993** A(1R) Arg(1,2R) **1994** E(1,2), NZ(1,2,3)
Points	Nil

Notable landmarks in rugby career: A serious knee injury ruled him out of World Cup contention, having been first-choice hooker in the first part of 1994, playing both home Tests against England and all three in the All Black dominated series against New Zealand. During that tour he also turned out against Counties, Wellington, Southland, Waikato and Canterbury. Glasgow-born John made his Springbok debut against Australia in Sydney on 31 July 1993 as a last-minute replacement for the great Uli Schmidt. South Africa won that game (19–12) – one of seven starts made by John in Oz – but he did not reappear in the Test side until the autumn tour to Argentina when starting the first Test and coming on as a 52nd minute replacement in the second, where the Springboks completed a 2-0 series sweep. John had returned to the Republic in the summer of 1992 to live with wife Claire, having collected the last of his nine Scotland caps in the World Cup third/fourth place play-off against New Zealand at Cardiff (30.10.91). Figured in five of Scotland's six Cup ties before

being usurped by perennial rival Kenny Milne for the '92 Five Nations Championship. Warmed replacements' bench throughout the latter, as he had done in 1990/91 season, when also replacement for Scotland B against Ireland and France, before making full-debut in first Test at Dunedin on summer tour of New Zealand (lost 16–31, 16.6.90). Five Nations debut came the following season against Wales (2.2.91)
Touchlines: Reading

Andrew, C. R. MBE   England

Full Name: Christopher Robert Andrew MBE
Club: Newcastle
Position: Outside-half
Height: 5ft 9in (1.76m)
Weight: 12st 8lb (80kg)
Occupation: Associate director with DTZ Debenham Thorpe (chartered surveyors)
Born: Richmond, Yorkshire, 18.2.63
Family: Sara (wife) and Emily (daughter)
Family links with rugby: Brothers (Richard and David) play for Headingley
Former clubs: Middlesbrough, Cambridge University (Blues: 1982,83,84), Nottingham, Gordon (Sydney, Aus), Toulouse (Fr)
International debut: England 22, Romania 15, 1985
Five Nations' debut: England 9, France 9, 1985
Best moment in rugby: Beating France 21–19 at Twickenham to win 1991 Five Nations' Grand Slam
Worst moment in rugby: Losing 1990 Grand Slam decider 13–7 to Scotland – losing the World Cup final was disappointing but in a different way; losing England place (1992/93)
Most embarrassing moment: Missing 9 out of 10 kicks at goal for Nottingham against London Welsh in fourth round of 1985 John Player Cup (lost 11–12)
Most respected opponent: Michael Lynagh (Australia)
Other sporting achievements: Played first-class cricket for Yorkshire 2nd XI and Cambridge Univ, 1984 and 1985 (as captain). Scored 101 n.o. for Univ against Notts at Trent Bridge (1984)
Notable landmarks in rugby career: World's most capped outside-half (69 of his 70 caps in the No.10 jersey) who won the inaugural Adidas golden boot

award for a spectacular goal-kicking campaign last season. Opened up with 24 points in 54–3 home defeat of Romania (12.11.94) but enjoyed his finest hour against Canada, again at Twickenham (10.12.94), when he kicked a perfect 12 out of 12 (six cons, six pens) for an English record 30 points – a total only ever exceeded at the time by the 50 points (10 tries) amassed by Hong Kong wing Ashley Billington in the 164–13 World Cup qualifier defeat of Singapore. Continued to plunder points through England's third Grand Slam in five years, most notably the 24 he claimed to win the championship decider against Scotland (Twickenham, 18.3.95). Totalled 53 in Five Nations series before steering England to fourth place in World Cup. Had only resumed the goal kicking duties for England after a five-year break during the 1994 Championship. Highlighted summer tour to South Africa with 27-point display in England's first Test win over cocksure Springboks, in so doing becoming first English player to achieve a 'full house' of try, conversion (2), penalty goal (5) and

England (1985)
Last Season	11 caps	186 pts
Career	70 caps	396 pts
Lions 1989	2 Tests	8 pts
1993	3 Tests	3 pts

Caps (70): **1985** Ro, F, S, I, W **1986** W, S, I, F **1987** I, F, W wc-J(R), US **1988** S, I(1,2), A(a1,a2), Fj, A(b) **1989** S, I, F, W, Ro, Fj. Lions-A(2,3) **1990** I, F, W, S, Arg(b) **1991** W, S, I, F, Fj, A(a) wc-NZ, It, US, F, S, A(b) **1992** S, I, F, W, C, SA **1993** F, W. Lions-NZ(1,2,3). NZ **1994** S, I, F, W, SA(1,2), R, C, I, F(a), W, S wc-Arg, It, A, NZ, F(b)

Points (396 – 2t,33c,86p,21dg): **1985** Ro(4p,2dg), F(2p,1dg), S(2p), I(2p), W(1c,2p,1dg) **1986** W(6p,1dg), S(2p), I(3c,1p) **1987** F(1dg) **1988** S(1dg), I(1:3c) **1989** S(2p), I(1c,2p), F(1p), W(2p,1dg), Ro(1dg), Fj(1c). Lions-A(2:1c,1p,1dg) **1991** F(1dg), Fj(1t,2dg) wc-NZ(1dg), S(1dg) **1993** Lions-NZ(2:1dg). NZ(1dg) **1994** F(5p,1dg), W(1c,1p), SA(1:1t,2c,5p,1dg), SA(2:3p), R(6c,4p), C(6c,6p) **1995** I(1c,1p), F(2c,4p), W(1c,2p), S(7p,1dg) wc-Arg(6p,2dg), It(1c,5p), A(1c,5p,1dg), NZ(3c,1p), F(3p)

dropped goal in a Test. World record holder for international dropped goals with 22 (20 for England, two for Lions). Replaced injured Paul Dean (13.6.89) on triumphant Lions tour of Australia and played in last two Tests (1c,1p,1dg in Brisbane second Test). Either side of trip Down Under captained England to win 58–3 in Romania (13.5.89) and British Lions XV to 29–27 success over France (4.10.89) in French Revolution Bicentennial match. Captained Wasps to 1989/90 Courage Championship and London to 1990 Divisional Championship (having represented North in 1985 and 1986). Moved family, work and rugby to Toulouse after 1991 World Cup but returned with job early in 1992/93 season. Subjected to 120-day re-qualification rule which prevented his playing League rugby and doubtless affected his form. Deposed by Stuart Barnes midway through 1993 Five Nations' Championship but gained his revenge when becoming first-choice No.10 for Lions in New Zealand that summer, playing in all three Tests.
Touchlines: Gardening and DIY

Andrews, K. S.   South Africa

Full Name: Keith Steven Andrews
Club: Villagers
Province: Western Province
Position: Tighthead prop
Height: 5ft 11in (1.80m)
Weight: 16st 7lb (105kg)
Occupation: Accountant
Born: Molteno, 3.5.62
International debut: England 33,
South Africa 16, 1992
Notable landmarks in rugby career:
Toured to New Zealand with
Springboks in 1994, playing in eight
of the 14 matches, the last of which
was the third and final Test, in
Auckland on 6 August, where the
South Africans avoided a whitewash
by snatching an 18–18 draw. Cousin
of fellow Springbok Mark Andrews,
Keith also turned out against
Counties, Wellington, Southland,
Taranaki, Manawatu, Otago and
Canterbury. Having made his debut
against England at Twickenham
(14.11.92), Keith's Test career went

South Africa (1992)

Last Season	1 cap	0 pts
Career	8 caps	0 pts

Caps (8): **1992** E **1993** F(1,2),
A(1R,2,3), Arg(2) **1994** NZ(3)
Points Nil

from strength to strength in 1993, with the only blip coming when he was one
of two Springboks sent-off during 40–12 tour triumph over Argentine province
Tucuman (2.11.93). Played in four of South Africa's six games in South
America (also against Cordoba and Rosario), having appeared eight times on
the summer tour of Australia – outings in each of the the three Tests plus starts
against South Australia, Victoria, NSW Country, Queensland and Queensland
Country. Although only a replacement first time against Argentina he took over
from Transvaal's Balie Swart for the second international in Buenes Aires
(13.11.93). Educated at Selbourne College in the South African district of East
London, Keith played 95 times for Western Province before being selected by
Boks to tour France and England in 1992, during which the Cape Town-based
player appeared in eight of the 13 games.

Andrews, M. G.   South Africa

Full Name: Mark Gregory Andrews
Province: Natal
Position: Lock
Height: 6ft 7in (2.0m)
Weight: 17st 5lb (112kg)
Occupation: Student
Born: Elliot, 21.2.72
Former club: Aurillac (Fra)
International debut: South Africa 27, England 9, 1994
Notable landmarks in rugby career:
A crucial player in South Africa's World Cup winning side, versatile Mark was moved to No 8 in the semi-final against France (Durban 17.6.95) to combat Laurent Cabannes at the tail of the lineout and remained there against All Black Zinzan Brooke as the Boks won a famous final victory in Johannesburg (24.6.95). South Africa's outstanding player on their 1994 tour of New Zealand, with former All Black lock Andy Haden opining: 'He is in the top-10 lineout ball winners in the world already and I'm sure he's going to get bigger, stronger and more clever.' Learned much of his trade in France, where cousin

South Africa (1994)

Last Season	13 caps	15 pts
Career	13 caps	15 pts

Caps (13): **1994** E(2), NZ(1,2,3), Arg(1,2), S, W **1995** WS(a) wc-A, WS(b), F,NZ

Points (15 – 3t): 1994 Arg(2:1t) **1995** WS(a:1t) wc-WS(b:1t)

stronger and more clever.' Learned much of his trade in France, where cousin Keith Andrews set up the raw 19-year-old to play in Aurillac. He survived 22 bone-crunching games in 25 weeks and returned home a man. Really came to the fore in '94, helping Natal beat England 21–6 in a try-less contest on May 21 and, after England took out their annoyance on the Springboks in a sensationally one-sided first Test, was then summoned to Cape Town to bolster the South African line-up in the second and final Test. England were beaten 27–9. However it was in New Zealand that the former water polo standout left an indelible mark. Targetted by the All Blacks, he shrugged off separate 'assaults' on his head and ankles to build a formidable tour CV, dominating the front of nearly every lineout he graced. Mark maintained his 100 per cent record in South Africa colours, playing in both Tests in Argentina, before helping the Springboks dispose of Wales and Scotland on a largely successful autumn tour of Britain.
Touchlines: Junior Springbok colours at water polo

Armary, L.   France

Full Name: Louis Armary
Club: Lourdes
Position: Prop, hooker
Height: 6ft (1.83m)
Weight: 16st 2lb (98kg)
Occupation: Business executive with Lyonnaise des Eaux
Family: Wife and two children
Born: Lourdes, 24.7.63
International debut: France 55, Romania 12, 1987
Five Nations' debut: Scotland 23, France 12, 1988
Notable landmarks in rugby career: Lost France loosehead berth to Laurent Benezech on the triumphant 1994 tour of New Zealand but still revelled in 2–0 Test series triumph as he came on as a replacement in both matches. Failed to regain first-choice jersey until coach Pierre Berbizier turned in desperation to experience to see off the Five Nations Wooden Spoon in Dublin (4.3.95). Moved to tighthead in South Africa last summer where Louis played against Tonga, Ireland and South Africa in a World Cup campaign which yielded a third place finish. Scored one and only international try for France in

France (1987)

Last Season	7 caps	0 pts
Career	47 caps	4 pts

Caps (47): **1987** wc-R(a). R(b) **1988** S, I, W, Arg(b1,b2), R **1989** W, S, A(1,2) **1990** W, E, S, I, A(1,2,3), NZ(1) **1991** W(b) **1992** S, I, R, Arg(a1,a2), SA(1,2), Arg(b) **1993** E, S, I, W, SA(1,2), R(b), A(1,2) **1994** I, W, NZ(1R,2R) **1995** I, R wc-T, I, SA
Points (4 – 1t): **1990** A(2:1t)

48–31 second Test reversal at hands of Australia in Brisbane (24.6.90). An unused member of France's 1991 World Cup squad, Louis bounced back to represent France in two different positions during 1991/92 season: at hooker against Wales in non-cap Test in Cardiff (4.9.91), and at loosehead prop at Murrayfield and in Paris against Ireland after first-choice Gregoire Lascube had been suspended for his dismissal against England. In 1992/93, however, he remained at loosehead throughout the ten-match campaign (including France's 1993 Five Nations title triumph) before missing Spring trip to Bucharest. Reinstated, Louis wore No.1 jersey throughout the South Africa and Australia Test series, neither of which France lost. Injury sidelined him for much of 1994 championship. Eleven of his 47 appearances have come at hooker, so his 36 propping caps leave him well short of the 55 gained by French record holder Robert Paparemborde.

Atherton, S.   South Africa

Full Name: Stephen Atherton
Province: Natal
Club: Pinetown
Position: Lock
Height: 6ft 7in (2.0m)
Weight: 18st 8lb (xkg)
Occupation: Self-employed in
building renovation business
Born: England, 17.3.65
International debut: Argentina 26,
South Africa 29, 1993
Notable landmarks in rugby career:
Full-time rugby player, having
played continuously for the last eight
years, spreading his time during the
last 16 'seasons' equally between
Natal and Italy. Steve started out as a
fullback at Pinetown boarding
school, moving to prop before
settling in the engine room.
However, he retains his kicking skills
and was frequently utilised by his
Italian club. A product of the
Crusaders club down Durban way,
Steve made his provincial debut for

South Africa (1993)

Last Season	5 caps	0 pts
Career	7 caps	0 pts

Caps (7): **1993** Arg(1,2) **1994** E(1,2),
NZ(1,2,3)
Points Nil

Natal in 1988 and had made 71 appearances when he was selected for the
reborn Springboks first tour in 1992. Steve made six appearances on the trip to
France and England without breaking into the Test side. That honour befell him
the former Junior Springbok the following year in Argentina, when he excelled
in both Test victories over the Pumas. Steve also turned out in the wins over
Cordoba and Tucuman. Maintained his progress the following year and
impressed in the shared Test series with England and the less successful three-
match series in New Zealand, a tour on which he also appeared in the wins over
Counties, Wellington, Southland, Manawatu and Canterbury. Partnered Natal
team mate Mark Andrews in the Test second row and, although he felt he had
a good campaign, he was discarded thereafter.

Bachop, G. T. M.   New Zealand

Full Name: Graeme Thomas Miro
Bachop
Club: Linwood
Province: Canterbury
Position: Scrum-half
Height: 5ft 10in (1.77m)
Weight: 13st (82kg)
Occupation: Sports trainer with Samix
Born: Christchurch, 11.6.67
Family links with rugby: Stephen
(brother) played for Western Samoa
(4 caps) and now New Zealand (5)
International debut: Wales 9, New
Zealand 34, 1989
Notable landmarks in rugby career:
Shares with Sid Going All Black
record for most caps won by a scrum-
half (29) having returned to Test side
in 1994 after night of long knives
removed many of those responsible
for allowing France to leave New
Zealand with 2–0 series win. Added
bonus for Graeme was that he was
partnered with brother Stephen in
Test side which kept the touring
South Africans at bay, winning the
first two Tests before sharing the
third in Auckland. Despite New

New Zealand (1989)

Last Season	10 caps	10 pts
Career	29 caps	18 pts

Caps (29): 1989 W,I **1990** S(1,2),
A(1,2,3), F(1,2) **1991** Arg(1,2),
A(a1,a2). wc-E, US, C, A(b), S
1992 Wd(1) **1994** SA(1,2,3), A
1995 C wc-I, W, S, E, SA

Points (18 – 4t): **1989** W(1t) **1990** A(2:1t)
1995 C(1t) wc-E(1t)

Zealand's subsequent Bledisloe Cup
loss to Australia, Graeme held onto the No.9 jersey through to the World Cup
where he formed an outstanding partnership with fly-half starlet Andrew
Mehrtens all the way through to extra-time of the final. In his former All Black
life, Graeme had toured Wales and Ireland with the class of '89, two years after
being a member of the New Zealand Colts team which beat their Australian
counterparts 37–12. Indeed, in 1987, he had toured with the All Blacks to
Japan, before even having made provincial bow for Canterbury, where he was
only third choice. Selected ahead of Canterbury team mate Bruce Deans for first
cap against Wales, at Cardiff, and celebrated with try in handsome win. Bagged
seven tries in six games on tour of Australia in 1988. Lost automatic place in
national side to Auckland's Ant Strachan after World XV won the first Test
28–14 of the centenary series at Christchurch in April 1992. Only outing
thereafter came against Australian Capital Territory in 45–13 win at Canberra
in July 1992, where he was voted man of the match.

Bachop, S. J.   New Zealand

Full Name: Stephen John Bachop
Province: Otago
Position: Fly-half
Height: 5ft 10in (1.78m)
Weight: 13st 3lb (79kg)
Born: 2.4.66
Family links with rugby: Brother
Graeme has been capped 29 times at
scrum-half by All Blacks
Former club: Blackrock College (Ire)
International debut (for W Samoa):
Wales 13, Western Samoa 16, 1991
International debut (for NZ): New
Zealand 20, France 23, 1994
Notable landmarks in rugby career:
Superb family occasion as Stephen
wins second cap, for brother Graeme
was his half-back partner. The
match was New Zealand's first Test
engagement against touring South
Africa (Dunedin, 9.7.94) and the
pair combined to steer the All Blacks
home 22–14. The celebrations were
a far cry from Stephen's debut the
previous week, in the second Test
against France at Auckland's Eden

Western Samoa (1991)		
Career	4 caps	7 pts
New Zealand (1994)		
Last Season	5 caps	0 pts
Career	5 caps	0 pts

Caps (5): **1994** F(2), SA(1,2,3), A
Points Nil

Park (3.7.94). New Zealand had looked good for a share of the series until
France ran the length of the field in the final minute and Jean-Luc Sadourny
touched down a sensational try. The shock of that that 2–0 series defeat
galvanised the All Blacks into sweeping aside the Boks, with the brothers
Bachop holding firm through the second and third Tests. However, a 16–20
Bledisloe Cup defeat to Australia (Sydney, 17.8.94) convinced the selectors to
think again and by the time the '95 All Blacks were unveiled Stephen had most
unluckily given way to young Canterbury prodigy Andrew Mehrtens. This
meant he missed out on the World Cup (Southland's Simon Culhane going
along as No.2), a tournament in which he had first surfaced, in 1991, as pivot
in the Western Samoa team which stunned Wales, winning 16–13 in Cardiff.
Played four times for Manu Samoa before declaring for New Zealand and
touring to Australia and South Africa in 1992, making seven appearances en
route.

Back, M.   Wales

Full Name: Matthew Back
Club: Bridgend
Position: Fullback
Height: 6ft (1.83m)
Weight: 14st (84kg)
Occupation: Schoolteacher at
Cwmlai Primary School, Tonyrefail
Born: 5.4.70
Family links with rugby: Uncle, Ian
Back, played for Wales against South
Africa in 1970; father Terry played
at scrum-half for Gilfach Goch
International debut: France 21,
Wales 9, 1995
Five Nations debut: As above
Notable landmarks in rugby career:
Matthew suffered from the shake-up
in Welsh rugby that followed only
the country's second ever Five
Nations whitewash. Having played
in all four matches, coming on
against France and England as
replacement for Simon Hill and
Tony Clement respectively, the

Wales (1995)

Last Season	4 caps	0 pts
Career	4 caps	0 pts

Caps (4): **1995** F(R), E(R), S, I
Points Nil

former Cardiff Institute and Pontypridd player won the starting berth against
Scotland and Ireland. The resignation of the Alan Davies-Bob Norster ticket,
however, combined with the return from injury of Clement, led to Matthew's
omission from Wales' World Cup squad, although that might one day be
viewed as a mixed blessing. He had risen to international prominence on the
Welsh Development tour to France and in 1993/94 represented Welsh Students
against England and also Wales A versus Japan and North of England.
Switched allegiance from Sardis Road to Bridgend last season.

Back, N. A.   England

Full Name: Neil Antony Back
Club: Leicester
Position: Openside flanker
Height: 5ft 10in (1.78m)
Weight: 14st 6lb (87kg)
Occupation: Senior pensions
supervisor with AXA Equity and
Law, Coventry
Born: Coventry, 16.1.69
Family: Single
Former club: Nottingham
International debut: Scotland 14,
England 15, 1994
Five Nations debut: As above
Other sporting achievements:
Cricket for Coventry and
Warwickshire Schools
Notable landmarks in rugby career:
Hamstring injury ruined Neil's
World Cup last summer just when he
seemed to be building up a head of
steam. Having come on as a 47th
minute replacement for Steve
Ojomoh against Argentina (won

England (1994)		
Last Season	3 caps	0 pts
Career	5 caps	0 pts

Caps (5): **1994** S,I **1995** wc-Arg,It,WS
Points Nil

24–18), Neil was moved to openside for the next two Pool B games against Italy
(won 27–20) and Western Samoa (won 44–22), where the injury was sustained.
It was a big shame for the little man, having waited so long for Test recognition,
then been discarded, then fought his way back to prominence. February 5, 1994
had seen the day when a player told he was too small to grace the international
stage did exactly that. He had won 12 caps in England's second XV dating back
to his B debut against the Emerging Wallabies in 1990, a year after claiming a
hat-trick of tries as England's first ever under-21 side walloped their Romanian
counterparts in sunny Bucharest. He had played, too, for England U-18s
(1985–87) and England Colts (1987/88), starred for the centenary Barbarians
against England (September 1990) and even scored a try for an England XV in
their 33–15 defeat of Italy in 1990. But what he hungered for more than
anything was a full cap. Nothing else would suffice. Hence the satisfaction that
February afternoon in Edinburgh when he finally achieved his goal. So
disappointed had he been to have missed the All Blacks visit to Twickenham the
previous November that he had taken the advice of three fitness advisors and
devised a programme that would have him in tip-top shape for 5 Feb. What a
shame after such a long wait that England should turn in such a poor
performance, despite Jon Callard's injury-time winner. If anything they were

worse on Neil's second outing, when Ireland won at Twickenham for the first time since 1982. The upshot was that England's management reverted to the 'big is beautiful' script, with Neil being dumped for the tour to South Africa, the country in which he was to make his return the following summer.

Touchlines: Training five days a week for rugby, golf, equestrian sports.

Bayfield, M. C. England

Full Name: Martin Christopher Bayfield
Club: Northampton
Position: Lock
Height: 6ft 10in (2.08m)
Weight: 18st 2lb (115kg)
Occupation: Police constable with the Bedfordshire Constabulary
Born: Bedford, 21.12.66
Family: Helena (wife), Rosanna (daughter) and Polly (daughter)
Former clubs: Metropolitan Police, Bedford
International debut: Fiji 12, England 28, 1991
Five Nations' debut: Scotland 7, England 25, 1992
Best moment in rugby: Lions' second Test defeat of New Zealand (1993)
Worst moment in rugby: Being dumped by England (1994)
Notable landmarks in rugby career: One of England's few genuinely outstanding players at last summer's World Cup. Ever-present in side throughout 1994/95 campaign, save for World Cup-tie against Western Samoa (Durban 4.6.95) when Richard West was given his debut.

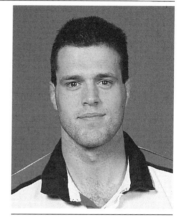

England (1991)		
Last Season	11 caps	0 pts
Career	27 caps	0 pts
Lions 1993	3 Tests	0 pts

Caps (27): **1991** Fj, A **1992** S, I, F, W, C, SA **1993** F, W, S, I. Lions-NZ(1,2,3) **1994** S, I, SA(1,2), R, C **1995** I, F, W, S wc-Arg, It, A, NZ, F
Points Nil

That apart, the tallest forward ever to play for England maintained a permanent vigil in the England engine room alongside Martin Johnson as the Lillywhites swept to their third Five Nations' Grand Slam in five seasons. Bayfs had graduated to British Lion status (on the '93 tour to New Zealand) after just two seasons as his country's first-choice lock, and he played in all three Tests of a series edged by the hosts. An injury to his neck and spine, sustained in a fall in New Zealand, kept him out of the 15–9 autumn defeat of those same All Blacks and, for a period, threatened his career. Previously made three appearances for England 18-Group, represented Midlands Division and British Police for three seasons, toured with British Police to Italy (1989) and broke into England's B set-up during 1990/91 season, playing against Emerging Australians (12–12, Wasps 4.11.90) and Italy (12-9, Waterloo 27.3.91). Progressed to England squad for 1991 tour to Fiji and Australia, playing in both Tests after Wade Dooley sustained hand injury. Missed out on the World Cup squad but, following Paul Ackford's retirement, booked a permanent berth alongside Dooley in England's 1992 Grand Slam XV. Reverted to England B for summer of '92 tour to New Zealand, where he played in both 'Tests' losses to the All Black XV (lost 18–24, Hamilton, 28.6.92; lost 18–26, Pukekohe, 5.7.92). Returned to the senior side once back in Blighty and played the full season, doubling his cap tally to a dozen, before being one of 16 Englishmen measured for Lions' blazers.

Touchlines: Weight training.

Bell, J. C.   Ireland

Full Name: Jonathan Charles Bell
Club: Ballymena
Position: Wing, centre
Height: 5ft 11in (1.80m)
Weight: 14st 7lb (94kg)
Occupation: Student at Loughborough University
Born: Belfast, 7.2.74
International debut: Australia 31, Ireland 13, 1994
Five Nations debut: Scotland 26, Ireland 13, 1995
Notable landmarks in rugby career: An Irish Schools cap just three years ago (1992), Jonathan has the hopes of much of Irish rugby invested in him. A swift promotion up the representative ladder has seen him turn out at fullback, centre and wing for Schools (three caps), Ireland Under-21s (victory over New Zealand in October 1993) and the national senior side. Toured to Australia in summer of 1994, playing against New South Wales, ACT, Queensland and an Australian

Ireland (1994)

Last Season	8 caps	5 pts
Career	8 caps	5 pts

Caps (8): **1994** A(1,2), US **1995** S, It wc-NZ, W(b), F(b)
Points (5 – 1t): **1995** S(1t)

XV before making his debut in the first Test at Ballymore (5.6.94). Returned home to captain Ireland Under-21s to victory over England and break into the Ulster side for the Inter-Pros. Moved to the left wing for Ireland's 26–15 home defeat of USA (5.11.94) and would have remained in the position for the Five Nations opener against England but for a hamstring injury which forced his withdrawl. Returned in place of Niall Woods a fortnight later, at Murrayfield, and celebrated with his first Test try in a match which Ireland could well have won, but Scotland did. Further injury hampered his international progress thereafter and he did not feature again until the eve of the World Cup when Ireland went to Treviso (8.5.95) and became the first major nation to lose to Italy (12–22). Fortunately, a place in the World Cup quarter-finals all but erased that memory.

Benazzi, A.   France

Full Name: Abdelatif Benazzi
Club: Agen
Position: No 8, flanker
Height: 6ft 6in (1.98m)
Weight: 17st 5lb (111kg)
Occupation: Sales representative with Astra-Calve
Born: Oujda, Morocco, 20.8.68
Family: Single
Former club: Cahors
International debut: Australia 21, France 9, 1990
Five Nations' debut: England 21, France 19, 1991
Other sporting achievements: Moroccan junior record holder for discus and shot
Notable landmarks in rugby career: One of the stars of the World Cup and an ever-present in France back row during 1994/95 season, save for the pre-World Cup trip to Bucharest. Abdel also played a notable role in the historic 2–0 series win in New Zealand (June-July 1994). Claimed his second Test try in the 54–18 World Cup defeat of Cote d'Ivoire (30.5.95), having bagged his first against England in 1994

France (1990)

Last Season	12 caps	5 pts
Career	38 caps	10 pts

Caps (38): **1990** A(1,2,3), NZ(1,2) **1991** E, US(1R,2) wc-Ro, Fj, C **1992** SA(1R,2), Arg(b) **1993** E, S, I, W, A(1,2) **1994** I, W, E, S, NZ(1,2), C(b) **1995** W, E(a), S(a), I(a), R wc-T, IC, S(b), I(b), SA, E(b)
Points (10 – 2t): **1994** E(1t) **1995** wc-IC(1t)

Championship, a Five Nations campaign in which he became the first player for 30 years to wear jerseys 6, 7 and 8. Less glorious had been his Test debut which lasted 14 minutes before he was sent off for stamping on a Wallaby in Sydney. But modest 14-day ban meant he was able to play in next two Tests of the series at flanker. Switched to second row for visit of All Blacks to Nantes (1990) and it was six internationals before he finally adopted his favoured No.8 berth. Came to France by way of Czechoslovakia where, while on tour with Morocco, he met up with a touring fourth division French club. On learning he wanted to play in France, they advised him to join Cahors. This he did before switching, a year later, to Agen, for whom he appeared in the 1990 French Cup final. Represented Morocco in the African zone of the 1991 World Cup qualifying rounds, against Belgium in Casablanca, and then France in the final stages. Became the first Moroccan to play at Twickenham when making Five Nations' debut for France in the 1991 Grand Slam decider. Suspended indefinitely during 1991/92 season by the French Federation after being sent-off for fighting with Eric Champ in an Agen-Toulon Cup match on 2 May 1991. The ban ruled him out of France's summer tour of Argentina but he was back in the engine room shortly afterwards, coming on as replacement for Jean-Marie Cadieu in the Test loss to South Africa, in Lyon on 17 October. Started the next six internationals, playing in disastrous home loss to Argentina but also in 1993 Championship triumph. Lost Test place on '93 summer tour to South Africa after an infected wound required a stay in hospital, but returned to side for Autumn series against Australia.

Benetton, P. France

Full Name: Philippe Benetton
Club: Agen
Position: Flanker, No 8
Height: 6ft 3in (1.90m)
Weight: 15st 6lb (98kg)
Occupation: Sports instructor with Agen council
Born: Cahors, 17.5.68
Family: Married with one child
Former club: Cahors
International debut: France 27, British Lions 29, 1989
Five Nations' debut: England 16, France 15, 1993
Notable landmarks in rugby career: World Cup campaign ended prematurely for Philippe when he sustained a broken arm 17 minutes

into France's thrilling 22–19 defeat of Scotland (Pretoria, 3.6.95). Had previously turned out against both Tonga and Cote d'Ivoire (as a replacement) in what was yet another consistently impressive campaign. For the second season running he was absent from only France's visit to Bucharest. Had marked his senior debut with a try against the 1989 British Lions, masquerading as a Home Unions XV, in the Paris

France (1989)

Last Season	10 caps	10 pts
Career	32 caps	29 pts

Caps (32): **1989** BL **1991** US(2) **1992** Arg(a1,a2R), SA(1R,2), Arg(b) **1993** E, S, I, W, SA(1,2), R(b), A(1,2) **1994** I, W, E, S, NZ(1,2), C(b) **1995** W, E, S(a), I wc-T, IC(R), S(b)

Points (29 – 6t): **1989** BL(1t) **1993** W(2t) **1994** I(1t), NZ(1:1t) **1995** C(b:1t)

floodlit international staged to mark the bicentenary of the French Revolution. In common with back row team mate Abdel Benazzi, he began his playing career with Cahors before switching to Agen in 1988. At international level Philippe graduated through Under-21 and B set-ups. He missed out on the 1990 and 1991 Five Nations' Championships, unable in the latter to displace Xavier Blond from the blindside berth. However, he re-emerged on France's 1991 tour to North America, winning the second cap in the 10-3 second Test win over the US Eagles. The match, staged in Colorado Springs, was abandoned at half-time due to lightning. Although included in the 26-man '91 World Cup squad, he remained redundant through France's four matches and, at first, continued in the same vein after former club mate Pierre Berbizier succeeded Jacques Fouroux as national coach. However, not only did he return to Test favour in 1992/93, he played in the last nine internationals, as France won the 1993 Championship and he scored two tries in the title-clinching 26–10 defeat of Wales (Paris, 20.3.93). Having found a home at No.8, Philippe toured with France to South Africa (1993) and New Zealand (1994), the latter culminating in an historic 2–0 series defeat of the All Blacks. And he was the star of the show, scoring the only try in the first Test and being acclaimed as one of the 1995 New Zealand Rugby Almanack's five players of the year.

Benezech, L.   France

Full Name: Laurent Benezech
Club: Racing Club de France
Position: Loosehead prop
Height: 6ft 1in (1.85m)
Weight: 17st 3lb (104kg)
Occupation: Company rep with Agence Audour
Born: Pamiers, 19.12.66
Family: Married
Former clubs: Ariege, Toulouse
International debut: France 18, England 14, 1994
Five Nations debut: As above
Notable landmarks in rugby career: Star of the forward show in New Zealand (1994) when France scored a 22–8 first Test triumph over the All Blacks (Christchurch, 26.6.94) en route to an historic 2–0 series win. Laurent started life as a second row forward but was unable to find a place in the Toulouse engine room during his teenage days. So he took the decision to 'bulk-up' and was rewarded with a place on the loosehead side of the front row. Four

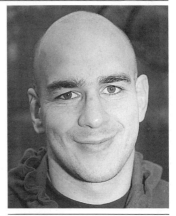

France (1994)

Last Season	6 caps	0 pts
Career	11 caps	0 pts

Caps (11): **1994** E, S, C(a), NZ(1,2), C(b) **1995** W, E(a) wc-IC, S(b), E(b)
Points Nil

years after joining Toulouse from Ariege in 1985, he again switched allegiances, this time to the capital and the flamboyant Racing Club de France. The move was immediately rewarded as Racing captured the French championship in 1990 and Laurent was selected for France A's tour to Namibia. It was not until 1993 that the senior selectors came calling, including yer man in the tour party for the historic trip to born-again South Africa. However, a foot injury meant that the former French Student and French Armed Forces player had to call-off, so missing another famous series win. No such rejections in 1993/94, though, when he was called into a French side, reeling after defeat in Cardiff, to pack down against arch-rivals England in Paris. He impressed, not least opposite number Victor Ubogu, and held his place for the Championship finale against Scotland in Edinburgh, before heading to Canada and New Zealand and widespread acclaim. Troubled by injury last season which confined his World Cup appearances to outings against Cote d'Ivoire, Scotland and England.

Bernat-Salles, P.   France

Full Name: Philippe Bernat-Salles
Club: Pau
Position: Wing
Height: 5ft 11½in (1.81m)
Weight: 11st 8lb (74kg)
Occupation: Clerical officer with STAP, Pau
Born: 17.2.70
International debut: France 20, Argentina 24, 1992
Five Nations' debut: England 31, France 10, 1995
Notable landmarks in rugby career: Earned his Five Nations debut against Ireland in Paris (15.1.94) but had to wait a year for his second Championship appearance, at Twickenham as a late call-up for the crocked Emile NTamack. Philippe's third Five Nations cap coincided with Scotland's first ever win at Parc des Princes, after which NTamack returned. The 'Pau Rocket', Philippe burst explosively onto the Test scene, scoring six tries in his first five internationals. But don't remind

France (1992)

Last Season	2 caps	0 pts
Career	10 caps	30 pts

Caps (10): **1992** Arg(b) **1993** R(a), SA(1,2), R(b), A(1,2) **1994** I **1995** E, S(a)
Points (30 – 6t): **1993** R(a:3t), R(b:3t)

Romania, as each of his two appearances against them yielded a try hat-trick: in Bucharest (won 37–20, 20.5.93) and Brive (won 51–0, 9.10.93). Established himself as a permanent fixture in the French side until injury curtailed his 1993/94 season, forcing him out of the last three Championship games. Philippe first earned full international recognition against Argentina, not in South America as he would have initially hoped – having toured there with France in the summer of '92 (scoring tries against Cordoba, Buenos Aires and Cuyo) – but at Nantes, where the Pumas came, saw and historically conquered on 14 November 1992. France lost 20–24, their first ever home loss to the Pumas, and Philippe was one of many who paid the price for team failure. He was dropped down a notch on the representative ladder and turned out on the right wing for France B at Leicester, on 15 January 1993, where England A triumphed 29–17 (11 months on from his B debut against Scotland in the 27–18 win in Albi). Reunited with Scotland in April 1993 as a member of the French team which contested the World Cup Sevens at Murrayfield

Bowen, S.   Australia

Full Name: Scott Bowen
State: New South Wales
Club: Southern Districts
Position: Outside-half
Height: 5ft 9in (1.76m)
Weight: 12st 10lb (76kg)
Occupation: Development officer
Born: 20.9.72
Family: Single
International debut: Australia 12, South Africa 19, 1993
Best moment in rugby: Being chosen for first Test against South Africa in 1993
Worst moment in rugby: Being plagued by hamstring injuries in 1992 – only playing 10 games
Most respected opponent: Hennie Le Roux (Transvaal & South Africa)
Best memory of 1993: Winning third Test against South Africa
Serious injuries: Hamstring (1992)
Notable landmarks in rugby career:

Australia (1993)

Last Season	1 cap	0 pts
Career	4 caps	0 pts

Caps (4): 1993 SA(1,2,3) 1995 wc-R
Points Nil

With Michael Lynagh's return to full fitness, Scott's only cap in 1994/95 came in the 42–3 World Cup win over Romania (Stellenbosch, 3.6.95). It was a far cry from 1993 when he held down the Wallabies No.10 jersey throughout the three-Test visit of the Springboks. Lynagh had started campaign at outside-half against Tonga before his late withdrawl from the Bledisloe Cup game against New Zealand in Dunedin gave Queensland's Pat Howard his chance. The result, a 10–25 loss, did him no favours while, the following week, Scott's contribution (partnering Nick Farr-Jones at half-back) to New South Wales' 29–28 defeat of the Springboks (Sydney, 24.7.93) did wonders for his cause. Despite Australia's shock defeat in the first Test (31.7.93), the selectors stood by him and their faith was repaid as the Wallabies bounced back to win the series. Scott then embarked on Australia's autumn tour of North America and France but, with Lynagh restored to rude health, found his opportunities limited. In all he made three appearances, starting with the 40–3 win over Canada A in freezing Calgary (6.10.93). He marked his debut in France with a try as Aquitaine's colours were lowered in Dax (won 30-15, 16.10.93) but had less to shout about at Grenoble where he failed to finish his third outing (26.10.93) when replaced by Jason Little during Australia's 24–23 win. Returned to favour last summer when included in Wallaby 26 for World Cup.

Tours: 1993 – North America and France.
Touchlines: Tennis, golf, beach, spending time with girlfriend

Bracken, K. P. P.   England

Full Name: Kyran Paul Patrick Bracken
Club: Bristol
Position: Scrum-half
Height: 5ft 11in (1.80m)
Weight: 12st 9lb (80kg)
Occupation: Trainee solicitor with Alsters Solicitors, College Green, Bristol
Born: Dublin, 22.11.71
Family: Single
Former club: Waterloo (minis)
International debut: England 15, New Zealand 9, 1993
Five Nations debut: Scotland 14, England 15, 1994
Best moment in rugby: Final whistle of New Zealand game (1993)
Worst moment in rugby: Getting dropped after Ireland game (1994)
Other sporting achievements: Tennis for Jersey Youths
Most respected opponent: Robert Jones (Swansea & Wales)
Serious injuries: Broken nose (when 18), ankle ligaments (v New Zealand, 1993)

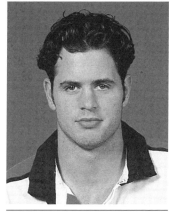

England (1993)

Last Season	7 caps	5 pts
Career	10 caps	5 pts

Caps (10): **1993** NZ **1994** S, I, C **1995** I, F, W, S wc-It, WS(R)
Points (5 – 1t): **1994** C(1t)

Notable landmarks in rugby career: Heel injury put paid to Kyran's World Cup even though Dewi Morris had already won back the No.9 jersey with combative performances against Argentina and Western Samoa. Kyran's solitary start came in the 27–20 defeat of Italy (Durban, 31.5.95), though he did come on as a replacement eight minutes from the end of the Western Samoa win. Prior to that he had scored his first try in the 60–19 win over Canada (Twickenham, 10.12.94) and then sampled his first Grand Slam as an ever present through the 1995 campaign. Kyran was thrust into the limelight after the late withdrawl of Morris prior to England's home international with New Zealand (27.11.93), having originally been selected as a first-time bench reserve. Responded with fairy tale performance, all the more impressive for the fact that he could hardly walk after having his right ankle stamped on by Jamie

Joseph in the early stages. Kyran, who had played for the South West and England A against the All Blacks earlier in the tour, forgot the obvious pain to celebrate England's 15–9 win before hobbling away from HQ on crutches. 'To be honest, I thought I was going to have to go off early in the game,' he recalled. 'Towards the end, I was just living on adrenalin.' His second and third caps coincided with far from satisfactory performances by England against Scotland and Ireland, the upshot of which was the return of Morris for the remainder of the championship. But Kyran, who graduated through Lancashire, North Schools and England 16-Group as an outside-half and captained England 18-Group in 1989/90, remained in the squad and was included in the summer tour squad to South Africa, although exams belatedly forced his withdrawl. Played for Bristol in 1992/93 UAU final at Twickenham prior to touring Canada with England A and Australia with England U-21s.

Touchlines: Cinema, football.

Bradley, M. T. Ireland

Full Name: Michael Timothy Bradley
Club: Cork Constitution
Position: Scrum-half
Height: 5ft 10in (1.78m)
Weight: 13st 2lb (83kg)
Occupation: Manager with Top Security Ltd (Cork)
Born: Cork, 17.11.62
Family: Gillian (wife)
Family links with rugby: Father (Austin) played for Cork Constitution; he also played amateur international soccer for Ireland
International debut: Ireland 9, Australia 16, 1984
Five Nations' debut: Scotland 15, Ireland 18, 1985

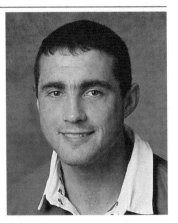

Best moment in rugby: Captaining Cork Constitution to 1990/91 All-Ireland League victory and beating England in Dublin (1993)
Worst moment in rugby: Ireland losing 3–35 to England at Twickenham in 1988, having led 3–0 at half-time
Most respected opponent: Nick Farr-Jones (NSW & Australia)
Serious injuries: Torn ankle ligaments (1990)
Notable landmarks in rugby career: Lost Ireland captaincy to Terry Kingston last season after France had destroyed Irish late on in Dublin (4.3.95). And retired after the same opponents put paid to Ireland's World Cup dream

in the quarter-final stage (Durban, 10.6.95). Skipper since succeeding Phil Danaher during 1992 tour to New Zealand, Michael struggled for form in 1995 and lost his place to Terenure's Niall Hogan for final Five Nations' game against Wales. His finest hour had come in the 17–3 win over England at Lansdowne Road (20.3.93), an occasion he marked by becoming Ireland's most-capped scrum-half (29). Reached the 40-cap milestone in South Africa in the

Ireland (1984)		
Last Season	4 caps	5 pts
Career	40 caps	21 pts

Caps (40): **1984** A **1985** S, F, W, E **1986** F, W, E, S, Ro **1987** E, S, F, W(a) wc-W(b), C, T, A **1988** S, F, W, E(a) **1990** W **1992** NZ(1,2) **1993** S, F, W, E, R **1994** F, W, E, S, A(1,2), US **1995** S, F wc-NZ

Points (21 – 5t): **1986** Ro(1t) **1987** F(1t) wc-C(1t) **1988** S(1t) **1994** US(1t)

creditable 19-43 loss to the All Blacks. Played four games for Irish Schools and captained them on 1980 tour of Australia. Captained Irish U-19s and U-21s. Completed journey up representative ladder with appearances for U-25s and B (1983 against Scotland). Chosen as replacement for Ireland in 1984 before having played provincial rugby for Munster. Played in Ireland's 1985 Triple Crown-winning side. Returned to Ireland's B team in 1990/91 and captained side to victories over Argentina (27–12, Limerick 20.10.90) and England (24–10, Old Belvedere 1.3.91). Scored try in defeat of touring Pumas. Led Cork Constitution to 1990/91 All-Ireland League title. Played in both Tests on '92 New Zealand tour, taking over the captaincy for the second match, in Wellington. Ireland lost 6–59 and Michael lost his place for next outing, against Australia in Dublin. However, he returned as skipper for the 1993 International Championship, leading the side to morale-boosting wins over Wales and England. Claimed fifth Test try last season in 26–15 dour home win over USA (5.11.94).

Touchlines: Golf, landscape gardening

Jeremy Guscott stretches the Scottish cover during England's Grand Slam win.

Brewer, M. R.   New Zealand

Full Name: Michael Robert Brewer
Province: Otago
Position: Flanker, No 8
Height: 6ft 5in (1.95m)
Weight: 16st 9lb (101kg)
Occupation: Marketing manager,
Canterbury International
Born: Pukekohe, 6.11.64
Family: Beverley (wife), Harrison (son)
International debut: New Zealand 18, France 9, 1986
Serious injuries: Damaged hip, foot, torn calf muscle
Notable landmarks in rugby career: 'Bruiser' returned to favour in 1994, after two years out of the All Black side, when playing against France and throughout the home series win over South Africa. Moved to No. 8 during the World Cup pool matches in South Africa, in the absence of Zinzan Brooke, playing against Ireland and Wales, reverting to the blindside berth for the semi-final (vs England) and final (vs South Africa). Injury has restricted Mike's All Black caps, since he marked his debut in

New Zealand (1986)
Last Season	11 caps	0 pts
Career	30 caps	4 pts

Caps (30): **1986** F(a), A(1,2,3), F(b1,b2) **1988** A(1) **1989** A, W, I **1990** S(1,2), A(1,2,3), F(1,2) **1992** I(2), A(1) **1994** F(1,2), SA(1,2,3), A **1995** C wc-I, W, E, SA
Points (4 – 1t): **1986** F(a:1t)

Christchurch with a try against the beaten French in 1986. Two World Cups have passed him by. On the day he was due to be named All Black captain on the eve of the 1991 finals, he was again crocked (torn calf muscle in final trial) and missed the three centenary Tests as well as the first test against Ireland. Captain of Otago in 1986 at the tender age of 21, Mike was also an everpresent in the New Zealand side that year, after making his debut for the baby All Blacks at No 8. He was transformed into a flanker on the 1987 tour to Japan. A hip injury ruled him out of the 1987 World Cup, and thus robbed him of a winners' medal when the All Blacks beat France 29–9 in the Auckland final. Toured Australia in 1988 and, the following year, Ireland and Wales. His openside wing-forward play won a host of British admirers and it was little wonder that he featured in all seven Tests in 1990. Controversially omitted from the 1991 World Cup squad after failing an early fitness test ordered by the NZRU. Returned in 1992 for second Test against Ireland, a 59–6 thumping of the tourists in Wellington, before his progress was again interrupted by injury after 65 minutes of the first match in the Bledisloe Cup series against Australia. Prior to that he had skippered the side to wins over South Australia (scoring a try) and ACT. Captained Otago to 1991 national championship before, at the end of the 1992 campaign, his eighth year in charge, he relinquished the reins.

Brooke, R. M.   New Zealand

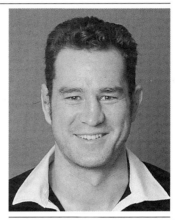

Full Name: Robin Brooke
Province: Auckland
Position: Lock
Height: 6ft 5½in (1.96m)
Weight: 18st 10lb (114kg)
Occupation: Self-employed builder
Born: Warkworth, 10.1.67
Family links with rugby: Zinzan (brother) plays for Auckland and New Zealand (32 caps, 43 pts); Martin (brother) a former New Zealand triallist
International debut: New Zealand 59, Ireland 6, 1992
Best moment in rugby: Getting named to play my first Test while visiting Zinzan in hospital
Worst moment in rugby: Losing to Australia 15–16 in first Test of 1992 Bledisloe Cup
Most embarrassing moment: Walking into a clear glass door in front of 500 people at Ellis Park while the speeches were on
Notable landmarks in rugby career: Injury has disrupted the last three

New Zealand (1992)

Last Season	7 caps	10 pts
Career	17 caps	10 pts

Caps (17): **1992** I(2),A(1,2,3), SA **1993** BL(1,2,3), A, WS **1994** SA(2,3) **1995** C wc-J, S, E, SA
Points (10 – 2t): **1995** wc-J(2t)

seasons for Robin. At the World Cup he sat out the Pool matches against Ireland and Wales, before returning with a two-try performance against Japan (4.6.95) and being paired with Ian Jones thereafter. In 1994, he played just twice for the All Blacks, in the second and third Tests against South Africa, and in '93, although touring to England and Scotland, he was unable to take any active part. His frustration was compounded by fact he had become first-choice All Black lock, alongside former North Auckland secondary schools team mate Jones, during the course of the year, playing all three Tests against the British Lions, helping wrestle the Bledisloe Cup back from world champions Australia, (25-10) in Dunedin on 17 July, and picking up his tenth cap in the 35–13 defeat of Western Samoa that same month. Had settled remarkably easily into the Test side in 1992 after being given his chance against Ireland in Wellington on 6 June. It might have come earlier for Robin had he not missed the national trials in favour of club commitments in Italy. As one of three All Black debutants that June day – along with Auckland prop Olo Brown and Waikato fullback Matthew Cooper – he helped rout the Irish 59–6. His performance earned him a berth on the tour to Australia where he played alongside Jones in all three matches of the Bledisloe Cup series. But it was in Johannesburg on 15 August that Robin enjoyed his finest hour. With brother Zinzan, he was the star performer as New Zealand beat South Africa for the first time on African soil, 27–24. In addition to the Tests he turned out in the wins over Western Australia (80–0), New South Wales (41–9) and Queensland (26–19), while in South Africa he enjoyed that winning feeling against Junior South Africa (25–10) in Pretoria. A member of the New Zealand Maoris since 1988.

Touchlines: Golf, family, travel, basketball

Brooke, Z. V. New Zealand

Full Name: Zinzan Valentine Brooke
Club: Marist
Province: Auckland
Position: No 8, flanker
Height: 6ft 3in (1.90m)
Weight: 16st 4lb (99kg)
Occupation: Broadcaster, SKY TV
Born: Waiuku, 14.2.65
Family links with rugby: Marty (brother) is a former New Zealand triallist; Robin plays for Auckland, Maoris and New Zealand (17 caps 10 pts)
International debut: New Zealand 46, Argentina 15, 1987
Serious injuries: Broken ankle (1991)
Notable landmarks in rugby career:
Ankle injury disrupted Zinzan's
World Cup, forcing him to miss the Ireland and Wales Pool matches, having also been sidelined for the pre-tournament romp against Canada. But came back strongly and stunned England with an outrageous 40-metre dropped goal in New Zealand's remarkable 45–29 semi-final win. Played in all but one international in 1994, scoring one of New Zealand's two tries in the series-clinching second Test against South Africa at Wellington (23.7.94). Confirmed himself as one of the world's great back rows on New Zealand's tour to England and Scotland in 1993. Yet only after starting off in the 'dirt trackers' XV, a result of having lost his Test following after the series win over the '93 British

Lions. Only a replacement, albeit a utilised one, for the third Test win in Auckland, he sat out the Bledisloe Cup victory over Australia before coming on as a replacement against Western Samoa, and scoring a try. On tour in the UK he captained the midweek XV but, after coming on in the first two Saturday games and then scoring four tries in the 84–5 defeat of South of Scotland, he won a Test place at openside flanker against both Scotland (scored try) and England. A product of the 1985 New Zealand Colts team, he has represented

New Zealand (1987)		
Last Season	9 caps	8 pts
Career	32 caps	43 pts

Caps (32): **1987** wc-Arg **1989** Arg(2R) **1990** A(1,2,3), F(1R) **1991** Arg(2), A(a1,a2). wc-E, It, C, A(b), S **1992** A(2,3), SA **1993** BL(1,2,3R), WS(R), S, E **1994** F(2), SA(1,2,3), A **1995** wc-J, S, E, SA

Points (43 – 9t,1dg): **1987** wc-Arg(1t) **1990** A(2:1t) **1991** Arg(2:1t). wc-It(1t), C(1t) **1992** SA(1t) **1993** WS(R:1t), S(1t) **1994** SA(2:1t) **1995** wc-E(1dg)

Auckland since 1986 and the All Blacks since scoring one of their six tries in the 46–15 win over Argentina on his debut in June 1987, at the inaugural World Cup. Came to the fore when succeeding captain Wayne Shelford at No 8 after the Scotland series in 1990. But although he played in all three Tests against Australia that year he was injured and replaced in the first Test against France in Nantes. Returned strongly in 1991, after recovering from a broken ankle, and was the All Black's first-choice No 8 through the World Cup, a personal campaign which featured tries against Italy and Canada. An impressive Sevens player, he captained New Zealand to victory in the 1989 and 1990 Hong Kong Sevens. Made ten appearances on the All Blacks' tour of Australia and South Africa in 1992, playing in three of the four Tests.
Touchlines: Competing at anything.

French lock Olivier Roumat seeks official approval.

161

Brouzet, O.   France

Full Name: Olivier Brouzet
Club: Grenoble
Position: Lock
Height: 6ft 8in (2.03m)
Weight: 18st 7lb (113kg)
Occupation: Student
Born: Beziers, 22.11.72
Family: Single
Former club: Seyssins
International debut: Scotland 12, France 20, 1994
Five Nations debut: As above
Notable landmarks in rugby career:
Started World Cup campaign in French second row, but after easy wins over Tonga and Cote d'Ivoire, Olivier lost out to the preferred combination of Olivier Roumat and Olivier Merle. Coach Pierre Berbizier alternated the trio throughout the 1994/95 campaign, depending on Roumat's fitness and Merle's disciplinary record. Msr Brouzet played against England and Scotland whilst Merle was suspended and against Ireland and

France (1994)

Last Season	8 caps	0 pts
Career	9 caps	0 pts

Caps (9): **1994** S,NZ(2R) **1995** E,S(a),I,R wc-T,IC,E(TR)
Points Nil

Romania in the absence of Roumat. Had made his debut against Scotland the previous season in a French team desperate to shake off the threat of a Wooden Spoon. After a Gallic win, Scotland took it instead. Olivier comes from a rich sporting lineage, his father Yves being the former French athletics champion who has held the national shot-putt record for 24 years. Olivier played alongside former lumberjack Merle in the Grenoble team that reached the 1992/93 French championship final, losing to Castres. He helped France win the 1992 Students World Cup and as recently as February 1993 was in the French Under-21 side which whipped their Scottish counterparts 67–9 in Dijon. Promoted to replacement for the 1994 Championship opener against Ireland in Paris (15.1.94), having been a member of the France A gold medal-winning side at the 1993 Mediterranean Games. Toured with France to New Zealand in 1994 and savoured glory of 2–0 series win after coming on as a last-minute substitute in the second Test. In the 60 seconds he was on the field France ran the length of the pitch for Jean-Luc Sadourny to sensationally score the match and series-clinching try.

Brown, O. M.   New Zealand

Full Name: Olo Max Brown
Province: Auckland
Position: Tighthead prop
Height: 6ft ½in (1.85m)
Weight: 15st 11lb (100kg)
Occupation: Chartered accountant, Price Waterhouse
Born: Western Samoa, 24.10.67
Family: Single
International debut: New Zealand 59, Ireland 6, 1992
Most respected player: Colin Meads
Notable landmarks in rugby career: Polynesian powerhouse who was regular All Black loosehead prop throughout 1994 and last summer's World Cup, missing only the world record romp against Japan. Claimed first international try on 18th appearance, in the 73–7 slaughter of Canada (Auckland, 22.4.95). Missed part of 1993 season (including 35–13 defeat of his country of origin, Western Samoa) with a neck injury. First represented the All Blacks in 1990 when, having been flown out to join the tour of France

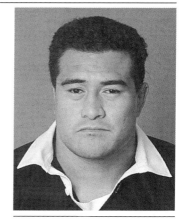

New Zealand (1992)

Last Season	12 caps	5 pts
Career	23 caps	5 pts

Caps (23): **1992** I(2),A(1,2,3),SA **1993** BL(1,2,3), A, S, E **1994** F(1,2), SA(1,2,3), A **1995** C wc-I, W, S, E, SA
Points (5 – 1t): **1995** C(1t)

as a replacement, he was thrust into the fray against France A in the Stade Marcel Deflandre, La Rochelle. The date was 6 November and the tourists won 22–15. Three months earlier he had helped Auckland beat the touring Australians 16-10 at Eden Park. Although overlooked for the Argentina tour and the World Cup in 1991, a fine display for the Saracens team which beat a New Zealand XV 20–15 in one of the national trial matches speeded his return to the big time. Having also helped Auckland destroy Ireland 62–7 at Eden Park (23 May), weighing in with one of his team's 11 tries, his Test debut followed soon after (6 June) when selected in place of Richard Loe for the second International against the Irish in Wellington, which resulted in a 59–6 win for the host nation. Auckland team mate Robin Brooke and Waikato's Matthew Cooper also made their debuts that day. After that Olo was retained for the tour of Australia and South Africa, figuring in the nine weekend engagements, including all four Test matches. Failed to score any points but his contribution in terms of strength enabled the All Blacks to achieve an edge over their Wallaby rivals in the scrum.

Bunce, F. E. — New Zealand

Full Name: Frank Eneri Bunce
Province: North Harbour
Position: Centre
Height: 6ft 1in (1.85m)
Weight: 14st 10lb (93kg)
Occupation: Brewery rep, Lion Breweries
Born: Auckland, 4.2.62
Family: Married, three children
Family links with rugby: Steve (brother) plays for Western Australia
Former nation: Western Samoa
Former province: Auckland
Former club: Manukau
International debut (NZ): New Zealand 24, Ireland 21, 1992
Worst moment in rugby: The death of my father before he could see me become an All Black
Most respected opponents: John Kirwan (Auckland & NZ) and Philippe Sella (Agen & France)
Notable landmarks in rugby career: Among the game's great midfield defenders, Frank also boasts a prolific strike rate with 15 tries in 28 Tests since switching allegiance from Western Samoa after the 1991 World Cup. Ever-present for the past three years, save for the World Cup romp against Japan. He scored New Zealand's only try in their first Test

Western Samoa (1991)		
Career	4 caps	4 pts
New Zealand (1992)		
Last Season	12 caps	25 pts
Career	28 caps	71 pts

Caps (28): **1992** Wd(1,2,3), I(1,2), A(1,2,3), SA **1993** BL(1,2,3), A, WS, S, E **1994** F(1,2), SA(1,2,3), A **1995** C wc-I, W, S, E, SA

Points (71 – 15t): **1992** I(1:2t), I(2:2t), A(1:1t), A(3:1t) **1993** BL(1:1t), BL(3:1t), A(1t), S(1t) **1994** F(1:1t) **1995** C(2t) wc-I(1t), S(1t)

defeat by France (Christchurch, 26.6.94) and a brace against Canada (Auckland, 22.4.95) before claiming World Cup touchdowns against Ireland (Johannesburg 27.5.95) and Scotland (Pretoria, 11.6.95). It is hard to believe that it took six years, after making his debut for Auckland in a Ranfurly Shield game against Horowhenua at Eden Park, for his All Black Test debut, against a World XV. But it was his two-try show against Ireland in the following series which confirmed him as a class act. Mind you, the 30-year old was no novice that day at Carisbrook. Frustrated at his lack of opportunities in the New Zealand national set-up he had declared his allegiance for Western Samoa in the '91 World Cup and featured strongly in each of their four games – against Wales, Australia, Argentina and Scotland – claiming a try in the 35–12 win over the Pumas. Any notion that his heroics in the 24–21 defeat of Ireland at Dunedin were a flash in the pan was dispelled in the second Test when he weighed in with another try-brace. Frank has since gone from strength to strength, playing in ten of the All Blacks' fixtures on their tour of Australia and South Africa (scoring five tries) and bagged tries in the All Blacks' first and third Test wins over the 1993 British Lions. His penetrative qualities, allied with his brick wall defending, make him a perennial target for the Rugby League scouts.

Burke, M. Australia

Full Name: Matthew Burke
State: New South Wales
Club: Eastwood
Position: Fullback, centre
Height: 6ft 1in (1.84m)
Weight: 15st 9lb (95kg)
Occupation: Eastwood rugby development officer
Born: 26.3.73
Family: single
International debut: Australia 19, South Africa 12, 1993
Notable landmarks in rugby career: Brave as a lion under the high ball, Matt made quite an impression at the World Cup. Sadly for him the Wallabies did not, falling to England in one of three games Matt played. He also turned out in the wins over Canada (Port Elizabeth 31.5.95) and Romania (Stellenbosch 3.6.95), scoring a try and two conversions in the 42–3 defeat of the Romanians. Utility back who greatly impressed during Australia's 1993 tour of North America and France,

Australia (1993)

Last Season	7 caps	19 pts
Career	9 caps	19 pts

Caps (9): **1993** SA(3R),F(1) **1994** I(1,2), It(1,2) **1995** wc-C, R, E
Points (19 – 3t,2c): **1994:** I(1:1t), It(1:1t) **1995** wc-R(1t,2c)

prompting Wallaby coach Bob Dwyer to describe him as 'a real investment for the future.' He added: 'Against Languedoc he gave one of the greatest displays of fullback play by a young man it's ever been my pleasure to witness.' Matt also appeared at centre, for New South Wales in their thrilling 29–28 defeat of the touring Springboks (24.7.93) – a performance that led to his first cap as a replacement in the decisive third Test victory over South Africa in Sydney (21.8.93) – and for the Wallabies in their 40–3 win against Canada A in Calgary (16.10.93). Controversially displaced Marty Roebuck in the Australia side for the first Test against France in Bordeaux (30.10.93). The Wallabies lost and Roebuck, with his superb goalkicking ability, was recalled to save the series. Returned to favour in 1994, scoring tries in the first Tests of the series against Ireland (Brisbane 5.6.94) and Italy (Brisbane 18.6.94).

Burke, P. A.   Ireland

Full Name: Paul Anthony Burke
Club: Cork Constitution
Position: Fly-half
Height: 5ft 8in (1.73m)
Weight: 12st (76kg)
Occupation: PE teacher, Christian Brothers College, Cork
Born: London, 1.5.73
Family: Single
International debut: Ireland 8, England 20, 1995
Five Nations debut: As above
Notable landmarks in rugby career: Anglo-Irishman who won his Test call-up last season on the back of an Inter-Provincial title-winning campaign in the colours of Munster, having previously represented England at Schools, Under-18, Colts and Under-21 level. But Galway-born father and Kildare-born mother allowed him to declare for the Emerald Isle in November 1992. Toured with the Irish development squad to Africa in 1993 before working his way through Ireland U-

Ireland (1995)

Last Season	5 caps	44 pts
Career	5 caps	44 pts

Caps (5): 1995 E, S, W(a:R),It wc-J
Points (44 – 7c,9p,1dg): 1995 E(1p),S(1p), W(a:1c,2p,1dg), It(4p) wc-J(6c,1p)

21 and 'A' teams to senior side, where he earned his call-up at the expense of Alan McGowan for the 1995 Five Nations opener against England (Dublin, 21.1.95). Despite defeat, he held his place for the Scotland game. However, a poor day's goalkicking contributed to Irish defeat and to his deselection. Fit-again Eric Elwood returned against France but Ireland looked little different. And the nation seemed on course for the Wooden Spoon when Elwood was clobbered by a late tackle in Cardiff (18.3.95) and Paul introduced to the fray. The former London Irish mini-player grabbed his chance superbly, dropping a neat goal to settle his nerves, before adding two penalties and the conversion of Brendan Mullin's try as Ireland ran out 16–12 winners. In spite of four penalty goals next time out, Ireland's 'feat' of becoming the first major nation to lose to

Italy (Treviso, 6.5.95) counted against Paul in the World Cup reckoning and although he went to South Africa he lost out to Elwood, playing only against Japan (Bloemfontein, 31.5.95), a game in which he contributed 15 points to a 50–28 win.

Burnell, A. P. Scotland

Full Name: Andrew Paul Burnell
Club: London Scottish
Position: Prop
Height: 6ft 1in (1.85m)
Weight: 16st 8lb (105kg)
Occupation: Director, Anglo-Scottish Finance Ltd
Born: Edinburgh, 29.9.65
Family: Single
Former clubs: Marlow, Harlequins, Leicester
International debut: England 12, Scotland 12, 1989
Five Nations' debut: As above
Best moment in rugby: Beating England to win 1990 Grand Slam
Worst moments in rugby: Scotland losing 3–19 to France in 1989; London Scottish getting relegated from English Second Division (1988/89); missing 1992 tour to Australia due to torn knee medial ligament sustained in 12–15 defeat by Wales in '92 Five Nations Championship finale
Most respected opponent: David Sole (ex-Edinburgh Acads & Scotland) – good scrummager, great ball player, superb captain

Scotland (1989)

Last Season	3 caps	5 pts
Career	39 caps	5 pts
Lions 1993		

Caps (39): **1989** E, I, F, Fj, Ro **1990** I, F, W, E, Arg **1991** F, W, E, I, Ro wc-J, Z, I, WS, E, NZ **1992** E, I, F, W **1993** I, F, W, E, NZ **1994** W, E, I, F, Arg(1,2), SA **1995** wc-IC, T(R)
Points (5 –1t): **1995** wc-IC(1t)

Serious injuries: Ruptured disc in back (1989, required surgery), acute tear in knee medial ligament (1992)
Notable landmarks in rugby career: Missed out on Scotland's revival in 1995, having lost his place after the 10–34 loss to South Africa (Murrayfield, 19.11.94). Remained on the edge of the team, however, and was rewarded for his continued loyalty with a World Cup appearance, and first ever Test try, in the 89–0 beating of Cote d'Ivoire (Rustenburg, 26.5.95). Also played the last six minutes of the 41–5 defeat of Tonga (Pretoria, 3.6.95). Those two caps took

him to within 11 of Sandy Carmichael's 50-cap national best for a prop. A British Lion in 1993, Paul played against North Harbour, Canterbury, Otago, Auckland and Waikato, but missed out on Test honours against All Blacks. Missed out on nothing in 1993/94 season, however, except league relegation after sterling end-of-season rally by London Scottish. Scored on first team debut for Leicester and Scotland B debut in 26–3 win over Italy in L'Aquila (1989). Twice helped London Scottish win promotion, as 1989/90 Third Division and 1991/92 Second Division champions, and featured in their triumphant 1990/91 Middlesex Sevens side. Toured with Scotland to Zimbabwe (1988), New Zealand (1990), having been ever-present tighthead in Grand Slam campaign, and Argentina (1994) but missed tours to Japan (1989) and Australia (1992) through injury.

Touchlines: Cinema-going.

Cabannes, L. France

Full Name: Laurent Cabannes
Club: Racing Club de France
Position: Flanker
Height: 6ft 2in (1.88m)
Weight: 15st 3lb (92kg)
Occupation: Public relations officer
Born: Reims, 6.2.64
Family: Married
Former club: Pau
International debut: France 12, New Zealand 30, 1990
Five Nations' debut: France 15, Scotland 9, 1991
Notable landmarks in rugby career: Dropped through lack of form midway through the 1995 Five Nations Championship, the enigmatic Laurent returned with a

vengeance at the World Cup, turning in outstanding displays, both in lineout and loose play. Ever-present in France's impressive run, he was particularly notable against Scotland (Pretoria, 3.6.95), Ireland (Durban, 10.6.95) and South Africa (Durban, 18.6.95). A seriously torn thigh muscle had ruined 1993/94 for Laurent, one of the most mobile and effective loose forwards in the game. Having helped France to their historic series win in South Africa (1993) he sustained the injury in September and was sidelined for the next five months. But he was recalled at the earliest possible opportunity and played final two championship matches, against England and Scotland before helping the French to an historic 2–0 series win over New Zealand Down Under. Made his senior debut for Pau at the age of just 17. In 1992/93, in addition to further enhancing his reputation with a hefty contribution to France's Five Nations' title triumph, he also turned out for France at Murrayfield in the World Cup Sevens tournament. Laurent, whose two international tries have come in spectacular style against Ireland, has travelled far in rugby pursuit, playing the club game in South Africa and in the south west region of France for Pau. But it was

France (1990)

Last Season	12 caps	0 pts
Career	41 caps	8 pts

Caps (41): 1990 NZ(2R) 1991 S, I, W, E, US(2), W wc-Ro, Fj, C, E 1992 W, E, S, I, R, Arg(a2), SA(1,2) 1993 E, S, I, W, R(a), SA(1,2) 1994 E, S, C(a), NZ(1,2) 1995 W, E(a), S(a), R wc-T(R), IC, S(b), I(b), SA, E(b)

Points (8 – 2t): 1991 I(1t) 1992 I(1t)

with Racing that his representative career burgeoned, scoring a try as the Paris side won the 1990 French Club Championship; their first success in 31 years. He was also on the side which finished runners-up in 1987, the year after he had begun playing France B rugby (against Wales B at Pontypridd) but it was only in November 1990 that he broke into the senior ranks as a replacement for Abdel Benazzi in the second Test against New Zealand in Paris.

Califano, C.   France

Full Name: Christian Califano
Club: Toulouse
Position: Tighthead Prop
Height: 5ft 11in (1.80m)
Weight: 16st 7lb (100kg)
Occupation: Army (military service)
Born: Toulon, 16.5.72
Family: Single
International debut: New Zealand 8, France 22, 1994
Five Nations debut: France 21, Wales 9, 1995
Notable landmarks in rugby career: Remarkable rise to prominence for Christian who was voted France's top tighthead prop at the end of the 1993/94 season and celebrated with his international debut on the

momentous summer tour of New Zealand. Had secured his berth with an outstanding display in the French championship final, in which Toulouse beat Montferrand, and went on to impress seasoned onlookers with his technical ability in the tour games against Northland, North Harbour and New Zealand A.

His Test bow came in Christchurch (26.6.94) and resulted in a remarkable 22–8 victory for France over the All Blacks. More notable still, France repeated the result on Christian's second appear-ance, clinching the series by virtue of a last-gasp 23–20 victory in Auckland (3.7.94). Since then he has missed just two games: the

France (1994)

Last Season	12 caps	0 pts
Career	12 caps	0 pts

Caps (12): **1994** NZ(1,2), C(b) **1995** W, E(a), S(a), I(a) wc-T, IC, S(b), I(b), SA, E(b)

Points Nil

pre-World Cup visit to Bucharest and the Cup opener against Tonga last summer. But his run of Test victories came to an end at Twickenham (4.2.95) where England (again) contrived to undo the French challenge. Another defeat followed, this time to Scotland (the first home loss to Ecosse for 26 years) but there was little question of Christian losing his place. Instead it was loosehead prop Laurent Benezech who paid the price, with Pierre Berbizier drafting the experience of Louis Armary into the front row to stave off further Five Nations disaster.

Callard, J. E. B.   England

Full Name: Jonathan Edward Brooks Callard
Club: Bath
Position: Full-back
Height: 5ft 10in (1.78m)
Weight: 12st 7lb (75kg)
Occupation: Schoolmaster, Downside
Born: Leicester, 1.1.66
Family: Gail (wife)
Family links with rugby: Brother (Nigel) plays for Newport
International debut: England 15, New Zealand 9, 1993
Five Nations debut: Scotland 14, England 15, 1994
Best moment in rugby: Beating All Blacks on debut
Worst moment in rugby: Being dropped after Ireland defeat (1994)
Most respected opponent: Gavin Hastings (Watsonians & Scotland)
Serious injuries: Fractured patella (1992)
Other sporting achievements: Junior cricket for Monmouthshire
Notable landmarks in rugby career: After his eventful 1993/94 campaign, last season was rather a comedown internationally-speaking for Jon. Having lost

the England fullback berth to Paul Hull in South Africa (1994) – and almost an eye in a vicious stamping incident against Eastern Province that required 25 stitches – he then saw Bath fly-half team mate Mike Catt jump to the head of the queue. Meanwhile, Jon sat patiently on the

England (1993)

Last Season	1 cap	21 pts
Career	4 caps	60 pts

Caps (4): **1993** NZ **1994** S, I **1995** wc-WS
Points (60 – 3c,18p): **1993** NZ(4p) **1994** S(5p), I(4p) **1995** wc-WS(3c,5p)

bench, making just the one appearance, as fullback in England's impressive 44–22 World Cup defeat of Western Samoa (Durban, 4.6.95). He at least marked the occasion with a thoroughly polished 21-point performance (3c,5p). But then again Jon had already shown England he was a man for the big match, having celebrated his Twickenham debut in 1990 with a try in Bath's Pilkington Cup final triumph, and marked his England debut at Twickenham, on 27 November 1993, with four penalty goals in the 15–9 defeat of New Zealand. Save for a wayward pass which gifted the Blacks a try against England A, Jon enjoyed their tour, as he landed eight penalty goals against them wearing the colours of South West Division and the national 'A' team. But he saved his finest hour for his Five Nations debut, at Murrayfield on 5 February 1994, when pulling the Calcutta Cup out of the fire with a last-gasp penalty goal from 40 metres. 'For a few awful seconds I wanted to run and hide,' remembers Jon of the moment when Will Carling turned to him and said 'Here, it's easy, get on with it'. 'But you can't hide, you have to conquer yourself,' added the former Newport player, who had made his debut as an 18-year-old against Bath. He dutifully obliged before embarking on a well-deserved celebratory jig. How fitting for a man who not so long ago had been 'lost' in the third team at Chipping Sodbury. However, Jon's season turned thereafter as he was one of the victims of the purge which followed Ireland's sensational Twickenham win. Joined England's tour of South Africa as emergency replacement for David Pears, making three appearances and contributing 17 points.

Touchlines: Bandit golfer.

Campbell, S. J.   Scotland

Full Name: Stewart Joseph Campbell
Club: Dundee HSFP
Position: Lock
Height: 6ft 6in (1.98m)
Weight: 16st 8lb (101kg)
Occupation: Architectural student, Dundee University (attached to Wellwood/Leslie Architects)
Born: Glasgow, 25.4.72
Family: Single
Former club: West of Scotland
International debut: Scotland 22, Canada 6, 1995
Five Nations debut: Scotland 26, Ireland 13, 1995
Notable landmarks in rugby career: One of Scotland's new kids on the block last season when coming into an ailing side and helping transform its fortunes. Prior to Stewart's debut against Canada at a freezing Murrayfield (21.1.95) Scotland had failed to win in nine internationals. Yet his debut ended in a 22–6 triumph, and five of his next seven

Scotland (1995)

Last Season	8 caps	0 pts
Career	8 caps	0 pts

Caps (8): **1995** C, I, F(a), W, E, R wc-IC, NZ(R)
Points Nil

caps also yielded victories. The sixth member of the Dundee High School Former Pupils club to be capped (following in the bootprints of George Ritchie, JS Wilson, Chris Rea, David Leslie and, most recently, Andy Nicol), Stewart represented Scotland at three age-groups before stepping out with Scottish Students. There then followed three winning outings for Scotland A: against France, Italy and, most notably, South Africa. The venue was Melrose, the date was 9 November 1994 and the result was 17–15 in the A-team's favour, thanks to Duncan Hodge's last-gasp dropped goal. It was the Springboks only defeat other than their tour-ending game against the Barbarians in Dublin. Stewart had also played against another touring side, the 1993 All Blacks, in the Scottish Development XV beaten 31–12 in Edinburgh (16.11.93). He next came across New Zealand in last summer's World Cup when coming on as a 62nd minute for Damian Cronin in Scotland's 48–30 quarter-final defeat (Pretoria, 11.6.95). It was his second outing of the tournament, having played all of the opening game against Cote d'Ivoire, a game in which Scotland registered the biggest win in their history, 89-0 (Rustenburg, 26.5.95).
Touchlines: Music

Campese, D. I.   Australia

Full Name: David Ian Campese
State: New South Wales
Clubs: Randwick (Aus: since 1986),
Mediolanum Milan (It: since 1988)
Position: Wing, fullback
Height: 5ft 10in (1.77m)
Weight: 14st 12lb (90kg)
Occupation: Partner in Campo's
Sports Store
Born: 21.10.62
Family: Tony (father), Joan
(mother), Mario (brother), Lisa
(sister), Corinne (sister)
Former clubs: Queanbeyan (1980-
86), Petrarca (Padua, It: 1984-87)
International debut: New Zealand
23, Australia 16, 1982
Best moments in rugby: Debut in
first Test vs New Zealand 1982 when scored try; 1989 Hong Kong Sevens
Player of Tournament; 1991 World Cup.
Worst moment in rugby: Being dropped for first Test vs France in 1990
Most embarrassing moment: Dropping ball at Cardiff vs 1988 Barbarians with
try line in sight
Most respected opponent: Hugo Porta (Argentina)
Serious injuries: Dislocated shoulder (1985), ankle (1987), knee (1992)
Other sporting achievements: 1981 ACT Schools Golf Championship
Suggestions to improve rugby: Allow playing the ball on the ground. Stop locks
marking wingers under current maul law. Install professional rugby
administrators
Notable landmarks in rugby career: The world's leading Test try-scorer with
63, Campo is also Australia's most-capped player, with 91 appearances to his
name ... and he refused to contemplate retirement after Australia's World Cup
defence ended in the quarter-finals against England (Cape Town, 11.6.95).
Shares with Greg Cornelsen the Aussie record for most tries scored in a single
Test, with his four against the United States Eagles in 1983. One of a growing
number of full-time rugby players, who follow the winter season around the
globe by playing their 'trade' in both hemispheres. Campo started with
Queanbeyan before joining Randwick in 1987. His State allegiance also
switched from Australian Capital Territory to New South Wales. Made his
international debut against New Zealand back in 1982 and has been a thorn in
opponents' flesh ever since; not least in the 1991 World Cup when six tries in
six appearances helped Australia win the Webb Ellis Cup and him to be
declared both the Player of the Tournament, the Australian Society of Rugby

Writers' Player of the Year and a similar accolade from the British Rugby Writers in the form of the Pat Marshall Memorial Award. He was an ever-present throughout Australia's eight-Test campaign in 1992, adding to his try-tally against Scotland, New Zealand (first Test), South Africa (No.50), Ireland and Wales. An unbroken run in 1993 included the third try hat-trick of his career, against Canada (won 43–16, Calgary, 9 October), having claimed two against Tonga (won 52–14, Brisbane 3 July). More of the same in 1994, with tries against Ireland, Italy and Western Samoa, before he bagged three in two Tests against Argentina pre-World Cup.

Touchlines: Golf.

Australia (1982)

Last Season	9 caps	25 pts
Career	91 caps	310 pts

Caps (91): **1982** NZ(1,2,3) **1983** US, Arg(1,2), NZ, It, F(1,2) **1984** Fj, NZ(1,2,3), E, I, W, S **1985** Fj(1,2) **1986** It, F, Arg(1,2), NZ(1,2,3) **1987** wc-E, US, J, I, F, W. NZ **1988** E(1,2), NZ(1,2,3), E, S, It **1989** BL(1,2,3), NZ, F(1,2) **1990** F(2,3), US, NZ(1,2,3) **1991** W, E, NZ(1,2). wc-Arg, WS, W, I, NZ, E **1992** S(1,2), NZ(1,2,3), SA, I, W **1993** T, NZ, SA(1,2,3), C, F(1,2) **1994** I(1,2), It(1,2), WS, NZ **1995** Arg(1,2) wc-SA, C, E

Points (310 – 63t,8c,7p,2dg): **1982** NZ(1:1t), NZ(2:1t) **1983** US(4t,1c), Arg(1:1p), Arg(2:1t,3c,1p), It(3c,1p), F(1:1c,1p), F(2:1p) **1984** Fj(1t), NZ(2:1p), NZ(3:1t,1p), S(2t) **1985** Fj(1:1dg), Fj(2:2t) **1986** It(2t), F(1t), Arg(1:1t), Arg(2:2t), NZ(1:1t), NZ(3:1t) **1987** wc-E(1t), US(1t), J(1t), F(1t) **1988** E(a2:1t), E(b:1t), S(2t), I(3t) **1989** NZ(1t), F(1:1t) **1990** F(2:1t), F(3:1t), US(1t,1dg) **1991** W(a:1t), E(a:2t). wc-Arg(2t), W(b:1t), I(2t), NZ(b:1t) **1992** S(1:2t), NZ(1:1t), SA(1t), I(1t), W(1t) **1993** T(2t), C(3t) **1994** I(1:1t), It(2:1t), WS(1t) **1995** Arg(1:1t), Arg(2:2t)

Carling, W. D. C.   England

Full Name: William David Charles Carling
Club: Harlequins
Position: Centre
Height: 5ft 11lb (1.81m)
Weight: 14st 2lb (89.5kg)
Occupation: Runs own management training/personal development company: Insight
Born: Bradford-on-Avon, Wiltshire, 12.12.65
Family: Julia (wife)
Family links with rugby: Father (Bill) played for Cardiff
Former club: Durham University
International debut: France 10, England 9, 1988
Five Nations' debut: As above
Best moments in rugby: England beating Australia 28–19 in my first game as captain; leading England to back-to-back Grand Slams; beating Australia in 1995 World Cup quarter-final
Worst moment in rugby: Losing 1990 Grand Slam decider to Scotland; being dropped by 1993 Lions; losing England captaincy (albeit temporarily)
Most respected opponent: Denis Charvet (Toulouse & France)
Serious injuries: Fracture of leg (1989)
Suggestions to improve rugby:

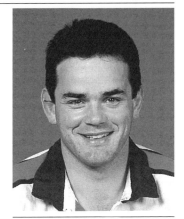

England (1988)

Last Season	11 caps	20 pts
Career	60 caps	49 pts
Lions 1993	1 Test	0 pts

Caps (60): **1988** F, W, S, I(1,2), A(a2), Fj, A(b) **1989** S,I,F,W,Fj **1990** I, F, W, S, Arg(a1,a2), Arg(b) **1991** W, S, I, F, Fj, A(a) wc-NZ, It, US, F, S, A(b) **1992** S, I, F, W, C, SA **1993** F, W, S, I. Lions-NZ(1). NZ **1994** S, I, F, W, SA(1,2), R, C **1995** I, F(a), W, S wc-Arg, WS, A, NZ, F(b)

Points (49 – 11t): **1989** F(1t) **1990** F(1t), W(1t) **1991** wc-US(1t), F(1t) **1992** W(1t), SA(1t) **1994** R(1t) **1995** I(1t) wc-NZ(2t)

Greater player involvement in law-changes and in the administration of the game. It seems so logical to me yet they ignore it. General level of coaching in English club rugby must be raised – still too stuck in our ways. We must learn from other countries. Better communication is needed and everyone, regardless of hemisphere, should play by the same rules

Notable landmarks in rugby career: Busy season for Will, who was one moment picking up his third England Grand Slam in five years and the next picking up the pieces of an apparently shattered career. The now infamous 'old farts' affair, in which he rather unwisely labelled the RFU's committee as old windbags and was sacked as skipper for his cheek, threatened to wreck all he had achieved in 55 Test appearances. But the country rallied behind him and public pressure, allied to the refusal of England's other players to accept the vacant captaincy, led to Will's reinstatement. He was thus able to lead the nation to the World Cup in South Africa. England's most-capped centre (60) and holder of world record for most international wins as captain (40 in 53 games), Will rebounded from disappointment of being dropped by 1993 Lions after first Test loss to All Blacks to lead England to victory over same opponents (27.11.93). Began playing career with Terra Nova School Under-11s as a six-year old. First fifth-former (15-year old) to play in Sedbergh's first XV (three years in team – experienced only two defeats), prior to captaining England 18-Group (1984) and moving on to Durham University on an Army scholarship (reading psychology) where switched to fullback. Northern Division selectors Geoff Cooke and Dave Robinson advised playing centre, where he has remained ever since. Rates a county performance for Durham against Lancashire as one of the most influential in shaping his future career. Bought himself out of Army (2nd Lt heading towards Royal Regiment of Wales) when told he would not be able to play representative rugby. Helped England B beat France B 22–9 (Bath, 20.2.87). England's youngest captain for 57 years (since P D Howard of Old Millhillians, 1931) when handed reins aged 22 years and 11 months for England's 28–19 win over Australia (5.11.88). Captain in two Grand Slams and 1991 run to World Cup final. Confessed, on Radio 4's Desert Island Discs (May 1992) that, if cast away, he would want with him Tolkein's book *The Hobbit*, Louis Armstrong's record 'What a Wonderful World', and a flotation tank.

Touchlines: Painting – sketching and inks, social golf.

England and Scotland tussle for possession during the Five Nations Grand Slam decider at Twickenham.

Catt, M. J.   England

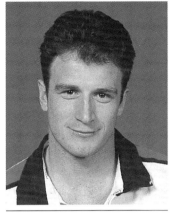

Full Name: Michael John Catt
Club: Bath
Position: Centre, outside-half
Height: 5ft 10in (1.78m)
Weight: 13st 2lb (79kg)
Occupation: Rugby union
player
Born: Port Elizabeth, 17.9.71
Family: Single
International debut: England 15,
Wales 8, 1994
Five Nations debut: As above
Other sporting achievements:
Triathlon for Eastern Province
(Under-21 champion)
Notable landmarks in rugby career:
Grabbed his England chance with
both hands last season after coming
on as a 27th minute replacement
against Romania (Twickenham,
12.11.94) for Paul Hull, England's
outstanding back on the tour to
South Africa only months earlier.
Mike scored two tries and has been
unchallenged since. Played in all four
rounds of England's '95 Grand Slam
and throughout World Cup

England (1994)

Last Season	11 caps	13 pts
Career	12 caps	13 pts

Caps (12): **1994** W(R), C(R) **1995** I,
F(a), W, S wc-Arg, It, WS, A, NZ,
F(b)

Points (13 – 2t,1dg): **1994** C(R:2t) **1995**
wc-WS(1dg)

campaign, including one game at fly-half when he dropped a goal in the 44–22
defeat of Western Samoa, and one game when this Catt was run over, literally,
by All Black sensation Jonah Lomu. Moved to Bath from Eastern Province, in
South Africa, in 1992, and immediately establishing himself as deputy to Stuart
Barnes. Born in Port Elizabeth he holds a British passport thanks to his English
mother. A stand-off by design, Mike has flourished at centre in the star-studded
Bath side. However, it was at No.10 that he appeared for South West England
against New Zealand (30.10.93), although he reverted to centre for England
A's challenge to the tourists at Gateshead the following weekend. Completed
his hat-trick of appearances against the All Blacks with stand-off outing for
England Emerging Players (Gloucester, 23.11.93). Returned to South Africa
with England in '94, having toured Australia with England's Under-21 side in
1993, scoring a try in their 'Test' win. Took him only nine domestic
appearances to get himself nominated for England's preliminary squad to play
New Zealand and although he didn't figure in the final 21, he was drafted into
the squad for the 1994 Five Nations Championship, warming bench in each

game before coming on in 76th minute of title decider against Wales as a replacement for Rob Andrew.

Cecillon, M. France

Full Name: Marc Cecillon
Club: Bourgoin-Jallieu
Position: No 8, flanker, lock
Height: 6ft 3in (1.90m)
Weight: 15st 2lb (96kg)
Occupation: Schoolmaster
Born: Bourgoin-Jallieu, 30.7.59
International debut: France 25, Ireland 6, 1988
Five Nations' debut: As above
Notable landmarks in rugby career: Indefatigable player who refuses to go quietly. In 1994 he set off on another tour, this time to Canada and New Zealand, after a season in which he turned 35 and picked up a further eight caps to take his tally to 40. Failed to make the team which inflicted an historic 2–0 series defeat on the All Blacks but was summoned to lend experience in the 1995 Five Nations, marking his return with a try against Ireland (Dublin, 4.3.95). Hung around for the World Cup in South Africa. Appointed captain for the 1992 Summer and Autumn Tests against Argentina (on tour in July) and Springboks (at Lyon and Paris in October) but was succeeded in that position by Jean-Francois Tordo thereafter. Still, Marc retained his place in the side at No 8 and played a full part in France's Championship triumph. Starting out, he had had to

France (1988)

Last Season	6 caps	5 pts
Career	46 caps	38 pts

Caps (46): **1988** I, W, Arg(a2), Arg(b1,b2), Ro **1989** Ro, I, E, NZ(1,2), A(1) **1990** S, I, E(R) **1991** Ro, US(1), W wc-E **1992** W, E, S, I, R, Arg(a1,a2), SA(1,2) **1993** E, S, I, W, R(a), SA(1,2), R(b), A(1,2) **1994** I, W **1995** I(a), R wc-T, S(b), I(b), SA

Points (38 – 9t): **1988** Arg(b1:1t), Arg(b2:1t) **1989** NZ(1:1t), NZ(2:1t) **1991** Ro(1t), US(1:1t) **1992** I(1t) **1993** R(a:1t) **1995** I(a:1t)

wait more than eight years between first representing France B – in December 1979 against Wales (won 33–12) in Bourg-en-Bresse – and making his full debut against Ireland in Paris in 1988. In between he busied himself with regular tours of duty for France A in the FIRA Championship, before embarking on a cap-less world tour with France in 1986. A Jack of virtually all scrummage trades and master of a good many. Before 1991 he appeared only sporadically, collecting four Championship caps in three seasons. All that changed in 1991/92 when he was recognised as a vital member of the French squad, as well as being the oldest. Indeed, so highly was he regarded that a place was made for him in the 26-man World Cup party despite then coach Jean Trillo knowing his torn thigh muscle would rule him out of the three Pool games.

Chalmers, C. M. Scotland

Full Name: Craig Minto Chalmers
Club: Melrose
Position: Outside-half
Height: 5ft 11in (1.80m)
Weight: 13st 6lb (85kg)
Occupation: Marketing advisor with Scottish Power
Born: Galashiels, 15.10.68
Family: Lucy (wife), Sam (son)
Family links with rugby: Father (Brian) coaches at Melrose
International debut: Scotland 23, Wales 7, 1989
Five Nations' debut: As above
Best moments in rugby: Winning 1990 Grand Slam by beating England; winning 1989/90, 1991/92, 1992/93 and 1993/94 Scottish Championships with Melrose
Worst moment in rugby: Being dropped by 1989 Lions, after playing in first Test against Australia (lost 12-30); breaking arm at Twickenham (6.3.93) to be ruled out of '93 Lions' selection; being dropped by Scotland (1994)
Most respected opponent: Michael Lynagh (Queensland & Australia)
Serious injuries: Torn knee cartilage, strained groin, dead leg, double break of right forearm (1993), partial torn cruciate knee ligament (1994)
Suggestions to improve rugby: Revise amateur laws. I don't see why

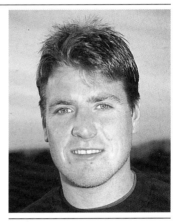

Scotland (1989)

Last Season	11 caps	11 pts
Career	46 caps	131 pts
Lions 1989	1 Test	6 pts

Caps (46): **1989** W, E, I, F. Lions-A(1). Fj **1990** I, F, W, E, NZ(1,2), Arg **1991** F, W, E, I, Ro wc-J, Z, I, WS, E, NZ **1992** E, I, F, W, A(1,2) **1993** I, F, W, E, NZ **1994** W, SA **1995** C, I, F(a), W, E, R wc-IC, T, F(b), NZ
Points (131 – 5t,7c,24p,8dg): **1989** W(1t,1dg). Lions-A(1:1p,1dg) **1990** I(1c,1p), F(2c,2p), W(3p), E(3p), Arg(1t) **1991** F(2p,1dg), W(1t,1c,1p,1dg), E(4p), I(2c,3p) wc-J(1t,1p), I(1dg) **1992** W(1dg,2p), A(2:1c,1p) **1993** E(1dg), NZ(1p)

we should not be paid for playing. Play game without flankers (give me more room to run).

Notable landmarks in rugby career: Succeeded John Rutherford as Scotland's most-capped fly-half when winning his 43rd cap in the 89-0 World Cup rout of Cote d'Ivoire (Rustenburg, 26.5.95). Marked the occasion with a try in Scotland's biggest win of all time. Everpresent in South Africa until suffering a 'dead thigh' in the quarter-final against New Zealand and limping off at half-time. With him went Scotland's hopes of staying in the tournament. Still, the season was something of a triumph for Craig after an awful 1993/94 campaign, during which he suffered the ignominy of being dropped for first time since Scotland debut in 1989, and being dogged by injury which ruled him out of summer tour to Argentina. Paid price for playing when less than 100% fit against Wales and was not required thereafter. A far cry from 6 March 1993 when he was considered odds-on to become British Lions' first-choice stand-off in New Zealand that summer. A double break of his right forearm, playing against England at Twickenham – the last Test hurdle for Scotland before selection was made – put paid to that. The injury also meant he was a spectator as Melrose were crowned Scottish club champions for the third time in four seasons. They won it again in 1993/94. Youngest player ever to represent Scotland B – as a 19-year old in the 18–12 defeat of France B at Chalon-sur-Saone (20.3.88) – having already turned out for Scottish Schools, Under-18, Under-19 and Under-21. Scored a try and dropped goal on full debut against Wales (21.1.89), having marked first XV debut for Melrose with three dropped goals against Harrogate. Earned selection to 1989 Lions tour of Australia and kicked six points in first Test before being replaced by Rob Andrew for remainder of series. Still, played in seven of the 12-match programme. Scotland's Grand Slam No.10 in 1990 who kicked three penalty goals in never-to-be-forgotten decider against England. Dropped two goals as England turned tables in 1995 Grand Slam decider (Twickenham, 18.3.95) and bagged a try in 62–7 non-cap Test win over Spain (Madrid, 6.5.95). Toured with Scotland to New Zealand (1990), North America (1991) and Australia (1992).
Touchlines: Golf (12-handicap), ten-pin bowling

Clarke, B. B.   England

Full Name: Benjamin Bevan Clarke
Club: Bath
Position: No 8
Height: 6ft 5in (1.95m)
Weight: 16st 13lb (107kg)
Occupation: Works for National
Power, Swindon
Born: Bishop's Stortford, 15.4.68
Family: Single
Family links with rugby: Father
(Bevan) played for Bishop's
Stortford and is now club chairman
Former clubs: Bishop's Stortford,
Saracens
International debut: England 33,
South Africa 16, 1992
Five Nations' debut: England 16,
France 15, 1993
Best moment in rugby: Lions' second
Test defeat of All Blacks; England's
win over All Blacks (both 1993)
Most respected opponent: Dean
Ryan (Wasps & England)
Other sporting achievements:
Swimming for Hertfordshire
Suggestions to improve rugby:
Revise amateur rules. Compensate
players or employers for time lost to
rugby. Talk to players before introducing new regulations

England (1992)		
Last Season	10 caps	5 pts
Career	21 caps	10 pts
Lions 1993	3 Tests	0 pts

Caps (21): **1992** SA **1993** F, W, S, I.
Lions-NZ(1,2,3). NZ **1994** S, F,
W, SA(1,2), R, C **1995** I, F, W,S
wc-Arg, It, A, NZ
Points (10 – 2t): **1994** SA(1:1t) **1995** I(1t)

Notable landmarks in rugby career: The outstanding British Lion in New
Zealand (1993), it is hard to believe that Ben still has only 21 England caps to
his credit, of which half came last season. Stalwart in England's Grand Slam
triumph and World Cup campaign, Ben had previously proved himself one of
the most dynamic and dependable of performers on England's 1994 tour to
South Africa. Within five caps of his England debut (14.11.92) he had been
snapped up by the Lions for their safari in New Zealand – a country he had
previously visited in 1992 with England B, though he did not pick up a 'Test'
scalp (lost 18–24, Hamilton, 28.6.92; lost 18-26, Pukekohe, 5.7.92). In his
formative years Ben represented Hertfordshire Colts, U-21 and full teams while
with Bishop Stortford. On joining Saracens at start of 1990/91, he was selected
for London Division, Public School Wanderers, Penguins, England Students
and England B. Toured Australia (1991) with London, and was a member of
the 1992 England B 'Grand Slam'-winning side which accounted for Spain,

Ireland B, France B and Italy B (scored tries v Sp,I). Helped Bath successfully defend Pilkington Cup last season.
Touchlines: Golf, squash, hockey.

Clement, A. Wales

Full Name: Anthony Clement
Club: Swansea
Position: Outside-half, fullback
Height: 5ft 9in (1.75m)
Weight: 13st 8lb (86kg)
Occupation: Leasing executive with C.M. Day Ltd, Swansea
Born: Swansea, 8.2.67
Family: Debra (wife)
Family links with rugby: Father (Malcolm) played for Bonymaen; brother (Michael) plays for Bonymaen
Former club: Morriston Youth
International debut: Wales 46, US Eagles 0, 1987
Five Nations' debut: England 3, Wales 11, 1988
Best moments in rugby: Scoring two tries for Wales on debut. Helping Wales beat Australia 16–10 in quarter-finals of 1990 Hong Kong Sevens. Beating Scotland (21.3.92) to end three-year winless run at Arms Park. Call-up to '93 Lions; Swansea beating Australia (Nov '92)
Serious injuries: Hamstring strain, shin fracture (Swansea v Australia, Nov '92 and didn't come off)
Notable landmarks in rugby career: Injury again disrupted his season, but not as badly as it did Mike

Wales (1987)		
Last Season	7 caps	0 pts
Career	37 caps	16 pts
Lions 1989		
1993		

Caps (37): **1987** US(R) **1988** E, NZ, WS(R), Ro **1989** NZ **1990** S(R), I(R), Na(1,2) **1991** S(R), A(a:R), F(b) wc-WS, A(b) **1992** I, F, E, S **1993** I(R), F, J, C **1994** S, I, F. wc(q)-Sp. C(R), T, WS. wc(q)-It. SA **1995** F, E wc-J, NZ, I(b)

Points (16 – 3t,1dg): **1987** US(R:2t) **1990** Na(2:1dg) **1993** J(1t)

Rayer, his rival for the Wales fullback slot. Rayer broke his leg horribly, having kept Clem out of the No 15 jersey in the World Cup qualifiers against Romania and Italy, and his season was over. So Swansea skipper Clem moved off the left wing, his position against Italy (12.10.94), to fullback where he remained until injury robbed him of appearances against Scotland and Ireland. But returned for ill-fated World Cup trip to South Africa, where he played in all three games.

A 1993 British Lion, having also toured with them to Australia in 1989, when the Wallabies were beaten. On neither trip was he 'capped'. Touring New Zealand with Lions, Clem turned out against North Auckland, Canterbury, Otago, Southland, Taranaki, Hawke's Bay and Waikato. Helped Swansea wallop the touring Wallabies 21–6 (14.11.92). Has appeared for Wales in four different positions (fullback, wing, fly-half and centre) and toured South Africa with World XV in 1989. But it was not until 1991/92 season that he finally secured much-cherished fullback slot, after returning from Wales' horrible tour of Australia. Turned out against Western Samoa and Australia during 1991 World Cup and proved a major success in 1992 Five Nations Championship. Equally impressive for Swansea who won 1991/92 Heineken Championship. Joined All Whites in 1985, having played six games for Welsh Youth the previous year. Captained Wales U-20s and also represented Wales U-21s and B (three times).

Touchlines: Soccer, cricket

Clohessy, P. M. N.   Ireland

Full Name: Peter Martin Noel Clohessy
Club: Young Munster
Position: Tighthead prop
Height: 5ft 11in (1.80m)
Weight: 16st (102kg)
Occupation: Director, Clohessy Couriers, Limerick
Born: Limerick, 22.3.66
Family: Anna (wife), Luke (son)
Family links with rugby: Grandfather (Peter O'Hallaran) won Munster Senior Cup medal with Garryowen
Former club: Garryowen
International debut: Ireland 6, France 21, 1993
Five Nations' debut: As above
Best moment in rugby: Beating 1992 Wallabies with Munster
Worst moment in rugby: Being suspended for 12 weeks after trial by video playing for Young Munster against St Mary's College in All-Ireland League
Most respected opponent: Louis

Ireland (1993)		
Last Season	5 caps	0 pts
Career	14 caps	5 pts

Caps (14): **1993** F, W, E **1994** F, W, E, S, A(1,2), US **1995** E, S, F, W
Points (5 – 1t): **1994** A(2:1t)

Armary (Lourdes & France)
Serious injuries: Slipped disc, broken leg and arm
Notable landmarks in rugby career: Missed World Cup last summer through work commitments, having been regular Ireland tighthead through 1995 Five Nations. Graduated through Irish Under-23 (1989 v Italy, Ravenhill) and B ranks to full side in 1992/93 season, after helping Munster beat touring Australians 22–19 at Thomond Park and Young Munster win All-Ireland Championship. Debut against France came three years after Ireland B debut in 22–22 draw with Scotland B at Murrayfield (9.12.89). Big breakthrough followed provincial appearances against Ulster, Leinster and Connacht and came in wake of Ireland's desperately poor defeat by Scotland at Murrayfield. Paul McCarthy was player to pass over tighthead duties. Peter retained No.3 jersey for the remainder of the Championship and should have been picked for 1993 British Lions tour to New Zealand. A ten-week suspension (for stamping) ruled him out of Ireland's 1993/94 Test opener against Romania (14.11.93). Regained jersey from Garrett Halpin by time of 1994 Five Nations Championship after which he toured Australia with Ireland, scoring his first international try in the 32–18 second Test. loss (Sydney, 11.6.94).
Touchlines: Waterskiing.

Coker, T. Australia

Full Name: Troy Coker
State: Queensland
Clubs: Southern Districts (Aus)
Position: Lock, back row
Height: 6ft 6in (1.98m)
Weight: 17st 13lb (114kg)
Occupation: Industrial Relations
Advocate with Carter Newell
Solicitors
Born: 30.5.63
Family: Single
Former clubs: GPS (Brisbane: 1981-
84), Western Districts (1985-91),
Oxford University (1988-89)
International debut: Australia 19,
England 6, 1987
Best moments in rugby: Winning
1991 World Cup and 1992 Bledisloe
Cup series

Worst moment in rugby: Snapping cruciate ligament in right knee (Argentina 1987) after full recovery from left knee operation the previous year
Most respected opponent: Ian Jones (North Auckland & New Zealand)

Serious injuries: Left knee reconstruction (1986), right knee reconstruction (1987-88)
Other sporting achievements: Oxford rowing 1990-91
Suggestions to improve rugby: Get referees to realise that they have had a good game if people/players did not notice they were there. They are there to administer the rules, not shove them down our throats!

Australia (1987)		
Last Season	1 cap	0 pts
Career	16 caps	0 pts

Caps (16): **1987** wc-E, US, F, W **1991** NZ(a2). wc-Arg, WS,NZ(b), E(b) **1992** NZ(1,2,3), W(R) **1993** T, NZ **1995** Arg(2)
Points Nil

Notable landmarks in rugby career: A familiar face to English audiences, having represented Oxford University (along with now retired Wallaby Brian Smith) in the 1988 and 1989 Varsity matches, and Harlequins since 1990 (helping them to a 1991 Pilkington Cup final victory over Northampton). Returned to Australia last season but injury wrecked his campaign, with only one outing against Argentina (Sydney, 6.5.95) to his credit. Embroiled in controversy during 1993/94 domestic season in England when he claimed to be the victim of a 'pre-meditated act' of foul play during the league clash between Quins and Bath. It was claimed he suffered eye gouging and that there were severe scratch marks around his eyes. First played for Australia in the 1987 World Cup, winning caps at No 8 against England, the United States, France and Wales. Thereafter despite touring in 1987 and 1990, did not add a fifth cap to his tally until 1991 when replacing Tim Gavin at No 8 against New Zealand in Auckland. Something of a utility forward in the Wallabies' triumphant World Cup campaign: employed at lock in the Pool victories over Argentina and Western Samoa, before reverting to No 8 for the semi-final defeat of New Zealand and the final win over England. His travels around the scrum continued when he opened 1992 at blindside in the 16–15 first Test defeat of the All Blacks in Sydney. From there he switched flanks to fill the openside berth for the remainder of the Bledisloe Cup-winning series. Displaced by a combination of Willie O and David Wilson thereafter, he nonetheless played against Wales in Cardiff.

Collins, R. G.   Wales

Full Name: Richard (Richie)
Graham Collins
Club: Pontypridd
Position: Flanker
Height: 6ft 1in (1.85)
Weight: 14st 7lb (87.5kg)
Occupation: Policeman
Born: Cardiff, 2.3.62
Family: Single
Former clubs: Pontypridd, Newport,
South Wales Police, Cardiff
International debut: Wales 19,
England 12, 1987
Five Nations' debut: As above
Best moment in rugby: Wales
winning 1988 Triple Crown in
Ireland
Worst moment in rugby: 1991 Wales
tour of Australia
Most embarrasing moment: Whole
of above tour
Most respected opponent: Finlay
Calder (Stewart's-Melville &
Scotland)
Other sporting achievements: Welsh
basketball international
Notable landmarks in rugby career:
Returned to Wales set-up in 1994

Wales (1987)		
Last season	7 caps	0 pts
Career	28 caps	9 pts

Caps (28): **1987** E(a:R), I(a), US wc-I(b),
E(b). NZ **1988** E, S, I, F, R **1990** E,
S, I **1991** A(a), F(b) wc-WS **1994**
C, Fj, T, WS wc(q)-R, It. SA **1995**
F, E, S, I(a)

Points (9 – 2t): **1991** F(b:1t) **1994** Fj(1t)

after three-year absence. Having rejoined Pontypridd from South Wales Police
he was seconded onto summer tour to Canada and South Seas, where claimed
openside berth and played in all four Tests, scoring his second Test try in the
23–8 defeat of Fiji (Suva, 18.6.94). Retained his place throughout 1995 Five
Nations Championship but white-washed Wooden Spoon led to him being
jettisoned along with coach Alan Davies. New broom, Alex Evans, omitted
Richie from World Cup trip to South Africa – the first of the three tournaments
he has missed. Played rugby initially to sharpen reflexes and bulk-up for
basketball. Spent a year playing Wellington club rugby in New Zealand before
returning to join Pontypridd, and Newport, with whom played in 1986 Welsh
Cup final. Scored try on Wales B debut in 24–12 win over Italy (1986). Made
full Wales debut as replacement at Cardiff in 1987. Returned to national set-up
for 1991 tour of Australia and played in 6–63 loss to host nation, before
opening try account in 9–22 loss to France in September 1991. World Cup duty
was restricted to a solitary appearance, in the 16–13 defeat by Western Samoa.

Cooksley, M. S.　　　　　　New Zealand

Full Name: Mark Cooksley
Province: Counties
Position: Lock
Height: 6ft 7½in (2.02m)
Weight: 18st 2lb (115kg)
Born: 11.4.71
International debut: New Zealand 14, World XV 28, 1992
Notable landmarks in rugby career: First-choice All Black lock alongside Ian Jones in 1994, appearing in five of New Zealand's six engagements. The biggest man in New Zealand's squad for the 1992 tour of Australia and South Africa, Mark made his Test debut in the first match of the centenary series in Christchurch (18 April). The good news ended there as the All Blacks were beaten 28-14 and Mark, although teaming up with Jones to get the better of Frenchmen Olivier Roumat and Marc Cecillon, sustained an injury. Fit for the aforementioned tour, he made seven appearances – against Western

New Zealand (1992)

Last Season	5 caps	0 pts
Career	9 caps	0 pts

Caps (9): 1992 Wd(1) 1993 BL(2,3R),A 1994 F(1,2),SA(1,2),A

Points Nil

Australia (scored try), ACT, Victoria, Queensland B, Sydney, Natal and Central Unions – improving the longer the trip progressed. Graduated through the age-group ranks at second division Counties, developing into a strong lock and number four jumper, though also well versed in the front-jumping duties. Represented New Zealand at Under-19 level and NZ Colts between 1990-91. One of his great memories is 11 August 1991 in Christchurch when he played on the Colts side which demolished their Australian counterparts 61–9. First All Black trial came in 1991 and helped Saracens trial team beat New Zealand XV 20–15 at Napier in 1992. Partook in New Zealand Maoris' two tours in 1992 (one internal, the other to the Pacific Islands) but had to wait until 1993 before adding to his cap tally when selected ahead of Jones for the second Test against the British Lions. Lasted only half of Wellington defeat before Jones replaced him. Roles reversed in deciding Test when Mark came on for Jones 20 minutes in New Zealand's 30–13 Auckland win. Kept place for Bledisloe Cup defeat of Australia (Dunedin, 17.7.93) but did not tour England and Scotland in autumn of '93. Not included in Kiwi squad for last summer's World Cup.

Cooper, M. J.   New Zealand

Full Name: Matthew James Cooper
Province: Waikato
Club: Marist (Hamilton)
Position: Fullback, centre, wing
Height: 6ft 2in (1.88m)
Weight: 14st 13lb (95kg)
Born: 10.10.66
Family links with rugby: Greg (brother) plays for Otago and New Zealand
Former provinces: Otago, Hawke's Bay
International debut: New Zealand 59, Ireland 6, 1992
Best memory in rugby: Ending Auckland's dominance of the Ranfurly Shield in 1993
Suggestions to improve rugby: Make goal posts wider or bend outwards at the top
Notable landmarks in rugby career: Paid the price for New Zealand's 2–0 series defeat by France in 1994, being replaced in All Black midfield by Alama Ieremia before Walter Little reclaimed his former glories. Matt had made a record-breaking start to international career in

New Zealand (1992)

Last Season	2 caps	18 pts
Career	8 caps	55 pts

Caps (8): **1992** I(2), SA(R) **1993** BL(1R,3TR), WS(TR), S **1994** F(1,2)
Points (55 – 2t,10c,9p): **1992** I(2:2t,6c,1p) **1993** S(4c,2p) **1994** F(1:1p), F(2:5p)

second Test against Ireland at Wellington in 1992. Having displaced brother Greg at fullback, he responded with 23 points in 59–6 win. His tally – two tries, six conversions and a penalty goal – represented a world record for a Test debutant (since improved to 45 by countryman Simon Culhane in South Africa last summer). Matt, who finished second to his fraternal rival in the 1992 New Zealand domestic charts, with 260 points (6t,59c,38p,1dg) to Greg's 291, at least had the satisfaction of taking national championship honours with Waikato, 40–5 against his brother's Otago side. His national squad involvement had begun as far back as 1987, when he represented the All Blacks as a centre in Tokyo against Japan B, where the tourists triumphed 94–0, and in Kyoto in the 96–3 win over the Asian Barbarians. He scored a total three tries. Returned to set-up in 1992 after Trial in which he contributed 23 points to a winning cause. Took to 11 his total All Black appearances with nine outings during the 1992 tour of Australia and South Africa, including his second cap as a temporary replacement against the Springboks. Ended tour as second top scorer (with 71 points), a feat he repeated in 1993 when bagging 76 points (11c,18p) in England and Scotland ('dirt tracker' Shane Howarth topped the charts with 81). Matt had already taken his cap haul to five with three more replacement outings (two temporary) against the Lions (whom he'd helped Waikato thrash) and Western Samoa, before a tour in which his brilliant kicking form suggested him to be the new Grant Fox. Landed 14 points (4c,2p) against Scotland (won 51–15, 20.11.93) but a groin injury (sustained in 78th minute at Murrayfield) kept him out of England game. It was perhaps no coincidence New Zealand lost (15–9).

Corkery, D. Ireland

Full Name: David Corkery
Club: Cork Constitution
Position: Flanker
Height: 6ft 4in
Weight: 14st 5lb
Occupation: Insurance clerk, James Bruen & Sons Ltd
Born: Cork, 6.11.72
International debut: Australia 31, Ireland 13, 1994
Five Nations debut: Ireland 7, France 25, 1995
Notable landmarks in rugby career: The biggest mistake surely Ireland's selectors made in 1994/95 was to drop this man. A cracking tour of Australia (1994) suggested at his potential and a wonderful World Cup in South Africa (1995) confirmed it. In between, the Murphy boys left him on the bench and, save for the face-saver against Wales, Ireland lost the lot. In Oz, David helped the Irish beat Western Australia and ACT and push Super-10 kings Queensland close

Ireland (1994)

Last Season	6 caps	10 pts
Career	8 caps	10 pts

Caps (8): **1994** A(1,2), US **1995** E wc-NZ, J, W(b), F(b)
Points (10 – 2t): **1995** wc-NZ(1t), J(1t)

(lost 26–29). The former Munster Schools, Under-20 and Ireland Under-21 player then appeared in both Tests against the Wallabies (lost 13–31 and 18–32). But on his return ... nothing. His aggression and blood red determination was absent from a colourless Five Nations campaign and he sat on the bench in Treviso while Ireland became the first major nation to lose to Italy (lost 12–20, Treviso 8.5.95). The Powers that be finally came to their senses in South Africa and were rewarded with try-scoring displays from David

189

against New Zealand (Johannesburg, 27.5.95) and Japan (Bloemfontein, 31.5.95). He was excellent too in the 24–23 defeat of Wales that booked the Emeral Isle's quarter-final berth. Made his Munster Inter-Provincial debut last season – and the province ended up kingpins.

Costes, A.   France

Full Name: Arnaud Costes
Club: Montferrand
Position: Flanker
Height: 1.86m
Weight: 102kg
Occupation: Student
Born: Tulle, 16.6.73
Family: Single
International debut: France 28, Canada 9, 1994
Five Nations debut: None
Notable landmarks in rugby career:
Unfortunate enough to surface at the same time as the powerful Philippe Benetton-Laurent Cabannes-Abdel Benazzi triumvirate, Arnaud nonetheless contributed fully to the French squad last season. His debut came in the No 6 jersey at Besancon (17.12.94) against Canada (won 28–9) in the absence of Cabannes. Thereafter the youngster warmed the replacements' bench throughout the 1995 Five Nations Championship

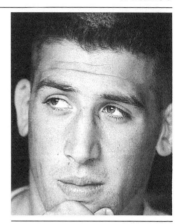

France (1994)

Last Season	3 caps	5 pts
Career	3 caps	5 pts

Caps (3): **1994** C(b) **1995** R wc-IC
Points (5 – 1t): **1995** wc-IC(1t)

before getting his second opportunity in the pre-World Cup trip to Bucharest. Again he contributed to a victory, this time 24–15 over Romania, in a game in which (not for the first time) Thierry Lacroix's boot (14 points) held sway. Selected in France's World Cup squad of 26, Arnaud took his chance in France's middle Pool D match against little Cote d'Ivoire at Rustenburg (won 54–18, 30.5.95) and, despite a thoroughly unsatisfactory team display, he impressed with a try-scoring performance.

Cronin, B.   Ireland

Full Name: Ben Cronin
Club: Garryowen
Position: No 8
Height: 6ft 5in
Weight: 16st 2lb
Occupation: Salesman, Gilbey's
Born: Charlesville, 13.7.68
International debut: Scotland 26,
Ireland 13, 1995
Five Nations debut: As above
Notable landmarks in rugby career:
Just one cap for Ben but for a while it
seemed he would not even get that,
such was his his misfortune with
injury. Originally selected for the
Autumn Dublin international
against United States (won 26–15,
5.11.94), he was forced to withdraw
with a cracked cheekbone which also
explained his absence from the
Development XV against the same
opposition. A player who had been
selected for the Irish Trial as long
ago as 1992/93 (injury again put

Ireland (1995)

Last Season	1 cap	0 pts
Career	1 cap	0 pts

Caps (1): **1995** S
Points Nil

paid to that) finally made it to the altar in one piece for the 1995 Five Nations
opener against Scotland (Murrayfield, 4.2.95). Unhappily, Ireland left their
game in the changing room at half-time and a side that looked destined for
victory crumbled to lose 13–26. Injury returned thereafter to haunt the former
pupil of Cistercian College, Roscrea, who had made his Munster debut in 1992
and played in the provincial side that defeated the '92 Wallabies a shade
controversially. Selection for Ireland A quickly followed against Scotland and
England as a prelude to a tour of southern Africa with an Irish Development
squad in the summer of 1993, which saw him play in two of the 'Tests'. Having
helped Garryowen win the All-Ireland title for the second time in three years,
Ben was drafted out to Australia to replace injured Roger Wilson in the full
squad and played against Australia B.

Cronin, D. F. Scotland

Full Name: Damian Francis Cronin
Club: Bourges (Fra)
Position: Lock
Height: 6ft 6in (1.98m)
Weight: 17st 10lb (112.5kg)
Occupation: Self-employed with Bourges reclamation
Born: Wegberg, West Germany, 17.4.63
Family: Annie (wife), Callum (son), Connie (daughter)
Family links with rugby: Father is a past-president of Ilford Wanderers
Former clubs: Ilford Wanderers, Bath
International debut: Ireland 22, Scotland 18, 1988
Five Nations' debut: As above
Best moment in rugby: Winning 1990 Grand Slam with Scotland; being selected for the 1993 Lions
Worst moment in rugby: Being dropped by Scotland during 1991 World Cup
Most embarrassing moment: Getting ball knocked out of my hands as I was going over to score a try against Wellington (1990)
Most respected opponent: Wade Dooley (Preston Grasshoppers & ex-England)

Scotland (1988)

Last Season	6 caps	10 pts
Career	35 caps	18 pts

Lions 1993

Caps (35): **1988** I, F, W, E, A **1989** W, E, I, F, Fj, Ro **1990** I, F, W, E, NZ(1,2) **1991** F, W, E, I, Ro wc-Z **1992** A(2) **1993** I, F, W, E, NZ **1995** C, I, F(a) wc-T, F(b), NZ
Points (18 – 4t): **1989** I(1t) **1990** W(1t) **1995** C(1t), I(1t)

Serious injuries: Ligament damage in both knees. Staple put in right knee
Other sporting achievements: Drove in celebrity race round Brands Hatch; won Victor Ludorum three years in a row at school
Suggestions to improve rugby: Do not change the lineout. It is a lottery which is half the fun. Those who survive are technicians who learn to survive. Better off working on keeping the game flowing more. Make people stay on their feet more and referees more aware of players, especially flankers, coming over the top.
Notable landmarks in rugby career: After a wretched 1993/94 campaign, 'Del' made yet another comeback, this time from the unlikely base of Bourges in northern France, where he had gone to set up business. And it proved to be one of his best, scoring tries in each of his 'comeback' Tests against Canada

(21.1.95) and Ireland (4.2.95) at Murrayfield. Scotland won both to end a nine-game winless period but a serious arm injury (ruptured tendon in bicep), sustained midway through Scots' historic win in Paris (18.2.95), required a two and a half hour operation and four and a half months recuperation. Returned in the 62–7 non-cap Test victory over Spain in Madrid (6.5.95) – a match staged at altitude to acclimatise the tartan army for South Africa's High Veldt – and held his place in the Pretoria-based World Cup games against Tonga, France and New Zealand. It was all a far cry from the previous season when Del's only Test outing had been in the record 51–15 loss to New Zealand (Murrayfield, 20.11.93) which, in turn, had followed on from a British Lions tour place in New Zealand, and appearances against North Auckland, NZ Maoris, Southland, Taranaki, Hawke's Bay and Waikato. Had done well to return to rugby after fracturing base of spine aged 22. Built reputation in Scotland with performances for Anglo-Scots, becoming eligible thanks to Lothian-based grandparents. Helped 1987 Anglo's beat French at Cupar and was included in Scottish XV which achieved a similar feat. Toured with Scotland to Zimbabwe in 1988 (captaining them against Mashonaland District), Japan (1989) and New Zealand (1990). Largely kept out of 1991 World Cup campaign and 1992 Championship by Doddie Weir and Neil Edwards. Lust for game returned on moving from Bath to London Scottish. Helped them win promotion back to division one in 1991/92 before touring Australia with Scotland in 1992 and recapturing Test place.
Touchlines: Antiques, DIY.

Crowley, D. J.   Australia

Full Name: Daniel (Dan) James Crowley
State: Queensland
Club: Southern Districts
Position: Tighthead prop
Height: 5ft 8in (1.73m)
Weight: 16st 3lb (103kg)
Occupation: Police officer, Queensland Police Service
Born: 28.8.65
Family: Lisa (wife), Jessica (daughter)
International debut: Australia 30, British Lions 12, 1989
Suggestions to improve rugby: No kicking out on the full from anywhere ... make the backs do some work

Notable landmarks in rugby career: Responsible for breaking up one of the great front row partnerships of all time when selected for the first Test versus Argentina (Brisbane, 29.4.95). After a world record 35 Test appearances together Tony Daly, Phil Kearns and Ewen McKenzie were split, with Daly making way for Dan

Australia (1989)

Last Season	3 cap	0 pts
Career	10 caps	0 pts

Caps (10): **1989** BL(1,2,3) **1991** wc-WS **1992** I, W **1993** C(R) **1995** Arg(1,2) wc-SA

Points Nil

in the 53–7 win. He retained his place in the next two games, against Argentina (Sydney, 6.5.95) and in the Wallabies' big World Cup tests (and defeats) against South Africa and England in Cape Town. Dan had been the man to present Her Majesty the Queen with a miniature football prior to Australia's World Cup final win over England in 1991, having made just the one tournament appearance against Western Samoa. Indeed, his links with the United Kingdom stretch back to 1989 when he made his debut against the British Lions and retained his place through the three-Test series. That same year he toured Canada and France but was stood down for the 1990 trip across the Tasman Sea. With Daly and McKenzie pretty much shoring up the Test propping duties his outings have been restricted to just four appearances since the 89' Lions left Oz in triumph. He was a reserve in all Tests in 1991. However, he ended 1992 on a high when, with Daly missing the tour to Ireland and Wales, he wore the loosehead's jersey in both internationals. Dan had himself been unavailable for the historic visit to South Africa in August, but once in Britain was one of the busiest players on duty: appearing also against Leinster, Munster, Ulster and Connacht on the Irish leg, and Wales B and Llanelli once the tourists switched their attentions to the Principality. Perhaps his proudest moment came with a try in the 30–20 defeat of the Barbarians at a packed Twickenham.

Irish passion: (from left) Conor O'Shea, David Corkery, Niall Hogan, Gabriel Fulcher and Eric Elwood.

Culhane, S.   New Zealand

Full Name: Simon Culhane
Province: Southland
Position: Fly-half
Height: 5ft 9in (1.75m)
Weight: 12st 7lb (75kg)
Occupation: Self employed carpenter
Born: 10.3.68
International debut: New Zealand 145, Japan 17
Notable landmarks in rugby career: Modest Test debut in last summer's World Cup. While the world was raving about Canterbury rival Andrew Mehrtens, Simon snuck in for one game against Japan (Bloemfontein, 4.6.95) and went on a record rampage. New Zealand won 145–17, a best for the World Cup finals, and Simon bagged 45 points. This constituted a world record for a debutant, beating Mehrtens' 28 points against Canada only weeks earlier. It also surpassed Gavin Hastings' 44 points against

New Zealand (1995)

Last Season	1 cap	45 pts
Career	1 cap	45 pts

Caps (1): **1995** wc-J
Points (45 – 1t,20c): **1995** wc-J(1t,20c)

Cote d'Ivoire, the previous World Cup finals high for an individual. He claimed one of a record 21 tries and his 20 conversions was a world record. Only Hong Kong wing Ashley Billington's 50 points (ten tries), in a 164–13 World Cup qualifier romp against hapless Singapore, denied Simon every record in the book. Perhaps we should not have been totally surprised, given the staggeringly prolific form Simon produced for Southland in the New Zealand second division in 1994. He smashed Grant Fox's season-scoring record with 180 points, including 37 against Manawatu. But he is not just about kicking as he possesses a rare ability to set a back division alight and is a deceptive runner and fearless tackler. Enough to make you sick, in fact.
Touchlines: Hunting and fishing.

Daly, A. J.   Australia

Full Name: Anthony (Tony) John Daly
State: New South Wales
Club: Randwick
Position: Loosehead prop
Height: 5ft 10in (1.78m)
Weight: 16st 3lb (103kg)
Occupation: Sales executive with Carmin Office Furniture
Born: 7.3.66
Family: Shannon (wife)
Former clubs: Wests (1985-86), Gordon (1987-90), Easts (1991-92)
International debut: New Zealand 24, Australia 12, 1989
Best moment in rugby: 1991 World Cup victory
Most respected opponent: Olo Brown (Auckland & New Zealand)
Serious injuries: Broken ankle (1988); disc protrusion (1992)
Suggestions to improve rugby: More investments for players; more media for the game
Notable landmarks in rugby career: Would have become Australia's most-capped last season, had front row pal Ewen McKenzie been dropped. In the event Tony lost his place just prior to the World Cup and McKenzie was first to edge

Australia (1989)

Last Season	8 caps	0 pts
Career	41 caps	17 pts

Caps (41): **1989** NZ,F(1,2) **1990** F(1,2,3), US, NZ(1,2,3) **1991** W(a), E(a), NZ(a1,a2) wc-Arg, W(b), I, NZ(b), E(b) **1992** S(1,2), NZ(1,2,3), SA **1993** T, NZ, SA(1,2,3), C, F(1,2) **1994** I(1,2), It(1,2), WS, NZ **1995** wc-C, R
Points (17 – 4t): **1990** F(3:1t),US(1t) **1991** wc-E(b:1t) **1993** C(1t)

ahead of Andy McIntyre (1982–89: 38). After a world record 35 Test appearances together the Daly-Phil Kearns-McKenzie front row was broken up and Dan Crowley brought in. Having played every international in 1994, Tony was axed from the Argentina series and, though he played in the World Cup ties against Canada and Romania, he missed the big 'uns against South Africa and England. Had scored his fourth try in the 43–16 defeat of Canada (Calgary, 9.10.93), though it won't go down as his most notable score. That, without doubt, came in the 1991 World Cup final when he scored the only try of Australia's 12–6 win. A breakaway wing-forward in his school days at St Joseph's College, he was transformed into a prop when playing under former Wallaby front-rower John Griffiths at Western Suburbs in Sydney. So well did he master the art that he was plucked from the relative obscurity of club rugby

in 1989 and asked to prop against Richard Loe in the All Black Test at Eden Park. He has since amassed 41 caps despite being unavailable to tour Ireland and Wales in the autumn of 1992. Among his other fond memories are the 1992 Bledisloe Cup series win against New Zealand (though not their one-off loss at Dunedin in '93) and the defeats of South Africa in 1992 (by a record 26–3 margin) and 1993 (a 2–1 series decision).
Touchlines: Tennis, movies, socialising.

Dalton, J. South Africa

Full Name: James Dalton
Province: Transvaal
Position: Hooker
Height: 5ft 11in (1.80m)
Weight: 15st 3lb (92kg)
Occupation: Company director
Born: 16.8.72
Family: Single
International debut: South Africa 42, Argentina 22, 1994
Notable landmarks in rugby career:
Earned infamy when being sent-off in the 'Battle of the Boet' along with Canucks, Gareth Rees and Rod Snow. The match was the Pool A decider between the Springboks and Canada (3.6.95) at the same Port Elizabeth stadium in which England's Tim Rodber had been dismissed the previous summer playing against Eastern Province. A scuffle quickly broke out following an overzealous tackle by Springbok wing Pieter Hendriks and a

South Africa (1995)

Last Season	2 caps	0 pts
Career	3 caps	0 pts

Caps (3): **1994** Arg(1R) **1995** wc-A, C
Points Nil

provocative late hit on Hendriks by Canadian fullback Scott Stewart (both later cited and banned). From there all hell broke loose, resulting in Irish ref David McHugh brandishing three red cards. 'I have a reputation and I seem to have been hanged for it this time,' said James. 'But I can honestly say that I went in to stop the fighting not to take part. I've been made a scapegoat. My whole life may be ruined by this decision.' The former Johannesburg night club bouncer later broke down in tears at a press conference. What a contrast with his previous appearance in the tournament opener at Newlands, Cape Town. After a memorable opening ceremony, the Boks beat world champions Australia in a classic and James played a full part. Toured with South Africa in 1994 to New

Zealand (playing against King Country, Wellington, Hanan Shield XV, Taranaki, Waikato, Manawatu, Otago and Bay of Plenty) and Wales, Scotland and Ireland (appearing versus Wales A, Neath, Scotland A, Scottish Select, Pontypridd and the Barbarians). In between, made his debut as 75th minute replacement for Uli Schmidt against in first Test Argentina (15.10.94) at guess where … Port Elizabeth.

Danaher, P. P. A.   Ireland

Full Name: Philip Paul Anthony Danaher
Club: Garryowen
Position: Centre
Height: 5ft 11in (1.81m)
Weight: 14st (84kg)
Occupation: Director of Premier Peat Products Ltd (Nenagh)
Born: Limerick, 5.10.65
Family: Married
Former clubs: Abbeyfeale, Lansdowne
International debut: Ireland 22, Scotland 18, 1988
Five Nations' debut: As above
Most embarrassing moment: Touching ball down behind line and conceding 5-yard scrum against Wales (ref was wrong!)
Most respected opponent: Jeremy Guscott (Bath & England)
Biggest influence on career: Don Spring (Dublin Univ & Ireland No.8, 1978-81)
Serious injuries: Broken both ankles, serious hamstring injuries

Ireland (1988)

Last Season	5 caps	0 pts
Career	28 caps	6 pts

Caps (28): **1988** S, F, W, WS, It **1989** F, NZ(R) **1990** F **1992** S, F, NZ(1), A **1993** S, F, W, E, R **1994** F, W, E, S, A(1,2), US **1995** E, S, F, W

Points (6 – 2p): **1988** It(2p)

Other sporting achievements: Badminton at national level while at school. Gaelic football for Limerick (helped them reach 1991 Munster Cup final against Kerry)
Notable landmarks in rugby career: Missed out on World Cup last summer due to business commitments but flew out to South Africa as a replacement later for crocked fullback Jim Staples, though he didn't get a game. Had also not been involved in 1991 tournament. Still searching for first Test try after 28 starts. Virtually everpresent in the No.12 jersey for the past two years. Succeeded Phil Matthews as Ireland captain for final game of 1992 Five Nations

Championship, against France in Paris (21.3.92). Ireland lost 44–12 to complete whitewashed Wooden Spoon. Then led side to New Zealand for summer tour, having previously toured to France and North America. Skippered Irish to sensational 12–0 lead over All Blacks in first Test at Dunedin. After he had gone off injured in the 35th minute New Zealand recovered, just, to scrape home 24–21. Missed second Test but recovered fitness in time to lead side in 17–42 loss to Australia (31.10.92). Subsequently relinquished captaincy to Michael Bradley. Collected first international honours in 1982 when represented Ireland Schools (v E,W). Left Garryowen for Lansdowne in 1984 but returned four years later. The 1987/88 season brought his Munster debut and first full cap (at fullback) against Scotland (16.1.88). Helped Garryowen win 1995 Munster Cup

Touchlines: Social golf, walking my pet English sheepdog Boris

Davies, A.   Wales

Full Name: Adrian Davies
Club: Cardiff
Position: Outside-half
Height: 5ft 10in (1.78m)
Weight: 12st 10lb (xkg)
Occupation: Surveyor with Chestertons
Born: Bridgend, 9.2.69
Family: Single
Family links with rugby: Brother (Graham) plays for Llanharan; brother (Lloyd) played for Cambridge University
Former clubs: Pencoed Youth, Neath
International debut: Wales 24, Barbarians 31, 1990
Five Nations' debut: None
Most respected opponent: Aled Williams (Swansea & Wales A)
Serious injuries: Neck problem for one and a half years
Other sporting achievements: Football Blue at Cambridge (offered trials with Leeds United and Sheffield Wednesday aged 16), having played for Wales U-15s
Suggestions to improve rugby: Don't

Wales (1990)

Last Season	2 caps	0 pts
Career	9 caps	22 pts

Caps (9): 1991 Ba(R), A 1993 Z(1,2), J, C 1994 Fj 1995 wc-J, I(b)
Points (22 – 2c,3p,3dg): 1991 A(1dg) 1993 Z(1:1dg) 1994 Fj (2c,3p) 1995 wc-I(b:1dg)

be afraid to listen to experienced international players. There is much benefit to be gained from hearing what the likes of Ieuan Evans and Will Carling think. It is irresponsible to ignore what the players have to say

Notable landmarks in rugby career: Still looking for first appearance in Five Nations Championship despite having won nine caps. Added three more last season, including two at the World Cup where Japan were summarily dispatched but Ireland put paid to Welsh hopes of a quarter-final berth. Had spent the summer of 1994 touring the South Seas with Wales, and kicked 13 points in the 23–8 win over Fiji (Suva, 18.6.94). Had played in both autumn Tests in 1993, but defeat by Canada prompted wholesale changes before start of '94 Five Nations, including switch of Neil Jenkins from centre to outside-half. Adrian captained Wales at U-18, U-19 and U-21 levels. Kicked four penalty goals for Wales B in 15–28 loss to France B at La Teste (12.11.89). Made full debut for Wales when coming on as 47th minute replacement for Mark Ring during 24–31 loss to Barbarians (6.10.91) and dropped a goal against Australia in Wales' 6–63 record reversal in Brisbane (21.7.91). Included in Welsh World Cup squad but talent was not utilised. Switched from Neath to Cardiff seeing 'a perfect opportunity, with their great back-division, to be in a position to take hold of a game and run the show'. Captained Cambridge to 17-11 win over Oxford in 110th Varsity Match (10.12.92), kicking nine points. Played also in 1990 and 1991 Varsity matches. Kicked one conversion and two penalty goals on one Wales A appearance in 1992/93, but still lost 28–29 loss to Ireland A at Newport (5.3.93). Toured with Wales to Africa in 1993 and dropped a goal in 35–14 first Test win over Zimbabwe (Bulawayo, 22.5.93) but outside-half berth again went to Jenkins after second Test in Harare. Helped Cardiff win 1993/94 Swalec Cup and 1994/95 Heineken League title.

Touchlines: Cricket, piano, trumpet

Brendan Mullin en route to the match winning try in Cardiff as Wales captain Mike Hall grabs a lift.

Davies, J. D.   Wales

Full Name: John David Davies
Club: Neath
Position: Tighthead prop
Height: 6ft (1.83m)
Weight: 16st 7lb (100kg)
Occupation: Farmer
Born: Carmarthen, 1.2.69
Family: Veronica (wife)
Former club: Crymych
International debut: Wales 21,
Ireland 21, 1991
Five Nations' debut: As above
Best moment in rugby: Beating
France and winning Five Nations
title (both 1994)
Worst moment in rugby: Losing
1992/93 Swalec Cup final to Llanelli
Most embarrassing moment: Being
given an aerial view of Paris during a
scrum against France
Most respected opponent: Jason
Leonard (Harlequins & England)
Other sporting achievements:
Winning 'Wales Strongest Man' in
1993
Notable landmarks in rugby career:

Wales (1991)

Last Season	8 caps	0 pts
Career	22 caps	5 pts

Caps (22): **1991** I, F **1993** F(R), Z(2), J,
C **1994** S, I, F, E. wc(q)-P, Sp. C,
WS. wc(q)-R, It. SA **1995** F, E wc-
J, NZ, I(b)

Points (5 – 1t): **1993** Z(2:1t)

Sent-off for clumsy footwork on Ben
Clarke 62 minutes into Wales' 9–23 loss to England in Cardiff by French referee
Didier Mene (18.2.95). Soiled his season in what was a wretched campaign for
Wales. Not only did they take the Wooden Spoon, they failed to reach the
World Cup quarter-finals, despite John's return for all three games in South
Africa. A far cry from 1994 when Wales were Five Nations champions, with
John as permanent tighthead. Toured with Wales to Zimbabwe and Namibia
in 1993, scoring his first inter-national try in 42–13 second Test win over
Zimbabwe (Harare, 29.5.93). Toured to Canada and South Pacific in '94 after
helping Wales qualify for World Cup with wins in Portugal and Spain. First
player from Crymych to represent Wales Youth, turning out against Ireland,
France and England in 1987 and same three opponents the following season.
Joined Neath in 1987 and was included in Wales B squad in his first senior
season. An Under-21 cap against Scotland in 1989 was followed by 'B'
recognition against Holland, in 34–12 win (1990/91) and against North of
England in 1992/93. Graduated to senior side in 1991
Touchlines: Gardening, renovating houses.

201

Davies, N. G.   Wales

Full Name: Nigel Gareth Davies
Club: Llanelli
Positions: Centre, wing
Height: 6ft 1in (1.86m)
Weight: 13st 10lb (87kg)
Occupation: Management
consultant with Dennis Morgans
Associates, Swansea
Born: Llanelli, 29.3.65
Family: Married
Family links with rugby: Father
played for Trimsaran
Former club: Trimsaran
International debut: New Zealand
54, Wales 9, 1988
Five Nations' debut: Scotland 23,
Wales 7, 1989
Other sporting achievements:
County tennis (member of Llanelli
LTC)
Notable landmarks in rugby career:
A key component in Wales' 1994
Five Nations Championship
triumph, Nigel experienced the other
side of life in 1995, being dropped
from the World Cup squad by
caretaker coach Alex Evans. His

Wales (1988)

Last Season	5 caps	5 pts
Career	19 caps	13 pts

Caps (19): **1988** NZ(2), WS **1989** S, I
1993 F **1994** S, I, E. wc(q)-P, Sp. C,
Fj, T(R), WS. wc(q)-R, It **1995** E,
S, I
Points (13 – 3t): **1988** WS(2t) **1994** wc(q)-
It(1t)

form in the '94 title surge had been
remarkable in that he had only been rescued from four years in Test wilderness
on 20 March 1993, when deployed against France. Thereafter, was forced to
pull out of summer tour to Zimbabwe and Namibia before departure.
Graduated from Trimsaran Youth to Wales Youth and passed through national
Student and B levels before breaking into Test side in 1988 on disastrous tour
to New Zealand. His debut came in second Test, a 54–9 thrashing in Auckland
which clinched one of most convincing 2-0 series results ever. On his return he
ran in two tries as Wales defeated Western Samoa 28–6 at Cardiff. Following
season made his Five Nations' debut against Scotland at Murrayfield in a game
Wales lost 23–7. Lost place after 19–13 home loss to Ireland that same season.
Nigel, who toured Italy with Wales B in 1986/87, is very highly regarded on the
club scene inside the Principality and was one of the central figures in Llanelli's
League and Cup double and victory over Australia in 1992/93.
Touchlines: Reading, music, motocross.

Davies, P. T.   Wales

Full Name: Philip Thomas Davies
Club: Llanelli
Position: No 8, lock, flanker
Height: 6ft 3in (1.90m)
Weight: 17st 3lb (109kg)
Occupation: Marketing Executive, M.R.J. Group Ltd (Cross Hands)
Born: Seven Sisters, 19.10.63
Family: Caroline (wife), Rebecca (daughter) and Danikka (daughter)
Family links with rugby: Wife Caroline is Jonathan Davies' sister
Former club: Sevens Sisters, South Wales Police
International debut: Wales 24, England 15, 1985
Five Nations' debut: As above
Best moments in rugby: Captaining Llanelli to three Schweppes Challenge Cup triumphs (1988, 1991 and 1992) against Neath, Pontypool and Swansea respectively
Worst moment in rugby: Wales' 1990 whitewash
Serious injuries: Broken cheekbone, misplaced disc in neck, dislocated elbow
Other sporting achievements: Swam for West Wales Schools
Suggestions to improve rugby: Talk to players before changing laws

Wales (1985)

Last Season	4 caps	0 pts
Career	46 caps	21 pts

Caps (46): **1985** E, Fj **1986** E, S, I, F, Fj, T, WS **1987** F, E(a), I wc-T, C, NZ **1988** WS, R **1989** S, I, F, E, NZ **1990** F, E, S **1991** I, F(a), A(a), F(b) wc-WS, Arg, A(b) **1993** F, Z(1), Na **1994** S, I, F, E, C, Fj(R), WS. wc(q)-R, It **1995** F, I

Points (21 – 5t): **1985** Fj(2t) **1986** I(1t) **1990** E(1t) **1993** Z(1:1t)

Notable landmarks in rugby career: Welsh rugby's great survivor and one of its finest and most loyal servants. Extended to 46 his record as the nation's most-capped forward (beating Graham Price's 41 caps) with appearances against France and Ireland either end of the 1995 Five Nations Championship. But with the resignation of coach Alan Davies went his chances of appearing in a third World Cup. Phil's return to the side in 1993 had coincided with Wales' resurgence (actually, it was no coincidence). His first three games all ended in wins as Wales clinched 1994 Five Nations Championship, and he then toured the South Seas and played in Wales' World Cup qualifying wins over Romania and Italy. A former policeman, who first played for Wales at 16-Group, Phil broke into full Welsh squad in 1984. Marked second cap with two tries in 40-3 win over Fiji at the National Stadium (9.11.85). Had jaw broken by punch in

controversial Five Nations' clash with England (Twickenham, 7.3.87). Dropped after playing in 1987 World Cup and became Wales B captain. Returned against Western Samoa in 1988 but missed that year's Championship. Retired from international arena when left out of team to play the centenary Barbarians (6.10.90) but returned during 1991 Five Nations and held place through 1992 Australia tour and World Cup before being replaced by Swansea's Stuart Davies for 1992 Championship campaign. Captained Llanelli to four Cup finals (three wins) in his five years in the job.
Touchlines: Golf.

Davies, S.   Wales

Full Name: Stuart Davies
Club: Swansea
Position: No 8
Height: 6ft 3in (1.90m)
Weight: 17st 4lb (110kg)
Occupation: Environmental Health Officer with Swansea City Council
Born: Swansea, 2.9.65
Family: Lorna (wife)
Family links with rugby: Father (Elwyn) played at centre for Swansea
Former club: South Glamorgan Institute
International debut: Ireland 15, Wales 16, 1992
Five Nations' debut: As above
Best moment in rugby: Leading Swansea to victory over 1992 Wallabies
Most embarrassing moment: Falling over when running out onto pitch for Swansea against All Blacks (21.10.89, lost 22–37)
Serious injuries: Cartilage operations on each knee, torn medial ligaments in left knee

Wales (1992)		
Last Season	3 caps	0 pts
Career	15 caps	9 pts

Caps (15): **1992** I, F, E, S, A **1993** E, S, I, Z(1R,2), Na, J **1995** F wc-J, I(b)
Points (9 – 2t): **1992** I(1t) **1993** Z(2:1t)

Notable landmarks in rugby career: Captained Swansea to 1995 Welsh Cup final triumph over Pontypridd having led the All Whites to the league title the previous season and a famous 21–6 win over Australia in 1992. Rewarded with return to Wales side under the direction of caretaker coach Alex Evans. Stuart was played at blindside in the World Cup, against Japan and Ireland. Wales were not required thereafter. Toured to Zimbabwe and Namibia in 1993, playing in all three internationals (scoring try in second Test against Zimbabwe) and skippering side against Zimbabwe B and Namibia B. Knee trouble prompted his late withdrawl from the 1994 tour to Canada and the South Pacific. Represented Wales at Under-15, Under-16 and Under-18 levels and was an Under-21 squad member (1987). Attended South Glamorgan Institute, where turned out for Welsh Colleges, Students and Academicals. Selected for Wales B squad in 1989 but the match against France coincided with his wedding. Called into Wales squad post-1991 World Cup and played full 1992 Championship season at No 8, marking debut with winning try against Ireland in Dublin.

Touchlines: Golf (22-handicap), seeing my wife, cinema, eating out.

Dawe, R. G. R.   England

Full Name: Richard Graham Reed Dawe
Club: Bath
Position: Hooker
Height: 5ft 11in (1.80m)
Weight: 13st 10lb (82.5kg)
Occupation: Farmer
Born: Plymouth, 4.9.59
Family: Liz (wife)
Former club: Launceston
International debut: Ireland 17, England 0, 1987
Five Nations' debut: As above
Worst moment in rugby: Being told that I had been banned by England after 1987 Wales match
Suggestions to improve rugby: Anything to speed up the game. Diminish value of conversion or get rid of it (takes up too much time). Somehow reduce my travelling. Arrange individual rates of compensation for players or employers for time committed to rugby
Notable landmarks in rugby career: Ended eight years in the international

England (1987)

Last Season	1 cap	0 pts
Career	5 caps	0 pts

Caps (5): **1987** I, F, W wc-US **1995** wc-WS
Points Nil

rugby wilderness when recalled to the England side for last summer's World Cup pool match against Western Samoa (Durban, 4.6.95). It was Graham's first outing since the first World Cup in 1987 when he turned out against the United States. That year the Cornwall farmer played four times for England but

205

his suspension after the notorious Wales match (Twickenham, 7.3.87) seemed to put paid to his long-term senior future. Contented himself instead as a vital member of England's second-string, making 11 appearances, and busied himself by continuing with his dedicated practice of 300-mile round-trips to get to Bath RFC from his Milton Abbott farm. His reward has been seven cup-winning medals. Took massive pride in Cornwall winning the 1990/91 ADT County Championship (29–20 v Yorks, 20.4.91) and reaching Twickenham again the following year. Started his career as a scrum-half or fullback at Launceston and reached 26 before making his first-class debut for Bath against London Welsh. Warmed bench throughout England's 1995 Five Nations Grand Slam drive.

Touchlines: Bell ringing, cycling, sheep shearing.

De Glanville, P. R.   England

Full Name: Philip Ranulph de Glanville
Clubs: Bath
Position: Centre
Height: 6ft (1.83m)
Weight: 13st 7lb (81kg)
Occupation: Marketing executive with Cow & Gate, Trowbridge
Born: Loughborough, 1.10.68
Family: Single
Family links with rugby: Father played for Loughborough and Rosslyn Park
Former clubs: Durham Univ, Oxford Univ
International debut: England 33, South Africa 16, 1992
Five Nations' debut: Wales 10, England 9, 1993
Best moment in rugby: Beating New Zealand (1993)
Worst moment in rugby: Being stamped on my face during South West game against 1993 All Blacks
Most embarrassing moment: Losing match for Durham Univ on

England (1992)

Last Season	3 caps	0 pts
Career	12 caps	0 pts

Caps (12): **1992** SA(R) **1993** W(R), NZ **1994** S, I, F, W, SA(1,2), C(R) **1995** wc-It, WS
Points Nil

Canadian tour when dropped a goalbound penalty effort beneath posts, and Univ of Victoria scored try from resultant scrum
Most respected opponent: Philippe Sella (Agen & France)

Serious injuries: Broken arm, dislocated collarbone, eye gash (required 15 stitches)

Suggestions to improve rugby: Appoint independent arbitrator to deal with matters of discipline. My eye injury in 1993, caused by a boot, highlighted fact that there is no procedure. We need a neutral body to examine such incidents. As for IRB themselves, we need a governing body which lays down the law. At present, Unions are split in way they handle their affairs

Notable landmarks in rugby career: Captained Bath to Pilkington Cup final glory last season, which made up for a quiet campaign with England. The return to full fitness of Jerry Guscott meant Phil had to make do with 16 minutes against Canada (Twickenham, 10.12.94) and World Cup outings against Italy (Durban, 31.5.95) and Western Samoa (Durban, 4.6.95). England won each game. Having earned his first two caps as a replacement, Phil came into his own in 1993/94. With the season-long injury to Guscott, the former Oxford Blue was given an extended run alongside Will Carling, growing in confidence as the season progressed. However, he was lucky; not in being selected, but in being fit enough to be considered. Representing South West England against the touring All Blacks (30.10.93), he suffered a horrifying eye injury at the bottom of a ruck. Fifteen stitches were required to keep his left eyelid intact and there was a deep wound above and below the eye. 'It wasn't an accident,' Phil insists. Amazingly, less than a month later, he faced up against the tourists again in the colours of England and enjoyed a sweet victory. Member of original England Under-21 side, scoring two tries against Romania U-21s (won 54–13, Bucharest 13.5.89). Made England B debut as a 20-year old in 44–0 defeat of Italy (19.3.89). Helped underdogs Oxford University win 1990 Varsity match (11.12.90) and favourites Bath to win 1991/92 Pilkington Cup. Toured New Zealand with England B in summer of '92, playing in both 'Test' losses to the All Black XV, scoring a try in the second. Took England B appearances into double figures with cap against South Africa (7.11.92). Toured Canada with England A (1993)

Touchlines: Golf, cricket

Delaigue, Y. France

Full Name: Yann Delaigue
Club: Toulon
Position: Fly-half, centre
Height: 5ft 11in (1.80m)
Weight: 12st 8lb (75kg)
Occupation: Shop keeper
Born: Toulon, 5.4.73
Family: Single
International debut: Scotland 12, France 20, 1994
Five Nations debut: As above
Notable landmarks in rugby career:
A season of contrasts for Yann. Brilliant in the 25–7 defeat of Ireland in Dublin (4.3.95), he failed to spark in South Africa and lost out in the World Cup selection stakes to first Christophe Deylaud, the player who had made way for him in Dublin, then Franck Mesnel. Son of Gilles Delaigues, also a centre, who won two caps during the 1973 season against Japan and Romania, Yann turned Toulon's back division into one of the most exciting around and was the guiding light behind the

France (1994)

Last Season	5 caps	11 pts
Career	7 caps	11 pts

Caps (7): **1994** S,NZ(2R), C(b) **1995** I, R wc-T, IC
Points (11 – 1t,2dg): **1994** C(b:1dg) **1995** I(1t) wc-T(1dg)

club's championship triumph in 1992. At 22, he was the second youngest (behind Arnaud Costes) member of France's World Cup squad. As a teenager he scored a try against England 18-Group at Franklin Gardens, having gone from school team straight into the Toulon side alongside Aubin Hueber. Played a hefty role in the 67–9 rout of Scotland Under-21s by France Under-21s, in Dijon (5.2.93) and helped France A defeat their England second-string counterparts 20–8 in Paris (5.3.94). A fortnight later, with France staring a Five Nations' Wooden Spoon square in the face, he was called upon to steer them clear of that unthinkable prospect. Given his debut in Edinburgh, Yann's upright elusive running was a feature of France's 20–12 win. Indeed, it was his break that made the opening try for Jean-Luc Sadourny. His reward was a place on France's ultra-successful tour to New Zealand where he appeared as a replacement in the second Test win which clinched a 2–0 series triumph.

Deylaud, C.   France

Full Name: Christophe Deylaud
Club: Toulouse
Position: Centre
Height: 5ft 9 ½in (1.76m)
Weight: 11st 11lb (75kg)
Occupation: Sports instructor
Born: Toulouse, 2.10.64
Family: Married with a child
International debut: France 25,
Romania 6, 1992
Five Nations' debut: France 21,
Wales 9, 1995
Notable landmarks in rugby career:
The man behind France's finest ever
Test series result – the 2–0 defeat of
New Zealand in their own backyard
in 1994 – Christophe failed to
reproduce the same brilliance at
home and, after indifferent displays
against Wales, England and
Scotland, he was dropped for the trip
to Dublin. It was quite a comedown
for a player who had shown genius
to dismantle the All Blacks. He
dropped two goals in the 22–8 first
Test triumph (Christchurch,
26.6.94) and landed five points in
the 23–20 series clincher at Eden

France (1992)
Last Season	9 caps	14 pts
Career	14 caps	21 pts

Caps (14): **1992** R, Arg(a1,a2), SA(1)
1994 C, NZ(1,2) **1995** W, E, S(a)
wc-IC(R), S(b), I(b), SA
Points (21 – 1t,2c,1p,3dg): **1992**
Arg(a1:1t,1c) **1994** NZ(1:2dg),
NZ(2:1c,1p) **1995** S(a:1dg)

Park (3.7.94). Won his place back with a polished display as a replacement
against Cote d'Ivoire (Rustenburg, 30.5.95) during the World Cup. But his
semi-final display against South Africa was abysmal and arguably cost France
a spot in the final. Franck Mesnel took over for third place play-off game against
England. Christophe had previously ended two years in the cold with a brilliant
display in 1994 French Championship final guiding Toulouse to victory.
(Repeated feat with 26 points in 1995 final). He was promptly included in
France's squad to tour Canada and New Zealand. However, in one-off Test
against Canucks, with Christophe at No.10, France crashed 18–16 (Ottawa,
5.6.94). Previously, this highly promising midfielder had failed to sustain his
challenge for a Test place in 1992 after being initially blooded in the 25–6 defeat
of Romania at Le Havre (28.5.92). He was retained for the summer tour to
Argentina, contributing a try and conversion to the 27–12 first Test win in
Buenos Aires (4.7.92), although he was later replaced by Christian Courveille,
and retained his berth alongside Courveille for the 33–9 second Test win the

following week. Returned home with the praise of Robert Paparemborde ringing in his ears. 'Christophe is going to become a magnificent player in our back division,' forecast the then team manager. 'He is an excellent link-man and his fast hands make him a very good distributor of the ball.' Yet the visit of South Africa to Lyon (17.10.92) marked the beginning of the end of his season as France were downed 15–20 and Thierry Lacroix was drafted in to partner Mesnel.

De Rougemont, M.   France

Full Name: Marc de Rougemont
Club: Toulon
Position: Hooker
Height: 5ft 9in
Weight: 14st 7lb
Occupation: Publican
Born: Marseille, 24.5.72
International debut: England 31, France 10, 1995
Five Nations debut: As above
Notable landmarks in rugby career:
A versatile front row man, being also a tried and trusted prop, Marc picked up three caps last season despite only starting and/or finishing one match. Before his first full Test he picked up two caps as blood-bin replacement in the 10–31 defeat by England (Twickenham, 4.2.95) and France's 24–15 win over Romania (Bucharest, 7.4.95). A member of the 1993/94 France A side that beat their England counterparts in Paris, Marc finally got his first full international start in South Africa. Coach Pierre

France (1995)

Last Season	3 caps	0 pts
Career	3 caps	0 pts

Caps (3): **1995** E(TR), R(TR) wc-IC
Points Nil

Berbizier was true to his pledge to give the whole 26-man squad a game and Marc got his chance against Cote d'Ivoire before an enthusiastic crowd in the rural outpost of Rustenburg (30.5.95). France won 54–18. He remained a valued member of the successful squad thereafter. Impressive performances for Toulon in the French club championship had earned him a place on France's tour to Canada and New Zealand (1994) but he broke a bone in the quarter-final against Montferrand and had to pull out. His place was taken by friend and rival Christian Califano, who has been the first-choice tighthead prop ever since. Marc recovered from his injury in time to warm the replacements' bench

against Canada in Besançon (17.12.94) in a match France won 28–9.
Touchlines: Deep sea diving

Dowd, C. New Zealand

Full Name: Craig Dowd
Province: Auckland
Club: Suburbs
Position: Loosehead prop
Height: 6ft 3¾in (1.91m)
Weight: 18st 11lb (115kg)
Occupation: Carpenter, AIT
Born: 26.10.69
International debut: New Zealand
20, British Lions 18, 1993
Best moment in rugby: Winning the
Gallagher Shield
Notable landmarks in rugby career:
The outstanding loosehead prop of
last summer's World Cup and an
avid pasta and potato eater, Craig
announced his Test intentions by
first relieving All Black Steve
McDowell of his place in the
Auckland scrum. That achieved he
set to work on the national slot and
achieved his goal in time for the visit
of the 1993 British Lions. Lost out
the following year, when Richard
Loe returned to favour, but got his
act together in 1995, playing in every

New Zealand (1993)

Last Season	7 caps	5 pts
Career	14 caps	5 pts

Caps (14): **1993** BL(1,2,3), A, WS, S, E
1994 SA(1R) **1995** C wc-I, W, J, E,
SA
Points (5 – 1t): **1995** wc-J(1t)

game – save for the World Cup quarter-final defeat of Scotland when he was
injured. A powerfully built, mobile player, Craig came up New Zealand's
representative ladder, playing for both New Zealand Colts (he was a team mate
of England and Lions lock Martin Johnson) and the New Zealand XV – he was
also a bench reserve against England B in 1992. An everpresent in the 2–1 series
defeat of the '93 Lions (his debut came in Christchurch on 12 June), Craig held
his place for the 25–10 Bledisloe Cup victory over Australia (Dunedin,
17.7.93). England's 15–9 win over the All Blacks (Twickenham, 27.11.93)
ended Craig's run of never having left the Test arena a loser. Broke his try-duck,
along with most others, in the 145–17 World Cup rout of Japan (Bloemfontein,
4.6.95).
Touchlines: Weight training, bodybuilding.

Du Randt, P.   South Africa

Full Name: Pieter du Randt
Province: Orange Free State
Position: Prop
Height: 1.90m
Weight: 113kg
Occupation: Diesel mechanic,
Barlows Equipment
Born: 8.9.72
International debut: South Africa 42,
Argentina 22, 1994
Notable landmarks in rugby career:
Surfaced internationally last season
after an impressive domestic
campaign for Orange Free State.
Helped his province to reach the
final of the Bankfin Currie Cup
(Bloemfontein, 1.10.94) and
although losing 56–33 to defending
champions Transvaal, Pieter's efforts
were almost immediately rewarded
with a Test debut the following
weekend against Argentina in Port
Elizabeth (8.10.94). The Boks won
42–22 and Pieter – nicknamed 'Ox'
or 'Oz' after his wrestling exploits as

South Africa (1994)
Last Season	9 caps	0 pts
Career	9 caps	0 pts

Caps (9): **1994** Arg(1,2), S, W **1995**
WS(a) wc-A, WS(b), F, NZ
Points Nil

a youngster – has not looked back since. Retained his place in the 46–26 second
Test defeat of the Pumas and then toured to Britain, turning out against Wales
A, Neath, Swansea, Scottish Combined Districts and the Barbarians, in
addition to appearing in the victories over Scotland (34–10, Murrayfield
19.11.94) and Wales (20–12, Cardiff 26.11.94). Continued in the same vein in
1995, a campaign of course highlighted by the World Cup, in which Pieter
played against Australia, Western Samoa, France and, particularly notably,
New Zealand in that never-to-be-forgotten final (Johannesburg, 24.6.95)

Eales, J. A.   Australia

Full Name: John Anthony Eales
State: Queensland
Club: Brothers
Position: Lock
Height: 6ft 7in (2.00m)
Weight: 17st 8lb (107kg)
Occupation: Promotions manager with G&E Hotels
Born: 27.6.70
Family: Jack (father), Rosa (mother), Bernadette (sister), Damian (brother), Antoinette (sister), Rosaleen (sister)
International debut: Australia 63, Wales 6, 1991
Most respected opponent: Ian Jones (North Auckland & New Zealand)
Notable landmarks in rugby career: One of the world's foremost lineout men, John demonstrated his versatility and his refound fitness when helping Queensland to Super-10 glory with two conversions and a penalty goal in the 30–16 final defeat of Transvaal (Johannesburg, 8.4.95). To prove it was no fluke, he slotted four conversions for Australia in her 42–3 World Cup defeat of Romania (Stellenbosch,

Australia (1991)		
Last Season	10 caps	13 pts
Career	29 caps	17 pts

Caps (29):	**1991** W(a), E(a), NZ(a1,a2). wc-Arg, WS, W(b), I, NZ(b), E(b) **1992** S(1,2), NZ(1,2,3), SA, I **1994** I(1,2), It(1,2), WS, NZ **1995** Arg(1,2) wc-SA, C, R, E
Points (17 – 2t,4c):	**1992** S(2:1t) **1995** Arg(1:1t) wc-R(4c)

3.6.95). Outstanding in below par Wallaby side at World Cup. Everpresent for Wallabies in 1994/95. Had announced himself in 1990 when winning the coveted Rothmans Medal Best-and-Fairest Award in Brisbane club rugby. His skills were appreciated by a wider audience when he toured Europe with the Emerging Wallabies, playing in the 12–12 draw with England B at Wasps. From there he was included in the Aussies' World Cup training squad and, having made his debut in the record rout of Wales at Ballymore, he played all six matches in the Cup-winning side. His astonishing rise continued in 1992 when he was selected to play for the World XV in the Centenary Series against New Zealand. Unfortunately, he damaged a shoulder in the second Test – an injury which forced him to miss the entire 1993 campaign and kept him out until visit of Ireland in June 1994. Started 1992 superbly when voted the Chivas Regal Man-of-the-Series against Scotland, having scored his first Test try in the 27–12 opening international win. Thereafter, toured South Africa – playing against

Northern Transvaal and the Republic itself – and took his cap tally to 17 when appearing in the 42–17 win over Ireland on 31 October. His other tour outings came against Leinster, Ulster (scored try), Swansea, Neath and Llanelli
Touchlines: Golf, cricket, reading.

Elwood, E. P. Ireland

Full Name: Eric Paul Elwood
Club: Lansdowne
Position: Outside-half
Height: 6ft (1.83m)
Weight: 13st 5lb (84kg)
Occupation: Sales representative with Irish Distillers
Born: Galway, 26.2.69
Family: Single
Former club: Galwegians
International debut: Wales 14, Ireland 19, 1993
Five Nations' debut: As above
Worst moments in rugby: Lansdowne's relegation from Division One of the 1991/92 All-Ireland League; losing semi-final of 1993 World Cup Sevens to Australia
Most respected opponent: Michael Lynagh (Queensland & Australia)
Serious injuries: Chipped vertebrae in neck (1987)
Other sporting achievements: Gaelic football and soccer for Galway
Suggestions to improve rugby: Referee maul law according to the spirit of the game and not to the letter of the law
Notable landmarks in rugby career: Prodigious goal-kicker who has

Ireland (1993)

Last Season	5 caps	27 pts
Career	14 caps	119 pts

Caps (14): **1993** W, E, R **1994** F, W, E, S, A(1,2) **1995** F(a), W(a) wc-NZ, W(b), F(b)

Points (119 – 10c,31p,2dg): **1993** W(1c,3p), E(2p,2dg), R(1c,6p) **1994** F(5p), W(5p), E(1c,2p), S(2p), A(1:1c,1p) **1995** F(a:1c) wc-NZ(2c), W(b:3c,1p), F(b:4p)

carried Ireland's strike threat virtually single-handed since his debut in 1993. His 14 starts have produced 119 points and inspired two wins against England. Slotted four penalties out of four against France in the World Cup quarter-final (Durban, 10.6.95) but unfortunately the rest of Ireland's game went to pot. Still, it was a personally satisfying way to end an injury-ravaged year. Having missed out on a Schools trial, Eric first wore an Ireland jersey on 30 September 1989 when on national U-21 side beaten 10-9 by Italian counterparts in

Treviso. Bench reserve for following match v New Zealand U-21s (D13–13, 19.11.89). Connacht debut came in the same year, v Ulster. Progressed up international ladder in 1992/93 after series of impressive displays for Connacht: v Australia and throughout Inter-Provincial Championship. Missed national trial but was drafted onto Ireland bench for the visit to Dublin of France, and subsequently succeeded Niall Malone as outside-half. Headlined in games v Wales and England, not least because Ireland won both. He contributed 23 of the 36 points scored by the men in green and was widely acclaimed. His omission from the Lions' squad, named 48 hours after England's defeat in Dublin, was contentious, but he put disappointment behind him and enjoyed a fine 1993/94 campaign, scoring 64 of Ireland's 74 points. He also kicked four penalty goals against the touring All Blacks for the Barbarians in a 25–12 loss (Cardiff, 4.12.93).

Touchlines: Gym, walking.

Evans, D. W. Wales

Full Name: David Wyn Evans
Club: Treorchy
Positions: Outside-half, centre
Height: 5ft 9in (1.75m)
Weight: 11st 8lb (85kg)
Occupation: Development officer for Sports Council of Wales
Born: Wootton Bassett, Wilts, 1.11.65
Family: Roberta (wife)
Former clubs: Swansea and Oxford Universities, Aberaman Youth, Cardiff
International debut: France 31, Wales 12, 1989
Five Nations' debut: As above
Best moment in rugby: Wales 12, England 9, 1989
Worst moment in rugby: England 34, Wales 6, 1990
Most respected opponent: Philippe Sella (Agen & France)
Serious injuries: Dislocated and fractured shoulder, concussion, tendon reattached to kneecap (out most of 1991/92 season)

Wales (1989)

Last Season	1 cap	0 pts
Career	12 caps	6 pts

Caps (12): **1989** F, E, NZ **1990** F, E, S, I, Ba **1991** A(a:R), F(b:R) wc-A(b:R) **1995** wc-J(R)
Points (6 – 2dg): **1990** F(1dg), Ba(1dg)

Suggestions to improve rugby: Reduce number of games played by top players.

More consistent refereeing. Leagues in Wales are not a good development. Enjoyment has gone out of the game and I don't think standards have improved as a result. The rules are trying to encourage a more open game but the need to win at all costs is counter-productive

Notable landmarks in rugby career: David's last two caps for Wales have spanned two World Cups, having continued an international career left in the 1991 tournament, against Australia (12.10.91), when he reappeared as a 56th minute replacement for Adrian Davies in the 57–10 defeat of Japan in the 1995 competition. Thereafter warmed bench as Wales lost to New Zealand and Ireland and beat a hasty retreat home from South Africa. Test career revived as a result of move to Treorchy. Had previously partnered Robert Jones at half-back three times for 1984 Welsh Schools, scoring 16 points in 20–0 defeat of France. Also represented Welsh Students, Welsh Universities, Swansea University (1988 UAU final) and Oxford University (1988 Blue). Toured Fiji, Australia, New Zealand and USA with Oxbridge, Japan with Oxford, and Canada with Wales B (where made B debut). Dropped goal for Wales in 24–31 early-season loss to Barbarians (1990/91) before fracturing left shoulder for second time. Overdue a decent innings in the Test arena as his last four appearances have produced a total of just 37 minutes action

Touchlines: Spanish guitar.

Evans, I. C   Wales

Full Name: Ieuan Cenydd Evans
Club: Llanelli
Position: Wing
Height: 5ft 10 ½in (1.79kg)
Weight: 13st 5lb (85kg)
Occupation: Marketing manager, Forthright Finance Ltd (Cardiff)
Born: Pontardulais, 21.3.64
Family: Single
Family links with rugby: Father (John) played for Aberavon
Former club: Carmarthen Quins
International debut: France 16, Wales 9, 1987
Five Nations' debut: As above
Best moments in rugby: Scoring tries that (i) clinched Test series for 1989 Lions in Australia and (ii) beat England in Cardiff (1992)

Worst moment in rugby: New South Wales 71, Wales 8, 1991
Most respected opponent: David Campese (Randwick & Australia)

Serious injuries: Recurring dislocated shoulder, broken leg

Notable landmarks in rugby career: Wales' record try scorer (23) and most-capped wing (an honour he shares with Ken Jones, 1947-57), Ieuan would have put up even more impressive numbers had he not broken his ankle badly playing for Llanelli and missed three internationals during the 1994/95 campaign. A remarkably speedy recovery enabled him to return in time for the second round of Five Nations matches, against England, and it was just a shame his hard work was not rewarded with something more fitting than a whitewashed Wooden Spoon. As a consequence, coach Alan Davies resigned to be replaced by Cardiff supremo Alex Evans, and he

Wales (1987)		
Last Season	7 caps	15 pts
Career	54 caps	107 pts
Lions 1989	3 Tests	4 pts
1993	3 Tests	0 pts

Caps (54): **1987** F, E(a), S, I(a) wc-I(b), C, E(b), NZ, A **1988** E, S, I, F, NZ(1,2) **1989** I, F, E. Lions-A(1,2,3) **1991** E, S, I, F(a), A(a), F(b) wc-WS, Arg, A(b) **1992** I, F, E, S, A **1993** E, S, I, F, J, C **1994** S, I, F, E. wc(q)-P, S. C, Fj, T, WS. wc(q)-R **1995** E, S, I(a) wc-J, NZ, I(b)

Points (107 – 23t): **1987** I(a:1t) wc-C(4t) **1988** S(1t), F(1t) **1989** Lions-A(3:1t) **1991** wc-WS(1t) **1993** E(1t), I(1t), J(2t) **1994** S(1t). wc(q)-P(3t), S(3t). C(1t) wc(q)-R(1t) **1995** wc-J(2t)

replaced Ieuan as captain with his club skipper Mike Hall for the ill-fated World Cup campaign. *Rugby World & Post* Player of the Year for 1992/93, Ieuan led Wales to 1994 Five Nations title. Wales' 103rd captain, when appointed prior to 1991 World Cup, he became Principality's longest-serving leader when taking charge of last May's World Cup qualifier in Portugal (celebrated with try hat-trick). Mission No.19 in charge, a 102–11 win, nudged him past Arthur 'Monkey' Gould. When he was replaced, Ieuan had led Wales 28 times. Early part of playing career severely hampered by injury – five dislocations and two operations. But played all three Tests in 1989 Lions series win (2–1) in Australia, scoring series-clinching try in final Test in Sydney (won 19–18, 15.7.89), and all three Tests in New Zealand with 1993 Lions. Missed whole of 1989/90 season through injury. Played in five matches in 1987 World Cup, scoring Welsh record-equalling four tries in 40–9 defeat of Canada, and contributed one (against Western Samoa) to Wales' 1991 Cup challenge and two (against Japan) in 1995. Scored six tries for Wales B in 1985 defeat of Spain (80–9) at Bridgend. National hero when running in winning try against England (6.2.93). Also crossed against Ireland, in next Test at Arms Park (6.3.93) to account for two thirds of Wales' entire try-tally in 1992/93 season. Domestically, scored winning try as Llanelli beat Australia 13–9 (14.11.92) and shared in Scarlets' 1992/93 League and Cup double.

Touchlines: Tennis, cricket, squash, golf.

Evans, R. L.   Wales

Full Name: Richard (Ricky) Lloyd
Evans
Club: Llanelli
Position: Loosehead prop
Height: 6ft 2in (1.88m)
Weight: 17st 3lb (109kg)
Occupation: Fireman in the Dyfed-
Powys Brigade
Born: Cardigan, 23.6.61
Family: Married with son and
daughter
Former clubs: Cardigan, Army
International debut: Wales 10,
England 9, 1993
Five Nations' debut: As above
Best moment in rugby: Beating
England on debut in Cardiff
Most embarrassing moment:
Coming on as replacement flanker
for Llanelli and using hands to push
ball back between legs at scrum
Serious injuries: Broken leg (twice)
Other sporting achievements: Long
boat rowing for Aberporth LBC
Suggestions to improve rugby:
Referees must hold tighter
disciplinary reins

Wales (1993)		
Last Season	6 caps	0 pts
Career	19 caps	0 pts

Caps (19): **1993** E, S, I, F **1994** S, I, F, E.
wc(q)-P, Sp. C, Fj, WS. wc(q)-R, It.
SA **1995** F wc-NZ, I(b)
Points Nil

Notable landmarks in rugby career: Victim of widely condemned head-butt by
France lock Olivier Merle (Paris, 21.1.95) which resulted in him falling
awkwardly and breaking a leg in two places. Missed remainder of 1995 Five
Nations season but returned in time for World Cup selection and played twice
in South Africa. Restored to national side in 1994, having been omitted from
1993 tour to Zimbabwe and Namibia and two autumn internationals, Ricky
played a full part in Wales' 1994 Five Nations title-winning run. Selectors
learned their lesson and kept him in situ for World Cup qualifiers and summer
tour to Canada and South Pacific. Spent nine years in Army (16–25) before
playing for two years in Pembrokeshire League with Cardigan. Other causes
represented are Army, Crawshays and both Wales and British Fire Brigades.
Broke leg against Cambridge University in only his sixth game for Llanelli.
Toured Canada with Wales B in 1989, making three appearances. Wore their
colours again in 21–13 victory over North of England (Pontypool, 14.10.92),
11–24 loss to Australia (Cardiff, 7.11.92), 61–5 defeat of Japan (Llanelli,
29.9.93) and 24-8 win against North of England (Pontypool, 13.10.93).

Helped Llanelli beat '92 Wallabies 13–9 win at Stradey en route to League and Cup double. Ricky, who finished fourth in the televised Strongest Man competition in 1992, made his Wales debut in 1993 Five Nations' Championship as a result of Mike Griffiths' freak cycling accident in Lanzarote, in which he broke a collarbone to put himself out for campaign.

Field, M. J.   Ireland

Full Name: Maurice John Field
Club: Malone
Position: Centre, wing, fullback
Height: 6ft (1.83m)
Weight: 13st 2lb (84kg)
Occupation: Firefighter
Born: Greenisland, 24.2.64
Family: Gillian (wife), Rebekah (daughter)
Former club: NIFC
International debut: England 12, Ireland 13, 1994
Five Nations debut: As above
Best moment in rugby: Beating England at Twickenham on debut
Worst moment in rugby: Not being selected for Ireland's tour to New Zealand (1992)
Most respected opponent: Scott Hastings (Watsonians & Scotland)
Suggestions to improve rugby: Revise amateur regulations to make sure we don't lose out financially through playing
Notable landmarks in rugby career:

Ireland (1994)

Last Season	4 caps	0 pts
Career	6 caps	0 pts

Caps (6): **1994** E, S **1995** F(R), It(R) wc-NZ(R), J
Points Nil

Won four more caps last season despite being unable to break the Mullin-Danaher midfield stranglehold. And when Jonathan Bell was switched inside from the wing it must have hurt Maurice, who seemed to have done everything that had been asked of him yet had to live off scraps. His one 80-minute stint came at the World Cup in the 50–28 defeat of Japan (Bloemfontein, 31.5.95). Had taken full advantage of his Test opportunity in 1993/94, helping Ireland to a two-match unbeaten run after they had started 1994 championship campaign with pair of losses. His promotion to centre berth followed injury to Vinnie Cunningham and selectors' decision to replace Bangor's Mark McCall after defeat by Wales in Dublin. So Maurice was given debut at Twickenham (19.2.94), where Ireland had not won since 1982. England were beaten 13–12 and yer man was suitably chuffed. He retained his place for drab 6–6 home draw with Scotland (5.3.94) and was then invited to tour Australia. Started out with NIFC, playing for Ulster at Under-20 level in 1983. Following year played for Ulster U-23s but then had to wait six years before senior provincial debut against Irish Exiles. Played in Ulster's defeat by Australia in 1992 and won first international honours in Ireland A side beaten 20–10 by Wales counterparts at Donnybrook (4.2.94)

Touchlines: Golf (17-handicap).

Fitzpatrick, S. B. T. New Zealand

Full Name: Sean Brian Thomas Fitzpatrick
Club: University
Province: Auckland
Position: Hooker
Height: 6ft (1.83m)
Weight: 14st 10lb (93kg)
Occupation: Marketing development manager, Coca-Cola
Born: Auckland, 4.6.63
Family: Bronwyn (wife) and child
Family links with rugby: Brian (father) won three caps as All Black five-eighth (1953 W; 1954 I, F)
International debut: New Zealand 18, France 9, 1986
Best memory in rugby: Beating Australia 30–16 in Sydney (25.7.87) – a great team performance

Earliest memory in rugby: Ball boy for my brother's team when I was 3½. My father was also coach of that team and no my brother was not captain!

Notable landmarks in rugby career: Most capped All Black of all time – his 69 caps putting him ten clear of Gary Whetton and John Kirwan, the previous co-record holders. All Black Test hooker since 1986 and world's most-capped player in that position (ahead of England's Brian Moore, 63). Succeeded Whetton as captain prior to the 1992 centenary series. Captaincy has rested well on his shoulders, adding a new dimension to his already immense performances. Sean, who is widely considered to be the world's premier lineout thrower, is the first Auckland hooker to pass the 100-appearance mark for the province, a total amassed since his debut in 1984. And he made his 100th All Black appearance in last summer's World Cup quarter-final defeat of Scotland (Pretoria, 11.6.95). Sean's Test debut came against France in 1986 in Christchurch, while the Cavaliers were away in South Africa. He was displaced by the returning Hika Reid for the second and third Tests against the Wallabies later in the year but reversed the roles for the tour of France and has since resisted each and every pretender to his throne. Equalled NZ record for a hooker when scoring two tries in the 30–16 win over Australia in 1987. He was selected for New Zealand Schools in 1981, progressing to NZ Colts, whom he represented in 1983 (along with John Kirwan, Grant Fox and Murray Mexted) and captained the following year. His 1984 charges included Bernie McCahill, Frano Botica (now Wigan RL) and Paul Henderson. Captained the All Blacks

New Zealand (1986)

Last Season	13 caps	10 pts
Career	69 caps	40 pts

Caps (69): **1986** F(a), A(1), F(b1,b2) **1987** wc-It, Fj, Arg, S, W, F. A **1988** W(1,2), A(1,2,3) **1989** F(1,2), Arg(1,2), A, W, I **1990** S(1,2), A(1,2,3), F(1,2) **1991** Arg(1,2), A(a1,a2). wc-E, US, It, C, A(b), S **1992** Wd(1,2,3), I(1,2), A(1,2,3), SA **1993** BL(1,2,3), A, WS, S, E **1994** F(1,2), SA(1,2,3), A **1995** C wc-I, W, J, S, E, SA

Points (40 – 9t): **1987** A(2t) **1989** F(2:1t) **1990** A(1:1t), A(2:1t) **1993** BL(3:1t), A(1t) **1994** F(2:1t) **1995** wc-S(1t)

on nine occasions during the 1992 tour to Australia (scoring two tries against NSW) and South Africa, in the process becoming the first New Zealander to skipper a winning side in the Republic. Despite the disappointment of Auckland finally relinquishing the Ranfurly Shield and England beating the Blacks at Twickenham, 1993 was generally another fine year for Sean. Auckland became national champions once more, New Zealand regained the Bledisloe Cup at Australia's expense, and they won 12 of 13 tour games in England and Scotland.

Touchlines: Golf, fishing, skin diving.

Garin Jenkins draws a crowd as he tries to shake off Christophe Deyland during Wales's 9–21 loss in Paris.

Foley, A. G.   Ireland

Full Name: Anthony Gerard Foley
Club: Shannon
Position: Flanker
Height: 6ft 3in (1.91m)
Weight: 16st 8lb (105kg)
Occupation: Student
Born: Limerick, 30.10.73
Family: Single
Family links with rugby: Father
(Brendan) won 11 caps in Ireland
second row (1976 F, E 1977 W(R)
1980 F, W 1981 F, E, S, SA(1,2),A)
International debut: Ireland 8,
England 20, 1995
Five Nations debut: As above
Best moment in rugby: Scoring debut
try against England (1995)
Notable landmarks in rugby career:
Boy's Own start to his international
career, scoring a try against the old
enemy, England, at Lansdowne
Road (21.1.95). The fairy tale ended
there as Ireland lost 8–20 and went
on to only narrowly avoid the Five
Nations' Wooden Spoon. However,

Ireland (1995)

Last Season	6 caps	5 pts
Career	6 caps	5 pts

Caps (6): **1995** E, S, F, W, It wc-J(TR)
Points (5 – 1t): E(1t)

Anthony continued to make an impression – as he had done in the Irish
championship-winning Shannon side – and kept his place right up to the World
Cup. He even played one game at No 8, against France (Dublin, 4.3.95) after
Paddy Johns' withdrawl at the 11th hour. His success in the Five Nations meant
that his failure to show in South Africa came as a surprise, the only addition to
his cap tally coming by virtue of a few minutes as a blood-bin replacement for
Dennis McBride in the defeat of Wales (Johannesburg, 4.6.95). However,
considering last season he was also turning out for Ireland Under-21s, he should
be proud of his progress. Made his Inter-Provincial debut in Munster's title-
winning side last season and has also represented Ireland at Schools (touring
New Zealand with them in 1992), Colleges and Students grades

Forster, S. T.   New Zealand

Full Name: Stuart (Stu) Thomas
Forster
Province: Otago
Club: Southern
Position: Scrum-half
Height: 5ft 6 3/4in (1.70m)
Weight: 11st 11lb (75kg)
Born: 12.2.69
Former province: Hawke's Bay
International debut: Scotland 15,
New Zealand 51, 1993
Worst moment in rugby: Getting
thrashed by Waikato in final of 1992
New Zealand Championship
Notable landmarks in rugby career:
Lost his All Black place after France
swept the 1994 series 2–0 in New
Zealand. Renowned as a top-notch
sevens player (he played in '92
World Cup at Murrayfield) well
before the British Lions' roar was
muted in Dunedin on 5 June 1993
thanks in no small measure to a
superb performance from Batman

New Zealand (1993)

Last Season	2 caps	0 pts
Career	4 caps	0 pts

Caps (4): **1993** S,E **1994** F(1,2)
Points Nil

(aka Michael Keaton) lookalike Stu, a one-time Hawke's Bay player. An Otago
side, also including current All Blacks Marc Ellis and Josh Kronfeld, won 37–24
and those English and Scottish players in the Lions XV took note. The reason
was that five months later they were once again opposing the diminutive but
devastating runner as he arrived in Britain for the All Blacks' autumn tour as
one of the two selected scrum-halves. A bench reserve (behind Waikato's Simon
Crabb) for the New Zealand XV which swept their 1992 series with England B,
Stu's form in the defeats of London (won 39–12, Twickenham 23.10.93),
North of England (won 27–21, Liverpool 2.11.93), England A (won 26–12,
Gateshead 7.11.93) and Scotland A (won 20–9, Glasgow 13.11.93) ensured
that he displaced Wellington's Jon Preston (first-choice in '93 against the Lions,
Australia and Western Samoa) from the No.9 berth for the two Tests against
Scotland (Edinburgh 20.11.93) and England (lost 9–15, Twickenham
27.11.93). He formed an all-Otago half-back partnership with Marc Ellis. A
1989 New Zealand Colt, Stu's team mates included Craig Innes (now Leeds
RL), Va'iga Tuigamala (now Wigan RL), John Timu (now Auckland Warriors
RL), Blair Larsen, Craig Dowd and English Lion Martin Johnson.
Touchlines: Boogie boarding, water skiing, mountain biking, skiing, golf,
tennis.

Francis, N. P. J.   Ireland

Full Name: Neil Patrick John Francis
Club: Old Belvedere
Position: Lock
Height: 6ft 6in (1.98m)
Weight: 17st 12lb (113kg)
Occupation: Self-employed
consultant to Equity Bank
Born: Dublin, 17.3.64
Family: Single
Former clubs: London Irish, Manly
(Aus)
International debut: Ireland 32,
Tonga 9, 1987
Five Nations' debut: Scotland 37,
Ireland 21, 1989
Serious injuries: Broken vertebrae
(out for two years)
Other sporting achievements: Javelin
for Ireland (national junior and
senior champion)
Notable landmarks in rugby career:
One of Ireland's star performers in
last summer's World Cup, Franno
was the catalyst in an exceptional
Irish forward effort which accounted
for nine of the 13 tries scored in four
games. His lineout understanding
with Gabriel Fulcher hinted at a
bright future and the present looked

Ireland (1987)

Last Season	6 caps	5 pts
Career	33 caps	14 pts

Caps (33): **1987** wc-T, A **1988** WS, It
1989 S **1990** E, F, W **1991** E, S,
Na(1,2) wc-Z, J, S, A **1992** W, E, S
1993 F, R **1994** F, W, E, S, A(1,2),
US **1995** E wc-NZ, J, W(b), F(b)
Points (14 – 21t): **1988** WS(1t) **1994**
A(2:1t) **1995** wc-J(1t)

pretty good too as he piled into the All Blacks on that unforgettable evening in
Johannesburg (27.5.95). Franno had returned to the front line in 1993/94 after
injury decimated the previous season from his viewpoint. Enigmatic player who
has been in and out of favour since debut in 1987 World Cup. Represented Irish
Schools five times (1981-82), but back injury meant no representative rugby for
four years from the age of 19, by which time he had already won Leinster Senior
Cup medal with Blackrock. Did not represent Leinster until 1986. Scored try
for Ireland Under-25s against Canada in 1986. Rejoined Blackrock from
London Irish in 1989 and moved on to Old Belvedere last season. After debut
in '87, not called upon again until October 1988 when scored only
international try to date against touring Western Samoans. Sole Irish
representative in Home Unions team which played Rest of Europe at
Twickenham in 1990 Romania Appeal match. Ever-present in 1991/92 season,
including each 1991 World Cup-tie, until final Five Nations' match in Paris

when Brian Rigney returned, thus breaking Neil's 11-game streak. Missed Ireland's tour to New Zealand in 1992, but visited Namibia (1991) and Australia (1994).

Fulcher, G. M.   Ireland

Full Name: Gabriel Mark Fulcher
Club: Cork Constitution
Position: Lock
Height: 6ft 5in (1.96m)
Weight: 17st (108kg)
Occupation: Sales representative, Micro-Bio (Ireland) Ltd
Born: England, 27.11.69
International debut: Australia 32, Ireland 18, 1994
Five Nations debut: Ireland 8, England 20, 1995
Notable landmarks in rugby career: Hugely impressive debut season in Test rugby, forming a convincing partnership with Neil Francis in the Irish engine room. Once Gabriel had proved that at 25 he was old enough for the job the selectors stopped advertising the post. Gabriel came on as a half-time replacement for the injured Mick Galwey against England (Dublin, 21.1.95) and was a permanent fixture thereafter, save for the Japan World Cup-tie

Ireland (1994)

Last Season	9 caps	0 pts
Career	10 caps	0 pts

Caps (10): **1994** A(2), US **1995** E(R), S, F(a), W(a), It wc-NZ, J, W(b), F(b)
Points Nil

(Bloemfontein, 31.5.95) when he was given the day off and Davy Tweed took a turn. Toured Australia with Irish Schools in 1986/87. Helped UC Dublin win the Under-19 McCorry Cup and played for the Munster Under-21s against Italy in Cork. Won two caps for the Ireland Under-21 team in 1990/91, against Netherlands and England, before graduating to Ireland B the following season. Joined Cork Con from UCD and was included in Ireland development squad which toured Zimbabwe, Namibia and South Africa in 1993. Spent the following summer Down Under – making his international debut in the second Test in Sydney (11.6.95) – before returning to South Africa for the World Cup last summer
Touchlines:

Gallart, P.   France

Full Name: Philippe Gallart
Club: Beziers
Position: Prop
Height: 6ft ½in (1.85m)
Weight: 17st 5lb (105kg)
Occupation: Commercial agent, Sarl
Usine a Gaz
Born: 18.12.62
Former club: Pezenas
International debut: France 6,
Romania 12, 1990
Five Nations' debut: Scotland 10,
France 6, 1992
Notable landmarks in rugby career:
Returned to international favour at
tail-end of 1994/95 season, playing
in France's World Cup warm-up
match against Romania in Bucharest
(won 24–15, 7.4.95) and then going
to South Africa with Pierre
Berbizier's side and playing in the
Tricolors' opening engagement
against Tonga (Pretoria, 26.5.95).
But that was that as Laurent
Benezech and Louis Armary shored
up the loosehead duties thereafter.

France (1990)		
Last season	2 caps	0 pts
Career	17 caps	0 pts

Caps (17): **1990** R, A(1,2R,3) **1992** S, I,
R, Arg(a1,a2), SA(1,2), Arg(b)
1994 I, W, E **1995** R wc-T
Points Nil

Recalled in 1992 in place of Philippe Gimbert against Scotland (7.3.92) for first
time since being sent-off by Clive Norling for punching Tim Gavin in the 48th
minute of the 28-19 third Test win against Australia in Sydney (30.6.90). For
that misdemeanour a four-month suspension was meted out, ensuring that he
played no part in the 1991 Five Nations campaign when only England stood
between France and a fifth Grand Slam. Despite touring to North America in
summer of '91 he was no less redundant, and failed to make the 26-man World
Cup squad. However, the Paris debacle, which wrote Gimbert and Lascube out
of the international script, allowed Gallart to restore a representative career
which had begun, in Stade Patrice Brocas, Auch, with defeat against Romania
(24.5.90). Injury forced him from the field prematurely, to be replaced by Pascal
Ondarts, although he returned Down Under to play in two and a half Tests
against the Wallabies. Having been voted 1992 Prop of the Year by French
rugby writers, he promptly lost his place to Merignac's Seigne for 1993 Five
Nations' Championship, but only because of a serious calf injury.

Galthie, F.   France

Full Name: Fabien Galthie
Club: Colomiers
Position: Scrum-half
Height: 5ft 10 ½in (1.80m)
Weight: 12st 4lb (78kg)
Occupation: Executive
Born: Cahors, 20.3.69
International debut: Romania 21,
France 33, 1991
Five Nations' debut: Wales 9, France
12, 1992
Former club: Tournefeuille
Notable landmarks in rugby career:
Called into France's World Cup
squad last summer as an emergency
replacement for Guy Accoceberry,
who broke his arm in the Pool D
decider against Scotland in Pretoria.
Coach Pierre Berbizier courted
controversy by picking Fabien ahead
of incumbent Aubin Hueber for the
semi-final with South Africa but his
decision was vindicated by a strong
show from the first Colomiers player
ever to be capped. Fabien was
similarly impressive in the play-off

France (1991)

Last Season	2 caps	0 pts
Career	16 caps	9 pts

Caps (16): **1991** R, US(1) wc-R, Fj, C, E **1992** W, E, S, R, Arg(b) **1993** I, W, E **1995** wc-SA, E(b)

Points (9 – 2t): **1992** R(1t), Arg(b:1t)

defeat of England (Pretoria, 22.6.95). Had succeeded Berbizier at No 9 in 1991.
Given his debut in Bucharest (22.6.91) and remained intact for eight of the next
ten internationals, before Hueber took over for Ireland's Championship visit to
Paris (21.3.92) following mounting criticism of the Fabien. In the latter's
defence, he was unable to settle into a half-back understanding because of the
constantly changing identity of his stand-off, with Didier Camberabero,
Thierry Lacroix and Alain Penaud all given a shot. He even captained France
for part of the Five Nations' game against England (15.2.92) when Philippe
Sella was injured. Saw little Test action in 1992/93 (prefereed to by Hueber)
though was a try scorer in both games he did play – against Romania (won
25–6, Le Havre, 28.5.92) and Argentina (lost 20–24, Nantes, 14.11.92). He
was one of eight casualties after the Pumas' historic first win on French soil.
Bench reserve for both Tests against South Africa in summer of 1993 and was
recalled for '94 Championship before again losing place, for final game against
Scotland, to Perpignan's Alain Macabiau. Not seen again in the Test arena until
last summer's World Cup.

227

Galwey, M. J.   Ireland

Full Name: Michael Joseph Galwey
Club: Shannon
Position: Lock, flanker
Height: 6ft 4in (1.95m)
Weight: 17st 5lb (110kg)
Occupation: Sales representative
with Hibernian Business Equipment
Born: County Kerry, 8.10.66
Family: Joan (wife)
Former club: Castle Island
International debut: Ireland 13,
France 21, 1991
Five Nations' debut: As above
Best moment in rugby: Scoring
winning try against England
(20.3.93)
Most respected opponent: Zinzan
Brooke (Auckland & New Zealand)
Serious injuries: Damaged Achilles
tendon, knee ligaments (1992)
Other sporting achievements:
Winner of All-Ireland Gaelic
Football medal with Kerry in 1986
Notable landmarks in rugby career:
Lost out in the Ireland selection
stakes last season after playing in the
first two games against USA (as an
injury-time replacement for Paddy

Ireland (1991)

Last Season	2 caps	0 pts
Career	21 caps	5 pts

Lions 1993

Caps (21): **1991** F, W, Na(2R) wc-J
1992 E, S, F, NZ(1,2), A **1993** F,
W, E, R **1994** F, W, E, S, A(1),
US(R) **1995** E
Points (5 – 1t): **1993** E(1t)

Johns) and England (Dublin, 21.1.95). British Lion status in 1993, though he
was unable to win a Test place, was fitting reward for a memorable 1992/93
season, highlighted by his match-winning try against England in Dublin. Nick
Popplewell was the only other Irishman in the original Lions selection. A
campaign which had begun with two Tests in New Zealand (1992) ended back
in the Land of the Long White Cloud, albeit as a flanker. Selected to play with
Munster U-20 whilst a member of Castle Island, he took possession of a
Munster Senior Cup medal in three successive seasons, and was awarded a
Shannon RFC cap for the achievement. Played for Ireland U-25s in wins over
US Eagles (12–10, Limerick 10.3.90) and Spain (36–17, Limerick 8.9.90). First
called into Irish squad for 1988 tour of France but did not break into the senior
team until the 1991 Five Nations Championship, playing against France and
Ireland having warmed bench in season-opener against Argentina. Made B
debut in 1989 against Scotland at Murrayfield (drew 22–22, 9.12.89) and
added caps against Argentina (scoring try), Scotland and England in 1990/91.

Toured with Ireland to Namibia (1991), New Zealand (1992) and Australia (1994)
Touchlines: Fishing the Kerry Lakes, golf.

Gavin, B. T.   Australia

Full Name: Bryant Timothy (Tim) Gavin
State: New South Wales
Clubs: Eastern Suburbs (Aus), Mediolanum Milan (It)
Position: No 8, Lock
Height: 6ft 5in (1.96m)
Weight: 16st 12lb (107kg)
Occupation: PR consultant
Born: 20.11.63
Family: Single
International debut: Australia 19, New Zealand 19, 1988
Worst moment in rugby: Sustaining knee injury in club game before 1991 World Cup which forced me to miss tournament
Most embarrassing moment: Being sidestepped by a grey-haired Italian at least ten years older than me
Most respected opponent: Wayne Shelford (New Zealand)
Serious injuries: Knee reconstruction (1991), 1992 thigh injury
Suggestions to improve rugby: Change tackle law as players are picked because of their ability to kill the ball
Notable landmarks in rugby career: Australia's most-capped No 8 with 40 of his 42 caps having come at the

Australia (1988)

Last Season	12 caps	5 pts
Career	42 caps	40 pts

Caps (42): **1988** NZ(2,3), S, It(R) **1989** NZ(R), F(1,2) **1990** F(1,2,3), US, NZ(1,2,3) **1991** W(a), E(a), NZ(a1) **1992** S(1,2), SA, I, W **1993** T, NZ, SA(1,2,3), C, F(1,2) **1994** I(1,2), It(1,2), WS, A **1995** Arg(1,2) wc-SA, C, R, E

Points (40 – 9t): **1990** F(2:1t), US(1t) **1991** W(a:2t), NZ(a1:1t) **1993** T(1t), F(1:1t), F(2:1t) **1994** WS(1t)

back of the scrum (other two came as replacement lock). Everpresent for Australia in 1994/95, playing in all 12 Tests and contributing a try to the 73–3 defeat of Western Samoa (Sydney, 6.8.94). Debut had come against 1988 All Blacks but it was a further two years before the second row-turned No 8 (with more than a little help from national coach Bob Dwyer) shook off the challenge of Steve Tuynman to secure a regular berth. Once ensconced he wasted little time attracting a host of admirers, not least the Australian Society of Rugby

229

Writers who voted him their Player of the Year in 1990. Tim was a racing certainty for the Aussies' 1991 World Cup squad before sustaining a knee injury in club colours and having to watch the crowning glory via satellite back home in Oz. Injury continued to frustrate him in 1992 when a bruised thigh kept him out of the 2–1 Bledisloe Cup series-win. he recovered in time to tour South Africa and made a wonderful start in the Republic – scoring two tries as the Wallabies downed Western Transvaal 46–13 in Potchefstroom. He did not reappear until the Test match, in Cape Town on 22 August, when the Wallabies handed the Springboks a frightful beating (26–3). From there he toured Ireland and Wales, playing in both internationals in addition to the wins over Leinster, Ulster (two tries), Wales B and the Barbarians, and the losses to Swansea and Llanelli. Stepped up his try-scoring rate in an injury-free 1993, touching down against Tonga and in both Tests of the shared autumn series against France
Touchlines: Fishing, skiing.

Geoghegan, S. P.   Ireland

Full Name: Simon Patrick Geoghegan
Club: Bath
Position: Wing
Height: 6ft 1in (1.86m)
Weight: 13st (83kg)
Occupation: Solicitor, Rosling King
Born: Barnet, Herts, 1.9.68
Family: Single
Former club: Wasps (Colts)
International debut: Ireland 13, France 21, 1991
Five Nations' debut: As above
Most respected opponent: David Campese (NSW & Australia)
Notable landmarks in rugby career: Groin injury robbed him of an everpresent campaign for Ireland in 1994/95 but spared him from any involvement in Italy's first ever win over one of the Big Eight nations (lost 12–22, Treviso, 8.5.95). That apart, Simon scored tries against USA, France and Japan and remained influential despite being frustrated by the lack of possession coming his way. Simon's return to

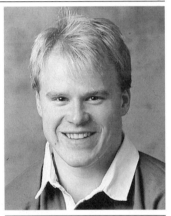

Ireland (1991)

Last Season	9 caps	15 pts
Career	30 caps	41 pts

Caps (30): **1991** F, W, E, S, Na(1) wc-Z, S, A **1992** E, S, F, A **1993** S, F, W, E, R **1994** F, W, E, S, US **1995** E, S, F(a), W(a) wc-NZ, J, W(b), F(b)
Points (41 – 9t): **1991** W(1t), E(1t), S(1t) wc-Z(1t) **1993** R(1t) **1994** E(1t), US(1t) **1995** F(a:1t) wc-J(1t)

form in 1993/94 had been Heaven-sent for Ireland. Without him the Irish wouldn't have scored a try all season. With him, they managed two – against Romania and England – and you don't need to be an Einstein to know which was the best received. Missed Ireland's tour to New Zealand in 1992 but returned to side for visit of world champions Australia to Dublin. Failed to emulate his previous scoring exploits in that game or in his subsequent outings in the 1993 Five Nations' Championship. Represented Ireland at Under-25, Students, B and Full level. Quickly rose to prominence, with try-scoring debuts for Ireland U-25 (36–17 v Spain, Limerick 8.9.90) and Ireland B (27–12 v Argentina, Limerick 20.10.90). Quality Inter-Provincial performances for Connacht sped his progress into the senior national XV, for whom he opposed the Bayonne Express, Patrice Lagisquet, on his debut against France at Lansdowne Road (2.2.91). Scored tries in next three internationals, against Wales, Ireland and Scotland. Toured Namibia (1991) and Australia (1994) and played in last two World Cups

Touchlines: Soccer (West Ham fan), Cinema, theatre.

Gibbs, A. Wales

Full Name: Andrew Gibbs
Club: Newbridge
Position: Flanker
Height: 6ft 3in
Weight: 16st 7lb
Occupation: Police officer, Gwent constabulary
Born: 20.3.72
International debut: Wales 12, Ireland 16, 1995
Five Nations debut: As above
Notable landmarks in rugby career: Became the 922nd player to be capped by Wales when selected by coach Alan Davies for the 1995 Five Nations visit of Ireland to Cardiff (18.3.95), two days before his 23rd birthday. It was a fitting tribute to a player who has overcome serious illness – he required a six-month course of officially sanctioned steroid treatment to cure his reactive arthritis. And his selection was seen as a good omen for the slumping Welsh as he had never been on the

Wales (1995)

Last Season	1 cap	0 pts
Career	1 cap	0 pts

Caps (1): **1995** I(a)
Points Nil

losing side in 15 appearances in a Wales jersey at Youth, under-19, under-21 and A levels. But such superstition counted for nought as Ireland won the match 16–12 to hand Wales only their second ever whitewashed Wooden Spoon, Davies resigned his post, and Andrew was consigned to the ranks of the forgotten men by new coach Alex Evans. The Gwent blindside had represented Newbridge at Under-13 to Under-16 levels before captaining Crumlin Youth for two seasons, during which time he was capped by Wales Youth against Ireland, France, Japan and England in 1991. A member of the brilliant Wales Under-19 side that toured Canada in '91, Andrew broke into the Newbridge league side in 1994 and represented Wales A (versus Ireland and France) that same year.

Gonzales, J.-M. France

Full Name: Jean-Michel Gonzales
Club: Bayonne
Position: Hooker, prop
Height: 5ft 9in (1.75m)
Weight: 16st 13lb (103kg)
Occupation: Company rep, Bridat Securite
Born: Bayonne, 10.7.67
Family: Married
International debut: Argentina 12, France 27, 1992
Five Nations' debut: France 35, Ireland 15, 1994
Former club: Cambo
Notable landmarks in rugby career: Jean-Michel's accurate lineout throwing was a feature of France's third place play-off victory over England (Pretoria, 22.6.95) in last summer's World Cup and capped a busy season for the Bayonne hooker – one in which he made the No2 jersey his own, missing only the 54–18 World Cup romp against Cote d'Ivoire. Yet until Jean-Francois Tordo's switch from flanker prior to the 1993 Five Nations' Championship, France had

France (1992)

Last Season	14 caps	0 pts
Career	29 caps	5 pts

Caps (29): 1992 Arg(a1,a2), SA(1,2), Arg(b) 1993 R(a), SA(1,2), R(b), A(1,2) 1994 I, W, E, S, C(a), NZ(1,2), C(b) 1995 W, E(a), S(a), I(a), R wc-T, S(b), I(b), SA, E(b)
Points (5 – 1t): 1992 Arg(b:1t)

seemed unsure as to who they wanted to perform their hooking duties. Jean-Pierre Genet, the Racing Club de France rake, lost the jersey on tour in

Argentina, having done the honours against Romania at Le Havre in May, and coach Pierre Berbizier instead invited Jean-Michel to put in a bid. He played in both Tests in Buenos Aires against a poor Pumas side and kept the job through the two-Test series with South Africa, despite the 15–20 loss France suffered at Lyon (17.10.92). But his time was nearly up. Had France not allowed Argentina, now themselves on tour, an historic first victory on French soil at Nantes on 14 November, he might have survived. As it was the Pumas won 24–20 and, in spite of the hooker scoring one of the home side's three tries, he was one of eight casualties as the selectors wielded the axe. He did not reappear again subsequently, although he was granted a place on the bench at Parc des Princes (20.3.93) to watch France beat Wales 26–10 and clinch the inaugural Five Nations' Cup. Reappeared at loosehead prop against Romania in Bucharest (20.5.93) where another serious injury to Tordo paved the way for Jean-Michel to reassert himself. He played the next nine Tests and then toured to Canada and New Zealand (1994), contributing fully in France's historic 2–0 series defeat of the All Blacks.

Gregan, G. Australia

Full Name: George Gregan
State: Australia Capital Territory
Position: Scrum-half
Height: 1.72m
Weight: 77kg
Occupation: Marketing trainee
Born: 19.4.73
International debut: Australia 23, Italy 20, 1994
Notable landmarks in rugby career:
Followed in the footsteps of David Campese by winning international recognition whilst playing for unfashionable Australian Capital Territory. But it was his last-minute tackle on All Black Jeff Wilson that won him worldwide acclaim. The 'hit' came in the Bledisloe Cup match under the Sydney floodlights 17.8.94) and won the Wallabies a match they had threatened to let slip through their hands. Australia had raced into a 17–3 lead but New Zealand powered back to 16–17 with just four minutes left. David

Australia (1994)
Last Season	10 caps	5 pts
Career	10 caps	5 pts

Caps (10): **1994** It(1,2), WS, NZ **1995** Arg(1,2) wc-SA, C, R, E
Points (5 – 1t): **1994** WS(1t)

Knox's penalty for the home side still made it a one-score game and when Wilson darted past four defenders he appeared to have that score. But wee George arrived from nowhere and put in a shuddering tackle (as he had done previously to stun giant All Black forwards Richard Loe and Mark Cooksley) to dislodge the ball from Golden Boy's grasps. The youngster made his debut in the home series against Italy, and opened his try-scoring account in the 73–3 rout of Manu Samoa (Sydney, 6.8.94). Retained his place in the Wallaby line-up in 1995 but was less effective in the World Cup as the defending champions stuttered their way to the quarter-finals before losing 25–22 to England in a last-minute thriller (Cape Town, 11.6.95).

Griffiths, M. Wales

Full Name: Michael Griffiths
Club: Cardiff
Position: Loosehead prop
Height: 5ft 11in (1.81m)
Weight: 16st 10lb (106kg)
Occupation: Brewery representative
Born: Tonypandy, 18.3.62
Family: Anne (wife), Joel Michael (son) and Luc Rhys (son)
Family links with rugby: Brother plays for Ystrad Rhondda
Former clubs: Ystrad Rhondda, Bridgend
International debut: Wales 24, Western Samoa 6, 1988
Five Nations' debut: Scotland 23, Wales 7, 1989
Best moment in rugby: Winning first Welsh cap against touring Samoans (12.11.88)
Worst moments in rugby: Wales losing 6–34 to England at Twickenham (18.2.90); breaking collarbone in freak cycling accident and missing 1992/93 international season
Most embarrassing moment: Twice having to change shorts against France (1991/92) in front of the Princess of Wales
Most respected opponents: Jeff Probyn (Wasps & England: for his technique)

Wales (1988)

Last Season	6 caps	5 pts
Career	34 caps	5 pts

Lions 1989

Caps (34): **1988** WS, R **1989** S, I, F, E, NZ **1990** F, E, Na(1,2), Ba **1991** I, F(a), F(b) wc-WS, Arg, A(b) **1992** I, F, E, S, A **1993** Z(1,2), Na, J, C **1995** F(R), E, S, I(a) wc-J, I(b)

Points (5 – 1t): **1995** wc-J(1t)

234

and Iain Milne (Heriot's FP & Scotland: for his size and strength)

Serious injuries: Broken ribs, fractured arm, twisted shoulder muscles, damaged ankle and knee ligaments

Other sporting achievements: Accomplished soccer player (centre-back)

Notable landmarks in rugby career: Benefited from the misfortune of Llanelli rival Ricky Evans in 1995, appearing in all four rounds of the Five Nations Championship after Ricky had broken his leg in two places against France (Paris, 21.1.95), falling awkwardly following a head-butt from French lock Olivier Merle. Mike took over in the eighth minute and remained until the end of the campaign, by which time, sadly, Wales had taken delivery of a white-washed Wooden Spoon. Happier times were ahead, with Mike's first Test try, in the 57–10 World Cup win over Japan (Bloemfontein, 27.5.95), but the celebrations were shortlived as Wales failed to make the quarter-finals as in 1991. Mike's penchant for mountain biking had wrecked his international hopes in 1992/93 when he suffered a broken collarbone as a result of colliding with Anthony Clement and Colin Stephens in a freak accident on Lanzarote's mountain roads during Wales' preparations for the 1993 Five Nations' campaign. His Test season was over until his 1994 summer tour to Zimbabwe and Namibia, where he appeared in all three Tests. Retained berth on return home, figuring against Japan and Canada, but was one of old guard swept from office following Canadian victory. Started career in back-row but moved to front of scrum shortly before joining Bridgend. Moved to Cardiff for new challenges and found them: playing for Crawshays, Wales B (in 12–18 loss to France B, Brecon 29.10.88), Wales and 1989 Lions. Despite failing to oust David Sole in Test side, he played in six of the Lions' 12 games, including the final game (as a replacement) against the ANZAC XV. Played at tighthead against Barbarians (6.10.90). Only Welsh representative in Home Unions' team which played Rest of Europe at Twickenham on behalf of Romania Appeal (won 43–18, 22.4.90). Missed the 1991 tour to Australia but was quickly recalled for the duration of the World Cup and 1992 Five Nations Championship

Touchlines: Mountain biking (!)

Guscott, J. C.   England

Full Name: Jeremy Clayton Guscott
Club: Bath
Position: Centre
Height: 6ft 1in (1.86m)
Weight: 13st 5lb (85kg)
Occupation: Marketing co-ordinator, British Gas
Born: Bath, 7.7.65
Family: Jayne (wife) and Imogen (daughter)
International debut: Romania 3, England 58, 1989
Five Nations' debut: England 23, Ireland 0, 1990
Best moment in rugby: Try scored for 1989 Lions v Australia in second Test
Worst moment in rugby: Being dropped by Bath for semi-finals of 1989/90 Pilkington Cup
Suggestions to improve rugby: Revise amateur regulations completely to allow players to earn money through off-field activities. Reduce amount of offences in lineout: there must be 100-odd, when there should be no more than five or six, and it is such an annoying part of the game
Notable landmarks in rugby career: By Jerry's Everest-high standards, 1994/95 constituted a slightly disappointing campaign. He was an influential member of an England side winning it's third Grand Slam in five seasons but the effects of the

England (1989)		
Last Season	11 caps	5 pts
Career	39 caps	78 pts
Lions 1989	2 Tests	4 pts
1993	3 Tests	0 pts

Caps (39): **1989** R, Fj. Lions-A(2,3) **1990** I, F, W, S, Arg(b) **1991** W, S, I, F, Fj, A(a) wc-NZ, It, F, S, A(b) **1992** S, I, F, W, C, SA **1993** F, W, S, I. Lions-NZ(1,2,3) **1994** R, C **1995** I, F(a), W, S wc-Arg, It, A, NZ, F(b)

Points (78 – 17t,2dg): **1989** R(3t), Fj(1t). Lions-A(2:1t) **1990** I(1t), F(1t), S(1t), Arg(b:2t) **1991** A(a:1t) wc-It(2t) **1992** S(1dg), I(1t), C(1t), SA(1t) **1993** W(1dg), S(1t) **1995** F(a:1t)

long-term groin injury which had ruled him out of entire 1993/94 season perhaps took the edge off his England performances. Jerry failed to score a try at the World Cup, nor did he dominate the midfield as of old. His only score of the season came in the 31–10 Five Nations' defeat of France (Twickenham, 4.2.95). An automatic selection for the 1993 Lions (playing in all three Tests) after super 1992/93 season in which he bagged tries against Canada, South Africa and Scotland and dropped a goal in defeat by Wales in Cardiff. For many, though, his most memorable contribution of the campaign was his part in the wonderful move which led to Rory Underwood's try against the Scots (6.3.93). Stuart Barnes' break and divine pass allowed Jerry to stretch his legs like the thoroughbred he is, unravel the tartan defence and then release Underwood. Started out with Bath's mini-section as a wing, aged seven. Meteoric rise in 1989 brought two caps for England B, three tries on full England debut in Bucharest, and one invitation from the British Lions (before capped by England). Scored crucial try in Brisbane (second Test: won 19–12, 8.7.89) to bring Lions back into the series which they went on to win 2–1. Ever-present throughout England's back-to-back Grand Slams (1991-92) and wore No.12 jersey in 1991 World Cup final, having previously toured Australia (1991). Toured New Zealand with World XV (April 1992), playing in first two Tests, including famous 28–14 first Test defeat of All Blacks. Collected fourth Pilkington Cup winners' medal in 1992 to add to those collected in 1987, '89 and '90

Touchlines: Golf.

Hall, M. R. Wales

Full Name: Michael Robert Hall
Club: Cardiff
Positions: Centre, wing
Height: 6ft 1in (1.86m)
Weight: 15st 3lb (96kg)
Occupation: Director (chartered surveyor), Steep Holm Property Advisors Ltd
Born: Bridgend, 13.10.65
Family: Single
Former clubs: Bridgend, Maesteg, Cambridge University
International debut: New Zealand 52, Wales 3, 1988
Five Nations' debut: Scotland 23, Wales 7, 1989
Worst moment in rugby: Every time I go to Twickenham!
Most embarrassing moment: England 34, Wales 6 (17.2.90, record defeat at Twickenham)
Most respected opponent: Philippe Sella (Agen & France)
Other sporting achievements: Schoolboy honours at county level in soccer, basketball and cricket
Notable landmarks in rugby career: Quit rugby union last summer after captaining Wales to World Cup failure in South Africa. Having skippered

Cardiff to Heineken League triumph he was given the keys to his country by caretaker coach Alex Evans (also Cardiff supremo). But it all went sour in Johannesburg where Wales lost to New Zealand and Ireland and failed to make the quarter-finals for the second straight World Cup. It was a far cry from a season earlier when he had captained Cardiff to Swalec Cup triumph and played a full part in Wales' 1994 Five Nations title triumph. And finished excellent campaign with try hat-trick in World

Wales (1988)		
Last Season	9 caps	0 pts
Career	42 caps	33 pts
Lions 1989	1 Test	0 pts

Caps (42): **1988** NZ(1R,2), WS, R **1989** S, I, F, E, NZ. Lions-A(1) **1990** F, E, S **1991** A(a), F(b) wc-WS, Arg, A(b) **1992** I, F, E, S, A **1993** E, S, I **1994** S, I, F, E wc(q)-P, Sp. C, T wc(q)-R, It. SA **1995** F, S, I(a) wc-J, NZ, I(b)

Points (33 – 7t): **1989** S(1t), E(1t) **1994** wc(q)-P(3t). C(2t)

Cup qualifier against Portugal (won 102–11, Lisbon, 17.5.94). 1989 Lion who failed to retain his place on 1993 tour, though not helped by being dropped by Wales for their final Five Nations' game in Paris. Past captain of British Universities, Welsh Students and Wales U-21s. Two Blues at Cambridge (1987,88). Wales B against France in 1987 (lost 0–26). Represented 1989 Lions against Australia in first Test (lost 12–30). Toured to New Zealand (1988) and Australia (1991) with Wales, and to South Africa (1989) with World XV. Scored winning try against England (Cardiff, 18.3.89, won 12-9) to deny them 1989 Five Nations' Championship
Touchlines: Golf.

Halpin, G. F. Ireland

Full Name: Garrett Francis Halpin
Club: London Irish
Position: Tight-head prop
Height: 6ft (1.83m)
Weight: 17st 6lb (111kg)
Occupation: Teacher, Woburn High School
Born: Dublin, 14.2.66
Family: Caroline (wife) and child
Former clubs: Rockwell College, Wanderers
International debut: England 23, Ireland 0, 1990
Five Nations' debut: As above
Most embarrassing moment: Scoring try on 22-metre line in 1991 at Ballymena

Other sporting achievements: Irish International hammer thrower – American Indoor Collegiate champion. Represented Ireland in 1987 in World Athletics Championships (Rome); hockey coach

Notable landmarks in rugby career: Enjoyed a cracking finish to the 1994/95 season after scoring a hat-trick of tries for the Barbarians in the Mobbs Memorial Match. Went on to claim the No1 Ireland jersey at the World Cup and stunned the mighty All Blacks by scoring the early try which gave Ireland the lead at Ellis Park, Johannesburg (27.5.95). Ireland bagged three tries in all and although they lost 19–43 their gutsy display provided a springboard for quarter-final qualification. Joined Wanderers on return from a sports scholarship with University of Manhattan in New York. Played four times for Ireland Schools (1983-84). Toured North America with Ireland (1989), scoring try in defeat of Mid West in Chicago. Won 1989/90 Leinster League and Cup double with Wanderers. Lost his place after debut against England at Twickenham (20.1.90) and had to be content with turning out in Ireland Under-25s' 36–17 win over Spain (Limerick, 8.9.90) and Ireland B's 27–12 win over Argentina (Limerick, 20.10.90). Everpresent on Irish replacements' bench during 1991 Five Nations Championship and failed to make Test team on summer tour to Namibia. Played against Japan in 1991 World Cup and toured to Australia in 1994, failing to make Test team but playing against New South Wales, ACT, Queensland, Australia B and NSW Country

Touchlines: Motor-biking, music

Ireland (1990)		
Last Season	4 caps	5 pts
Career	11 caps	5 pts

Caps (11): **1990** E **1991** wc-J **1992** E,S,F **1993** R **1994** F(R) **1995** It wc-NZ,W(b),F(b)

Points (5 – 1t): **1995** wc-NZ(1t)

Ian Hunter tags Jean-Luc Sadourny in that awful World Cup third-place play-off, in which France beat England.

Halvey, E. O.   Ireland

Full Name: Eddie Oliver Halvey
Club: Shannon
Position: Flanker
Height: 6ft 4in
Weight: 15st 8lb
Occupation: Airport employee, Aer Rianta
Born: Limerick, 11.7.70
International debut: Ireland 7, France 25, 1995
Five Nations debut: As above
Notable landmarks in rugby career: Assumed national hero status in Ireland after coming on as a bloodbin replacement for Denis McBride in the all-or-nothing World Cup-tie against Wales (Johannesburg, 4.6.95). Ireland's early lead was under severe threat when Eddie's fresh legs were introduced to the fray and he responded almost immediately with the try that effectively killed the contest. He then trotted off, McBride returned bandaged, Ireland

Ireland (1995)		
Last Season	6 caps	10 pts
Career	6 caps	10 pts

Caps (6): **1995** F(a), W(a), It wc-J, W(b:TR), F(b:R)
Points (10 – 2t): **1995** wc-J(1t), W(b:1t)

advanced to the quarter-finals and Wales went home. Eddie's performance was typical of an Ireland pack revitalised after an indifferent Five Nations series. Yet a year earlier he had only just broken into the Ireland A team, playing against Scotland and Wales. Named in the Irish Development squad at the start of last season he continued in the A side (turning out against England and Scotland) before getting his senior call-up against France at blindside, after Paddy Johns cried off at the 11th hour and Anthony Foley switched to No 8. Held his place against Wales and Italy, in his favoured openside berth, before marking his World Cup debut with a try in the 50–28 defeat of plucky Japan (Bloemfontein, 31.5.95). Came on as a replacement for Gabriel Fulcher in the 12–36 quarter-final loss to France (Durban, 10.6.95).

Hastings, A. G.   Scotland

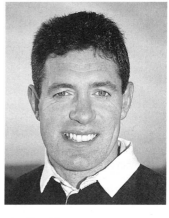

Full Name: Andrew Gavin Hastings
Club: Watsonians
Position: Fullback
Height: 6ft 2in (1.88m)
Weight: 14st 7lb (92kg)
Occupation: Sports marketing executive, The Carnegie Partnership
Born: Edinburgh, 3.1.62
Family: Diane (wife)
Family links with rugby: Clifford (father) played No.8 for Edinburgh XV and Watsonians; Scott (brother) plays for Watsonians, Scotland and British Lions; Graeme (brother) plays centre for Melbourne RFC and Victoria State (Australia); Ewan (brother) plays on wing for Watsonians
Former clubs: Cambridge University, London Scottish
International debut: Scotland 18, France 17, 1986
Five Nations' debut: As above
Best moments in rugby: Winning 1990 Grand Slam; 1989 British Lions' 2–1 series win in Australia; taking part in the 1992 New Zealand Rugby Football Union Centenary celebrations; captaining 1993 British Lions; beating France in Paris (1995)
Worst moment in rugby: Missing kick in front of posts against England in 1991 World Cup semi-final at Murrayfield (26.10.91)
Most embarrassing moment: Missing plane home from Ireland after B international
Most respected opponent: The All Blacks, because of their record – I've only beaten them twice in 13 attempts (NZ 14, World XV 28, 1992; NZ 7, British Lions 20, 1993)
Notable landmarks in rugby career: Retired from international arena after leading Scotland to World Cup quarter-finals last summer and breaking countless scoring records en route. His 44-point haul, including four tries, in the 89–0 rout of Cote d'Ivoire (Rustenburg, 26.5.95) eclipsed every previous single-international scoring feat in history bar Hong Kong wing Ashley Billington's little-known 50-point tally (ten tries) in a '95 World Cup qualifier against Singapore. Gavin then added 31 points (including world record equalling eight penalty goals) next time out against Tonga (Pretoria, 30.5.95), the second biggest haul ever by a Scotsman, and by the end of his World Cup (four matches) he had an incredible 104 points to his credit. No wonder his 227 World Cup career total (5t,14c,17p) is without peer. But 1995 was far from all

241

about events in South Africa for the Scotland skipper, who responded to calls for his sacking from the national side (after the 10–34 loss to South Africa, 19.11.94) by inspiring them to a Grand Slam showdown with England at Twickenham (lost 12–24, 18.3.95) and a first ever win over France in Parc des Princes (18.2.95). In all he scored a Scottish record 56 points in the 1995 Five Nations series and an astonishing 201 points in his 11-Test campaign (plus 22 points, 2t,6c, in the 62–7 non-cap defeat of Spain, 6.5.95). Became Scotland's most-capped player with 53rd cap against Ireland (Murrayfield, 4.2.95). Appointed captain of both Scotland and British Lions in 1992/93. Bowed out of Test rugby with northern hemisphere high 667 points (730 including Lions' points) to his credit. Won two Blues at Cambridge University (1984-85) and five caps for Scotland B before establishing then Scottish record with six penalty goals on full debut (17.1.86). Toured with Scotland to North America (1985), 1987 World Cup (where scored 62 points in four games), New Zealand (1990) and Australia (1992). Scored go-ahead try in second Test for 1989 Lions and 15 points in victorious decider. Kicked penalty for 1986 British Lions in 7–15 defeat by The Rest at Cardiff in match to celebrate centenary of IRFB. Played in '1989 Home Unions' 29–27 win over France (scored 22 points) and for 1989 Barbarians' against All Blacks. Led London Scottish to 1989/90 Courage League division three title, and Watsonians to promotion (1990/91) to McEwan's League division one. Captained Barbarians at 1991 Hong Kong Sevens. Represented 1992 World XV in three-Test series against All Blacks (NZRFU centenary celebrations), kicking penalty in 28–14 first Test win and scoring try in second

Touchlines: Golf.

Scotland (1986)		
Last Season	11 caps	201 pts
Career	61 caps	667 pts
Lions 1986		
1989	3 Tests	28 pts
1993	3 Tests	35 pts

Caps (61): **1986** F, W, E, I, R **1987** I, F, W, E wc-F, Z, R, NZ **1988** I, F, W, E, A **1989** Fj, R. Lions-A(1,2,3) **1990** I, F, W, E, NZ(1,2), Arg **1991** F, W, E(a), I(a) wc-J, I(b), WS, E(b), NZ **1992** E, I, F, W, A(1) **1993** I, F, W, E. Lions-NZ(1,2,3). NZ **1994** W, E, I, F, SA **1995** C, I, F(a), W, E, R wc-IC, T, F(b), NZ

Points (667 – 17t,86c,140p): **1986** F(6p), W(1t,1p), E(3c,5p), R(3c,5p) **1987** I(1c), F(1c,4p), W(2c,2p), E(1c,2p) wc-F(4p), Z(1t,8c), R(2t,8c,1p), NZ(1p) **1988** I(2c,2p), F(1t,4p), W(4p), E(2p), A(1t,1c,1p) **1989** Fj(1t,4c,2p), R(3c,2p). Lions-A(1:2p), A(2:1t,1p), A(3:5p) **1990** F(1p), NZ(1:2c), NZ(2:2c,2p), Arg(1t,5c,1p) **1991** W(1c,2p), I(a:1t,1p) wc-J(1t,5c,2p), I(b:2c,3p), WS(2c,4p), E(b:2p), NZ(2p) **1992** E(1p), I(2c,2p), F(2p), W(1p), A(1:1c,2p) **1993** I(1c,1p), F(1p), W(5p), E(3p). Lions-NZ(1:6p), NZ(2:4p), NZ(3:1c,1p). NZ(4p) **1994** W(2p), E(2p), I(2p), F(4p),SA(1c,1p) **1995** C(1c,5p), I(2c,4p), F(a:1t,2c,3p), W(2c,4p),E(2p), R(1t,4c,2p) wc-IC(4t,9c,2p), T(1t,1c,8p), F(b:1c,4p), NZ(3c,3p)

Hastings, S. Scotland

Full Name: Scott Hastings
Club: Watsonians
Positions: Centre, wing, full-back
Height: 6ft 1in (1.86m)
Weight: 14st 4lb (93kg)
Occupation: Advertising account executive, Barker's, Scotland
Born: Edinburgh, 4.12.64
Family: Jenny (wife), Corey (son)
Family links with rugby: Clifford (father) played No.8 for Edinburgh XV and Watsonians; Gavin (brother) plays for Watsonians and captains Scotland and British Lions; Graeme (brother) plays centre for Melbourne RFC and Victoria State (Australia); Ewan (brother) plays on wing for Watsonians
Former club: Newcastle Northern
International debut: Scotland 19, France 18, 1986
Five Nations' debut: As above
Best moment in rugby: 1989 Lions' Test series win; 1990 Grand Slam win with Scotland; playing in Hong Kong Sevens; receiving a pass from brother Gavin for Scotland against England; winning the Stockholm 10 a sides with New Zealand Warblers in August 1993
Worst moment in rugby: Sustaining hamstring injury on first appearance in 1987 World Cup (55–28 win v Romania)

Scotland (1986)		
Last Season	7 caps	10 pts
Career	57 caps	38 pts
Lions 1989 1993	2 Tests	0 pts

Caps (57): **1986** F, W, E, I, R **1987** I, F, W wc-R **1988** I, F, W, A **1989** W, E, I, F, Fj, R. Lions-A(2,3) **1990** I, F, W, E, NZ(1,2), Arg **1991** F, W, E(a), I(a) wc-J, Z, I(b), WS, E(b), NZ **1992** E, I, F, W, A(1,2) **1993** I, F, W, E, NZ **1994** E, I, F, SA **1995** W, E, R(R) wc-T, F(b), NZ

Points (38 – 9t): **1986** E(1t), R(1t) **1987** F(1t) **1988** I(1t) **1991** I(1t) wc-J(1t), Z(1t) **1995** wc-T(1t), NZ(1t)

Most embarrassing moment: Finding out Gavin was my brother
Most respected opponent: Brendan Mullin (Blackrock & Ireland) – played opposite him ever since we captained our respective countries in a Schools international; Tim Horan and Jason Little
Serious injuries: Torn hamstring, cartilage operation (1985), broken cheekbone (1987 v Wales), fractured jaw and cheekbone (Lions v Otago, 1993 – 4½ hour operation to rebuild face)
Suggestions to improve rugby: Pay players a £1,000 international match fee or a percentage of gate fees, sponsorship revenue and TV rights

Notable landmarks in rugby career: Scotland's most-capped centre having reclaimed his former kingdom towards the end of last season. Cast into the wilderness after Scotland's 34–10 humping by Springboks (Murrayfield, 19.11.94) he watched helplessly as Ian Jardine and Gregor Townsend successfully shored up the midfield duties in the 1995 Five Nations series. Only when Jardine was injured in Paris did Scott return but he took his chance well against Wales and England. However, he was again relegated to bench duties, this time behind the new combination of Tony Stanger and Graham Shiel, against Romania, Spain and Cote d'Ivoire before the selectors drew upon his experience for the remainder of Scotland's World Cup campaign. He responded with tries in Pretoria against Tonga (30.5.95) and New Zealand (11.6.95) – his first Test tries since the 1991 World Cup. Shares with Sean Lineen the world record for an international centre partnership of 28 games (Lineen retired after 1992 Australia tour). No such fond memories of 1993/94 campaign in which Scotland collected '94 Five Nations wooden spoon and Scott admitted to being 'humiliated' playing out of position as a winger in 51–15 defeat by New Zealand (20.11.93). Captaining Barbarians against same All Black tourists (Cardiff, 4.12.93) was a far more accurate reflection of his international stock. Took his tally of caps to 50 (against France, 19.3.94) on same day as brother Gavin. Pair had become first Scottish brothers to play together in a Lions' Test back in 1989. Selected to tour with 1993 Lions to New Zealand, under Gavin's captaincy, but returned early and in agony after sustaining a fractured cheekbone. Former Watsonians captain (1989/90) who helped Edinburgh to three Inter-District Championship 'grand slams' between 1986-88. Also ex-skipper of Scottish Schools. Played three times for Scotland U-21s and once for Scotland B (at fullback in 9–0 win over Italy B, Glasgow 7.12.85). Also played at outside-half, for Anglo-Scots, during time at Newcastle Polytechnic. Key cog in Scotland's 1990 Grand Slam machine, making famous try-saving tackle on England's Rory Underwood in Murrayfield decider.

Rob Andrew kicks Australia out of the World Cup in Cape Town.

Hattingh, H.   South Africa

Full Name: Hendrikus (Drikus) Hattingh
Club: Normaal College Pretoria
Province: Northern Transvaal
Position: Lock
Height: 6ft 4 ½in (1.94m)
Weight: 18st 3lb (116kg)
Occupation: Market agent
Born: Rustenburg, 21.2.68
International debut: South Africa 3, Australia 26, 1992
Other sporting achievements: Former Junior Springbok athlete
Notable landmarks in rugby career: Took cap-tally to five in 1994 when appearing in both home Test wins over Argentina, two years on from his previous international appearance at Twickenham. The Springboks won the first Test 42–22 in Port Elizabeth (8.10.94) and the second 46–26 in Johannesburg (15.10.94). Had risen to prominence in the Northern Transvaal side which completed a Currie Cup-Lion

South Africa (1992)

Last Season	2 caps	0 pts
Career	5 caps	0 pts

Caps (5): 1992 A(R), F(2R), E **1994** Arg(1,2)
Points Nil

Cup double in his first season on the team. A busy member of South Africa's 1992 European tour. Having had made his Test bow as a 64th minute replacement for Adri Geldenhuys in the 3–26 loss to Australia (Cape Town, 22.8.92), he featured in eight of the ten non-internationals played in France and England – against France B (lost 17–24, Bordeaux, 4.10.92), Aquitaine (won 29–22, Pau, 7.10.92), Midi-Pyrenees (won 18-15, Toulouse, 15.10.92), Langedoc-Roussillon (won 36–15, Beziers, 20.10.92), French Universities (lost 13–18, Tours, 28.10.92), the Midlands Division (won 32–9, Leicester, 4.11.92), England B (won 20–16, Bristol, 7.11.92) and the Northern Division (won 19–3, Leeds, 10.11.92) – scoring tries against France B, Languedoc-Roussillon and England B. In addition the former Junior Springbok athlete came on as a 49th minute replacement, again for Geldenhuys, in the 16–29 second Test defeat by France at the Parc des Princes, and then playing from start to finish against England at Twickenham (lost 16–33, 14.11.92).

Henderson, P. W.   New Zealand

Full Name: Paul William Henderson
Province: Southland
Position: Flanker
Height: 6ft 2in (1.88m)
Weight: 15st (95kg)
Occupation: Farmer
Born: Bluff, South Island, 21.9.64
Former Province: Otago
International debut: Argentina 14,
New Zealand 21, 1991
Serious injuries: Damaged knee
ligaments (vs Neath, 1989)
Notable landmarks in rugby career:
Captained All Blacks to world record
145–17 rout of Japan in World Cup
(Bloemfontein, 4.6.95) and
contributed one of the 21 tries. It
remained his one appearance of the
tournament, indeed his only cap for
three years, but what a memory. Had
announced himself as an
18-year-old with a stirring
performance for Southland in their
41–3 loss to the 1983 British Lions at
Invercargill. After turning out for the
Province for four seasons he moved to

New Zealand (1991)

Last Season	1 cap	5 pts
Career	7 caps	9 pts

Caps (7): 1991 Arg(1). wc-C **1992** Wd(1,2,3), I(1) **1995** wc-J
Points (9 – 2t): **1992** I(1:1t) **1995** wc-J(1t)

Dunedin in 1987 and played for Otago until reverting back to Southland at the start of 1992. Paul's international career began when he represented New Zealand Secondary Schools and, in 1983–84, NZ Colts. Team mates in 1983 included Sean Fitzpatrick, Grant Fox and Murray Mexted, while Fitzpatrick captained the '84 side which featured Bernie McCahill and Frano Botica. Toured with New Zealand to Wales and Ireland in 1989 but a knee ligament injury sustained against Neath forced him to return home after only three games. Luck finally changed in 1991 when, during the All Blacks' tour of Argentina he was awarded his first cap in the 28–14 win over the Pumas in Buenos Aires. Still, he only made the 1991 World Cup squad when Otago's Mike Brewer was withdrawn through injury. He collected his second cap, in the 29–13 quarter-final defeat of Canada in the pouring rain at Lille's Stade du Nord. Despite missing the final trial in 1992 because of a calf muscle strain, Paul made the All Black line-up for the centenary series, retaining his place in each of the three Tests against the World XV. although he failed to finish the second and third legs. It was not until Ireland's visit to Dunedin on 30 May that he finally made the scoresheet, crossing for the first of the Blacks' four tries as

Ireland, 100/1 no-hopers, had their remarkable 12–0 lead pegged back, eventually losing 24–21. Injury robbed him of further caps when, two games into the tour of Australia and South Africa, he broke his thumb against NSW and was forced to return home.

Hendriks, P. South Africa

Full Name: Pieter Hendriks
Club: Roodepoort
Position: Wing
Height: 6ft (1.82m)
Weight: 13st 8lb (86kg)
Occupation: Teacher
Born: Douglas, 13.4.70
International debut: South Africa 24, New Zealand 27, 1992
Other sporting achievements: Former South African junior hurdles champion
Notable landmarks in rugby career: Responsible for arguably the two most memorable moments of the 1995 World Cup, though for contrasting reasons. Pieter gave the clenched fist in triumph before touching down the first try of the tournament, for the Springboks against reigning champions Australia in the opening match, having left David Campese sprawling in his wake. But he was adjudged to have used the same fist (and his boot) for an

South Africa (1992)

Last Season	5 caps	5 pts
Career	7 caps	5 pts

Caps (7): 1992 NZ, A 1994 S, W 1995 wc-A, R, C
Points (5 – 1t): 1995 wc-A(1t)

altogether less acceptable activity when getting involved in the Battle of the Boet (Port Elizabeth, 3.6.95) during South Africa's 20–0 defeat of Canada. He was cited for his part in a brawl which led to three players being sent-off and banned for 90 days for 'kicking and punching', so ending his tournament and allowing back in the 'Black Pearl' Chester Williams, whose initial injury had presented the opportunity to Pieter. Prior to that Pieter had not toured with 1994 Springboks to New Zealand but did make the autumn trip to Scotland and Wales, winning his first caps for two years in the two Tests, and scoring two tries in the 78–7 rout of Swansea (5.11.94). Had set a South African record for tries scored in a season with 33 in the 1992 campaign as Transvaal marched to the Currie Cup final. Picked up his first two caps playing in the new Republic's comeback defeats by New Zealand (24–27, Johannesburg, 15.8.92) and

Australia (3–26, Cape Town, 22.8.92). Toured to France and England in '92, failing to make the Test side but turning out against the Midlands and North divisions.

Herbert, D. **Australia**

Full Name: Daniel Herbert
State: Queensland
Club: GPS (Brisbane)
Position: Centre
Height: 6ft 2in (1.87m)
Weight: 15st 7lb (94kg)
Occupation: Student
Born: 6.2.74
Family: Single
Family links with rugby: Brother Anthony played 10 times for Australia (1987-93)
International debut: Australia 32, Ireland 18, 1994
Notable landmarks in rugby career: Outstanding debut against Ireland (Sydney, 11.6.94) saw Danny claim try within three minutes of the start of his international career as the Wallabies ran out 32–18 winners. Added a second try on his second appearance, in the 23–20 defeat of Italy in Brisbane the following weekend. But that was where his scoring exploits ended as in his last

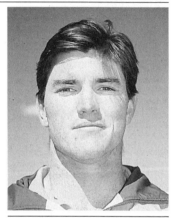

Australia (1994)

	Caps	Pts
Last Season	8 caps	10 pts
Career	8 caps	10 pts

Caps (8): **1994** I(2), It(1,2), WS(R) **1995** Arg(1,2) wc-SA,R
Points (10 – 2t): **1994** I(2:1t), It(1:1t)

six outings he has failed to cross the try-line. Proved a valuable deputy for Tim Horan while the latter battled to recover from an horrific knee injury. Partnered fellow Queenslander Jason Little in Wallaby midfield in both pre-World Cup Tests versus Argentina and got the nod ahead of Horan in the World Cup opener against South Africa (Cape Town, 25.5.95). Defeat in that game for the defending champions hastened Horan's return and Danny's only other outing thereafter in the new Republic came in the 42–3 win over Romania (Stellenbosch, 3.6.95).

Hill, S. D. Wales

Full Name: Simon David Hill
Club: Cardiff
Position: Wing
Height: 5ft 11in (1.81m)
Weight: 13st 2lb (83kg)
Occupation: Dental student, Cardiff Medical College
Born: Barry, South Glamorgan, 27.5.68
Family: Single
Former club: Headingley
International debut: Zimbabwe 14, Wales 35, 1993
Five Nations' debut: Ireland 15, Wales 17, 1994
Best moment in rugby: Scoring try on Wales debut
Notable landmarks in rugby career: Turned out on either wing for Wales last season, appearing first on the left in the 12–20 loss to South Africa (Cardiff, 26.11.94), then the right in the 9–21 defeat by France (Paris, 21.1.95). Also helped Cardiff win Heineken league title for first time.

Wales (1993)

Last Season	2 caps	0 pts
Career	7 caps	10 pts

Caps (7): **1993** Z(1,2), Na **1994** I(R), W, SA **1995** F
Points (10 – 2t): **1993** Z(1:1t), Na(1t)

Had been a late call-up into the Wales squad for the 1993 summer tour to Zimbabwe and Namibia but took his opportunity with both hands; playing in all six matches including the three internationals against Zimbabwe (two) and Namibia. To add to his joy, he bagged a try on his Test debut, in Bulawayo on 22 May, and added another in the 38–23 win over Namibia, in Windhoek on 5 June. Wales won all six matches with Simon also turning out against Zimbabwe B (try in 64–13 win, Harare, 25 May), Namibia B (won 47–10, Windhoek, 2 June) and the South African Barbarians (39th minute replacement for Wayne Proctor in 56-17 triumph). Played in two legs of Wales' 1994 Five Nations triumph, coming on as a 44th minute replacement for Proctor in Dublin and playing throughout famous 24–15 defeat of France in Cardiff (19.2.94). Previously represented Glamorgan and Headingley (while studying in Leeds). Included in Wales' preliminary 1991 World Cup squad. Bench reserve for Wales B during 34–12 win over Netherlands in Leiden (2.12.90). Finished 1993/94 season on a high after helping Cardiff beat Llanelli in Swalec Cup final
Touchlines: Lifeguards in summer.

Hilton, D. I. W.   Scotland

Full Name: David Ivor Walter Hilton
Club: Bath
Position: Loosehead prop
Height: 5ft 10in
Weight: 16st 4lb
Occupation: Butcher, Broadway Butchers (Bristol)
Born: Bristol, 3.4.70
International debut: Scotland 22, Canada 6, 1995
Five Nations debut: Scotland 26, Ireland 13, 1995
Notable landmarks in rugby career: A part of Scotland's new wave, having been introduced to the national side at a time of some despair. Scotland had failed to win a match in nine attempts when the Bristol butcher was called into the line-up to replace injured fellow West Countryman Alan Sharp against Canada at a frozen Murrayfield (21.1.95). The Canucks were beaten 22–6 and Scotland went

Scotland (1995)

Last Season	9 caps	5 pts
Career	9 caps	5 pts

Caps (9): **1995** C, I, F(a), W, E, R wc-T,F(b), NZ
Points (5 – 1t): **1995** W(1t)

onto enjoy a remarkable 1995, coming within 80 minutes of the Grand Slam and reaching the World Cup quarter-finals where they became the first side ever to score 30 points against New Zealand, and lose (Pretoria, 11.6.95). A member of the Scotland A side that beat South Africa and Italy in the autumn of 1994, Dave helped the Scottish Exiles win the Inter-District Championship in January 1995 but enjoyed his best moment when scoring a try in the 26–13 defeat of Wales (Edinburgh, 4.3.95). Also helped Bath win successive Pilkington Cups in 1994 (against Leicester) and 1995 (against Wasps). Qualifies for Scotland by virtue of paternal grandparent, Walter, who hails from Edinburgh.

Hogan, N. A.   Ireland

Full Name: Niall Andrew Hogan
Club: Terenure College
Position: Scrum-half
Height: 5ft 8in
Weight: 11st
Occupation: Doctor
Born: Dublin, 20.4.71
Family: Single
International debut: Ireland 8, England 20, 1995
Five Nations' debut: As above
Notable landmarks in rugby career: Pound for pound one of the toughest competitors around and perceived as a future Ireland captain. Indeed, took the place of skipper Michael Bradley in 1995, first when the latter was struck with a family tragedy, then purely professionally as Irish bosses looked for new blood to end a winless Five Nations campaign. The tactic worked as Ireland beat Wales 16–12 in Cardiff (18.3.95) and left the Wooden Spoon behind in the

Ireland (1995)

Last Season	5 caps	5 pts
Career	5 caps	5 pts

Caps (5): **1995** E, W(a) wc-J, W(b), F(b)
Points (5 – 1t): **1995** wc-J(1t)

Principality. Added his third cap in South Africa in the World Cup defeat of Japan, days before enjoying a wonderful weekend: receiving his doctorate in a ceremony at Ireland's Johannesburg hotel on the Saturday, booking a quarter-final place at the expense of the hapless Welsh on the Sunday. Tournament ended in slight disappointment for the Terenure terror as France rolled over the Irish in a one-sided quarter-final under the Durban sun. Captained Leinster at Schools, U-19 and U-20 levels and also represented Irish Colleges and Irish Students. Broke into Ireland U-21 team in 1990/91 on tour to Netherlands and was appointed captain in 1991/92 for the games against Wales (lost 15–22) and England (won 19–10).
Touchlines: Golf.

Horan, T. J.   Australia

Full Name: Timothy (Tim) James
Horan
State: Queensland
Club: Southern Districts
Position: Centre, five-eighth
Height: 6ft (1.83m)
Weight: 14st 8lb (88kg)
Occupation: Commercial leasing
consultant
Born: 15.5.70
Family: Katrina (wife), Lucy
(daughter)
Former clubs: None. Souths since
1988
International debut: New Zealand
24, Australia 12, 1989
Best moment in rugby: Winning
1991 World Cup
Worst moment in rugby: Losing to
New Zealand at Eden Park in second
Test of 1991 Bledisloe Cup series
Most embarrassing moment:
Answering just one question on *Sale
of the Century*
Most respected opponent: Jerry
Guscott (Bath & England)
Serious injuries: Knee (1990)
Suggestions to improve rugby:
Improve standards of refereeing
Notable landmarks in rugby career:
Made a stupendous recovery from
knee reconstruction after potentially
career-ending injury playing for

Australia (1989)

Last Season	3 caps	0 pts
Career	36 caps	70 pts

Caps (36): **1989** NZ, F(1,2) **1990** F(1),
NZ(1,2,3) **1991** W(a), E(a),
NZ(a1,a2). wc-Arg, WS, W(b), I,
NZ(b), E(b) **1992** S(1,2),
NZ(1,2,3), SA, I, W **1993** T, NZ,
SA(1,2,3), C, F(1,2) **1995** wc-C, R,
E

Points (70 – 16t): F(1:2t) **1990** NZ(2:1t)
1991 W(a:1t). wc-Arg(2t),
W(b:1t), NZ(b:1t) **1992** S(2:2t),
NZ(1:1t), I(1t) **1993** NZ(1t),
SA(2:1t), SA(3:1t), C(1t)

Queensland in 1994 Super-10 final against Transvaal and regained his midfield
position in last summer's World Cup, playing against Canada, Romania and
England. In his two-year absence Danny Herbert, Richard Toombs and Pat
Howard had vied for the vacant berth next to Queensland team mate and long-
term midfield foil Jason Little. Tim's injury had come as a cruel blow after
establishing himself as the world's premier centre with quite outstanding
campaigns for 1992–93. Tim has proved a highly capable performer since being
given his debut as a teenager against the All Blacks in 1989 – two years after
helping Australia Under-17s beat their New Zealand counterparts 16–3. A
World Cup winner in 1991 and an everpresent since. His glorious '92 included

tries in the 16–15 first Test win over New Zealand, and another in the 42–17 defeat of Ireland. Prior to those, he had represented the World XV against New Zealand in the first and third Tests of the '92 Centenary Series.
Touchlines: Golf and family.

Howard, P. Australia

Full Name: Patrick William Howard
Club: Queensland University
State: Queensland
Position: Outside-half, five-eighth, inside-centre
Height: 5ft 10in (1.78m)
Weight: 14st 6lb (87kg)
Occupation: Pharmacy Student
Born: 14.11.73
Family: Single
Family links with rugby: Father (Jake) coached Irish club Wanderers
International debut: New Zealand 25, Australia 10, 1993
Best moment in rugby: Debut Test against All Blacks (1993)
Worst moment in rugby: Getting dropped after above match
Most respected opponent: Grant Fox (ex-Auckland & New Zealand)
Suggestions to improve rugby: Change the new rules back to the old rules so that there are less back rowers clogging the backline

Australia (1993)		
Last Season	3 caps	0 pts
Career	3 caps	0 pts

Caps (3): 1993 NZ 1994 WS,NZ
Points (5 – 1t): 1994 WS(1t)

Notable landmarks in rugby career: Delighted Dublin when replacing the injured Scott Hastings 47 minutes into the Barbarians' famous 23–15 defeat of the touring Springboks (3.12.94). His free-running and eye for an opening tormented the Boks and it was his interception that presented local hero Simon Geoghegan with his match-winning try. Such talent earned Pat a place in the Wallaby midfield, during Tim Horan's enforced absence, and he marked his return – a year after his debut – with a try in the extraordinary 73–3 rout of Western Samoa (Sydney, 6.8.94). Retained his place in the thrilling 20–16 Bledisloe Cup victory over New Zealand (Sydney, 17.8.94) but come 1995 he had been usurped by Queenslander Daniel Herbert alongside Jason Little. Had made his debut as a late call-up in the 1993 Bledisloe Cup game against New Zealand in Dunedin (17.7.93). Captain Michael Lynagh withdrew at the 11th hour through illness and young Pat was drafted in at fly-half. But New Zealand

won 25–10 and the No.10 jersey was taken over by New South Wales' Scott Bowen. Nonetheless, Pat kept himself busy. He represented Queensland in their 17–3 defeat by the touring Springboks at Ballymore (8.8.93) and was then invited on Australia's Autumn tour of North America and France. His first outing came as a centre in the non-cap Test against the United States Eagles and he bagged a try in Australia's 26–22 win, played in severe heat at Riverside, California (2.10.93). From there he made four appearances in France
Touchlines: Travelling and surfing.

Hueber, A. France

Full Name: Aubin Hueber
Club: Toulon
Position: Scrum-half
Height: 5ft 8in (1.73m)
Weight: 12st 12lb (77kg)
Occupation: PR officer, Var Regional Council
Born: Tarbes, 5.4.67
Family: Married with a child
International debut: Australia 19, France 28, 1990
Five Nations' debut: France 44, Ireland 12, 1992
Notable landmarks in rugby career: Driven to tears when made a scapegoat for France's ineffectual back line display against Ireland (Durban 10.6.95) in last summer's World Cup quarter-final. Fabien Galthie (who had pipped him to 1991 World Cup selection), only called into the squad as an emergency replacement after Guy Accoceberry broke his arm, got the nod from coach Pierre Berbizier and Aubin was furious. He (rightly, it has to be said) felt half-back partner Christophe Deylaud was the main offender against the Irish, though,

France (1990)

Last Season	3 caps	5 pts
Career	22 caps	18 pts

Caps (22): **1990** A(3), NZ(1) **1991** US(2) **1992** I **1992** Arg(a1,a2), SA(1,2), Arg(b) **1993** E, S, I, W, R(a), SA(1,2), R(b), A(1,2) **1995** wc-T, S(b:R), I(b)

Points (18 – 3t,1dg): **1992** Arg(a2:1t,1dg) **1993** A(2:1t) **1995** wc-T(1t)

Aubin would surely admit to not being anywhere near his best either. Had played second fiddle to Accoceberry throughout 1994 before coming in for the World Cup opener against Tonga (Pretoria, 26.5.95) and responding with a try in the 38-10 win. Came on as a 33rd minute replacement against Scotland after

Accoceberry had suffered his tournament-ending injury. Damaged knee ligaments had restricted Aubin to Test appearances in only the first part of 1993/94 season. He played six times before the turn of the year (Romania twice, South Africa twice and Australia twice) and not all after it. The highlight of his season was the try he scored in France's shock 16–13 defeat of the world champion Wallabies, in Bordeaux (30.10.93). Had been France's first-choice scrum-half since making his Five Nations' debut in 44–12 rout of Ireland in Paris (21.3.92). Although rested for subsequent engagement against Romania at Le Havre, he played the next nine games – three against Argentina (two on tour in July 1992), two against South Africa and all four in France's triumphant 1993 Five Nations' campaign. Had succeeded Henri Sanz as France B scrum-half at Brecon (29.10.88) when Wales B were defeated 18-12. Again partnered Thierry Lacroix at half-back when the second string were undone 14–12 by Scotland B at Melrose (18.2.89), and was captain when Wales B were beaten 28–15 in La Teste (12.11.89). A year earlier he had appeared at Auch in a non-cap match against Ireland and moved a step nearer cap-recognition when selected to represent the Rest of the Europe against the Four Home Unions (lost 43–18) at Twickenham. He again understudied Sanz when France toured Australia in 1990 but was given his long-awaited chance in the third Test.

Hull, P. A.   England

Full Name: Paul Anthony Hull
Club: Bristol
Position: Fullback, outside-half, wing, centre
Height: 5ft 10in (1.78m)
Weight: 11st 11lb (70kg)
Occupation: RAF physical training instructor
Born: London, 17.5.68
Former club: Milton Keynes
International debut: South Africa 15, England 32, 1994
Five Nations debut: None
Best moment in rugby: Meeting president Nelson Mandela at Ellis Park prior to my debut and then beating South Africa

Worst moment in rugby: Missing 1988 John Player Cup final epic between Harlequins and Bristol through injury
Serious injuries: Torn ankle ligaments
Advice for International Board: Make game more professional
Notable landmarks in rugby career: Hard to think of a less fortunate

255

international player in 1994/94. Paul had been arguably England's star player on the 1994 tour to South Africa, proving his mettle both in attack and defence, yet when he was injured 27 minutes into England's second autumn engagement, against

England (1994)
| Last Season | 2 caps | 0 pts |
| Career | 4 caps | 0 pts |

Caps (4): **1994** SA(1,2),R,C
Points Nil

Canada (Twickenham 10.12.94), Mike Catt came on, scored two tries and retained the No 15 jersey thereafter. Paul was even overlooked for a return to South Africa for last summer's World Cup, his consolation being the captaincy of England's A tour to Australia and Fiji, during which he led the side to a notable 27–19 win over an Australia XV (Brisbane, 7.6.95). Had been selected ahead of Jonathan Callard for the 1994 visit to the new Republic after incumbent Ian Hunter withdrew from original selection, and such swift progress did he make that coach Jack Rowell deployed him in the first Test, a record-breaking occasion in Pretoria on 4 June 1994. He proved utterly dependable on his debut – impressing with his strategic positioning and his confidence under the high ball – and it was no surprise he was retained for the second Test, where his defence was, if possible, even better. It was easy to forget that Paul had been waiting patiently in the wings for his chance for four years, having been taken to Argentina with England's senior party back in 1990 and given outings against Buenos Aires, Cuyo and Cordoba. His England A debut had come the same year, in the 20–12 home loss to Fiji. Paul was also member of England's original Under-21 side which panned their Romanian counterparts 54–13 in Bucharest (13.5.89). Paul's stock rose in 1993 with no less than four impressive showings against the touring All Blacks. On tour in South Africa he also turned out against Orange Free State, Western Transvaal, Transvaal and Eastern Province, scoring two tries in the latter contest, since dubbed 'the Battle of Port Elizabeth'
Touchlines: Soul music, nightlife.

Ieremia, A.   New Zealand

Full Name: Alama Ieremia
Province: Wellington
Position: Centre
Height: 6ft 1in (1.86m)
Weight: 14st 1lb (85kg)
Occupation: Bank officer, National
Bank of New Zealand
Born: 27.10.70
Family: Single
International debut: New Zealand
22, South Africa 14, 1994
Notable landmarks in rugby career:
A member of the 1993 Western
Samoan side which wreaked havoc
in New Zealand, winning seven of its
nine matches and giving the All
Blacks much food for thought in a
13–35 Test loss (Auckland, 31.7.93),
Alama threw his hand in with the
Kiwis soon after and was rewarded
with a place in the centres, alongside
another ex-Samoan, Frank Bunce, in
the 1994 series defeat of South
Africa. His debut came in Dunedin
(9.7.94) and he held his place for the

New Zealand (1994)

Last Season	4 caps	5 pts
Career	4 caps	5 pts

Caps (4): **1994** SA(1,2,3) **1995** wc-J
Points (5 – 1t): **1995** wc-J(1t)

13–9 second Test win in Wellington, his place of residence (23.7.94), and the
18–18 third Test draw at Eden Park, Auckland (6.8.94). Walter Little's return
to prominence relegated Alama to the replacements' bench thereafter, though
he did get one outing during last summer's World Cup – and what a day it
proved to be. Japan were jettisoned 145–17 (Bloemfontein, 4.6.95) and Alama
weighed in with one of the 21 tries. Likens himself to a snake …'slippery, sly
and shy, but lethal.'

Jardine, I. C. — Scotland

Full Name: Ian Carrick Jardine
Club: Stirling County
Position: Centre
Height: 6ft 1in (1.85m)
Weight: 13st 7lb (81kg)
Occupation: Secondary maths teacher, Larbert HS
Born: Dunfermline, 20.10.64
Family: Ann (wife), Megan (daughter)
Family links with rugby: Four brothers (Stephen, Neil, Colin and Aitken) play at Stirling
International debut: Scotland 15, New Zealand 51, 1993
Five Nations debut: Wales 29, Scotland 6, 1994
Worst moment in rugby: Scotland's record defeat coinciding with my debut
Most embarrassing moment: Accidentally drinking my wife's contact lenses, which she had left in a glass of water by our bed in hotel room, after a Scotland B game when I was worse for wear

Scotland (1993)		
Last Season	6 caps	0 pts
Career	11 caps	0 pts

Caps (11): 1993 NZ 1994 W, E(R), Arg(1,2) 1995 C, I, F(a) wc-T, F(b:R), NZ(R)
Points Nil

Suggestions to improve rugby: Revise maul law because it encourages forwards to hang off scrums, so cluttering midfield
Notable landmarks in rugby career: Promoted to first-choice centre after Scotland's hammering by South Africa and played a key role in the nation's revival, until fracturing his cheekbone in the final seconds of France's historic home burial in Parc des Princes (18.2.95). Returned in time for Scotland's altitude-training trip to Spain, coming on as a 65th minute replacement in the 62–7 non-cap defeat of the Spaniards (6.5.95) and thereafter appearing in all but one of the Scots' World Cup matches. Helped Stirling win Scottish championship for first time in their history in 1994/95. Had seemingly waited years for his Test chance only to get the call for Scotland's record defeat (51–15 vs New Zealand). Retained place for 1994 Five Nations opener against Wales but that result was little better and he was relegated back onto bench to accomodate Doug Wyllie's return. Picked up third cap as a 71st minute replacement for Scott Hastings against England (5.2.94). Replacement for Scotland U-21s (1986) and Scotland B in Italy (1988/89). Made B debut in 22–22 draw with Ireland B (9.12.89) and, after being only bench reserve in

0–16 loss to Ireland B (22.12.90), made A-team's No.12 jersey his own in 1992/93, turning out against Ireland B at Murrayfield (lost 19–29, 28.12.91) and in Albi against France B (3.2.92) where he scored try in 18–27 defeat. Helped Glasgow win 1989/90 Inter-District Championship. Toured with Scotland to Canada, the United States (1991) and Argentina (1994).
Touchlines: Hill walking, cycling.

Jenkins, G. R.   **Wales**

Full Name: Garin Richard Jenkins
Club: Swansea
Position: Hooker
Height: 5ft 10in (1.78m)
Weight: 15st 2lb (96kg)
Occupation: Schools liason officer, Swansea RFC
Born: Ynysybwl, 18.8.67
Family: Helen (wife)
Family links with rugby: Father's uncle played for Wales. Mother's cousin propped for Wales and Lions
Former clubs: Ynysybwl, Pontypridd, King Country (NZ), Pontypool
Best moments in rugby: Scoring try for Swansea in win over 1992 Wallabies
Other sporting achievements: Marbles champion at Treobart Junior School
Notable landmarks in rugby career: Lost Wales No2 jersey for first time in three seasons when displaced by Jonathan Humphreys during last summer's World Cup. Having been everpresent through Wales' dismal Five Nations campaign, Garin

Wales (1991)

Last Season	10 caps	0 pts
Career	27 caps	5 pts

Caps (27): **1991** F(b) wc-WS(R), Arg, A(b) **1992** I, F, E, S, A **1993** C **1994** S, I, F, E. wc(q)-P, Sp. C, T, WS wc(q)-R, It. SA **1995** F, E, S, I(a) wc-J
Points (5 – 1t): **1994** wc(q)-Sp(1t)

played the World Cup opener versus Japan (won 57–10, Bloemfontein, 27.5.95) but then sat out the defeats by New Zealand and Ireland. It was a far cry from the previous year when, for many, he had been the heart and soul of Wales' Five Nations title run. He celebrated his maiden Test try in 54–0 World Cup qualifying win against Spain (Madrid, 21.5.94). Had lost place in Welsh side during 1992/93 after performing hooking duties in 43–12 win over Italy XV at Cardiff (7.10.92) and 6–23 loss to Australia (21.11.92) also in National

Stadium. Between two outings he helped Swansea to a famous win over Wallabies at St Helens, scoring one of All Whites' two tries in 21–6 victory (4.11.92). But come the 1993 Five Nations' Championship Pontypool's Nigel Meek earned vote, with Llanelli's Andrew Lamerton his bench deputy. Garin, a former coal miner, represented Boys Clubs of Wales U-18s and Glamorgan U-23s. He started his career with Ynysybwl, the birthplace of ex-national coach Alan Davies, and in 1990 toured Kenya with Pontypool, having represented Pooler against 1989 All Blacks. Broke into Wales team at the start of 1991/92 season when Davies was appointed coach following catastrophic 1991 Australia tour, and played in all eight games spanning the French 'floodlit' game, the 1991 World Cup and 1992 Five Nations' Championship (pack leader). Helped Swansea win 1991/92 and 1993/94 Heineken League title and 1995 SWALEC Cup.

Touchlines: Soccer, cricket, weightlifting.

Jenkins, N. R. Wales

Full Name: Neil Roger Jenkins
Club: Pontypridd
Position: Fly-half
Height: 5ft 10in (1.78m)
Weight: 13st 5lb (80kg)
Occupation: PR consultant, Just Rentals Ltd
Born: Church Village, Pontypridd, 8.7.71
Family: Single
International debut: Wales 6, England 25, 1991
Five Nations' debut: As above
Best moment in rugby: Winning 1994 Five Nations title
Worst moment in rugby: Being sent-off in 39th minute of 6–27 1991/92 Schweppes Cup semi-final against Llanelli at Arms Park

Most respected opponents: Philippe Sella (Agen & France)
Notable landmarks in rugby career: Another staggering year of points scoring saw Neil succeed Paul Thorburn (304 in 37 matches, 1985-91) as Wales' record points scorer. Neil ended the season with 95 points more than Thorburn, having still played one less Test. How sad that apart from retaining his Welsh Player of the Year title, he had little else to show for his 153-point campaign. A year after claiming the Five Nations title Wales were whitewashed and they fared little better at the World Cup, failing to reach the knockout stages. Still,

he contributed 38 of Wales' 43 Five Nations points, and 41 of the 99 scored in South Africa. On the home front Neil's Pontypridd finished runners-up in both league and cup with him breaking all club scoring records. Had been central to Wales' 1994 championship win. Buoyed by his world record haul of eight penalty goals in 24–26 defeat by Canada (Cardiff, 10.11.93), Neil bagged 14 points against Scotland, all 17 against Ireland, 14 against France and three against England for a 48-point haul. Perhaps more significantly was that he missed hardly any. An ever-present for Wales in last five Five Nations' campaigns yet, remarkably, until 1993/94 had appeared in no other Tests (including 1991 World Cup). Represented Wales A team in 21–13

Wales (1991)		
Last Season	12 caps	153 pts
Career	36 caps	399 pts

Caps (36): **1991** E, S, I, F **1992** I, F, E, S **1993** E, S, I, F, Z(1,2), Na, J, C **1994** S, I, F, E. wc(q)-P, Sp. C, T, WS. wc(q)-R, It. SA **1995** F, E, S, I(a) wc-J, NZ, I(b)

Points (399 – 4t,46c,93p,3dg): **1991** E(1p), I(1t,1dg) **1992** I(3p), F(3p), S(1c,3p) **1993** E(1c,1p), I(3p), F(1c,1p), Z(1:3c,2p), Z(2:1t,3c,2p), Na(2c,3p), J(1t,5c), C(8p) **1994** S(1c,4p), I(1t,4p), F(1c,4p), E(1p). wc(q)-P(11c), Sp(5c,3p). C(3c,4p), T(6p), WS(3p). wc(q)-R(1c,3p), It(7p,1dg). SA(4p) **1995** F(3p), E(3p), S(1c,2p), I(a:4p) wc-J(5c,4p), NZ(2p,1dg), I(b:2c,2p)

win over North of England at Pontypool (14.10.92) in which he contributed 11 points (1c,3p) and again last season at centre in 61–5 defeat of Japan at Llanelli (claiming 19 points: 2t,3c,1p). Played for East Wales Under-11s v West Wales, East Glamorgan and Wales Youth (1989/90). Having broken into Wales U-21s into 1990/91 – playing against New Zealand Under-21 XV (14pts:4c,2p) and Scotland U-21 (15pts: 1t,1c,3p) – added a second cap and ten points in 22–15 win over Ireland U-21 in 1991/92 (2c,2p). Abandoned plans to play for Northern Transvaal last summer due to 'exhaustion'.
Touchlines: Golf

Ian Jardine powers his way through the French defence during Scotland's historic win at the Parc des Princes.

John, S. C.   Wales

Full Name: Spencer Courtney John
Club: Llanelli
Position: Tighthead Prop
Height: 6ft 1in (1.85m)
Weight: 17st (103kg)
Occupation: Mechanical engineer in family firm
Born: 19.10.73
International debut: Scotland 26, Wales 13, 1995
Five Nations debut: As above
Notable landmarks in rugby career: Handed Wales No3 jersey after Neath incumbent John Davies was sent-off for kicking in the 9–23 loss to England (Cardiff, 18.2.95) and subsequently obliged to serve a 60-day suspension. His absence allowed the former Wales under-18 (9 caps), under-19 (1 cap) and under-21 (5 caps) player to make his full debut against Scotland (Murrayfield, 4.3.95), a match which ended in 13–26 defeat. His second appearance (Cardiff, 18.3.95)

Wales (1995)		
Last Season	2 caps	0 pts
Career	2 caps	0 pts

Caps (2): 1995 S,I(a)
Points Nil

proved equally fruitless with Ireland winning the Wooden Spoon decider 16–12, so condemning Wales to only their second ever Five Nations whitewash. Spencer survived the changing of the guard, with Alex Evans succeeding Alan Davies as coach, but failed to keep his place in South Africa where Davies returned for all three World Cup-ties. An occasional No8 at Neath College, Spencer represented Llanelli in the Scarlets' 12–30 loss to the touring Springboks (Stradey Park, 29.10.94) only ten days after his 21st birthday.

Johns, P. S.   Ireland

Full Name: Patrick Stephen Johns
Club: Dungannon
Position: Lock, No 8
Height: 6ft 6in (1.98m)
Weight: 16st 11lb (102kg)
Occupation: Dentist
Born: Portadown, 19.2.68
Family: Kirsty (wife)
Former clubs: Newcastle Univ, Gosforth, Dublin Univ
International debut: Ireland 20, Argentina 18, 1990
Five Nations' debut: Scotland 15, Ireland 3, 1993
Worst moment in rugby: Waiting two years for second cap
Serious injuries: Neck injury, broken wrist, knee cartilage (1992), two operations (1993/94) on left knee
Notable landmarks in rugby career: Saved his best performance of 1994/95 for the match which really mattered. Paddy was a revelation in the 24–23 defeat of Wales (Johannesburg, 4.6.95), a result which booked Ireland's place in the World Cup quarter-finals and sent Wales home to an uncertain future.

Ireland (1990)

Last Season	9 caps	0 pts
Career	24 caps	0 pts

Caps (24): **1990** Arg **1992** NZ(1,2), A **1993** S, F, W, E, R **1994** F, W, E, S, A(1,2), US **1995** E, S, W(a), It wc-NZ, J, W(b), F(b)
Points Nil

Indeed, Paddy appeared in all four of Ireland's matches in South Africa including the last-eight tie against France, an opponent whom he had missed in the 1995 Five Nations campaign after contracting appendicitis on the eve of combat. Only switched from lock to No 8 midway through 1993/94 season as Ireland moved to change their fortunes for the better, after a 35–15 loss in Paris where Paddy sustained an eye injury which required an operation and forced him to take a week off work. Impressed in his new position as England were beaten at Twickenham and Scotland held at Lansdowne Road. Along with Nick Popplewell has been an ever-present in Irish side for past two seasons (from 1992 New Zealand tour through to 1994 Australia tour). Represented Ulster against 1989 All Blacks (lost 3–21, Ravenhill 21.11.89) and Ireland Schools in 1986, against Japan (twice), Australia, England and Wales. Toured Canada with Dungannon (1989). Played for Ireland at Under-21 and Under-25 level (twice) in 1988/89 season. Also turned out for Irish Students and Universities while at Dublin University. Represented Ireland B in 22–22 draw with Scotland B at Murrayfield (9.12.89)

and twice against England B – in 24–10 win at Old Belvedere (scoring try, 1.3.91) and at Richmond (No.8 in 15–47 loss, Richmond 31.1.92). First capped by Ireland against touring Argentina Pumas (27.20.90)
Touchlines: Painting, making wine.

Johnson, G. K. South Africa

Full Name: Gavin Keith Johnson
Province: Transvaal
Club: Pirates
Position: Fullback
Height: 6ft 1in (1.85m)
Weight: 14st 12lb (90kg)
Occupation: Aircraft parts supplier
Born: Louis Trichardt, 17.10.66
Family: Single
International debut: Argentina 23, South Africa 52, 1993
Notable landmarks in rugby career: Unsung Springbok hero, averaging over 12 points per game for the world champions. Can play equally well in any back position. Made a record-equalling international debut when scoring 22 points in the Springboks' second Test victory over Argentina (Buenos Aires, 13.11.93). Gavin (nicknamed 'Magic') plundered a try, four conversions and three penalty goals to equal Gerald Bosch's South African single-Test points-scoring record. Moreover, he was within one point of equalling the then world record for points scored on a Test debut (since raised to 45 by All Black

South Africa (1993)

Last Season	6 caps	22 pts
Career	7 caps	86 pts

Caps (7): **1993** Arg(2) **1994** NZ(3), Arg(1) **1995** WS(a) wc-R, C, WS(b)
Points (86 – 5t,14c,11p): **1993** Arg (2:1t,4c,3p) **1994** NZ(3:1t,1c,2p) **1995** WS(a:3t,5c,1p) wc-R(1c,3p), WS(b:3c,2p)

Simon Culhane in 145–17 defeat of Japan, Bloemfontein 4.6.95). Gavin had only journeyed to South America as a late call-up replacing the injured Chris Dirks, who broke his hand in the 'battle of Tucuman' (Gavin was on tour in the UK with the SA Barbarians at the time). From there it was on to Buenos Aires and his tour de force which silenced 30,000 home hopefuls. Recalled to Bok side for third Test (dead rubber) versus New Zealand (Auckland, 6.8.94) and claimed 13 points in an 18–18 draw. But his most prolific day came at his home Ellis Park where he plundered 28 points (3t,5c,1p) in the 60–8 defeat of Western

Samoa. Collected 12 points versus the same opposition at the same JoBurg venue (10.6.95), in the quarter-finals of a triumphant World Cup campaign in which he also bagged 11 against Romania (Cape Town, 30.5.95). Unused replacement in World Cup final win over Kiwis (JoBurg, 24.6.95).

Johnson, M. O.   England

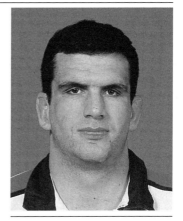

Full Name: Martin Osborne Johnson
Club: Leicester
Position: Lock
Height: 6ft 7in (2.01m)
Weight: 17st 12lb (109kg)
Occupation: Bank officer, Midland Bank (Market Harborough)
Born: Solihull, 9.3.70
Family: Single
Former clubs: Wigston, College Old Boys (NZ)
International debut: England 16, France 15, 1993
Five Nations' debut: As above
Suggestions to improve rugby: Beware not to alter too much of the game. If we try to make too many changes, in an attempt to pander to television etc, we stand the chance of changing the face of the game, and that would be diastrous
Notable landmarks in rugby career: A rock in the England scrum, Martin played in all 12 of his country's matches in 1994/95, partnering Martin Bayfield in the engine room in all but the 44–22 defeat of

England (1993)		
Last Season	12 caps	0 pts
Career	18 caps	0 pts
Lions 1993	2 Tests	0 pts

Caps (18): **1993** F. Lions-NZ(2,3). NZ **1994** S, I, F, W, R, C **1995** I, F(a), W, S wc-Arg, It, WS, A, NZ, F(b)

Points Nil

Western Samoa, when Richard West deputised for Bayfs. Spent 18 months playing out in New Zealand for College Old Boys (1990-91) and for King Country in Division Two of inter-Provincial Championship, during which time he also represented NZ Colts against Australia counterparts on a two-week tour. Team mates included All Blacks Va'aiga Tuigamala, John Timu and Blair Larsen. Planned to remain only 12 months but niggling shoulder complaint prolonged his stay. Had previously represented England Schools (1987-88) and 1989 England Colts (along with Damien Hopley and Steve Ojomoh) prior to heading Down Under. On his return played for England U-21 – partnering Gloucester's David Sims in 94–0 rout of Belgium (1.9.91), before turning out, again alongside Sims, in England B's away wins against France B (15.2.92) and Italy B (7.3.92). But it was in 1992/93 season that he really hit the big-time. Expecting to play for England A against France A at Leicester (15.1.93), he was diverted to Twickenham where Wade Dooley had withdrawn from senior side with thigh injury. At less than 24 hours notice Martin was thrust into Five Nations' opener against France and acquitted himself well, especially in second half. Returned to A-team thereafter, playing in wins over Italy A, Spain and Ireland A before touring to Canada and playing in both internationals. So impressive was he that when Dooley returned home early from the clashing British Lions tour to New Zealand, Martin was quickly switched summoned and played in final two Tests. Ever-present in England side in 1993/94 but came home early from summer tour to South Africa after being concussed in 24–21 loss to Transvaal.

Joiner, C. A. Scotland

Full Name: Craig Alexander Joiner
Club: Melrose
Position: Wing
Height: 5ft 10in (1.78m)
Weight: 13st 12lb (83.5kg)
Occupation: Chemical engineering student
Former club: Eastern Suburbs (Sydney, Aus)
Born: Glasgow, 21.4.74
International debut: Argentina 16, Scotland 15, 1994
Five Nations debut: Scotland 26, Ireland 13, 1995
Notable landmarks in rugby career: Everpresent for Scotland in 1994/95, save for the autumn loss to South Africa (on the bench) which made it nine games without a win for the national side. Once Craig came aboard, the team won its next four games and went to Twickenham for the most improbable of Grand Slam deciders. The former Scottish Schools sprint and rugby star had made his debut on the dismal tour of Argentina in 1994, appearing in both Test defeats as well as three of the four other games. But it was his second coming that was of greater note. The son of a national triathlon specialist (Mike) and

Scotland (1994)

Last Season	10 caps	10 pts
Career	12 caps	10 pts

Caps (12): **1994** Arg(1,2) **1995** C, I, F(a), W, E, R wc-IC, T, F(b), NZ
Points (10 – 2t): **1995** I(1t), R(1t)

brother of a Scottish Schools hockey international (Kerry), Craig marked his Five Nations debut with a try in the 26–13 defeat of Ireland (Murrayfield, 4.2.95). He added a second on the same ground in the 49–16 win over Romania (22.4.95) and a fortnight later went try-mad in Spain, bagging one hat-trick against a Spanish XV and another in the 62–7 non-cap Test victory (Madrid, 6.5.95). All of which made his failure to score a try in four World Cup outings rather disappointing, though he did twice run rings around tournament star Jonah Lomu in Scotland's 30–48 quarter-final loss to the All Blacks (Pretoria, 11.6.95).

Jones, D.   Wales

Full Name: Derwyn Jones
Club: Cardiff
Position: Lock
Height: 6ft 10in (2.08m)
Weight: 18st 7lb (113kg)
Occupation: Police officer, Gwent Constabulary (Newport)
Born: Pontarddulais, 14.11.70
International debut: Wales 12, South Africa 20, 1994
Five Nations debut: France 21, Wales 9, 1995
Former clubs: Neath, Llanelli, Loughborough Univ, Northampton
Family links with rugby: Rhodri (brother) plays for Bridgend
Notable landmarks in rugby career: Shares with England lock Martin Bayfield the distinction of being the tallest player in international rugby and is also a police officer. Derwyn's route to the top took him via Neath, Llanelli and Loughborough University, with whom he won two UAU Cup victories, to Northampton

Wales (1994)		
Last Season	7 caps	0 pts
Career	7 caps	0 pts

Caps (7): **1994** SA **1995** F, E, S wc-J, NZ, I(b)

Points Nil

and then Cardiff, where he shared in the 1994 SWALEC Cup triumph and the 1994/95 Heineken League title. His Test debut came against South Africa (Cardiff, 26.11.94), tourists against whom he had already appeared for both Cardiff and Wales A. Derwyn also earned Wales A honours versus North of England, Ireland and France in 1993/94, having graduated from the Under-21 side with whom he turned out against Ireland (1991) and Scotland (1992). Dropped by the senior side for the 1995 Five Nations finale against Ireland

(Cardiff, 18.3.95), which Wales lost to complete only their second ever whitewash, he was restored by new coach (and Cardiff supremo) Alex Evans for Wales' truncated World Cup campaign, playing in the three games against Japan, New Zealand and Ireland.

Jones, I. D.   New Zealand

Full Name: Ian Donald Jones
Province: North Harbour
Club: Kamo
Position: Lock
Height: 6ft 6in (1.98m)
Weight: 16st 8lb (105kg)
Occupation: Sponsorship manager, All Black Club
Family: Single
Born: Whangarei, 17.4.67
International debut: New Zealand 31, Scotland 16, 1990
Notable landmarks in rugby career: Outstanding lineout display in last summer's World Cup final could not prevent New Zealand suffering a shock extra-time loss to the host nation Springboks (Johannesburg, 24.6.95). Nonetheless it completed a satisfying campaign for the Kamo Kid who had switched clubs from North Auckland to North Harbour after the 1993 autumn tour of England and Scotland. Represented Whangarei Schools (1979) and North Island Under-18s. The teenage Jones broke into both the Kamo first XV and North Auckland Colts side in 1986, and two years later made his bow for North

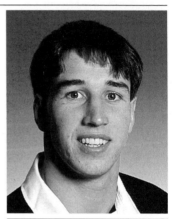

New Zealand (1990)
Last Season	10 caps	0 pts
Career	42 caps	12 pts

Caps (42): **1990** S(1,2), A(1,2,3), F(1,2) **1991** Arg(1,2), A(a1,a2). wc-E, US, It, C, A(b), S **1992** Wd(1,2,3), I(1,2), A(1,2,3), SA **1993** BL(1,2R,3), WS, S, E **1994** F(1,2), SA(1,3), A **1995** C wc-I, WS, E, SA
Points (12 – 3t): **1990** S(1:1t) **1991** A(1:1t) **1992** I(2:1t)

Auckland. Having marked his inaugural season of provincial rugby (1988) with four tries in eight matches, he played in the 1989 All Black Trials and was included in the squad for their tour to Wales and Ireland. Failed to make the Test side but did make a lot of friends and consequently returned to Britain the following year as an invited guest of the centenary Barbarians, playing against England, Wales and Argentina. By then he had made his Test debut against Scotland at Dunedin, following the retirement of Murray Pierce, and celebrated

with a try in the 31–16 win. Ian appeared in all seven All Black Tests in 1990 and toured Argentina the following year, starting both Tests. A try in the 21–12 Bledisloe Cup first Test defeat by Australia. An everpresent in the World Cup he maintained his place throughout the nine-Test schedule in 1992, claiming his third international try in the second Test romp over Ireland. Enjoyed an impressive tour of Australia and South Africa in 1993, edging highly-rated Wallaby John Eales in the lineout. Made ten appearances on the tour, including one (a formidable display) as captain against Orange Free State at Bloemfontein. Extended his unbroken run in the New Zealand side to 29 caps with appearances in each of the three Tests in the 2–1 series win over the '93 Lions (though he was a half-time replacement in the middle match).
Touchlines: Golf, water skiing, swimming.

Jones, M. N.   New Zealand

Full Name: Michael Niko Jones
Province: Auckland
Position: Flanker, No 8
Height: 5ft 11in (1.80m)
Weight: 15st 2lb (96kg)
Born: Auckland, 8.4.65
Former country: Western Samoa
International debut: Western Samoa 14, Wales 32, 1986
International debut (NZ): New Zealand 70, Italy 6, 1987
Serious injuries: Damaged knee (1989)
Notable landmarks in rugby career: Michael's 1994/95 campaign was restricted to two Test outings: the first as a 44th minute replacement for Blair Larsen in the 18–18 third

Test draw with South Africa (Auckland, 6.8.94), the second against Australia in the Wallabies' thrilling 20–16 Bledisloe Cup win (Sydney, 17.8.94). Missed World Cup selection because of religious beliefs which forbid him from playing on a Sunday. Injury had robbed him of a place on the 1993 All Blacks' tour to England and Scotland after he broke his jaw in three places in a training accident shortly prior to departure. Auckland-born Michael, one of the greatest wing forwards of all time, had first caught the eye playing in the colours of Western Samoa against Wales at Suva in 1986. By the following year New Zealand had snapped him up and he was included in their World Cup-winning squad, scoring a try against Italy at Eden Park 30 minutes into his debut and claiming the All Blacks' first, after 17 minutes of their 29–9 World Cup final win over

France on the same Auckland field. Had been marked out as something special ever since his provincial debut in 1985 when he scored three tries against South Canterbury. However, his climb to the very pinnacle of the world game was abruptly halted in 1989 when he sustained a serious knee injury playing against Argentina, having scored two tries in the 60–9 first Test defeat of the Pumas at Dunedin. The injury was described by his specialist as 'the equivalent of being hit by a truck doing 60mph'. As a consequence he missed the tour to Wales and Ireland but returned, 18 months later, for the 1990 tour of France, during which he crossed for a try in the 30–12 second Test victory in Paris. Made headlines on and off the paddock at the 1991 World Cup, scoring the only try of the tournament opener as England were beaten 18–12 in their own Twickenham backyard, before declining to play in the quarter-final and semi-final ties against Canada and Australia respectively as the games fell on a Sunday. This refusal to compromise his religious beliefs also led to him missing the Brisbane Test against Australia in the 1992 Bledisloe Cup series. Prior to that training injury in '93, Michael had helped the Blacks beat the Lions, over three matches, and the Aussies, to recapture the Bledisloe Cup.

Western Samoa (1986)		
Career	1 cap	0 pts
New Zealand (1987)		
Last Season	2 caps	0 pts
Career	35 caps	36 pts

Caps (35): **1987** wc-It,Fj,S,F. A **1988** W(1,2), A(2,3) **1989** F(1,2), Arg(1,2) **1990** F(1,2) **1991** Arg(1,2), A(1,2). wc-E, US, S **1992** Wd(1,3), I(2), A(1,3), SA **1993** BL(1,2,3), A, WS **1994** SA(3R), A

Points (36 – 9t): **1987** wc-It(1t), F(1t) **1988** W(2:1t), A(2:1t) **1989** Arg(1:2t) **1990** F(2:1t) **1991** Arg(2:1t). wc-E(1t)

Tony Underwood comes to Will Carling's assistance in Dublin.

Jones, R. N.   Wales

Full Name: Robert Nicholas Jones
Club: Swansea
Position: Scrum-half
Height: 5ft 8in (1.73m)
Weight: 11st 8lb (74kg)
Occupation: Development
consultant, Heath Wales Insurance
Brokers
Born: Trebanos, 10.11.65
Family: Megan (wife)
Family links with rugby: Father-in-
law (Clive Rowlands) played for
Wales and Lions. Brother (Rhodri)
plays for Neath
International debut: England 21,
Wales 18, 1986
Five Nations' debut: As above
Best moments in rugby: Captaining
Wales. 1989 Lions winning decisive
third Test against Australia
Worst moments in rugby:
Captaining Wales in 1990
whitewash – very, very despondent.
Defeat by New Zealand in 1987
World Cup
Most embarrassing moment:
Attempted dropped goal for Wales
against Ireland, hit ground before
ball and sent it three yards. Paul
Dean collected and initiated move
which led to Irish try
Other sporting achievements:
Cricket for Wales at three age-
groups

Wales (1986)			
Last Season		6 caps	5 pts
Career		54 caps	14 pts
Lions	1989	3 Tests	0 pts
	1993		

Caps (54): **1986** E, S, I, F, Fj, T, WS
1987 F, E(a), S, I(a), US wc-I(b), T,
E(b), NZ,A **1988** E, S, I, F, NZ(1),
WS, R **1989** I, F, E, NZ. Lions-
A(1,2,3) **1990** F, E, S, I **1991** E, S,
F(b) wc-WS, Arg, A(b) **1992** I, F, E,
S, A **1993** E, S, I **1994** I(R). wc(q)-P
1995 F, E, S, I(a) wc-NZ, I(b)
Points (14 – 3t): **1987** wc-E(1t) **1994**
wc(q)-P(1t) **1995** S(1t)

Suggestions to improve rugby: Reduce worth of penalty goal, rather than
increase value of try which has only served to make for a greater disparity
between the major and the developing nations, discouraging the latter.
Notable landmarks in rugby career: Succeeded the great Gareth Edwards as
Wales' most-capped scrum-half when winning his 54th cap in the disastrous
World Cup loss to Ireland (Johannesburg, 4.6.95). Both he and Ieuan Evans are
now within one cap of JPR Williams' 55-cap national best. Reclaimed the No 9
jersey from Rupert Moon in 1995 after carrying out bench duties in the three
autumn Tests. Claimed his third international try two minutes into Wales'

13–26 loss to Scotland (Murrayfield, 4.3.95). Had joined Western Province, in South Africa, in Spring of 1994 after a campaign spent watching Wales' Five Nations title triumph, save for nine minutes of action in Dublin as a replacement for Nigel Davies during Wales' 17–15 victory (5.2.94). Started first Test of season against Portugal (won 102–11) in World Cup qualifier in Lisbon (17.5.94). Celebrated with first try in seven years. Former captain of Swansea and Wales. Having been ommitted from final game of 1993 Championship in Paris, Robert's morale was boosted by Lions' selectors who drafted him for New Zealand tour, after his good friend Gary Armstrong, withdrew with a groin injury. Turned out against North Auckland, Canterbury, Southland, Taranaki, Hawke's Bay and Waikato. First played for Swansea whilst still at Cwmtawe School, having already played for West Wales U-11s and Wales 12-Group. Represented Welsh Schools for two seasons before graduating, by way of Wales B in 1985, to senior XV for 1986 Five Nations Championship. Enjoyed outstanding World Cup (1987) and equally magnificent tour, to Australia, with 1989 Lions. Partnered Jonathan Davies in 22 internationals before latter switched codes. Missed Welsh tour of Namibia in 1991 through injury but did go to Fiji, Tonga and Western Samoa (1986), New Zealand (1988) and Australia (1991)
Touchlines: Golf.

Joseph, J. W.   New Zealand

Full Name: Jamie Joseph
Province: Otago
Position: Flanker
Height: 6ft 5in (1.96m)
Weight: 16st 8lb (105kg)
Born: Blenheim, 21.11.69
Family links with rugby: Jim (father) played for New Zealand Maoris in 1960s
International debut: New Zealand 54, World XV 26, 1992
Notable landmarks in rugby career: Controversy has dogged Jamie from the start of his Test career. On his international debut he was spotted stamping by television – for which he later received a four-week suspension from the Union's judiciary committee – against the World XV, in the second Test of the 1992 centenary series. A year on, dateline 27 November 1993 (his sixth Tour appearance), he was again guilty of stamping. Twickenham was the venue,

England the opposition, and Kyran Bracken the victim, his ankle crunched by Jamie's studs while the game was still in its infancy. The fact the All Blacks' management failed to make known any punishment prolonged the dissatisfaction over the incident. In between these two unsavoury incidents Jamie made news, for the right reasons, on the All

New Zealand (1992)

Last Season	6 caps	0 pts
Career	19 caps	5 pts

Caps (19): **1992** Wd(2,3R), I(1), A(1R,3), SA **1993** BL(1,2,3), A, WS, S, E **1995** C wc-I, W, J(R), S, SA(R)

Points (5 – 1t): **1992** A(3:1t)

Black tour of Australia and South Africa. Lost out in selection stakes to first Mike Brewer, his Provincial skipper, then Andy Earl in the first two tests against Australia, although he came on as a 65th minute replacement for Brewer in Sydney. But he was awarded the start in the 'dead rubber' and scored a wonderful try. Against South Africa, too, he impressed. In all he made nine appearances on the trip, bagging a try in the 80–0 defeat of Western Australia. His other outings were against New South Wales, Victoria, Queensland, Natal, Junior South Africa. A latecomer to top-grade rugby, having completed only two seasons of First Division rugby at Otago, the 1991 national champions. He was acclaimed the Province's most improved player in 1992 and in the same year, excelled in two national trials at Napier, finishing on the winning side for Fitzpatrick's XV and the Saracens team which beat a New Zealand XV 20–15. Completed an excellent campaign by following in his father's studprints and representing the New Zealand Maoris on their tour of the Pacific Islands. Injury sidelined him in 1994 but he returned with a vengeance in '95, playing in six of New Zealand's seven Tests, including the World Cup final, albeit as a replacement for Mike Brewer.

Will Carling gets enveloped by Scots Kenny Logan, Doddie Weir and Peter Wright at Twickenham.

273

Joubert, A. J. — South Africa

Full Name: Andre Johan Joubert
Province: Natal
Position: Fullback
Height: 6ft 3in (1.90m)
Weight: 14st 6lb (87kg)
Occupation: Money trader, NBS
Born: Ladysmith, 15.4.64
Family: Married
International debut: Australia 19, South Africa 12, 1993
Former province: Orange Free State
Notable landmarks in rugby career: Arguably the world's premier fullback, Andre played a pivotal role in South Africa's World Cup triumph last summer, not least because he played in the semi-final and final nursing a broken bone in his hand (suffered in the quarter-final versus Western Samoa). Brilliant on the 1994 Springboks' tour of Wales and Ireland, Andre's finest moment came with a national-high 38 points (4t,9c) in the 78–7 rout of Swansea (5.11.94). Had been hugely influential in Natal's defeat of England (21.5.94), kicking four penalty goals in the famous 21–6 win, having earlier scored 33 points

South Africa (1993)

Last Season	11 caps	23 pts
Career	16 caps	56 pts

Caps (16): **1989** Wd(1R) **1993** A(3), Arg(1) **1994** E(1,2), NZ(1,2R,3), Arg(2) S, W **1995** wc-A, C, WS(b), F, NZ

Points (56 – 3t,4c,11p): **1993** Arg(1:1t) **1994** E(1:5p), E(2:1t,1c,2p), NZ(1:3p), S(3c,1p), W(1t)

in a '94 Super-10 match against Western Samoa. Claimed 28 points in two-Test series against England. Andre had first come to the notice of British audiences when turning out for centenary Barbarians against Scotland at Murrayfield (7.9.91) and setting up the most glorious try in final minute. From underneath his own posts he broke deep into the Scottish half to set up a spectacular match-saving score. Had to wait a further two years to gain Test recognition on the Springboks' tour of Australia. Andre scored two tries and two conversions in the 65–5 defeat of Queensland Country (Mackay, 11.8.93) and two conversions and four penalty goals in the 31–20 victory against Sydney (Penrith, 18.8.93). He was then selected to play fullback in the decisive third Test (Sydney, 21.8.93). Unhappily, for him and his compatriots, the Wallabies won 19–12.

Kearns, P. N.   Australia

Full Name: Philip (Phil) Nicholas Kearns
State: New South Wales
Club: Randwick
Position: Hooker
Height: 6ft (1.83m)
Weight: 17st (108kg)
Occupation: Business development manager, Tooheys Ltd
Born: 27.6.67
International debut: New Zealand 24, Australia 12, 1989
Serious injuries: Not enough room in this book
Suggestions to improve rugby: Get rid of the maul law. Change positional names back to the old way
Notable landmarks in rugby career: Most-capped hooker in Australian history, having moved five caps past previous record-holder, P G Johnson (42: 1959-71) in 1995, Phil was awarded the Wallaby captaincy last summer after the retirement of Michael Lynagh. Dogged by a troublesome Achilles injury, Phil nonetheless was everpresent through 1994, scoring a crucial try against New Zealand as the Wallabies just retained the Bledisloe Cup (Sydney, 6.5.94), and appeared in three of the four World Cup engagements in South Africa, where England ended

Australia (1989)
Last Season	11 caps	10 pts
Career	47 caps	34 pts

Caps (47): **1989** NZ, F(1,2) **1990** F(1,2,3), US, NZ(1,2,3) **1991** W(a), E(a), NZ(a1,a2). wc-Arg, WS, W(b), I, NZ(b), E(b) **1992** S(1,2), NZ(1,2,3), SA, I, W **1993** T, NZ, SA(1,2,3),C,F(1,2) **1994** I(1,2), It(1,2), WS, NZ **1995** Arg(1,2) wc-SA, C, E

Points (34 – 8t): **1989** F(2:1t) **1990** US(1t), NZ(3:1t) **1991** W(a:2t) wc-Arg(1t) **1994** NZ(1t) **1995** wc-SA(1t)

the champions' term in office. Skippered the side during Lynagh's absence in 1994, against Italy, Western Samoa and the All Blacks, as he had done in 1992 versus Wales, just three years after having been a Randwick reserve grade player. In 1989 he sprung from obscurity to hook against the All Blacks and has remained in the line-up ever since. The Test captaincy, in the absence of injured Lynagh, capped a fine season in which he packed down alongside Randwick team mate Ewen McKenzie throughout, as he did in '93.
Touchlines: Golf, surfing, reading

Kingston, T. J.   Ireland

Full Name: Terence John Kingston
Club: Dolphin
Position: Hooker
Height: 5ft 10in (1.78m)
Weight: 15st (90kg)
Occupation: Director, Computer Accessories & Systems Ltd
Born: Cork, 19.9.63
Family: Single
Former Club: Lansdowne
International debut: Ireland 6, Wales 13, 1987
Five Nations' debut: Ireland 22, Scotland 18, 1988
Best moment in rugby: Being awarded Ireland captaincy (1995)
Worst moment in rugby: Being dropped from Irish team and Dolphin's failure to qualify for National League in 1989/90 play-off match
Suggestions to improve rugby: An extra five metres should be added to all penalties as an increased deterrent and to encourage team benefiting to take fast, running ball while opposition is retreating

Ireland (1987)

Last Season	7 caps	0 pts
Career	25 caps	8 pts

Caps (25): 1987 wc-W, T, A 1988 S, F, W, E(a) 1990 F, W 1991 wc-J 1993 F, W, E, R 1994 F, W, E, S 1995 F(a), W(a), It wc-NZ, J(R), W(b), F(b)

Points (8 – 2t): 1988 W(1t) 1990 W(1t)

Notable landmarks in rugby career:
Started 1994/95 season as understudy to Garryowen starlet Keith Wood and ended it as Ireland captain. Turnaround came midway through 1995 Five Nations campaign when selectors rested Wood, troubled by a back problem. Terry took over the No2 jersey against France (Dublin, 4.3.95) and despite a defeat was made captain next time out. Kingston celebrated by leading his side to 16–12 victory over Wales in the Wooden Spoon decider (Cardiff, 18.3.95), though his next mission ended in embarrassment as Ireland became the first major rugby nation to lose to Italy (Treviso, 8.5.95). Rebounded well to reach the World Cup quarter-finals under Terry's marshalling. Particularly satisfying for the Munsterman was the performance in South Africa of the forwards, a unit he had led on and off for the previous two seasons. Of Ireland's 13 World Cup tries, the back division accounted for only two. Had re-established himself as Ireland's premier hooker in 1993 Five Nations' Championship, having previously been a regular member of the side five years before. Terry's finest domestic hour came when he skippered Munster to a 22–19 victory over the

touring Australians (Cork, 21.10.92). Had captained Ireland to a 32–16 World Cup win over Japan (Dublin, 9.10.91) in a 1991/92 season which he otherwise viewed from the bench, as Steve Smith monopolised the No 2 jersey. In all, Terry has represented Irish Schools (1982), Ireland Under-21s (1984), Ireland Under-25s (1987, three caps), Ireland B (beat Argentina 27–12, Limerick 20.10.90) and, on 25 occasions since his debut in the 1987 World Cup (in place of injured Harry Harbison), Ireland Full. Toured with Ireland to Namibia (1991), New Zealand (1992) and Australia (1994).
Touchlines: Golf.

Kronfeld, J. New Zealand

Full Name: Josh Kronfeld
Province: Otago
Position: Openside flanker
Height: 6ft ½in (1.84m)
Weight: 16st 6lb (100kg)
Occupation: Teacher, Kings High School
Born: 20.6.71
Family: Single
International debut: New Zealand 73, Canada 7, 1995
Notable landmarks in rugby career: One of the sensations of last summer's World Cup, Josh proved small can be beautiful in a rugby context (in the process giving fellow tiny terrors Neil Back and Denis McBride untold amounts of encouragement). His shaven head bobbed about all over every pitch he played on, always first to the breakdown, always in the face of oppsion half-backs. Wales coach Alex Evans said that but for Jonah Lomu, Josh would have been the All

New Zealand (1995)

Last Season	6 caps	15 pts
Career	6 caps	15 pts

Caps (6): **1995** C wc-I, W, S, E, SA
Points (15 – 3t): **1995** wc-I(1t), W(1t), E(1t)

Black superstar and, in all probability, also player of the tournament. Hard to believe he only made his full debut in late April, in the 73–7 rout of Canada (Auckland, 22.4.95), especially as he had so impressed observers during Otago's 37–24 defeat of the 1993 British Lions (Dunedin, 5.6.93), a match in which Scott Hastings smashed his cheekbone trying to tackle the Kiwi wingforward. Formerly with Hawke's Bay, Josh made his name in Sevens rugby, and enhanced it tenfold with try-scoring performances against Ireland, Wales and

England in South Africa. A great admirer of English entertainer Michael 'Awright' Barrymore.

Touchlines: Surfing.

Kruger, R. J. South Africa

Full Name: Ruben Jacobus Kruger
Province: Northern Transvaal
Club: Oostelikes
Position: Flanker
Height: 6ft 2in (1.88m)
Weight: 16st 9lb (101kg)
Occupation: Market agent
Born: Vrede, 30.3.70
Family: Married
Family links with rugby: Brother-in-law is fellow Springbok Drikus Hattingh
International debut: Argentina 26, South Africa 29, 1993
Notable landmarks in rugby career: Deserved the Jacques Cousteau award for services to underwater rugby when splashing over for South Africa's World Cup semi-final-winning try against France in *that* Durban monsoon (17.6.95). It was a deserved reward for a largely unheralded but hugely effective openside flanker. Of his display in the final win over New Zealand (Johannesburg, 24.6.95), former

South Africa (1994)

Last Season	8 caps	5 pts
Career	10 caps	5 pts

Caps (10): **1993** Arg(1,2) **1994** S, W **1995** WS(a) wc-A, R, WS(b), F, NZ

Points (5 – 1t): **1995** wc-F(1t)

England fly-half Stuart Barnes described Ruben as 'the one man who encapsulated Springbok efforts more than any other.' Bok manager Morne du Plessis added: 'He is an exceptional player. He gets the side an extra yard in front of the advantage line.' Ruben represented South Africa at Schools and B levels while playing out of Orange Free State. In 1993 he toured Australia and Argentina, scoring a try hat-trick versus Queensland Country, and making his Test debut in the 29–26 first Test defeat of the Pumas (Buenos Aires, 6.11.93). Toured New Zealand in 1994 (albeit as a replacement) and Britain, appearing in both international wins over Scotland and Wales, and claiming tries against Swansea, Combined Scottish Districts and the Barbarians. Really made the No 7 jersey his own in 1995.

Lacroix, T.   France

Full Name: Thierry Lacroix
Club: Dax
Position: Outside-half, centre
Height: 5ft 11in (1.80m)
Weight: 13st (78kg)
Occupation: Physiotherapist
Born: Nogaro, 2.3.67
Family: Married
International debut: France 15,
Australia 32, 1989
Five Nations' debut: France 36,
Wales 3, 1991
Notable landmarks in rugby career:
Top scorer in 1995 World Cup. His
116 points from six matches
(average: 19.3) broke down thus:
Tonga (25), Cote d'Ivoire (24),
Scotland (17), Ireland (26), South
Africa (15) and England (9). And it
nudged him ahead of Gavin
Hastings, who had shot out of the
traps with 75 points in his first two
games for Scotland. Overall,
Thierry's tally rose to 349, lifting
him to within five points of France's
record points scorer Didier
Camberabero (354 in 36 matches:
1982–93). It was his perfect
goalkicking (six out of six) which
allowed France to steal past Scotland
in injury time (Pretoria, 3.6.95) and
he hardly missed a kick thereafter. It
was a far cry from Paris (18.2.95)
where Scotland won at Parc des
Princes for the first time largely
because Lacroix couldn't hit his hat.
However he later revealed his
mother had been involved in a life-

France (1989)

Last Season	11 caps	159 pts
Career	35 caps	349 pts

Caps (35): **1989** A(1R,2) **1991** W(a:R),
W(b:R). wc-R(b), C(R), E(b) **1993**
SA(2) **1993** E, S, I, W, SA(1,2),
R(b), A(1,2) **1994** I, W, E, S, C(a),
NZ(1,2), C(b) **1995** W, E(a), S(a),
R wc-T, IC, S(b), I(b), SA, E(b)

Points (349 – 6t,32c,84p,1dg): **1989**
A(2:1c,5p) **1991** wc-C(2p), E(2p)
1992 SA(2:2c,5p) **1993** S(1t),
W(3p), SA(1:5p), SA(2:4p,1dg),
R(b:6c,3p), A(1:1c,1p), A(2:1p)
1994 I(1t,3c,3p), W(1c,1p), E(3p),
S(1c,2p), C(a:1c,3p), NZ(1:1c,2p),
NZ(2:1c,2p), C(b:2c,2p) **1995**
W(1c,3p), E(a:1c,1p), S(a:1p),
R(1c,4p) wc-T(2t,3c,3p),
IC(2t,4c,2p), S(b:1c,5p),
I(b:1c,8p), SA(5p), E(b:3p)

threatening car smash and his mind, understandably enough, was not wholly
focused on kicking a pig's bladder. Goalkicking apart, Thierry enjoyed a
magnificent World Cup in the Gallic midfield, and would have had an even
better time had his half-backs been any good. Most observers included him in
their teams of the tournament. Proved his versatility when appearing on the left

wing in New Zealand (1994), having also represented France at fly-half on numerous occasions. Had also been a big contributor to French success in 1993/94, bagging 101 points in nine starts and being largely responsible for the historic Test series defeat of South Africa (1993) (though also France's first loss to Wales in 12 years). Helped France win 1992 Students World Cup in Italy prior to turning out for France Espoirs in 24–17 win over touring Springboks in Bordeaux (4.10.92). In that game Thierry accounted for most of the points – kicking four penalty goals and converting one of Pierre Hontas' two tries. Scored winning try against Scotland (6.2.93) three penalty goals against Wales (20.3.93) as France won 1993 Five Nations' Championship. Had burst onto international scene with 17 points – five penalty goals and a conversion – on his first start in France's 25–19 defeat of Australia in the second Test in Lille. His debut had come in the first Test as a replacement for Camberabero. In spite of his prolific start he had to wait until the 1991 Five Nations Championship for his third cap, when replacing Philippe Sella in the 36–3 win over Wales (2.3.91).

Larsen, B. P. New Zealand

Full Name: Blair Larsen
Province: North Harbour
Position: Lock
Height: 6ft 6in (1.98m)
Weight: 18st 5lb (112kg)
Occupation: Police officer
Born: 20.1.69
Family: Single
International debut: New Zealand 54, World XV 26, 1992
Notable landmarks in rugby career: Switched to blindside flanker after losing his position as a Test lock to Robin Brooke. Change came on '93 All Blacks' tour of Britain, having been called up as a replacement for the aforementioned Brooke. Played so well he was rewarded with the final match against the Barbarians. First choice New Zealand No6 throughout 1994, excelling in the 13–9 second Test defeat of South Africa (Wellington, 23.7.94), but lost out to Jamie Joseph and Mike Brewer in 1995 and, ironically, had

New Zealand (1992)

Last Season	8 caps	4 pts
Career	11 caps	4 pts

Caps (11): 1992 Wd(2,3),I(1) 1994 F(1,2),SA(1,2,3) 1995 wc-I,W,J
Points (4 – 1t): 1992 Wd(2:1t)

to return to the second row for his three caps in the World Cup. Voted North

Harbour's most promising player in 1991, he went on to make a favourable impression in the 1992 national trials (after just 14 Provincial outings), from where a full debut in the second leg of the the centenary series was his next stop. One of six changes to the side beaten 28–14 by the World XV in the first Test, he claimed one of the ten tries scored by the revived All Blacks in a 54–26 win. Blair retained his place for the next two Tests, the victorious centenary decider and New Zealand's decidedly uncomfortable 24–21 first Test win over Ireland. As a result of such a close squeak the selectors made widespread alterations to the side for the second Test, with Blair one of the casualties. Nevertheless, he kept his spot in the squad for the tour to Australia and South Africa, and figured in seven of the 16 engagements. His one try came in the second match against South Australia, at Adelaide, where the visitors won 48–18.

Laubscher, T. G. South Africa

Full Name: Tommie Laubscher
Province: Western Province
Club: Northerns
Position: Prop
Height: 6ft 1½ft in (1.86m)
Weight: 18st 3lb (111kg)
Occupation: Mechanic
Born: Vredenburg, 8.10.63
International debut: South Africa 42, Argentina 22, 1994
Notable landmarks in rugby career:
A Springbok reserve as far back as 1989, Tommie finally broke into the Test side in 1994 when Argentina were the visitors to Port Elizabeth (8.10.94). He came in at loosehead for Transvaal rival Balie Swart, the same player who replaced him 63 minutes into the 46–26 second Test defeat of the Pumas at Ellis Park the following week. Tommie's selection was remarkable on two counts. It came on his 31st birthday and at a time when he representing no greater side than Western Province B.

South Africa (1994)

Last Season	4 caps	0 pts
Career	4 caps	0 pts

Caps (4): 1994 Arg(1,2), S, W
Points Nil

Maintained his pre-eminence on the '94 Springboks' autumn tour of Wales, Scotland and Ireland, turning out in the wins over Wales A, Llanelli, Swansea, Combined Scottish Districts and Irish Provinces XV, in addition to both Test victories. But 1995 proved less fruitful for one of the most awkward props in

South Africa, as Swart, Pieter du Randt, Garry Pagel and Marius Hurter shored up the propping duties.

Le Roux, H. P.   South Africa

Full Name: Hendrik (Hennie) Pieter Le Roux
Province: Transvaal
Club: RAU
Position: Centre, fly-half
Height: 5ft 10in (1.78m)
Weight: 12st 8lb (80kg)
Occupation: Manager, TVC Rugby Union
Born: Grahamstown, 10.7.67
Family: Single
Former Province: Eastern Province
International debut: South Africa 20, France 20, 1993
Notable landmarks in rugby career: Mr Versatility, having in 1994/95 been moved from fly-half to centre mid-season to accommodate South Africa's World Cup winner Joel Stransky in the side. Everpresent for Springboks in triumphant summer of '95. Hennie really made his name in Transvaal's 24–21 defeat of England (28.5.94), with a brilliant running performance. The former Junior Springbok, went over in Ellis Park's left corner for Transvaal's opening try as England were beaten 24–21. A

South Africa (1993)

Last Season	15 caps	19 pts
Career	17 caps	19 pts

Caps (17): **1993** F(1,2) **1994** E(1,2), NZ(1,2,3), Arg(2), S, W **1995** WS(a) wc-A, R(R), C, WS(b), F, NZ
Points (19 – 1t,1c,4p): **1994** E(2:1t,3p), W(1c,1p)

fortnight later he helped beat England again, this time contributing 14 points to the Springboks' 27–9 Newlands rout. Had also played in England the previous season on a Springbok tour which also took in France. He made six appearances and scored five points (one try). However, he had to wait for his Test chance until France visited the Republic in June and July of 1993. Selected to fill the No.10 jersey in the absence of retired legend Naas Botha, Hennie played in both Tests (first: drew 20–20, Durban 26.6.93; second: lost 17–18, Johannesburg 3.7.93). But South Africa's failure to even share the series led to changes at outside-half, with Natal's Joel Stransky taking over. Still, Hennie made six appearances on tour in Australia (against South Australia, New South Wales, NSW Country, ACT, Queensland Country and Sydney) and scored 14 points

(2t,2c). His tries came against South Australia and NSW. Played four out of the Springboks' six games on their Autumn tour of Argentina – against Cordoba, Buenos Aires, Tucuman and Rosario – scoring tries against Cordoba and Rosario. Helped Transvaal win 1993 and 1994 Currie Cups, against Natal and Orange Free State respectively.

Leonard, J.   England

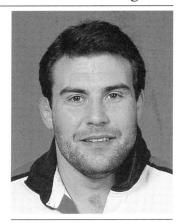

Full Name: Jason Leonard
Club: Harlequins
Position: Loosehead prop
Height: 5ft 10in (1.78m)
Weight: 17st 2lb (109kg)
Occupation: Sales rep, Services UK Ltd
Born: Barking, London, 14.8.68
Family: Single
Former clubs: Barking, Saracens
International debut: Argentina 25, England 12, 1990
Five Nations' debut: Wales 6, England 25, 1991
Best moment in rugby: New Zealand 7, British Lions 20, 1993
Worst moment in rugby: Losing third decisive Test with Lions against All Blacks (13–30)
Most embarrassing moment: Being made songmaster on '93 Lions tour – I can't sing to save my life
Most respected opponent: Jeff Probyn (Wasps & England) – superb technique and physical abilities
Biggest influences on career: Mixture of Jeff Probyn, Paul Rendall, Gary Pearce, Brian Moore and John Olver
Serious injuries: Ruptured disc in neck (1991/92)

England (1990)		
Last Season	11 caps	0 pts
Career	43 caps	0 pts
Lions 1993	3 Tests	0 pts

Caps (43): **1990** Arg(a1,a2), Arg(b) **1991** W, S(a), I, F(a), Fj, A(a) wc-NZ, It, US, F(b), S(b), A(b) **1992** S, I, F, W, C, SA **1993** F, W, S,I. Lions-NZ(1,2,3). NZ **1994** S, I, F, W, SA(1,2), R,C **1995** I, F(a), W, S wc-Arg, It, A, NZ, F(b)

Points Nil

Suggestion to improve rugby: Law makers must consult players. That is rugby's biggest problem.
Notable landmarks in rugby career: England's decision to field a weaker team in last summer's World Cup-tie against Western Samoa (4.6.95) brought to an end Jason's amazing run of 40 consecutive international appearances (all at

loosehead save for Italy, 31.5.95), an unbroken run dating back five years to his debut against Argentina (28.7.90). In that period he played on three Grand Slam sides, in a World Cup campaign which culminated in a Final appearance against Australia, and for the 1993 Lions throughout a three-Test series in New Zealand (two at tighthead). The period did not feature a try but it did include an injury which seriously threatened his playing career. After the 1992 Championship a neck injury required delicate surgery, including a muscle graft, and forced him to take three months off work. He had experienced problems at Murrayfield against Scotland (18.1.92) and it finally ruptured against Wales (7.3.92). Surgeons replaced the ruptured disc with piece of bone, then waited for it to bond with existing vertebra. He was off work for three months but, with no England tour, was able to recover in good time before returning for Test against Canada at Wembley (17.10.92). Jason started his career at Barking, helping them win Essex Colts Cup before tasting success at Twickenham with Eastern Counties winning U-21 County Championship. Won 1989/90 Courage League division two title with Saracens and sat on England U-21 bench in Romania (1989). Broke into England B ranks in 1989/90, winning caps against Fiji and France and warming bench against USSR before being promoted to senior status on '90 tour of Argentina when he made his debut in Buenos Aires.

Lewis, E. W.   Wales

Full Name: Emyr Wyn Lewis
Club: Cardiff
Position: Flanker, No 8
Height: 6ft 4in (1.93m)
Weight: 16st 8lb (101kg)
Occupation: Police officer, Gwent Constabulary
Born: Carmarthen, 29.8.68
Family: Single
Former Club: Carmarthen Athletic
International debut: Wales 21, Ireland 21, 1991
Five Nations' debut: As above
Best moments in rugby: Llanelli's defeat of 1992 Wallabies; winning first cap; Wales' 1994 Five Nations triumph
Worst moments in rugby: Missing England game in 1992 due to food poisoning on eve of game (I had wanted to play in an England game since I was a little boy and had to wait until the following season); losing to England (1994) when Grand Slam and Triple

Crown was at stake

Most embarrassing moment: Running down sidelines in support of attack, playing against Northampton (1990/91) and falling over, twisting ankle in process

Most respected opponent: Dean Richards (Leicester & England)

Serious injuries: 1993/94 was a nightmare season – suspected broken back v Pontypool (lost all feeling in feet and arms); strained knee ligaments v England; popped rib cartilage

Wales (1991)

Last Season	9 caps	0 pts
Career	37 caps	15 pts

Caps (37): **1991** I,F(a),A(a),F(b) wc-WS,Arg,A(b) **1992** I,F,S,A **1993** E,S,I,F,Z(1,2),Na,J,C **1994** S,I,F,E wc(q)-P,Sp. Fj,WS wc(q)-R,It. SA **1995** F,E,S,I(a) wc-J,I(b)

Points (15 – 3t): **1993** Na(2t),J(1t)

Notable landmarks in rugby career: Joined Cardiff in 1994/95 and helped new team mates to Heineken League title. It was a bright moment in a fairly dismal season, as Wales were humbled in Five Nations and World Cup and Emyr looked a shadow of his former international self, being dropped for the New Zealand game (Johannesburg, 31.5.95). Had discovered art of Test try-scoring in 1993/94. After 17 internationals without crossing goal line, he bagged a try-brace in Wales' 38–23 win against Namibia (Windhoek, 5.6.93) and added a third as Wales crushed Japan 55-5 (Cardiff, 16.10.93). He played at No 8 that day, as he did against Canada (10.11.93) but was moved to blindside flanker for 1994 Five Nations Championship to accomodate Scott Quinnell at base of pack. Wales' 1991/92 Player-of-the-Year also figured in Llanelli's 13–9 defeat of the touring Wallabies at Stradey (14.11.92) and in their 1992/93 League and Cup double. In the latter case, victory over Neath in the Swalec final was due to him, an improbable hero, as he dropped a late goal to clinch victory. Missed playing for Welsh Schools because he was too old by two days. Could not play for Wales Youth either because still at school, but on leaving represented Wales at Under-20, Under-21 and B (for two minutes as replacement in 34–12 defeat of the Netherlands at Leiden, 2.12.90) before graduating to senior level. Emerged from disastrous 1991 (tour to Australia and World Cup) with reputation enhanced. Having played for less than a minute of Llanelli's 1989 Schweppes Cup final loss to Neath (after coming on as a replacement), he embarked on a hat-trick of Cup wins with the Scarlets in 1990/91 (scoring a try in defeat of Pontypool), 1991/92 and 1992/93.

Touchlines: fishing (river spinning), shooting.

Little, J. S. Australia

Full Name: Jason Sidney Little
State: Queensland
Club: Southern Districts
Position: Centre
Height: 6ft 1in (1.86m)
Weight: 14st 12lb (90kg)
Occupation: Marketing manager, Queensland Cotton Corp.
Born: 26.8.70
International debut: France 15, Australia 32, 1989
Best moment in rugby: Test debut vs France
Worst moment in rugby: Breaking ankle vs United States prior to 1990 New Zealand tour
Most embarrassing moment: Accused of enhancing a potential moustache whilst playing in Japan
Most respected opponent: Frank Bunce (North Harbour & New Zealand)
Other sporting achievements: Limited!
Suggestions to improve rugby: Correct the maul rule
Notable landmarks in rugby career: Missed early part of 1994 recovering from serious knee injury suffered in Super-10 final against Natal, which Queensland won 21–10 (Durban,

Australia (1989)

Last Season	7 caps	15 pts
Career	36 caps	47 pts

Caps (36): **1989** F(1,2) **1990** F(1,2,3), US **1991** W(a), E(a), NZ(a1,a2). wc-Arg, W(b), I, NZ(b), E(b) **1992** NZ(1,2,3), SA, I, W **1993** T, NZ, SA(1,2,3), C, F(1,2) **1994** WS, NZ, Arg(1,2) wc-SA, C, E

Points (47 – 10t): **1990** F(2:1t), US(1t) **1991** W(a:1t) **1992** I(1t) **1993** T(1t), SA(2:2t) **1994** WS(2t), NZ(1t)

14.5.94). Returned in time for Western Samoa's trip to Sydney, scoring two tries in 73–3 win (6.8.94), and followed up with a first-minute try in the 20–16 Bledisloe Cup defeat of New Zealand (Sydney, 17.8.94). That got the Rugby League agents back on his tail and they pestered him thereafter. Partnered Danny Herbert in Wallaby midfield until club and state colleague Tim Horan returned from the same sort of knee injury suffered also in the '94 Super-10 final. Jason's rise to prominence was helped in no small measure by a strong showing for Australia Under-17s in their 16–3 over New Zealand in 1987. Two years later he was in Britain with the Emerging Wallabies – playing in the 12–12 draw with England B at Wasps – and the same year he broke into the Test side at Strasbourg in the first match against France during a Wallabies' tour which also took in Canada. Featured in the 1991 World Cup final at Twickenham, and played an equally full role in the 1992 Bledisloe Cup triumph over holders New Zealand. Jason, who was reared in the Darling Downs region of Queensland, was an ever-present in the '92 Wallabies XV, scoring his fourth Test try in the 42–17 rout of Ireland in Dublin (31 October), and also fitting in tour appearances against northern Transvaal, Leinster, Ulster (one try), Swansea, Neath (one try), Llanelli and the Barbarians. Retained centre berth throughout 1993, scoring tries against Tonga and South Africa (two in vital second Test at Ballymore). Turned out in three of Australia's four World Cup matches last summer.

Touchlines: Golf, movies, reading.

Little, W. K.   New Zealand

Full Name: Walter Kenneth Little
Province: North Harbour
Club: Glenfield
Position: Centre, wing, outside-half
Height: 5ft 10½in (1.79m)
Weight: 12st (76kg)
Occupation: Brewery technician, Lion Breweries
Born: Takapuna, 14.10.69
Family: Single, two children
Former Province: Auckland
International debut: New Zealand 31, Scotland 16, 1990
Notable landmarks in rugby career: Brilliant return from medial ligament injury at end of 1994, playing a starring role in New Zealand's narrow Bledisloe Cup loss to Australia (Sydney, 17.8.94). From there Walter lit up the All Black midfield at the World Cup with his straight lines of elusive running. It was his break that set up New Zealand's crucial second try in their stunning semi-final defeat of England (Cape Town, 18.6.95), having dismantled Scotland with two tries in Pretoria the previous weekend. Mr Versatile in the Kiwi

New Zealand (1990)		
Last Season	8 caps	15 pts
Career	31 caps	24 pts

Caps (31): **1990** S(1,2),A(1,2,3),F(1,2) **1991** Arg(1,2),A(a1). wc-It,S **1992** Wd(1,2,3),I(1,2),A(1,2,3),SA **1993** BL(1),WS(R) **1994** SA(2R),A **1995** C wc-I,W,S,E,SA

Points (24 – 5t): **1991** wc-S(1t) **1992** A(3:1t) **1995** wc-W(1t),S(2t)

set-up, having appeared at outside-half, centre and wing in consecutive Tests in 1993. Walter was seen as the heir apparent to Grant Fox's No.10 jersey until the Auckland man decided his career was far from over. When Fox was dropped after New Zealand's first test beating at the hands of the World XV, Walter moved from centre into the vacant half-back berth and guided the team to a centenary series win. He retained his job description for the 2–0 series defeat of Ireland before being selected again at centre for the tour of Australia and South Africa as Fox returned to conduct affairs at first-five. His excellent 1992 was sandwiched in between two relatively disappointing years. In '91 he was replaced in the Test side by Bernie McCahill, following the 21–12 Bledisloe Cup loss to Australia, after a run of ten consecutive Tests. And in '93 a last-minute injury in the first Test defeat of the British Lions put him out of contention for the rest of the series and although he returned as a replacement for Lee Stensness during the victory over Western Samoa (31 July) in Auckland, he was not selected to tour England and Scotland in the autumn. Indeed, Britain has not been the happiest of hunting grounds for Walter, who made only two appearances in the 1991 World Cup, scoring the winning try as the All Blacks clinched third place in Cardiff at the expense of Scotland, whom Walter had come up against on his international debut at Dunedin in 1990. A year earlier, as the youngest member of the touring party to Wales and Ireland, 20-year old Walter did not make the Test side, though he was picked for bench duties at Cardiff and featured against the Barbarians at Twickenham – three months after having helping New Zealand Colts beat their Australian counterparts 38–15.

Llewellyn, G. O.   Wales

Full Name: Gareth Owen Llewellyn
Club: Neath
Position: Lock
Height: 6ft 6in (1.98m)
Weight: 16st 8lb (105kg)
Occupation: Fitter/turner, British Steel (Port Talbot)
Born: Cardiff, 27.2.69
Family: Single
Family links with rugby: Brother (Glyn) plays for Neath and Wales; father (David), who was in Army with Will Carling's dad, is a qualified WRU coach
Former Club: Llanharan
International debut: Wales 9, New Zealand 34, 1989
Five Nations' debut: England 34, Wales 6, 1990

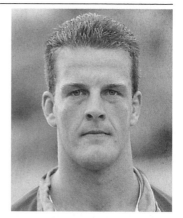

Worst moment in rugby: Twice being dropped by Wales

Most embarrassing moment: Almost tripping over when running out at Cardiff for first cap

Most respected opponent: Bob Norster (ex-Cardiff & Wales)

Notable landmarks in rugby career: Captained Wales three times in 1994/95 (vs Italy, South Africa and France) after Ieuan Evans suffered his horrendous ankle injury. It was a

Wales (1989)
Last Season	10 caps	5 pts
Career	40 caps	19 pts

Caps (40): **1989** NZ **1990** E, S, I **1991** E, S, A(a:R) **1992** I, F, E, S, A **1993** E, S, I, F, Z(1,2), Na, J, C **1994** S, I, F, E. wc(q)-P, Sp. C, T, WS wc-R, It. SA **1995** F, E, S, I(a) wc-J, NZ, I(b)

Points (19 – 4t): **1990** I(1t) **1993** Z(2:2t) **1994** wc(q)-P(1t)

fitting tribute to a player who was consistently outstanding, as well as everpresent, for his faltering national XV, even if his switch to blindside flanker for the World Cup clash with New Zealand was an act of folly on the management's part. Had previously skippered Wales on 1993 tour to Zimbabwe and Namibia, where he played in all three Tests (scoring two tries in 42–13 second Test defeat of Zimbabwe in Harare). The Neath skipper's performance had been central in the famous 10–9 victory over England (Cardiff, 6.2.93) and his line-out exploits, in particular, took him to the threshold of Lions' selection. To his credit, did not let his standards slip one iota in 1993/94, playing in all eight internationals and captaining side with great distinction in Wales' glorious 24-15 defeat of France (Cardiff, 19.2.94). Added a fourth international try in Wales' 102–11 World Cup qualifying rout of Portugal (Lisbon, 17.5.94). Capped three times by Wales Youth. Toured New Zealand with Welsh U-19 team (1987), playing at No 8. Also played for Crawshays and Barbarians. Represented Wales against England and Scotland in 1990/91 before losing place to Paul Arnold. Has previously partnered brother Glyn in second row both for Neath and Wales. Toured Australia with Wales in 1991, coming on as a 20th minute replacement for Phil Davies in 6–63 Test defeat to Wallabies. Omitted from Wales' World Cup squad in 1991 but recalled for 1992 Five Nations Championship, as lock partner for Llanelli's Tony Copsey, and has remained ever since.

Touchlines: Golf, squash, weights

Loe, R. W.   New Zealand

Full Name: Richard Wyllie Loe
Club: Frazer-Tech
Province: Waikato
Position: Prop
Height: 6ft 1in (1.85m)
Weight: 17st (108kg)
Occupation: Farmer
Born: Christchurch, 6.4.60
Family: Felicity (wife) and Jessica
(daughter)
Family links with rugby: Nephew of
former New Zealand coach Alex
'Grizz' Wyllie
Former club/Province: Lyon
(France), Canterbury (1980),
Marlborough (1982)
International debut: New Zealand
70, Italy 6, 1987
Notable landmarks in rugby career:
Returned to international rugby in
1994 after six-month ban, incurred
for eye-gouging Otago's New
Zealand fullback Greg Cooper.
Proved how effective a performer he
can be by roaming everpresent
through New Zealand's '94
campaign and making three
appearances at last summer's World
Cup, including coming on as
replacement for Craig Dowd in the
final (Johannesburg, 24.6.95). That

New Zealand (1987)

Last Season	9 caps	5 pts
Career	47 caps	25 pts

Caps (47): **1987** wc-It,Arg **1988** W(1,2),
A(1,2,3) **1989** F(1,2), Arg(1,2), A,
W, I **1990** S(1,2), A(1,2,3), F(1,2)
1991 Arg(1,2), A(a1,a2). wc-E, It,
C, A(b), S **1992** Wd(1,2,3), I(1),
A(1,2,3), SA **1994** F(1,2),
SA(1,2,3), A **1995** wc-J, S, SA(R)
Points (25 – 6t): **1989** A(1t) **1990** S(2:1t)
1992 Wd(2:2t), Wd(3:1t) **1995**
wc-J(1t)

outing made him the most-capped All Black prop, surpassing Steve McDowell
(46: 1985–92). Prior to suspension, Richard had successfully adapted to the
loosehead propping role, after more than 50 All Black outings and 34 Tests on
the other side, but seriously incurred the wrath of Australia during the 1992
Bledisloe Cup series. During the second Test Richard was seen to break Wallaby
match-winning wing Paul Carozza's nose with an elbow smash, having been
accused of inflicting damage to Sam Scott-Young's head in the first Test. A
member of what was the world's most-capped front row combination (with
McDowell and Fitzpatrick), his international career began out of the blue in
1986 when he was recruited from Lyon, where he was playing club rugby, to
bolster an injury-plagued All Black touring side in France. His test debut came
the following year in the 1987 World Cup rout of Italy and in the ensuing tour

of Japan he succeeded John Drake as regular tighthead. Played for centenary Barbarians against England in 1990 and in eight of New Zealand's nine Tests in 1992, the exception being the second match against Ireland when the calf muscle he had aggravated in the Dunedin opener failed to recover in time to prevent Olo Brown taking over. The highlight of his season was his two-try display in the second Test victory over the World XV.

Logan, K. M. Scotland

Full Name: Kenneth (Kenny) McKerrow Logan
Club: Stirling County
Position: Wing, fullback
Height: 6ft 1in (1.85m)
Weight: 13st 9lb (82kg)
Occupation: Farmer, James Logan and Co.
Born: 3.4.72, Stirling
Family: Single
International debut: Australia 37, Scotland 13, 1992
Five Nations' debut: England 26, Scotland 12, 1993
Worst moment in rugby: Scotland 'A' 9, All Blacks 20 (Glasgow, 13.11.93): Tuigamala went through me three times – everyone thought I was playing touch rugby
Most embarrassing moment: Gregor Townsend dummying me in the Gala-Stirling game. Every time he is shown on TV that moment is replayed
Biggest influence on career: Hamish Logan (cousin) who played ten years for West of Scotland
Other sporting achievements:

Scotland (1993)		
Last Season	11 caps	20 pts
Career	20 caps	20 pts

Caps (20): **1992** A(2) **1993** E(R), NZ(TR) **1994** W, E, I, F, Arg(1,2), SA **1995** C, I, F, W, E, R wc-IC, T, F, NZ
Points (20 – 4t): **1994** Arg(2:1t) **1995** R(1t) wc-IC(2t)

Turned down soccer trials (goalkeeper) with Dundee United and Hearts to pursue rugby career
Notable landmarks in rugby career: Emerged last season as one of Scotland's outstanding players, three years after becoming the first Stirling County player to be capped when selected at fullback in place of the injured Gavin Hastings for 13–37 second Test defeat by Australia (Brisbane, 21.6.92). Scotland's first-choice left wing in last 17 matches, Kenny had to wait nine internationals for

his first try, in the 17–19 loss to Argentina (Buenos Aires, 11.6.94). He added three more in 1995, two in Scotland's 89-0 World Cup opening romp against Cote d'Ivoire (Rustenburg, 26.5.95), in addition to helping Stirling win their first Scottish League title. Had played in seven of the eight games (four as wing, three as fullback) on Scotland's '92 tour of Oz (picked before playing in any national trial), thoroughly enjoying the experience, especially the acclaim which followed his try/match-saving tackle on Paul Carozza in the 15–15 draw with Queensland. Cemented his place in Scotland side in 1993/94, playing in all five games, although only as a temporary replacement (again for Gavin) against New Zealand. Represented Scotland U-18, U-19 (fullback v '91 Aussie Schools) and U-21 level and captained Glasgow to 1991/92 U-21 Championship. Won three Scotland A caps during 1992/93 campaign (scoring try in each game against Spain, Ireland and France) and again in 1993/94 (against New Zealand, Italy and, as fullback, Ireland). Toured with Scotland to Fiji, Tonga and Western Samoa (1993) – playing in all three non-cap internationals – and Argentina (1994).

Touchlines: Squash, weights, running 400-acre farm, golf (handicap 20).

Lomu, J.   New Zealand

Full Name: Jonah Lomu
Province: Counties
Position: Wing
Height: 6ft 5in (1.95m)
Weight: 19st (116kg)
Occupation: Bank officer, ASB Bank of New Zealand
Born: Mangere, 12.5.73
Family: Single
International debut: New Zealand 8, France 22, 1994
Notable landmarks in rugby career:
A big presence in every sense of the word, Jonah had a whale of a time at the World Cup where he was heralded as a true superstar. The statistics supported the hype. At 6ft 5in and 19st (making him the biggest ever All Black back), having weighed a colossal 11lb at birth, he could have played in just about any position save hooker. But a 100 metres time of 10.7 seconds clinched a wing berth in the New Zealand

New Zealand (1994)

Last Season	7 caps	35 pts
Career	7 caps	35 pts

Caps (7): **1994** F(1,2) **1995** wc-I, W, S, E, SA
Points (35 – 7t): **1995** wc-I(2t), S(1t), E(4t)

side in only his second season playing the position. Joint top try-scorer in South Africa (matching team mate Marc Ellis' seven), thanks chiefly to four-try destruction of England (Cape Town, 18.6.95) in awesome 45–29 semi-final win. An athlete par excellence, he holds records at home in sprint, hurdles, shot and discus and became the youngest ever capped All Black when making his debut in Christchurch against France (26.6.94) aged 19 years and six weeks. Rugby league wanted him, so too did American football in the form of the Dallas Cowboys who were willing to turn him into a six milion dollar man. A juggernaut presence in attack, witnessed first by his 70-yard run through four tackles during an awesome two-try display against Ireland (and subsequently versus Scotland and England), he is not quite so impressive in defence and was exposed by France during the All Blacks' stunning two-Test whitewash in 1994. Repaired his reputation with a brilliant campaign at the Hong Kong Sevens where he was player of the tournament in New Zealand's victory. Jonah played rugby league as a schoolboy, not switching codes until his fourth year at school, when he was played at flanker.

Lynagh, M. P.   Australia

Full Name: Michael Patrick Lynagh
State: Queensland
Clubs: Queensland Univ (Aus), Benetton Treviso (It)
Position: Fly-half
Height: 5ft 10in (1.78m)
Weight: 12st 8lb (80kg)
Occupation: Commercial Real Estate consultant
Born: 25.10.63
Family: Single
International debut: Fiji 3, Australia 16, 1984
Best moments in rugby: 1984 Grand Slam tour; 1991 World Cup victory
Worst moment in rugby: 1987 World Cup
Most embarrassing moment:
Running into the goal posts whilst trying to catch a kick in an under-age match
Most respected opponent: Grant Fox (ex-Auckland & New Zealand)
Serious injuries: Broken collarbone (1983), dislocated shoulder (1992)
Other sporting achievements: Cricket for Queensland Schoolboys
Notable landmarks in rugby career: Bowed out of international rugby after 1995 World Cup as Australia's captain and the world's all-time leading scorer with 911 points. His total comprises 17 tries, 140 conversions, 176 penalty

goals and nine dropped goals. Central to Australia's 1991 World Cup triumph, Michael handled himself marvellously last summer as the Wallabies failed to advance beyond the quarter-finals. He was every bit as gracious in defeat (to both South Africa and England) as he had been in victory four years previously. Michael began international life as a centre versus Fiji (Suva, 9.6.84). He marked the occasion with three penalty goals and has been popping them over ever since. He missed the Bledisloe Cup series that year but toured Great Britain and Ireland where he appeared at centre in all four Tests of the renowned '84 Aussies' Grand Slam. His 21-point haul in the defeat of Scotland equalled the Wallaby single-match record held by Paul McLean. He upped it a couple of notches on his first Test appearance at outside-half against Canada (15.6.85) when he registered 23 points (7c,3p) and by the end of 1990 he had twice enjoyed 24-point afternoons. Michael, who spends his Australian summers playing with Treviso in Italy, passed the 100-point barrier playing against the Italians (1.6.86). Has bagged 148 points in two World Cup tournaments, the second of which yielded a winners' medal. Helped Australia regain Bledisloe Cup from New Zealand in 1992 and succeeded Nick Farr-Jones as national skipper after the historic 26–3 rout of South Africa in Cape Town on 22 August. First Test in charge saw him last only 40 minutes against Ireland (won 42–17, Dublin, 31.10.92) before dislocating left shoulder and having to miss Cardiff

Australia (1984)

Last Season	8 caps	128 pts
Career	72 caps	911 pts

Caps (72): 1984 Fj,E,I,W,S 1985 C(1,2), NZ 1986 It, F, Arg(1,2), NZ(1,2,3) 1987 wc-E, US, J, I, F, W. Arg(1,2) 1988 E(a1,a2), NZ(1,3R), E(b), S, It 1989 BL(1,2,3), NZ, F(1,2) 1990 F(1,2,3), US, NZ(1,2,3) 1991 W(a), E(a), NZ(a1,a2). wc-Arg, WS, W(b), I, NZ(b), E(b) 1992 S(1,2), NZ(1,2,3), SA,I 1993 T, C, F(1,2) 1994 I(1,2), It(1) 1995 Arg(1,2) wc-SA, C, E

Points (911 – 17t,140c,176p,9dg): 1984 Fj(3p), E(1t,2c,1p), I(1p,1dg), W(1t), S(3c,5p) 1985 C(1:7c,3p), C(2:3c,2p,1dg), NZ(1c,1p) 1986 It(6c,1p), F(1c,6p,1dg), Arg(1:4c,5p), Arg(2:1c,4p), NZ(1:1c,1p), NZ(2:3p,1dg), NZ(3:1c,4p) 1987 wc-E(1c,3p), US(6c,1p), J(5c), I(4c,3p), F(2c,3p,1dg), W(2c,2p,1dg). Arg(1:1t,2c,1p), Arg(2:1c,3p) 1988 E(a1:6p), E(a2:1t,3c,2p), NZ(1:1p), NZ(3:1c), E(b:2c,1p), S(3c,2p), It(1t,8c,1p) 1989 BL(1:4c,1p,1dg), BL(2:1c,2p), BL(3:1c,4p), NZ(1c,2p), F(1:2c,4p), F(2:1c,3p) 1990 F(1:1c,5p), F(2:6c,4p), F(3:1c,2p,1dg), US(2t,8c), NZ(1:2p), NZ(2:2p,1dg), NZ(3:1c,5p) 1991 W(a:2t,6c,1p), E(a:4c,4p), NZ(a1:2c,3p), NZ(a2:1p). wc-Arg(3c,2p), WS(3p), W(b:1t,4c,2p), I(1t,2c,1p), NZ(b:1c,2p), E(b:1c,2p) 1992 S(1:1t,1c,3p), S(2:1c,5p), NZ(1:2p), NZ(2:3p), NZ(3:2c,3p), SA(1c,3p) 1993 T(1c), C(2c,3p), F(1:1c,2p) 1994 I(1:1t,1c,1p), I(2:1c,5p), It(1:1c,2p) 1995 Arg(1:2t,3c,4p), Arg(2:5p) wc-SA(1t,1c,2p), C(1t,3c,2p), E(1c,5p)

Test. Having resumed the captaincy in the 1993 season-opener against Tonga, injury robbed him of his participation in the Bledisloe Cup match, which New

Zealand won, and in South Africa's first visit to Oz since 1971. Missed another three games through injury in 1994 yet still racked up 128 points in eight games, including an Aussie-record 28 in the 53–7 first Test defeat of Argentina (Brisbane, 29.4.95)

Touchlines: Surfing, golf, fishing, music, films.

McBride, W. D.   Ireland

Full Name: William Denis McBride
Club: Malone
Position: Flanker
Height: 5ft 11in (1.80m)
Weight: 13st 10lb (87kg)
Occupation: Mechanical engineer, Ballylumford Power Ltd
Born: Belfast, 9.9.64
Family: Catrina (wife), Stephanie Denise (daughter)
Family links with rugby: Brother also plays
Former Club: Queen's University Belfast
International debut: Ireland 9, Wales 12, 1988
Five Nations' debut: As above
Best moments in rugby: Beating England in 1993 and 1994
Worst moment in rugby: Second half of Ireland's 3–35 defeat by England in 1988 when we conceded 35 points without reply
Most embarrassing moment: Ireland v England (1988)
Most respected opponents: David Wilson (Queensland & Australia)
Other sporting achievements: Completed the 1982 Belfast City Marathon

Ireland (1988)

Last Season	5 caps	10 pts
Career	22 caps	18 pts

Caps (22): 1988 W, E, WS, It 1989 S 1990 F, W, Arg 1993 S, F, W, E, R 1994 W, E, S, A(1R) 1995 S, F(a) wc-NZ, W(b), F(b)
Points (18 – 4t): 1988 WS(1t) 1990 W(1t) 1995 wc-NZ(1t), W(b:1t)

Notable landmarks in rugby career: Outstanding World Cup displays against New Zealand and Wales, each featuring tries, rubbished a home-based claim that Denis was an 'irrelevance' to Test rugby. His score against Wales (Johannesburg, 4.6.95) came after a lineout take and 40-yard burst through the Welsh defence. It knocked Wales out of the tournament. Irrelevant eh?! Had failed to make a Test place his own in Australia (1994), although he did come on as a replacement in the first Test. Still, it was a more successful trip than New

Zealand 1992, his last tour, when he returned after just one game – the victim of a freak training accident when he broke a toe after catching a stud in Kelvin Leahy. Malone and Ulster captain who returned to the Test arena after a three-year gap in 1993 Five Nations' Championship. First representative honours came for Ulster and Irish Schools sides in 1983. Graduated to Ulster Under-20s and Combined Provinces Under-21s in 1984/85 before making his senior Ulster bow against Connacht in 1987. Having impressed on summer tour to France, which featured a 19–18 non-cap victory against the French, he was given his Test debut in the '88 Championship against Wales. Collected his first try third time out against Western Samoa but lost his place after win over Italy. In and out of favour for next four years before firmly taking possession of the No 7 jersey in 1992/93.

Touchlines: Athletics (400 metres).

McCall, R. J. Australia

Full Name: Roderick (Rod) James McCall
State: Queensland
Club: Brothers (Brisbane)
Position: Lock
Height: 6ft 6in (1.98m)
Weight: 17st 5lb (110kg)
Occupation: Sales director with Walmac Printing Ltd
Born: 20.9.63
Family: Lorelle (wife), Megan (daughter)
International debut: France 15, Australia 32, 1989
Best moment in rugby: Winning 1987 Brisbane Grand Final and 1991 World Cup
Worst moment in rugby: Losing 3–6 to New Zealand at Eden Park in 1991 which cost us Bledisloe Cup
Most respected opponent: Paul Ackford (ex-Harlequins & England)
Serious injuries: Left knee dislocation (1988), left shoulder a/c (1991)
Other sporting achievements: Several centuries in golf
Suggestions to improve rugby: Lose

Australia (1989)

Last Season	6 caps	0 pts
Career	40 caps	5 pts

Caps (40): **1989** F(1,2) **1990** F(1,2,3), US, NZ(1,2,3) **1991** W(a), E(a), NZ(a1,a2). wc-Arg, W(b), I, NZ(b), E(b) **1992** S(1,2), NZ(1,2,3), SA, I, W **1993** T, NZ, SA(1,2,3), C, F(1,2) **1994** It(2) **1995** Arg(1,2) wc-SA, R, E

Points (5 – 1t): **1992** W(1t)

maul law and get rid of archaic rugby administrators who change rules without asking players and who uphold those which need changing

Notable landmarks in rugby career: Joined Steve Cutler as Australia's most-capped lock when winning his 40th cap in the Wallabies' 22–25 World Cup quarter-final loss to England (Cape Town, 11.6.95). On his previous outing had skippered his country for the first time in the 42–3 defeat of Romania (Stellenbosch, 3.6.95). Waited three years for his Test debut after first touring with Australia in 1986 to New Zealand. His call finally came in 1989 when he was given a chance in the first Test victory over France in Strasbourg. He needed no second invitation and has since been a Test regular, since 1991 alongside John Eales, although the latter's absence through injury in 1993 meant Rod teaming up with fellow Queenslander Garrick Morgan. His honours have included a 1991 World Cup winners' medal and a share in the 1992 Bledisloe Cup series win over the All Blacks. A full schedule in '92 saw him play all eight Tests – scoring his maiden international try in the 23–6 defeat of Wales in Cardiff – in addition to appearances against Northern Transvaal, Leinster, Ulster, Wales B, Neath, Llanelli, Monmouthshire (as a replacement) and the Barbarians. His omnipresence last season took him to New Zealand, North America and France on Test business. But return of Eales in 1994 ended his run.

Touchlines: Spending time with family.

McGowan, A. N.   Ireland

Full Name: Alan Noel McGowan
Club: Blackrock College
Position: Fly-half
Height: 5ft 10in (1.78m)
Weight: 12st 3lb (78kg)
Occupation: Trainee Accountant with Craig Gardner & Co.
Born: Dublin, 2.1.72
Family: Single
International debut: Ireland 26, USA 15, 1994
Five Nations debut: None
Notable landmarks in rugby career: An Irish squad member since 1993, Alan had to wait a year for his international debut, preferred to 'unfit' Eric Elwood for the visit of the United States Eagles on 5 November

1994. A lukewarm team showing was compensated somewhat by a 13-point display by the Leinster star. Alan converted both Irish tries, scored by Simon Geoghegan and Michael Bradley, and added three penalty goals. His

international career hit a snag thereafter as Anglo-Irishman Paul Burke, who had steered Munster to the Inter-Provincial title, was given his chance. He survived the first two Five Nations engagements before Elwood was considered fit enough to

Ireland (1994)		
Last Season	1 cap	13 pts
Career	1 cap	13 pts

Caps (1): **1994** US
Points (13 – 2c,3p): **1994** US(2c,3p)

return. This relegated Alan to third in the national rankings, hence he missed out on selection for the World Cup. As a student at Blackrock College he had won a Junior Cup medal in 1987, followed by a Senior Cup version three years later. He graduated from Leinster Schools, through Under-20 (1991) to the senior side, for whom he played against the 1992 Wallabies. His Ireland Under-21 debut followed in 1992/93. Earned a place on the full Ireland bench versus Romania in '93, before making his A-team debut (against Scotland the following month. Retained his place in the squad throughout the '94 Five Nations. Scored nine points for the Combined Provinces against South Africa in November 1994 and added 16 points in two Ireland A appearances against England and Scotland.

McKenzie, E. J. A.   Australia

Full Name: Ewen James Andrew McKenzie
State: New South Wales
Clubs: Randwick (Aus: since 1985), Paris Univ (Fr: since 1993)
Position: Tighthead prop
Height: 6ft (1.82m)
Weight: 18st 5lb (112kg)
Occupation: Project manager
Born: 21.6.65
Family: Sally (wife)
Former clubs: Harlequins (Melbourne, 1984),
International debut: France 9, Australia 21, 1990
Best moments in rugby: Beating NZ in 1991 World cup semi-final; beating NZ in Wellington (1990); beating South Africa (1992); winning Bledisloe Cup (1992)
Worst moment in rugby: Losing Grand Final to Parramatta (1986); missing selection for 1986 Scotland Test; being dropped by NSW selectors in 1989
Most embarrassing moment: Tony Daly and I doing our Fat Percentage tests prior to the 1991 World Cup. PS I should also mention that Phil Kearns

managed, with Tony Daly alongside, to lose a tighthead in a sixth grade trial match in 1993. Just in case they forget to mention it!

Most respected opponents: Entertainer – Tony Daly; story telling – Peter Fatialofa; scrummaging – Frederico Mendez; athleticism – Steve McDowell; demeanor/ornament to the position – David Sole; dancing – Olo Brown; drinking games – Jeff Probyn; singing – Pascal Ondarts/ Geoff Didier; most like to have a drink with – Jason Leonard (our paths have not crossed post-match despite three games against him)

Australia (1990)		
Last Season	12 caps	0 pts
Career	44 caps	9 pts

Caps	(44): 1990 F(1,2,3), US, NZ(1,2,3) 1991 W(a), E(a), NZ(a1,a2). wc-Arg, W(b), I, NZ(b), E(b). 1992 S(1,2), NZ(1,2,3), SA, I, W 1993 T, NZ, SA(1,2,3), C, F(1,2) 1994 I(1,2), It(1,2), WS, NZ 1995 Arg(1,2) wc-SA, C(R), R, E
Points	(9 – 2t): 1990 US(1t) 1992 I(1t)

Serious injuries: Posterior cruciate tear left knee (1987), medial ligament strain (1989), numerous other arthritic-causing ailments that medicine has been unable to cure

Suggestions to improve rugby: Exotic sevens tournament for tight-five only. More Barbarian-type fixtures. Regular Northern Hemisphere vs Southern Hemisphere fixtures. Reduce dropped goal value to one point. Universal trial by video. Standardised elegibility for national teams. Improve refereeing standards. Get rid of the new maul turnover rule as it encourages negative play. More efforts to improve situations for wives and children. They suffer more from the effects of time given up to rugby

Notable landmarks in rugby career: Australia's most-capped prop, having succeeded Andy McIntyre (38 caps: 1982–89) in the 53–7 first Test defeat of Argentina (Brisbane, 29.4.95). Everpresent in Wallaby No 3 jersey through 1994/95, although he only came on as a replacement in the World Cup contest with Canada. The first born and bred Victorian since 1932 to represent Australia, Ewen moved to Sydney club Randwick in 1985 to further his rugby career and, five years later, was rewarded with his first cap on the tour to France. Since those early days – a knee injury in 1989 had delayed his Test debut – he has built one of the most respected front row partnerships in world rugby with fellow New South Walians Phil Kearns and Tony Daly. A measure of the esteem in which he is held was that the World XV included him in their side to play the All Blacks in the 1992 Centenary Series, a year after he had picked up a World Cup winners' medal at Twickenham. A Test ever-present since, scoring his second international try in the 42–17 win over Ireland in Dublin in 1992, Ewen was awarded the captaincy during 1993 in the absence of Michael Lynagh. Ewen skippered the Wallabies in the 25–10 Bledisloe Cup loss to New Zealand and, rather more memorably, throughout the home series win over South Africa. Lynagh returned thereafter.

Touchlines: Trying to find ways to spend more time with my wife.

McKenzie, K. D.   Scotland

Full Name: Kevin Duncan McKenzie
Club: Stirling County
Position: Hooker
Height: 5ft 6in (1.68m)
Weight: 14st 1lb (85kg)
Occupation: Sales executive, Taylor Maxwell Timber Ltd
Born: Stirling, 22.1.68
Family: Fiona (wife)
International debut: Argentina 16, Scotland 15, 1994
Five Nations debut: None
Notable landmarks in rugby career: Captain of Scotland A side that inflicted last-gasp 17–15 defeat on touring Springboks (Melrose, 9.11.94), thanks to dropped goal from fly-half Duncan Hodge, Kevin's loyalty and commitment to the sport was suitably rewarded in 1994/95: both on the home front, with Stirling County winning it's first Scottish League title, and internationally. Five years after

Scotland (1994)

Last Season	2 caps	0 pts
Career	4 caps	0 pts

Caps (4): **1994** Arg(1,2) **1995** R wc-IC
Points Nil

making his Scotland B debut in the 22–22 draw with Ireland, he was selected to tour Argentina (1994) and played in both Tests: his debut coming in Buenos Aires on 4 June. Reluctantly surrendered No 2 jersey to Heriot's FP rival Kenny Milne on return, but won it back at end of season, for 49–16 defeat of Romania (Murrayfield, 22.4.95) and for the 89–0 World Cup opener against Cote d'Ivoire (Rustenburg, 26.5.95). In between, he appeared in the 62–7 non-cap defeat of Spain (Madrid, 6.5.95). Has played for Scotland at every level from Schools (1985), captaining the side twice, versus Wales and England), Under-19, Under-21, B and A. Captained Glasgow in 1994/95 Inter-District Championship.
Touchlines: Golf, weight training

Mehrtens, A.   New Zealand

Full Name: Andrew Mehrtens
Province: Canterbury
Position: Fly-half
Height: 5ft 10½in (1.79m)
Weight: 13st 9lb (82kg)
Occupation: Student
Born: Durban (SA), 28.4.73
Family: Single
Family links with rugby: Father
Terry played for Junior All Blacks
(1965); grandfather George played
for All Blacks (1928)
International debut: New Zealand
73, Canada 7, 1995
Notable landmarks in rugby career:
One of the stars of the World Cup,
Andrew made a record-breaking
start to his Test career by bagging 28
points on debut for All Blacks
against Canada (22.4.95). New
Zealand ran out 73–7 winners and
he claimed one try, seven
conversions and three penalty goals.
The previous best for a player
making his international bow was
the 23 scored by fellow Kiwi
Matthew Cooper against Ireland in

New Zealand (1995)

Last Season	6 caps	115 pts
Career	6 caps	115 pts

Caps (6): **1995** C wc-I, W, S, E, SA
Points (115 – 2t,21c,18p,3dg): **1995**
C(1t,7c,3p) wc-I(3c,4p),
W(2c,4p,1dg), S(1t,6c,3p),
E(3c,1p,1dg), SA(3p,1dg)

1992. (Unfortunately for Andrew, another All Black, Simon Culhane had
bettered his record inside two months with 45 points on his debut versus Japan,
4.6.95.) Despite his wonderful start in Auckland (22.4.95), Andrew arrived in
South Africa, the country of his birth, virtually unknown. But he quickly
rectified that, succeeding with seven kicks at goal (three conversions and four
penalties) from 10 attempts in the 43–19 defeat of Ireland (Johannesburg,
27.5.95). Next up, against Wales, also in Ellis Park, the former New Zealand
Colt was the star of the show, turning in a prodigious tactical kicking display.
He amassed 19 points, from two conversions, four penalties and a dropped
goal, as New Zealand cruised to a 34–9 win. In New Zealand's 48–30 quarter-
final defeat of Scotland he unleashed his electrifying pace to claim a try in his
23-point haul, and he added a further 12 in the semi-final win over England, a
figure he matched in the final against the Springboks but the match ended in
disappointment for South African-born Andrew, who missed with a dropped
goal attempt two minutes from time that would have won the cup. On the
domestic stage Andrew, who had left South Africa for New Zealand aged 18

months, helped Canterbury win and retain Ranfurly Shield, having made provincial bow in 1993 and toured Britain with them last season (scoring 63 points).

Merle, O. France

Full Name: Olivier Merle
Club: Grenoble
Position: Lock
Height: 6ft 6in (1.98m)
Weight: 20st (124kg)
Occupation: Rugby development officer with Isere Council
Born: Chamalieres, 14.11.65
Former clubs: Blanzat, Montferrand, Vichy
International debut: South Africa 20, France 20, 1993
Five Nations debut: France 35, Ireland 15, 1994
Notable landmarks in rugby career: Controversial season for Olivier, who was banned from the France side for one match for head-butting Wales prop Ricky Evans during the 1995 Five Nations opener (Paris, 21.1.95), an incident which resulted in Evans falling awkwardly and breaking his leg in two places. But Olivier continued to be highly valued in his homeland and returned to play a full part in France's march to third place in the World Cup. An extra-

France (1993)

Last Season	9 caps	0 pts
Career	21 caps	10 pts

Caps (21): **1993** SA(1,2), R(b), A(1,2) **1994** I, W, E, S, C(a), NZ(1,2), C(b) **1995** W, I(a), R wc-T, S(b), I(b), SA, E(b)

Points (10 – 2t): **1993** R(b:1t) **1994** I(1t)

ordinary athletic specimen, Olivier only took up rugby five years ago, having been one of his country's most promising shot putters. He boasts at being able to achieve an 80cm standing jump in full gear. Weighing in at an even 20 stones, and the owner of size 17 boots, his progress up rugby's representative ladder was swift. Joining Grenoble at the start of the 1992/93 season he powered them to the French Club Championship final, where they lost 14–11 to Castres (Paris, 5.7.92), and he was promptly invited to bolster France's challenge in South Africa during the summer of 1993. The former lumberjack proved invaluable, playing in both Tests as the French won a series in the Republic for the first time since 1958. Thereafter, he was a regular, playing in all of France's Test matches in 1993/94 – the shared series with world champions Australia, the 51–0 thrashing of Romania and the 1994 Five Nations Championship – before touring New Zealand and helping France to an historic 2–0 series win.

Mesnel, F. France

Full Name: Franck Mesnel
Club: Racing Club de France
Position: Centre/outside-half
Height: 5ft 11in
Weight: 14st 2lb
Occupation: Architect
Born: Neuilly-sur-Seine, 30.6.61
Former Club: St Germain-en-Laye
International debut: France 7, New Zealand 19, 1986
Five Nations' debut: France 16, Wales 9, 1987
Notable landmarks in rugby career: Restored to France side by coach Pierre Berbizier for final 1995 Five Nations campaign encounter versus Ireland (Dublin 4.3.95). France won 25–7 and scored four tries. Retained for winning visit to Bucharest (7.4.95) and then appeared twice at World Cup: once at centre, in 54–18 defeat of Cote d'Ivoire (Rustenburg, 30.5.95) and once at fly-half, in 19–9 third place play-off win over arch-rivals England (Pretoria, 22.6.95). Since missing the 21–9 first Test loss to Australia at Sydney (9.6.90), Franck was a permanent fixture in the French line-up up until Murrayfield 1992, appearing in all 20 matches. Of his 56 career caps, 24 have been won at outside-half, the position he occupied in 1987 when France won the Grand Slam and

Scotland (1990)
France (1986)

Last Season	4 caps	0 pts
Career	56 caps	41 pts

Caps (56): **1986** NZ(1R,2) **1987** W, E, S(a), I wc-S(b), Z, Fj, A, NZ. R(b) **1988** E, Arg(a1,a2), Arg(b1,b2), R **1989** I, W, E, S, NZ(1), A(1,2) **1990** E, S, I, A(2,3), NZ(1,2) **1991** S, I, W(a), E(a), R(a), US(1,2), W(b) wc-R(b), Fj, C, E(b) **1992** W, E, S, I, SA(1,2) **1993** E(R), W **1995** I, R wc-IC, E(b)

Points (41 – 8t,3dg): **1987** W(1t), E(1dg), S(a:1dg) **1989** W(1dg) **1990** I(2t), A(3:1t) **1991**

reached the World Cup final, and 32 at centre. His first cap came against New Zealand when replacing the injured Jean-Patrick Lescarboura two minutes from the end of the All Black's 19–7 triumph in Toulouse (8.11.86). He kept his place for the second Test the following week, in Nantes when France scored a famous 16–3 win.

Milne, K. S.   Scotland

Full Name: Kenneth Stuart Milne
Club: Heriot's FP
Position: Hooker
Height: 6ft (1.83m)
Weight: 15st 12lb (101kg)
Occupation: Sales manager, P.E.C.
Barr, Printers of Leith
Born: Edinburgh, 1.12.61
Family: Eleanor (wife), Stuart (son)
and Jenny (daughter)
Family links with rugby: Iain
(brother) played for Heriot's,
Scotland and British Lions. David
(brother) plays for Heriot's and
Scotland
International debut: Scotland 23,
Wales 7, 1989
Five Nations' debut: As above
Best moment in rugby: 1990 Grand
Slam
Worst moment in rugby: Losing
15–51 to New Zealand, 1993
Most embarrassing moment:
Accidentally flooring the referee
when the front rows of Heriot's and
Jed-Forest squared up. He let me off
Most respected opponents: Gary
Callender (Kelso & Scotland)
Biggest influence on career: Brothers
Iain and David

Scotland (1989)		
Last Season	9 caps	0 pts
Career	39 caps	12 pts
Lions 1993	1 Test	0 pts

Caps (39): **1989** W, E, I, F, Fj, Ro **1990** I,
F, W, E, NZ(2), Arg **1991** F, W, E
wc-Z **1992** E, I, F, W, A(1) **1993** I,
F, W, E. Lions-NZ(1). NZ **1994**
W, E, I, F, SA **1995** C, I, F(a), W, E
wc-T, F(b), NZ
Points (12 – 3t): **1989** Fj(1t) **1990** Arg(2t)

Suggestions to improve rugby: Leave rules alone. Make penalties between goal-line and 22 worth 3 points, between 22 and 10-metre line 2 points, and beyond 10-metre line 1 point. It seems stupid you can lose game on technical offence 45 metres out. People would be encouraged to run ball more and make for more exciting spectacle. Then you wouldn't get an ordinary side with a good kicker winning the game. Scottish Inter-District Championship should be broadened to include likes of Bath and Leicester. A British League of sorts, with stronger opposition, must be the way forward

Notable landmarks in rugby career: Scotland's most-capped hooker behind Colin Deans (52), Kenny maintained his virtual monopoly of the No2 jersey in 1994/95, save for two Tests at the tail end of the campaign when Stirling rival Kevin McKenzie got a look-in. Had earned British Lions recognition on 1993 tour to New Zealand when beating English rival Brian Moore to hooking berth

304

for first Test, an occasion marred from a British standpoint by Grant Fox's controversial injury-time penalty winner (lost 20–18, Christchurch 12.6.93). Played in eight of Lions' 13 games. Emigration to South Africa of long-time Scottish rival John Allan, after 1991 World Cup (in which Kenny made only one appearance), left way clear for Kenny to take cap tally to 39 in six-year period since debut in 1989. Scored first international try against Fiji in October 1989 and became first Scotland hooker to score two tries in an international when bagging a brace in 49–3 defeat of Argentina (Murrayfield, 10.11.90), in same year as he had been ever-present through triumphant Grand Slam campaign. Toured with Scotland to North America (1985 & 1991), New Zealand (1990) and Australia (1992). On tour to Oz, Kenny lasted just ten minutes in the 12–27 first Test defeat in Sydney before injury forced him out of fray. He was an absentee the following week as the Aussies completed a 2–0 series win at Ballymore and was again missing when a shadow Scotland side warmed up for 1993 Five Nations' campaign with a 22–17 win over Italy A at Melrose. However he was in situ by time of Championship. The youngest of the three-capped Milne brothers (they once played together for Barbarians in Mobbs Memorial Match), Kenny has six Scotland B appearances to his name (five wins) plus two in Scotland A colours.
Touchlines: Fly fishing (salmon & trout).

Moon, R. H. St J. B. Wales

Full Name: Rupert Henry St.John Barker Moon
Club: Llanelli
Position: Scrum-half
Height: 5ft 11in (1.81m)
Weight: 13st 7lb (86kg)
Occupation: TV researcher/presenter, Rugby Vision Ltd (Cardiff)
Born: Birmingham, 1.2.68
Family: Single
Family links with rugby: Brother (Richard) played scrum-half for Rosslyn Park. Sister (Estelle) plays scrum-half/back row for Wasps Ladies
Former clubs: Walsall, Abertillery, Neath

International debut: France 26, Wales 10, 1993
Five Nations' debut: As above
Best moments in rugby: Kicking conversion from each touchline playing for

Barbarians at 1991 Hong Kong Sevens; captaining Barbarians against Cork Constitution on centenary tour; selection to Wales team (1993); being shouldered off Stradey Park after Llanelli beat 1992 Wallabies

Worst moment in rugby: Head-high tackle by Gloucester's Dave Sims which dislocated my shoulder

Wales (1993)		
Last Season	4 caps	0 pts
Career	18 caps	15 pts

Caps (18): **1993** F, Z(1,2), Na, J, C **1994** S, I, F, E. wc(q)-Sp. C, Fj, WS wc(q)-R, It. SA **1995** E(R)

Points (15 – 3t): **1993** Z(1:1t), Na(1t), J(1t)

Most embarrassing moments: Saying my full name on national television; losing kicking competition to Llanelli club mates Phil Davies and Gary Jones

Biggest influence on career: Alfie 'the fruitbat' Brickell (Abertillery coach) – inspired to me go further at age of 18

Serious injuries: Popped rib cartilage, shoulder dislocation

Other sporting achievements: Cricket for Walsall. Soccer for Midlands Schools

Suggestions to improve rugby: Remember that rugby is a game for players not committees. Give all Student rugby players free food vouchers (but never money). Organise cheap nose jobs for people with big noses, when finished playing career

Notable landmarks in rugby career: Paid the highest price for Robert Jones' return to form in 1994/95, being relegated to bench duties during 1995 Five Nations Championship and then being omitted from last summer's World Cup (though, with hindsight, that was perhaps a blessing in disguise). Three tries and a full part in Wales' 1994 Five Nations title triumph had represented a pretty good return for Rupert in 1993/94. But anything less would have seen him slip from the heights of 1992/93. Two of his tries came on 1993 summer tour of Zimbabwe and Namibia, one against each nation, and the third was all but lost in the points avalanche that submerged hapless Japan (Cardiff, 16.10.93). Other career highs include being shouldered off Stradey Park after captaining Llanelli to a 13–9 defeat of the touring Wallabies (14.11.92), and then leading Scarlets to 1992/93 league and cup double. Declaring his allegiance to Wales in 1991/92 – having sat on bench for England Schools and stood on pitch for England Colts, Under-21s (scored try in inaugural match: Romania 13, England 54, Bucharest 13.5.89), Students (as captain and in 1988 Students World Cup) and B grades – led to his Test debut (20.3.93) when displacing British Lion Jones for the match against France in Paris (lost 10–26). Had been everpresent bench reserve prior to that. Joined Llanelli in 1990/91 and was promptly selected for four England B games against Emerging Australians, Ireland B, France B and Spain. Scored two tries in Kingsholm defeat of Spain. Picked up Man-of-the-Match awards in both 1990/91 and 1991/92 Schweppes Challenge Cup finals when Llanelli beat Pontypool and Swansea respectively. Captained England Students against pre-World Cup England XV. Selected to England's development squad but then switched to Wales, saying: 'After six years of living in Wales I have found myself being deeply affected by the passion for, and commitment to the game as shown by the whole community.'

Touchlines: Watching educational videos, eating out, ballet, theatre, star gazing, grass counting.

Moore, B. C.   England

Full Name: Brian Christopher Moore
Club: Harlequins
Position: Hooker
Height: 5ft 9in (1.76m)
Weight: 14st 3lb (90kg)
Occupation: Commercial litigation partner, Edward Lewis and Co.
Born: Birmingham, 11.1.62
Former clubs: Old Crossleyans, Nottingham
International debut: England 21, Scotland 12, 1987
Five Nations' debut: As above
Best moment in rugby: 1991 Grand Slam decider against France
Most embarrassing moment: Being forced to watch pre-match team talks on video
Biggest influence on career: Alan Davies (Nottingham coach)
Serious injuries: Fractured ego v Scotland, Murrayfield 17.3.90
Other sporting achievements: Intermediate swimming certificate
Suggestions to improve rugby: Desperate need for more consistent refereeing and, even more importantly, more consistent refereeing selections so that experienced officials always handle big matches and so that referees serve their time going up a proper ladder. What we have at present are

England (1987)			
Last Season		11 caps	0 pts
Career		63 caps	4 pts
Lions	1989	3 Tests	0 pts
	1993	2 Tests	0 pts

Caps (63): **1987** S wc-A, J, W(b) **1988** F, W, S, I(1,2), A(a1,a2), Fj, A(b) **1989** S, I, F, W, Ro, Fj. Lions-A(1,2,3) **1990** I, F, W, S, Arg(a1,a2) **1991** W, S(a), I, F(a), Fj, A(a) wc-NZ, It, F(b), S(b), A(b) **1992** S, I, F, W, SA **1993** F, W, S, I. Lions-NZ(2,3). NZ **1994** S, I, F, W, SA(1,2), R, C **1995** I, F(a), W, S wc-Arg, It, A, NZ, F(b)
Points (4 – 1t): **1989** I(1t)

referees taking charge of Pilkington Cup semi-finals, then Old Haberdashers, then a school game, then an International. That shouldn't happen. Redefine the role of the IB, but don't disband. Somewhere has to be found for our senile geriatrics. Nothing wrong with IB structure that couldn't be corrected by the right people. It's become a dumping ground for old administrators who have an

307

artificial perception of the game because they don't speak to players and coaches. Look at their decision to keep maul law, the practical consequences of which are totally counter-productive. Once the maul is stationary the defence's job is complete and they can spread out across the field, so negating the whole purpose of the exercise

Notable landmarks in rugby career: England's most-capped hooker (63) and second only in the world order to New Zealand captain Sean Fitzpatrick (69). Became northern hemisphere's most experienced No2 with 53rd cap (versus Romania, Twickenham, 12.11.94) taking him past Scotland's Colin Deans. Well clear of previous English record holder John Pullin's mark (42 caps, 1966-76). Brian, nicknamed 'Pitbull', continued to be the picture of menace in England's pack in 1994/95, as the side won it's third Grand Slam in five seasons. World Cup campaign came as a big disappointment to Brian and team mates. Counts as one of his career highlights the 15–9 Twickenham defeat of New Zealand (27.11.93), opponents to whom he had lost out with '93 British Lions and in 1995 World Cup semi-finals (Cape Town, 18.6.95). Has only missed five of England's last 68 internationals dating back to his debut against Scotland in 1987. Former captain of Nottingham and England B (on first appearance) who represented England Students in 1982 and toured Romania and Spain with England U-23s. First played for Nottingham in 1981 and left them for Quins prior to 1990/91 season. Voted 1990/91 Whitbread/Rugby World 'Player of Year'. Ever-present in 1989 Lions' 2–1 series win over Australia. Toured with England to Australia/Fiji (1988), Argentina (1990), Fiji/Australia (1991) and South Africa (1994)

Touchlines: Opera, theatre, cooking, training, tennis, golf

Pleased to be back: Springbok wing Chester Williams after returning from injury in time to pick up a World Cup winners' medal.

Morris, C. D.   England

Full Name: Colin Dewi Morris
Club: Orrell
Position: Scrum-half
Height: 6ft (1.83m)
Weight: 13st 7lb (86kg)
Occupation: Sales executive, Hallbridge of Warrington, Sport and Leisure Wear
Born: Crickhowell, Wales, 9.2.64
Family: Penny (wife)
Former clubs: Brecon, Crewe & Alsager College, Winnington Park, Liverpool St Helens
International debut: England 28, Australia 19, 1988
Five Nations' debut: England 12, Scotland 12, 1989
Best moments in rugby: Scoring try on England debut and winning. Scoring winning try for North in 15–9 defeat of Australia (Oct 1988). Winning 1992 Grand Slam. 1993 Lions selection
Worst moment in rugby: Losing 9–12 to Wales at Cardiff (March 1989) and being dropped thereafter
Most embarrassing moment: Being dropped by North for match against US Eagles after five consecutive international caps and five consecutive divisional caps

England (1988)
Last Season	7 caps	0 pts
Career	26 caps	21 pts
Lions 1993	3 Tests	0 pts

Caps (26): **1988** A **1989:** S, I, F, W **1992** S, I, F, W, C, SA **1993** F, W, S, I. Lions-NZ(1,2,3) **1994** F, W, SA(1,2), R **1995** S(TR) wc-Arg, WS, A, NZ, F(b)

Points (21 – 5t): **1988** A(1t) **1992** S(1t), I(1t), F(1t), SA(1t)

Biggest influence on career: Mickey Skinner (Blackheath & England) – for his team talks
Serious injuries: Broken nose (three times), serious ligament damage to left shoulder, both knees and right ankle, dislocated finger, damaged shoulder (1993)
Other sporting achievements: Gwent Schools Under-19 County cricket finalists
Suggestions to improve rugby: All we in England ask is to be treated like everyone else.
Notable landmarks in rugby career: Rejected Rugby League move to Workington after bowing out of union following last summer's World Cup, a campaign in which he was England's undoubted star. His success could not have been more deserved, having quit his job to concentrate on rugby only to

then lose his place to Kyran Bracken. Missed England's '95 Five Nations Grand Slam triumph but returned in South Africa, playing in all but the Italian job. A first-choice British Lion in 1993, playing in all three Tests versus New Zealand, 1993/94 was up-and-down for Dewi. He returned home from Kiwi land and promptly fell off a scrambler, so missing the North of England's contest with the touring All Blacks. Looked to have recovered in time for international itself but went down with flu in week of game and had to pass jersey over to Bracken. A brave performance by his Bristol rival meant Dewi taking his tally of bench reserve 'caps' to 22 before being recalled after England's dismal defeat against Ireland. Immediately re-established himself with strong showing in Paris, where England yet again beat France, and followed up by helping bury Wales' Grand Slam hopes. An unused replacement throughout 1991 World Cup, he replaced Richard Hill for 1992 Five Nations Championship and responded with tries in first three games, against Scotland, Ireland and France. Disappeared as quickly as he rose when dropped by England after 1989 Five Nations' loss in Wales. Dewi had graduated from junior rugby to international level in six months, via Winnington Park, Liverpool St Helens, Lancashire, the North and England B. Scored three tries to inspire Lancashire to 32–9 victory over Middlesex in 1990 County Championship final. Toured with England to Argentina (1990), Australia (1991) and South Africa (1994)
Touchlines: Motocross, holidays spent on lazy beaches.

Morrison, I. R. Scotland

Full Name: Iain Robert Morrison
Club: London Scottish
Position: Flanker
Height: 6ft 1in (1.86m)
Weight: 15st 7lb (98kg)
Occupation: Money broker, Director of Bond Sales, Swiss Bank Corporation
Born: Linlithgow, 14.12.62
Family: Courtenay (child)
Family links with rugby: Father captain Melville College FP
Former clubs: Linlithgow, Cambridge Univ
International debut: Scotland 15, Ireland 3, 1993
Five Nations' debut: As above
Best moment in rugby: Winning 1991 Middlesex Sevens

Most respected opponent: Stuart Barnes (Bath & England)

Biggest influence on career: Tony Rodgers (Cambridge Univ coach)
Serious injuries: Broken right leg (plate attached with ten screws); Knee cartilage operation (1993); broken left leg (two places, 1994)
Notable landmarks in rugby: Integral part of Scotland's outstanding back row in 1995, Iain produced arguably

Scotland (1993)
Last Season	10 caps	0 pts
Career	15 caps	0 pts

Caps (15): **1993** I, F, W, E **1994** W, SA **1995** C, I, F(a), W, E, R wc-T, F(b), NZ
Points Nil

his best ever rugby in his final season before retiring after last summer's World Cup. Appeared in every Scottish game save the Cote d'Ivoire slaughter, yet his one try did not count as it came in the 62–7 non-cap Test defeat of Spain (Madrid, 6.5.95), so condemning him to ending his career without an international point to his name. Career ravaged by injury, his jinx striking again in 1993/94 when he broke his left leg in two places in opening quarter of Scotland's 29–6 defeat by Wales in Cardiff (15.1.94). To make matters worse it was the Anglo's first international appearance of that season, having been mighty unlucky to have missed out on a place on the 1993 British Lions tour to New Zealand following impressive debut series in '93 Five Nations. Such a bad break ensured that Iain missed remainder of campaign, not to mention summer tour to Argentina. A latecomer to international rugby, he had turned 30 when making his first appearance for Scotland A, in the 22–13 win over Ireland A on 28 December 1992. He then played in his first Scotland Trial and was promptly given his full debut (16.1.93) in the 15–3 defeat of Ireland. He retained his openside berth for duration of Championship. Yet during his formative days at Glenalmond School he had represented Scotland 16-Group at Sevens and toured with them to Zimbabwe. Joined Linlithgow aged 16. Varsity appearances ensued for Cambridge in 1983 and 1984, during which time he also toured to Japan and the USA. Regular for London Scottish and Anglo-Scots since 1985. Scored try in Anglo Scots' 19–16 win over touring French in 1987. Helped London Scottish to five London Floodlit Sevens titles in addition to twice being on winning sides at Dubai Sevens, most recently in 1992/93 with Scotland.
Touchlines: Collect antique glasses.

Mulder, J. C.　　　　　　　　　　　　South Africa

Full Name: Jacobus (Japie)
Cornelius Mulder
Province: Transvaal
Position: Centre
Height: 6ft ½in (1.84m)
Weight: 14st 11lb (89kg)
Occupation: Self employed
Born: 18.10.69
Family: Single
International debut: New Zealand
13, South Africa 9, 1994
Family links with rugby: Nephew of
former Springbok Boet Mulder
Notable landmarks in rugby career:
Partnered Hennie le Roux in South
Africa's World Cup-winning
midfield last summer, turning out in
the wins over Australia (Cape Town,
25.5.95), Western Samoa
(Johannesburg, 10.6.95), France
(Durban, 17.6.95) and the never-to-
be-forgotten 15–12 extra-time final
versus New Zealand (JoBurg,
24.6.95). Benefited from the neck
injury suffered by Natal rival Pieter

South Africa (1994)
Last Season	9 caps	5 pts
Career	9 caps	5 pts

Caps (9): **1994** NZ(2,3), S, W **1995**
　　　WS(a) wc-A, WS(b), F, NZ
Points (5 – 1t): **1994** S(1t)

Müller on 1994 tour to New Zealand, being called up as an emergency
replacement and going straight into the second Test. His strong tackling and
equally powerful running ensured his continued presence in the Springbok side,
though he had to wait for the 34–10 defeat of Scotland (Murrayfield, 19.11.94)
for his first international try, during an autumn tour in which he also appeared
against Wales A, Llanelli, Swansea and the Barbarians. Had emerged of a player
of substance in Britain the previous year, whilst on tour with the South African
Barbarians, for whom he turned out in five matches, scoring tries versus
Northampton and Ulster. Added further touchdowns in New Zealand against
Waikato (Hamilton, 16.7.94) and Canterbury (two: Christchurch, 30.7.94).
Transvaal's continued success (1993-94 Currie Cup winners) kept Japie in the
public eye and after starting 1995 in the side against Western Samoa (won
60–8) he was set fair for World Cup glory.

Müller, P. G.   South Africa

Full Name: Pieter Gysbert Müller
Club: College Rovers
Province: Natal
Position: Centre
Height: 6ft 3in (1.90m)
Weight: 14st 2lb (90kg)
Occupation: Sales executive
Born: Bloemfontein, 5.5.69
Family links with rugby: Brother
(Helgard) played for Orange Free
State and won two caps – 1986
Cv(4R) 1989 Wd(1R)
Former Province: Orange Free State
International debut: South Africa 24,
New Zealand 27, 1992
Notable landmarks in rugby career:
Missed most of 1994 after sustaining
bad neck injury in 14–22 first Test
loss to New Zealand (Dunedin,
9.7.94), against whom he had also
made his debut in 1992, when South
Africa emerged from the
international sporting wilderness.
Indeed, up until the injury he was
one of only two players (James Small
being the other) to have played in all
14 Tests since the Springboks'

South Africa (1992)

Last Season	3 caps	0 pts
Career	15 caps	10 pts

Caps (15): **1992** NZ, A, F(1,2), E **1993**
F(1,2), A(1,2,3), Arg(1,2) **1994**
E(1,2), NZ(1)
Points (10 – 2t): **1992** NZ(1t) **1993**
A(2:1t)

return. Returned for autumn tour to Wales and Scotland, appearing against
Cardiff, Neath, Swansea, Combined Scottish Districts (scored two tries) and
the Barbarians (one try), but injury again sidelined him in early part of '95,
condemning him to miss out on World Cup glory. Pieter had been acclaimed as
the best player in South African rugby in '92. A big and powerful midfield
presence, he claimed his second international try in the 28–20 second Test
reversal at the hands of Australia (Brisbane, 14.8.93) during a season in which
he was permanently partnered in the centres by Heinrich Fuls. On tour in
Australia, he also turned out against South Australia, New South Wales and
Queensland, while he featured in five of the six Autumn engagements in
Argentina. Born and educated in Bloemfontein he represented South African
Schools before making his Provincial bow for Orange Free State in 1990. After
27 matches for OFS he switched allegiances to Natal, with whom he picked up
a Currie Cup winners' medal in '92, following the 14–13 final win over
Transvaal at Ellis Park, Johannesburg on 12 September. It was in the same
arena that he had made his international debut a month earlier, in the 24–27

defeat by New Zealand. His place in the XV which took the Springboks back into genuine Test rugby for the first time in 11 years was won with a fine performance for Natal in the 25–43 loss to the All Blacks at Kings Park, Durban (1.8.92). He marked his debut in South African colours with a try to go with the two bagged by fellow centre Danie Gerber. The following week he was required at Newlands in Cape Town for the visit of Australia, who ran riot with an historic 26–3 win. Pieter retained his berth alongside Gerber throughout the tour of France and England, playing in all three Tests.

Mullin, B. J. Ireland

Full Name: Brendan John Mullin
Club: Blackrock College
Position: Centre
Height: 6ft 1in (1.85m)
Weight: 13st 3lb (84kg)
Occupation: Stockbroker, Davy Stockbrokers
Born: Isreal, 31.10.63
Family: Sharon (wife)
Former clubs: Trinity College Dublin, Oxford Univ, London Irish
International debut: Ireland 9, Australia 16, 1984
Five Nations debut: Scotland 15, Ireland 18, 1985
Best moment in rugby: Selection for 1989 Lions
Worst moment in rugby: Ireland's dreadful campaign at 1987 World Cup
Biggest influence on career: Jim Burns (school hurdles coach)
Other sporting achievements: International hurdling for Ireland
Suggestions to improve rugby: Administration of rugby must be conducted on a more accurate and professional basis. IRB must offer direction and leadership. Rugby has long since outgrown what archaic IRB was set up to administer
Notable landmarks in rugby career: Came out of 33 months of retirement to bolster Irish midfield in 1994/95 and extend his national try-scoring record to 17 with touchdowns against Scotland (Edinburgh, 4.2.95) and Wales (Cardiff, 18.3.95). The latter score was absolutely critical as it decided the Wooden Spoon decider, giving Ireland her one and only win of the 1995 Five Nations campaign. Played throughout Ireland's run to the World Cup quarter-finals, becoming one of a select band to have appeared in all three tournaments dating back to the first in 1987. Had opted out of international rugby three-quarters

of the way through the 1992 Championship, citing business and personal reasons, so apparently ending a proud career that had begun with six Irish Schools caps in 1981–82, three as captain. Made B debut against Scotland in 1983 and following season broke into full team. Played for 1986 Lions against Rest of World in Cardiff to mark centenary of IRB. Scored three tries against Tonga in '87 World Cup, having previously won two Oxford Blues (1986–87). Voted 1988/89 Irish Player of Year and was leading try-scorer (7) for 1989 British Lions, for whom he played in 12–30 first Test loss to Australia. Represented 1989 Home Unions XV in 29–27 defeat of

Ireland (1984)

Last Season	10 caps	10 pts
Career	55 caps	72 pts
Lions 1986		
1989	1 Test	0 pts

Caps (55): **1984** A **1985** S, W, E **1986** F, W, E, S, R **1987** E, S, F, W(a) wc-W(b), C, T, A **1988** S, F, W, E(a,b), WS. It **1989** F, W, E, S, NZ. Lions-A(1) **1990** E, S, W,Arg **1991** F, W, E, S(a), Na(1,2) wc-J, S(b), A **1992** W, E, S **1994** US **1995** E, S, F(a), W(a), It wc-NZ, J, W(b), F(b)

Points (72 – 17t,1c): **1985** E(1t) **1986** E(1t), R(2t) **1987** W(1t) wc-T(3t) **1988** S(1t), WS(1t) **1989** F(1t), S(2t) **1991** W(1t), S(1t), Na(1:1c) **1995** S(1t), W(a:1t)

France in Paris and set Irish try-scoring record with his 15th in 25–28 loss to Scotland (Murrayfield, 16.3.91), six years after claiming his first against England on his fourth appearance. Sequence of 29 consecutive caps broken when missing 1990 Paris match.

NTamack, E.   France

Full Name: Emile NTamack
Club: Toulouse
Position: Fullback, wing
Height: 6ft 2in (1.88m)
Weight: 14st 3lb (90kg)
Occupation: Student
Born: Lyon, 25.6.70
Family: Single
International debut: Wales 24, France 15, 1994
Five Nations debut: As above
Best moment in rugby: Scoring first Test try v Canada (1994); helping Toulouse win 1994 French championship
Former clubs: Meyzieu, Lavaur
Notable landmarks in rugby career: A true world star and heart breaker

par excellence. Emile it was who muscled over for the try, four minutes into injury-time, that earned France a crucial 22–19 World Cup victory over Scotland (Pretoria, 3.6.95). He then repeated the feat in the 36–12 quarter-final defeat of Ireland (Durban, 10.6.95), waiting until stoppage time to run an interception back virtually the length of the field. And very little time remained when

France (1994)
Last Season	9 caps	30 pts
Career	13 caps	40 pts

Caps (13): **1994** W, C(a), NZ(1,2), C(b) **1995** W, I(a), R wc-T, S(b), I(b), SA, E(b)

Points (40 – 7t,1c,1p): **1994** C(a:1t), NZ(2:1t) **1995** W(1t), I(a:1t,1c,1p) wc-S(b:1t), I(b:1t), E(b:1t)

the Toulouse star scored the decisive try in the otherwise dreary 19–9 third place play-off win over England (Pretoria, 22.6.95). But that was only half the story as Emile, who helped Toulouse complete back-to-back French title wins in 1995, also claimed scores against Ireland, Wales and New Zealand, the latter coming in a 23–20 win (Auckland, 3.7.94) that gave France an historic 2–0 series win. The only disappointment for the ex-Meyzeieu Lavau player was his clueless goal-kicking versus Ireland (Dublin, 4.3.95). Emile had claimed his first Test try against Canada (Ottawa, 4.6.94), but there was little celebrating as France crashed to a shock 18–16 defeat. His debut had also ended in disappointment in the cauldron of Cardiff Arms Park. A trapped nerve in Philippe Bernat-Salle's neck gave the Toulouse flier his chance but he didn't receive another once the game got underway as a marvellous performance handed France their first defeat by Wales in 13 contests. Lost his place to Bordeaux University's William Techoueyres for the '94 championship closer against Scotland but was included in France's summer tour squad (while the garcon Techoueyres was not). Regarded by many as the new Serge Blanco.

Jonah Lomu ties up England's defence ... and keeps going.

Ofahengaue, V.   Australia

Full Name: Viliame Ofahengaue
State: New South Wales
Club: Manly
Position: Flanker, No 8
Height: 6ft 4in (1.93m)
Weight: 16st 7lb (105kg)
Occupation: Pile driver, Emanon Pty Ltd (Manly, NSW)
Born: 3.5.68
Family: Heleni (wife), Lavinia (mother), Sione (father), Sione Kata (brother), Epalahame (brother), Talia (sister)
International debut: New Zealand 21, Australia 6, 1990
Best moments in rugby: Being picked to play for Wallabies and winning 1991 World Cup
Worst moment in rugby: Being left in Australia by the New Zealand team when I toured Oz with them in 1988
Notable landmarks in rugby career: 'Willie O' returned strongly from the serious injury which had sidelined him throughout 1993, reclaiming his place in the Test side from Queensland's Ilie Tabua, following the winning series against Ireland and Italy. The star of Australia's 1992 tour to Ireland and Wales marked his

Australia (1990)
Last Season	7 caps	10 pts
Career	24 caps	26 pts

Caps (24): 1990 NZ(1,2,3) 1991 W(a), E(a), NZ(a1,a2). wc-Arg, W(b), I, NZ(b), E(b) 1992 S(1,2), SA, I, W 1994 WS, NZ 1995 Arg(1,2R) wc-SA, C, E
Points (26 – 6t): 1990 NZ(2:1t) 1991 W(a:1t), E(a:2t) 1994 WS(1t) 1995 Arg(1:1t)

comeback with a try in the 73–3 rout of Western Samoa (Sydney, 6.8.94) though, to be fair, most Wallabies did score that day. His sixth Test score came in the 53–7 first Test win over Argentina (Brisbane, 29.4.95) and he went onto play in three of the four World Cup matches that constituted Australia's brief defence of their crown. Auckland-educated, he toured New Zealand in 1990 as a late inclusion for Jeff Miller. Two years earlier he had been in the New Zealand Schools side but because of visa difficulties he was refused re-entry into the land of the Kiwi and headed back to Oz to live with his uncle. New Zealand's loss was Australia's gain as he has quickly amassed 17 caps and developed a fearsome reputation as an explosive runner and bone-crunching defender. Represented the World XV against New Zealand in the 1992 Centenary Series and helped Australia reach the 1993 World Cup Sevens final in Edinburgh
Touchlines: Music, movies.

317

Ojomoh, S. O.   England

Full Name: Stephen Oziegbe
Ojomoh
Club: Bath
Position: No 8, flanker
Height: 6ft 3in (1.90m)
Weight: 16st 7lb (100kg)
Occupation: Promotions officer,
Johnson's News, Bath
Born: Benin City, Nigeria, 25.5.70
Family: Single
International debut: England 12,
Ireland 13, 1994
Five Nations debut: As above
Best moment in rugby: Walking out
onto Parc des Princes pitch in
England jersey
Worst moment in rugby: Final
whistle of 1994 defeat to Ireland
Most respected opponent: Chris
Sheasby (Harlequins & England A)
Serious injuries: Ankle and knee
ligament damage
Other sporting achievements: South
West decathlon champion (1988).
Runner-up in 1988 English Schools

England (1994)

Last Season	6 caps	0 pts
Career	10 caps	0 pts

Caps (10): **1994** I, F, SA(1R,2), R **1995**
S(R) wc-Arg, WS, A(TR), F(b)
Points Nil

discus championship. South-West long-jump and triple-jump champion. Third
in All-England decathlon championship
Notable landmarks in rugby career: An outstanding campaign for England in
South Africa (1994), during which he appeared in both Tests, ensured Steve
started the new Test season versus Romania (Twickenham, 12.11.94). But he
was less than convincing in England's 54–3 win, playing in the openside flanker
berth, and was relegated to bench duties thereafter as Dean Richards' return for
the Five Nations' Grand Slam campaign allowed coach Jack Rowell to move
Ben Clarke to No 7. On the home front Steve continued to ply his trade in Bath's
second string but remained in the England squad and shared in the last half-
hour of the championship, coming on as a 51st minute replacement for
Richards in the 24–12 defeat of Scotland (Twickenham, 18.3.95). Further
injury to Deano allowed Steve to win three of his four caps at last summer's
World Cup, the exception being in the game against Western Samoa when he
tried his hand at blindside. England won 44–22. A brilliant natural athlete, he
has worked the skills that brought him schoolboy honours in the decathlon
disciplines into his rugby and become a very dynamic performer. Drafted into
England side for visit of Ireland (19.2.94) and although England lost his

performance earned praise. So much so, in fact, that he retained his place for the trip to Paris a fortnight later and played central role in fine win. When Richards then announced himself fit again the selectors only reluctantly moved Steve onto the bench for title decider against Wales. Previously played for England at 18-Group, Colts and Under-21 levels and joined Bath from Rosslyn Park in 1989. Toured with England A to New Zealand (1992) and Canada (1993). **Touchlines:** Basketball.

O'Shea, C. M. P. Ireland

Full Name: Conor Michael Patrick O'Shea
Club: Lansdowne
Position: Fullback, outside-half
Height: 6ft 2in (1.88m)
Weight: 14st 6lb (92kg)
Occupation: Lending executive, Ulster Investment Bank
Born: Limerick, 21.10.70
Family: Single
Family links with rugby: Brothers (Donal and Diarmid) play for Terenure College
International debut: Ireland 25, Romania 3, 1993
Five Nations debut: France 35, Ireland 15, 1994
Suggestions to improve rugby: Nothing. Game is running well
Notable landmarks in rugby career: Benefited from rival Jim Staples' misfortune at last summer's World Cup, having travelled to South Africa as back-up. Harlequin Staples broke his hand in Ireland's thunderous opener against New Zealand (JoBurg, 27.5.95) and

Ireland (1993)

Last Season	6 caps	3 pts
Career	13 caps	14 pts

Caps (13): **1993** R **1994** F, W, E, S, A(1,2), US **1995** E, S wc-J, W(b), F(b)

Points (14 – 1c,3p,1dg): **1994** A(1:1p), A(2:1c,1p,1dg), US(1p)

Conor stepped in for the remainder of the campaign, against Wales, Japan and France. Had only established himself in Ireland side during 1993/94, three years after making his Irish Under-21 debut against Netherlands (lost 7–21, Leiden 21.9.90) and England. Took his Under-21 cap-tally to four the following season with appearances against Wales (lost 15–22, Newport 16.10.91) and England (won 19–10, Dublin 23.10.91), scoring try in latter. Broke into Leinster senior side in 1992/93, having previously represented province at

Under-19 (two years) and Under-20 (two years). Came on as 22nd minute replacement for Staples in 1993 Irish trial and responded with a try. But cracked left ankle the following week ruled him out of Test contention until embarking on Irish development squad's summer tour to Zimbabwe, Namibia and South Africa. Tour displays earned him starting spot in 1993/94 Irish side, displacing Colin Wilkinson and Ciaran Clarke who had shared duties in the previous campaign, and his penetrating running combined with sound defence ensured that he remained a permanent member of the side through five internationals. Broke his Test scoring famine with 11 points in two internationals against 1994 Wallabies after Eric Elwood had dried up but after starting 1994/95 with three caps, he was edged out by your man Staples.
Touchlines: Golf, tennis.

Osborne, G. M.   New Zealand

Full Name: Glen Matthew Osborne
Province: North Harbour
Position: Fullback
Height: 6ft (1.83m)
Weight: 13st 3lb (84kg)
Occupation: Life agent, NZI Life
Born: Wanganui, 27.8.71
Family: Single
Family links with rugby: Brother Charles plays for Wanganui; uncle Bill Osborne played for All Blacks (1975-82)
International debut: New Zealand 73, Canada 7, 1995
Notable landmarks in rugby career: Scored 15 tries in 19 outings for North Harbour to earn World Cup selection by All Blacks and go onto make a big impression in South Africa. Voted Player of the Tournament at the 1994 Hong Kong Sevens (his third visit), Glen proceeded to represent New Zealand Maoris (against Mid Canterbury and Fiji) and the NZ Barbarians before

New Zealand (1995)

Last Season	6 caps	25 pts
Career	6 caps	25 pts

Caps (6): **1995** C wc-I, W, J, E, SA
Points (25 – 5t): **1995** C(2t) wc-I(1t), J(2t)

breaking into the New Zealand side against Canada (Auckland, 22.4.95). Two tries in the 73–7 rout of the Canucks marked Glen out for special attention on reaching the World Cup but he took it in his stride, looking both assured and dangerous in the All Blacks' Pool C matches against Ireland (one try), Wales and

Japan (two tries in world record hammering). A recurring ankle injury put him out of the quarter-final tie against Scotland, with Otago golden boy Jeff Wilson moving to fullback, but he was quickly restored for the England semi-final and looked a million dollars. Glen made his first-class debut in 1990 as an 18-year-old, playing at fly-half for Wanganui against Wellington. He moved from wing to fullback before representing the All Black Colts in '91 and then joining North Harbour in 1992, the year in which he represented New Zealand in the World Cup Sevens in Edinburgh. Won special acclaim in 1994 for his brilliant try-scoring performance in North Harbour's 27–23 defeat of France (Auckland, 12.6.94). Describes his most enjoyable tackle as Jonah Lomu … 'Because it's there!'

Patterson, D. W.   Scotland

Full Name: Derrick William Patterson
Club: West Hartlepool
Position: Scrum-half
Height: 5ft 9½in (1.76m)
Weight: 13st 11lb (83kg)
Occupation: Joiner, Heritage Homes, the Yuille Group
Born: Hawick, 6.7.68
Family: Single
International debut: Scotland 10, South Africa 34, 1994
Five Nations debut: None
Former clubs: Hawick, Edinburgh Academicals
Notable landmarks in rugby career: Bruising introduction to international rugby, having been overshadowed by Springbok counterpart Joost van der Westhuizen on his debut (Murrayfield, 19.11.94), an occasion on which he became Hawick's 53rd player to be capped, and then knocked all over the shop by an

Scotland (1994)

Last Season	2 caps	0 pts
Career	2 caps	0 pts

Caps (2): **1994** SA **1995** wc-T
Points Nil

over-zealous Tongan side in Scotland's 41–5 World Cup win at the tail end of the season (Pretoria, 30.5.95). However, he proved his worth in the latter game with a combative display on what resembled a battlefield. In between his two Test engagements, Derrick quit Hawick for English first division outfit West Hartlepool, having spent the summer of 1994 on tour in Argentina with

Scotland, appearing in the games against Buenos Aires and Rosario. First played for Hawick in 1987 and went on to represent both South, Edinburgh and Scottish Exiles in the Inter-District Championship. Moved to Edinburgh Accies in 1991, from where he graduated to the Scotland B side (vs France, 1992) and would have turned out for Scotland A against Spain the same year but for injury forcing his withdrawl. But played for Scottish Development XV in 12–31 loss to touring All Blacks (Edinburgh, 16.11.93).
Touchlines: Golf.

Pene, A. R. B. New Zealand

Full Name: Arran Rawi Brett Pene
Province: Otago
Position: No 8
Height: 6ft 3¼in (1.91m)
Weight: 16st 6lb (104kg)
Occupation: Student
Born: 26.10.67
International debut: New Zealand 14, World XV 28, 1992
Most embarrasing moment in rugby: Trying to chip kick down the line and missing ball altogether
Notable landmarks in rugby career: Captained New Zealand Maoris' tour to South Africa in 1994 but had lean time of it in All Black colours. In the absence of fellow Maori Zinzan Brooke, he operated at No 8 in the first Test against France (Christchurch, 26.6.94) but defeat cost him his place and he has not started a Test since, though he did add to his cap tally with two appearances as a replacement. The previous season he had been one of the stars of New Zealand's series-clinching third Test win over the

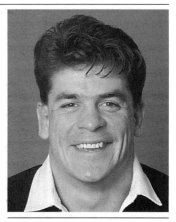

New Zealand (1992)

Last Season	3 caps	0 pts
Career	15 caps	16 pts

Caps (15): **1992** Wd(1R,2,3), I(1,2), A(1,2R) **1993** BL(3), A, WS, S, E **1994** F(1,2R), SA(1R)
Points (16 – 4t): **1992** Wd(2:1t), Wd(3:1t), I(2:2t)

British Lions (Auckland, 3.7.93). Kept his place thereafter on autumn tour to England and Scotland, in addition to both Tests turning out in the Saturday games against London, South West England, England A, Scotland A and the Barbarians. A member of Otago's outstanding All Black back row which took Otago to the 1992 National Championship final, Arran was one of a number of players who owed his All Black jersey to an outstanding '92 trial perfomance.

Ultimately, though, his Test selection was down to Mike Brewer, his Provincial captain and fellow back rower, whose calf injury ruled him out of selection and the national captaincy. Arran grabbed his chance with both hands and, after coming on as a 35th replacement for Michael Jones in the 14–28 first Test defeat by the World XV, monopolised the No 8 berth throughout the rest of the centenary series and two-Test visit of Ireland. Four tries in his first four Tests did his cause no harm. Little surprise that he won selection to the '92 All Black squad for Australia and South Africa, but injuries – in particular a broken hand – led to him losing his first-choice spot to the aforementioned Brooke for the second Test against Australia. Despite coming on as a replacement for Kevin Schuler in that game, he failed to win back his place for the third 'dead' leg of the Bledisloe Cup series or for the victory over South Africa in Johannesburg.

Peters, E. W. Scotland

Full Name: Eric William Peters
Club: Bath
Position: No 8
Height: 6ft 5½in (1.95m)
Weight: 16st 10lb (101kg)
Occupation: Chartered surveyor, King Sturge and Co, Bath
Born: Glasgow, 28.1.69
Family: Single
International debut: Scotland 22, Canada 6, 1995
Five Nations debut: Scotland 26, Ireland 13, 1995
Former clubs: Old Brentwoodians, Loughborough Univ, Cambridge Univ, Saracens
Notable landmarks in rugby career: Outstanding newcomer to international scene in 1994/95, Eric played in a Scottish back row (along with Wainwright and Morrison) which bore comparison with the legendary Jeffrey-Calder-White Grand Slam triumverate five years previously. He scored a brilliant try against Wales which took the new lid off Murrayfield (4.3.95) and he repeated the five-point trick in the 41–5 World Cup win over Tonga (Pretoria, 30.5.95). It is hard to believe Eric only broke into Test match rugby in January, such has been his progress. Remember that

Scotland (1995)

Last Season	9 caps	15 pts
Career	9 caps	15 pts

Caps (9): **1995** C, I, F(a), W, E, R wc-T, F(b), NZ
Points (15 – 3t): **1995** W(1t), R(1t) wc-T(1t)

323

Scotland had failed to win their nine internationals prior to his debut against Canada (21.1.95). But the Scots won that and reeled off four straight victories before losing the Grand Slam decider to Eric's former country (Twickenham, 18.3.95). Having captained Cambridge to Varsity glory in 1992, he represented England Under-21s and Students, as well as the Barbarians and Penguins. After moving to Bath, and making his first XV debut in October 1993, he quickly progressed further up the representative ladder, helping Scottish Exiles roam unbeaten through the 1994/95 Inter-District Championship, playing in a Scottish Select's 10–35 loss to the touring Springboks (Aberdeen, 15.11.94), and turning out in Scotland A's defeat of Italy in January 1995.
Touchlines: Training.

Pienaar, J. F.   South Africa

Full Name: Jacobus François Pienaar
Province: Transvaal
Position: Flanker
Height: 6ft 4in (1.92m)
Weight: 17st 1lb (104kg)
Occupation: Self-employed businessman
Born: Port Elizabeth, 2.1.67
Family: Single
International debut: South Africa 20, France 20, 1993
Notable landmarks in rugby career:
A quite remarkable man, having teamed up with South African president Nelson Mandela to give us the enduring memory of the 1995 World Cup. The sight of Mandela in Francois' No 6 Springbok jersey presenting him with the Webb Ellis trophy on that magical afternoon at Ellis Park, Johannesburg (24.6.95) will surely never be forgotten. He led by splendid example both on and off the pitch, but especially off the pitch. He not only said the right things at all time, he convinced us that he meant every word of them. He even

South Africa (1993)

Last Season	14 caps	5 pts
Career	21 caps	5 pts

Caps (21): **1993** F(1,2), A(1,2,3), Arg(1,2) **1994** E(1,2), NZ(2,3), Arg(1,2), S, W **1995** WS(a) wc-A, C, WS(b), F, NZ

Points (5 – 1t): **1993** A(3:1t)

organised for the cash-strapped Romanians to be given a set of brand new Adidas kit before flying home. Francois was a wonderful ambassador for the new Republic and deserved everything he got. Unhappily, the Transvaal RFU

324

were probaby thinking the same, at the time of going to press, when Francois was leading a walkout of leading players demanding better pay terms and was under threat of the sack by a province whom he skippered to back-to-back Currie Cup wins (1993-94) and the 1993 Super Ten triumph, not to mention a stunning 24–21 victory over the '94 England tourists. Appointed to skipper South Africa on his Test debut against France (Durban, 26.6.93), so becoming only the third Springbok to be so honoured (after Basil Kenyon and Des Van Jaarsveld). The game ended in a 20–20 draw and France went on to nick the series with an 18–17 win in Johannesburg the following week. Toured Argentina and Australia in 1993, his only international try thus far coming in Australia's 19–12 third Test win in Sydney (21.8.93). In 1994, concussion suffered against Wellington forced him to miss the first five matches of a largely unsuccessful New Zealand tour, including the first Test. But did not miss an international thereafter, save for the midweek World Cup-tie against Romania.

Pini, M. Australia

Full Name: Matthew Pini
State: Queensland
Club: Wests (Brisbane)
Position: Fullback
Height: 5ft 11½in (1.82m)
Weight: 14st 13lb (90kg)
Occupation: Plumber
Born: 21.3.69
International debut: Australia 33, Ireland 13, 1994
Notable landmarks in rugby career:
Went to 1995 World Cup as Australia's first-choice full-back but was quickly usurped by Matt Burke, following the Wallabies' opening day loss to South Africa (Cape Town, 25.5.95). Appeared just once thereafter, and that fleetingly as a bloodbin replacement for Danny Herbert during Australia's 42–3 win over Romania (Stellenbosch, 3.6.95). The former Australia Under-21 standout had made his debut in the 33–13 first Test defeat of Ireland (Brisbane, 5.6.94) only to strain a hamstring in training for the second Test. Returned against Italy

Australia (1994)		
Last Season	8 caps	10 pts
Career	8 caps	10 pts

Caps (8): **1994** I(1), It(2), WS, NZ **1995** Arg(1,2) wc-SA, R(TR)

Points (10 – 2t): **1994** WS(1t) **1995** Arg(1:1t)

(Melbourne, 26.6.94) after Burke was crocked and was a fixture in the next six matches, spanning 11 months. He claimed his first try in the extraordinary 73–3 rout of Western Samoa (Sydney, 6.8.94) and added a second in the 53–7 first Test defeat of Argentina (Brisbane, 29.4.95).

Popplewell, N. J.　　　　　　　　　Ireland

Full Name: Nicholas James Popplewell
Club: Wasps
Position: Loosehead prop
Height: 5ft 10in (1.78m)
Weight: 17st 3lb (105kg)
Occupation: Broker, Garban Europe
Born: Dublin, 6.4.64
Family: Rachel (wife)
Former clubs: Gorey, Greystones
International debut: Ireland 6, New Zealand 23, 1989
Five Nations' debut: Ireland 15, Wales 16, 1992
Best moment in rugby: 1993 Lions second Test win over New Zealand
Worst moment in rugby: Grant Fox's controversial late penalty winner in first Test for All Blacks against '93 Lions
Most respected opponent: Olo Brown (Auckland & New Zealand)
Serious injuries: Broken ribs (twice), cruciate knee ligaments (operation, May 1994)
Other sporting achievements: Hockey for Irish Schools (three caps)
Suggestions to improve rugby: Decrease value of penalty goal to two points. Scrap 90-degree scrum wheel law. Don't pay players a wage for playing

Ireland (1989)

Last Season	9 caps	5 pts
Career	32 caps	13 pts

Caps (32): **1989** NZ **1990** Arg **1991** Na(1,2) wc-Z,S,A **1992** W, E, S, F, NZ(1,2), A **1993** S, F, W, E, R **1994** F, W, E, S, US **1995** E, S, F(a), W(a) wc-NZ, J, W(b), F(b)

Points (13 – 3t): **1991** wc-Z(2t) **1995** wc-W(b:1t)

Notable landmarks in rugby career: Scored crucial try against Wales (Johannesburg, 4.6.95) which set Ireland on their way to gaining a place in the World Cup quarter-finals. Had captained his country in the previous match, a 50–28 win over Japan (Bloemfontein, 31.5.95), fitting for a player who in only his second full season as Ireland's first-choice loosehead prop had gained selection for 1993 British Lions (the Emerald Isle's solitary representative in the

Test side (for all three engagements). An ever-present in 1993/94 campaign, also turning out for Barbarians in 12–25 loss to touring All Blacks (Cardiff, 4.12.93), Poppy missed 1994 tour to Australia to have an operation on cruciate knee ligaments. Fully repaired, and having crossed the Irish Sea from Greystones to north-west London (Wasps), he was an everpresent in 1994/95, sharing with Brendan Mullin the distinction of starting all 10 internationals. Had taken over the Irish No1 jersey during 1991/92 season following 1991 tour to Namibia where he played in both Tests. Made great start to 1991 World Cup when scoring two tries in 55–11 Pool win over Zimbabwe in Dublin (6.10.91). In 1991/92 was one of only three permanent fixtures in the Irish side (along with Vinnie Cunningham and Paddy Johns) throughout seven-Test Irish programme. Previously, Nick had been a member of Irish party which toured France (May 1988) and North America (1989: playing in 24-21 defeat of Canada). Retired injured after 20 minutes of full debut against 1989 All Blacks and lost place for 1990 Championship. Redundant thereafter, except for 1990 Argentina (won 20–18) game, before heading off to Namibia. Helped train Presentation Juniors Bray U-15s to two Leinster Junior Cups in three years. Represented Ireland U-25s v US Eagles (1990). Scored one of Ireland B's four tries in 24–10 win over England B (Old Belvedere, 1.3.91)

Touchlines: Golf (18-handicap), tennis, squash.

Proctor, W. T.   Wales

Full Name: Wayne Thomas Proctor
Club: Llanelli
Position: Wing, fullback
Height: 6ft (1.83m)
Weight: 13st (78kg)
Occupation: Student, Swansea Institute of Higher Education
Born: Bridgend, 12.6.72
Family: Single
Former Club: Cardigan Youth
International debut: Wales 6, Australia 23, 1992
Five Nations' debut: Wales 10, England 9, 1993
Best moment in rugby: Beating England on Five Nations' debut (6.2.93)

Worst moment in rugby: Broken jaw suffered against Ireland (1994)
Most embarrassing moment: Being interviewed by the BBC for the first time
Most respected opponent: Tony Underwood (Leicester & England)

Other sporting achievements: Represented Wales 11 times at athletics; third in 1988 British Schools 400m hurdles
Serious injuries: Broken jaw (1994)
Suggestions to improve rugby: Introduce alternative to the scrum to help quicken up the game. Sell the game better. Televise more live games at different levels

Wales (1992)		
Last Season	6 caps	0 pts
Career	17 caps	10 pts

Caps (17): **1992** A **1993** E, S, Z(1,2), Na, C **1994** I, C, Fj, WS, R, It, SA **1995** S, I(a) wc-NZ

Points (10 – 2t): **1993** Z(1:1t), Na(1t)

Notable landmarks in rugby career: Wayne's three-year battle with Nigel Walker for the Wales left wing berth was resolved in his favour last summer when he alone was selected in the World Cup squad by caretaker coach Alex Evans, ironically Walker's club coach at Cardiff. It proved a chastening experience for Wayne, who made just one appearance, and that opposite Jonah Lomu in New Zealand's 34–9 win (Johannesburg, 4.6.95). Much to Wayne's obvious amusement (honest), the All Blacks switched Lomu onto his wing moments before kick-off. Mind you, it was the one and only game Lomu played in which he was anonymous. Wayne's cause was not helped by the three-try debut of Gareth Thomas against Japan, who returned for the catastrophic Ireland defeat (JoBurg, 4.6.95) which condemned Wales to an early flight home. But at least Wayne returned with his health, unlike in 1993/94 when he suffered a broken jaw in Dublin (5.2.94). It was only his second start of the campaign (Having also figured in 24–26 pre-Christmas loss to Canada) and promptly ended his season. It was a shame as he had discovered try-scoring knack on 1993 tour of Zimbabwe and Namibia, claiming a try against each host. Rapidly progressed into Wales senior side in 1992/93, only seven months after having made debut for Welsh Under-21s in 28–19 win over Scotland (Stirling, 18.4.92). Made his Test debut in the 6–23 loss to Australia (Cardiff, 21.11.92). Wayne, who had previously won four Welsh Youth caps and three Wales Under-19 caps (touring with the latter to Canada), kept his place for the first two matches of the 1993 Five Nations' Championship, sharing in the euphoria which surrounded the 10–9 defeat of England at Cardiff and then the dejection which followed their 0–20 shutout at Murrayfield. Partook in Llanelli's league and cup double in 1992/93, having turned out in 16–7 Final defeat of Swansea the previous season
Touchlines: Athletics, tennis, badminton.

Rayer, M. A. Wales

Full Name: Michael Anthony Rayer
Club: Cardiff
Position: Fullback
Height: 5ft 10in (1.78m)
Weight: 13st 3lb (78kg)
Occupation: Sales representative, Dimex Ltd, Manchester
Born: Cardiff, 21.7.65
Family: Debra (wife), Abigail (4) and Lloyd (2)
Family links with rugby: Father (Alec) played for Penarth, Cardiff Athletic and Llandaff North
Former Club: Llandaff North
International debut: Wales 13, Western Samoa 16, 1991
Five Nations' debut: England 24, Wales 0, 1992
Best moment in rugby: Landing dropped goal in extra-time of 1987 Schweppes Cup final against Swansea to put Cardiff in winning position; scoring a try in Cardiff's 15–8 Swalec Cup final win over Llanelli (1994)
Worst moment in rugby: Being robbed of Lions chance when dropped by Wales (1993)

Wales (1991)		
Last Season	2 caps	0 pts
Career	21 caps	23 pts

Caps (21): **1991** wc-WS(R), Arg, A(R) **1992** E(R), A **1993** E, S, I, Z(1), Na, J(R) **1994** S(R), I(R), F, W wc(q)-P. C, Fj, WS wc(q)-R, It
Points (23 – 4t,1p): **1991** wc-Arg(1p) **1993** J(R:1t) **1994** S(R:2t), Fj(1t)

Most respected opponent: Jean-Baptiste Lafond (Begles & France)
Serious injuries: Dislocated elbow (1988), broken leg (1994), sprung shoulder joint, damaged ribs, torn hamstring, ankle and knee ligaments
Other sporting achievements: Captained Wales B baseball team (1990/91)
Suggestions to improve rugby: Somehow get the International Board to discuss law changes with the players. We should be more involved and develop a more professional attitude. In short, disband 'old school tie' committees and stop living in past
Notable landmarks in rugby career: Wretched 1994/95 for Mike, who returned from a summer spent touring the South Seas to play in Wales' two World Cup play-off qualifying matches against Romania and Italy, before breaking his leg so badly playing for Cardiff that he was forced to write off the rest of the season, including the 1995 World Cup. Yet had topped Five Nations try-scoring charts (along with compatriot Nigel Walker and Frenchman Philippe Saint-Andre) in 1994 thanks to two touchdowns after coming on as a replacement against

Scotland (Cardiff, 15.1.94). Had started 1993/94 as second-choice fullback behind Tony Clement and it was not until last two games (against France and England) that he finally displaced his Swansea rival. Not that Mike missed out as he was also deployed as a replacement against Japan (scoring try) and Ireland. More of a disappointment to him was being dropped for final International of 1993 Five Nations' campaign against France, as it wrecked his Lions ambitions. Instead Clem was picked and Mike spent summer with Wales in Zimbabwe and Namibia. Captained Wales Youth (1983–85) at fullback prior to joining Cardiff in 1984/85, he played twice for Wales B, as a replacement against France B at Begles (lost 0–26, 17.10.87) and then from the start against the same opposition at La Teste two years later (won 28–15, 12.11.89). Toured Namibia with Wales (1990) but was unable to shift Paul Thorburn from fullback slot, despite scoring 28 points in 67–9 defeat of North Region (Tsumeb, 6.6.90). Top scored on tour with 64 points in three appearances. Knee surgery in August 1991 further delayed his entry into big time, but day finally arrived when replacing Clement during World Cup defeat by Western Samoa. Third and fourth Wales B appearances came in 1992/93 against North of England (scoring try in 21–13 win at Pontypool, 14.10.93) and Australia (7.11.92).

Redpath, B. W.　　　　　　　　Scotland

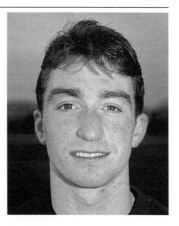

Full Name: Bryan William Redpath
Club: Melrose
Position: Scrum-half
Height: 5ft 7in (1.70m)
Weight: 11st 4lb (67kg)
Occupation: Self-employed joiner
Born: Galashiels, 2.7.71
Family: Single
Family links with rugby: Andrew (brother) has played for Melrose and Scotland U-21s; Craig (brother) for Melrose, Scotland U-21s and B; Lynne (sister) for Scotland Women U-21s
International debut: Scotland 15, New Zealand 51, 1993
Five Nations debut: Scotland 14, England 15, 1994
Most respected opponent: Gary Armstrong (Jedforest & Scotland)
Biggest influence on career: Rob Moffat
Other sporting achievements: Represented South of Scotland at cricket (also St Boswells) and athletics

Suggestions to improve rugby: Allow players to cash in on their talent: anything short of being paid to play. Reduce value of penalty goal to make for more entertaining spectacle
Notable landmarks in rugby career: Matured into a top-class international scrum-half during 1994/95 to such a degree that in his two outings against France he appeared reminiscent of the great Gary Armstrong. Ironically, it was the serious injury suffered by Armstrong, and by his understudy Andy Nicol, that gave the opportunity to Bryan, the youngest of three brothers in the Melrose side. Graduated into Scotland side on back of consistently outstanding displays in Melrose's back-to-back championship winning years (1992/93 and 1993/94). First two caps came courtesy of new temporary replacement ruling. His debut (Murrayfield, 20.11.93), followed an injury to Nicol which required medical treatment off the field. And Bryan was again required to temporarily fill the breach when Armstrong popped off for attention during Scotland's heartbreaking 14–15 Calcutta Cup loss to England (5.2.94). Finally, the diminutive Borderer won selection in his own right, for the 1994 Wooden Spoon decider against France, again in Edinburgh (19.3.94). Scotland lost 12–20, but his services were retained for the summer tour to Argentina, on which he played in both Test defeats. Bryan also turned out in 1993/94 for Scotland A against New Zealand, Italy A and France A, as well as for South of Scotland on the day they were slaughtered 84–5 by the touring All Blacks. Originally surfaced on representative scene as a replacement for Scotland Under-18s and Under-19s, he made his Under-21 debut in loss to Wales at Llanelli (20.4.91). Added second cap against Welsh at Bridgehaugh, Stirling (lost 19–28, 18.4.92). First played for Melrose as an 18-year old in October 1989.
Touchlines: Golf, cricket.

Scotland (1993)

Last Season	9 caps	0 pts
Career	14 caps	0 pts

Caps (14): **1993** NZ(TR) **1994** E(TR), F, Arg(1,2) **1995** C, I, F(a), W, E, R wc-IC, F(b), NZ

Points Nil

Reed, A. I.   Scotland

Full Name: Andrew Ian Reed
Club: Bath
Position: Lock
Height: 6ft 7in (2.00m)
Weight: 17st 10lb (108kg)
Occupation: Marketing executive,
Western Freights, Bristol
Born: St Austell, Cornwall, 4.5.69
Family: Sarah (wife)
Family links with rugby: Father
played in Royal Navy. Brother (Alec)
played for Hong Kong Islanders
Former clubs: Bodmin, Camborne,
Plymouth Albion
International debut: Scotland 15,
Ireland 3
Five Nations' debut: As above
Worst moment in rugby: Cornwall's
two County Championship final
defeats v Durham (1988/89) and
Lancashire (1991/92); second half of
the Lions Tour. Lost place in Test
side after playing badly.
Most embarrassing moment:
Dropping ball in front of clubhouse,
playing for Bath United, when over

Scotland (1993)		
Last Season	1 cap	0 pts
Career	10 caps	0 pts
Lions	1993	

Caps (10): 1993 I,F,W,E 1994 E,I,F,Arg(1,2),SA
Points Nil

for try. Club captain John Hall was standing in the crowd and he was first
person I saw when I looked up
Most respected opponent: Olivier Roumat (Agen & France)
Serious injuries: Torn ankle ligaments, a/c shoulder joint, torn quadricep
tendon in both knees (Right knee – Jan '93, left knee – June '93, first Test with
Lions), back injury (1994/95)
Other sporting achievements: Goalkeeper for Cornwall Schools
Suggestions to improve rugby: Everyone should receive some form of
compensation for time lost. Why shouldn't we benefit from off the field
activities. Murrayfield can house nearly 70,000, all paying around £20.00 a
ticket. What do the players get? A load of free kit which doesn't even fit. The
Unions make an absolute fortune out of the players. There must be a realistic
appreciation of how much time and effort is put into playing top-level rugby. I
don't want to make money from playing rugby – I enjoy playing and building
friendships through the sport – but I want to see that our commitment is
appreciated. It takes me more than six hours to get Murrayfield for training ...
and I still have to get home. Administrators must not change any more rules

without consulting the players

Notable landmarks in rugby career: Serious upper back injury sidelined Andy for almost entire 1994/95, although he did play in Scotland's horrible 10–34 loss to South Africa (Murrayfield, 19.11.94). Meteoric rise up representative ladder had seen him advance from second-choice club player at start of 1992/93 season to British Lion by the end. Touring with the Lions in New Zealand, Andy played in first Test defeat (Christchurch, 12.6.93) as well as turning out against North Auckland, Canterbury, Southland, Hawke's Bay and Waikato. The following summer he captained Scotland on tour of Argentina. Played in Cornwall's County Championship side in three Twickenham finals in four years from 1989–92 (beating Yorkshire 29–20 in 1990/91). Prior to his Scotland debut in 1993, Andy's only international experience had come in the colours of England Colts. All that changed when a series of impressive televised displays for Bath alerted first the Anglo-Scots, for whom he turned out in the 1992/93 Inter-District Championship, then Scotland. His switch of allegiances came courtesy of an Edinburgh-born mother and a Hearts football scarf which a Scottish spy spotted him wearing watching a rugby match in Plymouth. The news was relayed back up north and on 16 January 1993, having played in Scotland A's 22–13 'A' win in Dublin, the former Bodmin Town goalkeeper (South Western League), made his debut in the 15–3 win over Ireland at Murrayfield, a 1,200-mile round trip from his home. A member of Bath, whom he joined for their 1990 tour to Australia, Andy shared in their 1993/94 league and cup double, a season in which he also became Scotland's pack leader.

Touchlines: Watersports.

Richards, D. England

Full Name: Dean Richards
Club: Leicester
Position: No 8
Height: 6ft 4in (1.93m)
Weight: 17st 8lb (107kg)
Occupation: Police officer
Born: Nuneaton, 11.7.63
Family: Nicky (wife)
Family links with rugby: Father (Brian) played for Nuneaton
Former Club: Roanne (France)
International debut: England 25, Ireland 20, 1986
Five Nations' debut: As above
Best moment in rugby: Winning decisive third Test with 1989 Lions
Worst moments in rugby: Losing four

front teeth whilst in action; England
losing to Wales in Cardiff (1989)
Most respected opponent: Brian
Moore (Harlequins & England)
Biggest influence on career: My work
Serious injuries: Recurring dislocated
shoulder
Suggestions to improve rugby: IRB
must redefine their role, for all our
sakes. Home Unions must guard
against taking on new laws just
because they suit the Southern Hemisphere nations. Reduce maximum
age of committee men to 55
Notable landmarks in rugby career:
One of the Herculean figures of world

England (1986)

Last Season	8 caps	0 pts
Career	45 caps	24 pts
Lions 1989	3 Tests	0 pts
1993	3 Tests	0 pts

Caps (45): **1986** I, F 1987 S wc-A, J, US,
W **1988** F, W, S, I(1), A(a1,a2), Fj,
A(b) **1989** S, I, F, W,Ro. Lions-
A(1,2,3) **1990** Arg **1991** W, S, I, F,
Fj, A(a) wc-NZ, It, US **1992** S(R),
F, W, C **1993** Lions-NZ(1,2,3).
NZ **1994** W, SA(1), C **1995** I, F(a),
W, S wc-WS, A, NZ
Points (24 – 6t): **1986** I(2t) 1987 wc-J(1t)
1988 A(a2:1t) **1989** I(1t), Ro(1t)

rugby, Deano is the most-capped No 8 of all time, having exceeded the 46 caps
won by the great Mervyn Davies between 1969–76. His 45 England caps, allied
to six Lions Tests, give him a grand total of 51. Remarkably, his career has been
badly disrupted by injury, not least in 1995 when he had to sit out England's
World Cup-ties against Argentina, Italy and France. But his reputation has
never diminished. Oh yes, some did say he wouldn't be able to play on fast
grounds and at altitude, but then he masterminded England's 32–15 rout of
South Africa (Pretoria, 4.6.94). They don't say that any more. Selected to tour
with 1993 British Lions despite not figuring in England's plans for '93 Five
Nations' Championship, Dean played in all three Tests against New Zealand
and then, much to their chagrin, returned to England's side to inspire a 15–9
defeat of the touring All Blacks. Injury to Deano spared Scotland, Ireland and
France but he was back for the 1994 championship decider against Wales and,
although there had been some concerns as to his match fitness, he produced a
typically dictatorial performance to snuff out Wales' Grand Slam aspirations.
Had lost jersey in 1993 to Ben Clarke whose ultra-mobile style of play was
perfectly suited to new laws, but returned after Clarke was turned into an
openside flanker. Deano joined Leicester in 1982 after season playing in France.
Played for England Schools at lock, before graduating to England U-23s
(against Romania). Has also represented Leicestershire and Midlands Division.
Scored two tries on international debut against Ireland 'but it was one of my
worst performances'. Played in 1987 World Cup and returned to Australia with
1989 Lions, playing in all three Tests of 2–1 series win. Shoulder injury ruled
out 1989/90 season. Lynchpin of England's 1991 Grand Slam success. Scored
one of England XV's two tries in 18–16 defeat of centenary Barbarians at
Twickenham (29.9.90). Voted 1990/91 Whitbread/Rugby World Player of
Year and played in three World Cup Pool games in 1991 before Mike Teague
took over at No 8 for knock-out stages. Marked his return in 1992 Five Nations
Championship by steering England to another Grand Slam.
Touchlines: Squash, five-a-side soccer.

Richter, A.   South Africa

Full Name: Adriaan Richter
Club: Harlequins (Pretoria)
Province: Northern Transvaal
Position: No 8
Height: 6ft 4in (1.93m)
Weight: 15st 6lb (98kg)
Occupation: Insurance broker
Born: Roodepoort, 10.5.66
Former Province: Transvaal
International debut: France 15, South Africa 20, 1992
Notable landmarks in rugby career: Enjoyed a cracking World Cup last summer, scoring all four of South Africa's tries in the two games he started at No 8, against Romania (Cape Town, 30.5.95) and Canada (Port Elizabeth, 3.6.95). To ice the cake he was made skipper for the 21–8 defeat of Romania. Lost out in the knockout stages of the tournament as coach Kitch Christie gambled on playing 6ft 7in lock Mark Andrews at No 8 to give the Boks greater height at the tail of the

South Africa (1992)

Last Season	7 caps	20 pts
Career	10 caps	20 pts

Caps (10): **1992** F(1,2), E **1994** E(2), NZ(1,2,3) **1995** wc-R, C, WS(b:R)
Points (20 – 4t): **1995** wc-R(2t), C(2t)

lineout. Had returned to South African team for second Test against England in 1994, a move which contributed to the Springboks turning a 32–15 first Test reversal into a 27–9 win (Cape Town, 11.6.94). Two years previously had started the Springboks' tour to France and England as a flanker, played a game at lock, and finished up as No 8 in the Test against England. During the course of the trip he developed into a first-choice player, deposing Transvaal's Ian MacDonald as breakaway wing-forward in the two internationals against France – the 20–15 win in Lyon (17.10.92) and the 16–29 loss in Paris' Parc des ' Princes the following weekend. Scored try in 20–16 defeat of England B (Bristol, 7.11.92). Missed out on selection for the two home Tests against New Zealand and Australia (August 1992), he did captain Northern Transvaal against the All Blacks (lost 17–24) at Loftus Versfeld (14.8.92), four years after having had made his provincial debut for rivals Transvaal, with whom he played 27 times.

Rodber, T. A. K.　　　　　　England

Full Name: Timothy Andrew Keith Rodber
Clubs: Northampton & Army
Position: Flanker, No 8
Height: 6ft 6in (1.98m)
Weight: 16st 7lb (100kg)
Occupation: Army officer, Green Howards
Born: Richmond, Yorkshire, 2.7.69
Family: Single
Family links with rugby: Father played
Former clubs: Oxford Old Boys, Petersfield
International debut: Scotland 7, England 25, 1992
Five Nations' debut: As above
Best moment in rugby: Beating South Africa in first Test (1994)
Worst moment in rugby: Being sent-off against Eastern Province (1994)
Most respected opponent: Dean Richards (Leicester & England) – awesome in every department
Serious injuries: Popped ribs
Other sporting achievements: Hampshire Schools County hockey and cricket

England (1992)		
Last Season	12 caps	5 pts
Career	20 caps	10 pts

Caps (20): **1992** S, I **1993** NZ **1994** I, F, W, SA(1,2), R, C **1995** I, F(a), W, S wc-Arg, It, WS(R), A, NZ, F(b)
Points (10 – 2t): **1994** W(1t), R(1t)

Suggestions to improve rugby: Anything to take away stagnant play
Notable landmarks in rugby career: Tim enjoyed a mighty season for England in 1994/95, being in the vanguard of all their best work, and constantly pestering the gain line with his bullish runs. He appeared in all 12 of England's games and his whole-hearted displays did much to erase the unhappy memory of his dismissal, for fighting (retaliation), against Eastern Province (Port Elizabeth, 7.6.94) during England's tour to South Africa (the only other player ever to be sent-off in an English jersay was Mike Burton back in 1975). But Tim remains an officer and a gentleman, and is the logical successor to the England captaincy as and when Will Carling's post becomes vacant. Having been selected as a No 8 in his first two international outings, against Scotland and Ireland during England's 1992 Grand Slam run, Tim was moved to blindside flanker in 1993/94. An impressive showing against the touring All Blacks secured his place but a ripped hamstring then put him out of the Calcutta Cup clash and a return to where he had made his debut (18.1.92). However, once fit John Hall was dropped to accomodate his return. Had represented England's

inaugural Under-21 side in 54–13 defeat of Romania in Bucharest (13.5.89) and, after helping an England XV beat Italy 33–15 in May 1990 (won 33–15), toured with full England squad to Argentina that summer, turning out against Tucuman Selection (won 19–14), Cuyo Selection (lost 21–22) and Cordoba Selection (won 15–12). In 1990/91 he scored tries for England B in 31–16 defeat of Namibia and in 10–24 loss to Ireland B, and represented Northampton in 1991 Pilkington Cup final, losing to Harlequins in extra time. On a happier note he helped England win 1993 World Cup Sevens title in Edinburgh and scored one of England's paltry two tries in entire 1993/94 campaign as Wales were beaten (19.3.94).

Roumat, O.   France

Full Name: Olivier Roumat
Club: Dax
Position: Lock
Height: 6ft 6in (1.98m)
Weight: 17st 5lb (111kg)
Occupation: Surveyor
Born: Mont-de-Marsan, 16.6.66
Family links with rugby: Father played in Mont-de-Marsan back row
International debut: New Zealand 34, France 20, 1989
Five Nations' debut: Wales 19, France 29, 1990
Notable landmarks in rugby career: Within seven caps of succeeding Jean Condom as France's most-capped lock of all time, Olivier gave us one of the most poignant memories of last summer's World Cup when collapsing in tears after France's agonising semi-final defeat by South Africa (Durban, 17.6.95). His cure was the best one imaginable for a Frenchman, the winning try against England, as France ended a run of eight straight defeats at the hands of their long-standing foe with 19–9 victory in a frankly dreadful third place play-off (Pretoria, 22.6.95). Olivier had captained France to their first series win in South Africa since

France (1989)

Last Season	9 caps	5 pts
Career	55 caps	23 pts

Caps (55): **1989** NZ(2R), BL **1990** W, E, S, I, R, A(1,2,3), NZ(1,2) **1991** S, I, W, F, R, US(1), W wc-R, Fj, C, E **1992** W(R), E(R), S, I, SA(1,2), Arg(b) **1993** E, S, I, W, R(a), SA(1,2), R(b), A(1,2) **1994** I, W, E, C(a), NZ(1,2), C(b) **1995** W, E(a), S(a) wc-IC, S(b), I(b), SA, E(b)

Points (23 – 5t): **1991** W(1t) wc-R(1t) **1992** SA(2:1t) **1994** W(1t) **1995** wc-E(b:1t)

1958 during summer of 1993, after 'regular' skipper Jean-Francois Tordo had been stamped out of the tour. France drew first Test 20–20 (Durban, 26.6.93) before winning second Test 18–17 (Johannesburg, 3.7.93). 'Olivier was magnifique, both as a player and a captain,' opined Tordo generously. He retained captaincy on return home, leading France to 51–0 rout of Romania and to a share of home series against world champions Australia (after Wallabies had slumped to shock 13–16 loss in Bordeaux, 30.10.93). His fortunes dipped during 1994 Five Nations Championship when, having scored a try in defeat by Wales (Cardiff, 19.2.94), he was dropped after England won again in Paris (5.3.94). However, he returned in time to share in France's historic tour of New Zealand, which realised a 2–0 series win over the stunned All Blacks. The first French forward to score a five-point try when touching down against South Africa (Paris, 24.10.92). His feat partially made up for his dismissal playing against New Zealand for a World XV in Wellington that summer. Kiwi referee David Bishop dismissed him for illegal use of the shoe after only nine minutes. He was banned for four weeks and missed the tour to Argentina. Formerly a flanker, his position against the British Lions XV who helped celebrate the bicentenary of the French Revolution in 1989, he built himself an impressive reputation in the 1988 Student World Cup and helped France B beat Wales B 28–15 in La Teste (12.11.89), four months after replacing Marc Cecillon against New Zealand in Auckland for his first cap.

Roux, J. South Africa

Full Name: Johan Roux
Province: Transvaal
Position: Scrum-half
Height: 5ft 11in (1.80m)
Weight: 14st 1lb (85kg)
Occupation: Stockbroker, Edhern Rudolph
Born: 25.2.69
Family: Married
International debut: South Africa 27, England 9, 1994
Notable landmarks in rugby career:
Given his debut after an impressive showing for Transvaal in their 24–21 defeat of England (Johannesburg, 28.5.94), and for South Africa B in their 19–16 defeat of the same tourists (Kimberley, 31.5.94), Johan promptly helped turn around the fortunes of the national side. England had recovered from their Transvaal defeat to stun South Africa the

following weekend, winning 32–15 in the first Test (Pretoria, 4.6.94). One of the Boks to pay the price was scrum-half Joost van der Westhuizen, Johan came in and South Africa breezed to 27–9 victory in the second Test. The Transvaal terror hung onto his place through the tour to New Zealand, operating in all three Tests (none of them wins) and also turning out against Counties (scored two tries), Wellington, Waikato, Otago (as a replacement) and Canterbury. Opened his try-scoring account with a brace in South Africa's 42–22 first Test defeat of Argentina (Port Elizabeth, 8.10.94) but did not then tour to Wales, Scotland and Ireland, Natal's Kevin Putt instead going along as back-up to van der Westhuizen. Johan re-emerged at last summer's World Cup, appearing in three games as South Africa surged towards ecstasy.

South Africa (1994)		
Last Season	8 caps	10 pts
Career	8 caps	10 pts

Caps (8): **1994** E(2), NZ(1,2,3), Arg(1)
1995 wc-R, C, F(R)
Points (10 – 2t): **1994** Arg(1:2t)

Rowntree, G. C. England

Full Name: Graham Christopher Rowntree
Club: Leicester
Position: Prop
Height: 6ft (1.83m)
Weight: 17st 2lb (104kg)
Occupation: Insurance broker, P&G Bland, Leicester
Born: Stockton-on-Tees, 18.4.71
Family: Single
International debut: England 24, Scotland 12, 1995
Five Nations debut: As above
Notable landmarks in rugby career: The youngest member of Leicester's 1993 Pilkington Cup-winning side, Graham nonetheless had to exercise patience before gaining his first cap as a temporary replacement for Jason Leonard during the 1995 Grand Slam decider in which England beat Scotland 24–12 (Twickenham, 18.3.95). An England Colts team mate of Martin Johnson and Steve Ojomoh, he toured with

England (1995)		
Last Season	3 caps	0 pts
Career	3 caps	0 pts

Caps (3): **1995** S(TR) wc-It,WS
Points Nil

England A to Canada in 1993, playing in both 'Tests', and then traipsed around South Africa with the full England squad in 1994, appearing against Orange Free State (lost 11–22), Western Transvaal (won 26–24), South Africa B (lost 16–19) and Eastern Province (won 31–13), but failing to get a look-in on Test match days. Enjoyed better fortune when returning to the new Republic for last summer's World Cup, Graham was awarded starts in the wins against Italy (Durban, 31.5.95) and Western Samoa (Durban, 4.6.95), and made a favourable impression on both occasions. Joined Leicester from Hinckley, where he was educated, in 1990 and three years later broke into the Midlands and England A sides.

Sadourny, J.-L.   France

Full Name: Jean-Luc Sadourny
Club: Colomiers
Position: Wing, fullback
Height: 6ft 1in (1.86m)
Weight: 13st 9lb (86.5kg)
Occupation: Company manager, Mag Pub L'Espace
Family: Married with two children
Born: Toulouse, 26.8.66
International debut: Wales 9, France 22, 1991
Five Nations' debut: France 13, England 31, 1992
Notable landmarks in rugby career: Given the keys to France after rounding off what captain Philippe Saint-Andre termed 'the try from the end of the world' in New Zealand. France had won the first Test 22–8 but were trailing in the second Test with seconds to go. From under their own posts France launched an audacious counter-attack. Most of the team got a touch before Jean-Luc rounded off the match and series-clinching try at the other end of the Eden Park (3.7.94). Has since added tries against Canada (17.12.94), Scotland (18.2.95) and Romania (7.4.95) but none came close to giving him the same buzz. One of

France (1991)

Last Season	11 caps	23 pts
Career	33 caps	35 pts

Caps (33): **1991** W(R) wc-C(R) **1992** E(R), S, I, Arg(a1R,a2), SA(1,2) **1993** R(a), SA(1,2), R(b), A(1,2) **1994** I, W, E, S, C(a), NZ(1,2), C(b) **1995** W, E(a), S(a), I(a), R wc-T, S(b), I(b), SA, E(b)

Points (35 – 6t,2dg): **1992** I(1t) **1993** A(1:1dg) **1994** S(1t), NZ(1:1dg), NZ(2:1t), C(b:1t) **1995** S(a:1t), R(1t)

four fullbacks employed by France during 1992/93, Jean-Luc had to wait until 1993/94 to finally establish himself as the successor to Serge Blanco, playing in all ten Tests (scoring a try against Scotland, 19.3.94, and a dropped goal in the 16–13 defeat of Australia at Bordeaux, 30.10.93). Had deposed Stephane Ougier on the 1992 summer tour of Argentina, after coming on as a 42nd minute replacement for the Toulouse played in the 27–12 first Test win in Buenos Aires (4.7.92). Retained his place for second Test the following week and took his cap-tally to nine with appearances in both legs of the drawn series with South Africa back home in October. However, Sebastien Viars was preferred against Argentina in Nantes and Jean-Baptiste Lafond took over after that humiliating loss. Being dropped was not the first knock-out blow Jean-Luc had suffered in his Test career. For he suffered concussion in the 10–6 win over England B at Bristol in 1991, having previously marked his B debut with a try in the 31–10 win over Scotland at Hughenden. Lightning struck twice as he lasted just nine minutes on his Five Nations' debut against England in Paris (15.2.92) before running straight into Alain Penaud needing to be led groggily from the arena. His first cap came as a 76th minute replacement for Blanco in the floodlit international against Wales at the Arms Park (4.9.91).

Saint-Andre, P.   France

Full Name: Philippe Saint-Andre
Club: Montferrand
Position: Wing, centre
Height: 5ft 11in (1.80m)
Weight: 13st 6lb (85kg)
Occupation: Marketing executive, Media Standre
Family: Married
Born: Romans, 19.4.67
Former clubs: Romans, Clermont-Ferrand
International debut: France 6, Romania 12, 1990
Five Nations' debut: Ireland 13, France 21, 1991
Notable landmarks in rugby career: Maintained his prolific strike rate in international rugby with seven tries

in the maximum 12 Tests last season. If ever a captain led by example it was Philippe, whose tenure as skipper has seen France win in Scotland for the first time in 16 years and inflict the first ever 2–0 series beating on New Zealand (1994). It has also seen Scotland win in France for the first time in 26 years and France lose to Canada for the first time ever, but enough of that. Appointed

France captain for 1994 Five Nations finale against Scotland (won 20–12, Murrayfield 19.3.94) in succession to Olivier Roumat, who was dropped after defeat by England a fortnight previously. In so doing, Philippe, nicknamed *le goret* (the piglet), became the first wing to captain France since Christian Darrouy 27 years ago. Celebrated with second try of the championship, his first having come against Ireland (won 35–15, Paris 15.1.94). Has become one of world rugby's most potent finishers with 22 Test tries in the past three years. His finest moment came, at Twickenham (16.1.91), when scoring *The Try* against England in a thrilling Grand Slam decider. The move was

France (1990)

Last Season	12 caps	35 pts
Career	50 caps	102 pts

Caps (50): **1990** R, A(3), NZ(1,2) **1991** I(R), W(a), E(a), US(1,2), W(b) wc-R(b), Fj, C, E(b) **1992** W, E, S, I, R, Arg(a1,a2), SA(1,2) **1993** E, S, I, W, SA(1,2), A(1,2) **1994** I, W, E, S, C(a), NZ(1,2), C(b) **1995** W, E(a), S(a), I(a), R wc-T, IC, S(b), I(b), SA, E(b)

Points (102 – 22t): **1991** W(a:1t), E(a:1t), US(1:1t), W(b:1t) wc-R(b:1t), C(1t) **1992** W(1t), R(1t), Arg(a2:1t) **1993** E(2t), I(1t), SA(1:1t) **1994** I(1t), S(1t) **1995** W(1t), S(a:2t), I(a:1t) wc-T(1t), IC(1t), I(b:1t)

initiated by Serge Blanco and fed, via Jean-Baptiste Lafond, Didier Camberabero, Philippe Sella and then Camberabero's boot behind enemy lines where Philippe, who has clocked 10.9sec over 100m, scorched through to apply the *coup de grace*. It was bettered only by Jean Luc-Sadourny's try 'from the end of the world' which accounted for the All Blacks on a 1994 tour that saw Philippe play both Tests at centre. Claimed championship-high three tries – against England (two) and Ireland – as France won 1993 Five Nations' Cup. He also toured to Argentina with the French side, crossing in the 33–9 second Test win in Buenos Aires (11.7.92), and turned out on both occasions against South Africa (in Lyon and Paris). The owner of an Irish pub in Clermont-Ferrand, Philippe represented France A and B before stepping into the top flight at Stade Patrice Brocas, Auch (24.5.90) as a centre for the visit of Romania, who triumphed (12–6) on French soil for the first time.

Sella, P.   France

Full Name: Philippe Sella
Club: Agen
Position: Centre
Height: 5ft 11in (1.80m)
Weight: 13st 4lb (84kg)
Occupation: Business manager,
Protesports & Sella Communicat
Family: Married with two children
Born: Clairac, 14.2.62
International debut: Romania 13,
France 9, 1982
Five Nations' debut: England 15,
France 19, 1983
Notable landmarks in rugby career:
World's most-capped player, taking
his tally to an astonishing 111 caps
with 10 out of a maximum 12
outings in 1994/95. His 30th Test try
came against Canada (Besancon,
17.12.94) and showed what he
thought of being controversially
sent-off against the same opponents
six months earlier (5.6.94) on his
99th international appearance for
(allegedly) punching as France
slumped to a shock 18–16 defeat at
Elms Park, Ontario. Philippe, who
had captained France between
February and May 1992, was
subsequently banned for one match.
Dropped for France's tour to
Argentina in 1992, but reclaimed
midfield berth (14.11.92) for
disastrous return against Pumas in
Nantes. His only consolation in a
game which saw Argentina secure
their first ever win on French soil
was his 26th Test try. Philippe
succeeded compatriot Serge Blanco
(93) as world's most-capped player
during 1993/94 campaign, his tally
having been amassed since his debut
in the 1982 defeat by Romania. On

France (1982)
Last Season	10 caps	5 pts
Career	111 caps	125 pts

Caps (111): **1982** Ro,Arg(1,2) **1983** E, S,
I, W, A(1,2), Ro **1984** I, W, E, S,
NZ(1,2), Ro **1985** E, S, I, W,
Arg(1,2) **1986** S, I, W, E, Ro(a),
Arg(1,2), A, NZ, Ro(b), NZ(1,2)
1987 W, E, S, I wc-S, Ro, Z(R), Fj,
A, NZ **1988** E, S, I, W, Arg(a1,a2),
Arg(b1,b2), Ro **1989** I, W, E, S,
NZ(1,2), BL, A(1,2) **1990** W, E, S,
I, A(1,2,3) **1991** W, E, Ro, US(1,2),
W, Fj, C, E **1992** W, E, S, I, Arg(b)
1993 E, S, I, W, R(a), SA(1,2),
R(b), A(1,2) **1994** I, W, E, S, C(a),
NZ(1,2), C(b) **1995** W, E(a), S(a),
I(a) wc-T, S(b), I(b), SA, E(b)

Points (125 – 30t): **1982** Arg(1:2t) **1983**
E(1t) **1984** I(1t), W(1t), E(1t),
Ro(1t) **1986** S(1t), I(1t), W(1t),
E(1t), Ro(a:1t), Arg(2:1t), A(1t),
NZ(1:1t) **1987** E(1t), wc-S(1t),
Ro(1t), A(1t) **1988** I(1t), Arg(4:1t)
1990 W(1t) **1991** W(1t), Fj(2t)
1992 Arg(b:1t) **1993** I(1t), R(b:1t)
1994 W(1t), C(b:1t)

343

his next appearance, in the first Test against Argentina, he scored the first two of his 30 international tries. He played 45 consecutive Tests until injury ruled him out of the 49–3 win over Romania, a match played on his own Agen pitch (11.11.87). It was but a temporary blip for a man who had also represented France at Schools, Juniors and Universities grade. In 1986 he scored a try in every Championship match, equalling a feat achieved only by compatriot Patrick Esteve (1983), Johnny Wallace (Scotland, 1925) and Carston Catcheside (England, 1924). That same year he was alone in playing all 12 French internationals and represented the Five Nations in a 13–32 defeat by the Overseas Unions in the IRB Centenary match at Twickenham (19.4.86). The next season he played a key role in France's run to the 1987 World Cup final. A torn thigh muscle accounted for his absence from the 1991 World Cup opener against Romania but, typically, he returned with two dazzling tries in the following match against Fiji.

Sharp, A. V. Scotland

Full Name: Alan Victor Sharp
Club: Bristol
Position: Loosehead prop
Height: 5ft 10in (1.78m)
Weight: 16st 7lb (100kg)
Occupation: Builder, Alan Richardson Construction (Bedminster)
Born: Bristol, 17.10.69
Family: Zoe (daughter)
International debut: Scotland 14, England 15, 1994
Five Nations debut: As above
Best moment in rugby: Winning first cap
Worst moment in rugby: Having to pull out of Scotland team to play Ireland (1993) less than 48 hours before what would have been my debut when found I had a broken leg
Most respected opponent: Paul Burnell (London Scottish & Scotland)
Biggest influence on career: Derek Eves (Bristol)
Serious injuries: Broken leg

Scotland (1994)

Last Season	1 cap	0 pts
Career	6 caps	0 pts

Caps (6): **1994** E, I, F, Arg(1,2), SA
Points Nil

Suggestions to improve rugby: More money must be pumped into grass roots

344

rugby to give everyone a chance of coming through

Notable landmarks in rugby career: Began his representative life as a Scotsman (playing for the Under-21s), then became an Englishman (winning England B honours against Spain as a 20-year-old in 1989 and being included in England's Development Squad), then switched back to the land of the kilt, 'a decision I have not regretted for one minute'. Qualified by virtue of having a grandmother in Brechin. A Scottish Exile, Alan was chosen to play for his adopted nation without representing the second-string XV but had to postpone his debut after learning he had a broken leg, two days before ireland visited Murrayfield. Had declared himself fit but a hard midweek scrummaging session resurrected his uncertainty and an Edinburgh Hospital X-ray, after dye had been injected into the bone, revealed a crack. No matter, he satisfied himself with 'A' team appearances against Italy and Ireland in '93 before hitting the big time in 1994; replacing Boroughmuir's Peter Wright in the No 1 jersey after Scotland's heavy defeat in Cardiff, and wearing it with distinction against England, Ireland and France. Toured Argentina last summer, playing in both Tests, as well as in the 24–24 draw with Buenos Aires (25.5.94). Last season was effectively washed out through injury, but only after he had appeared in the 10–34 loss to South Africa (Murrayfield, 19.11.94).

Touchlines: Coaching Southmead RFC.

Shiel, A. G. Scotland

Full Name: Andrew Graham Shiel
Club: Melrose
Position: Outside-half, centre
Height: 5ft 10lb (1.78m)
Weight: 12st 10lb (81kg)
Occupation: Junior site manager, J&R Elliot of Hawick
Born: Galashiels, 13.8.70
Family: Single
Family links with rugby: Father (Andrew) played for Melrose GS
Former Club: Manly (Aus)
International debut: Scotland 24, Ireland 15, 1991
Five Nations' debut: Scotland 15, Ireland 3, 1993
Best moment in rugby: Scoring winning try against Ireland on

Scotland debut after coming on as 43rd minute replacement in 1991 World Cup match at Murrayfield

Worst moment in rugby: Missing majority of 1993/94 season through injury

Most embarrassing moment: Ball toppled over in front of posts before I kicked it during 1990 Hawick Sevens
Most respected opponent: Sean Lineen (ex-Boroughmuir & Scotland)
Biggest influences on career: Ian McGeechan and Jim Telfer
Serious injuries: Straining inner and exterior quadriceps and adductor muscle (1988/89) and missing over four months rugby. Pelvic strain (Nov 1990) – three months out; knee ligaments (1993/94) – six months out; flaked bone in ankle trapping nerve

Scotland (1991)
Last Season	5 caps	10 pts
Career	14 caps	14 pts

Caps (14): **1991** wc-I(R), WS **1993** I, F, W, E, NZ **1994** Arg(1,2), SA **1995** R wc-IC, F, NZ
Points (14 – 3t): **1991** wc-I(R:1t) **1994** R(1t) **1995** wc-IC(1t)

Other sporting achievements: Athletics for Borders Schools and Borders AAA
Suggestions to improve Scottish rugby: Playing standards need to be improved at club level – inferior to England and Wales. Still too forward orientated in Scotland (lack of running ability)
Notable landmarks in rugby career: The one Scotland centre truly capable of unlocking international midfields, Graham impressed in last summer's World Cup calling the tune against Cote d'Ivoire (and scoring a try), and troubling both France and New Zealand. It was only a shame he had to move to fly-half midway through the quarter-final against the All Blacks (Pretoria, 3.6.95) because the Melrose combination between him and Craig Chalmers (before being dazed) was definitely making the Kiwis think. It was an especially brave performance as he had sustained a fractured nose cartilage against France (Pretoria, 3.6.95) which, safe to assume, hurt like hell. Injury had blighted 1993/94 for Graham, who reckons he only played in 3 ½ out of 12 months due to damaged anterior cruciate ligaments in left knee (caused him to miss Scotland's 1992 tour to South Seas) and a trapped nerve in his ankle caused by a flaked bone. In between injuries he fitted in one Test cap, as centre in 51–15 loss to New Zealand (Murrayfield, 20.11.93). Run of bad luck started at the end of a season in which he had established himself as heir-apparent to Sean Lineen alongside Scott Hastings in Scottish midfield. He played in all four legs of the 1993 Five Nations' Championship after a Trial in which he started for the Possibles and finished with the Probables. Represented Scottish Schools three times, Scotland U-19s and U-21s (twice). Scored six points in 1989/90 defeat (10–24) by Wales Under-21 and played in 15–23 loss to same opposition (1990/91). Toured with Scotland to New Zealand (1990), North America and Canada (1991), Australia (1992) and Argentina (1994), the latter trip ending his injury nightmare as he appeared at centre in both Tests. Having been included in Scotland's 1991 World Cup squad, he was given debut against Ireland as a 43rd minute replacement for outside-half Craig Chalmers. A fairytale scenario saw him score a try as Scotland came from behind to win. Seven days later he won second cap (as centre) in quarter-final against Western Samoa when knee injury ruled out Lineen. Remained in Australia after 1992 tour to spend summer playing with Manly.
Touchlines: Social golf, cricket, swimming.

Slattery, P. J.   Australia

Full Name: Peter John Slattery
State: Queensland
Club: Queensland University
Position: Scrum-half
Height: 5ft 9in (1.76m)
Weight: 12st 4lb (78kg)
Occupation: Sports administrator
Born: 6.6.65
Family: Single
Former clubs: Wests (1983-86). Queensland Univ since 1987
International debut: Australia 67, USA 9, 1990
Best moment in rugby: Winning 1991 World Cup; beating Wales (1992)
Worst moment in rugby: Pre-season training
Serious injuries: Broken arm (1987)
Suggestions to improve rugby: Ban kicking ball out on full inside your own 22
Notable landmarks in rugby career: Lost out to ACT starlet George Gregan in the Wallaby selection stakes during 1994 after playing in both Test victories over touring Ireland. Went to World Cup as back-

Australia (1990)

Last Season	5 caps	0 pts
Career	17 caps	8 pts

Caps (17): **1990** US(R) **1991** W(a:R), E(a:R). wc-WS(R), W(b), I(R) **1992** I, W **1993** T, C, F(1,2) **1994** I(1,2), It(1R) **1995** wc-C, R(R)

Points (8 – 2t): **1990** US(1t) **1991** wc-W(b:1t)

up but did pick up two caps along the way, in the wins over Canada and Romania (as a replacement). Three years previously he had been assigned the considerable task of filling the Wallaby No 9 jersey worn by Nick Farr-Jones, after the long-time skipper and inspiration hung up his boots in 1992. But after successfully steering the Wallabies past Ireland and Wales that autumn, Peter sustained broken ribs playing against Tonga in the curtain-opener for the 1993 Test campaign (Brisbane, 3.7.93). The upshot was the recall from retirement of Farr-Jones for the Bledisloe Cup match and three-Test home series with South Africa. A fit-again Slattery returned for the autumn tour to North America and France but did not produce his best form, notably in the first Test defeat by France in Bordeaux when he spilled two scoring passes. A Test reserve on and off since 1985, he bagged a try on his international debut in 1990 after coming on as a replacement for Farr-Jones in the 67–9 defeat of the United States Eagles. The following year he replaced his perennial rival on a further four occasions, twice during the Wallabies' triumphant World Cup campaign. In 1992 he

captained Queensland to victory in the prestigious Super Six Championship and skippered the Aussies twice on tour in South Africa.
Touchlines: Sleeping, eating and surfing.

Small, J. T. South Africa

Full Name: James Terence Small
Province: Natal
Club: Wits
Position: Wing
Height: 6ft (1.82m)
Weight: 13st 3lb (84kg)
Occupation: Self-employed
Born: Cape Town, 10.2.69
Family links with sport: Son of former Springbok soccer player Vernon Small (1956)
Former Province: Transvaal
International debut: South Africa 24, New Zealand 27, 1992
Notable landmarks in rugby career: James badly let himself down with ill-discipline, on and off the field, in 1994 but partially salvaged his reputation with a tremendous defensive display on New Zealand bulldozer Jonah Lomu in last summer's World Cup final (Johannesburg, 24.6.95). Had been sent-off for verbally abusing English referee Ed Morrison during South Africa's 20–28 second Test defeat against Australia (Brisbane, 14.8.94) and confessed: 'The Springboks' blazer means more to me than most things in life and I let it down. I've also let down my team mates. It will be a while

South Africa (1992)

Last Season	11 caps	5 pts
Career	23 caps	45 pts

Caps (23): **1992** NZ, A, F(1,2), E **1993** F(1,2), Arg(1,2), A(1,2,3) **1994** E(1,2), NZ(1,2,3TR), Arg(1) **1995** WS(a) wc-A, R, F, NZ

Points (45 – 9t): **1992** F(1:1t) **1993** F(2:1t), Arg(1:2t), Arg(2:1t), A(1:2t), A(3:1t) **1995** WS(a:1t)

before I can look them in the eye.' But he continued to play over-aggressive rugby and then started getting himself in trouble away from the pitch. His tour to Australia (1994) was particularly unhappy. It was such a shame as James had been the most prolific try-scorer in world rugby during 1993, with seven scores in six-Test spell, and is worshipped by the youth of South Africa. Petulance got the better of him in the first Test against England (4.6.94) and he was fortunate to last the duration. Formerly a superb soccer player, which he inherited from his father, a 1956 international, James was included in the first Springbok side selected after the ending of the international boycott. Not only did he play against New Zealand but Australia also the following week before turning out for Transvaal in the 1992 Currie Cup final. Unhappily for the player, victory went to Natal by the odd point in 27 (he then moved to Natal in 1993 and, would you believe, lost to Transvaal in the 1993 final), but his smile was restored when he scored one of South Africa's two tries in their 20–15 victory over France (Lyon, 17.10.92). in addition to retaining his place for the next two Test engagements, against France (lost 16–29, Paris, 24.10.92) and England (lost 16–33, Twickenham, 14.11.92). Everpresent through 1993 campaign, scoring a try against France in the second Test of the home series (lost 17–18, Johannesburg 3.7.93) and bagging three tries in the two away Test wins over Argentina in the autumn.

Smith, D. P. P. Australia

Full Name: Damien Paul Peter Smith
State: Queensland
Club: Southern Districts
Position: Wing
Height: 6ft 2in (1.88m)
Weight: 14st 9lb (93kg)
Occupation: Property consultant, Colliers Jardine
Born: 1.2.69
International debut: Australia 12, South Africa 19, 1993
Worst moment in rugby: Kicking a ball 20 metres backwards with a gale-force wind behind me against Welsh Students on 1992 Wales/Ireland Tour
Most respected opponent: James Small (Natal & South Africa)
Serious injuries: Broken wrist and arm (1990)
Notable landmarks in rugby career: Scored a brilliant try in Australia's quarter-final defeat by England at last summer's World Cup (Cape Town, 11.6.95), leaping high to take an up-and-under then, in the same movement, rolling over the line for the score. It capped a prolific year for

Australia (1993)		
Last Season	11 caps	30 pts
Career	16 caps	35 pts

Caps (16): **1993** SA(1,2,3), C, F(2) **1994** I(1,2), It(1,2), WS, NZ **1995** Arg(1,2) wc-SA, R, E
Points (35 – 7t): **1993** C(1t) **1994** I(1:1t), WS(2t) **1995** Arg(1:1t) wc-R(1t), E(1t)

the strong-running Queenslander who claimed six tries in just 11 Tests. Broke

into Queensland side in 1992 and quickly graduated into the Wallaby squad which toured Wales and Ireland. Having missed the 1990 season with a broken arm, he was not about to let his chance slip and he responded with eight starts out of a possible 13, scoring three tries. However, a Test place eluded him until 1993 when he was drafted in for the three-match home series against South Africa – their first visit Down Under since 1971. Damien occupied the right wing berth in each of the Tests as Australia came from behind to edge a 2–1 decision. Next goal to be fulfilled was his first international try, achieved during Canada's 43–16 beating in Calgary (9.10.93) in the early throes of an autumn tour which also incorporated two Tests against France. Damian lost out to young NSW flier Alistair Murdoch in the first Test selection stakes but, after France triumphed 16–13 in Bordeaux, was recalled for the second match, which yielded a 24–3 series-levelling scoreline. He retained his Test place throughout 1994 and in three of the Wallabies' four World Cup engagements.
Touchlines: Water skiing, mountineering, surfing and parachuting.

Smith, I. R. Scotland

Full Name: Ian Richard Smith
Club: Gloucester
Position: Flanker
Height: 6ft (1.83m)
Weight: 14st (89kg)
Occupation: Civil engineer, Sir William Halcrow Ltd
Born: Gloucester, 16.3.65
Family: Karen (wife) and two children
Family links with rugby: Father (Dick) was an England trialist who captained Gloucester and the Barbarians
Former Club: Longlevens, Wollongong (Aus, 1988)
International debut (Scotland): Scotland 7, England 25, 1992
Five Nations' debut: As above
Best moment in rugby: Running out at Murrayfield for first Scotland cap against England
Worst moment in rugby: Losing 1989/90 Pilkington Cup final 6–48 to Bath

Scotland (1992)		
Last Season	1 caps	0 pts
Career	11 caps	0 pts

Caps (11): **1992** E, I, W, A(1,2) **1994** E(R), I, F, Arg(1,2) **1995** wc-IC
Points Nil

Most embarrassing moment: Above match – we were humiliated

Most respected opponent: Lyn Jones (Treorchy & Wales)
Biggest influences on career: Father and Derek Cook (coach at Longlevens)
Suggestions to improve rugby: I'm in favour of setting up refereeing seminars where they can get together with players and coaches to work things out
Notable landmarks in rugby career: The success of the Wainwright-Morrison-Peters back row combination shut the international door on 'Smudge' in 1994/95 and he to make do with one outing in Scotland's World Cup opener against Cote d'Ivoire (won 89–0, Rustenburg, 26.595). Had only been recalled to the side in 1993/94 after injury forced out Rob Wainwright. Ian replaced him 66 minutes into 1994 Calcutta Cup clash at Murrayfield (5.2.94), a match which England won 15–14 with last kick of game, and he held place for the final two games of the Wooden Spoon campaign, against Ireland and France, prior to departing for summer tour to Argentina where he appeared in both Test defeats. Two years previously he had toured Australia, appearing at openside in both Test losses. A former England 18-Group trialist, who played his 200th game for Gloucester in 1990 Pilkington Cup final, Ian spent the 1988 Australian season playing in Wollongong. Toured Spain with England B (1990) and was selected to England's 1991 World Cup squad, having spent 1990 off-season on standby for Argentina tour. But he opted to switch allegiance to Scotland (Scottish grandparents on father's side) and played twice for Scotland B in 1990/91 (v Ireland and France) before leading side in 19–29 home loss to Ireland in 1991/92, a season in which also captained Gloucester (as in 1992/93) and broke into Scotland team for Five Nations' Championship. He missed only the French visit to Murrayfield, due to a badly cut hand, but was absent throughout 1993 Championship, displaced by another Anglo-Scot, London Scottish's Iain Morrison. Ian, prior to losing place, had been tipped in some quarters as a successor to national captain David Sole; after all, he did skipper Scotland against New South Wales (lost 15–35, Sydney, 6.6.92). But a place in the shadow Scotland XV which struggled to beat Italy (Melrose, 19.12.92) was as near as he came to the national side in any capacity.
Touchlines: Shooting, squash, trout fishing.

Stanger, A. G.   Scotland

Full Name: Anthony George Stanger
Club: Hawick
Position: Centre, wing
Height: 6ft 2in (1.88m)
Weight: 15st 2lb (96kg)
Occupation: New Business representative, RoyScot Trust (Edinburgh)
Born: Hawick, 14.5.68
Family: Bridget (wife)
Family links with rugby: Peter (brother) plays for Hawick
Former Club: Warringah (Aus)
International debut: Scotland 38, Fiji 17, 1989
Five Nations' debut: Ireland 10, Scotland 13, 1990
Best moment in rugby: Scoring winning try in 1990 Grand Slam decider against England
Worst moment in rugby: Getting dropped by Scotland on 1992 Australia tour
Other sporting achievements: Hawick High School athletics champion (three times)
Suggestions to improve rugby: Make everyone play by the same rulebook. So many people are bending the laws at present and we get upset because we're being made to look stupid

Scotland (1989)

Last Season	3 caps	20 pts
Career	38 caps	81 pts

Caps (38): **1989** Fj, Ro **1990** I, F, W, E, NZ(1,2), Arg **1991** F, W, E, I, Ro wc-J, Z, I, WS, E, NZ **1992** E, I, F, W, A(1,2) **1993** I, F, W, E, NZ **1994** W, E, I, F, SA **1995** R wc-IC

Points (81 – 18t): Fj(2t), Ro(3t) **1990** E(1t), NZ(2:1t), Arg(2t) **1991** I(1t) wc-J(1t), Z(1t), WS(1t) **1992** I(1t) **1993** I(1t) **1994** SA(1t) **1995** R(2t) wc-IC(1t)

Notable landmarks in rugby career: Tony's 38-cap haul would constitute a Scottish record for a wing, had he not switched to centre at the start of 1993/94. His most recent two caps came in midfield so he needs another appearance on the wide outside if he is to tie Iwan Tukalo (37: 1985–92). An ever-present in Scotland's side for 35 matches since his debut against Fiji in 1989 before missing the 1994 tour to Argentina through unavailability. Left the limelight to hone his skills as a centre and looked to have emerged as the genuine article when claiming two tries against Romania (Murrayfield, 22.4.95). But despite another try-scoring display, this time in the World Cup opener against Cote d'Ivoire, his was not a convincing performance and Scott Hastings was brought back. Still, Tony's 18 Test tries has moved him to within six of Scottish record scorer I S Smith (24 in 32 matches: 1924-33). Indeed, the Hawick flier scored

six tries in first six internationals (two on debut against Fiji, three against Romania and one against England in 1990 Grand Slam decider). Toured with Scotland to Japan (1989), New Zealand (1990), North America (1991) and Australia (1992). Made debut for Hawick while 17-year old student. Earned five caps for Scottish Schools at centre in 1985/86, followed by two for Scotland U-21s. Began 1990/91 season with two tries in 49–3 defeat of Argentina, taking try-tally to nine in as many games. Could not sustain that prolific pace through 1991/92 season's 11-game schedule but did not do badly, managing four tries: three in World Cup and one against Ireland in Championship for second consecutive season. Also turned out for Scotland A in 36–16 win over Spain (Murrayfield, 28.12.91). Made second A-team appearance in 22–13 win over Ireland (28.12.92), scoring two tries to book his Five Nations' place. Celebrated with great try in Championship opener against Ireland.
Touchlines: Social golf.

Staples, J. E. Ireland

Full Name: James (Jim) Edward Staples
Club: Harlequins
Position: Fullback, wing
Height: 6ft 2in (1.88m)
Weight: 13st 9lb (86kg)
Occupation: Bank officer, Societe Generale
Born: London, 20.10.65
Family: Single
Family links with rugby: Younger brother (David) plays for Westcombe Park
Former clubs: St Mary's, Bromley, Sidcup, London Irish
International debut: Wales 21, Ireland 21, 1991
Five Nations' debut: As above
Worst moments in rugby: Michael Lynagh's last-gasp try for Australia in our 1991 World Cup quarter-final. Missing out on promotion to English First Division with London Irish in 1988/89 after losing 22–21 to last-minute dropped goal by Blackheath, having led 21–0 at half-time

Ireland (1991)

Last Season	4 caps	0 pts
Career	18 caps	21 pts

Caps (18): **1991** W, E, S, Na(1,2) wc-Z, J, S, A **1992** W, E, NZ(1,2), A **1995** F, W, It wc-NZ
Points (21 – 4t,2c): **1991** W(1t), Na(2:1t,2c) wc-J(1t) **1992** NZ(1:1t)

353

Most embarrassing moment: Missing flight home from Spain on first county senior trip

Most respected opponent: Gavin Hastings (Watsonians & Scotland) – strong, fast and always a threat

Biggest influence on career: John O'Driscoll (Connacht: got me involved in the provincial scene)/Roy White (schoolteacher: took me along to Sidcup where he was captain)

Serious injuries: Prolapsed disc in back, broken nose, damaged knee ligaments (missed whole of 1993/94 season), broken hand (1995)

Other sporting achievements: Played in same Greenwich Borough forward line as Arsenal and England striker Ian Wright

Suggestions to improve rugby: Unions should pay a third of players' working salaries to employers to reduce stress in workplace. They must realise that without sympathetic employers we could not afford to play. But I don't want to be paid to play. It doesn't matter if game is professional or amateur as long as rules are same for everyone

Notable landmarks in rugby career: Test career blighted by injury ever since damaging knee in Irish trial preceding 1993 Five Nations' campaign. Prior to that had been first-choice fullback. Missed whole of 1993/94 campaign with damaged knee ligaments and after returning for 1994 tour of Australia (playing in five of the eight non-Test matches) and switching allegiances from London Irish to neighbouring Harlequins, he got injured again. This time it happened just half an hour into his World Cup campaign, when he collided with All Black wing Jeff Wilson under a high ball (Johannesburg, 27.5.95), suffered a broken hand and his tournament was over. It was a crying shame as Jim had looked back to near his best in Five Nations outings against France and Wales. Prior to all this he had toured to New Zealand in 1992, weighing in with one of the three tries which so nearly proved good enough to beat the All Blacks in the first Test (Dunedin, 30.5.92). Also played in second Test in Wellington and against Australia in Dublin (31.10.92). Took over from former Ireland fullback Hugo MacNeill at No 15 in London Irish team and followed his footsteps into Ireland side in 1991. Represented Connacht against 1989 All Blacks and Irish Wolfhounds in 1988/89 Hong Kong Sevens. Played twice for Ireland Under-25s before reaching B grade in 1989/90 with appearance in 22–22 draw with Scotland. Selected for senior bench against France in 1991 Five Nations' opener before playing in next three games, scoring try in 21–21 draw with Wales.

Touchlines: Soccer, most other sports.

Strachan, A. D.   New Zealand

Full Name: Anthony (Ant) Strachan
Province: North Harbour
Position: Scrum-half
Height: 5ft 9in (1.75m)
Weight: 13st (82kg)
Born: Te Awamutu, 7.6.66
Former Provinces: Otago, Auckland
International debut: New Zealand 54, World XV 26, 1992
Serious injuries: Dislocated shoulder (1992)
Notable landmarks in rugby career:
Made the All Black scrum-half position his own with a brilliant 1992 campaign but then lost out to Jon Preston and Stu Forster in '93 and, the revitalised Graeme Bachop in 1994/95. Ant's prodigious clearance speed earned him a national call-up after just eight first-class games for Auckland, where he was back-up to Jason Hewett. It was an injury to Hewett which gave him his ticket to the big time, ahead of Paul McGahon and Kevin Putt. And although his squad selection was as

New Zealand (1992)

Last Season	2 caps	0 pts
Career	11 caps	8 pts

Caps (11): **1992** Wd(2,3), I(1,2), A(1,2,3), SA **1993** BL(1) **1995** wc-J, SA(TR)
Points (8 – 2t): **1992** Wd(2:1t), I(2:1t)

second string scrum-half, he was given his Test debut as early as the second leg of the centenary series, following New Zealand's 14–28 first Test defeat in Christchurch. Brought in for Bachop he responded with a try in the 54–26 Wellington win. A product of Auckland Grammar School, Ant kept his place as New Zealand completed their come-from-behind series win in Auckland and through the two-Test Ireland visit, contributing another try in the 59–6 second Test victory in Wellington. In Australia and South Africa, on New Zealand's three-month tour, no-one surpassed Ant's tally of ten appearances and his standard of performance. His one disappointment came in the 27–24 defeat of South Africa in Johannesburg, where he dislocated his shoulder. Ant reassumed control at the start of the Lions series in 1993 but lost his place after an unconvincing performance in the first Test at Christchurch and did not re-emerge until last summer's World Cup when contributing to New Zealand's sensational 145–17 defeat of Japan (Bloemfontein, 4.6.95) and then coming on as a temporary replacement for Bachop in the World Cup final (JoBurg, 24.6.95). A member of New Zealand's Student World Cup-winning squad in 1988, Ant's surname is pronounced 'Strawn'.

Straeuli, R. A. W. South Africa

Full Name: Rudolph August Wilkens
Straeuli
Province: Transvaal
Position: No 8, flanker
Height: 6ft 4in (1.93m)
Weight: 17st (103kg)
Occupation: Attorney clerk
Born: 20.8.63
Family: Married
International debut: New Zealand
22, South Africa 14, 1994
Family links with rugby: Father
(Hans) played for Northern
Transvaal; brother-in-law of
Springbok Johan Roux
Former Club: Penarth (Wales)
Notable landmarks in rugby career:
Well-known to Welsh rugby
observers even before he burst onto
the international stage in 1994 with
a try on his debut against the All
Blacks in the first Test (Dunedin,
9.7.94). Had a spell at Penarth,
helping the Seasiders' to some
notable results including a cherished
victory over Swansea. Started

South Africa (1994)

Last Season	9 caps	20 pts
Career	9 caps	20 pts

Caps (9): **1994** NZ(1), Arg(1,2), S, W
1995 WS(a) wc-A, WS(b), NZ(R)
Points (20 – 4t): **1994** NZ(1:1t),
Arg(2:1t), S(1t), W(1t)

provincial life with Northern Transvaal (1986), a product of the Tukkies club
in Pretoria, he became the 612th player to be capped by South Africa, having
previously been involved in the national Schools, University and Defence sides.
Switched allegiance to Transvaal in time to help them beat England (JoBurg,
28.5.94) and to share in the Currie Cup final victory over Orange Free State.
Once ensconced he set about building his international career. His try-scoring
debut was matched by repeat performances in three of his next four outings,
against Argentina, Scotland and Wales. He also bagged touchdowns on the '94
British tour against Wales A, Swansea, Combined Scottish Districts and
captained the Boks in the wins over Cardiff and combined Irish Provinces.
Appeared in three of South Africa's World Cup wins last summer, including the
final when he came on for Mark Andrews.

Stransky, J. T.   South Africa

Full Name: Joel Stransky
Province: Western Province
Club: College Rovers
Position: Fly-half
Height: 5ft 11in (1.80m)
Weight: 13st 5lb (80kg)
Occupation: Restaurant owner
Family: Married
Born: Pietermaritzburg, 16.7.67
International debut: Australia 12,
South Africa 19, 1993
Former Province: Natal
Notable landmarks in rugby career:
Hero of South Africa after kicking
them to World Cup final victory over
All Blacks (Johannesburg, 24.6.95).
In an absorbing and memorable
game, Joel landed three penalty kicks
and dropped two goals, the second in
the second period of extra-time as the
Boks edged home 15–12. His 15-
point haul completed an excellent
year's work, having bagged 106
points in just eight outings. Vied with
Transvaal's Hennie le Roux for South
Africa's No10 jersey throughout
1993. Le Roux got first shot but when
the Springboks won neither Test
against France at which he was at the
helm, Joel was brought in for the
country's first tour to Australia in 22
years. His debut (Sydney, 31.7.93)

South Africa (1993)

Last Season	8 caps	106 pts
Career	12 caps	132 pts

Caps (12): **1993** A(1,2,3), Arg(1) **1994**
Arg(1,2) **1995** WS(a) wc-A, R(TR),
C, F, NZ

Points (132 – 5t,19c,20p,3dg): **1993**
A(2:1t,2c,2p), A(3:1c),
Arg(1:3c,1p) **1994**
Arg(1:1t,4c,3p), Arg(2:1t,4c,1p)
1995 WS(1t,1c) wc-
A(1t,1c,4p,1dg), C(2c,2p),
F(1c,4p), NZ(3p,2dg)

resulted in a famous 19–12 win for the visitors against shell-shocked world
champions. Joel took over the goalkicking duties for the second Test (Brisbane,
14.8.93), after Theo van Rensburg had been forced to return home for
emergency surgery on a groin hernia, and responded with 15 points (1t,2c,2p)
yet Australia still won 28–20. One Stransky conversion in the deciding third
Test was insufficient to stop the series staying in Oz. Still, he finished the tour
with 58 points (1t,22c,3p). Joel then kicked five penalty goals in the Currie Cup
final (Kings Park, Durban 16.10.93) but Natal, his former province, lost 15–21
to Transvaal, before heading off to Argentina, where he lost his Test place after
kicking nine points (3c,1p) in a 29–26 first Test defeat of the Pumas (Buenos
Aires, 6.11.93).

Strauss, C. P. South Africa

Full Name: Christiaan (Tiaan) Petrus Strauss
Province: Western Province
Club: Northerns-Tygerberg-College
Position: No 8
Height: 6ft 1in (1.86m)
Weight: 15st 6lb (98kg)
Occupation: Articled clerk with Cape Town law firm
Born: Upington, 28.6.65
International debut: France 15, South Africa 20, 1992
Notable landmarks in rugby career: Star of South African team in 1993, Tiaan was dropped after England stunned Boks 32–15 (Pretoria, 4.6.94). Things have not been the same since, although ironically he did return as captain for the first Test against New Zealand (Dunedin, 9.7.94) when François Pienaar was away nursing concussion. But Tiaan was regarded more as a stop-gap. He made three further appearances, scoring a try in the 42–22 first Test defeat of Argentina (Port Elizabeth, 8.10.94), but did not figure in South

South Africa (1992)

Last Season	5 caps	5 pts
Career	15 caps	20 pts

Caps (15): **1992** F(1,2), E **1993** F(1,2), A(1,2,3), Arg(1,2) **1994** E(1), NZ(1,2), Arg(1,2)
Points (20 – 4t): **1992** E(1t) **1993** Arg(2:2t) **1994** Arg(1:1t)

Africa's World Cup triumph last summer. Tiaan had been one of only two Springbok forwards to play in all seven Tests during 1993 (the other being skipper Pienaar), saving his most productive performance for last when bagging two tries in the 52–23 defeat of Argentina (Buenos Aires, 13.11.93) which completed a 2–0 series whitewash away from home. He had also claimed a try hat-trick in the opening 55–37 victory over Cordoba (27.10.93) and finished the six-match tour as top try-scorer. Appeared in all six big tour games in Australia and skippered the side to their biggest win of that tour: a 90–3 rout of hapless South Australia (Adelaide, 17.7.93). Had captained Junior Springboks side which played against both Namibia and New Zealand (lost 15–20) in 1992, a year in which he made a favourable impression on the tour of France and England when playing in all three Tests and five other games besides. A powerful man, the legacy of his days on the family farms in the Kalahari and Namibia, he was pulled from the under-20 ranks to make his senior debut for Western Province in 1986. Scored South Africa's only try in 16–33 loss to England (14.11.92). Capped 120 times by his union before the accomplished

Jannie Breedt retired, vacating a berth in the back row for him to make his Test bow in the 20–15 defeat of France in Lyon on 17 October 1992. Spent the late 1980s and early 1990s in Italy playing with Noceto, a second division outfit to be found near Parma.

Strydom, H. — South Africa

Full Name: Hannes Strydom
Province: Transvaal
Position: Lock
Height: 6ft 6½in (1.99m)
Weight: 18st 5lb (112kg)
Occupation: Chemist, Roussel Labs
Family: Married with one child
Born: 13.7.65
International debut: South Africa 17, France 18, 1993
Notable landmarks in rugby career: One of three forwards drafted in to bolster South Africa's flagging challenge against France, after the 1993 tourists had sent shockwaves throughout the Republic by sharing the first Test 20–20 (Durban, 26.6.93), the injection of new blood made no odds as South Africa crashed 18–17 in Ellis Park, Johannesburg (3.7.93). Hannes was retained despite the setback, and played the full three-Test complement in Australia over the next two months, on each occasion

South Africa (1993)

Last Season	5 caps	0 pts
Career	12 caps	0 pts

Caps (12): **1993** F(2), A(1,2,3), Arg(1,2)
1994 E(1) **1995** wc-A, C, F, NZ
Points Nil

in second row partnership with Western Province's Nico Wegner. He remained first-choice lock throughout the tour, turning out in the other 'biggies' against South Australia (won 90–3, Adelaide 17.7.93), New South Wales (lost 28–29, Sydney 24.7.93) and Queensland (won 17–3, Brisbane 8.8.93). Less active in 1994, dropped after England's shock 32–15 win in Pretoria (4.6.94), Hannes returned in last summer's World Cup, partnering Mark Andrew and, latterly, Transvaal team mate Kobus Wiese in the Bok engine room. On a provincial note, 1993 had been a Red Letter year for Transvaal who captured both prestigious Super-10 trophy (beating Auckland 20–7 in final at Ellis Park, Johannesburg on 22.5.93) and Currie Cup (as they did again in 1994). After the latter, Hannes departed with Springboks for Argentina where he played in four of the six tour missions: both Test wins, the 28–27 loss to Buenos Aires and the

359

40–12 'battle' of Tucuman. The latter contest (2.11.93) brought shame on the player as he was one of four dismissed. However, Lady Luck treated him kindly as he, and fellow Springbok Keith Andrews, were handed nothing more than suspended sentences and so were free to play in the first Test a mere four days later.

Swart, B. South Africa

Full Name: Balie Swart
Province: Transvaal
Position: Prop
Height: 6ft ½in (1.84m)
Weight: 18st 6lb (113kg)
Occupation: Marketing manager, Kohler Corrugated
Family: Single
Born: 18.5.64
International debut: Australia 12, South Africa 19, 1993
Notable landmarks in rugby career: World Cup winner last summer, Balie performed impressively on the tighthead, especially in the 15–12 final defeat of New Zealand, one of four ties in which he was selected. Beneficiary of Johan le Roux's mega suspension for ear biting All Black skipper Sean Fitzpatrick in 1994, as it vacated the No 3 jersey. Balie also helped Transvaal complete back-to-back Currie Cup wins at the expense of Orange Free State. Had enjoyed a triumphant debut in Sydney (3.7.93) when South Africa celebrated their return to Australia after a 22-year absence with a 19–12 defeat of the Wallabies.

South Africa (1993)

Last Season	10 caps	0 pts
Career	14 caps	0 pts

Caps (14): **1993** A(1,2,3), Arg(1) **1994** E(1,2), NZ(1,3), Arg(2R) **1995** WS(a) wc-A, WS(b), F, NZ
Points Nil

Balie would almost certainly have made his bow earlier but for an emergency appendectomy which forced him out of the reckoning for the two-Test series with France in June and July of the same year. Still, he made up for lost time in Australia, turning out in eight of the 13 engagements, including each leg of the three Test-series which the world champions came from behind to win (Sydney, 31.8.93), in a third Test in which Balie departed after 45 minutes with a broken nose. A member of the Transvaal side which won the inaugural Super-10 tournament (beating Auckland 20–7 in final, Johannesburg 22.5.93), he also toured with the Boks to Argentina in the Autumn but was replaced by Western

Province's Keith Andrews at tighthead for the second Test in Buenos Aires, a city in which he had appeared in the first international the previous weekend, and against whom he had played on a Springboks side beaten 28–27 (30.10.93). Despite his South American omission, he was restored to the Test side for the visit of England (1994) and was superb in second Test once switched to favoured tighthead berth.

Tabua, I.   Australia

Full Name: Ilie Tabua
State: Queensland
Club: Brothers
Position: Flanker, No 8
Height: 6ft 5in (1.96m)
Weight: 16st 4lb (104kg)
Occupation: Student, marketing rep
Born: Fiji, 30.9.64
Family: single
International debut: Australia 28, South Africa 20, 1993
Best moment in rugby: Test debut against South Africa at Ballymore; World Cup Sevens in Edinburgh when I made my Australia debut
Worst moment in rugby: Canterbury verses Old (Christchurch) in 1992. Nearly died of hypothermia
Suggestions to improve rugby: Legalise lifting in the line out
Notable landmarks in rugby career:
Ilie first came to notice of British audiences when playing for Australia in World Cup Sevens in Edinburgh (16-18.4.93). The Fijian-born Brothers flanker, then uncapped in

Australia (1993)
Last Season	6 caps	5 pts
Career	10 caps	15 pts

Caps (10): 1993 SA(2,3), C, F(1) 1994 I(1,2), It(1,2) 1995 wc-C, R
Points (15 – 3t): 1994 I(1:1t), I(2:1t) 1995 wc-C(1t)

the XV-man sphere, helped the Wallabies reach the final, where he was spared the agony of losing 21–17 to unfancied England. Among his team mates in that tournament were David Campese and Matt Burke, with whom he made his Test debut against South Africa in Brisbane (14.8.93). His call-up was prompted by the Wallabies' shock 12–19 loss in the first Test in Sydney and his arrival more than redressed the balance. The world champions won the next two Tests. Ilie then embarked on the Autumn tour to North America and France, scoring a try in the 26–22 non-cap Test victory over the United States in sweltering California (2.10.93) before appearing against Canada and then France in the

surprise 13–16 first Test loss in Bordeaux. It was an especially painful afternoon for Ilie as he broke his left arm midway through the game and was put out of action for the remainder of the season. Typically positive return in 1994 when scoring a try in each of the two Test wins over Ireland, confirming himself a powerhouse in the 'Willie O' mould. Added his third try at last summer's World Cup in the Wallabies' 27–11 defeat of Canada (Port Elizabeth, 31.5.95).
Touchlines: Relaxing, reading, sleeping.

Taylor, H. T. Wales

Full Name: Hemi Takatou Taylor
Club: Cardiff
Position: Flanker, No 8
Height: 6ft 2in (1.88m)
Weight: 14st 7lb (87.5kg)
Occupation: Rugby development officer, Cardiff RFC
Born: Morrinsville, New Zealand, 17.12.64
Family: Wife and child
Former provinces/clubs: Waikato (NZ), Wairarapa Bush (NZ), Newbridge (Wal), East Brisbane (Aus)
International debut: Portugal 11, Wales 102, 1994
Five Nations debut: Wales 9, England 23, 1995
Notable landmarks in rugby career: Became first New Zealander to represent Wales at Test level when given debut in World Cup qualifier against Portugal (Lisbon, 17.5.94). The former New Zealand Colt, whose allegiances in the Land of the Long White Cloud were to Waikato and Wairarapa Bush, celebrated the

Wales (1994)		
Last Season	8 caps	5 pts
Career	13 caps	10 pts

Caps (13): **1994** wc(q)-P. C, Fj, T, WS(R) wc(q)-R, It. SA **1995** E, S wc-J, NZ, I(b)

Points (10 – 2t): **1994** wc(q)-P(1t) **1995** wc-I(b:1t)

occasion with a try in the 102–11 rout. Although he did not play in the second leg of the Iberian trip, against Spain four days later, he was included in the national squad for the summer tour of Canada, Fiji, Tonga and Western Samoa (turning out in all three Tests), and picked up his second cap in the 33–15 'revenge' victory over the Canucks in Toronto (11.6.94). Serious hand injury robbed Wales of his talents mid-season and although he returned against England (making his Five Nations debut in his ninth appearance), he failed to impress in South Africa last summer, sadly in keeping with most of his team mates. An ever-present in Wales A's 1994 5-match 'Grand Slam', he appeared in the wins over Japan (won 61-5, Llanelli 29.9.93), North of England (scored try in 24–8 win, Pontypool 13.10.93), Ireland A (won 20–10, Donnybrook 4.2.94), Canada A (won 42–11, Cardiff, 12.3.94) and France A (won 21–8, Cardiff 18.3.94). Cardiff fans voted him their Player of the Year in 1992/93 and it was with the same club that he picked up a Swalec Cup winners medal (1993/94) and league champions medal (1994/95).

Taylor, M. Wales

Full Name: Mark Taylor
Club: Pontypool
Position: Centre
Height: 6ft 1in (1.85m)
Weight: 13st 10lb (82kg)
Occupation: Trainee accountant, Moore Stephens, London
Born: 27.2.73
Family: Single
Family links with rugby: Father (Ivor) is Pontypool team manager; brother (Paul) plays for Pontypool
International debut: Wales 12, South Africa 20, 1994
Five Nations debut: France 21, Wales 9, 1995
Notable landmarks in rugby career: Deserves praise for breaking into Wales side in 1994/95 in spite of playing for a Pontypool XV regularly getting thumped in the Heineken Leagues. Mark had scored a try in the relegation decider against Dunvant to spare Ponty's blushes in

Wales (1994)

Last Season	3 caps	0 pts
Career	3 caps	0 pts

Caps (3): **1994** SA **1995** F, E
Points Nil

1993/94, but for all his best efforts, the former legends of the Welsh game were relegated last term. Mark's Test debut came in a commendable Welsh performance, albeit a losing one, versus South Africa (Cardiff, 26.11.94). He retained his midfield slot alongside Cardiff captain Mike Hall for the Five Nations opener against France (Paris, 21.1.95) but was dropped after Wales crashed 9–23 at home to England (Cardiff, 18.2.95). Being London-based through his work as a trainee accountant, the fears are that Mark will take his rugby to the Big Smoke. Wales could do with the former Under-21 international hanging around.

Techoueyres, W.   France

Full Name: William Techoueyres
Club: Bordeaux University
Position: Wing
Height: 6ft ½in (1.84m)
Weight: 13st 6lb (80.7kg)
Occupation: Cafe owner
Born: Bordeaux, 12.2.66
Family: Single with one child
International debut: France 14,
England 18, 1994
Five Nations debut: As above
Best moments in rugby: Getting
capped; helping Begles win 1991
French Championship
Notable landmarks in rugby career:
William's debut proved to be a
baptism of fire as it coincided with
England's 1994 defeat of France in
Paris. Being a winger, he was an easy
target for Parc des Princes crowd
looking to vent their displeasure.
Not that he deserved the abuse, a
point confirmed by the selectors who
retained his services for the next

France (1994)

Last Season	1 cap	5 pts
Career	3 caps	5 pts

Caps (3): **1994** E, S **1995** wc-IC
Points (5 – 1t): **1995** wc-IC(1t)

international, against Scotland (Murrayfield, 19.3.94). That game ended on a
happier note for France as a 20–12 victory staved off the dreaded Wooden
Spoon. William, who did not tour to Canada and New Zealand that summer,
is the first Bordeaux University player since Michael Celaya, 33 years ago, to
receive full international recognition. He joined the club in 1993/94 after a
lengthy spell at Begles (Bordeaux's other major club), with whom he won a
French Championship medal in 1991, when Toulouse were sent packing after
losing the final 19–10. Ended 14 months in the international wilderness when
given his third cap at the World Cup. France beat Cote d'Ivoire 54–18
(Rustenburg, 30.5.95) and William weighed in with one of the Tricolors' eight
tries.

Townsend, G. P. J.   Scotland

Full Name: Gregor Peter John Townsend
Club: Gala
Position: Outside-half, centre
Height: 5ft 11in (1.81m)
Weight: 12st 7lb (75kg)
Occupation: History/politics student, Edinburgh University
Born: Edinburgh, 26.4.73
Family: Single
Family links with rugby: Father (Peter) played twice for South of Scotland
International debut: England 26, Scotland 12, 1993
Five Nations' debut: As above
Best moment in rugby: Playing in Australia for Warringah; beating France in Paris (1995)
Worst moment in rugby: 1993 World Cup Sevens – I was looking forward to it so much and then played terribly and got dropped; damaging ligaments and missing 1995 World Cup

Scotland (1993)		
Last Season	5 caps	5 pts
Career	12 caps	11 pts

Caps (12): **1993** E(R) **1994** W, E, I, F, Arg(1,2) **1995** C, I, F(a), W, E
Points (11 – 1t,2dg): **1994** E(1dg), Arg(2:1dg) **1995** F(a:1t)

Most embarrassing moment: Giving try-scoring 'pass' to French winger Philippe Saint-Andre at Murrayfield (1994)
Most respected opponent: Rob Andrew (Wasps & England)
Biggest influence on career: My father (Peter)
Serious injuries: Sprung ribs at 1992 Hong Kong Sevens, damaged knee ligaments in 1993 Scotland Trial; broken bone in hand (Sept 1993 v Boroughmuir out for 12 weeks)
Suggestions to improve rugby: Consult players before introducing new laws. Greater integration between top and bottom level of game (massive difference between club and international level in terms of facilities etc)
Notable landmarks in rugby career: Exciting prospect but rather prone to errors as he continued to learn his trade. A case in point was last summer when Scotland coach Dougie Morgan directly blamed the Gala youngster's decision-making for Argentina's 16–15 first Test win (Buenos Aires, 4.6.94). Nonetheless, Gregor's have-a-go style brightened up a largely tedious international stage in 1994 and in 1995 it inspired the Scots to their first ever win at Parc des Princes (18.2.95). In a thriller, Gregor scored Scotland's first try and then, after his failute to find touch had gifted Philippe Saint-Andre the go-ahead score,

provided the classy inside flick to unlock the French midfield and put Gavin Hastings away for the last-minute winning score. It was a fitting reward for a player who has endured more than his fair share of heartache – in 1994 he had a dropped goal against Wales ruled out by French referee Patrick Robin, who didn't think it had gone over. Then he looked to have won Scotland the Calcutta Cup (Murrayfield, 5.2.94), only for Jon Callard to steal his glory with an injury-time strike from 40 metres. Knee-ligament damage, sustained in the final trial, wrecked his 1993 campaign and another tear robbed him of a place in Scotland's 1995 World Cup squad. Toured Fiji, Tonga and Western Samoa (1993: playing in latter two Tests and top-scoring on tour with 30 points), and Australia (1992), appearing in eight games. Then helped Scotland win Dubai Sevens and turned out for Scotland A in against Spain, Italy and Ireland. Turned out for Irish Wolfhounds at 1992 Hong Kong Sevens, having quickly progressed through Gala U-14, U-15 and U-16 ranks and, in 1991/92, played for Scotland U-21 and Scotland B.

Touchlines: Golf (9-handicap).

Tweed, D. A. Ireland

Full Name: Davy Alexander Tweed
Club: Ballymena
Position: Lock
Height: 6ft 5in (1.96m)
Weight: 18st 2lb (115kg)
Occupation: Machine operator, Northern Ireland Railways
Born: Ballymoney, 13.11.59
Family: Married with four children
International debut: Ireland 7, France 25, 1995
Five Nations debut: As above
Notable landmarks in rugby career: Became the oldest ever Irish debutant (aged 35) when called up at the 11th hour for Ireland's 7–25 loss to France (Dublin, 4.3.95) after Paddy Johns pulled out with appendicitis. Tweedy responded with a wonderful lineout performance in tandem with Gabriel Fulcher. In fact, despite the lopsided scoreline, Ireland ruled the touchlines and the father of four proud kids retained his place for the

Ireland (1995)		
Last Season	4 caps	0 pts
Career	4 caps	0 pts

Caps (4): 1995 F, W, E wc-J
Points Nil

16–12 victory over Wales (Cardiff, 18.3.95) and the rather embarrassing 12–22 loss to Italy (Treviso, 8.5.95). Tweedy, who made his Ulster debut in 1989 and his Ireland A bow three years later (taking his tally of A caps to eight last season), represented Irish Combined Provinces in defeat against touring Northern Transvaal (Donnybrook, 3.3.95). He continued his South African connection last summer when touring with Ireland to the World Cup, where he played in the 50–28 win over Japan (Bloemfontein, 31.5.95).
Touchlines: Basketball.

Ubogu, V. E. England

Full Name: Victor Eriakpo Ubogu
Club: Bath
Position: Tighthead prop
Height: 5ft 9in (1.76m)
Weight: 16st 2lb (102.5kg)
Occupation: Company director, Cobrawatch (family-owned security firm); owner of London sports bar, Shoeless Joe's
Born: Lagos, Nigeria, 8.9.64
Family: Single
Former clubs: Moseley, Richmond
International debut: England 26, Canada 13, 1992
Five Nations' debut: Scotland 14, England 15, 1994
Best moments in rugby: Being capped by England; Bath beating Toulouse in 1989/90
Worst moment in rugby: England losing 21–6 to Natal in Durban (1994)
Suggestions to improve rugby: Rules must be redefined so we have same game in either hemisphere. Too many vague interpretations of what is, and is not, okay, and no consistency in refereeing. The IRB have basically made a hash of the laws

England (1992)

Last Season	11 caps	5 pts
Career	20 caps	5 pts

Caps (20): **1992** C, SA **1993** NZ **1994** S, I, F, W, SA(1,2), R, C **1995** I, F(a), W, S wc-Arg, WS, A, NZ, F(b)

Points (5 – 1t): **1995** W(1t)

Notable landmarks in rugby career: Landed a healthy wager when backing himself to score the first try against Wales (Cardiff, 18.2.95) and doing precisely that. Victor's five-pointer helped England to a 23–9 win en route to their third Grand Slam in five years, though Shoeless Joe's first. He had high hopes of adding a World Cup winner's medal but despite five appearances in South

Africa, Victor was unable to stir the England pack sufficiently to deal with the All Black machine (Cape Town, 18.6.95) on that extraordinary afternoon at Newlands. Wembley debuts are few and far between but Victor, a member of Oxford's beaten Varsity team in 1987, was lucky enough to make his in the shadow of the twin towers when selected ahead of Jeff Probyn against Canada (17.9.92). Twickenham, needless to say, was unavailable due to reconstruction. Although the school wing-turned international prop lost his place to Probyn for the 1993 Five Nations' campaign, his time came in 1993/94 when he was everpresent throughout. Adept on either side of the scrum, he has won three Pilkington Cup winners' medals: in 1990 (helping demolish arch-rivals Gloucester 48–6), 1994 and 1995.

Underwood, R.   England

Full Name: Rory Underwood
Club: Leicester & RAF
Position: Wing
Height: 5ft 9in (1.76m)
Weight: 14st (84kg)
Occupation: RAF pilot
Born: Middlesbrough, 19.6.63
Family: Wendy (wife), Rebecca (daughter) and Alexandra (daughter)
Family links with rugby: Brother (Tony) plays for Leicester, England and British Lions
Former club: Middlesbrough
International debut: England 12, Ireland 9, 1984
Five Nations' debut: As above
Best moment in rugby: Winning first (1991) Grand Slam with England
Worst moment in rugby: England's 9–12 loss to Wales at Cardiff (1989)
Most embarrassing moment: Making error which led to Wales scoring crucial try against England in above match
Most respected opponent: Patrice Lagisquet (ex-Bayonne & France)
Biggest influence on career: Geoff Cooke (ex-England manager)
Other sporting achievements: Swam and played cricket for same Barnard Castle School as England team-mate Rob Andrew attended
Suggestions to improve rugby: IRB must make unambiguous rulings concerning amateurism. A lot of them seem to be out of touch with reality
Notable landmarks in rugby career: England's most-capped player (79) and record try-scorer (47) having added another chapter to his glorious career in 1994/95 when bagging another ten tries in 12 appearances (including braces

versus Canada, Western Samoa and, in an extraordinary World Cup semi-final, New Zealand. It had all begun with two tries for Leicester against the 1983 Barbarians. Three months later Rory was in the England team. Missed tour to Argentina in summer of 1990, due to RAF commitments, having already become England's most-capped back and highest try-scorer during 1989/90 season. RAF duties also took precedence over tours to South Africa (1984) and New Zealand (1985). Equalled Dan Lambert's 1907 England record of five tries in an international, against Fiji (won 58–23, Twickenham 4.11.89). Previously played for England Colts, U-23 and B teams. Toured Australia with 1989 Lions, playing in all three Tests. Held his place on 1993 tour to New Zealand, where he scored winning try in second Test. Rates his 26th Test try (scored in 16–7 defeat of Ireland during 1991 Grand Slam run) as most important of career. Also scored in 21–19 win over France (1991 Grand Slam decider). In 1991/92 he notched a further eight tries: including four en route to World Cup final and three in 1992 Grand Slam campaign. Retired from international arena once back-to-back Grand Slams were safely stowed in the bag but did a Frank Sinatra and returned in 1992/93 after missing Wembley opener against Canada. Tony and he are first brothers to appear in same England championship side since the Wheatley brothers packed down against Scotland in 1938.
Touchlines: Crosswords, reading.

England (1984)		
Last Season	12 caps	50 pts
Career	79 caps	200 pts
Lions 1986		
1989	3 Tests	0 pts
1993	3 Tests	5 pts

Caps (79): **1984** I, F, W, A **1985** Ro, F, S, I, W **1986** W, I, F **1987** I, F, W, S wc-A, J, W **1988** F, W, S, I(1,2), A(a1,a2), Fj, A(b) **1989** S, I, F, W. Lions-A(1,2,3). Ro, Fj **1990** I, F, W, S, Arg(b) **1991** W, S, I, F, Fj, A wc-NZ, It, US, F, S, A **1992** S, I, F, W, SA **1993** F, W, S, I. Lions-NZ(1,2,3). NZ **1994** S, I, F, W, SA(1,2), R, C **1995** I, F(a),W,S wc-Arg, It, WS, A, NZ, F(b)

Points (200 – 47t): **1984** F(1t) **1985** I(1t) **1987** wc-J(2t) **1988** I(1:2t), I(2:1t), A(a1:1t), A(a2:1t), Fj(2t), A(b:2t) **1989** Fj(5t) **1990** I(1t), F(1t), W(2t), Arg(b:3t) **1991** I(1t), F(1t), Fj(1t) wc-It(1t), US(2t), F(1t) **1992** S(1t), I(1t), F(1t) **1993** S(1t). Lions-NZ(2:1t) **1994** W(1t), R(1t), C(2t) **1995** W(2t) wc-It(1t), WS(2t), NZ(2t)

Underwood, T.   England

Full Name: Tony Underwood
Clubs: Leicester, Cambridge Univ
Position: Wing
Height: 5ft 9in (1.76m)
Weight: 13st 7lb (81kg)
Occupation: Equity broker, Crosby Securities
Born: Ipoh, Malaysia, 17.2.69
Family: Single
Family links with rugby: Brother Rory is England's record try-scorer and most-capped player (79 caps – 47 tries, 200 points)
International debut: England 26, Canada 13, 1992
Five Nations' debut: England 26, Scotland 12, 1993
Best moments in rugby: 1993 Lions' selection; South Africa 15, England 32, 1994
Worst moments in rugby: England's 12–13 loss to Ireland (1994); England 29, New Zealand 45, 1995
Most embarrassing moment: Post-try behaviour following my late score in 1991 Varsity match
Most respected opponents: Ian Hunter (Northampton & England B) and David Campese (Randwick & Australia)

England (1992)

Last Season	10 caps	40 pts
Career	20 caps	50 pts

Lions 1993

Caps (20): **1992** C, SA **1993** S, I, NZ **1994** S, I, W, SA(1,2), R, C **1995** I, F(a), W, S wc-Arg, It, A, NZ
Points (50 – 10t): **1992** SA(1t) **1993** S(1t) **1994** R(2t), C(1t) **1995** I(1t), F(a:2t) wc-It(1t), A(1t)

Biggest influence on career: My mother (Anne)
Serious injuries: Broken jaw, torn hamstring and damaged knee cartilage - all in second half of 1989/90 season
Notable landmarks in rugby career: Like older brother Rory, Tony enjoyed a prolific 1994/95 campaign, running in eight tries, the most memorable being the score against Australia that dumped the holders out of the World Cup in a simply fabulous quarter-final (Cape Town, 11.6.95). But he won't want to dwell too long on the semi-final, the following weekend on the same Newlands pitch. England were stuffed and Tony's marker, Jonah Lomu, bulldozed his way to four tries. It had been against the All Blacks that Tony had made his name in 1989, uncapped and playing for the Barbarians. And against them that he celebrated victory with England in 1993. Toured South Africa (1994), having been dropped after England's shock home defeat by Ireland (19.2.94).

Replaced by Ian Hunter against France and Wales but in case of latter, scrambled back in through back door. Injury to Stuart Barnes got Tony onto bench from where subsequent injury to David Pears in run-up to game led to Hunter moving to fullback and Tony being reprieved. A midweek British Lion in 1993, Tony had returned home to make England No.14 jersey his own against All Blacks, Scotland and Ireland. But shared in criticism of England's try-scoring failure – ironic as he has been such a prolific scorer at B and A level. Played for England Schools (18-Group) before graduating to England team for inaugural Student World Cup (1988) and for senior England side in 18–16 non-cap win over Barbarians (1990/91). Went on to represent Combined Students, North of England, England B (13 times) and, latterly, England in traumatic 1990 summer tour of Argentina. Tony's Test debut came against Canada (Wembley, 17.10.92) and his first top-level try arrived in the 33–16 defeat of South Africa (Twickenham, 14.11.92). Helped Leicester win 1992/93 Pilkington Cup and 1994/94 Courage league title.

Touchlines: Cricket, squash, golf, tennis.

Van der Westhuizen, J. H.   South Africa

Full Name: Joost Heystek van der Westhuizen
Province: Northern Transvaal
Position: Scrum-half
Height: 6ft 1½in (1.86m)
Weight: 13st 9lb (82kg)
Occupation: Student
Born: Pretoria, 20.2.71
Family: Single
International debut: Argentina 26, South Africa 29, 1993
Other sporting achievements: 'Korf bal' (like netball) for South Africa
Notable landmarks in rugby career:
Started 1994/95 in contention for a
Test place and finished it as arguably
the world's premier scrum-half. A
combative, in-your-face sort of No 9
(like Dewi Morris), Joost's finest hour (to date) was probably his display at Murrayfield (19.11.94) when he tore Scotland apart with two magnificent first half tries. That took his try-tally to five in six Tests, though that shouldn't have surprised anyone, given the fact he has always scored tries for by the bucket-load for Northern Transvaal. Moreover, his Springbok debut saw him bag four tries against Western Australia. Granted the opposition was not up to much, they crashed 71–8 (WACA, 14.7.93), but his remained an outstanding opening

effort. And he continued in the same prolific vein, crossing New South Wales' line during the 29–28 defeat (Waratah, 24.7.93), repeating the feat against NSW Country (won 41–7, Orange, 31.7.93) and bagging try-braces against both Australian Capital Territory (won 57–10, Bruce Stadium, 4.8.93) and Queensland Country (won 63–5, Mackay, 11.8.93). He completed a cracking first tour with a try on his final outing against Sydney (Penrith, 18.8.93), to return home top try-scorer with 11. Little wonder he was promptly redirected to Argentina for the Springboks' Autumn visit, and little wonder either that he graduated into the Test XV during the trip. The Pumas could not contain Joost either as he claimed a try in each game (first Test: won 29–26, Buenos Aires 6.11.93; second Test: won 52–23, Buenos Aires 13.11.93) as South Africa completed a 2–0 series whitewash. He retained his place in 1994 for South Africa's opening mission against England (Pretoria, 2.6.94) and, despite looking lively, was dropped for the Cape Town return as the management changed the gameplan, preferring Johan Roux's more orthodox style. Still, he picked up his cap, as a 30th minute replacement for injured wing Chester Williams. Toured New Zealand (1994), scoring three tries in five outings but being unable to shift Roux from the Test berth. But after a try-scoring return in the second Test against Argentina (JoBurg, 15.10.94) he won back first-choice recognition on the Autumn tour to Britain. Linked with a £500,000 move to Leeds RLFC throughout last summer's World Cup, a tournament in which he was magnificent.

South Africa (1993)		
Last Season	11 caps	15 pts
Career	13 caps	25 pts

Caps (13): **1993** Arg(1,2) **1994** E(1,2R), Arg(2), S, W **1995** WS(a) wc-A, C(R), WS(b), F, NZ

Points (25 – 5t): **1993** Arg(1:1t), Arg(2:1t) **1994** Arg(2:1t), S(2t)

Wales wing Ieuan Evans shunts flying Scotsman Kenny Logan into the sidings.

Viars, S.   France

Full Name: Sebastien Viars
Club: Brive
Position: Wing, fullback
Height: 6ft ½in (1.84m)
Weight: 13st 5lb (80kg)
Occupation: Commercial agent
Family: Single
Born: Aurillac, 24.6.71
International debut: Wales 9, France 12, 1992
Five Nations' debut: As above
Notable landmarks in rugby career: Impressive points scorer for France, though unable to establish a regular place in the Test side, Sebastien rounded off a belter of a score against England (isn't it always) during 10–31 defeat in the 1995 Five Nations (Twickenham, 4.2.95), having come on as a 38th minute replacement for Jean-Luc Sadourny. His next outing was the World Cup mission against Cote d'Ivoire (Rustenburg, 30.5.95) and he again responded with a try in the 54–18 win. Had ended a year in the international wilderness when coming on as a replacement for captain Philippe Saint-Andre against Canada (lost 16–18, Ontario, 5.6.94) at the start of France's

France (1992)

Last Season	2 caps	10 pts
Career	14 caps	115 pts

Caps (14): **1992** W, E, I, R, Arg(a1,a2), SA(1,2R), Arg(b) **1993** R(a) **1994** C(a:R), NZ(1TR) **1995** E(a:R) wc-IC

Points (115 – 7t,16c,17p): **1992** W(1p), E(1t,1c,1p), I(2t,5c,2p), Arg(a1:1t,4p), Arg(a2:1t,3c,3p), SA(1:1c,1p), Arg(b:1c,1p) **1993** R(a:4c,3p) **1995** E(a:1t) wc-IC(1t)

summer tour to Canada and New Zealand, a trip which was to yield an historic 2–0 series win over the All Blacks. Previously, he had been France's find of 1992, marking his debut in Cardiff with a penalty goal in the 12–9 win over Wales before notching his first try (as well as a penalty and conversion) on his Paris debut against England (lost 13–31) a fortnight later. Topped it all by then claiming a Five Nations record 24 points in the 44–12 win over Ireland on a delightful sunny afternoon in Parc des Princes. His history-making haul included two tries, five conversions and two penalty goals. Sebastien had hinted at this potential when scoring a quite outstanding try in France B's 10–6 win over England B at Bristol (15.3.91), having represented French second string in the 31–10 win over Scotland B at Hughenden, two weeks earlier. Not required for duty during the 1991 World Cup – although he toured to North America in

July 1991, scoring four tries against Western Unions and USA B. His very early career featured Schools caps in 1989, Junior honours in 1990 (landing four goals against Wales Youth) and appearance at 1991 Hong Kong Sevens with France.

Wainwright, R. I.   Scotland

Full Name: Robert Iain Wainwright
Club: West Hartlepool
Position: Flanker
Height: 6ft 5in (1.95m)
Weight: 15st 4lb (97kg)
Occupation: Army doctor
Born: Perth, 22.3.65
Family: Romayne (wife), Douglas (son)
Family links with rugby: Father (J.F.Wainwright) a 1956 Cambridge Blue
Former clubs: Cambridge University, Edinburgh Academicals
International debut: Ireland 10, Scotland 18, 1992
Five Nations' debut: As above
Most respected opponent: John Jeffrey (Kelso & ex-Scotland)
Other sporting achievements: Boxing Blue at Cambridge Univ
Serious injuries: Broken cheekbone (Jan 1990), ankle (Sept 1990)
Notable landmarks in rugby career: Injury prevented him from captaining Scotland on 1994 tour to Argentina, but rebounded strongly

Scotland (1992)

Last Season	10 caps	5 pts
Career	17 caps	14 pts

Caps (17): **1992** I(R), F, A(1,2) **1993** NZ **1994** W, E **1995** C, I, F(a), W, E, R wc-IC, T, F(b), NZ

Points (14 – 3t): **1992** A(1:1t) **1994** E(1t) **1995** wc-F(b:1t)

from that disappointment to underline his leadership potential during Scotland's revival in 1995. Scored only one try, in the heartbreaking World Cup defeat by France (Pretoria, 3.6.95), though did bag a brace in the 62–7 non-cap Test win over Spain (Madrid, 6.5.95). Everpresent throughout 11 engagements in '95, combining with Iain Morrison and Eric Peters to form an outstanding back row combination. Had sustained broken cheekbone 66 minutes into 15–14 Calcutta Cup defeat by England (5.2.94), a Murrayfield match in which he scored the solitary try on 28 minutes. One of Scotland's most versatile players, his 17 caps have come at No 8 (four), flanker (12) and replacement lock (one, on debut). Representative career really took off in 1991/92 season when

he captained Scotland B, broke into senior side and toured Australia in summer, playing in both Tests and claiming Scotland's only try in 12–27 Sydney loss (13.6.92). First cap had come four months earlier when replacing Neil Edwards for last two minutes against Ireland in Dublin (15.2.92). He then played the full 80 minutes in the 10–6 win over France (7.3.92). Injury deprived him of a Test run on his return from Down Under in 1992. Having appeared in three consecutive Varsity matches (1986-88), he made his Scotland B debut in 26–3 win over Italy at L'Aquila. Won further B caps against Ireland (lost 0–16, 22.12.90) and, as captain, against France (lost 18–27, Albi 3.2.92). He scored a try in latter contest. Other career landmarks include participation on Barbarians Easter tour (1988), Hong Kong Sevens (1988,89) and 1989 tour to Japan with Scotland (two games, two tries).
Touchlines: Wildlife, fishing, photography, whisky.

Walker, N. K.   Wales

Full Name: Nigel Keith Walker
Club: Cardiff
Position: Wing
Height: 5ft 11in (1.81m)
Weight: 12st 9lb (75kg)
Occupation: Development officer with Sports Council of Wales; part-time Radio Wales presenter of Walker-ound Sport
Born: Cardiff, 15.6.63
Family: Mary (wife), Rebecca (daughter)
International debut: Wales 14, Ireland 19, 1993
Five Nations' debut: As above
Best moment in rugby: Scoring try vs France (1994)
Worst moments in rugby: Conceding try in 1994 Swalec Cup final (thankfully Cardiff still won); being helped off pitch with concussion against Scotland (1994); missing out on World Cup 1995 selection
Most respected opponent: Ieuan Evans (Llanelli & Wales)
Serious injuries: Torn ankle ligaments, sprained wrist, concussion (1994)
Other sporting achievements: 110m hurdles semi-finalist in 1984 Los Angeles

Wales (1993)

Last Season	2 caps	0 pts
Career	10 caps	40 pts

Caps (10): **1993** I, F, J **1994** S, F, E wc(q)-P, Sp **1995** F, E
Points (40 – 8t): **1993** F(1t) **1994** F(1t), E(1t). wc(q)-P(4t), Sp(1t)

Olympics having clocked 14.07sec in heat

Notable landmarks in rugby career: Unhappy 1994/95 season for former Olympic hurdler Nigel who had equalled Welsh try-scoring record when bagging four in 102–11 World Cup qualifying defeat of Portugal in Lisbon (17.5.94). The shoulder injury, which had forced him out of the summer tour to Canada and the South Seas, kept him out of the pre-Christmas internationals and, after returning for the Tests against France and England, he again went missing from the national team. However, it was his failure to make the World Cup squad that caused most upset, not least (one suspects) as his club coach, Alex Evans, had a hand in selecting the 26. Reached the top in a second sport when capped against Ireland (6.3.93) at Cardiff. The following Test, against France, he became the first Welshman to cross the try-line at Parc des Princes since Jeff Squire ten years earlier. Returned to rugby at the age of 29, following conversation with Mark Ring, having gained a Welsh Schools trial in 1981. Made an immediate impression in 1993/94, getting among the try leaders in the Heineken Championship, appearing in the East-West match at Cardiff in December and scoring a try hat-trick in Den Bosch as Wales A walloped Holland 57–12 (6.2.94). Initial ambition was 'to maximise my potential and to become an automatic choice in the Wales side.' And he went some way to achieving goal in 1994 when marking his recall to Test arena with tries in last two games against France and England. The first, a match-sealing effort against France, all but lifted roof off the Arms Park, while the second, at Twickenham (19.3.94) ensured that Wales clinched the 1994 Five Nations title. Nigel, who had been unable to tour with Wales to Zimbabwe and Namibia in the summer of '93, also turned out against Japan and Scotland, but was injured in the latter. Ended 1993/94 on a high when helping Cardiff lift Swalec Cup, after beating holders Llanelli in final.

Touchlines: No time.

Scrum-half Robert Jones contemplates the future during Wales' ill-fated World Cup campaign.

Wallace, R. M.   Ireland

Full Name: Richard Michael
Wallace
Club: Garryowen
Position: Wing
Height: 5ft 11in (1.80m)
Weight: 13st 7lb (86kg)
Occupation: Financial consultant
partner, K Walshe & Associates
Born: Cork, 16.1.68
Family: Single
Former club: Cork Constitution
International debut: Namibia 15,
Ireland 6, 1991
Five Nations' debut: Ireland 15,
Wales 16, 1992
Best moment in rugby: 1993 Lions
call-up and defeat of England
Most respected opponent: Philippe
Saint-Andre (Montferrand &
France)
Serious injuries: Broken right leg
(1994)
Other sporting achievements: Sailed
(Laser class) for Ireland at 1990
European Championships (France)
Notable landmarks in rugby career:
Disappointing 1994/95 campaign
for Richard, precipitated by leg-

Ireland (1991)

Last Season	5 caps	0 pts
Career	20 caps	13 pts

Lions 1993

Caps (20): **1991** Na(1R) **1992** W, E, S,
F, A **1993** S, F, W, E, R **1994** F, W,
E, S **1995** W(a), It wc-NZ, J, W(b)
Points (13 – 3t): **1991** W(1t), S(1t) **1992**
A(1t)

break, suffered playing for Garryowen vs Shannon at end of previous season,
which forced him to miss '94 summer tour of Australia. Finally returned to
national side for Wooden Spoon decider against Wales (Cardiff, 18.3.95) but
Ireland's 16–12 victory was about as good as it got. Followed up by playing in
Irish side beaten in Italy (Treviso, 8.5.95) and although he played in all three
World Cup pool matches, Richard was clearly out of form. Dropped for
quarter-final against France, with uncapped Darragh O'Mahony getting the
nod. Spent 1992 and 1993 'off' seasons in New Zealand, each trip providing a
tale of the unexpected. In 1992 he had only just overcome the jet-lag following
the trip out with Ireland when he was punched, playing against Canterbury,
sustained a hair-line fracture of the jaw, and was flown home. In 1993 he was
minding his own business in Moscow when Ian Hunter was injured in the
British Lions' first engagement against North Auckland and he was summoned
post haste as a replacement. Once in place he turned out against Canterbury,
Taranaki, Southland, Hawke's Bay and Waikato. Richard had taken his first

step up the representative ladder when appearing for Munster Under-18s and Under-21s (1988). A member of the 1987/88 Irish Colleges XV, he scored a try in the 24–10 defeat of England B at Old Belvedere on only his second outing for Ireland B (1.3.91). Broke into Ireland senior XV on 1991 tour of Namibia, when replacing Simon Geoghegan in 74th minute of first Test (Windhoek, 20.7.91). Scored tour-high five tries in Namibia. Marked Five Nations' debut with try in Dublin loss to Wales (18.1.92), and retained place throughout Championship (also crossing against Scotland) before ill-fated trip to the land of the All Black. Third and most recent Test try came in 17–42 loss to Australia (Dublin, 31.10.92) prior to him helping Ireland reach semi-finals of inaugural World Cup Sevens (Murrayfield, April 1993)

Touchlines: Flying (hold private licence), sailing, reading, music.

Walton, P.   Scotland

Full Name: Peter Walton
Club: Newcastle
Position: Flanker, No 8
Height: 6ft 3in (1.90m)
Weight: 18st (110kg)
Occupation: Livestock fieldsman
Born: Alnwick, 3.6.69
Family: Diana (wife)
Family links with rugby: Brother (Michael) played for Scottish Schools
Former clubs: Alnwick, Gosforth
International debut: Scotland 14, England 15, 1994
Five Nations debut: As above
Worst moment in rugby: Losing to England on debut to last kick of game
Most embarrassing moment: Passing to Leicester's Rory Underwood in Cup quarter-final. I thought he was a team mate; you know, similar hooped shirt, that sort of thing. Cost us scoring position
Most respected opponent: Dean

Scotland (1994)

Last Season	1 cap	10 pts
Career	6 caps	10 pts

Caps (6): 1994 E, I, F, Arg(1,2) 1995 wc-IC

Points (10 – 2t): 1995 wc-IC(2t)

Richards (Leicester)/Tim Rodber (Northampton)
Biggest influence on career: Brother Michael, who had to give up rugby aged 22 through injury after playing for Scotland Schools and England Colts
Serious injuries: Shoulder operation, five years ago, after which told I couldn't

play rugby again. Returned to the game three months later

Notable landmarks in rugby career: Lost out in Scotland blindside stakes to fit-again Rob Wainwright in 1995, having taken his tally to five caps when appearing in both Tests on largely unsuccessful tour of Argentina in 1994. Included in World Cup squad but made just the one appearance. However, he marked the occasion, against Cote d'Ivoire (Rustenburg, 26.5.95), with two tries in a national record 89–0 victory. Previously played for and captained Scotland Schools six times (1986–87) in sides which also included Tony Stanger, Craig Chalmers, Andy Nicol and Carl Hogg. But then played at prop for England Colts in 1988, as no Scottish alternative, playing alongside Neil Back and fellow Scot Andy Reed. First represented Northumberland in 1989 but it was in colours of 1993/94 Scottish Exiles (against Leinster, Munster and Auckland) that he earned his Test call-up. Bench replacement for Scotland A against touring All Blacks (Glasgow, 13.11.93), a fine display three days later in Edinburgh for Scottish Development XV against same opposition (lost 12–31) won him starts in A-team against Italy (lost 15–18, Rovigo 18.12.93) and Ireland A (won 24–9, Ayr 28.12.293). After Scotland's dismal showing against Wales in 1994 Five Nations opener, Peter was among newcomers drafted in for Calcutta Cup clash. England were given shock of their lives and Peter retained blindside berth throughout remainder of campaign.

Touchlines: Horse racing (Newcastle & Kelso).

Waugh, W. W. Australia

Full Name: Warwick William Waugh
State: New South Wales
Club: Randwick
Position: Lock
Height: 6ft 7in (2.01m)
Weight: 18st 8lb (118kg)
Occupation: Accounts executive
Born: 17.9.68
Family: Single
International debut: Australia 12, South Africa 19, 1993
Best moment in rugby: Scoring in my first Wallaby game with my first touch of the ball, Western Transvaal versus Australia '92.
Worst moment in rugby: Breaking my leg (New South Wales v Wales '91)
Most respected opponent: Ian Jones

Suggestions to improve rugby:
Actively encourage more ex-players to become referees

Notable landmarks in rugby career:
Failed to break up the John Eales-Rod McCall second row combination, after Garrick Morgan had turned

Australia (1993)
Last Season	1 cap	0 pts
Career	2 caps	0 pts

Caps (2): 1993 SA(1) 1995 wc-C
Points Nil

professional in 1994. And had to wait until the 1995 World Cup to win his second cap, fully two years after his first against South Africa. His second outing came in the 27–11 defeat of the Canucks (Port Elizabeth, 31.5.95). Warwick's debut had actually come two years later than had been widely anticipated after breaking his leg playing for New South Wales against touring Wales in 1991. He had formed a highly successful partnership with Steve Cutler, soon after making his debut for the state in Argentina, and was seen as a genuine international contender. However, the leg break put such thoughts on hold. A powerful scrummager and noted line-out jumper, he was selected to tour South Africa in the summer of 1992 and marked his debut with a try against Western Transvaal (won 46–13, Potchefstroom, 11 August). He also turned out in the 34–8 victory over Eastern Province in Port Elizabeth seven days later. On to Wales and Ireland where he gained further experience with starts against Munster, Connacht, Swansea, Monmouthshire and Welsh Students. His apprenticeship complete, Wallaby coach Bob Dwyer finally gave him his first cap on 31 July 1993 in the first Test against South Africa in Sydney. Unhappily for Warwick, the Springboks won 19–12 and it was back to bench duties for the remainder of the series.

Touchlines: Cars, music, skiing, running, golf.

All Blacks at play. New Zealand eye up their next victims at the World Cup.

Weir, G. W.   Scotland

Full Name: George Wilson (Doddie) Weir
Club: Melrose
Position: No 8, lock
Height: 6ft 6in (1.98m)
Weight: 16st 2lb (98kg)
Occupation: Sales executive, Carlsberg/Tetley, Alloa
Born: Edinburgh, 4.7.70
Family: Single
Family links with rugby: Father (John) played for Gala. Brother (Tom) plays for Gala. Brother (Christopher) plays for Melrose
International debut: Scotland 49, Argentina 3, 1990
Five Nations' debut: Scotland 7, England 25, 1992
Best moment in rugby: Scoring two tries against 1995 All Blacks
Most embarrassing moment: Trying to kick clear and then dive on a loose ball, and missing it both times, in 1991 Melrose Sevens first round loss to Hawick
Most respected opponents: John Eales (Queensland & Australia) and Ian Jones (North Auckland & New Zealand)

Scotland (1990)

Last Season	9 caps	10 pts
Career	32 caps	14 pts

Caps (32): **1990** Arg **1991** Ro wc-J, Z, I, WS, E, NZ **1992** E, I, F, W, A(1,2) **1993** I, F, W, E, NZ **1994** W(R), E, I, F, SA **1995** F(a:R), W, E, R wc-IC, T, F(b), NZ
Points (14 – 3t): **1991** wc-Z(1t) **1995** wc-NZ(2t)

Biggest influence on career: Jim Telfer (Melrose coach) – told me what to do, when and how
Other sporting achievements: Stow sprint champion. Completing Thirlestone cross-country (horses); 1991 Scottish Horse Trials (intermediate class)
Suggestions to improve rugby: Sort out lineout. There is supposed to be a one-metre gap but no-one bothers with it. Better education of referees to allow game to flow better. Abolish conversions and instead increase worth of tries
Notable landmarks in rugby career: Would have assumed national hero status when scoring two tries against New Zealand in 1995 World Cup quarter-final (Pretoria, 11.6.95), had not the All Blacks won 48–30. Nonetheless it was a marvellous effort and confirmed how far Doddie has come as an international force. Moved from No 8 to engine room following home whipping by South Africa (Murrayfield, 19.11.94), but had to wait for Damian Cronin to get injured midway through away win in France to return to favour. Thereafter, he

was everpresent, a seven Test run which culminated in his heroics against the Kiwis. Had not been selected for '94 Five Nations opener either, but came on against Wales as 18th minute replacement after Iain Morrison had broken his left leg in two places and was unmoved thereafter. Toured New Zealand with Scottish Schools (1988) and Scotland (1990). Represented South of Scotland in Inter-District Championship, Scotland U-19, Scotland U-21s (v Wales, 1990 and 1991) and Scotland B, becoming youngest forward to represent them (at 19) in 22–22 draw with Ireland B (Murrayfield, 9.12.89). Also played in annual Scotland A game against Spain for three years (1990-93) and for full Scotland side masquerading as A-team against Italy (19.12.92). Made full debut against touring Pumas (10.11.90). Toured North America with Scotland (1991), playing in all six matches (including two non-cap Tests against US Eagles and Canada), Australia (1992), appearing at lock in both Tests, South Pacific (1993 – playing in non-cap Tests against Fiji, Tonga and Western Samoa), and Argentina (1994). Helped Melrose win McEwan's Scottish Club Championship for fourth time in five seasons in 1993/94.

Touchlines: Horse riding (one-day eventing), clay pigeon shooting, training six days per week.

Wiese, J. J. South Africa

Full Name: Jakobus (Kobus) Johannes Wiese
Province: Transvaal
Position: Lock
Height: 6ft 6in (1.98m)
Weight: 20st 1lb (125kg)
Occupation: Insurance broker
Born: 16.5.64
International debut: South Africa 20, France 20, 1993
Notable landmarks in rugby career:
Returned to form with a vengeance in 1995, and was a powerful force in South Africa's World Cup-winning side. Yet had begun tournament as second-choice lock as Hannes Strydom and Mark Andrews shored up the duties in the big opener
against defending champions Australia. Toured to both New Zealand and Great Britain and Ireland in 1994, but without appearing in the Test arena. Down Under his one outing came against Southland, while in Britain he at least had six starts. Ironically, had made a big impression on England's tourists in 1994, with his bullish runs and immense strength guiding both Transvaal and

South Africa B to accomplished wins. Indeed, such an impact did he make that he was conspicuous by his absence in the two Tests. Had been one of the victims of the selectors' purge after France had the temerity to draw the first Test of the 1993 series 20–20 in Durban (26.6.93). Along

South Africa (1993)

Last Season	6 caps	0 pts
Career	7 caps	0 pts

Caps (7): 1993 F(1) 1995 WS(a) wc-R, C, WS(b), F, NZ

Points Nil

with engine room partner, Natal's Rudie Visagie, he was given his cards and replaced by Strydom and Nico Wegner for the second Test, which France proceeded to win. A member of the 1993 Transvaal side that won the inaugural Super-10 tournament (beating Auckland 20–7 in the final at Ellis Park, Johannesburg 22.5.93) and the Currie Cup (beating Natal 21–15 in the final at Kings Park, Durban 16.10.93). Between the two he toured Australia with the Springboks, turning out against Western Australia (won 71–8, Perth 14.7.93), Victoria (won 78–3, Melbourne 21.7.93); NSW Country (won 41–7, Orange 27.7.93), ACT (won 57–10, Canberra 4.8.93), Queensland Country (won 65–5, Mackay 11.8.93) and Sydney (won 31–20, Penrith 18.8.93). But he was not required when the selectors took an inexperienced party to Argentina in the Autumn.

Williams, C. M.   South Africa

Full Name: Chester Williams
Province: Western Province
Position: Wing
Height: 5ft 8½in (1.74m)
Weight: 13st 4lb (80kg)
Occupation: Development officer, Western Province RFU
Born: 9.8.70
Family: Single
International debut: Argentina 23, South Africa 52, 1993
Notable landmarks in rugby career:
The darling of South African rugby, Chester (nicknamed the Black Pearl) was the talk of the World Cup when withdrawing injured on the eve of competition, then returning when Pieter Hendriks was banned for foul

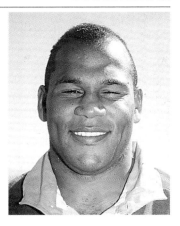

play and marking his comeback with a South African record four tries in the 42–14 quarter-final defeat of Western Samoa (Johannesburg, 10.6.95). Organisers used Chester's face to promote the tournament, with the slogan

'The Waiting's Over', so it was something of a relief for them when his waiting ended. Had impressed greatly on the Boks 1994 tour of Britain, scoring tries in the Test defeats of Scotland and Wales. Not that him scoring was anything out of the ordinary, as he bagged ten in a six-match run between the first Test against Argentina (Port Elizabeth, 8.10.94) and the Samoan rout the following year. Emerged on 1993 tour of Australia, playing in seven of the 13 matches and contributing seven tries, including a hat-trick against Victoria. His services were retained on the Autumn trip to Argentina where the hosts were handed a 2–0 series whitewash in the first ever official Tests between the sides. Chester was deployed in four of the six games and responded with three tries. One of these came on his international debut in the second Test against the Pumas in Buenos Aires (13.11.93), as South Africa ran out convincing 52–23 winners. Collected his second cap (4.6.94) when England won 32–15 in Pretoria but was stretchered off with neck injury 30 minutes into second Test (Cape Town, 11.6.94). However returned in time for the tour to New Zealand and played in all three Tests.

South Africa (1993)

Last Season	12 caps	50 pts
Career	13 caps	55 pts

Caps (13): **1993** Arg(2) **1994** E(1,2), NZ(1,2,3), Arg(1,2), S, W **1995** WS(a) wc-WS(b), F, NZ

Points (55 – 11t): **1993** Arg(2:1t) **1994** Arg(1:1t), Arg(2:1t), S(1t), W(1t) **1995** WS(a:2t) wc-WS(b:4t)

Wilson, D. J.   Australia

Full Name: David John Wilson
State: Queensland
Club: Eastern Districts
Position: Flanker
Height: 6ft 2in (1.88m)
Weight: 14st 11lb (94kg)
Occupation: Area manager, BP Oil
Born: 4.1.67
International debut: Australia 27, Scotland 12, 1992
Best moment in rugby: Second Test win over All Blacks which secured 1992 Bledisloe Cup series
Worst moment in rugby: Missing the 1990 tour to New Zealand due to broken ankle
Most respected opponent: Michael Jones (Auckland & New Zealand)

Serious injuries: Knee reconstruction (1987), broken ankle (1990), broken

collarbone (1992)
Other sporting achievements:
Bettering 105 for a round of golf
Suggestions to improve rugby:
Penalty and dropped goal should be
worth only two points
Notable landmarks in rugby career:
Influential performer in 1994 as
Australia impressively lived up to
their billing as world champions with
six wins out of six. David played in all

Australia (1992)

Last Season	11 caps	15 pts
Career	27 caps	20 pts

Caps (27): **1992** S(1,2), NZ(1,2,3), SA, I,
W **1993** T, NZ, SA(1,2,3), C,
F(1,2) **1994** I(1,2), It(1,2), WS, NZ
1995 Arg(1,2) wc-SA, R, E

Points (20 – 4t): **1992** W(1t) **1994** I(2:1t)
1995 Arg(2:1t) wc-R(1t)

games and retained his place in 1995 in the World Cup warm-up series against
Argentina. Indeed, he scored a try in the 30–13 second Test win (Sydney,
6.5.95). Played in three of the Wallabies' four World Cup ties, which meant he
was on hand when England's Rob Andrew dropped the goal that ended
Australia's tenure as Cup holders (Cape Town, 11.6.95). Had emerged on the
1989 tour to Canada and France, though his ensuing progress was slowed by a
fractured ankle which kept him out of the 1990 tour to New Zealand. However,
he had recovered in time to tour Europe with the Emerging Wallabies later that
year. Everpresent in 25 Tests up until sitting out the Canada Cup-tie (31.5.95),
David was a dual winner in 1989 and 1991 of the Queensland Rothmans
Medal.
Touchlines: Surfing, golf, fishing.

Wilson, J. W.   New Zealand

Full Name: Jeffrey (Jeff) William
Wilson
Province: Otago
Position: Wing, full-back
Height: 5ft 11¼in (1.81m)
Weight: 14st 6lb (91kg)
Occupation: Sales and marketing
rep, Nike
Born: 24.10.73
Family: Single
International debut: Scotland 15,
New Zealand 51, 1993
Best moment in rugby: Scoring hat-
trick of tries on Test debut
Most respected player: Serge Blanco
(ex-Biarritz & France), the greatest
full-back to ever play the game
Notable landmarks in rugby career: It

was always going to be a struggle to live up to the standards he set in 1993 and so it proved as Jeff played just once in 1994. That said it was almost enough to win him the freedom of New Zealand as he came with inches of scoring the Bledisloe Cup-winning try against world champions Australia (Sydney, 17.8.94), only to

New Zealand (1993)

Last Season	7 caps	20 pts
Career	9 caps	46 pts

Caps (9): **1993** S, E **1994** A **1995** C wc-I, J, S, E, SA

Points (46 – 7t,1c,3p): **1993** S(3t,1c), E(3p) **1995** C(1t) wc-J(3t)

be hit by The Tackle from Wallaby wonder George Gregan. Played a fuller part in Test matters in 1995, scoring a try in the 73–7 pre-World Cup romp against Canada (Auckland, 22.4.95) before playing in five of the six ties in South Africa. A heavy knock sustained against Ireland saw him rested against Wales but he returned against Japan and scored three tries, just as he had done on his debut against Scotland in 1993. Moved to his favoured position of fullback for the quarter-final versus Scotland (Pretoria, 11.6.95) but was less than awesome (by his own standards) and so was restored to the right wing thereafter. At the age of 16 Jeff clocked 11sec over 100 metres. While still at High School he played provincial rugby and cricket, and he finished the 1992 season as the star of the New Zealand Secondary Schools rugby side. Let's not forget either that in June '92 he scored 66 points (nine tries and 15 conversions) for Cargill High School, Invercargill – in ONE match. But all that was nothing on 1993. He began the year with a call-up to the New Zealand one-day cricket side against Australia and, after an impressive bowling performance, stroked the winning runs. Swapping flannels for Black, he became an All Black at the age of 19, scoring two tries on his first start against London (won 39–12, Twickenham 23 October). His Test bow against Scotland yielded a try hat-trick and a touchline conversion for good measure. 'My aim was to get through the game without making a mistake,' he said. His bubble deflated a little on his second Test outing when, due to an injury to first-choice goalkicker Matthew Cooper, he was assigned the duties against England at Twickenham. Five penalty misses out of eight effectively cost New Zealand the match. But it was a rare off-day for a young man who moved from Invercargill to Dunedin to attend teachers' college and joined Otago.

Touchlines: Cricket, basketball.

Wood, K. G. M.   Ireland

Full Name: Keith Gerald Mallinson Wood
Club: Garryowen
Position: Hooker
Height: 6ft (1.83m)
Weight: 15st 12lb (101kg)
Occupation: Customer advisor, Irish Permanent PLC
Born: Limerick, 27.1.72
Family links with rugby: Father (Gordon) played for Ireland (29 times: 1954-61) and 1959 British Lions (first and third Tests v New Zealand)
International debut: Australia 33, Ireland 13, 1994
Five Nations debut: Ireland 8, England 20, 1995
Notable landmarks in rugby career: Recurring shoulder problem ruined 1994/95 campaign for Keith, who had been Ireland's most valuable player on '94 tour of Australia. Having played in both Tests Down Under and impressed, despite the

Ireland (1994)

Last Season	4 caps	0 pts
Career	6 caps	0 pts

Caps (6): **1994** A(1,2), US **1995** E, S wc-J
Points Nil

defeats, with his pace and mobility, huge things were expected of the Limerick man last term. But nagging injury hampered his form and he was relegated to bench duties midway through the Five Nations Championship. To make matters worse his replacement, Terry Kingston, was handed the captaincy. Keith returned to the Ireland jersey in South Africa but his World Cup lasted but nine minutes before his shoulder went again against Japan (Bloemfontein, 31.5.95). A bench replacement since 1992, his path to progress blocked at both provincial (Munster) and national level by Dolphin's Kingston, Keith had helped Garryowen win 1991/92 and 1993/94 All-Ireland League titles. As recently as the 1992/93 he was playing for the Ireland Under-21s. A year previous he had been selected for the senior bench against the '92 Wallabies, but an injury frustrated him over the remainder of the season. The next time he encountered Australia, in their own backyard, he opposed them on the field, first at Ballymore, in Brisbane (5.6.94) and then in Sydney (11.6.94) when the Wallabies wrapped up a 2–0 series win with a 32–18 victory. Gerry Murphy, Ireland's coach, said of Keith: 'He has been our outstanding player in both Tests and has the potential to be world class.' His other tour outings came against Western Australia and Queensland, scoring a try in 29–26 loss to the latter.

Wright, P. H. Scotland

Full Name: Peter Hugh Wright
Club: Boroughmuir
Position: Prop
Height: 6ft (1.83m)
Weight: 17st 2lb (109kg)
Occupation: Blacksmith,
MacDonald & Ross
Born: Bonnyrigg, 30.12.67
Family: Audrey (wife)
Family links with rugby: Graham
(brother) and David (brother) play
for Lasswade
Former club: Lasswade
International debut: Australia 27,
Scotland 12, 1992
Five Nations' debut: France 11,
Scotland 3, 1993
Best moment in rugby: Being told I
was in the 1993 British Lions squad
Worst moment in rugby: Tearing
medial and cruciate knee ligaments
Most respected opponent: Tony
Daly (NSW & Australia) and most
French props
Biggest influence on career: Bruce
Hay (Boroughmuir coach)
Serious injuries: Torn medial and
cruciate knee ligaments (October 1989: out for 18 months)

Scotland (1992)

Last Season	10 caps	5 pts
Career	16 caps	5 pts

Lions 1993

Caps (16): **1992** A(1,2) **1993** F, W, E
1994 W **1995** C, I, F(a), W, E, R
wc-IC, T, F(b), NZ
Points (5 – 1t): **1995** wc-IC(1t)

Suggestions to improve rugby: Stop chopping and changing rules. It is difficult to keep adapting. When you've decided on them make sure every nation adheres to them

Notable landmarks in rugby career: Enjoyed a notable return to form in 1994/95, following the disappointment of a largely unhappy Lions experience in 1993 and equally unimpressive 1994. But just as his critics were writing him out of Scotland's script, Peter returned a revitalised player. Autumn defeat by South Africa prompted the selectors to change the props and Peter and David Hilton were the beneficiaries. The Boroughmuir blacksmith, switched to the tighthead side, was ever-present in 1995, helping Scotland to second place in the Five Nations series before claiming his maiden Test try in the 89–0 World Cup rout of Cote d'Ivoire (Rustenburg, 26.5.95). The seventh player to be capped from the Boroughmuir club, Peter appeared on both sides of the Scottish front row in 1992/93 – making his debut on the tour to Australia in the first Test defeat in Sydney (13.6.92). Retained place the following week at Ballymore

when the world champion Wallabies ran out 37–13 winners, but was deposed by Paul Burnell for the 1993 Five Nations' Championship. That would have been that but for the fact that the Scots were having something of a crisis at loosehead in the wake of David Sole's retirement. Bristol's Alan Sharp was picked but withdrew injured and after one cap his replacement, GHK's Alan Watt, also pulled out of contention. Peter was offered the job and did so well against France, Wales and England that he was picked to tour New Zealand with the Lions, playing against North Auckland, NZ Maoris, Southland, Taranaki, Hawke's Bay and Waikato. During previous Lions tour in 1989 he was to be found in Japan with Scotland, where he made appearances against Kanto and Japan Under-23. Indeed, Peter is no stranger to representative rugby, having played for Scotland at Under-15, Under-18, Under-19 and Under-21 levels. He also skippered Edinburgh Under-21s. He played his first senior game for Boroughmuir at the age of 18 and his Scotland B bow in the 14–12 win over France B at Melrose in 1989.
Touchlines: Golf, all sports.

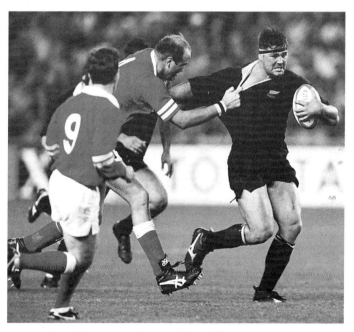

All Black Craig Dowd is tagged by Welshman Derwyn Jones, watched by Robert Jones.

APPENDIX

BADENHORST, Chris. **Country:** South Africa. **Position:** Wing. **Province:** Orange Free State. **Debut:** South Africa 46, Argentina 26, 1994. **Caps:** 2. **Points:** 10 (2t). 1994/95: 2. **Notes:** Played 7 games in NZ (1994), top-scoring with seven tries, versus Southland (3), Hanan Shield (2) and Manawatu (2). Two tries on debut against Pumas at Ellis Park (15.10.94). **Record** (2–10:2t): 1994 Arg(2:2t) 1995 WS(a:R)

BENNETT, Mark. **Country:** Wales. **Position:** Flanker. **Club:** Cardiff. **Debut:** Wales 9, New Zealand 34, 1995. **Caps:** 1. **Points:** 0. 1994/95: 1. **Born:** 26.1.68. **Height:** 6ft 1in. **Weight:** 15st 3lb. **Occupation:** Technical representative. **Notes:** Helped Cardiff win 1994/95 Heineken league title; Wales debut at openside against All Blacks (Johannesburg, 31.5.95). **Record** (1): 1995 wc-NZ

BLOND, Xavier. **Country:** France. **Position:** Flanker. **Club:** Racing Club de France. **Debut:** Australia 19, France 28, 1990. **Caps:** 6. **Points:** 0. 1994/95: 1. **Born:** 28.8.67. **Height:** 6ft 3in. **Weight:** 15st 3lb. **Occupation:** Sales rep. **Notes:** Collected sixth cap as a 73rd minute replacement for Philippe Benetton in series-clinching 23–20 win over New Zealand (3.7.94). **Record** (6): 1990 A(3) 1991 S, I, W(a), E 1994 NZ(2R)

BRINK, Robbie. **Country:** South Africa. **Position:** Flanker. **Province:** Western Province. **Debut:** South Africa 21, Romania 8, 1995. **Caps:** 2. **Points:** 0. 1994/95: 2. **Born:** 21.7.71. **Height:** 6ft 5in. **Weight:** 17st 10lb. **Occupation:** Student. **Notes:** One of three uncapped Boks in World Cup-winning squad, he played in the wins over Romania and Canada. **Record** (2): 1995 wc-R,C

CIGAGNA, Albert. **Country:** France. **Position:** No 8. **Club:** Toulouse. **Debut:** France 19, England 9, 1995. **Caps:** 1. **Points:** 0. 1994/95: 1. **Born:** 25.9.60. **Height:** 6ft 1 1/2in. **Weight:** 16st 6lb. **Notes:** Called up as emergency replacement after Philippe Benetton broke arm in last summer's World Cup. Made debut in third place play-off defeat of England (22.6.95). **Record** (1): 1995 wc-E(b)

FOLEY, Michael. **Country:** Australia. **Position:** Hooker. **State:** Queensland. **Debut:** Australia 27, Canada 11, 1995. **Caps:** 2. **Points:** 5 (1t). 1994/95: 2. **Born:** 7.6.67. **Height:** 6ft. **Weight:** 17st 2lb. **Occupation:** Student. **Notes:** Made debut at World Cup, as 70th minute replacement for Phil Kearns (Port Elizabeth, 31.5.95). Then try versus Romania on first start. **Record** (2 – 5:1t): 1995 wc-C(R), R(1t)

HEWITT, Norm. **Country:** New Zealand. **Position:** Hooker. **Province:** Southland. **Caps:** 2. **Points:** 0. 1994/95: 2. **Born:** 11.11.68. **Height:** 5ft 10in. **Weight:** 17st 10lb. **Occupation:** Marketing director. **Notes:** Outstanding for NZ Maoris and Hawke's Bay v '93 Lions, but had to wait for Test debut until last summer's World Cup, against Ireland and Japan. **Record** (2): 1995 wc-I(TR), J

HOPLEY, Damian Paul. **Country:** England. **Position:** Centre. **Debut:** England 44, Western Samoa 22, 1995. **Caps:** 1. **Points:** 0. 1994/95: 1. **Club:** Wasps. **Born:** 12.4.70. **Height:** 6ft 3in. **Weight:** 15st 7lb. **Occupation:** Repro broker. **Notes:** Long-awaited debut came as 70th minute repl for Will Carling (Durban, 4.6.95). Helped England win 1993 World Cup Sevens. **Record** (1): 1995 wc-WS(R)

HOWARTH, Shane Paul. **Country:** New Zealand. **Position:** Full-back. **Province:** Auckland. **Debut:** New Zealand 22, South Africa 14, 1994. **Caps:** 4. **Points:** 54 (1t,2c,15p). 1994/95: 4. **Born:** 8.7.68. **Height:** 5ft 10in. **Weight:** 14st 1lb. **Notes:** Lost out to Glen Osborne in World Cup selection after being first-choice in '94. Top scorer on NZ's '93 tour of Eng/Scot (81 pts). **Record** (4 – 54: 1t,2c,15p): 1994 SA(1:1c,5p), SA(2:1p), SA(3:6p), A(1t,1c,3p).

HUMPHREYS, Jonathan. **Country:** Wales. **Position:** Hooker. **Club:** Cardiff. **Debut:** Wales 9, New Zealand 34, 1995. **Caps:** 2. **Points** 5 (1t). 1994/95: 2. **Born:** 27.2.69. **Height:** 6ft. **Weight:** 15st 10lb. **Occupation:** Rugby Development officer. **Notes:** Ended World Cup as Wales' first-choice hooker, scoring try on second outing in 23–24 loss to Ireland (Johannesburg, 4.6.95). **Record** (2): 1995 wc-NZ, I(b:1t)

HURTER, Marius. **Country:** South Africa. **Position:** Prop. **Province:** Northern Transvaal. **Debut:** South Africa 21, Romania 8, 1995. **Caps:** 2. **Points:** 0. 1994/95: 2. **Born:** 8.10.70. **Height:** 6ft 2in. **Weight:** 18st 1lb. **Occupation:** Student. **Notes:** One of three uncapped Boks in World Cup-winning squad, making appearances versus Romania and Canada. **Record** (2): 1995 wc-R, C

JUNEE, Darren. **Country:** Australia. **Position:** Wing, centre. **State:** New South Wales. **Debut:** France 15, Australia 32, 1989. **Caps:** 4. **Points:** 5 (1t). 1994/95: 2. **Born:** 2.7.69. **Height:** 5ft 10in. **Weight:** 12st 4lb. **Notes:** All four caps as replacements. Opened Test scoring account in 73–3 rout of Western Samoa (Sydney, 6.8.94). Son of Kangaroo RL legend Kevin Junee. **Record** (4 – 5:1t): 1989 F(1R), F(2R) 1994 WS(R:1t), NZ(R)

KEBBLE, Guy. **Country:** South Africa. **Position:** Prop. **Province:** Natal. **Debut:** Argentina 26, South Africa 29, 1993. **Caps:** 4. **Points:** 0. 1994/95: 2. **Age:** 28. **Height:** 6ft 1in. **Weight:** 20st. **Notes:** Doubled cap tally in first two Tests versus New Zealand (1994) having represented Springboks twice against Pumas in Argentina (1993). **Record** (4): 1993 Arg(1,2) 1994 NZ(1R,2)

KIRWAN, John Joseph MBE. **Country:** New Zealand. **Position:** Wing. **Debut:** New Zealand 10, France 9, 1984. **Caps:** 63. **Points:** 143 (35t). 1994/95: 5 (1t). **Born:** 16.12.64. **Height:** 6ft 3in. **Weight:** 14st 7lb. **Occupation:** Professiona Rugby League player. **Notes:** All Black record try-scorer before switching codes to see out his career with Auckland Warriors. **Record** (63 – 143:35t): 1984 F(1,2) 1985 E(1), E(2:1t), A, Arg(1:2t), Arg(2:2t) 1986 F(a),A(1,2,3), F(b1,b2) 1987 wc-It(2t), Fj(1t), Arg, S, W(2t), F(1t). A(1t) 1988 W(1:4t), W(2:2t), A(1:2t), A(2:1t), A(3:1t) 1989 F(1,2), Arg(1:2t), Arg(2:1t)A 1990 S(1:2t), S(2), Arg(1:1t), Arg(2,3), F(1,2) 1991 Arg(2:1t), A(a1,a2). wc-E, It, C(1t), A(b), S 1992 Wd(1,2), Wd(3:1t), I(1), I(2:1t), A(1), A(2:1t), A(3), SA(1t) 1993 BL(2,3), A, WS 1994 F(1,2), SA(1:1t), SA(2,3)

KNOX, David. **Country:** Australia. **Position:** Fly-half. **Debut:** Australia 73, Western Samoa 3, 1994. **Caps:** 2. **Points:** 28 (8c,4p). 1994/95: 2. **Notes:** Marked debut with 18 points (Sydney, 6.8.94) but his scoring of 10 points in the 20–16 Bledisloe Cup defeat of All Blacks (Sydney, 17.8.94) were the more precious. **Record** (2 – 28:8c,4p): 1994 WS(6c,2p), NZ(2c,2p)

LE ROUX, Johan. **Country:** South Africa. **Position:** Prop. **Debut:** South Africa 27, England 9, 1994. **Caps:** 3. **Points:** 0. 1994/95: 3. **Notes:** Gained notoriety when chomping on ear of All Black skipper Sean Fitzpatrick during second Test (Wellington, 23.7.94) and getting 19-month ban. Took appeal to High Court in Wellington in March 1995, but lost. **Record** (3): 1994 E(2), NZ(1,2)

McBRYDE, Robin Currie. **Country:** Wales. **Position:** Hooker. **Club:** Swansea. **Debut:** Fiji 8, Wales 23, 1994. **Caps:** 2. **Points:** 0. 1994/95: 2. **Born:** 3.7.70. **Height:** 6ft. **Weight:** 14st 7lb. **Occupation:** Overhead linesman. **Notes:** TV's 1992 'Strongest Man in Wales' who made Test debut in Suva (18.6.94) before coming on as a temporary rep versus Springboks (26.11.94). **Record** (2): 1994 Fj, SA(TR)

MacDONALD, Ian. **Country:** South Africa. **Position:** Flanker. **Province:** Transvaal. **Debut:** South Africa 24, New Zealand 27, 1992. **Caps:** 6. **Points:** 0. 1994/95: 1. **Born:** 22.2.68. **Height:** 6ft 5in. **Weight:** 17st 5lb. **Occupation:** Teacher. **Notes:** Solitary Test appearance last season came as replacement for Kobus Wiese in 60–8 defeat of Western Samoa (JoBurg, April '95). **Record** (6): 1992 NZ, A 1993 F(1), A(3) 1994 E(2) 1995 WS(a:R)

McIVOR, David John. **Country:** Scotland. **Position:** Flanker. **Club:** Edinburgh Academicals. **Debut:** Scotland 7, England 25, 1992. **Caps:** 6. **Points:** 0. 1994/95: 1. **Born:** 29.6.64. **Height:** 6ft 1in. **Weight:** 16st 9lb. **Occupation:** Computer technician. **Notes:** Picked up sixth cap in 10-34 loss to South Africa (Edinburgh, 19.11.94) after which he was not required. **Record** (6): 1992 E, I, F, W 1993 NZ 1994 SA

MALONE, Niall Gareth. **Country:** Ireland. **Position:** Fly-half. **Club:** Leicester. **Debut:** Scotland 15, Ireland 3, 1993. **Caps:** 3. **Points:** 9 (3p). 1994/95: 1. **Born:** 30.4.71. **Height:** 5ft 11in. **Weight:** 13st. **Occupation:** Student. **Notes:** Added third cap as half-time replacement for Brendan Mullin versus USA (Dublin, 5.11.94), almost two years after winning first two caps. **Record** (3 – 9:3p): 1993 S(1p), F(2p) 1994 US(R)

MALLETT, John. **Country:** England. **Position:** Prop. **Club:** Bath. **Debut:** England 44, Western Samoa 22, 1995. **Caps:** 1. **Points:** 0. 1994/95: 1. **Born:** 28.5.70. **Height:** 6ft 2in. **Weight:** 17st 6lb. **Occupation:** Student teacher. **Notes:** Ex-England Colts captain (1989), who made senior debut at '95 World Cup as 24th minute replacement for Graham Rowntree (Durban, 4.6.95). **Record** (1): 1995 wc-WS(R)

MANSON, John. **Country:** Scotland. **Position:** Prop. **Club:** Dundee HSFP. **Debut:** England 24, Scotland 12, 1995. **Caps:** 1. **Points:** 0. 1994/95: 1. **Born:** 22.6.68. **Height:** 6ft. **Weight:** 17st 11lb. **Occupation:** Electrician. **Notes:** Unused in last summer's World Cup having made Test debut as 45th minute replacement for Dave Hilton in Grand Slam decider at Twickers. **Record** (1): 1995 E(R)

MANU, Daniel. Country: Australia. **Position:** Flanker. **State:** New South Wales. **Debut:** Australia 42, Romania 3, 1995. **Caps:** 1. **Points:** 0. 1994/95: 1. **Born:** 4.6.70. **Height:** 6ft 5in. **Weight:** 18st 11lb. **Notes:** Emergency call-up to replace Troy Coker at World Cup, where he earned his first cap as a temporary replacement for David Wilson (Stellenbosch, 3.6.95). **Record** (1): 1995 wc-R(TR)

MOORE, Andrew. Country: Wales. **Position:** Scrum-half. **Club:** Cardiff. **Debut:** Wales 57, Japan 10, 1995. **Caps:** 1. **Points** 5 (1t). 1994/95: 1. **Born:** 6.9.68. **Height:** 5ft 9in. **Weight:** 13st 11lb. **Occupation:** Surveyor. **Notes:** Welsh league title winner with Cardiff who marked full Wales debut with try versus Japs at World Cup (Bloemfontein, 27.5.95). Benched thereafter. **Record** (1 – 5:1t): 1995 wc-J(1t)

O'CONNOR, Michael. Country: Australia. **Position:** Centre. **State:** Australian Capital Territory. **Club:** Royals. **Debut:** Australia 33, Ireland 13, 1994. **Caps:** 1. **Points:** 0. 1994/95: 1. **Age:** 24. **Height:** 5ft 8in. **Weight:** 14st 4lb. **Occupation:** Rugby League. **Notes:** Switched codes after making Wallaby debut in first Test defeat of Ireland (Brisbane, 5.6.94). **Record** (1): 1994 I(1)

O'HARA, Patrick Thomas. Country: Ireland. **Position:** Flanker. **Club:** Cork Constitution. **Debut:** Ireland 49, Western Samoa 22, 1988. **Caps:** 15. **Points:** 4 (1t). 1994/95: 1. **Born:** Essex, 4.8.61. **Height:** 6ft 2in. **Weight:** 15st. **Occupation:** Sales director. **Notes:** Won 15th cap at blindside in 26-15 defeat of USA (Dublin, 5.11.94). **Record** (15 – 4:1t): 1988 WS(R) 1989 F, W, E, NZ 1990 E, S, F, W 1991 Na(1) wc-J 1993 F, W, E 1994 US

O'MAHONY, Darragh. Country: Ireland. **Position:** Wing. **Club:** Blackrock. **Debut:** Ireland 12, France 36, 1995. **Caps:** 1. **Points:** 0. 1994/95: 1. **Born:** 18.8.72. **Height:** 5ft 10in. **Weight:** 13st 11lb. **Occupation:** Student. **Notes:** Handed debut in World Cup quarter-final (Durban, 10.6.95) after selectors dropped off-form Richard Wallace. One of two uncapped in squad. **Record** (1): 1995 F(b)

O'MAHONY, David. Country: Ireland. **Position:** Scrum-half. **Club:** University College Dublin. **Debut:** Italy 22, Ireland 12, 1995. **Caps:** 1. **Points:** 0. 1994/95: 1. **Occupation:** Student. **Notes:** Surprise call-up for Treviso mission (8.5.95), ahead of Michael Bradley and Niall Hogan, in which Ireland became Italy's first major scalp. **Record** (1): 1995 It

PROSSER, Greg. Country: Wales. **Position:** Lock. **Club:** Pontypridd. **Debut:** Wales 9, New Zealand 34, 1995. **Caps:** 1. **Points:** 0. 1994/95: 1. **Born:** 21.5.66. **Height:** 6ft 6in. **Weight:** 17st 4lb. **Occupation:** South Wales Police officer. **Notes:** Made debut in Johannesburg (31.5.95) having risen to prominence with Wales A and in Pontypridd's impressive 1994/95 campaign. **Record** (1): 1995 wc-NZ

RICHARDSON, Jeremy. Country: Scotland. **Position:** Lock. **Club:** Edinburgh Acads. **Debut:** Scotland 10, South Africa 34, 1994. **Caps:** 1. **Points:** 0. 1994/95: 1. **Born:** 7.9.63. **Height:** 6ft 6in. **Weight:** 16st 13lb. **Occupation:** Company director. **Notes:** Capped (19.11.94) eight years after first making Scotland squad, for 1987 World Cup. Unused also at 1995 World Cup. **Record** (1): 1994 SA

ROFF, Joe. **Country:** Australia. **Position:** Wing. **State:** Australian Capital Territory. **Debut:** Australia 27, Canada 11, 1995. **Caps:** 2. **Points:** 15 (3t). 1994/95: 2. **Born:** 20.9.75. **Height:** 6ft 3½in. **Weight:** 16st 2lb. **Occupation:** Student. **Notes:** Big, strong and the target of just about every Rugby League scout after impressive World Cup in which he scored 3 tries. **Record** (2 – 15: 3t): 1995 wc-C(1t), R(2t)

ROLLAND, Alain Colm Pierre. **Country:** Ireland. **Position:** Scrum-half. **Club:** Blackrock. **Debut:** Ireland 20, Argentina 18, 1990. **Caps:** 3. **Points:** 0. 1994/95: 2. **Born:** 22.8.66. **Height:** 5ft 10in. **Weight:** 11st 9lb. **Occupation:** Financial consultant. **Notes:** Replacement caps versus USA (Dublin, 5.11.94) and Italy (Treviso, 8.5.95) either end of last season. **Record** (3): 1990 Arg 1994 US(R) 1995 It(R)

ROSSOUW, Chris. **Country:** South Africa. **Position:** Hooker. **Province:** Transvaal. **Debut:** South Africa 60, Western Samoa 8, 1995. **Caps:** 5. **Points:** 10 (2t). 1994/95: 5. **Born:** 14.9.68. **Height:** 5ft 11 1/2in. **Weight:** 17st 5lb. **Occupation:** Importer/exporter. **Notes:** Came into Bok World Cup team after James Dalton's sending-off. Try on debut (JoBurg, 13.4.95). **Record** (5 – 10: 2t): 1995 WS(a:1t) wc-R, WS(b:1t), F, NZ

ROY, Stuart. **Country:** Wales. **Position:** Lock. **Club:** Cardiff. **Debut:** Wales 57, Japan 10, 1995. **Caps:** 1. **Points:** 0. 1994/95: 1. **Born:** 25.12.68. **Height:** 6ft 6in. **Weight:** 17st 8lb. **Occupation:** Medical practitioner. **Notes:** Given debut as 72nd minute replacement for Derwyn Jones (Bloemfontein, 27.5.95), having helped Cardiff win Heineken League title. **Record** (1): 1995 wc-J(R)

RUSH, Eric James. **Country:** New Zealand. **Position:** Wing. **Province:** North Harbour. **Debut:** New Zealand 43, Ireland 19, 1995. **Caps:** 2. **Points:** 15 (3t). 1994/95: 3. **Born:** 11.2.65. **Height:** 6ft. **Weight:** 13st 5lb. **Family:** Married, 3 children. **Occupation:** Solicitor. **Notes:** Made debut at World Cup (as repl), and scored three tries in 145-17 rout of Japan (4.6.95). **Record** (2): 1995 wc-I(R), J(3t)

SCHMIDT, Uli. **Country:** South Africa. **Position:** Hooker. **Province:** Northern Transvaal. **Debut:** South Africa 21, NZ Cavaliers 15, 1986. **Caps:** 17. **Points:** 9 (2t). 1994/95: 4. **Born:** 10.7.61. **Height:** 5ft 11in. **Weight:** 14st 8lb. **Occupation:** Doctor. **Notes:** One cap shy of becoming most-capped Bok hooker, Uli added four caps to his tally in 1994. **Record** (17 – 9:2t): 1986 Cv(1,2,3:1t,4) 1989 Wd(1,2) 1992 NZ, A 1993 F(1:1t,2), A(1,2,3) 1994 Arg(1,2), S, W

SCHOLTZ, Christiaan. **Country:** South Africa. **Position:** Centre. **Province:** Transvaal. **Debut:** South Africa 42, Argentina 22, 1994. **Caps:** 4. **Points:** 0. 1994/95: 4. **Born:** 22.10.70. **Height:** 6ft 1 1/2in. **Weight:** 15st 5lb. **Occupation:** Antique dealer. **Notes:** Helped Transvaal beat England (28.5.94). Bok debut in Port Elizabeth (8.10.94). Started three games in World Cup. **Record** (4): 1994 Arg(1) 1995 wc-R,C,WS(b)

SCHULER, Kevin. **Country:** New Zealand. **Position:** No8, flanker. **Province:** North Harbour. **Debut:** New Zealand 27, Australia 17, 1990. **Caps:** 4. **Points:** 0. 1994/95: 2. **Born:** 21.3.67. **Height:** 6ft 3in. **Weight:** 16st 6lb. **Occupation:** Japan-based. **Notes:** Made first Test start in 145-17 rout of Japan (Bloemfontein, 4.6.95), almost five years after winning first cap. **Record** (4): 1990 A(2R) 1992 A(R) 1995 wc-I(R),J

SCHUTTE, Philipus Jacobus. **Country:** South Africa. **Position:** Lock. **Province:** Transvaal. **Debut:** Scotland 10, South Africa 34, 1994. **Caps:** 2. **Points:** 0. 1994/95: 2. **Born:** 7.10.69. **Height:** 6ft 7 1/2in. **Weight:** 18st 12lb. **Occupation:** Student. **Notes:** Toured France/England (1992) and Scotland/Wales (1994), scoring two tries vs Combined Irish Provinces (29.11.94). **Record** (2): 1994 S,W

SEIGNE, Laurent. **Country:** France. **Position:** Prop. **Club:** Merignac. **Debut:** France 27, British Lions 29, 1989. **Caps:** 14. **Points:** 0. 1994/95: 2. **Born:** 12.8.60. **Height:** 5ft 10in. **Weight:** 16st 9lb. **Occupation:** Travelling salesman. **Notes:** Lost loosehead berth in France side to Laurent Benezech in 1994/95, starting only the home loss to Scotland (18.2.95). **Record** (14): 1989 BL, A(1) 1990 NZ(1) 1993 E, S, I, W, R(a), A(1,2) 1994 S, C(a) 1995 E(a), S(a)

THOMAS, Gareth. **Country:** Wales. **Position:** Wing, centre. **Club:** Bridgend. **Debut:** Wales 57, Japan 10, 1995. **Caps:** 3. **Points:** 15 (3t). 1994/95: 3. **Born:** 25.7.74. **Height:** 6ft 3in (1.91m). **Weight:** 15st 3lb. **Occupation:** Postal worker. **Notes:** Great potential. Try hat-trick on debut (Bloemfontein, 27.5.95) but failed to spark in other World Cup ties vs NZ and Ireland. **Record** (3): 1995 wc-J(3t), NZ, I(b)

TIMU, John Kahukura Raymond. **Country:** New Zealand. **Position:** Fullback. **Province:** Otago. **Debut:** Argentina 14, New Zealand 28, 1991. **Caps:** 27. **Points:** 26 (6t). **Born:** 8.5.69. **Height:** 5ft 11in. **Weight:** 13st 10lb. **Occupation:** Rugby League professional. **Notes:** Everpresent All Black fullback in 1994 before switching codes at end of year. **Record** (27 – 26:6t): 1991 Arg(1), A(a1,a2) wc-E, US(1t), C(2t), A(b) 1992 Wd(2), I(1), I(2:1t), A(1), A(2:1t), A(3), SA 1993 BL(1,2,3), A, WS, S, E 1994 F(1,2), SA(1), SA(2:1t), SA(3), A

TOMBS, Richard Craig. **Country:** Australia. **Position:** Centre. **State:** New South Wales. **Debut:** Australia 27, Scotland 12, 1992. **Caps:** 4. **Points:** 0. 1994/95: 2. **Born:** NZ, 4.1.68. **Height:** 5ft 10in. **Weight:** 13st 1lb. **Notes:** One of Tim Horan's deputies in 1994, playing in 32–18 win over Ireland (Sydney, 11.6.94) and 23-20 defeat of Italy (Brisbane, 18.6.94). **Record** (4): 1992 S(1,2) 1994 I(2), It(1)

VAN DER BERGH, Elandre. **Country:** South Africa. **Position:** Flanker. **Province:** Eastern Province. **Debut:** South Africa 46, Argentina 26, 1994. **Caps:** 1. **Points:** 0. 1994/95: 1. **Born:** 9.12.66. **Height:** 6ft 5 1/2in. **Weight:** 16st 7lb. **Occupation:** Company director. **Notes:** Debut at Ellis Park as 42nd minute replacement for Tiaan Strauss. Toured Wales/Scotland (1994). **Record** (1): 1994 Arg(2R)

VAN HEERDEN, Fritz. **Country:** South Africa. **Position:** Flanker. **Province:** Western Province. **Debut:** South Africa 32, England 15, 1994. **Caps:** 2. **Points:** 0. 1994/95: 2. **Notes:** From the same province as national hero Chester Williams, he made his debut in defeat by England at Loftus Versfeld (4.6.94) and lost his starting place to Adriaan Richter for return match. **Record** (2): 1994 E(1,2R)

VAN RENSBURG, Jan Theo Jansen. **Country:** South Africa. **Position:** Fullback. **Province:** Transvaal. **Debut:** South Africa 24, New Zealand 27, 1992. **Caps:** 7. **Points:** 40. 1994/95: 1 (9pts). **Born:** 26.8.67. **Height:** 5ft 10in. **Weight:** 12st 4lb. **Notes:** Kicked Transvaal to 24–21 win over England (28.5.94) and claimed all nine points in 9–13 2nd Test loss to NZ (23.7.94). **Record** (7 – 40: 2c,12p): 1992 NZ,A,E 1993 F(1:5p), F(2:4p), A(1:2c) 1994 NZ(2:3p)

VENTER, Brendan. **Country:** South Africa. **Position:** Centre. **Province:** Orange Free State. **Debut:** South Africa 15, England 32, 1994. **Caps:** 11. **Points:** 5 (1t). 1994/95: 11. **Born:** 29.12.69. **Height:** 6ft 1/2in. **Weight:** 14st 4lb. **Occupation:** Doctor. **Notes:** Emerged on back of Free State's run to 1994 Currie Cup final. Replaced James Small in World Cup final. **Record** (11 – 5: 1t): 1994 E(1,2), NZ(1,2,3:1t), Arg(1,2) 1995 wc-R, C, WS(b:R), NZ(R)

WALLACE, Paul. **Country:** Ireland. **Position:** Prop. **Club:** Blackrock. **Debut:** Ireland 50, Japan 28, 1995. **Caps:** 1. **Points:** 0. 1994/95: 1. **Born:** 30.12.71. **Height:** 6ft. **Weight:** 16st 11lb. **Occupation:** Building society marketing employee. **Notes:** One of only two uncapped Irishman in last summer's World Cup squad prior to Bloemfontein debut (31.5.95). **Record** (1): 1995 wc-J

WALLACE, Timothy Mark. **Country:** Australia. **Position:** Fly-half, centre. **State:** New South Wales. **Debut:** Australia 23, Italy 20, 1994. **Caps:** 2. **Points:** 20 (1c,6p). 1994/95: 2. **Born:** 29.3.69. **Height:** 5ft 9in. **Weight:** 13st 1lb. **Occupation:** Student. **Notes:** Kicked five points on debut after coming on as 60th minute replacement for Michael Lynagh (Brisbane, 18.6.94). **Record** (2 – 20:1c,6p): 1994 It(1R:1c,1p), It(2:5p)

WEST, Richard. **Country:** England. **Position:** Lock. **Club:** Gloucester. **Debut:** England 44, Western Samoa 22, 1995. **Caps:** 1. **Points:** 0. 1994/95: 1. **Born:** 28.3.71. **Height:** 6ft 11in. **Weight:** 20st. **Occupation:** Business/property manager, Hartpury Agricultural College. **Notes:** Surprise World Cup pick ahead of Nigel Redman, but impressed on debut (Durban, 4.6.95). **Record** (1): 1995 wc-WS

WILLIAMS-JONES, Hugh. **Country:** Wales. **Position:** Prop. **Club:** Llanelli. **Debut:** Scotland 23, Wales 7, 1990. **Caps:** 16. **Points:** 0. 1994/95: 1. **Born:** 10.1.63. **Height:** 5ft 11in. **Weight:** 16st 6lb. **Occupation:** Police sergeant. **Notes:** Controversial tactical front row replacement for flanker Hemi Taylor vs England (Cardiff, 18.2.95) after prop John Davies was sent-off. **Record** (16): 1989 S(R) 1990 F(R), I 1991 A(a) 1992 S, A 1993 E, S, I, F, Z(1), Na 1994 Fj, T, WS(R) 1995 E(R)

WOODS, Niall. **Country:** Ireland. **Position:** Left wing. **Club:** Blackrock. **Debut:** Australia 33, Ireland 13, 1994. **Caps:** 4. **Points:** 0. 1994/95: 2. **Born:** 21.6.71. **Height:** 5ft 11in. **Weight:** 11st 8lb. **Notes:** Made debut at Ballymore (5.6.94) and added caps last season versus England and France. Toured Zimbabwe/Namibia/SA (1993) and Australia (1994) with Ireland. **Record** (4): 1994 A(1,2) 1995 E, F

WORLD CUP FINALS 1995

ONE Nation, One Team, One World Cup: three things South Africa did not have going for it when the rugby people of the world gathered four years earlier, that it can proudly boast today.

When the Five Nations hosted the 1991 World Cup, the Boks were an irrelevance. One nation? No, apartheid was still a way of life. One team? No, a collection of inter-provincial rivalries with no common cause to fight thanks to civilisation's repulsion of the Old Republic's racist values. One World Cup? Forget it. The Boks were not permitted to participate in the 1991 tournament, hosted by the Five Nations, let alone get their mitts on the William Webb Ellis Trophy.

Try to imagine then the feeling, a heady cocktail of elation and disbelief, when François Pienaar stepped onto the podium at Ellis Park on 24 June 1995 to receive the World Cup from beloved President Nelson Mandela. Both men were sporting Springbok No 6 jerseys but had so much more in common. No, said Pienaar, it did not feel great to have 65,000 supporters behind him. 'We had 43 million behind us.'

On that glorious afternoon in Johannesburg, South Africa celebrated as one. True, the majority black community still harbours deep doubts, and no little suspicion, but the process of reconciliation is now assuredly underway. On this day the Rainbow Nation radiated unity. They danced in the rugby strongholds of Jo'Burg, Pretoria, Durban and Cape Town, but in the townships too.

Why then did Louis Luyt, President of the South African Rugby Football Union, have to roll back the clock only hours after the final whistle? The official banquet allowed him the platform to gloat and display all the worst characteristics of the white-ruled Old Republic. The All Blacks stormed out and flanker Mike Brewer reflected the outrage when branding Luyt a 'fat Afrikaner bastard'.

As if words had not been wounding enough, Luyt took it upon himself to present a gold watch to Derek Bevan, the Welsh referee who had presided over the South Africa–France final in that Durban monsoon. It was an act of grave folly, not least because Bevan, renowned as the world's best official, did not have one of his better games and the Springboks won.

Then again, he was put under disgraceful pressure to play the game in conditions wholly unsuitable for an occasion of such import. Luyt,

TV bosses and World Cup officials were all breathing down his neck, and an announcement over the tannoy told of how all evening flights out of Durban would be delayed an hour. Bevan's biggest concern, however, was that a player could drown if a scrum or maul went down.

The contrast 24 hours later could not have been more marked. For driving rain read glorious sunshine, for tight forward play read Jonah Lomu. The giant All Black wing, the World Cup's star turn, destroyed England with four tries in one of the most devastating periods of play ever put together by a team.

New Zealand were awesome, their first half performance unrivalled throughout the tournament. But when they got to the final they could not reproduce anything even similar. The Boks suffocated Lomu and Co, and in a match so incredibly rich in tension, Joel Stransky won the battle of the goalkickers against Andrew Mehrtens.

Just as South Africa had utilised the emotion of Mandela's opening day visit to them in Cape Town, where they deposed holders Australia, so Pienaar's men tapped into the nation's heartbeat on closing day at Ellis Park. Well done them.

Jonah Lomu walks all over England: this time Mike Catt is his victim.

Rugby Union Who's Who Team of the Tournament

Fullback:	Andre Joubert (South Africa)
Right wing:	Emile NTamack (France)
Centre:	Walter Little (New Zealand)
Centre:	Thierry Lacroix (France)
Left wing:	Jonah Lomu (New Zealand)
Fly-half:	Andrew Mehrtens (New Zealand)
Scrum-half:	Joost van der Westhuizen (South Africa)
L Prop:	Craig Dowd (New Zealand)
Hooker:	Federico Mendez (Argentina)
R Prop:	Patricio Noriega (Argentina)
Lock:	John Eales (Australia)
Lock:	Ian Jones (New Zealand)
B Flanker:	Abdelatif Benazzi (France)
O Flanker:	Josh Kronfeld (New Zealand)
No 8:	Zinzan Brooke (New Zealand)

WORLD CUP SQUADS

ARGENTINA: D Albanase (San Isidro) E; L Arbizu (Belgrano) E(1t,1c,1p), WS, It; N Bossicovich (Gimnasia y Esgrima); P Buabse (Los Tarcos); M Corral (San Isidro) E, WS, It(1t); R Crexell (Jockey Club) E(1p), WS(1t), It; D Cuesta Silva (San Isidro) E, WS, It; F del Castillo (Jockey Club); G del Castillo (Jockey Club); J L Cilley (San Isidro) WS(2c,4p), It(1t,1c,1p); F Garcia (Alumni); S Irazoqui (Palermo Bajo) E(R); E Jurado (Jockey Club) E, WS, It; R Le Fort (Tucuman); G Llanes (La Plata) E, WS, It; R Martin (San Isidro) E, WS, It(1t); F Mendez (Mendoza) E, WS, It; P Noriega (Hindu) E(1t), WS, It; A Pichot (Atletico San Isidro); S Salvat (Alumni) E*, WS*, It*; J Santamarina (Tucuman) E, WS, It; P Sporleder (Curupayti) E, WS, It; M Sugasti (Jockey Club); M Teran (Tucuman) E, WS, It; M Urbano (Buenos Aires C&RC); C Viel (Newman) E, WS, It. *Penalty tries:* 2. **Manager:** L Chaluleu. **Coach:** A Petra. **Summary:** Fourth in Pool B.

AUSTRALIA: S Bowen (NSW) R; M Burke (NSW) C, R(2c,2t), E; D Campese (NSW) SA, C, E; D Crowley (Queensland) SA, E; T Daly (NSW) C, R; J Eales (Queensland) SA, C, R(4c), E; M Foley (Queensland) C(R), R(1t); T Gavin (NSW) SA, C, R, E; G Gregan (ACT) SA, C(R), R, E; M Hartill (NSW) C; D Herbert (Queensland) SA, R; T Horan (Queensland) C, R, E, P Kearns (NSW) SA(1t), C, E; J Little (Queensland) SA, C, E; M Lynagh (Queensland) SA*(1t,1c,2p), C*(1t,3c,2p), E*(1c,5p); R McCall (Queensland) SA, R*, E; E McKenzie (NSW) SA, C(R), R, E; D Manu (NSW) R(TR); W Ofahengaue (NSW) SA, C, E; M Pini (Queensland) SA, R(TR); J Roff (ACT) C(1t), R(2t); P Slattery (Queensland) C, R(R); D Smith (Queensland) SA, R(1t), E(1t); I Tabua (Queensland) C(1t), R; W Waugh (NSW) C; D Wilson (Queensland) SA, R(1t), E. **Manager:** P Falk. **Coach:** R Dwyer. **Summary:** Runners-up in Pool A. **Quarter-final:** lost England 22–25.

CANADA: R Bice (Vancouver); M Cardinal (James Bay) R, SA; A Charron (Ottawa Irish) R(1t), A(1t), SA; G Ennis (Kats) R, A(R), SA; E Evans (UBCOB) R, A, SA; I Gordon (James

Bay) R, SA; J Graf (UBCOB) R, A, SA; S Gray (Kats) R, A, SA; J Hutchinson (UBCOB) A, SA(R); M James (Burnaby Lake) R, A; P Leblanc (Kats); D Lougheed (Toronto Welsh) R, A, SA; S Lytton (Meraloma); G MacKinnon (Brittania Lions) A, SA; C McKenzie (UBCOB) R(1t), SA; C Michaluk (Rowing Club) SA(R); G Rees (Oak Bay Castaways) R*(2c,4p,1dg), A*(2p), SA*(off); B Ross (James Bay); G Rowlands (Velox Valhallians) A; R Snow (Dogs) R, A, SA(off); W Stanley (UBC) R, A, SA; C Stewart (Western Province) R, A, SA; S Stewart (UBCOB) R, A, SA(cited); K Svoboda (Ajax Wanderers) A; R Toews (Meraloma); A Tynan (UBC). **Manager:** R Skett. **Coach:** I Birtwell. **Summary:** Third in Pool A.

COTE d'IVOIRE: B Aka (Burotic) F; E Angoran (Rodez) S, F(R), T; G Bado (Cognac) S, T; E Bley (ASPAA) S, F(R), T; P Bouazo (Burotic) S, F(R); M Brito (Biscarosse) S(R), F, T; A Camara (ASPAA) S(R), F(1t), T; F Dago (ASPAA); A Dali (Clamart) S*, T(R:2p); T Djehi (Millau) S, F, T; F Dupont (Nimes) S, F, T; J-P Ezoua (ASPAA) F; A Kone (Soustons) S, F(R), T; S Kone (Burotic); T Kouame (ASPAA) T(R); V Kouassi (Burotic) S, F(1c,2p), T; I Lassissi (Burotic) S, F, T; L Niakou (Niort) S, F, T; L N'Gbala (Cahors) S; A Niamien (Bouake) F; A Okou (Poitiers) S(R), F, T(1t); P Pere (ACBB Paris) S, F, T; D Quansah (ASPAA) T(R); D Sanoko (Biarritz) S, F, T(R); J Sathicq (CASG) S, F*, T*; A Soulama (Burotic) F(1t), T. **Manager:** P Cassagnet. **Coach:** C-A Ezoua. **Summary:** Fourth in Pool D.

ENGLAND: R Andrew (Wasps) Arg(6p,2dg), It(1c,5p), A(1c,5p,1dg), NZ(3c,1p), F(3p); N Back (Leicester) Arg(R), It, WS(1t); M Bayfield (Northampton) Arg, It, A, NZ, F; K Bracken (Bristol) It, WS(R); J Callard (Bath) WS(3c,5p); W Carling (Harlequins) Arg*, WS*, A*, NZ*(2t), F*; M Catt (Bath) Arg, It, WS, A, NZ, F; B Clarke (Bath) Arg, It, A, NZ, F; G Dawe (Bath) WS; P de Glanville (Bath) It, WS; J Guscott (Bath) Arg, It, A, NZ, F; D Hopley (Wasps) WS(R); I Hunter (Northampton) WS, F; M Johnson (Leicester) Arg, It, WSA, NZ, F; J Leonard (Harlequins) Arg, It, A, NZ, F; J Mallett (Bath) WS(R); B Moore (Harlequins) Arg, It, A, NZ, F; D Morris (Orrell) Arg, WS, A, NZ, F; S Ojomoh (Bath) Arg, WS, A(TR), F; D Richards (Leicester) WS, A, NZ; T Rodber (Northampton) Arg, It, WS(R), A, NZ, F; G Rowntree (Leicester) It, WS; V Ubogu (Bath) Arg, WS, A, NZ, F; R Underwood (Leicester) Arg, It(1t), WS(2t), A, NZ(2t), F; T Underwood (Leicester) Arg, It(1t), A(1t), NZ; R West (Gloucester) WS. *Penalty try:* 1. **Manager/Coach:** J Rowell. **Summary:** Fourth. Winners Pool B. **Quarter-final:** beat Australia 25–22. **Semi-final:** lost New Zealand 29–45. **Play-off:** lost France 9–19.

FRANCE: G Accoceberry (Dax) IC(1t), S; L Armary (Lourdes) T, I, SA; A Benazzi (Agen) T, IC(1t), S, I, SA, E; P Benetton (Agen) T, IC(R), S; L Benezech (Racing Club) IC, S, E; O Brouzet (Grenoble) T, IC, E(TR); L Cabannes (Racing Club) T(R), IC, S, I, SA, E; C Califano (Toulouse) IC, S, I, SA, E; M Cecillon (Toulouse) T, S(R), I, SA; A Cigagna (Toulouse) E; A Costes (Montferrand) IC(1t); Y Delaigue (Toulon) T(1dg), IC; M de Rougemont (Toulon) IC; C Deylaud (Toulouse) IC(R), S, I, SA; P Gallart (Beziers) T; F Galthie (Colomiers) SA, E; J-M Gonzales (Bayonne) T, S, I, SA, E; A Hueber (Toulon) T(1t), S(R), I; T Lacroix (Dax) T(2t,3c,3p), IC(2t,4c,2p), S(1c,5p), I(1c,8p), SA(5p), E(3p); O Merle (Grenoble) T, S, I, SA, E; F Mesnel (Racing Club) IC, E; E N'Tamack (Toulouse) T, S(1t), I(1t), SA,E(1t); O Roumat (Dax) IC, S, I, SA, E(1t); J-L Sadourny (Colomiers) T, S, I, SA, E; P Saint-Andre (Montferrand) T*(1t), IC*(1t), S*, I*(1t), SA, E; P Sella (Agen) T, S, I, SA, E; W Techoueyres (Bordeaux University) IC(1t); S Viars (Brive) IC(1t). **Manager:** G Laporte. **Coach:** P Berbizier. **Summary:** Third. Winners Pool D. **Quartet-final:** beat Ireland 36–12. **Semi-final:** lost South Africa 15–19. **Play-off:** beat England 19–9.

IRELAND: J Bell (Ballymena) NZ, W, F; M Bradley (Cork Constitution) NZ; P Burke (Cork Constitution) J(6c,1p); S Byrne (Blackrock College); D Corkery (Cork Constitution) NZ(1t), J(1t), W, F; P Danaher (Garryowen); E Elwood (Lansdowne) NZ(2c), W(3c,1p), F(4p); M Field (Malone) NZ(R), J; A Foley (Shannon)J(TR); N Francis (Old Belvedere)

NZ, J(1t), W, F; G Fulcher (Cork Constitution) J, W, F; S Geoghegan (Bath) NZ, J(1t), W, F; G Halpin (London Irish) NZ(1t), W, F; E Halvey (Shannon) J(1t), W(TR:1t), F(R); N Hogan (Terenure College) J(1t), W, F; H Hurley (Old Wesley); P Johns (Dungannon) NZ, J, W, F; T Kingston (Dolphin) NZ*, J(R), W*, F*; D McBride (Malone) NZ(1t), W(1t), F; B Mullin (Blackrock College) NZ, J, W, F; D O'Mahony (Blackrock College) F; C O'Shea (Lansdowne) J, W, F; N Popplewell (Wasps) NZ, J, W*, F; J Staples (Harlequins) NZ; D Tweed (Ballymena) J; P Wallace (Blackrock College) J; R Wallace (Garryowen) NZ, J, W; K Wood (Garryowen) J. *Penalty tries:* 2. **Manager:** N Murphy. **Coach:** G Murphy. **Summary:** Runners-up in Pool C. **Quarter-final:** lost South Africa 12–36.

ITALY: O Arancio (Amatori Catania) WS, E, Arg; M Bonomi (Milan) WS; S Bordon (Ciabatta Rovigo) E, Arg; M Capuzzoni (Milan); A Castellani (L'Aquila); C Checchinato (Ciabatta Rovigo) WS; Massimo Cuttitta (Milan) WS*, E*(1t), Arg*; Marcello Cuttitta (Milan) WS(1t); M Dal Sie (Lafert San Dona); D Dominguez (Milan) WS(1c,1p,1dg), E(2c,2p), Arg(1t,2c,4p); R Favaro (Benetton Treviso) WS; I Francescato (Benetton Treviso) WS, E, Arg; J Gardner (MDP Roma) WS, E, Arg; M Gerosa (Piacenza) E, Arg(1t); M Giacheri (Benetton Treviso) E,Arg; F Mazzariol (Benetton Treviso); C Orlandi (Lyons Piacenza) WS, E, Arg; P Pedroni (Milan) WS, E, Arg; M Platania (Milan); F Properzi-Curti (Milan) WS, E, Arg; M Ravazzolo (Fly Flot Calvisano) WS; A Sgorlon (Lafert San Dona) E, Arg; M Trevisiol (Benetton Treviso); L Troiani (L'Aquila) E,Arg; A Troncon (Milan) WS, E,Arg; P Vaccari (Milan) WS(1t), E(1t), Arg(1t). **Manager:** G Dondi. **Coach:** G Coste. **Summary:** Third in Pool B.

JAPAN: T Akatsuka (Meiji University) NZ(R); B Ferguson (Hino Motor) W, I, NZ; K Hamabe (Kinki Nippon Railway); T Haneda (World); S Hirao (Kobe Steel) W, I(1t); K Hirose (Kyoto Sangyo University) NZ; E Hirotsu (Kobe Steel); M Horikoshi (Kobe Steel) W, I; K Imazumi (Suntory); K Izawa (Daito Bunka University) I(R:1t), NZ; H Kajihara (Katsunuma) W, I, NZ; M Kunda (Toshiba Fuchu) W*, I*, NZ*; Sione Latu (Daito Bunka University) W, I; Sinali Latu (Sanyo Electric) W, I(1t), NZ; T Masuho (Kobe Steel) W; T Matsuda (Toshiba Fuchu) W, I, NZ; K Matsuo (World); Y Motoki (Kobe Steel) W, I, NZ; W Murata (Toshiba Fuchu) NZ; O Ota (NEC) W, I, NZ; L Oto (Daito Bunka University) W(2t), I, NZ; Y Sakuraba (Nippon Steel Kamaishi) W, I, NZ; K Takahashi (Toyota) W, NZ; M Takura (Mitsubishi Motor Co) I(1t); A Yoshida (Kobe Steel) W, I, NZ; Y Yoshida (Isetan) I(4c), NZ. **Manager:** Z Shirai. **Coach:** O Koyabu. **Summary:** Fourth in Pool C.

NEW ZEALAND: G Bachop (Canterbury) I, W, S, E(1t), SA; M Brewer (Canterbury) I, W, E, S, SA; R Brooke (Auckland) J(2t), S, E, SA; Z Brooke (Auckland) J, S, E(1dg), SA; O Brown (Auckland) I, W, S, E, SA; F Bunce (North Harbour) I(1t), W, S(1t), E, SA; S Culhane (Southland) J(1t,20c); C Dowd (Auckland) I, W, J(1t), E, SA; M Ellis (Otago) I(R), W(1t), J(6t), S, SA(R); S Fitzpatrick (Auckland) I*, W*, S*(1t), E*, SA*; P Henderson (Southland) J*(1t); N Hewitt (Southland) I(TR), J; A Ieremia (Wellington) J(1t); I Jones (North Harbour) I, W, S, E, SA; J Joseph (Otago) I, W, J(R), S, SA(R); J Kronfeld (Otago) I(1t), W(1t), S, E(1t), SA; B Larsen (North Harbour) I, W, J, E(R); R Loe (Canterbury) J(1t), S, SA(R); J Lomu (Counties) I(2t), W, S(1t), E(4t), SA; W Little (North Harbour) I, W(1t), S(2t), E, SA; A Mehrtens (Canterbury) I(3c,4p), W(2c,4p,1dg), S(1t,6c,2p), E(3c,1p,1dg), SA(3p,1dg); G Osborne (North Harbour) I(1t), W, J(2t), E, SA; E Rush (North Harbour) W(R), J(3t); K Schuler (North Harbour) I(R), J; A Strachan (North Harbour) J, SA(TR); J Wilson (Otago) I, J(3t), S, E, SA. **Manager:** E Kirton. **Coach:** L Mains. **Summary:** Runners-up. Winners Pool C. **Quarter-final:** beat Scotland 48–30. **Semi-final:** beat England 45–29. **Final:** lost South Africa 12–15 (aet).

ROMANIA: V Brici (Farul) SA, A; T Brinza (U.Cluj) SA*, A*; S Ciorascu (Auch) C*, SA, A; C Cojocariu (Bayonne) C, SA, A; L Costea (Steaua) C; C Draguceanu (Steaua); V Flutur

403

(U.Cluj) C(R), SA, A; R Fugigi (CSM Foresta Sibiu); A Gealapu (Steaua) C, SA, A; R Gontineac (U.Cluj) C, SA, A; A Guranescu (Dinamo) SA(1t), A; I Ivanciuc (Suceava) C(R), SA(1p), A(1dg); G Leonte (Vienne) C, SA, A; V Lucaci (Remin Baia Mare); A Lungu (Castres) A(R); D Neaga (Dinamo) C; I Negreci (CFR Constanta) C, SA, A; N Nichitean (U.Cluj) C(1p); D Niculae (Steaua); T Oroian (Steaua) C; N Racean (U.Cluj) C, SA, A; I Rotaru (Dinamo) C; O Slusariuc (Dinamo) C; G Solomie (Timisoara) C, SA, A; G Vlad (Dinamo) C, SA, A; V Tufa (Dinamo) SA(R), A(R). **Manager:** T Radulescu. **Coach:** M Paraschiv. **Summary:** Fourth in Pool A.

SCOTLAND: P Burnell (London Scottish) IC(1t), T; S Campbell (Dundee HSFP) IC, NZ(R); C Chalmers (Melrose) IC(1t), T, F, NZ; D Cronin (Bourges) T, F, NZ; C Glasgow (Heriot's FP); G Hastings (Watsonians) IC(4t,9c,2p), T(1t,1c,8p), F(1c,4p), NZ(3c,3p); S Hastings (Watsonians) T(1t), F,NZ(1t); D Hilton (Bath) T, F, NZ; I Jardine (Stirling County) T, F(R), NZ(R); C Joiner (Melrose) IC, T, F, NZ; K Logan (Stirling County) IC(2t), T, F, NZ; J Manson (Dundee HSFP); K McKenzie (Stirling County) IC; K Milne (Heriot's FP) T, F, NZ; I Morrison (London Scottish) T, F, NZ; D Patterson (West Hartlepool) T; E Peters (Bath) T(1t), F, NZ; B Redpath (Melrose) IC, F, NZ; J Richardson (Edinburgh Academicals); G Shiel (Melrose) IC(1t), F, NZ; I Smith (Gloucester) IC; T Stanger (Hawick) IC(1t); R Wainwright (West Hartlepool) IC, T, F(1t), NZ; P Walton (Northampton) IC(2t); G Weir (Melrose) IC, T, F, NZ(2t); P Wright (Boroughmuir) IC(1t), T, F, NZ. **Manager:** D Paterson. **Coach:** D Morgan. **Summary:** Runners-up in Pool D. **Quartet-final:** lost New Zealand 30–48.

Springbok fans celebrate as François Pienaar hoists aloft the World Cup, to the obvious delight of President Nelson Mandala.

SOUTH AFRICA: M Andrews (Natal) A, WS(1t), F, NZ; R Brink (Western Province) R, C; J Dalton (Transvaal) A,C(off); N Drotske (OFS) WS(R); P du Randt (OFS) A,WS,F,NZ; P Hendriks (Transvaal) A(1t),R,C; M Hurter (Northern Transvaal) R, C; G Johnson (Transvaal) R(1c,3p), C,WS(3c,2p); A Joubert (Natal) A, C, WS, F, NZ; R Kruger (Northern Transvaal) A, R, WS, F(1t), NZ; H le Roux (Transvaal) A, R, C(R), WS, F, NZ; J Mulder (Transvaal) A, WS, F, NZ; K Otto (Northern Transvaal) A(R), R, C(R), WS(R); G Pagel (Western Province) R, C, NZ(R); F Pienaar (Transvaal) A*, C*, WS*, F*, NZ*; A Richter (Northern Transvaal) R*(2t), C(2t), WS(R); C Rossouw (Transvaal) R, WS(1t), F, NZ; J Roux (Transvaal) R, C, F(R); C Schultz (Transvaal) R, C, WS; J Small (Natal) A, R, F, NZ; R Straeuli (Transvaal) A, WS, NZ(R); J Stransky (Western Province) A(1t,1c,4p,1dg), R(TR), C(2c,2p), F(1c,4p) NZ(3p,2dg); H Strydom (Transvaal) A, C, F, NZ; B Swart (Transvaal) A, WS, F, NZ; J van der Westhuizen (Northern Transvaal) A, C(R), WS, F, NZ; K Wiese (Transvaal) R, C, WS, F, NZ; C Williams (Western Province) WS(4t), F, NZ; B Venter (OFS) R, C, WS(R), F(R). **Manager:** M du Plessis. **Coach:** K Christie. **Summary:** Champions. Winners Pool A. **Quartet-final:** beat Western Samoa 42–14. **Semi-final:** beat France 19–15. **Final:** beat New Zealand 15–12 (aet).

TONGA: I Afeaki (Wellington) F(R), S, IC; F Fakaongo IC(R); S Fe'ao (Queensland) F, S; I Fenukitau (Queenbeyan & ACT) F, S(1t); T Fukofuka (Grammar OB) F, S, IC; T 'Isitolo (Kolofo'ou) IC(R); P Latu (Vaheloto) F, S, IC; P Latukefu (Canberra Royals & ACT) S, IC(1t); W Lose (North Harbour) F, S, IC; T Lutua (Police RFC) S(R), IC(R); A Mafi (Queenbeyan); F Mafi (Queenbeyan & ACT) F, IC; S Mafile'o IC; F Mahoni (Fasi/Ma'ufanga) F(off); F Masila (Kolomotu'a) F; M 'Otai (Kia-Toa) F*, S*, IC*(1t); E Talakai (Auckland) IC; A Taufa (Wellington Harlequins) F, S; N Tufui (Kolomotu'a) S(R), IC; S Tu'ipuloto (Manly & NSW) F(1c,1p), S, IC(1t,3c,1p); T Va'enuku (Police RFC) F(1t), S, IC; U Va'enuku (Toloa OB) F, S, IC; E Vunipola (Toa-Ko-Ma'afu) F, S, IC; F Vunipola (Toa-Ko-Ma'afu) F(R), S, IC; M Vunipola (Toa-Ko-Ma'afu) F, S. *Penalty try:* 1. **Manager:** H Mailefihi. **Coach:** S Taumoepeau. **Summary:** Third in Pool D.

WALES: M Bennett (Cardiff) NZ; A Clement (Swansea) J, NZ, I; A Davies (Cardiff) J, NZ(1dg); J Davies (Neath) J, NZ, I; S Davies (Swansea) J, I; D Evans (Treorchy) J(R); I Evans (Llanelli) J(2t), NZ, I; R Evans (Llanelli) NZ, I(R); S Ford (Cardiff); M Griffiths (Cardiff) J(1t), I; M Hall (Cardiff) J*, NZ*, I*; J Humphreys (Cardiff) NZ, I(1t); G Jenkins (Swansea) J; N Jenkins (Pontypridd) J(5c,4p), NZ(2p,1dg), I(2c,2p); S John (Llanelli); D Jones (Cardiff) J, NZ, I; R Jones (Swansea) NZ, I; E Lewis (Cardiff) J, I; G Llewellyn (Neath) J, NZ, I; A Moore (Cardiff) J(1t); W Proctor (Llanelli) NZ; G Prosser (Pontypridd) NZ; S Roy (Cardiff) J(R); H Taylor (Cardiff) J, NZ, I(R); G Thomas (Bridgend) J(3t), NZ, I; J Thomas (Cardiff). **Manager:** G Evans. **Coach:** A Evans. **Summary:** Third in Pool C.

WESTERN SAMOA: T Fa'amasino It, Arg, E(2c,1p), SA(2c); L Falaniko (Marist) It, Arg, E, SA; P Fatialofa (Manurewa) It, E(R), SA(R); G Harder It(1t), Arg(1t), SA; M Iupeli (Marist) E(R); S Kaleta (Suburbs); D Kellett (Counties) It(1t,3c,2p), Arg(1c,5p); P Lam (Auckland/Marist) Arg*(1t), E*, SA*; G Latu (Vaimoso) Arg, E, SA; L Leaupepe (Papakura & Counties) Arg(R:1t), E; P Leavasa (Apia) It(R), Arg, E; T Leiasamaivao (Moataa) It, Arg, E, SA; B Lima (Marist) It(3t), Arg, E, SA; S Lemanea (SCOPA) E(R), SA; M Mika (Otago) It, Arg, E, SA; T Nu'uali'itia (Auckland) It, Arg, E, SA(1t); J Paramore (Manurewa) It, Arg, SA; E Puleitu E; B Reidy (Marist) SA(R); F Sini (Marist) A(R), E(R:2t), SA; S Tatupu (Ponsonby & Auckland) It(1t), Arg, E, SA(1t); F Tuilagi (Marist) E(R), SA(R); M Umaga (Wellington) It, Arg, E(1t), SA; T Vaega (Moataa) It, Arg, E, SA; S Vaifale (Marist) It, SA(R); V Vitale (Vaiala) Arg(R); D Williams (Colomiers) It, E. **Manager:** L T Simi. **Coach:** S P Schuster. **Summary:** Runners-up in Pool B. **Quarter-final:** lost South Africa 14–42.

POOL MATCHES

POOL A

What the World Cup needs is a belting good start to make the globe sit up and take notice, and South Africa and Australia do not disappoint. An electric atmosphere at Newlands is rewarded with a shock result, in most people's book. After sitting out the first two World Cups the Springboks are intent on making a statement and Pieter Hendriks' clenched fist, as he left David Campese sprawling in his wake, does nicely. Victory over the reigning world champions gives South Africa Pool glory, though not without a fight. This comes in the closing game against Canada, and results in three players being sent-off in one international for the first time. In addition, two more are cited and sent home including your man Hendriks. That apart, Canada can consider themselves unlucky to have been drawn in the Group of Death. Their fearless running deserves a platform in the knockout phase.

Pool highlight: Canada's second half effort against South Africa
Pool lowlight: Brawl between Springboks and Canucks.

Joost van der Westhuizen snaps at the heels of his Western Samoan rival during South Africa's quarter-final win.

Australia 18, South Africa 27
Cape Town, 25 May 1995

Australia: Pini; Smith, Herbert, Little, Campese; Lynagh (capt), Gregan; Crowley, Kearns, McKenzie, McCall, Eales, Ofahengaue, Wilson, Gavin.
  Scorers – *Tries:* Lynagh, Kearns. *Conversion:* Lynagh. *Penalty goals:* Lynagh 2.

South Africa: Joubert; Small, Mulder, le Roux, Hendriks; Stransky, van der Westhuizen; du Randt, Dalton, Swart (Otto 65), Andrews, Strydom, Pienaar (capt), Kruger, Straeuli.
  Scorers – *Tries:* Hendriks, Stransky. *Conversion:* Stransky. *Penalty goals:* Stransky 4. *Dropped goal:* Stransky.

Referee: D Bevan (Wales).

Series score: Played 33, Australia 10, South Africa 23.

Canada (11) 34, Romania (3) 3
Port Elizabeth, 26 May 1995

Canada: S Stewart; Stanley, C Stewart, Gray, Lougheed; Rees (capt), Graf; Evans, Cardinal, Snow, Ennis, James, Charron, Gordon, McKenzie.
  Scorers – *Tries:* Charron, Snow, McKenzie. *Conversions:* Rees 2. *Penalty goals:* Rees 4. *Dropped goal:* Rees.

Romania: Solomie; Colceriu, Raceanu, Gontineac, Rotaru; Nichitean (Ivanciuc 67), Neaga (Flutur 52); Leonte, Negreci, Vlad, Ciorascu (capt), Cojocariu, Oroian, Gealapu, Slusariuc.
  Scorer – *Penalty goal:* Nichitean.

Referee: C Hawke (New Zealand).

Series score: Played 2, Canada 2, Romania 0.

South Africa (8) 21, Romania (0) 8
Cape Town, 30 May 1995

South Africa: Johnson; Small, Scholtz, Venter (Stransky TR), Hendriks; le Roux, Roux; Pagel, Rossouw, Hurter, Wiese, Otto, Kruger, Brink, Richter (capt).
  Scorers – *Tries:* Richter 2. *Conversion:* Johnson. *Penalty goals:* Johnson 3.

Romania: Brici; Colceriu, Raceanu, Gontineac, Solomie; Ivanciuc, Flutur; Leonte, Negreci (Tufa 62), Vlad, Ciorascu, Cojocariu, Guranescu, Gealapu, Brinza (capt).
  Scorers – *Try:* Guranescu. *Penalty goal:* Ivanciuc.

Referee: K McCartney (Scotland).

Series score: PLayed 1, South AFrica 1, Romania 0.

Australia (20) 27, Canada (6) 11
Port Elizabeth, 31 May 1995

Australia: Burke; Roff, Little, Horan, Campese; Lynagh (capt), Slattery (Gregan 80); Daly, Kearns (Foley 70), Hartill (McKenzie 56), Waugh, Eales, Ofahengaue, Tabua, Gavin.
  Scorers – *Tries:* Tabua, Roff, Lynagh. *Conversions:* Lynagh 3. *Penalty goals:* Lynagh 2.

Canada: S Stewart; Stanley, C Stewart, Gray, Lougheed; Rees (capt), Graf; Evans, Svoboda, Snow, James, Rowlands (Ennis 69), Hutchinson, MacKinnon, Charron.
  Scorers – *Try:* Charron. *Penalty goals:* Rees 2.

Referee: P Robin (France).

Series score: Played 4, Australia 4, Canada 0.

Australia (14) 42, Romania (3) 3
Stellenbosch, 3 June 1995

Australia: Burke; Smith, Herbert (Pini TR), Horan, Roff; Bowen, Gregan (Slattery 70); Daly, Foley, McKenzie, McCall (capt), Eales, Tabua, Wilson (Manu TR), Gavin.
    Scorers – Tries: Foley, Roff 2, Burke, Smith, Wilson. Conversions: Burke 2, Eales 4.

Romania: Brici; Colceriu, Raceanu, Gontineac (Lungu 56), Solomie; Ivanciuc, Flutur; Leonte, Negreci (Tufa 73), Vlad, Ciorascu, Cojocariu, Guranescu, Gealapu, Brinza (capt).
    Scorer – *Dropped goal:* Ivanciuc.

Referee: N Saito (Japan).

Series score: Played 1, Australia 1, Romania 0.

Canada 0, South Africa (17) 20
Port Elizabeth, 3 June 1995

Canada: S Stewart; Stanley, C Stewart, Gray, Lougheed; Rees (capt), Graf; Evans, Cardinal, Snow, Charron, Ennis (Hutchinson 65), Gordon, MacKinnon, McKenzie (Michaluk 79). Sent-off: Rees, Snow (both 30-day bans). Cited: S Stewart (60-day ban).

South Africa: Joubert; Johnson (van der Westhuizen 18), Scholtz, Venter, Hendriks; Stransky (H le Roux 59), Roux; Pagel, Dalton, Hurter, Wiese, Strydom (Otto 71), Pienaar (capt), Brink, Richter. Sent-off: Dalton (30-day ban). Cited: Hendriks (90-day ban).
    Scorers – *Tries:* Richter 2. *Conversions:* Stransky 2. *Penalty goals:* Stransky 2.

Referee: D McHugh (Ireland).

Series score: Played 1, Canada 0, South Africa 1.

	P	W	L	F	A	Pts
South Africa	3	3	0	68	26	9
Australia	3	2	1	87	41	7
Canada	3	1	2	45	50	5
Romania	3	0	3	14	97	3

POOL B

One of the mysteries of the World Cup is how Argentina return home early with nothing to show for their campaign. Here is a side who push England's famed forwards to breaking point, inflict two unanswered tries on the European champions and lose only because Lisandro Arbizu has left his goalkicking boots at home on the Pampas. Next up against Western Samoa, Argentina are cruising to victory only to concede 19 points without reply in the last half-hour. No surprise then that the Pumas lead Italy 25–24 with two minutes remaining … and lose. England prove to be the master under-achievers of the Pool phase, floundering in the aforementioned match, shading Italy by no more than a converted score before virtually their second string restores some respect in the Pool decider against a Western Samoa side nonetheless repeating their 1991 feat of reaching the last eight.

Pool highlight: Argentina's forward effort against England.
Pool lowlight: Argentina's lack of reward against England.

Western Samoa (12) 42, Italy (11) 18
East London, 27 May 1995

Western Samoa: Umaga; Lima, Vaega, Fa'amasino, Harder; Kellett, Nu'uali'itia; Mika; Leiasamaivao, Fatialofa (capt), Falaniko (Leavasa 58), Williams, Vaifale, Paramore, Tatupu.

Scorers – *Tries:* Lima 3, Harder, Tatupu, Kellett. *Conversions:* Kellett 3. *Penalty goals:* Kellett 2.

Italy: Vaccari; Ravazzolo, Francescato, Bonomi, Marcello Cuttitta; Dominguez, Troncon; Massimo Cuttitta (capt), Orlandi, Properzi-Curti, Favaro, Pedroni, Arancio, Gardner, Checcinato.

Scorers – *Tries:* Marcello Cuttitta, Vaccari. *Conversion:* Dominguez. *Penalty goal:* Dominguez. *Dropped goal:* Dominguez.

Referee: J Dume (France).

Series score: Played 1, Western Samoa 1, Italy 0.

England (12) 24, Argentina (0) 18
Durban, 27 May 1995

England: Catt; T Underwood, Carling (capt, de Glanville 78), Guscott, R Underwood; Andrew, Morris; Leonard, Moore, Ubogu, Johnson, Bayfield, Rodber, Ojomoh, Clarke.

Scorer – *Penalty goals:* Andrew 6. *Dropped goals:* Andrew 2.

Argentina: Jurado; Albinese, Cuesta-Silva, Salvat (capt), Teran; Arbizu, Crexell; Corral, Mendez, Noriega, Llanes, Sporleder, Martin, Viel, Santamarina.

Scorers – *Tries:* Noriega, Arbizu. *Conversion:* Arbizu. *Penalty goals:* Arbizu 2.

Referee: J Fleming (Scotland).

Series score: Played 6, England 4, Argentina 1, Drawn 1.

Western Samoa clear their lines against England despite the attentions of Dewi Morris and Neil Back.

Western Samoa (10) 32, Argentina (16) 26
East London, 30 May 1995

Western Samoa: Umaga; Lima, Vaega, Fa'amasino, Harder (Leaupepe 51); Kellett (Sini 78), Nu'uali'itia; Mika, Leiasamaivao, Latu, Leavasa, Falaniko, Tatupu, Paramore, Lam (capt).
    Scorers – *Tries:* Harder, Leaupepe, Lam. *Conversion:* Kellett. *Penalty goals:* Kellett 5.

Argentina: Jurado; Cuesta-Silva, Arbizu, Salvat (capt), Teran; Cilley, Crexell; Corral, Mendez, Noriega, Llanes, Sporleder, Martin, Viel, Santamarina.
    Scorers – *Tries:* penalty try, Crexell. *Conversions:* Cilley 2. *Penalty goals:* Cilley 4.

Referee: D Bishop (New Zealand).

Series score: Played 1, Western Samoa 1, Argentina 0.

England (16) 27, Italy (10) 20
Durban, 31 May 1995

England: Catt; T Underwood, de Glanville, Guscott, R Underwood; Andrew, Bracken; Rowntree, Moore, Leonard, Johnson, Bayfield, Rodber, Back, Clarke.
    Scorers – *Tries:* T Underwood, R Underwood. *Conversion:* Andrew. *Penalty goals:* Andrew 5.

Italy: Troiani; Vaccari, Bordon, Francescato, Gerosa; Dominguez, Troncon; Massimo Cuttitta (capt), Orlandi, Properzi-Curti, Pedroni, Giacheri, Arancio, Sgorlon, Gardner.
    Scorers – *Tries:* Vaccari, Cuttitta. *Conversions:* Dominguez 2. *Penalty goals:* Dominguez 2.

Referee: S Hilditch (Ireland).

Series score: Played 2, England 2, Italy 0.

Argentina (12) 25, Italy (12) 31
East London, 4 June 1995

Argentina: Jurado; Cuesta-Silva, Arbizu, Salvat (capt), Teran; Cilley, Crexell; Corral, Mendez, Noriega, Llanes, Sporleder, Martin, Viel, Santamarina.
    Scorers – Tries: Martin, penalty try, Corral, Cilley. Conversion: Cilley. Penalty goal: Cilley.

Italy: Troiani; Vaccari, Bordon, Francescato, Gerosa; Dominguez, Troncon; Massimo Cuttitta (capt), Orlandi, Properzi-Curti, Pedroni, Giacheri, Arancio, Sgorlon, Gardner.
    Scorers – *Tries:* Vaccari, Gerosa, Dominguez. *Conversions:* Dominguez 2. *Penalty goals:* Dominguez 4.

Referee: C Thomas (Wales).

Series score: Played 2, Argentina 0, Italy 2.

England (21) 44, Western Samoa (0) 22
Durban, 4 June 1995

England: Callard; Hunter, Carling (capt, Hopley 70), de Glanville, R Underwood; Catt, Morris; Rowntree (Mallett 24), Dawe, Ubogu, Johnson, West, Ojomoh, Back (Rodber 32), Richards (Bracken 72).
    Scorers – *Tries:* Back, R Underwood 2, penalty try. *Conversions:* Callard 3. *Penalty goals:* Callard 5. *Dropped goal:* Catt.

Western Samoa: Umaga; Lima, Vaega, Fa'amasino, Leaupepe; Puleitu (Sini 41), Nu'uali'itia; Mika, Leiasamaivao, Latu (Fatialofa 72), Williams, Falaniko, Leavasa (Iupeli 28, Lemanea 67), Tatupu, Lam (capt).

410

Scorers – *Tries:* Sini 2, Umaga. *Conversions:* Fa'amasino 2. *Penalty goal:* Fa'amasino.
Referee: P Robin (France).
Series score: Played 1, England 1, Western Samoa 0.

	P	W	L	F	A	Pts
England	3	3	0	95	60	9
Western Samoa	3	2	1	96	88	7
Italy	3	1	2	69	94	5
Argentina	3	0	3	69	87	3

POOL C

It's just like the old days in Pool C with New Zealand back to their best and Wales back to their worst. The All Blacks 'recover' from conceding three tries to Ireland (they still win 43-19) to breeze past Wales and then annihilate Japan by a world record 145-17. Jonah Lomu, the 6ft 5in, 19st wing juggernaut assumes superstar status with 84 interview requests in one day, while play-anywhere back Marc Ellis smashes the World Cup try-scoring record with six of the best against Japan. Wales, under the caretaker coaching of Wallaby Alex Evans, show promise against the hapless Japs, but nothing else thereafter. Team selection against New Zealand is bizarre, with predictable consequences, while the quality of performance in the crunch match with Ireland is such that Wales cannot escape to the airport fast enough. By contrast, the Irish take the challenge to all their opponents and are suitably rewarded.

Pool highlight: Jonah Lomu's 70-yard, four-tackle busting run against Ireland.
Pool lowlight: Wales' desperate first 20 minutes against Ireland.

Wales (34) 57, Japan (0) 10
Bloemfontein, 27 May 1995

Wales: Clement; I Evans, Hall (capt), N Jenkins, Thomas; A Davies (D Evans 56), Moore; Griffiths, G Jenkins, J Davies, D Jones (Roy 72), Llewellyn, S Davies, Taylor, Lewis.
    Scorers – *Tries:* Thomas 3, I Evans 2, Moore, Griffiths. *Conversions:* N Jenkins 5. *Penalty goals:* N Jenkins 4.

Japan: Matsuda; Oto, Yoshida, Motoki, Masuho; Hirao, Horikoshi; Ota, Kunda (capt), Takahashi, Sakuraba, Ferguson, Kajihara, Sinali Latu, Sione Latu.
    Scorer – *Tries:* Oto 2.

Referee: E Sklar (Argentina).
Series score: Played 2, Wales 2, Japan 0.

New Zealand (20) 43, Ireland (12) 19
Johannesburg, 27 May 1995

New Zealand: Osborne, Wilson (Ellis 31), Bunce, Little, Lomu; Mehrtens, Bachop; Dowd, Fitzpatrick (capt, Hewitt TR), Brown, Jones, Larsen, Joseph, Kronfeld, Brewer (Schuler 74).
    Scorers – *Tries:* Lomu 2, Bunce, Kronfeld, Osborne. *Conversions:* Mehrtens 3. *Penalty goals:* Mehrtens 4.

Ireland: Staples (Field 36); R Wallace, Mullin, Bell, Geoghegan; Elwood, Bradley; Popplewell, Kingston (capt), Halpin, Fulcher, Francis, Corkery, McBride, Johns.
    Scorers – Tries: Halpin, McBride, Corkery. Conversions: Elwood 2.

411

Referee: W Erickson (Australia).
Series score: Played 13, New Zealand 12, Ireland 1.

Ireland (19) 50, Japan (14) 28
Bloemfontein, 31 May 1995
Ireland: O'Shea; R Wallace, Mullin, Field, Geoghegan; Burke, Hogan; Popplewell, Wood (Kingston 9), P Wallace, Tweed, Francis, Corkery, Halvey (Foley TR), Johns.
    Scorers – *Tries:* Corkery, Francis, Geoghegan, penalty try 2, Halvey, Hogan. *Conversions:* Burke 6. *Penalty goal:* Burke.

Gavin Hastings sets his sights on more glory during his wonderful World Cup campaign

Japan: Matsuda; Oto, A Yoshida, Motoki, Y Yoshida; Hirao, Horikoshi; Ota, Kunda (capt), Takura, Sakuraba, Ferguson, Kajihara, Sinali Latu, Sione Latu (Izawa 9).
    Scorers – *Tries:* Sinali Latu, Izawa, Hirao, Takura. *Conversions:* Y Yoshida 4.

Referee: S Neethling (South Africa).

Series score: Played 4, Ireland 4, Japan 0.

New Zealand (20) 34, Wales (6) 9
Johannesburg, 31 May 1995

New Zealand: Osborne; Ellis, Bunce, Little, Lomu (Rush 70); Mehrtens, Bachop; Dowd, Fitzpatrick (capt), Brown, Jones, Larsen, Joseph, Kronfeld, Brewer.
    Scorers – *Tries:* Little, Ellis, Kronfeld. *Conversions:* Mehrtens 2. *Penalty goals:* Mehrtens 4. *Dropped goal:* Mehrtens.

Wales: Clement; I Evans, Hall (capt), Thomas, Proctor; N Jenkins, R Jones; R Evans, Humphreys, J Davies, D Jones, Prosser, Llewellyn, Taylor, Bennett.
    Scorers – *Penalty goals:* N Jenkins 2. *Dropped goal:* N Jenkins.

Referee: E Morrison (England).

Series score: Played 16, New Zealand 13, Wales 3.

New Zealand (84) 145, Japan (3) 17
Bloemfontein, 4 June 1995

New Zealand: Osborne; Wilson, Ellis, Ieremia, Rush; Culhane, Strachan; Dowd, Hewitt, Loe, R Brooke, Larsen (Joseph 15), Schuler, Henderson (capt), Z Brooke.
    Scorers – *Tries:* Ellis 6, Rush 3, Wilson 3, Osborne 2, R Brooke 2, Loe, Ieremia, Dowd, Culhane, Henderson. *Conversions:* Culhane 20.

Japan: Matsuda; Oto, A Yoshida, Motoki, Y Yoshida; Hirose, Murata; Ota, Kunda (capt), Takahashi, Sakuraba, Ferguson, Kajihara, Izawa, Sinali Latu (Akatsuka 55).
    Scorers – *Tries:* Kajihara 2. *Conversions:* Hirose 2. *Penalty goal:* Hirose.

Referee: G Gadjovich (Canada).

Series score: Played 1, New Zealand 1, Japan 0.

Ireland (14) 24, Wales (6) 23
Johannesburg, 4 June 1995

Ireland: O'Shea; R Wallace, Mullin, Bell, Geoghegan; Elwood, Hogan; Popplewell, Kingston (capt), Halpin, Fulcher, Francis, Corkery, McBride (Halvey TR), Johns.
    Scorers – *Tries:* Popplewell, McBride, Halvey. *Conversions:* Elwood 3. *Penalty goal:* Elwood.

Wales: Clement; I Evans, Hall (capt), N Jenkins, Thomas; A Davies, R Jones; Griffiths, Humphreys, J Davies (R Evans 83), D Jones, Llewellyn, S Davies, Taylor, Lewis.
    Scorers – *Tries:* Humphreys, Taylor. *Conversions:* N Jenkins 2. *Penalty goals:* N Jenkins 2. *Dropped goal:* A Davies.

Series score: Played 99, Ireland 35, Wales 58, Drawn 1.

	P	W	L	F	A	Pts
New Zealand	3	3	0	222	45	9
Ireland	3	2	1	93	94	7
Wales	3	1	2	89	68	5
Japan	3	0	3	55	252	3

Star of the Pool is Gavin Hastings, with 89 in his three outings. He opens up with a World Cup finals best of 44 against Cote d'Ivoire, adds 31 against an over-physical Tonga, and concludes with 14 against France. Not enough in the latter case, however, as Thierry Lacroix's perfect kicking display, allied to Emile NTamack's last-gasp try gives France Pool glory and the plum quarter-final tie (Ireland rather than New Zealand). Scotland's solace is having played a full part in one of the great Tests of all time in front of 39,000 at Loftus Versfeld. Cote d'Ivoire (don't call them Ivory Coast) provide the innocence as Black Africa's first-ever qualifiers, but also the tragedy when 24-year-old Paris-based wing Max Brito breaks his neck against Tonga and is confirmed as a quadraplegic. Having rallied from the humiliation of an 89-0 loss to Scotland, to score two tries against mighty France, it is an awful way to end their campaign.

Pool highlight: NTamack's winning try against Scotland, four minutes into stoppage time.
Pool lowlight: Brito's tragic injury at Rustenburg.

Scotland (34) 89, Cote d'Ivoire 0
Rustenburg, 26 May 1995

Scotland: G Hastings; Joiner, Stanger, Shiel, Logan; Chalmers, Redpath; Burnell, McKenzie, Wright, Campbell, Weir, Walton, Smith, Wainwright.
   Scorers – *Tries:* G Hastings 4, Walton 2, Logan 2, Chalmers, Stanger, Burnell, Wright, Shiel. *Conversions:* G Hastings 9. *Penalty goals:* G Hastings 2.

Cote d'Ivoire: Kouassi; Bouazo, Sathicq, Niakou, N'Gbala (Brito 40); Dali (capt, Camara 27), Dupont; Bley, Angoran, Djehi, Kone, Bado, Pere, Sanoko, Lassissi.

Referee: F Vito (Western Samoa).

Series score: Played 1, Scotland 1, Cote d'Ivoire 0.

France (6) 38, Tonga (0) 10
Pretoria, 26 May 1995

France: Sadourny; NTamack, Sella, Lacroix, Saint-Andre (capt); Delaigue, Hueber; Gallart, Gonzales, Armary, Merle, Brouzet, Benetton, Benazzi, Cecillon (Cabannes 58).
   Scorers – *Tries:* Lacroix 2, Hueber, Saint-Andre. *Conversions:* Lacroix 3. *Penalty goals:* Lacroix 3. *Dropped goal:* Delaigue.

Tonga: Tu'ipulotu; Taufa, U Va'enuku, Latu, T Va'enuku; E Vunipola, M Vunipola; Fe'ao, Masila (F Vunipola 10), Fukofuka, Lose, Mafi (Afeaki 76), Mahoni, Fenukitau, Otai (capt). Sent-off: Mahoni.
   Scorers – *Try:* T Va'enuku. *Conversion:* Tu'ipulotu.

Referee: S Lander (England).

Series score: Played 1, France 1, Tonga 0.

France (28) 54, Cote d'Ivoire (3) 18
Rustenburg, 30 May 1995

France: Viars; Techoueyres, Mesnel, Lacroix, Saint-Andre (capt); Delaigue (Deylaud 40), Accoceberry; Benezech, de Rougemont, Califano, Brouzet, Roumat, Costes, Cabannes, Benazzi (Benetton 71).
   Scorers – *Tries:* Lacroix 2, Benazzi, Accoceberry, Viars, Techoueyres, Costes, Saint-Andre. *Conversions:* Lacroix 4. *Penalty goals:* Lacroix 2.

Cote d'Ivoire: Kouassi; Soulama (Bouazo 80), Sathicq (capt), Niakou, Brito; Camara,

Dupont; Ezoua (Bley 43), Niamien, Djehi (Angoran 73), Aka, Sanoko (Dago 54), Pere, Okou, Lassissi (Kone 71).

Scorers – *Tries:* Camara, Soulama. *Conversion:* Kouassi. *Penalty goals:* Kouassi 2.

Referee: H Moon Soo (Korea).

Series score: Played 1, France 1, Cote d'Ivoire 0.

Scotland (18) 41, Tonga (5) 5
Pretoria, 30 May 1995

Scotland: G Hastings; Joiner, S Hastings, Jardine, Logan; Chalmers, Patterson; Hilton, Milne, Wright (Burnell 74), Cronin, Weir, Wainwright, Morrison, Peters.

Scorers – *Tries:* Peters, G Hastings, S Hastings. *Conversion:* G Hastings. *Penalty goals:* G Hastings 8.

Tonga: Tu'ipulotu; Taufa, U Va'enuku, Latu, T Va'enuku; E Vunipola, M Vunipola (Tufui 54); Fe'ao, F Vunipola, Fukofuka, Lose, Latukafu, Afeaki, Fenukitau, Otai (capt).

Scorer – *Try:* Fenukitau.

Referee: B Leask (Australia).

Series score: Played 1, Scotland 1, Tonga 0.

Tonga (24) 29, Cote d'Ivoire (0) 11
Rustenburg, 3 June 1995

Tonga: Tu'ipulotu; Latu, Mafile'o, U Va'enuku ('Isitolo 67), T Va'enuku; E Vunipola, Tufui; Fukofuka (Latua 50), F Vunipola, Talakai, Latukefu, Mafi, Afeaki (Fakaongo 63), Lose, Otai (capt).

Scorers – *Tries:* penalty try, Latukefu, Otai, Tu'ipulotu. *Conversions:* Tu'ipulotu 3. *Penalty goal:* Tu'ipuloyu.

Cote d'Ivoire: Kouassi; Soulama, Sathicq (capt), Niakou, Brito (Kouame 5); Camara (Dali 39), Dupont; Bley (Ezoua 40), Angoran (Sanoko 40), Djehi, Bado, Kone, Pere, Okou, Lassissi.

Scorers – *Try:* Okou. *Penalty goals:* Dali 2.

Series score: Played 1, Tonga 1, Cote d'Ivoire 0.

Scotland (13) 19, France (3) 22
Pretoria, 3 June 1995

Scotland: G Hastings (capt); Joiner, S Hastings, Shiel (Jardine 45), Logan; Chalmers, Redpath; Hilton, Milne, Wright (Burnell 68), Cronin, Weir, Wainwright, Morrison, Peters.

Scorers – Try: Wainwright. Conversion: G Hastings. Penalty goals: G Hastings 4.

France: Sadourny; NTamack, Sella, Lacroix, Saint-Andre (capt); Deylaud, Accoceberry (Hueber 33); Benezech, Gonzales, Califano, Merle, Roumat, Benazzi, Cabannes, Benetton (Cecillon 17).

Scorers – *Try:* NTamack. *Conversion:* Lacroix. *Penalty goals:* Lacroix 5.

Referee: W Erickson (Australia).

Series score: Played 67, Scotland 31, France 33, Drawn 3.

	P	W	L	F	A	Pts
France	3	3	0	114	47	9
Scotland	3	2	1	149	27	7
Tonga	3	1	2	44	90	5
Ivory Coast	3	0	3	29	172	3

A match of zero tension goes the way of the French despite their not managing a try until the 78th minute. Less than half of the 51,000 seats are taken and there is little to shout about for those who do show. This is a match for the goalkicking connoisseur, with Eric Elwood landing four out of four to put Ireland ahead on each occasion, but Thierry Lacroix responding in kind to tie the scores at 12–12 at half-time. Frenchman Lacroix goes on to equal the world record with eight successes, and converts the late tries from wings Philippe Saint-Andre and, following a 90-metre interception run, Emile NTamack. France deserve victory by virtue of a 2:1 ratio of lineout ball and 3:1 ratio of loose ball. But frustrated coach Pierre Berbizier moans: 'We can play champagne rugby if only we could get the cork out of the bottle.'

France (12) 36, Ireland (12) 12
Durban, 10 June 1995

France: Sadourny; NTamack, Sella, Lacroix, Saint-Andre (capt); Deylaud, Hueber; Armary, Gonzales, Califano, Merle, Roumat, Benazzi, Cabannes, Cecillon.
  Scorers – Tries: Saint-Andre, NTamack. *Conversion:* Lacroix. *Penalty goals:* Lacroix 8.

Ireland: O'Shea; D O'Mahony, Mullin, Bell, Geoghegan; Elwood, Hogan; Popplewell, Kingston (capt), Halpin, Fulcher (Halvey 60), Francis, Corkery, McBride, Johns.
  Scorer – Penalty goals: Elwood 4.

Referee: E Morrison (England).

Series score: Played 69, France 39, Ireland 25, Drawn 5.

*Rob Andrew drops the goal that knocks out World Champions Australia.
Michael Lynagh can only admire his footwork.*

South Africa (23) 42, Western Samoa (0) 14
Johannesburg, 10 June 1995

A match steeped in controversy, with referee Jim Fleming widely criticised for his laissez-faire attitude towards late tackles, belongs to the 'Black Pearl' Chester Williams who marks his eagerly-awaited debut in the tournament with four tries. However, his performance is overshadowed by continuous rough-house tactics, highlighted by the dangerous tackle by Samoan fullback Mike Umaga which puts opposite number Andre Joubert out of the game with a broken hand. Umaga is later cited by competition chiefs and handed a 90-day ban, reduced on appeal to 60..

South Africa: Joubert (Venter 19); Johnson, Scholtz, Mulder, Williams; le Roux, van der Westhuizen; du Randt, Rossouw, Swart, Wiese (Drotske 76), Andrews (Otto 70), Pienaar (capt), Kruger (Richter 48), Straeuli.
Scorers – Tries: Williams 4, Rossouw, Andrews. *Conversions:* Johnson 3. *Penalty goal:* Johnson 2.

Western Samoa: Umaga; Lima, Vaega, Fa'amasino, Harder (Tuilagi 40); Sini, Nu'uali'itia; Mika (Reidy 74), Leiasamaivao, Latu (Fatialofa 64), Lemanea, Falaniko, Tatupu, Paramore (Vaifale 71), Lam (capt). Cited: Umaga (90-day ban).
Scorers – Tries: Nu'uali'itia, Tatupu. *Conversions:* Fa'amasino 2.

Referee: J Fleming (Scotland).

Series score: Played 2, South Africa 2, Western Samoa 0.

England (13) 25, Australia (6) 22
Cape Town, 11 June 1995

'The biggest day for English rugby and a great day for England' is how manager Jack Rowell greets the dramatic defeat of world champions Australia, courtesy of Rob Andrew's dropped goal, two minutes 36 seconds into stoppage time. England, who had surged 13-3 ahead with Tony Underwood's cracking try, fall 19-16 behind when Damian Smith leaps to spectacularly take an up-and-under and roll over the try-line, and Michael Lynagh's boot does the rest. But Albion steadfastly refuse to succumb to their 1991 final conquerors and when Andrew levels the scores with his fifth penalty four minutes from time the scene is set for a glorious finale.

England: Catt; T Underwood, Carling (capt), Guscott, R Underwood; Andrew, Morris; Leonard, Moore, Ubogu, Johnson, Bayfield, Rodber, Clarke, Richards (Ojomoh TR).
Scorers – Try: T Underwood. *Conversion:* Andrew. *Penalty goals:* Andrew 5. *Dropped goal:* Andrew.

Australia: Burke; Smith, Little, Horan, Campese; Lynagh (capt), Gregan; Crowley, Kearns, McKenzie, McCall, Eales, Ofahengaue, Wilson, Gavin.
Scorers – Try: Smith. *Conversion:* Lynagh. *Penalty goals:* Lynagh 5.

Referee: D Bishop (New Zealand).

Series score: Played 19, England 7, Australia 12.

New Zealand (17) 48, Scotland (9) 30
Pretoria, 11 June 1995

Scotland become the first side ever to inflict 30 points on the All Black machine...and lose. Despite their scoring heroics a woeful tartan defence allows New Zealand to advance to the semi-finals. Jonah Lomu knocks down the door with two storming runs that yield two tries and thereafter the straight running of Walter Little, allied to some great opportunism and powder-puff defending, sees New Zealand home comfortably. Andrew Mehrtens is again outstanding, despite missing five penalty kicks at goal, and seals a 23-point day with an electrifying 50-metre burst and touch down. Scotland still haven't beaten New Zealand.

New Zealand: Wilson; Ellis, Bunce, Little, Lomu; Mehrtens, Bachop; Loe, Fitzpatrick (capt), Brown, Jones, R Brooke, Joseph, Kronfeld, Z Brooke.

Scorers – Tries: Little 2, Lomu, Mehrtens, Bunce, Fitzpatrick. *Conversions:* Mehrtens 6. *Penalty goals:* Mehrtens 2.

Scotland: G Hastings (capt); Joiner, S Hastings, Shiel, Logan; Chalmers (Jardine 40), Redpath; Hilton, Milne, Wright, Cronin (Campbell 62), Weir, Wainwright, Morrison, Peters.

Scorers – Tries: Weir 2, S Hastings. *Conversions:* G Hastings 3. *Penalty goals:* G Hastings 3.

Referee: D Bevan (Wales).

Series score: Played 18, New Zealand 16, Scotland 0, Drawn 2.

SEMI-FINALS

France (6) 15, South Africa (10) 19
Durban, 17 June 1995

Never in the field of Rugby World Cup conflict have so many been so soaked. They say it doesn't rain much in Durban, which is why most of the 52,000-seater King's Park is not under cover. No-one who survives this remarkable afternoon wants to hear that any more. Referee Derek Bevan delays the game by an hour an a half, fearing a player could actually 'drown' if trapped under a ruck or collapsed scrum on the sodden surface. But cometh the hour (finally) cometh the men and 31 players produce a gripping encounter. South Africa lead from the second minute, when Joel Stransky kicks the first of his four penalty goals (from seven attempts), and try as France do (with Thierry Lacroix landing five of his six penaltiy shots) they never get even. But unlucky they certainly are. Emile NTamack is denied what looks a pucka try and in the same second-half Abdel Benazzi comes up inches short. The thing is you can only go to the well so often. A stoppage time try to beat Scotland, two more in the last minute against Ireland: the French can't really complain ... and to his credit coach Pierre Berbizier does not. As for South Africa, it's party time.

France: Sadourny; NTamack, Sella, Lacroix, Saint-Andre (capt); Deylaud, Galthie; Armary, Gonzales, Califano, Merle, Roumat, Benazzi, Cabannes, Cecillon.

Scorer – Penalty goals: Lacroix 5.

South Africa: Joubert; Small, Mulder, le Roux, Williams; Stransky, van der Westhuizen (Roux 51); du Randt, Rossouw, Swart, Wiese, Strydom, Pienaar (capt), Kruger, Andrews.

Scorers – Try: Kruger. *Conversion:* Stransky. *Penalty goals:* Stransky 4.

Referee: D Bevan (Wales).

Series score: Played 24, France 5, South Africa 14, Drawn 5.

New Zealand (25) 45, England (3) 29
Cape Town, 18 June 1995

New Zealand produce one of the great All Black performances in the first half to blow away the much vaunted England side. Stung by criticism of their slipshod display in dispatching Scotland (still by 48 points), the Kiwis go on the rampage led, predictably, by the marauding Jonah Lomu. Juggernaut Jonah blasts over in only the second minute for the first of his stunning four tries and shell-shocked England go on to concede more points than they have ever before in an international. Josh Kronfeld and Zinzan Brooke, who claims an outrageous dropped goal from fully 40 metres, are also outstanding. So powerful is New Zealand's opening burst that they are 12–0 up after four minutes, 25–0 clear in 26 minutes. England battle back gamely to 'win' the second-half 26–20, with Rory Underwood nabbing two tries to make him the World Cup's all-time leading try scorer (with 11) and Will Carling also bagging a brace of touchdowns, but the affect is purely cosmetic. The contest is long since over.

New Zealand: Osborne; Wilson, Bunce, Little, Lomu; Mehrtens, Bachop; Dowd, Fitzpatrick (capt), Brown, Jones, R Brooke, Brewer, Kronfeld, Z Brooke (Larsen 63).
    Scorers – Tries: Lomu 4, Kronfeld, Bachop. *Conversions:* Mehrtens 3. *Penalty goal:* Mehrtens. *Dropped goals:* Z Brooke, Mehrtens.

England: Catt; T Underwood, Carling (capt), Guscott, R Underwood; Andrew, Morris; Leonard, Moore, Ubogu, Johnson, Bayfield, Rodber, Clarke, Richards.
    Scorers – Tries: R Underwood 2, Carling 2. *Conversions:* Andrew 3. *Penalty goal:* Andrew.

Referee: S Hilditch (Ireland).

Series score: Played 17, England 3, New Zealand 14.

THIRD PLACE PLAY-OFF

France (3) 19, England (3) 9
Pretoria, 22 June 1995

It could be said that anyone attending a third place play-off deserves what he or she gets. But in this case such an observation would be harsh. Only days after suffering the acute disappointment of semi-final defeat, and playing for nothing more tangible than the right not to pre-qualify for the 1999 tournament, the pride of the northern hemisphere serve up

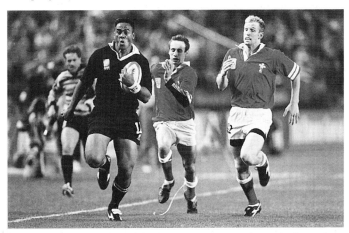

Jonah Lomu leads Wales' backs Wayne Proctor and Gareth Thomas a merry dance in Johannesburg.

419

a feast that would not satisfy a gnat. And no excuses can explain this one away. If ever there is a game in which England can throw caution to the wind, realise the running potential they are forever harping on about, it is in front of 45,000 hungry fans in Loftus Versfeld. Just as there is precious little to gain from victory, there is next to nothing to lose ... unless you produce the lifeless performance England do. France are only marginally more ambitious but that is easily enough. The excellent Olivier Roumat – rivalled for man of the match by Abdel Benazzi, Laurent Cabannes and Dewi Morris – scores France's first try with burly wing Emile NTamack popping up for his customary late score.

France: Sadourny; NTamack, Sella, Lacroix, Saint-Andre (capt); Mesnel, Galthie; Califano, Gonzales, Benezech, Merle, Roumat, Benazzi, Cabannes, Cigagna.
  Scorers – Tries: Roumat, NTamack. *Penalty goals:* Lacroix 3.

England: Catt; Hunter, Carling (capt), Guscott, R Underwood; Andrew, Morris; Leonard, Moore, Ubogu, Johnson, Bayfield, Rodber, Clarke, Ojomoh.
  Scorer – Penalty goals: Andrew 3.

Referee: D Bishop (New Zealand).
Series score: Played 72, France 25, England 40, Drawn 7.

FINAL

South Africa (6) 15, New Zealand (6) 12
(aet. 12-12 after 80 minutes) Johannesburg, 24 June 1995

Ultimately, the destiny of the William Webb Ellis Trophy comes down to two dropped goal attempts. The first, from All Black fly-half Andrew Mehrtens two minutes from the end of normal time, with the scores locked at 12-12, is missed. The second, 12 minutes into extra time from Springbok No10 Joel Stransky, is as measured as Mehrtens' had been rushed. The ball splits the uprights, Ellis Park erupts, and the Rainbow Nation, President Nelson Mandela included, goes absolutely beserk. Eight long minutes later English whistler Ed Morrison blows for time and inspirational Springbok captain Francois Pienaar, his face awash with tears, calls his team mates to prayer. Amid the cacophony of sound, South Africa's heroes each go down on one knee and thank the Lord. The mood in the All Black camp does not bear consideration. They can only reflect on the intense frustration of an afternoon spent caged up, Juggernaut Jonah included, by the Boks. Having scaled unimaginable heights the previous week against England, the pain of failure is excruciating. All this the day after the announcement of a £366 million deal to give the Southern Hemisphere it's three-country equivalent of the Five Nations Championship. But if any cynic sees a link between that and the first try-less contest of World Cup '95, forget it. This is a contest beyond compare. This is one of the truly great rugby matches. Absorbing, gripping, utterly compelling. The might of New Zealand against the emotion-charged host nation. Bookies make the All Blacks favourites, by a ten-point margin, but their calculations fail to take into account the Springboks' hunger. Just as England had underestimated New Zealand the week before, so the Kiwis set to much store in their apparent strengths. Perhaps they forget they had not previously come up against Southern Hemisphere opposition. They will certainly be reminded of it for the next four years.

South Africa: Joubert; Small (Venter 98), Mulder, le Roux, Williams; Stransky, van der Westhuizen; du Randt, Rossouw, Swart (Pagel 69), Wiese, Strydom, Pienaar (capt), Kruger, Andrews (Straeuli 90).
  Scorer – Penalty goals: Stransky 3. *Dropped goals:* Stransky 2.

New Zealand: Osborne; Wilson (Ellis 56), Bunce, Little, Lomu; Mehrtens, Bachop (Strachan TR, 66-71); Dowd (Loe 83), Fitzpatrick (capt), Brown, Jones, R Brooke, Brewer

(Joseph 40), Kronfeld, Z Brooke.
  Scorer – Penalty goals: Mehrtens 2. *Dropped goal:* Mehrtens.
Referee: E Morrison (England).
Series score: Played x, South Africa x, New Zealand x, Drawn x.

WORLD CUP ROLL OF HONOUR

1987 – New Zealand (beat France 29-9)
1991 – Australia (beat England 12-6)
1995 – South Africa (beat New Zealand 15-12 aet)
Series score: Played 3, Southern Hemisphere 3, Northern Hemisphere 0.

WORLD CUP RECORDS

Leading points scorers in 1995 World Cup

	Tries	Cons	Pens	Drops	Total
Thierry Lacroix (France)	4	7	26	–	112
Gavin Hastings (Scotland)	5	14	17	–	104
Andrew Mehrtens (NZ)	1	14	14	3	84
Rob Andrew (England)	–	5	26	3	78
Michael Lynagh (Australia)	2	5	9	–	47
Joel Stransky (South Africa)	1	4	13	3	61
Simon Culhane (NZ)	1	20	–	–	45
Neil Jenkins (Wales)	–	7	8	1	41

Leading try scorers in 1995 World Cup

Jonah Lomu	(New Zealand)	7
Marc Ellis	(New Zealand)	7
Rory Underwood	(England)	5
Gavin Hastings	(Scotland)	5
Chester Williams	(South Africa)	4
Thierry Lacroix	(France)	4
Adriaan Richter	(South Africa)	4

Most points in World Cup rugby:

227 Gavin Hastings (Scotland)
195 Michael Lynagh (Australia)
170 Grant Fox (New Zealand)

Most points in a match:

145 New Zealand v Japan (1995)
 89 Scotland v Cote d'Ivoire (1995)
 74 New Zealand v Fiji (1987)

Most points in a match (individual):

 45 Simon Culhane (1t, 20c: New Zealand v Japan, 1995)
 44 Gavin Hastings (4t, 9c, 2p: Scotland v Cote d'Ivoire, 1995)
 31 Gavin Hastings (1t, 1c, 8p: Scotland v Tonga, 1995)

Most tries:
- 11 Rory Underwood (England)
- 10 David Campese (Australia)
- 9 Gavin Hastings (Scotland)
- 7 Jonah Lomu, Marc Ellis, John Kirwan (all New Zealand), Iwan Tukalo (Scotland)

Most tries in a match:
- 21 New Zealand v Japan (1995)
- 13 Scotland v Cote d'Ivoire (1995)
  France v Zimbabwe (1987)

Most tries in a match (individual):
- 6 Marc Ellis (New Zealand v Japan, 1995)
- 4 Jonah Lomu (New Zealand v England, 1995), Chester Williams (South Africa v Western Samoa, 1995), Brian Robinson (Ireland v Zimbabwe, 1991), Ieuan Evans (Wales v Canada, 1987), Craig Green (New Zealand v Fiji, 1987), John Gallagher (New Zealand v Fiji, 1987)

Most conversions:
- 39 Gavin Hastings (Scotland)
- 37 Grant Fox (New Zealand)
- 36 Michael Lynagh (Australia)

Most conversions in a match:
- 20 Simon Culhane (New Zealand v Japan, 1995)
- 10 Grant Fox (New Zealand v Fiji, 1987)
- 9 Gavin Hastings (Scotland v Cote d'Ivoire, 1995); Didier Camberabero (France v Zimbabwe, 1987)

Most penalty goals (individual):
- 36 Gavin Hastings (Scotland)
- 33 Michael Lynagh (Australia)
- 31 Grant Fox (New Zealand)
- 30 Thierry Lacroix (France)
- 26 Rob Andrew (England)

Most penalty goals in a match (individual):
- 8 Gavin Hastings (Scotland v Tonga, 1995); Thierry Lacroix (France v Ireland, 1995)
- 6 Rob Andrew (England v Argentina, 1995); Grant Fox (New Zealand v Scotland, 1987),
  Grant Fox (New Zealand v Argentina, 1987)

Most dropped goals (individual):
- 5 Rob Andrew (England)
- 3 Joel Stransky (South Africa), Abdrew Mehrtens (New Zealand), Jonathan Davies (Wales)

Most dropped goals in a match (team):
- 3 Fiji v Romania (1991)

THE YEAR'S RESULTS

SOUTH AFRICA TO NEW ZEALAND
June-August 1994: P14 W10 D1 L3 F345 A241.

The sixth Springbok tour to New Zealand is an unhappy experience for the visitors who come preciously close to becoming the first ever South African side to be whitewashed in a Test series. They do become the first Springbok side to fail to win at least one Test and suffer the disgrace of having prop Johan le Roux banned for biting the ear of All Black skipper Sean Fitzpatrick during the second Test. Off the park South Africa's efforts are undermined by disharmony amongst the hierarchy, culminating in SARFU president Louis Luyt threatening to quit if 'has-beens', tour manager Jannie Engelbrecht and coach Ian McIntosh, don't fall on their swords. They have little choice. By contrast New Zealand, having suffered the ignominy of losing a first ever home Test series to France, and 2–0 at that, can be well satisfied with their series.

PARTY: J Allan (Natal – 2,3R,4,8,10,12,14); K Andrews (Western Province – 2,3R,4,7,9,11,12,14); M Andrews (Natal – 2,3,6,8,10,12,14); S Atherton (Natal – 2,3,4R,6,9,10,12,14); C Badenhorst (OFS – 2,4,5,7,9,11,13); W Bartmann (Natal – 2*); J Claassens (Northern Transvaal – 1,4,5,7,9,11,13); J Dalton (Transvaal – 1,3,5,7,8R,9,11,13); A Geldenhuys (Eastern Province – 7,8R,9,11,13); G Johnson (Transvaal – 13,14); A Joubert (Natal – 2,4,6,8,10R,11,12,14); G Kebble (Natal – 2,4,5,7,8,10,13; R Kruger (Northern Transvaal – 4,5,7,9,11,13); H le Roux (Transvaal – 2,3,6,8,10,11,12,14); J le Roux (Transvaal – 1,3,5,8,10); O le Roux (OFS – 8R,9,11,13); F A Meiring (Northern Transvaal – 1,3R,4,5,7,9,13); J Mulder (Transvaal – 8,10,11,12,14); P Muller (Natal – 2,3,6); K Otto (Northern Transvaal – 1,4,5,7,8,); F Pienaar (capt, Transvaal – 1*,3*,9*,10*,12*,14*); A Richter (Northern Transvaal – 2,4*,5,6,9,10,12,14); J Roux (Transvaal – 2,3,6,8,10,11R,12,14); L Sherrell (Northern Transvaal – 1,4,5,7,9,13); J Small (Natal – 1,3,6,8,10,12); R Straeuli (Transvaal – 1,2R,3,5R,6,7*,8,12); T Strauss (Western Province – 1,3,5,6*,7R,8*,10,11*,13*); B Swart (Transvaal – 1,3); T van Rensburg (Transvaal – 1,3,4R,5,7,9,10); B Venter (OFS – 2,3,6,8,10,12,14); N Wegner (Western Province – 11,13); C van der Westhuizen (Natal – 1,2,3,7,9,11,13); J van der Westhuizen (Northern Transvaal – 1,2R,4,5,7,8R,9,11,13); F van Heerden (Western Province – 2,3R,4,57,9,11,13,14); K Wiese (Transvaal – 4); C Williams ((Western Province – 4,5,6,8,10,12,14).

RESULTS: (1) King Country 10, Springboks 46 (Taupo, 23 June); (2) Counties 26, Springboks 37 (Pukekohe, 25 June); (3) Wellington 26, Springboks 36 (Wellington, 28 June); (4) Southland 15, Springboks 51 (Invercargill, 2 July); (5) Hanan Shield XV 19, Springboks 67 (Timaru, 5 July); (6) first Test: New Zealand 22, South Africa 14 (Dunedin, 9 July); (7) Taranaki 12, Springboks 16 (New Plymouth, 13 July); (8) Waikato 17, Springboks 38 (Hamilton, 16 July); (9) Manawatu 21, Springboks 47 (Palmerston North, 19 July); (10) second Test: New Zealand 13, South Africa 9 (Wellington 23 July); (11) Otago 19, Springboks 12 (Dunedin, 27 July); (12) Canterbury 11, Springboks 21 (Christchurch, 30 July); (13) Bay of Plenty 12, Springboks 33 (Rotorua, 2 August); (14) third Test: New Zealand 18, South Africa 18 (Auckland, 6 August).

King Country 10, Springboks 46
Taupo, 23 June 1994

Canterbury: W Te Huia; J Wells, J Sim, L Langkilde, M Seavill; R Daly, C Wills; J Veitayaki, P Mitchell, P Coffin (capt), G Stanton, F Fakaongo, H Morgan, D Anglesey, H Nelson.
    Scorers – *Try:* penalty try. *Conversion:* Te Huia. *Penalty goal:* Daly.

Springboks: van Rensburg; C van der Westhuizen, Claassens, Meiring, Small; Sherrell, J van der Westhuizen; Swart, Dalton, J le Roux, Wiese, Otto, Pienaar (capt), Straeuli, Strauss.
    Scorers – *Tries:* Otto, Straeuli, Strauss, C van der Westhuizen, Small, penalty try. *Conversions:* van Rensburg 3, Sherrell 2. *Penalty goals:* Sherrell 2.

Referee: D Bishop (Otago).

Counties 26, Springboks 37
Pukekohe, 25 June 1994

Counties: D Sheppard; D Henare, G Millington, T Marsh, L Foai; D Love, M Scott; T Barchard, A Roose, L Lidgard, J Coe, C Rose, J Atuahiva, J Paramore, E Brain (capt).
    Scorers – *Tries:* Foai, Barchard. *Conversions:* Love 2. *Penalty goals:* Love 4.

*Chester Williams heads for one of his four tries in South Africa's
World Cup quarter-final defeat of Western Samoa.*

424

Springboks: Joubert; C van der Westhuizen, Venter, Muller, Badenhorst; H le Roux, Roux (J van der Westhuizen 73); Kebble, Allan, K Andrews, M Andrews, Atherton, Bartmann (capt, Straeuli 76), F van Heerden, Richter.

    Scorers – *Tries:* Roux 2, le Roux, Venter, Straeuli. *Conversions:* Joubert 3. *Penalty goals:* Joubert 2.

Referee: R Hill.

Wellington 26, Springboks 36
Athletic Park, 28 June 1994

Wellington: S Doyle; T Umaga, S Cottrell, A Ieremia, A Taufa; S Mannix (capt), E Moncrieff; M Edwards, T Mannix, S McDowell, M Russell, C Trevaskis, D Tuiavii, G Simpson, F Tiatia.

    Scorers – *Tries:* Doyle 2, Umaga. *Conversion:* Moncrieff. *Penalty goals:* Moncrieff 3.

Springboks: van Rensburg; C van der Westhuizen, Venter, Muller (Meiring), Small; H le Roux, Roux; Swart, Dalton (Allan), J le Roux (K Andrews), M Andrews, Atherton, Pienaar (capt, van Heerden), Straeuli, Strauss.

    Scorers – *Tries:* van Rensburg 2, Venter, Strauss, Allan. *Conversion:* van Rensburg. *Penalty goals:* van Rensburg 3.

Referee: P O'Brien (Southland).

Southland 15, Springboks 51
Invercargill, 2 July 1994

Southland: E Todd; R Stodart, G Beardsley, P Johnston, P Dynes; S Culhane, J Marshall; R Borland (S Hay 72), D Heaps, C Corbett, W Miller, M Tinnock, B Morton, B Shepherd, S Harvey (capt).

    Scorers – *Tries:* Todd, Stoddart. *Conversion:* Culhane. *Penalty goal:* Culhane.

Springboks: Joubert (van Rensburg 70); Williams, Claassens, Meiring, Badenhorst; Sherrell, J van der Westhuizen; Kebble, Allan, K Andrews, Wiese (Atherton 57), Otto, Kruger, van Heerden, Richter (capt).

    Scorers – *Tries:* Richter 2, Claasens, Kruger, Badenhorst 3, Atherton. *Conversions:* Joubert 4. *Penalty goal:* Joubert.

Referee: J Taylor.

Hanan Shield XV 19, Springboks 67
Timaru, 5 July 1994

Hanan Shield XV: D Hunter; S Todd, S Tarrant, B Laney, H Hunt; C Gard, B Matthews; R Morgan, R McArthur, D McCrea, T Gresham, V Muir, J Simpson, S Wills, J Mawhinney (J Smith).

    Scorers – *Tries:* Todd 2, penalty try. *Conversions:* Laney 2.

Springboks: van Rensburg; Williams, Claassens, Meiring, Badenhorst; Sherrell, J van der Westhuizen; Kebble, Dalton, J le Roux, van Heerden, Otto, Kruger, Richter, Strauss (capt, Straeuli).

    Scorers – *Tries:* Williams, Sherrell 2, Claassens, Badenhorst 2, J van der Westhuizen, van Rensburg 2, Strauss, Meiring. *Conversions:* van Rensburg 6.

Referee: D Ross (North Harbour).

New Zealand 22, South Africa 14
first Test: Dunedin, 9 July 1994

New Zealand: S Howarth; J Kirwan, F Bunce, A Ieremia, J Timu; S Bachop, G Bachop; R

Loe, S Fitzpatrick (capt), O Brown, M Cooksley, I Jones (A Pene 10, C Dowd 74), B Larsen, M Brewer, Z Brooke.
  Scorers – Try: Kirwan. Conversion: Howarth. Penalty goals: Howarth 5.

South Africa: Joubert; Small, Muller, Venter, Williams; H le Roux, Roux; J le Roux, Allan, Swart (Kebble 23), Atherton, M Andrews, Richter, Straeuli, Strauss (capt).
  Scorers – Try: Straeuli. Penalty goals: Joubert 3.

Referee: B Stirling (Ireland).

Series score: Played 39, New Zealand 17, South Africa 20, Drawn 2.

Taranaki 12, Springboks 16
New Plymouth, 13 July 1994

Taranaki: K Crowley; T Wolfe, D Asi, K Eynon, F Mahoni; J Cameron, R Yarman; M Allen (capt), S McDonald, G Slater, J Roache, S Lines, R Wheeler, S Tiatia, A Slater.
  Scorer – Penalty goals: Crowley 4.

Springboks: van Rensburg; C van der Westhuizen, Claassens, Meiring, Badenhorst; Sherrell, J van der Westhuizen; Kebble, Dalton, K Andrews, Geldenhuys, Otto, Kruger (Strauss 58), van Heerden, Straeuli (capt).
  Scorer – Try: van Rensburg. Conversion: van Rensburg. Penalty goals: van Rensburg 3.

Referee: B Smallridge (Auckland).

Waikato 17, Springboks 38
Hamilton, 16 July 1994

Waikato: A Strawbridge; W Warlow, R Ellison, M Cooper, J Walters; I Foster, S Crabb; C Stevenson, W Gatland, P Martin, M Cooksley, S Gordon (T Coventry), R Jerram, D Monkley, J Mitchell (capt).
  Scorers – Tries: Warlow, Cooksley. Conversions: Cooper 2. Penalty goal: Cooper.

Springboks: Joubert; Williams, Venter, Mulder, Small; H le Roux, Roux; Kebble (O le Roux), Allan (J van der Westhuizen), J le Roux, M Andrews (Dalton), Otto, van Heerden, Straeuli (Geldenhuys), Strauss (capt).
  Scorers – Tries: Small 2, Venter, Mulder, Allan. Conversions: Joubert 5. Penalty goal: Joubert.

Referee: C Hawke (Canterbury).

Manawatu 21, Springboks 47
Palmerston North, 19 July 1994

Manawatu: J Smith; C Fowler, W Furnell, C Izatt, J Whyte; J Holland, G Baines; G Nesdale, P Doyle (capt), G Hurunui (S Halford 53), M 'Otai, A McKellar, B Hansen, D Rowe, K Williams.
  Scorers – Tries: Izatt, Hurunui. Conversion: Holland. Penalty goals: Holland 3.

Springboks: van Rensburg; C van der Westhuizen, Claassens, Meiring, Badenhorst; Sherrell, J van der Westhuizen; O le Roux, Dalton, K Andrews, Geldenhuys, Atherton, Pienaar (capt), Kruger, Richter.
  Scorers – Tries: Badenhorst 2, C van der Westhuizen, Claassens, J van der Westhuizen, O le Roux. Conversions: van Rensburg 4. Penalty goals: van Rensburg 3.

Referee: S Walsh (Wellington).

New Zealand (10) 13, South Africa (6) 9
second Test: Wellington, 23 July 1994

New Zealand: S Howarth; J Kirwan, F Bunce (W Little 73), A Ieremia, J Timu; S Bachop,

G Bachop; R Loe, S Fitzpatrick (capt), O Brown, M Cooksley, R Brooke, B Larsen, M Brewer, Z Brooke.
Scorers – *Tries:* Z Brooke, Timu. Penalty goal: Howarth.

South Africa: van Rensburg (Joubert 74); Small, Mulder, Venter, Williams; H le Roux, Roux; Kebble, Allan, J le Roux, Atherton, M Andrews, Strauss, Pienaar (capt), Richter.
Scorer – Penalty goals: Van Rensburg 3.

Referee: B Stirling (Ireland).

Series score: Played 40, New Zealand 18, South Africa 20, Drawn 2.

Otago 19, Springboks 12
Dunedin, 27 July 1994

Otago: J Timu; P Cooke, J Leslie, M Ellis, J Wilson; S Bachop, S Forster; R Lawton, D Latta (capt), N Moore, A Campbell, A Rich, J Joseph, J Kronfeld, A Pene.
Scorers – *Try:* Leslie. *Conversion:* Wilson. *Penalty goals:* Wilson 4.

Springboks: Joubert; C van der Westhuizen, Claassens, Mulder, Badenhorst; H le Roux, J van der Westhuizen (Roux 78); O le Roux, Dalton, K Andrews, Geldenhuys, Wegner, Kruger, van Heerden, Strauss (capt).
Scorers – *Tries:* H le Roux, J van der Westhuizen. *Conversion:* H le Roux.

Referee: G Wahlstrom.

Canterbury 11, Springboks 21
Christchurch, 30 July 1994

Canterbury: S Forrest; A Prince, M Mayerhofler, T Matson, P Bale; A Mehrtens, G Bachop; S Loe, M Sexton, R Loe, M McAtamney, G Kelly, T Blackadder, M Brewer (capt), R Penney.
Scorers – *Try:* Mayerhofler. *Penalty goals:* Mehrtens 2.

Springboks: Joubert; Williams, Venter, Mulder, Small; H le Roux, Roux; Swart, Allan, K Andrews, Atherton, M Andrews, Pienaar (capt), Straeuli, Richter.
Scorers – *Tries:* Mulder 2. *Conversion:* Joubert. *Penalty goals:* Joubert 3.

Referee: A Riley (Waikato).

Bay of Plenty 12, Springboks 33
Rotorua, 2 August 1994

Bay of Plenty: D Kaui; S Whareaorere, W Clark (K Pryor 72), C Bidois, D Menzies; D Stone, J Tauiwi; S Simpkins, R George (capt), W Morehu, S Axtens, P Weedon, J Winiata, B Sinkinson, M McGregor.
Scorers – *Tries:* Winiata, Sinkinson. *Conversion:* Stone.

Springboks: Johnson; C van der Westhuizen, Claassens, Meiring, Badenhorst; Sherrell, J van der Westhuizen; O le Roux, Dalton, Kebble, Geldenhuys, Wegner, Kruger, van Heerden, Strauss (capt).
Scorers – *Tries:* Meiring, Sherrell, J van der Westhuizen, Kebble. *Conversions:* Johnson 2. *Penalty goals:* Johnson 3.

Referee: Mike Fitzgibbons (Canterbury).

New Zealand (9) 18, South Africa (12) 18
third Test: Auckland, 6 August 1994

New Zealand: S Howarth; J Kirwan, F Bunce, A Ieremia, J Timu; S Bachop, G Bachop; R Loe, S Fitzpatrick (capt), O Brown, R Brooke, I Jones, B Larsen (M Jones 44), M Brewer, Z Brooke.

Scorer – Penalty goals: Howarth 6.

South Africa: A Joubert; G Johnson, J Mulder, B Venter, C Williams; H le Roux, J Roux; B Swart, J Allan, K Andrews, S Atherton, M Andrews, F Pienaar (capt), F van Heerden, A Richter.

Scorers – *Try:* Johnson, Venter. *Conversion:* Johnson. *Penalty goals:* Johnson 2.

Referee: R Yemen (Wales).

Series score: Played 41, New Zealand 18, South Africa 20, Drawn 3.

ITALY TO AUSTRALIA
June 1994: P8 W6 D0 L2 F268 A133

World Cup-bound Italy enhance their credentials as a global force with an impressive tour Down Under. A maximum six wins in the warm-up matches, including a 21–19 defeat of Super Ten champions Queensland, serve as a prelude to two tight Tests against the world champion Wallabies. Australia only sneak home by three points at Ballymore in the first match.

RESULTS: (1) Northern Territory 6, Italy 37; (2) South Australia 12, Italy 60; (3) Sydney 20, Italy 36; (4) Queensland 19, Italy 21; (5) Queensland Country 13, Italy 57; (6) first Test: Australia 23, Italy 20; (7) NSW Country 20, Italy 30; (8) second Test: Australia 20, Italy 7.

Wales captain Mike Hall breaks the Japanese cover.

Australia 23, Italy 20
first Test: Brisbane, 18 June 1994

Australia: M Burke; D Smith, D Herbert, R Tombs, D Campese; M Lynagh (capt, T Wallace 60), G Gregan; T Daly, P Kearns (capt), E McKenzie, G Morgan, J Eales, I Tabua, D Wilson, T Gavin.

Scorers – *Tries:* Herbert, Burke. *Conversions:* Lynagh, Wallace. *Penalty goals:* Lynagh 2, Wallace.

Italy: P Vaccari; Marcello Cuttitta, E Filizzola (S Bordon), M Bonomi, M Gerosa; L Troiani, A Troncon; F Propertzi, C Orlandi, Massimo Cuttitta, M Giancheri, R Favaro, M Giovanelli (capt), O Arancio, C Checchinato.

Scorers – *Try:* Bonomi. *Penalty goals:* Troiani 5.

Referee: I Rogers (South Africa).

Series score: Played 4, Australia 4, Italy 0.

Australia 20, Italy 7
second Test: Melbourne, 26 June 1994

Australia: M Pini; D Smith, D Herbert, M Burke, R Tombs, D Campese; T Wallace, G Gregan; T Daly, P Kearns (capt), E McKenzie, R McCall, J Eales, I Tabua, D Wilson, T Gavin.

Scorers – *Try:* Campese. *Penalty goals:* Wallace 5.

Italy: P Vaccari; Marcello Cuttitta, S Bordon, M Bonomi, M Gerosa; L Troiani, A Troncon; F Propertzi, C Orlandi, Massimo Cuttitta, M Giancheri, R Favaro, M Giovanelli (capt), O Arancio, C Checchinato.

Scorers – *Try:* Orlandi. *Conversion:* Troiani.

Referee: I Rogers (South Africa).

Series score: Played 5, Australia 5, Italy 0.

WESTERN SAMOA TO AUSTRALIA
July-August 1994: P5 W4 D0 L1 F147 A152.

Australia produce a stunning performance to annihilate Western Samoa 73–3, a winning score and margin that surpasses their previous record 67–9 defeat of the US Eagles in 1990. The result is all the more remarkable for the fact the Samoans have beaten Super Ten champions Queensland only a week earlier. The Wallabies spread 11 tries among nine players.

RESULTS: (1) Victoria 26, Western Samoa 60; (2) Australian Capital Territory 3, Western Samoa 39; (3) Queensland 22, Western Samoa 24; (4) New South Wales XV 18, Western Samoa 21; (5) Test: Australia 73, Western Samoa 3.

Australia (23) 73, Western Samoa (3) 3
Sydney, 6 August 1994

Australia: M Pini (D Junee 64); D Campese, J Little (D Herbert 70), P Howard, D Smith; D Knox, G Gregan; T Daly, P Kearns (capt), E McKenzie, G Morgan, J Eales, W Ofahengaue, D Wilson, T Gavin.

Scorers – *Tries:* Little 2, Ofahengaue, Howard, Campese, Gavin, Pini, Junee, Smith 2, Gregan. *Conversions:* Knox 6. *Penalty goals:* Knox 2.

Western Samoa: A Aiolupo; B Lima, T Vaega, F Tuilagi, T Samamia; D Kellett, V Vitale (T

Nu'uali'ita); P Fatialofa (capt), S To'omalatai, G Latu, M Keenan, M Birtwhistle, D Mika, S Vaifale, P Lam (M Tupeli 51).

Scorer – Penalty goal: Kellett.

Referee: G Wahlstrom (New Zealand).

Series score: Played 2, Australia 2, Western Samoa 0.

BLEDISLOE CUP

Australia 20, New Zealand 16
Sydney, 17 August 1994 (Australia regain Bledisloe Cup)

In the end it all comes down to one tackle. New Zealand, down 16–20 having recovered from 3–17, are poised to reclaim the Bledisloe Cup under the floodlit Sydney night sky. Golden boy Jeff Wilson, he of the debut try hat-trick against Scotland in 1993, romps past four Wallaby defenders. With time up on referee Ed Morrison's clock and the Aussies' unbeaten year similarly about to expire, the smallest player on the park flashes into view and thunders into Wilson. The ball spills and George Gregan, a scrum-half with everything to prove, transforms himself from zero to hero in one fell swoop.

Australia: M Pini (D Junee 69); D Smith, J Little, P Howard, D Campese; D Knox, G Gregan; T Daly, P Kearns (capt), E McKenzie, G Morgan, J Eales, W Ofahengaue, D Wilson, T Gavin.

Scorers – *Tries:* Little, Kearns. *Conversions:* Knox 2. *Penalty goals:* Knox 2.

New Zealand: S Howarth; J Wilson, F Bunce, W Little, J Timu; S Bachop, G Bachop; R Loe, S Fitzpatrick (capt), O Brown, M Cooksley, I Jones, M Brewer, M Jones, Z Brooke.

Scorer – *Try:* Howarth. *Conversion:* Howarth. *Penalty goals:* Howarth 3.

Referee: E Morrison (England).

Series score: Played 98, Australia 27, New Zealand 66, Drawn 5.

WORLD CUP QUALIFIERS

Wales emerge as leading European qualifier after hard fought defeats of Romania and Italy. In Bucharest, Welsh skipper Ieuan Evans breaks national try-scoring record with his 21st try. Daniel Dominguez, captaining Italy for first time, equals world record with eight penalty goals in defeat of Romania, but has to play second fiddle in Cardiff to Neil Jenkins whose 24 points equal the Welsh record for a single match and takes his overall tally (308) beyond Paul Thorburn (304) to make him his country's all-time leading points scorer.

Romania 9, Wales 16
Bucharest, 17 September 1994

Romania: V Brici; L Colceriu, N Racean, N Fulina, G Solomie; N Nichitean, D Neaga; G Leonte (C Gheorghe 71), G Ion, J Vlad, S Ciorascu, C Cojocariu, T Oroian, A Guranescu, T Brinza (capt, C Branescu 63).

Scorer – *Penalty goals:* Nichitean 3.

Wales: M Rayer (Cardiff); I Evans (Llanelli, capt), M Hall (Cardiff), N Davies, W Proctor (both Llanelli); N Jenkins (Pontypridd), R Moon; R Evans (both Llanelli); G Jenkins (Swansea), J Davies (Neath), P Davies (Llanelli), G Llewellyn (Neath), H Taylor (Cardiff), R Collins (Pontypridd), E Lewis (Cardiff).

Scorers – *Try:* I Evans. *Conversion:* N Jenkins. *Penalty goals:* N Jenkins 3.

Referee: D McHugh (Ireland).

Series score: Played 3, Romania 2, Wales 1.

Italy 24, Romania 6
Catania, 1 October 1994

Italy: P Dotto; P Vaccari, S Bordon, I Francescato, M Gerosa; D Dominguez (capt), A Troncon; M del Sie, C Orlandi, G Grespan, R Favaro, D Scaglia (D Sesenna), O Arancio, C Checchinato, A Scorglon (F de Rossi 58).

Scorer – Penalty goals: Dominguez 8.

Romania: V Brici; L Colceriu, N Fulina (Temp: I Tofan), G Solomie, R Cioca; N Nichitean, D Neaga; G Vlad, G Ion (capt), G Leonte, C Branesco (T Brinza), C Cojocariu, T Oroian, C Draguceanu, A Gealapu.

Scorer – Penalty goals: Nichitean 2.

Referee: E Sklar (Argentina).

Wales 29, Italy 19
Cardiff, 12 October 1994

Wales: M Rayer (Cardiff); W Proctor (Llanelli), M Hall (Cardiff), N Davies (Llanelli), A Clement (Swansea); N Jenkins (Pontypridd), R Moon; R Evans (both Llanelli); G Jenkins (Swansea), J Davies (Neath), P Davies (Llanelli), G Llewellyn (Neath), H Taylor (Cardiff), R Collins (Pontypridd), E Lewis (Cardiff).

Scorers – Try: N Davies. *Penalty goals:* N Jenkins 7. *Dropped goal:* N Jenkins.

Italy: P Vaccari; I Francescato, S Bordon, M Bonomi, M Gerosa; D Dominguez, A Troncon; M Cuttitta (capt), C Orlandi, G Grespan (M Dal-Sie 66), R Favaro, D Scaglia, O Arancio, C Checchinato.

Scorers – Try: Francescato. *Conversion:* Dominguez. *Penalty goals:* Dominguez 4.

Referee: K McCartney (Scotland).

Series score: Played 1, Wales 1, Italy 0.

14TH ASIAN CHAMPIONSHIP
(Asian Group qualifier for 1995 World Cup)

FINAL: Japan 26, Korea 15 (Japan qualify for World Cup).

Third place play-off: Hong Kong 80, Chinese Taipei 26.

POOL A: Malaysia 23, Sri Lanka 18; Japan 56, Chinese Taipei 5; Sri Lanka 3, Japan 67; Chinese Taipei 23, Malaysia 15; Malaysia 9, Japan 98; Chinese Taipei 25, Sri Lanka 9.

    Standings: (1) Japan 9pts, (2) Chinese Taipei 7, (3) Malaysia 5, (4) Sri Lanka 3.

POOL B: Singapore 5, Thailand 69; Hong Kong 17, Korea 28; Thailand 0, Hong Kong 93; Korea 90, Singapore 3; Singapore 13, Hong Kong 164 (World Cup record score); Korea 65, Thailand 13.

    Standings: (1) Korea 9pts, (2) Hong Kong 7, (3) Thailand 5, (4) Singapore 3.

ARGENTINA TO SOUTH AFRICA
September-October 1994: P6 W3 D0 L3 F216 A216

More a fact-finding mission ahead of the World Cup than a scalp-gaining tour, Argentina are nonetheless encouraged by their progress under the captaincy of 34-year-old Marcelo

Loffreda. Hugo Porta, Argentine ambassador to the new Republic, is especially pleased with the forwards. Individual tour highlight is provided by 21-year-old Jose Cilley who arrives in Johannesburg as a replacement three hours before the second Test and marks his debut by equalling Porta's record 21-point haul against the Springboks.

RESULTS: (1) SA Development XV 20, Argentina 51 (Wellington, 27.9.94); (2) Border 25, Argentina 41 (East London, 30.9.94); (3) South Africa A 56, Argentina 12 (Brakpan, 4.10.94); (4) first Test: South Africa 42, Argentina 22 (Port Elizabeth, 8.10.94); (5) Northern Free State 27, Argentina 64 (Welkom, 11.10.94); (6) second Test: South Africa 46, Argentina 26 (Johannesburg, 15.10.94).

SA Development XV 20, Argentina 51
Wellington, 27 September 1994

SA Development XV: P Rossouw; S Geduld, J Thomson, T Linee, C Breda; P O'Neil, S Raubenheimer; G Pagel, D Santon, R Kempson (P Froneman), H Jacobs, R Minty (R Britton), J Paarwater (capt), A Naebezi, H Karele.
  Scorers – *Tries:* Thomson, Breda, O'Neil. *Conversion:* O'Neil. *Penalty goal:* O'Neil.

Pumas: S Salvat; L Bouza, M Loffreda (capt), D Cuesta Silva, M Teran; G Camardon, R Bullrich; M Corral, F Mendez, E Noriega, G Ugartemendia, G Llanes, R Martin, C Viel Temperley, N Bossicovich.
  Scorers – *Tries:* Camardon 2, Corral, Mendez, Noriega, Bossicovich, 2 penalty tries. *Conversions:* Bouza 4. *Penalty goal:* Bouza.

Referee: S Neethling (Boland).

Border 25, Argentina 41
East London, 30 September 1994

Border: W Weyer; A Alexander, A Claasen, G Gelderbloom, T Hahn; R Henry, J Verwey, C van Zyl (G Hunter), W Scott (R van Zyl), P Froneman, R Minty, A Heuer, A Human (capt), A Botha (B Jacobs), R Weppelman.
  Scorers – *Tries:* Alexander, Claasen, Gelderbloom. *Conversions:* Henry 2. *Penalty goals:* Henry, Gelderbloom.

Pumas: S Salvat (capt); M Pfister, F Del Castillo, F Garcia, M Teran; G Del Castillo, C Barrea; M Corral, F Mendez, E Noriega, P Sporleder, G Llanes, R Martin, S Irazoqui, G Ugartemendia.
  Scorers – *Tries:* Salvat, Pfister 2, Martin. *Conversions:* Del Castillo 3. *Penalty goals:* Del Castillo 5.

Referee: P Lombaard (Natal).

South Africa A 56, Argentina 12
Brakpan, 4 October 1994

South Africa A: A Joubert; P Hendriks, C Scholtz, T Linee, C Badenhorst; E Herbert, J van der Westhuizen; B Swart (capt), O le Roux (M Visser), I Hattingh, R Opperman (K Wiese), P Schutte, R Kruger, E van der Bergh, G Teichmann.
  Scorers – *Tries:* Joubert 2, Badenhorst 2, Linee, Swart, Kruger. *Conversions:* Herbert 6. *Penalty goals:* Herbert 3.

Pumas: S Salvat; M Pfister, F Garcia, D Cuesta Silva, M Teran; G Camardon, R Bullrich; R Grau, C Promanzio, E Noriega, C Barrea, G Llanes, M Viola (R Martin), S Irazoqui, C Viel Temperley.
  Scorer – Penalty goals: Garcia 4.

Referee: I Rogers (Natal).

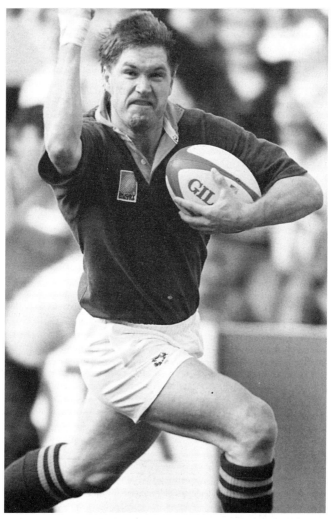

Springbok wing Pieter Hendriks raises a clenched fist to celebrate his try against Australia. South Africa downed the world champions in the Newlands curtain-raiser to World Cup 1995.

South Africa (20) 42, Argentina (15) 22
first Test: Port Elizabeth, 8 October 1994

South Africa: G Johnson; J Small, C Scholtz, B Venter, C Williams; J Stransky, J Roux; P du Randt, U Schmidt, T Laubscher, M Andrews, D Hattingh, F Pienaar (capt), R Straeuli, T Strauss.

Scorers – *Tries:* Roux 2, Stransky, Strauss, Williams. *Conversions:* Stransky 4. *Penalty goals:* Stransky 3.

Argentina: S Salvat; M Pfister, M Loffreda (capt), D Cuesta Silva (F Garcia 60), M Teran; G Del Castillo, R Bullrich; M Corral, F Mendez, E Noriega, P Sporleder, G Llanes, C Viel-Temperley, R Martin, G Ugartemendia.

Scorers – *Tries:* Loffreda, Pfister, Teran. *Conversions:* Del Castillo 2. *Penalty goal:* Del Castillo.

Referee: G Wahlstrom (New Zealand).

Series score: Played 3, South Africa 3, Argentina 0.

Northern Free State 27, Argentina 64
Welkom, 11 October 1994

NFS: K Kleyn; F Broodryk, B Brits, P Steenkamp (J Vermeulen), B Burrows; N Roeland, J Jerling (capt); D Gerson, O Wagener, A Michau, A Fouche, S Nieuwenhuizen, B Cronje, T Badenhorst, A Gebhardt.

Scorers – *Tries:* Jerling, Fouche, Badenhorst. *Conversions:* Roeland 3. *Penalty goals:* Roeland 2.

Pumas: G Camardon; F Garcia, M Loffreda (capt), F Del Castillo, M Teran; G Del Castillo (R Bullrich), C Barrea; M Corral, F Mendez, E Noriega, G Ugartemendia, G Llanes, R Martin, S Irazoqui, N Bossicovich.

Scorers – *Tries:* Camardon, Teran 2, Loffreda, Corral, Martin 2, Ugartemendia, Bossicovich, Bullrich. *Conversions:* G Del Castillo 4, Loffreda 2, Garcia.

Referee: M Franken (Griqualand-West).

South Africa (27) 46, Argentina (9) 26
second Test: Johannesburg, 15 October 1994

South Africa: A Joubert; C Badenhorst, H le Roux, B Venter, C Williams; J Stransky, J van der Westhuizen; P du Randt, U Schmidt, T Laubscher (B Swart 63), M Andrews, D Hattingh, T Strauss (E van der Bergh 42), R Straeuli, F Pienaar (capt).

Scorers – *Tries:* Badenhorst 2, Stransky, Andrews, Straeuli, Williams, van der Westhuizen. *Conversions:* Stransky 4. *Penalty goal:* Stransky.

Argentina: Salvat; Teran, Garcia, Loffreda (capt), Pfister; Cilley, Bullrich; Corral, Mendez, Noriega, Sporleder, Llanes, Viel-Temperley, Martin, Ugartemendia.

Scorers – *Tries:* Llanes, Cilley. *Conversions:* Cilley 2. *Penalty goals:* Cilley 4.

Referee: G Wahlstrom (New Zealand).

Series score: Played 4, South Africa 4, Argentina 0.

SOUTH AFRICA TO WALES, SCOTLAND AND IRELAND
(October-December 1994: P13 W11 D0 L2 F375 A151)

Springbok coach Kitch Christie gives a realistic evaluation of his charges' tour of three of the four Home Unions when declaring "I don't say we're on top of the world, I don't say we're going to win the World Cup, but we're back on the highway." South Africa lose two of their 13 engagements, at Melrose against a spirited Scotland A side (by virtue of a last-gasp Duncan Hodge dropped goal), and in their final outing against the Barbarians at Lansdowne Road, Dublin. But the success of tours is measured on Test results and both Scotland and Wales are put to the sword, though Wales not without a fight. Back rowers Rudi Straeuli, Ruben Kruger and Springbok captain Francois Pienaar, later named International Player of the Year, are the pick of the tourists along with brilliant fullback Andre Joubert, who leads the scoring charts with 75 points, including a South African record 38 in one game (against Swansea).

PARTY: M Andrews (Natal – 1,3,5,7,9,11,13); C Badenhorst (OFS – 1,3,4); J Claassens (Northern Transvaal – 12); P du Randt (OFS – 2,4,5,7,13); J Dalton (Transvaal – 2,4,6,8,10,13); D Hattingh (Northern Transvaal – 1,3,4,6); I Hattingh (Transvaal – 1,3,4,6,8,10,12); P Hendriks (Transvaal – 2,5,7,9,11,12),; G Johnson (Transvaal – 2,4,6,7R,8,10,12,13); A Joubert (Natal – 1,3,4R,5,7,9,11,13); R Kruger (Northern Transvaal – 1,2,5,7,9,11,13); T Laubscher (Western Province – 2,3R,5,7,9,11,12); H le Roux (Transvaal – 2,5,7,13); M Linee (Western Province – 2,6,8,10); J Mulder (Transvaal – 2,3,5,9,11,13); H Muller (OFS – 8,10,12); P Muller (Natal – 1,4,5,7,9,11,13); J Olivier (Northern Transvaal – 2,4,6,8,10); K Otto (Northern Transvaal – 8,10,12); F Pienaar (Transvaal, capt – 3*,5*,7*,9*,11*,13*); K Putt (Natal – 2,4,6,8,10,12); U Schmidt (Transvaal – 1,3,5,7,9,11,12); P Schutte (Transvaal – 2,5,7,9,11,12); R Straeuli (Transvaal – 1*,2,5,7,9,11,12*,13R); J Stransky (Western Province – 1,3,4,6,8,10,12,13R); C Strauss (Western Province – 4*,6*,8*,10*,13); B Swart (Transvaal – 1,3,6,8,10,12); G Teichmann (Natal – 1,3,4,6,8,10,12); E van den Bergh (Eastern Province – 2,3,4,6,8,10,12); B Venter (OFS – 1,3,4,6,7); C van der Westhuizen (Natal – 6,8,10,12); J van der Westhuisen (Northern Transvaal – 1,3,5,7,9,11,13); K Wiese (Transvaal – 2,4,6,8,10,13); C Williams (Western Province – 1,3,5,7,9,11,13).

Results: (1) Cardiff 6, Springboks 11 (22 October); (2) Wales A 13, Springboks 25 (Newport, 26 October); (3) Llanelli 12, Springboks 30 (29 October); (4) Neath 13, Springboks 16 (2 November); (5) Swansea 7, Springboks 78 (5 November); (6) Scotland A 17, Springboks 15 (Melrose, 9 November); (7) Combined Scottish Districts XV 6, Springboks 33 (Glasgow, 12 November); (8) Scottish Select XV 10, Springboks 35 (Aberdeen, 15 November); (9) Test: Scotland 10, South Africa 34 (Edinburgh, 19 November); (10) Pontypridd 3, Springboks 9 (22 November); (11) Test: Wales 12, South Africa 20 (Cardiff, 26 November); (12) Irish Combined Provinces XV 19, Springboks 54 (Belfast, 29 November); (13) Barbarians 23, South Africa 15 (Dublin, 3 December).

Scorers (375 – 50t,31c,21p): 75 – Joubert (6t,18c,3p); 69 – Johnson (3t,9c,12p); 26 – Stransky (3t,1c,3p); 25 – Straeuli (5t), J van der Westhuizen (5t); 20 – le Roux (1t,3c,3p); 15 – Kruger (3t), Muller (3t), Otto (3t), Schmidt (3t), Williams (3t); 10 – I Hattingh (2t), Hendriks (2t); 5 – van der Bergh (1t), H Hattingh (1t), Linee (1t), Mulder (1t), Pienaar (1t), Putt (1t), Strauss (1t), Venter (1t).

Cardiff 6, Springboks 11
Cardiff, 22 October 1994

Cardiff: C John; S Ford, M Hall (capt), C Laity, N Walker; A Davies, A Moore, M Griffiths, J Humphreys, L Mustoe, S Roy, D Jones, H Taylor, E Lewis, O Williams.
   Scorers – *Penalty goals:* Davies, John.

Springboks: Joubert; Williams, Venter, Muller, Badenhorst; Stransky, van der Westhuizen; Swart, Schmidt, I Hattingh, M Andrews, D Hattingh, R Kruger, R Straeuli (capt), G Teichmann.
   Scorers – *Try:* van der Westhuizen. *Penalty goals:* Stransky 2.

Referee: J Fleming (Scotland).

Wales A 13, Springboks 25
Newport, 26 October 1994

Wales A: M Back; D Manley, S Lewis (all Pontypridd), M Taylor (Pontypool), N Walker (Cardiff); A Davies (Cardiff), P John (Pontypridd, capt); I Buckett (Swansea), B Williams (Neath), L Mustoe (Cardiff), P Arnold (Swansea), D Jones (Cardiff), S Davies, R Appleyard (both Swansea), S Williams (Neath). Repl: M Griffiths (Cardiff) for Mustoe, 68 mins.

Scorers – *Try:* Walker. *Conversion:* Davies. *Penalty goals:* Davies 2.

Springboks: Johnson; Olivier, Mulder, Linee, Hendriks; le Roux, Putt; du Randt, Dalton, Laubscher, Wiese, Schutte, Kruger (Teichmann 56), van den Bergh, Straeuli (capt).

Scorers – *Tries:* Putt, Linee, Straeuli. *Conversions:* le Roux 2. *Penalty goals:* le Roux 2.

Referee: A Spredbury (England).

Llanelli 12, Springboks 30
Stradey Park, 29 October 1994

Llanelli: I Jones; W Proctor, N Boobyer, N Davies, M Wintle; C Stephens (J Strange 76), R Moon (capt); R Evans, R McBryde, S John, P Davies, A Copsey, P Jones, M Perego, J Williams.

Scorers – *Tries:* Wintle, Proctor. *Conversion:* Stephens.

Springboks: Joubert; Badenhorst, Mulder, Venter, Williams; Stransky, van der Westhuizen; Swart (Laubscher 40), Schmidt, I Hattingh, M Andrews, D Hattingh, van den Bergh, Pienaar (capt), Teichmann.

Scorers – *Tries:* Stransky, van den Bergh, Joubert, Pienaar. *Conversions:* Joubert 2. *Penalty goals:* Stransky, Joubert.

Referee: D McHugh (Ireland).

Springbok centre Japie Mulder eludes Scots Graham Shiel (right) and Scott Hastings.

Neath 13, Springboks 16
Gnoll, 2 November 1994

Neath: P Thorburn; C Higgs, J Bird, H Woodland, L Davies; A Thomas, R Jones; Brian Williams, Barry Williams, J Davies, G Llewellyn (capt), C Wyatt, A Kembury, C Scott, S Williams.

 Scorers – *Try:* Jones. *Conversion:* Thomas. *Penalty goals:* Thomas 2.

Springboks: Johnson; Badenhorst (Joubert 21), Muller, Venter, Olivier; Stransky, Putt; du Randt, Dalton, I Hattingh, K Wiese, D Hattingh, G Teichmann, E van der Bergh, C Strauss.

 Scorers – *Try:* Strauss. *Conversion:* Joubert. *Penalty goals:* Johnson 2, Joubert.

Referee: R Megson (Scotland).

Swansea 7, Springboks 78
St Helens, 5 November 1994

Swansea: A Clement (capt); Simon Davies, R Boobyer, D Weatherley, S Marshall; A Williams, R Jones; I Buckett, G Jenkins, K Colclough, P Arnold, R Moriarty (M Evans 53), A Reynolds, R Appleyard (Stuart Davies 61), I Davies.

 Scorers – *Try:* Simon Davies. *Conversion:* Williams.

Springboks: Joubert; Hendriks, Mulder, Muller, Williams; le Roux, van der Westhuizen; du Randt, Scmhidt, Laubscher, Andrews, Schutte, Pienaar (capt), Kruger, Straeuli.

 Scorers – *Tries:* Joubert 4, Hendriks 2, Williams, le Roux, Schmidt, van der Westhuizen, Straeuli, Kruger. *Conversions:* Joubert 9.

Referee: S Hilditch (Ulster).

Scotland A 17, South Africa 15
Melrose, 9 November 1994

Scotland A: R Shepherd (Edinburgh Academicals); C Joiner (Melrose), S Nichol (Selkirk), I Jardine (Stirling County), C Glasgow (Heriot's FP); D Hodge (Watsonians), B Redpath (Melrose); D Hilton (Bath), K McKenzie (Stirling County, capt), P Wright (Boroughmuir), D Cronin (Bourges), S Campbell (Dundee HSFP), F Wallace (Glasgow High/Kelvinside), I Smith (Gloucester), R Wainwright (West Hartlepool).

 Scorers – *Try:* Wallace. *Penalty goals:* Shepherd 2. *Dropped goals:* Hodge 2.

Springboks: Johnson; C van der Westhuizen, Linee, Venter, Olivier; Stransky, Putt; I Hattingh, Dalton, Swart, Wiese, D Hattingh, Teichmann, van der Bergh, Strauss (capt).

 Scorers – *Tries:* Venter, D Hattingh. *Conversion:* Stransky. *Penalty goal:* Johnson.

Referee: P Thomas (France).

Scottish Districts 6, Springboks 33
Glasgow, 12 November 1994

Scottish Districts: N Mardon; H Gilmour (Heriot's FP), A McRobbie, S Lineen (Boroughmuir, capt), J Kerr (Watsonians); M McKenzie (Stirling County), G Burns (Stewart's-Melville FP); G Wilson (Boroughmuir), G Ellis, B Robertson (Stirling County), B Ward (Currie), A Watt, S Munro (both Glasgow High/Kelvinside), S Reid (Boroughmuir), G Mackay.

 Scorer – *Penalty goals:* McKenzie 2.

Springboks: Joubert; Hendriks, Muller, Venter, Williams; le Roux, J van der Westhuizen; du Randt, Schmidt, Laubscher, Andrews, Schutte, Pienaar (capt), Kruger, Straeuli.

 Scorers – *Tries:* J van der Westhuizen, Muller 2, Straeuli, Kruger. *Conversions:* Johnson 4.

Referee: C Thomas (Wales).

Scottish Select 10, Springboks 35
Aberdeen, 15 November 1994

Scottish Select: M Dods (Gala); G Sharp (Bristol), F Harrold, R Erikkson (both London Scottish), M Appleson (Sale); S Welsh, G Oliver (capt, Hawick); J Manson (Dundee HSFP), M Scott (Dunfermline), D'Herrington (Dundee HSFP), R Brown (Melrose), R Scott (London Scottish), D Turnbull (Hawick), R Kirkpatrick (Jedforest), E Peters (Bath). Repl: B Renwick (Hawick) for Turnbull, 44 mins.

Scorers – *Try:* Oliver. *Conversion:* Welsh. *Penalty goal:* Welsh.

Springboks: Johnson; Oliver, H Muller, Linee, C van der Westhuizen; Stransky, Putt; Swart, Dalton, I Hattingh, Otto, Wiese, Teichmann, van den Bergh, Strauss (capt).

Scorers – *Tries:* Otto, Johnson, Hattingh. *Conversion:* Johnson. *Penalty goals:* Johnson 6.

Referee: G Simmonds (Wales).

Scotland 10, South Africa 34
Test: Edinburgh, 19 November 1994

Scotland: G Hastings (Watsonians, capt); A Stanger (Hawick), S Hastings (Watsonians), G Shiel (Melrose), K Logan (Stirling County); C Chalmers (Melrose), D Patterson (West Hartlepool); A Sharp (Bristol), K Milne (Heriot's FP), P Burnell (London Scottish), J Richardson (Edinburgh Academicals), A Reed (Bath), D McIvor (Edinburgh Academicals), I Morrison (London Scottish), G Weir (Melrose).

Scorers – *Try:* Stanger. *Conversion:* G Hastings. *Penalty goal:* G Hastings.

South Africa: Joubert; Hendriks, P Muller, Mulder, Williams; le Roux, J van der Westhuizen; du Randt, Schmidt, Laubscher, Andrews, Schutte, Pienaar (capt), Kruger, Straeuli.

Scorers – *Tries:* van der Westhuizen 2, Williams, Straeuli, Mulder. *Conversions:* Joubert 3. *Penalty goal:* Joubert.

Referee: O Doyle (Ireland).

Series score: Played 9, Scotland 3, South Africa 6.

Pontypridd 3, Springboks 9
Sardis Road, 22 November 1994

Pontypridd: G Jones; D Manley, J Lewis, S Lewis, O Robbins; C Cormack, Paul John; N Bezani (capt), Phil John, A Metcalfe, G Prosser, M Rowley, M Spiller, P Thomas, M Lloyd.

Scorer – *Penalty goal:* Cormack.

Springboks: Johnson; Oliver, H Muller, Linee, C van der Westhuizen; Stransky, Putt; Swart, Dalton, I Hattingh, Otto, Wiese, Teichmann, van den Bergh, Strauss (capt).

Scorer – *Penalty goals:* Johnson 3.

Referee: B Campsall (Yorkshire).

Wales (6) 12, South Africa (10) 20
Test: Cardiff, 26 November 1994

Wales: A Clement (Swansea); W Proctor (Llanelli), M Hall (Cardiff), M Taylor (Pontypool), S Hill (Cardiff); N Jenkins (Pontypridd), R Moon; R Evans (both Llanelli); G Jenkins (Swansea), J Davies (Neath), D Jones (Cardiff), G Llewellyn (Neath, capt), H Taylor (Cardiff), R Collins (Pontypridd), E Lewis (Cardiff). Temp Repl: R McBryde (Llanelli) for G Jenkins.

Scorer – *Penalty goals:* N Jenkins 4.

South Africa: Joubert; Hendriks, P Muller, Mulder, Williams; le Roux, J van der Westhuizen; du Randt, Schmidt, Laubscher, Andrews, Schutte, Pienaar (capt), Kruger, Straeuli.

Scorers – *Tries:* Straeuli, Joubert, Williams. *Conversion:* le Roux. *Penalty goal:* le Roux.

Referee: D Mene (France).

Series score: Played 8, Wales 0, South Africa 7, Drawn 1.

Combined Irish Provinces 19, Springboks 54
Belfast, 29 November 1994

Combined Provinces: J Bell (Ballymena); P Gavin (Old Belvedere), P Danaher (Garryowen), M Field (Malone), R Wallace (Garryowen); A McGowan, A Rolland (both Blackrock); J Fitzgerald (Young Munster), T Kingston (Dolphin, capt), G Halpin (London Irish), M Galwey (Shannon), N Francis (Old Belvedere), E Halvey (Shannon), D Corkery (Cork Constitution), S McKiinty (Bangor).

Scorers – *Tries:* Bell, Fitzgerald. *Penalty goals:* McGowan 3.

Springboks: Johnson; Hendriks, H Muller, J Classens, C van der Westhuizen; Stransky, Putt; I Hattingh, Schmidt, Laubscher, Otto, Schutte, Teichmann, van den Bergh, Straeuli (capt).

Scorers – *Tries:* Stransky 2, Otto 2, Schmidt 2, Hattingh, Johnson. *Conversions:* Johnson 7.

Referee: R Yemen (Wales).

Barbarians 23, South Africa 15
Dublin, 3 December 1994

Barbarians: J Callard; S Geoghegan (both Bath), M Hall (Cardiff), S Hastings (Watsonians), P Saint-Andre (Montferrand); C Chalmers (Melrose), R Jones (Swansea, capt); N Popplewell (Wasps), K Wood (Garryowen), P Clohessy (Young Munster), I Jones (North Harbour), S Shaw (Bristol), A Charron (Ottawa Irish), N Back (Leicester), R Wainwright (West Hartlepool). Repls: G Manson-Bishop (Newport) for Charron, 26 mins; P Howard (Queensland) for Hastings, 46 mins.

Scorers – *Tries:* Saint-Andre, Geoghegan. *Conversions:* Callard 2. *Penalty goals:* Callard 2. Dropped goal: Chalmers.

South Africa: Joubert; Johnson, P Muller, Mulder, Williams (Stransky 22); le Roux, J van der Westhuizen; du Randt, Dalton, Swart, Wiese, Andrews, Pienaar (capt, Straeuli 79), Kruger, Strauss.

Scorers – *Tries:* Kruger, Muller, Johnson.

Referee: D Bevan (Wales).

Ireland (9) 26, United States (3) 15
Dublin, 5 November 1994

Eagles coach Jack Clark describes the Lansdowne Road experience as 'awesome' which does much for America's reputation as the world capital of hyperbole. Ireland are booed by their impatient and bored fans inside the first half-hour when electing to kick at goal. The Americans might be inexperienced but lacking fitness they are not. Which brings us to Ireland. Line-out service provides no more comfort with Irish coach Gerry Murphy acknowledging: 'Against England (six weeks hence) our lineouts would need to improve 300 per cent.' At least fly-half Alan McGowan has the satisfaction of marking his debut with 13 points. In contrast, Brendan Mullin's long awaited return lasts only 40 minutes before the British Lion limps off with a thigh strain.

Ireland: C O'Shea (Lansdowne); S Geoghegan (Bath), B Mullin (Blackrock), P Danaher (Garryowen), J Bell (Ballymena); A McGowan (Blackrock), M Bradley (Cork Constitution, capt); N Popplewell (Wasps), K Wood (Garryowen), P Clohessy (Young Munster), G Fulcher (Cork Constitution), N Francis (Old Belvedere), P O'Hara, D Corkery (both Cork Constitution), P Johns (Dungannon). Repls: N Malone (Leicester) for Mullin, 39 mins; A Rolland (Blackrock) for Bradley, 73 mins; M Galwey (Shannon) for Johns, 79 mins.

Scorers – *Tries:* Geoghegan, Bradley. *Conversions:* McGowan 2. *Penalty goals:* McGowan 3, O'Shea.

USA: M Sika (Rhinos); C Schlereth (St Louis Bombers), T Takau (Rhinos), R Green (Univ of California), V Anitoni (Olympic); M Williams (Gentlemen of Aspen), A Bachelet (Old Blues, capt); C Lippert (OMBAC), T Billups, D James (both Old Blues), B Leversee (OMBAC), R Randell (United), D Lyle (Aspen), R Tardits (Mystic River), R Lumkong (Old Blues).

Scorers – *Tries:* Anitoni, Bachelet. *Conversion:* Williams. *Penalty goal:* Williams.

Referee: J-L Rolandi (Argentina).

Series score: Played 1, Ireland 1, USA 0.

England 54, Romania 3
Twickenham, 12 November 1994

When Romania crash 16–26 to Oxford University just seven days before their big day, the writing is on the wall. Whatever possessed the tourists to travel without a number of their leading lights, goodness only knows. Shorn of experience and possession they are forced to tackle and then tackle some more as England scrum-half Dewi Morris takes delivery of the ball on no fewer than 71 occasions. For all that, England manage only six tries and would not have cracked the half-century but for Rob Andrew's goalkicking brilliance. From 11 attempts, he misses once, otherwise landing four penalties and all six conversions.

England: P Hull (Bristol & RAF); T Underwood (Leicester), W Carling (Harlequins, capt), J Guscott (Bath), R Underwood (Leicester & RAF); R Andrew (Wasps), D Morris (Orrell); J Leonard, B Moore (both Harlequins), V Ubogu (Bath), M Johnson (Leicester), M Bayfield, T Rodber (both Northampton), S Ojomoh, B Clarke (both Bath).

Scorers – *Tries:* T Underwood 2, Carling, penalty try, Rodber, R Underwood. *Conversions:* Andrew 6. *Penalty goals:* Andrew 4.

Romania: V Brici (Farul Constanta); G Solomie, M Vioreanu (both Univ Timisoara), S Tofan, R Cioca (both Dinamo Bucharest); I Ivanciuc (Univ Petrosani), D Neaga (Dinamo Bucharest); L Costea (Steaua Bucharest), I Negreci (Railways, Constanta), J Vlad (Grivita Bucharest), C Cojocariu (Bayonne), C Branescu (Farul Constanta), T Oroian, A Gealapu (both Steaua Bucharest), T Brinza (Univ Cluj, capt). *Repl:* C Draguceanu (Steaua Bucharest) for Oroian, 51 mins; F Marioara (Dinamo Bucharest) for Costea, 52 mins; C Gheorghe (Grivita Bucharest) for Negreci, 65 mins; A Guranescu (Dinamo Bucharest) for Branescu, 78 mins.

Scorer – *Penalty goal:* Ivancuic.

Referee: S Neethling (South Africa).

Series score: Played 3, England 3, Romania 0.

England (15) 60, Canada (0) 19
Twickenham, 10 December 1994

Having doubtless chastised himself for missing one out of 11 goal kicks against Romania, Rob Andrew perfects the science on the same park. Canada are manifestly better than

Romania and indeed only lose the try count on a 2:1 ratio (six to three). Not since France in 1991 has a Twickenham visitor bagged three touchdowns. But they have no answer to Andrew who lines up 12 kicks and gets the lot (six conversions and six penalty goals) for a England-high 30-point haul. England's 42-point second half performance, including all six tries, is memorable, though not to Paul Hull. England's summer hero in South Africa retires from the fray after 27 minutes, to be replaced by Mike Catt, not to be seen again this side of the World Cup.

England: P Hull (Bristol & RAF); T Underwood (Leicester), W Carling (Harlequins, capt), J Guscott (Bath), R Underwood (Leicester & RAF); R Andrew (Wasps), K Bracken (Bristol); J Leonard, B Moore (both Harlequins), V Ubogu (Bath), M Johnson (Leicester), M Bayfield, T Rodber (both Northampton), S Ojomoh, B Clarke (both Bath). Repls: M Catt (Bath) for Hull, 27 mins; P de Glanville (Bath) for T Underwood, 64 mins.

Scorers – *Tries:* T Underwood, R Underwood 2, Bracken, Catt 2. *Conversions:* Andrew 6. *Penalty goals:* Andrew 6.

Canada: S Stewart (UBC Old Boys); R Toews (Meralomas), C Stewart (Rovigo & Western Province), I Stuart (Vancouver RC, capt), D Lougheed (Toronto Welsh); G Rees (Oxford Univ & Newport); J Graf (UBC Old Boys); E Evans (IBM Tokyo), M Cardinal (James Bay), D Jackart (UBC Old Boys), N Hadley (Wasps), I Gordon (James Bay), G MacKinnon (EX-Brittania Lions), C McKenzie (UBC Old Boys). Repl: S Gray (Kats) for Stuart, 56 mins.

Scorers – *Tries:* Lougheed 2, Evans. *Conversions:* Rees 2.

Referee: W Erickson (Australia).

Series score: Played 2, England 2, Canada 0.

England's Rob Andrew evades an Argentinian tackle watched by Ben Clarke.

France 28, Canada 9
Besancon, 17 December 1994

France atone for their summer blemish against the Canucks, a match marred by the shock dismissal of Philippe Sella, by giving their visitors a good spanking in the Stade Leo Lagrange. Sella crosses for the last of France's three unanswered tries.

France: J-L Sadourny (Colomiers); E NTamack (Toulouse), P Sella (Agen), T Lacroix (Dax), P Saint-Andre (Montferrand, capt); Y Delaigue (Toulon), G Accoceberry (Begles-Bordeaux); L Benezech (Racing Club), J-M Gonzalez (Bayonne), C Califano (Toulouse), O Merle (Montferrand), O Roumat (Dax), A Costes (Montferrand), A Benazzi, P Benetton (both Agen).

Scorers – *Tries:* Benetton, Sadourny, Sella. *Conversions:* Lacroix 2. *Penalty goals:* Lacroix 2. *Dropped goal:* Delaigue.

Canada: S Stewart (UBC Old Boys); W Stanley (Univ of BC), C Stewart (Rovigo), S Gray (Kats), D Lougheed (Toronto Welsh); G Rees (Oxford Univ & Newport, capt), J Graf (UBC Old Boys); E Evans (IBM Tokyo), K Svoboda (Ajax Wanderers), D Jackart (UBC Old Boys), M James (Burnaby Lake), N Hadley (Wasps), I Gordon (James Bay), G MacKinnon (EX-Brittania Lions), C McKenzie (UBC Old Boys). Repl: M Cardinal (James Bay) for Svoboda, 75 mins.

Scorer – *Penalty goals:* Rees 3.

Referee: B Leask (Australia).

Series score: Played 3, France 2, Canada 1.

Scotland (12) 22, Canada (6) 6
Edinburgh, 21 January 1995

When you have not won for nine internationals and almost two years, any crumb of comfort represents something of a feast. Canada are dreadful, the weather is abominable but the complaints could be counted on the fingers of a mitt. 'Gavin Hastings should be dropped', is a popular school of thought pre-match. Strange that no-one hammers home the point after the big man's 17-point match-winning contribution, from five penalty goals and the conversion of Damian Cronin's 61st minute try.

Scotland: G Hastings (Watsonians, capt); C Joiner (Melrose), G Townsend (Gala), K Logan (Stirling County); C Chalmers, B Redpath (both Melrose); D Hilton (Bath), K Milne (Heriot's FP), P Wright (Boroughmuir), D Cronin (Bourges), S Campbell (Dundee HSFP), R Wainwright (Edinburgh Academicals), I Morrison (London Scottish), E Peters (Bath).

Scorers – *Try:* Cronin. *Conversion:* Hastings. *Penalty goals:* Hastings 5.

Canada: S Stewart (UBC Old Boys); W Stanley (Univ of BC), C Stewart (Rovigo), S Gray (Kats), R Toews (Meralomas); G Rees (Oxford Univ & Newport, capt), J Graf (UBC Old Boys); E Evans (IBM Tokyo), M Cardinal (James Bay), D Jackart (UBC Old Boys), M James (Burnaby Lake), I Gordon (James Bay), K Whitley (Capilano), G MacKinnon (EX-Brittania Lions), C McKenzie (UBC Old Boys).

Scorer – *Penalty goals:* Rees 2.

Referee: C Thomas (Wales).

Series score: Played 1, Scotland 1, Canada 0.

1995 FIVE NATIONS CHAMPIONSHIP

Will Carling becomes the first man to captain a side to three Grand Slams as England make it three in five years. Jack Rowell's first championship as supremo culminates in a 24–12 defeat of Scotland in the winner-takes-all decider at Twickenham, a result which goes some way to erasing the painful memory of Murrayfield 1990. England are clearly the outstanding side in the Five Nations but Scotland deserve untold credit for hauling themselves off their knees, with more than a little help from captain Gavin Hastings and coach Dougie Morgan. Philippe Saint-Andre, the French captain, can reflect on a cracking campaign personally, though he will wince at the memory of Scotland ending their 26-year bogey in Paris, surely the performance of the championship.

France (15) 21, Wales (6) 9
Paris, 21 January 1995

France are profligate, Wales totally lacking a cutting edge. In both respects the result is satisfactory. But 24 hours after the final whistle comes the reverse camera angle of a seventh minute maul. Olivier Merle is spotted head-butting Ricky Evans who, in the act of falling awkwardly, breaks the tibula and fibia bones in his left leg. Wales protest, and although a French disciplinary commission clears their man, French coach Pierre Berbizier drops the giant lock, thus claiming the moral high ground – a spot hardly packed with rugby administrators. The little man also threatens to sue former England manager Geoff Cooke for branding Merle a "hit-man" on television. The Five Nations Championship is up and running.

France: J-L Sadourny (Colomiers); E NTamack (Toulouse), P Sella (Agen), T Lacroix (Dax), P Saint-Andre (Montferrand, capt); C Deylaud (Toulouse), G Accoceberry (Begles-Bordeaux); L Benezech (Racing Club), J-M Gonzalez (Bayonne), C Califano (Toulouse), O Merle (Montferrand), O Roumat (Dax), A Benazzi (Agen), L Cabannes (Racing Club), P Benetton (Agen).

Scorers – *Tries:* N'Tamack, Saint-Andre. *Conversion:* Lacroix. *Penalty goals:* Lacroix 3.

Wales: A Clement (Swansea); S Hill, M Hall (both Cardiff), M Taylor (Pontypool), N Walker (Cardiff); N Jenkins (Pontypridd), R Jones (Swansea); R Evans (Llanelli), G Jenkins (Swansea), J Davies (Neath), D Jones (Cardiff), G Llewellyn (Neath, capt), S Davies (Swansea), R Collins (Pontypridd), P Davies (Llanelli). Repl: M Griffiths (Cardiff) for Evans, 8 mins; M Back (Pontypridd) for Hill, 32 mins.

Scorer – *Penalty goals:* N Jenkins 3.

Referee: J Pearson (England).

Series score: Played 69, France 29, Wales 37, Drawn 3.

Ireland (3) 8, England (12) 20
Dublin, 21 January 1995

Disaster for Rob Andrew as the ball topples over as he attempts a first-half penalty kick at goal, so ending a run of 22 successful kicks for England. The shock fails to perturb his team mates who stroll to victory, so preventing Ireland completing a hat-trick of wins against their favourite enemy. Rory Underwood's 70th appearance makes him the most-capped Home Unions player, while Ben Clarke makes history for the wrong reason, becoming the first international player to receive a yellow card for a stamp on Simon Geoghegan.

Ireland: C O'Shea (Lansdowne); S Geoghegan (Bath), B Mullin (Blackrock, capt), P Danaher (Garryowen), N Woods (Blackrock); P Burke (Cork Constitution), N Hogan (Terenure); N Popplewell (Wasps), K Wood (Garryowen), P Clohessy (Young Munster), M Galwey (Shannon), N Francis (Old Belvedere), A Foley (Shannon), D Corkery (Cork Constitution), P Johns (Dungannon). Repl: G Fulcher (Cork Constitution) for Francis, 40 mins.

Scorers – *Try:* Foley. *Penalty goal:* Burke.

England: M Catt (Bath); T Underwood (Leicester), W Carling (Harlequins, capt), J Guscott (Bath), R Underwood (Leicester & RAF); R Andrew (Wasps), K Bracken (Bristol); J Leonard, B Moore (both Harlequins), V Ubogu (Bath), M Johnson (Leicester), M Bayfield, T Rodber (both Northampton), B Clarke (Bath), D Richards (Leicester).

Scorers – *Tries:* Carling, Clarke, T Underwood. *Conversion:* Andrew. *Penalty goal:* Andrew.

Referee: P Thomas (France).

Series score: Played 108, Ireland 38, England 62, Drawn 8.

England (13) 31, France (3) 10
Twickenham, 4 February 1995

A match traditionally associated with malicious thoughts, if not deeds, has been defused by Pierre Berbizier's banishing of Merle and with the French coach insisting that England are the kingpins of European rugby, the suspicion is of a Gallic backlash lurking in the undergrowth. But no, France are a crashing disappointment, although nothing should detract from the English effort as they surge to their eighth straight win in the fixture. The customary brilliant French try comes from Sebastien Viars and although it reduces the deficit to 13–10 on 55 minutes, England's authority is not genuinely threatened. Two outstanding Tony Underwood tries in the last seven minutes merely underscores the point.

England: M Catt (Bath); T Underwood (Leicester), W Carling (Harlequins, capt), J Guscott (Bath), R Underwood (Leicester & RAF); R Andrew (Wasps), K Bracken (Bristol); J Leonard, B Moore (both Harlequins), V Ubogu (Bath), M Johnson (Leicester), M Bayfield, T Rodber (both Northampton), B Clarke (Bath), D Richards (Leicester).

Scorers – *Tries:* Guscott, T Underwood 2. *Conversions:* Andrew 2. Penalty goals: Andrew 4.

France: J-L Sadourny (Colomiers); P Bernat-Salles (Pau), P Sella (Agen), T Lacroix (Dax), P Saint-Andre (Montferrand, capt); C Deylaud (Toulouse), G Accoceberry (Begles-Bordeaux); L Benezech (Racing Club), J-M Gonzalez (Bayonne), C Califano (Toulouse), O Brouzet (Grenoble), O Roumat (Dax), A Benazzi (Agen), L Cabannes (Racing Club), P Benetton (Agen). *Repls:* L Seigne (Brive) for Benezech, 23 mins; S Viars (Grenoble) for Sadourny, 38 mins. *Temp:* M de Rougemont (Toulon) for Gonzalez.

Scorers – *Try:* Viars. *Conversion:* Lacroix. *Penalty goal:* Lacroix.

Referee: K McCartney (Scotland).

Series score: Played 71, England 40, France 24, Drawn 7.

Scotland (9) 26, Ireland (8) 13
Edinburgh, 4 February 1995

Gavin Hastings (get used to the name) celebrates becoming Scotland's most-capped player (53) by winning the race to be the first European to top 500 points for his country. The big man pops over his first six kicks, including the conversions of tries by Damian Cronin and Craig Joiner, for a 16 point haul. Ireland lose for the sixth successive time at Murrayfield, with debutant fly-half Paul Burke lacking the poise of predecessor Eric Elwood. Had he kicked his goals the Irish would surely have hammered home the winning position given them early in the second half by tries from Jonathan Bell and Brendan Mullin. Instead, from the depths of despair only three weeks previously, it is Scotland who are whispering 'revival'.

Scotland: G Hastings (Watsonians, capt); C Joiner (Melrose), G Townsend (Gala), K Logan (Stirling County); C Chalmers, B Redpath (both Melrose); D Hilton (Bath), K Milne (Heriot's FP), P Wright (Boroughmuir), D Cronin (Bourges), S Campbell (Dundee HSFP),

R Wainwright (Edinburgh Academicals), I Morrison (London Scottish), E Peters (Bath).

Scorers – *Tries:* Cronin, Joiner. *Conversions:* Hastings 2. *Penalty goals:* Hastings 4.

Ireland: C O'Shea (Lansdowne); S Geoghegan (Bath), B Mullin (Blackrock), P Danaher (Garryowen), J Bell (Ballymena); P Burke (Cork Constitution), M Bradley (Cork Constitution, capt); N Popplewell (Wasps), K Wood (Garryowen), P Clohessy (Young Munster), P Johns (Dungannon), G Fulcher (Cork Constitution), A Foley (Shannon), D McBride (Malone), B Cronin (Garryowen).

Scorers – *Tries:* Mullin, Bell. *Penalty goal:* Burke.

Referee: D Bevan (Wales).

Series score: Played 107, Scotland 56, Ireland 45, Drawn 5, Abandoned 1.

Wales (3) 9, England (10) 23
Cardiff, 18 February 1995

Rory Underwood comes into the game on a dreaded hat-trick. In 1989 and 1993 he has boobed in Cardiff, on each occasion making a match-winning contribution to the Welsh cause. How he could do with wiping the slate clean with a couple of tries that give England only their second win in Wales since the War. And so it comes to pass. England move to within 80 minutes of the Grand Slam while Wales are left to rue the sending off (and resultant 60-day ban) of prop John Davies for kicking Ben Clarke. Skipper Ieuan Evans challenges the law makers by illegally substituting flanker Hemi Taylor for prop Hugh Williams-Jones citing the very real danger of having a non-prop in the front row for half an hour. His move wins support and the relevant regulation is swiftly amended.

Wales: A Clement (Swansea); I Evans (Llanelli, capt), M Taylor (Pontypool), N Davies (Llanelli), N Walker (Cardiff); N Jenkins (Pontypridd), R Jones (Swansea); M Griffiths (Cardiff), G Jenkins (Swansea), J Davies (Neath), D Jones (Cardiff), G Llewellyn (Neath), H Taylor (Cardiff), R Collins (Pontypridd), E Lewis (Cardiff). Repls: M Back (Bridgend) for Clement, 11 mins; R Moon (Llanelli) for Walker, 46 mins; H Williams-Jones (Llanelli) for H Taylor, 65 mins. Sent-off: J Davies, 62 mins.

Scorer – *Penalty goals:* N Jenkins 3.

England: M Catt (Bath); T Underwood (Leicester), W Carling (Harlequins, capt), J Guscott (Bath), R Underwood (Leicester & RAF); R Andrew (Wasps), K Bracken (Bristol); J Leonard, B Moore (both Harlequins), V Ubogu (Bath), M Johnson (Leicester), M Bayfield, T Rodber (both Northampton), B Clarke (Bath), D Richards (Leicester).

Scorers – *Tries:* Ubogu, R Underwood 2. *Conversion:* Andrew. *Penalty goals:* Andrew 2.

Referee: D Mene (France).

Series score: Played 101, Wales 48, England 41, Drawn 12.

France (5) 21, Scotland (13) 23
Paris, 18 February 1995

As home bankers go, France-Scotland is one to put the mortgage on. Never having won at Parc des Princes, and not anywhere in Paris since 1969, Scotland cannot even entertain the notion of ending their drought with a side barely adept at winning in their own back yard. Well Gavin Hastings does and manages to transmit his belief through the team. Surely the captaincy performance of the year sees Hastings weigh in with 18 points, including the match-winning conversion of his dramatic last-ditch try, in the match of the championship. France, who edge the try stakes 3–2, are gobsmacked and prepare the guillotine for five of their number, including hapless fly-half Christophe Deylaud. Jubilant Scotland return to the field for a lap of honour to celebrate their highest ever score on French soil and the breaking of a 26-year jinx.

France: J-L Sadourny (Colomiers); P Bernat-Salles (Pau), P Sella (Agen), T Lacroix (Dax), P Saint-Andre (Montferrand, capt); C Deylaud (Toulouse), G Accoceberry (Begles-Bordeaux); L Benezech (Racing Club), J-M Gonzalez (Bayonne), C Califano (Toulouse), O Brouzet (Grenoble), O Roumat (Dax), A Benazzi (Agen), L Cabannes (Racing Club), P Benetton (Agen).

Scorers – *Tries:* Saint-Andre 2, Sadourny. *Penalty goal:* Lacroix. *Dropped goal:* Deylaud.

Scotland: G Hastings (Watsonians, capt); C Joiner (Melrose), G Townsend (Gala), I Jardine, K Logan (both Stirling County); C Chalmers, B Redpath (both Melrose); D Hilton (Bath), K Milne (Heriot's FP), P Wright (Boroughmuir), D Cronin (Bourges), S Campbell (Dundee HSFP), R Wainwright (Edinburgh Academicals), I Morrison (London Scottish), E Peters (Bath). Repl: G Weir (Melrose) for Cronin, 40 mins.

Scorers – *Tries:* Townsend, Hastings. *Conversions:* Hastings 2. Penalty goals: Hastings 3.

Referee: D McHugh (Ireland).

Series score: Played 66, France 31, Scotland 32, Drawn 3.

Will Carling celebrates another Grand Slam triumph.

Scotland (20) 26, Wales (7) 13
Edinburgh, 4 March 1995

A year after Wales annihilated Scotland in the Cardiff rain, it is the rampant Scots who reign at Murrayfield. All season long the tartan dream of another Grand Slam decider with England, *à la* 1990, has been laughed out of sight. But not now. Woeful Wales sign their own death warrant with a hopelessly inadequate performance, despite having led through Robert Jones' second minute try. Scotland surge past them on a tide of self-belief, with Hastings' boot once again the catalyst and tries by Bath's Anglo-Scots, Eric Peters and Dave Hilton, providing the glitz.

Scotland: G Hastings (Watsonians, capt); C Joiner (Melrose), G Townsend (Gala), S Hastings (Watsonians), K Logan (Stirling County); C Chalmers, B Redpath (both Melrose); D Hilton (Bath), K Milne (Heriot's FP), P Wright (Boroughmuir), G Weir (Melrose), S Campbell (Dundee HSFP), R Wainwright (Edinburgh Academicals), I Morrison (London Scottish), E Peters (Bath).

Scorers – *Tries:* Peters, Hilton. *Conversions:* G Hastings 2. *Penalty goals:* G Hastings 4.

Wales: M Back (Bridgend); I Evans (Llanelli, capt), M Hall (Cardiff) N Davies, W Proctor (both Llanelli); N Jenkins (Pontypridd), R Jones (Swansea); M Griffiths (Cardiff), G Jenkins (Swansea), S John (Llanelli), D Jones (Cardiff), G Llewellyn (Neath), H Taylor (Cardiff), R Collins (Pontypridd), E Lewis (Cardiff).

Scorers – *Try:* R Jones. *Conversion:* N Jenkins. *Penalty goals:* N Jenkins 2.

Referee: S Lander (England).

Series score: Played 99, Scotland 43, Wales 54, Drawn 2.

Ireland (0) 7, France (3) 25
Dublin, 4 March 1995

A contest of mind-numbing tedium assures Ireland a berth in the Wooden Spoon decider with Wales a fortnight later and France a measure of self-respect after what has been, by their standards, a dreadful campaign. Pierre Berbizier's decision to bring back the golden oldies – Marc Cecillon, Louis Armary and Franck Mesnel – gives his team a stability hitherto lacking. What they need now is a goalkicker as Emile N'Tamack, a brilliant free runner, seems not to have the faintest idea when it comes to striking the ball. Ireland, for whom ageing debutant Davy Tweed is almost alone in escaping criticism, trail only 3–0 at half-time. Yet with the wind at their backs they promptly concede four tries, the first to accomplished fly-half Yann Delaigue.

Ireland: J Staples (London Irish); S Geoghegan (Bath), B Mullin (Blackrock), P Danaher (Garryowen), N Woods (Blackrock); E Elwood (Lansdowne), M Bradley (Cork Constitution, capt); N Popplewell (Wasps), T Kingston (Dolphin), P Clohessy (Young Munster), D Tweed (Ballymena), G Fulcher (Cork Constitution), E Halvey (Shannon), D McBride (Malone), A Foley (Shannon). Repl: M Field (Malone) for Mullin, 40 mins.

Scorers – *Try:* Geoghegan. *Conversion:* Elwood.

France: J-L Sadourny (Colomiers); E N'Tamack (Toulouse), P Sella (Agen), F Mesnel (Racing Club), P Saint-Andre (Montferrand, capt); Y Delaigue (Toulon), G Accoceberry (Begles-Bordeaux); L Armary (Lourdes), J-M Gonzalez (Bayonne), C Califano (Toulouse), O Brouzet (Grenoble), O Merle (Montferrand), P Benetton, A Benazzi (both Agen), M Cecillon (Bourgoin).

Scorers – *Tries:* Delaigue, Cecillon, N'Tamack, Saint-Andre. *Conversion:* N'Tamack. *Penalty goal:* N'Tamack.

Referee: C Thomas (Wales).

Series score: Played 68, Ireland 25, France 38, Drawn 5.

England (12) 24, Scotland (6) 12
Twickenham, 18 March 1995

England scoop all the prizes with their comfortable if unimpressive defeat of Scotland: Championship, Grand Slam, Triple Crown, Calcutta Cup and the big mouth award for Brian Moore's ingracious summary of events at Twickenham. 'Pitbull' slams 'disgraceful' Scotland for 'killing the ball and the game at all costs'. The visitors are livid. Rob Andrew, however, is exempt from the Scots' wrath, commanding only respect after kicking all 24 of England's points, with seven penalties and a dropped goal from nine attempts. His haul matches Frenchman Sebastien Viars' Five Nations record for a single game and lifts him 21 points above Jon Webb (296) to become the country's leading points scorer. Gavin Hastings' six points gives him 56 for the Championship, extending his own record by four points.

England: M Catt (Bath); T Underwood (Leicester), W Carling (Harlequins, capt), J Guscott (Bath), R Underwood (Leicester & RAF); R Andrew (Wasps), K Bracken (Bristol); J Leonard, B Moore (both Harlequins), V Ubogu (Bath), M Johnson (Leicester), M Bayfield, T Rodber (both Northampton), B Clarke (Bath), D Richards (Leicester). Repl: S Ojomoh (Bath) for Richards, 51 mins. Temps: G Rowntree (Leicester) for Leonard; D Morris (Orrell) for Bracken.

    Scorer – *Penalty goals:* Andrew 7. *Dropped goal:* Andrew.

Scotland: G Hastings (Watsonians, capt); C Joiner (Melrose), G Townsend (Gala), S Hastings (Watsonians), K Logan (Stirling County); C Chalmers, B Redpath (both Melrose); D Hilton (Bath), K Milne (Heriot's FP), P Wright (Boroughmuir), G Weir (Melrose), S Campbell (Dundee HSFP), R Wainwright (Edinburgh Academicals), I Morrison (London Scottish), E Peters (Bath). Repl: J Manson (Dundee HSFP) for Hilton, 45 mins.

    Scorers – *Penalty goals:* G Hastings 2. *Dropped goals:* Chalmers 2.

Referee: B Stirling (Ireland).

Series score: Played 112, England 56, Scotland 39, Drawn 17.

Wales (6) 12, Ireland (13) 16
Cardiff, 18 March 1995

If England and Scotland fall short of serving up a spectacle worthy of the unprecedented £1,000-per Black Market ticket prices, Wales and Ireland comfortably do justice to their match's billing as the Wooden Spoon decider. This is dreadful, just when the beleaguered Welsh management desperately require a filip. It later transpires that JPR Williams and Geoff Evans quit from the Welsh selection panel over the choice of line-up. The XV picked at a stormy seven-hour meeting were not the XV that took to the field. Coach Alan Davies fails to weather the storm from a nation traditionally trigger happy over such matters, and he resigns along with assistant Gareth Jenkins and team manager Robert Norster. Ireland, by comparison, are laughing, thanks to the performance of Paul Burke who comes on for Eric Elwood and promptly takes the game by the scruff of the neck. The result leaves Wales with only their second ever Five Nations whitewash.

Wales: M Back (Bridgend); I Evans (Llanelli, capt), M Hall (Cardiff) N Davies, W Proctor (both Llanelli); N Jenkins (Pontypridd), R Jones (Swansea); M Griffiths (Cardiff), G Jenkins (Swansea), S John, P Davies (both Llanelli), G Llewellyn (Neath), A Gibbs (Newbridge), R Collins (Pontypridd), E Lewis (Cardiff).

    Scorer – *Penalty goals:* N Jenkins 4.

Ireland: J Staples (London Irish); S Geoghegan (Bath), B Mullin (Blackrock), P Danaher, R Wallace (both Garryowen); E Elwood (Lansdowne), N Hogan (Blackrock); N Popplewell (Wasps), T Kingston (Dolphin, capt), P Clohessy (Young Munster), D Tweed (Ballymena),

G Fulcher (Cork Constitution), A Foley, E Halvey (both Shannon), P Johns (Dungannon).
Repl: P Burke (Cork Constitution) for Elwood, 18 mins.
   Scorers – *Try:* Mullin. *Conversion:* Burke. *Penalty goals:* Burke 2. *Dropped goal:* Burke.
Referee: R Megson (Scotland).
Series score: Played 98, Wales 58, Ireland 34, Drawn 6.

1995 FIVE NATIONS CHAMPIONSHIP TABLE

(1994 positions in brackets)

		P	W	D	L	F	A		Pts			+/-
England	(2)	4	4	0	0	98	(9t,4c,14p,1dg)	39	(2t,1c,7p,2dg)	8	+59
Scotland	(5)	4	3	0	1	87	(6t,6c,13p,2dg)	71	(6t,1c,11p,2dg)	6	+16
France	(3)	4	2	0	2	77	(10t,3c,6p,1dg)	70	(6t,5c,10p)	4	+7
Ireland	(4)	4	1	0	3	44	(5t,2c,4p,1dg)	83	(9t,4c,10p)	2	-39
Wales	(1)	4	0	0	4	43	(1t,1c,12p)	86	(8t,5c,11p,1dg)	0	-43

1995 SUPER TEN TOURNAMENT

Transvaal 16, Queensland 30
Final: Johannesburg, 8 April 1995

Transvaal: G Johnson; J van der Walt, C Scholtz (J Mulder 1), H le Roux, P Hendriks; J de Beer, J Roux; B Swart, Chris Rossouw, I Hattingh, K Wiese, H Strydom, G Combrinck, Charles Rossouw, R Straeuli.
   Scorers – *Try:* Roux. *Conversion:* De Beer. *Dropped goals:* De Beer 3.

Queensland: M Pini; D Smith, D Herbert, J Little, P Carozza; P Kahl, P Slattery (B Johnstone 54); D Crowley (M Ryan 23–28), M Foley (D Barrett 25-30), A Blades, R McCall, J Eales, B Wilson, I Tabua, T Coker (M Connors 9).
   Scorers – *Tries:* Connors, Johnstone, Little, Herbert. *Conversions:* Eales 2. *Penalty goal:* Eales. *Dropped goal:* Kahl.
Referee: E O'Brien (New Zealand).

Romania 15, France 24
Bucharest, 8 April 1995

France: J-L Sadourny (Colomiers); E N'Tamack (Toulouse), F Mesnel (Racing Club), T Lacroix (Dax), P Saint-Andre (Montferrand, capt); Y Delaigue (Toulon), G Accoceberry (Begles-Bordeaux); L Armary (Lourdes), J-M Gonzales (Bayonne), P Gallart (Beziers), O Brouzet (Grenoble), O Merle (Montferrand), A Costes (Montferrand), L Cabannes (Racing Club), M Cecillon (Bourgoin). Temp Repl: M de Rougemont (Toulon) for Armary.
   Scorers – *Tries:* Sadourny, penalty try. *Conversion:* Lacroix. *Penalty goals:* Lacroix 4.
Series score: Played 41, Romania 8, France 31, Drawn 2.

Fiji 10, Canada 22
Nadi, 8 April 1995

Fiji **scorers** – Try: Sorovaki. Conversion: Sorovaki. Dropped goal: Turueva.
Canada **scorers** – *Tries:* C Stewart, Rees, Evans. *Conversions:* Rees 2. Penalty goal: Rees.

South Africa 60, Western Samoa 8
Johannesburg, 13 April 1995

South Africa: G Johnson (Transvaal); J Small (Natal), J Mulder, H le Roux (both Transvaal), C Williams; J Stransky (both Western Province), J van der Westhuizen (Northern Transvaal); P du Randt (OFS), C Rossouw, B Swart (both Transvaal), K Wiese (Northern Transvaal), M Andrews (Natal), F Pienaar (capt, Transvaal), R Kruger (Northern Transvaal), R Straeuli (Transvaal). Repls: C Badenhorst (OFS) for Williams; I MacDonald (Transvaal) for Wiese; H Honiball (Natal) for Johnson; M Visser for Andrews.

    Scorers – *Tries:* Johnson 3, Williams 2, Small, Andrews, Stransky, Rossouw. *Conversions:* Johnson 5, Stransky. *Penalty goal:* Johnson.

Western Samoa: M Umaga; G Leaupepe, T Vaega, F Sini, G Harder; E Puleitu, T Nu'ualiita; M Mika, T Leiamaivao, P Fatialofa (capt), L Falaniko, D Williams, S Vaifale, M Iupeli, P Lam. Repl: B Lima.

    Scorers – *Try:* Lima. *Penalty goal:* Umaga.

New Zealand 73, Canada 7
Auckland, 22 April 1995

All Black fly-half Andrew Mehrtens sets a world record for an international debutant with 28 points as Canada are thrashed at Eden Park. The Canterbury player bags one of New Zealand's ten tries, converts seven of them and lands three penalty goals. Fellow newcomer, North Harbour fullback Glen Osborne, claims two tries, as does Marc Ellis, who toured Britain in 1993 as a scrum-half.

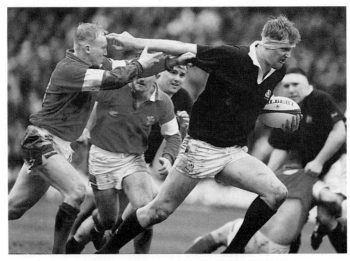

*Scotland's Doddie Weir hands off Wales fly half
Neil Jenkins at Murrayfield.*

New Zealand: G Osborne (North Harbour); J Wilson (Otago), F Bunce, W Little (both North Harbour), M Ellis (Otago); A Mehrtens, G Bachop (both Canterbury); C Dowd, S Fitzpatrick (capt), O Brown (all Auckland), I Jones (North Harbour), R Brooke (Auckland), J Joseph (Otago), M Brewer (Canterbury), J Kronfeld (Otago).

Scorers – *Tries:* Osborne 2, Bunce 2, Ellis 2, Wilson, Mehrtens, Bachop, Brown. *Conversions:* Mehrtens 7. *Penalty goals:* Mehrtens 3.

Canada: S Stewart; B Ebl (A Tynan 27), S Gray (C Stewart 25), G Rees (capt), D Lougheed; B Ross, J Graf; E Evans, M Cardinal, P Le Blanc (R Snow 52), A Charron, G Ennis, M James (G Rowlands 56), G MacKinnon, C McKenzie.

Scorers – *Try:* C Stewart. *Conversion:* Ross.

Series score: Played 2, New Zealand 2, Canada 0.

Scotland 49, Romania 16
Edinburgh, 22 April 1995

A standing ovation for Gavin Hastings as he leaves the park prematurely (dead leg) on his final appearance at Murrayfield. Yet again the Lions captain has led by splendid example, scoring the first of Scotland's seven tries in the opening minute and then adding 14 points with his trusty peg against a none too scruffy Romanian outfit. Most heartening for the tartan management is the performance of the 'new' centre partnership. Former wing star Tony Stanger marks his Test return with a try brace (taking his tally to 18) and Graham Shiel also crosses for a touchdown.

Scotland: G Hastings (Watsonians, capt); C Joiner (Melrose), A Stanger (Hawick), G Shiel (Melrose), K Logan (Stirling County); C Chalmers, B Redpath (both Melrose); D Hilton (Bath), K McKenzie (Stirling County), P Wright (Boroughmuir), G Weir (Melrose), S Campbell (Dundee HSFP), R Wainwright (Edinburgh Academicals), I Morrison (London Scottish), E Peters (Bath). Repl: S Hastings (Watsonians) for G Hastings, 78 mins.

Scorers – *Tries:* G Hastings, Stanger 2, Shiel, Peters, Joiner, Logan. *Conversions:* G Hastings 4. *Penalty goals:* G Hastings 2.

Romania: V Brici; R Cioca, N Racean, R Gontineac, G Solomie; N Nichitean, D Neaga; G Leonte, V Tufa, L Costea, S Ciorascu, C Cojocariu, T Oroian, A Gealapu (C Draguceanu 48), T Brinza (capt).

Scorers – *Try:* Racean. *Conversion:* Nichitean. *Penalty goals:* Nichitean 3.

Referee: N Lasaga (France).

Series score: Played 7, Scotland 5, Romania 2.

ARGENTINA TO AUSTRALIA
April 1995

Australia 53, Argentina 7
first Test: Brisbane, 29 April 1995

Australia: M Pini; D Smith, J Little, D Herbert, D Campese; M Lynagh (capt), G Gregan; D Crowley, P Kearns, E McKenzie (M Hartill), R McCall, J Eales, W Ofahengaue, D Wilson, T Gavin.

Scorers – *Tries:* Lynagh 2, Eales, Pini, Ofahengaue, Smith, Campese. *Conversions:* Lynagh 3. *Penalty goals:* Lynagh 4.

Argentina: S Meson; M Teran, S Salvat, F Garcia, G Camardon; L Arbizu, A Pichot; M Corral, F Mendez, P Noriega, P Sporleder, G Llanes, R Martin, C Viel, J Santamarina.

Scorers – *Try:* Pichot. *Conversion:* Arbizu.

Series score: Played 10, Australia 6, Argentina 3, Drawn 1.

Australia 30, Argentina 13
second Test: Sydney, 6 May 1995

Australia: M Pini; D Smith, J Little, D Herbert, D Campese; M Lynagh (capt), G Gregan; D Crowley, P Kearns, E McKenzie, R McCall, J Eales, D Wilson, T Gavin, T Coker (W Ofahengaue).

Scorers – *Tries:* Campese 2, Wilson. *Penalty goals:* Lynagh 5.

Argentina: S Meson (L Arbizu); E Jurado, S Salvat, F Garcia, M Teran; G del Castillo, R Crexell, M Corral, F Mendez, P Noriega, P Sporleder, G Llanes, R Martin, C Viel, J Santamarina.

Scorers – *Try:* Arbizu. *Conversion:* Crexell. *Penalty goals:* Meson, Crexell.

Series score: Played 11, Australia 7, Argentina 3, Drawn 1.

Italy (9) 22, Ireland (12) 12
Treviso, 6 May 1995

Italy: P Vaccari; M Ravazzolo, I Francescato, M Bonomi (S Bordon), Marcello Cuttitta; D Dominguez, A Troncon; Massimo Cuttitta (capt), C Orlandi, F Properzi-Curti, R Favaro, M Giacheri (M Capuzzoni), O Arancio, J Gardner, P Pedroni.

Scorers – *Try:* Vaccari. *Conversion:* Dominguez. *Penalty goals:* Dominguez 4. *Dropped goal:* Dominguez.

Ireland: J Staples (M Field); R Wallace, B Mullin, J Bell, Daragh O'Mahoney; P Burke, David O'Mahoney (A Rolland); N Popplewell, T Kingston (capt), G Halpin, G Fulcher, D Tweed, A Foley, E Halvey, P Johns.

Scorer – *Penalty goals:* Burke 4.

Series score: Played 2, Italy 1, Ireland 1.

SCOTLAND TO SPAIN
May 1995: P2 W2 D0 L0 F89 A23

PARTY: P Burnell (London Scottish – 1); S Campbell (Dundee HSFP – 1,2R); C Chalmers (Melrose – 2); D Cronin (Bourges – 2); C Glasgow (Heriot's FP – 1); G Hastings (Watsonians – 2); S Hastings (Watsonians – 1,2R); D Hilton (Bath – 1); I Jardine (Stirling County – 1,2R); C Joiner (Melrose – 1,2); K Logan (Stirling County – 2); J Manson (Dundee HSFP); K McKenzie (Stirling County – 1*,2); I Morrison (London Scottish – 2); D Patterson (West Hartlepool – 1); E Peters (Bath – 1,2); B Redpath (Melrose – 2); J Richardson – Edinburgh Academicals – 1); M Scott (Orrell – 2R); G Shiel (Melrose – 1,2); I Smith (Gloucester – 1); A Stanger (Hawick – 1,2); P Walton (Northampton – 1); R Wainwright (West Hartlepool – 2); G Weir (Melrose – 2); P Wright (Boroughmuir – 2).

Results: (1) Madrid Invitation XV 16, Scotland 27 (Madrid, 2.5.95); (2) non-cap Test: Spain 7, Scotland 62.

Scorers (89 – 15t, 7c) – Joiner 30 (6t), G Hastings 22 (2t, 6c), Wainwright 10 (2t), Chalmers 5 (1t), Logan 5 (1t), Morrison 5 (1t), Richardson 5 (1t), penalty try 5 (1t), Shiel 2 (1c).

Madrid Invitation XV (13) 16, Scotland (5) 27
Madrid, 2 May 1995

Madrid Invitation XV: F Puertas; D Saenz, N Duboscq, P Polidori, R Robles; A Kovalenko, J Hernandez; L Lelievre, J Aguiar (capt), A Sanz, A Ravier, T Nicaudie, P Monzon, J Gutierrez, S Samalo.

Scorers – Try: Duboscq. *Conversion:* Duboscq. *Penalty goals:* Duboscq 2. *Dropped goal:* Kovalenko.

Scotland: S Hastings; Joiner, Stanger, Jardine, Glasgow; Shiel, Patterson; Manson, McKenzie (capt), Burnell, Richardson, Campbell, Walton, Smith, Peters.

Scorers – *Tries:* Joiner 3, Richardson, penalty try. *Conversion:* Shiel.

Referee: J-L Mostaza (Spain).

Spain (0) 7, Scotland (36) 62
non-cap Test: Madrid, 6 May 1995

Spain: F Puertas; D Saenz, J Fernandez, A Mino (P Calderon 40), P Gutierrez; X Gerediaga, J Hernandez Gil (J Torres Morote 60); J Alvarez, F de la Calle, J Diez (I de Lazaro 65), J Villau, J Escobar (I Laskurain 40), A Malo, J Etxebarria, J Gutierrez (capt).

Scorers – Try: P Gutierrez. *Conversion:* Gerediaga.

Scotland: G Hastings; Joiner, Stanger (S Hastings 65), Shiel (Jardine 65), Logan; Chalmers, Redpath; Hilton, McKenzie, Wright, Cronin (Campbell 27), Weir, Wainwright, Morrison (Scott 73), Peters.

Scorers – *Tries:* G Hastings 2, Joiner 3, Wainwright 2, Morrison, Logan, Chalmers. *Conversions:* G Hastings 6.

Referee: J Dune (France).

MAJOR FIXTURES 1995/96

September 1995

  2   South Africa v Wales   Johnannesburg

October

 25   Neath v Fiji   Neath
 28   Cardiff v Fiji   Cardiff

November

1	French Barbarians v New Zealand	Toulon
	Treorchy v Fiji	Treorchy
4	Beziers v New Zealand	Beziers
	Pontypridd v Fiji	Pontypridd
7	Bayonne v New Zealand	Toulouse
	Wales v Fiji	Llanelli
11	FRANCE v NEW ZEALAND	Toulouse
	Wales v Fiji	Cardiff
12	ITALY v SOUTH AFRICA	Rome
14	Connacht v Fiji	Galway
	Nancy v New Zealand	Nancy
18	ENGLAND v SOUTH AFRICA	Twickenham
	SCOTLAND v WESTERN SAMOA	Murrayfield
	FRANCE v NEW ZEALAND	Paris
	IRELAND v FIJI	Landsdowne Road
21	Oxford University v Western Samoa	Iffley Road
25	Cambridge University v Western Samoa	Grange Road

December

5	Northern Division v Western Samoa	Huddersfield
9	South West Division v Western Samoa	Gloucester
12	England A v Western Samoa	Gateshead
16	ENGLAND v WESTERN SAMOA	Twickenham

January 1996

20	France A v England A	Paris
	FRANCE v ENGLAND	Paris
	IRELAND v SCOTLAND	Dublin

February

3	ENGLAND v WALES	Twickenham
	SCOTLAND v FRANCE	Murrayfield
17	FRANCE v IRELAND	Paris
	WALES v SCOTLAND	Cardiff

March

2	SCOTLAND v ENGLAND	Murrayfield
	IRELAND v WALES	Dublin
15	England A v Ireland A	Richmond
16	ENGLAND v IRELAND	Twickenham
	WALES v FRANCE	Cardiff
30/31	Cathay Pacific Hong Kong Sevens	Hong Kong

May

11	Middlesex Seven-a-side Finals	Twickenham

INDEX

Gregan, George (Australia)
Griffiths, Mike (Wales)
Guscott, Jerry (England)

Hall, Mike (Wales)
Halpin, Garrett (Ireland)
Halvey, Eddie (Ireland)
Hastings, Gavin (Scotland)
Hastings, Scott (Scotland)
Hattingh, Drikus (South Africa)
Hendriks, Peter (South Africa)
Herbert, Danny (Australia)
Hewitt, Norm (New Zealand)
Hill, Simon (Wales)
Hilton, David (Scotland)
Hogan, Niall (Ireland)
Hopley, Damian (England)
Howard, Pat (Australia)
Howarth, Shane (New Zealand)
Hueber, Aubin (France)
Hull, Paul (England)
Humphreys, Jonathan (Wales)
Hunter, Ian (England)

Ieremia, Alama (New Zealand)

Jardine, Ian (Scotland)
Jenkins, Garin (Wales)
Jenkins, Neil (Wales)
John, Spencer (Wales)
Johns, Paddy (Ireland)
Johnson, Gavin (South Africa)
Johnson, Martin (England)
Joiner, Craig (Scotland)
Jones, Derwyn (Wales)
Jones, Ian (New Zealand)
Jones, Michael (New Zealand)
Jones, Robert (Wales)
Joseph, Jamie (New Zealand)
Joubert, Andre (South Africa)
Junee, Darren (Australia)

Kearns, Phil (Australia)
Kebble, Guy (South Africa)
Kingston, Terry (Ireland)
Kirwan, John (New Zealand)
Knox, David (Australia)
Kronfeld, Josh (New Zealand)
Kruger, Rudi (South Africa)

Lacroix, Thierry (France)

Larsen, Blair (New Zealand)
Laubscher, T (South Africa)
Leonard, Jason (England)
Le Roux, Hennie (South Africa)
Le Roux, John (South Africa)
Lewis, Emyr (Wales)
Little, Jason (Australia)
Little, Walter (New Zealand)
Llewellyn, Gareth (Wales)
Loe, Richard (New Zealand)
Logan, Kenny (Scotland)
Lomu, Jonah, (New Zealand)
Lynagh, Michael (Australia)

McBride, Denis (Ireland)
McBryde, Robin (Wales)
McCall, Rod (Australia)
McGowan, Alan (Ireland)
McIvor, David (Scotland)
McKenzie, Ewen (Australia)
McKenzie, Kevin (Scotland)
MacDonald, Ian (South Africa)
Mallett, John (England)
Malone, Niall (Ireland)
Mannix, Simon (New Zealand)
Manson, John (Scotland)
Mehrtens, Andrew (New Zealand)
Merle, Olivier (France)
Mesnel, Franck (France)
Milne, Kenny (Scotland)
Moon, Rupert (Wales)
Moore, Andy (Wales)
Moore, Brian (England)
Morris, Dewi (England)
Morrison, Iain (Scotland)
Mulder, Japie (South Africa)
Muller, Peter (South Africa)
Mullin, Brendan (Ireland)

NTamack, Emile (France)

O'Connor, Michael (Australia)
O'Hara, Pat (Ireland)
O'Mahony, David (Ireland)
O'Mahony, Darragh (Ireland)
O'Shea, Conor (Ireland)
Ofahengaue, Willie (Australia)
Ojomoh, Steve (England)
Osborne, Glen (New Zealand)

Patterson, Derrick (Scotland)

Pene, Arran (New Zealand)
Peters, Eric (Scotland)
Pienaar, Francois (South Africa)
Pini, Matt (Australia)
Popplewell, Nick (Ireland)
Proctor, Wayne (Wales)
Prosser, Greg (Wales)

Rayer, Mike (Wales)
Redpath, Bryan (Scotland)
Reed, Andy (Scotland)
Richards, Dean (England)
Richardson, Jeremy (Scotland)
Redpath, Brian (Scotland)
Richter, Adrian (South Africa)
Rodber, Tim (England)
Roff, Joe (Australia)
Rolland, Alain (Ireland)
Rossouw, Chris (South Africa)
Roumat, Olivier (France)
Roux, Johan (South Africa)
Rowntree, Graham (England)
Roy, Stuart (Wales)
Rush, Eric (New Zealand)

Sadourny, Jean-Luc (France)
Saint-Andre, Philippe (France)
Schmidt, Uli (South Africa)
Scholtz, Christian (South Africa)
Schuler, Kevin (New Zealand)
Schutte, Philip (South Africa)
Seigne, Laurent (France)
Sella, Philippe (France)
Sharp, Alan (Scotland)
Shiel, Graham (Scotland)
Slattery, Peter (Australia)
Small, James (South Africa)
Smith, Damian (Australia)
Smith, Ian (Scotland)
Stanger, Tony (Scotland)
Staples, Jim (Ireland)
Strachan, Ant (New Zealand)
Straeuli, Rudi (South Africa)

Stransky, Joel (South Africa)
Strauss, Christian (South Africa)
Strydom, J (South Africa)
Swart, Balie (South Africa)

Tabua, Ilie (Australia)
Taylor, Hemi (Wales)
Taylor, Mark (Wales)
Techoueyres, William (France)
Thomas, Gareth (Wales)
Timu, John (New Zealand)
Toombs, Richard (Australia)
Townsend, Gregor (Scotland)
Tweed, Davy (Ireland)

Ubogu, Victor (England)
Underwood, Rory (England)
Underwood, Tony (England)

Van der Bergh, Eleandre (South Africa)
Van der Westhuizen, Joost (South Africa)
Van Heerden, Fritz (South Africa)
Van Rensburg, Theo (South Africa)
Venter, Brendan (South Africa)
Viars, Sebastien (France)

Wainwright, Rob (Scotland)
Walker, Nigel (Wales)
Wallace, Paul (Ireland)
Wallace, Richard (Ireland)
Wallace, Tim (Australia)
Walton, Peter (Scotland)
Weir, George (Scotland)
West, Richard (England)
Wiese, Kobus (South Africa)
Williams, Chester (South Africa)
Williams-Jones, Hugh (Wales)
Wilson, David (Australia)
Wilson, Jeff (New Zealand)
Wood, Keith (Ireland)
Woods, Niall (Ireland)
Wright, Peter (Scotland)

NOTES

NOTES

NOTES

NOTES

NOTES